Introduction to Philosophy
Knowledge, God, Mind, Morality

David E. Ohreen
Mount Royal College
University of Lethbridge

NELSON / EDUCATION

NELSON EDUCATION

Introduction to Philosophy:
Knowledge, God, Mind, Morality

by David E. Ohreen

**Associate Vice President,
Editorial Director:**
Evelyn Veitch

Editor-in-Chief:
Anne Williams

Acquisitions Editor:
Bram Sepers

Developmental Editor:
Heather Parker

Permissions Coordinator:
Sandra Mark

Content Production Manager:
Christine Gilbert

Production Service:
Macmillan Publishing Solutions

Copy Editor:
Wendy Yano

Proofreader:
Macmillan Publishing Solutions

Indexer:
Macmillan Publishing Solutions

Manufacturing Coordinator:
Ferial Suleman

Design Director:
Ken Phipps

Managing Designer:
Katherine Strain

Interior Design:
Tammy Gay

Cover Design:
Peter Papayanakis

Cover Image:
Jessie Parker/First Light

Compositor:
Macmillan Publishing Solutions

Printer:
Thomson West

**Library and Archives Canada
Cataloguing in Publication**

Ohreen, David E., 1968-
    An introduction to
philosophy : knowledge,
God, mind and morality /
David E. Ohreen.

Includes bibliographical references
and index.
ISBN 978-0-17-644257-6

    1. Philosophy—Introductions.
2. Philosophy—Textbooks.
I. Title.

BD21.O47 2008
100   C2007-907367-0

ISBN-13: 978-0-17-644257-6
ISBN-10: 0-17-644257-X

For Paula, Isaac, and Rachel

Contents

Chapter 4: The Mind–Body Problem 195

Chapter 5: Morality: Searching for Right and Wrong 280

Preface

An Introduction to Philosophy was born out of professional frustration in trying to find a text that would meet my pedagogical needs. Most anthology-based texts pose a challenge to students in three ways. First, traditional anthology-based texts are difficult for many students to read because they are filled with philosophical "isms" and they have been written by and for other philosophers. Even for professionals, philosophy can be a difficult subject, akin to trying to decipher the Dead Sea scrolls. Second, because philosophy is not easy to understand, traditional texts require a lot of exegetical work by students (and instructors), which first-year students especially find difficult. Third, many anthologies are too long for the one-semester (four-month) introductory philosophy course found across many North American colleges and universities. This means large portions of texts go unread. Over the years, students have expressed their dismay at spending money on a book of which they have only read half or three quarters.

An Introduction to Philosophy is specifically designed and written to meet these problems. First, as mentioned, reading original philosophical work can be arduous for the beginner student. I have tried to find historical and contemporary readings that are easy to understand and of high philosophical quality. The articles have been edited to ensure students get the most salient philosophical ideas without having to read superfluous details. In some cases, this meant selecting secondary sources rather than original work. For example, I have opted for an article on identity theory by William Lyons rather than U. T. Place's "Is Consciousness a Brain Process?" or J. J. C. Smart's "Sensation and Brain Processes." Place's and Smart's works are extremely important in philosophy of mind, but, from a pedagogical perspective, they require careful exegesis beyond the scope of an introductory course. Moreover, my experience in teaching philosophy of mind is that students often find the articles too philosophically technical and miss the main points of identity theory. Unfortunately, many academics scoff at the notion of using secondary sources as primary reading material, because the original ideas and arguments can potentially be watered down. However, the secondary sources in this text are from well-respected authorities in their fields so that philosophical integrity remains intact, while at the same time providing students easy access to key ideas.

Second, each chapter starts with a comprehensive introduction or commentary on the readings, setting out the main philosophical themes and concepts. I have tried to avoid as many "isms" as possible, and those that are used are explained in detail. Admittedly, the introductions are more or less detailed depending on the reading. However, the introductions are not intended to supplant the original work but support—and in some cases, offer guidance through—the readings. Although the introductions are intended to help students as they read the articles, I have tried to avoid forcing my own philosophical positions on students. The text is intentionally structured to give students contrasting and critical views regarding knowledge, God, mind, and morality. It is hoped that students will come to their own philosophical conclusions instead of merely pandering to mine.

Most significantly, An Introduction to Philosophy is intended to bring the relevance of philosophical issues to light for students in interesting and important ways. Getting students to see philosophy's relevance is difficult because the subject is poorly marketed, so to speak. Most students new to philosophy usually have no idea what philosophy is or have misguided conceptions that it is "navel gazing" and without value. Students also tend not to know why they ought to study philosophy, unlike, say, biology, mathematics, chemistry, or history. An Introduction to Philosophy is devoted to uncovering that purpose.

Third, this text offers students a unique set of readings focusing on five core issues in philosophy: What is the value of philosophy? Does God exist? What can we know? How does the mind relate to the body? And, what is morally right and wrong? The readings have been selected to focus on philosophical depth, not breadth, regarding these issues. Moreover, the total number of readings has been reduced, in comparison to other texts, to maximize text usage for students.

There is one notable omission in *An Introduction to Philosophy*: logic. Unlike other philosophy texts on the market, *An Introduction to Philosophy* does not have a logic section. Logic is an important part of philosophy, but my experience in teaching it in an introductory course is mixed. Some students get it, others do not, and still others do not see the point. Students new to college or university, in particular, seem to have the most trouble with logic. Instead, counterexamples and thought experiments are used in this text as a way of getting students engaged in critical thinking. Moreover, it is important for students not take things for granted, not to accept things at face value—to ask "why" questions and think critically. I, personally, have never been convinced logic was the best way to instill this kind of critical thinking in beginner students. Logic just seems to confuse and confound them. Hence, no section on logic is included.

Moreover, I have tried to make a book that students will actually read. The readings, introductions, boxes, discussion questions, and so forth are designed so that students will understand philosophy's relevance, learn, grow intellectually and personally, and ultimately enjoy their journey.

Organization and Pedagogical Features

The pedagogical features of *An Introduction to Philosophy* have been developed to get students thinking philosophically about the world in which they live. To do this, each chapter is organized in the same way and contains the same features. *An Introduction to Philosophy* includes the following features:

- *Quotations*: Quotations accompany each chapter heading and major subheading as a way of stimulating thought and debate.
- *"What Do You Think?"*: These boxes are designed to help students formulate their own opinions about a specific issue. It is hoped that students will use the boxes to assess their initial beliefs on particular issues. Then, once they go through the philosophical process, they will revisit their original beliefs to see if they are supported or rejected.
- *Discussion Questions*: Discussion questions have been designed to help students gain a better understanding of specific issues and to help instructors create a dialogue with their classes. Discussion questions are also flexible enough to be used before or after students have read the target article(s). In some cases, discussion questions are written to offer a criticism of a specific philosophical position. I have intentionally tried to make the discussion questions current and controversial to help generate debate and create a lively classroom setting.
- *Introductions*: A comprehensive introduction or commentary outlines the specific philosophical issue at hand and gives, in most cases, a detailed overview of each reading.
- *Boxes*: Boxes do not have a designated purpose, but are used in a variety of ways, including asking questions, defining important concepts, offering alternative views, or highlighting a newsworthy event. They are intended to help students and instructors generate dialogue in class and to stimulate philosophical thought.
- *Key Terms and Concepts*: Each chapter ends with a listing of reading-based "key terms and concepts." Key terms and concepts are highlighted in **bold** throughout the text to help students recognize their importance.
- *Study Questions*: Study questions are written to help students prepare for exams.
- *Further Reading*: A list of additional readings accompanies each chapter. These lists are intended to help students with any assigned papers and also to act a reference for further study in the area.
- *Internet Resources*: Reputable resources are listed to aid students with papers or further study.
- *Picture and Biography*: Every reading has an author picture, along with a biographical sketch.

How to Use This Text

Although many texts are designed to appeal to specific instructor areas of expertise (political philosophy, aesthetics, and so on). *An Introduction to Philosophy* takes a more focused approach. The text is divided into five chapters which can easily be covered by instructors in a 12- to 16-week semester with approximately three hours of lecture time per week. Given the range of topics discussed, certain areas may be omitted depending on time constraints. The course syllabus might look like the following:

Week 1   Plato – Apology (optional)

Bertrand Russell – The Value of Philosophy

Week 2   Rene Descartes – Meditations on First Philosophy (First and Second Meditations)

John Locke – Essay Concerning Human Understanding

George Berkeley – A Treatise Concerning the Principles of Human Knowledge

David Hume – Enquiries Concerning Human Understanding (optional)

Week 3   Georg Henrik von Wright – Wittgenstein on Certainty (optional)

Lorraine Code – Is the Sex of the Knower Epistemologically Significant?

Week 4   Saint Thomas Aquinas – Summa Theologiae

Theodore Schick Jr. – The "Big Bang" Argument for the Existence of God

Week 5   William Paley – Natural Theology

David Hume – Dialogues Concerning Natural Religion (optional)

Richard Dawkins – The Improbability of God

Week 6   St. Anselm – Proslogium (selection)

Yeager Hudson – The Ontological Argument

Week 7   William Rowe – The Problem of Evil

Week 8   Simon Blackburn – Infini–Rien (optional)

Natalie Angier – Sorry…I'm No Believer

Week 9   Rene Descartes – Meditations on First Philosophy (Sixth Meditation)

Patricia Churchland – Substance Dualism (optional)

Week 10   William Lyons – Nothing but the Brain

Jerry Fodor – Materialism

John Searle – Can Computers Think?

Week 11   Paul Churchland – Eliminative Materialism

Week 12   Plato – Euthyphro

James Rachels – The Challenge of Cultural Relativism

Week 13   John Stuart Mill – Utilitarianism

Richard Brandt – Moral Obligation and General Welfare

Immanuel Kant – Groundwork for the Metaphysics of Morals (optional)

Week 14   Joshua Glasgow – Kant's Principle of Universal Law

Alison Jaggar – Feminist Ethics

If instructors think that it is unrealistic to cover all the articles in one semester, there is sufficient depth and range of topics that they may pick and choose what to use or omit as time allows.

Acknowledgments

I would like to extend my deepest thanks to the reviewers who read and made valuable comments and suggestions on my manuscript. Their eye towards philosophical clarity and pedagogy has improved this book immensely. I took the reviewers' comments to heart and have tried to incorporate as many of their suggestions as possible. In some cases, their remarks were so perspicuous they were used verbatim. I appreciate the comments from the following reviewers: Guillermo Barron, Red Deer College; Robert Doede, Trinity Western University; David C. Flagel, University of New Brunswick at Saint John; Martin Lin, University of Toronto; Colleen Mahy, George Brown College; and others who wish to remain anonymous.

I would also like to thank everyone at Nelson Education who has helped with the production of this text. In particular, thanks to Bram Sepers for seeing a need and market for this text, and Heather Parker for her encouragement and patience, even when I failed to meet deadlines.

My students have also played a significant role in the development of this text. I have learned much from them over the years and their questions and comments have been incorporated as much as possible.

And finally, this text would have never come to fruition without the support, patience, and love of my wife Paula, son Isaac, and daughter Rachel. They are an inspiration, and without them, I would be a lesser man.

David E. Ohreen

Introduction

Some people would rather die than think.
— Bertrand Russell

Philosophy is a battle against the bewitchment of our intelligence by means of language.
— Ludwig Wittgenstein

The Problem with Philosophy

In today's society, philosophy suffers from a serious problem: visibility. In a culture increasingly dominated by instant communication, fast food, celebrity worship, and an unhealthy obsession with acquiring instant wealth, philosophy's visibility and its importance to everyday life have been marginalized. Superficial distractions shaped by the virtual reality of instant communication make the relevance of philosophy ever harder to see. Society, it seems, is increasingly concerned with instant happiness, easy money, and quick-fix solutions to life's problems. This might explain why students entering university go into the sciences and business rather than philosophy.[1] After all, business can make us lots of money quickly and science can give us facts about the world. Science can also discover medical breakthroughs that improve our overall health and extend our lives. What does philosophy offer? Not much. Philosophy, it is said, has made little progress (philosophers are still arguing over the same topics), never agrees on anything (lack of consensus about philosophical conclusions), and offers no practical value or benefit to humankind.

Let's consider the difference between philosophy and science, however, while taking each of the previous points in turn. First, is it true that philosophy has made little progress over the past millennia? It could be argued that, as a discipline, philosophy creates no new knowledge or facts; it merely argues over the same issues (e.g., knowledge, God, mind, and morality) *ad nauseum*. Science, in contrast, has made considerable progress in regard to biology and chemistry, to name only two disciplines. Molecular biology, for example, has discovered that genetically modified plants can resist pesticides and, thereby, increase crop yields and feed more people. In 1921, Canadian scientists Frederick Banting and Charles Best discovered insulin, thereby leading to treatment for millions of people with diabetes. And today, chemistry is being used to develop antiviral medicines to help those with HIV and AIDS to live longer, healthier lives. Science, it could be said, is the epitome of progress; philosophy is not.

Although it might be true that science is, at heart, a progressive discipline, we should remember that philosophy is not intended to create new knowledge or facts about the world. One goal of philosophy is to investigate, through philosophical analysis, how such scientific facts and knowledge affect human experience, human nature, and the world in which we live. Philosophers do not discover anything; they analyze what is discovered. This makes the objectives of philosophy radically different than those of science.

Second, does philosophy, unlike the sciences, lack consensus? A quick search in any philosophy journal will quickly tell you that 2,000 years of philosophizing has yielded little, if any, consensus about whether God exists, what we know, the relation between mind and body, and what is considered right or wrong. Science, in contrast, has achieve general agreement on a host of issues. For example, there is now a general scientific consensus that climate change (the warming of the earth's temperature due do human causes) is a real phenomenon with potential dire consequences for humankind.

It would be a mistake, however, to say that philosophers have never achieved consensus. There is, for instance, considerable consensus regarding the rules of logic, good and bad reasoning, and the interpretation of some historical works. This aside, the apparent lack of philosophical consensus has to do with the subject matter itself. The hypercritical nature of philosophy means that philosophers tend to focus on disagreement, not agreement. Philosophers tend to pick out weakness in each other's arguments, but this does not necessarily mean there is no consensus regarding conclusions.

Third, is philosophy too obscure or esoteric for practical use and value? For critics, a philosophical analysis of the nature of love, proper names, metaphor, propositional attitudes, perception, colour, personal identity, time, causation, mind, and so forth, has limited practical application to real life. Philosophy is merely unjustified navel-gazing, a kind of childish intellectual game the majority of people do not have the luxury to play. Most people are too busy trying to put food on the table, pay bills, and spend time with family and friends. Philosophical contemplation is a "nice to have" but not a necessity. Science, on the other hand, has provided considerable practical value to humankind including vaccinations, cancer medications, communication networks, air travel, and computer technology. Generally speaking, science has radically changed most human lives for the better; the same cannot be said for philosophy.

Although there are indirect benefits of philosophy, such as enhancing critical thinking skills, direct benefits may be found as well. Consider two previous examples. Although genetically modified food can increase crop production, there are social and ethical concerns related to genetic manipulation including the long-term effects of genetically modified foods on human health; its effects on farmers in developing countries; and the considerations of patenting life-forms for commercial use. These kinds of issues can be sorted out only by philosophical analysis. Similarly, significant antiviral drugs have been discovered that can prevent people with HIV from developing AIDS. But when it comes to making choices about one's lifestyle or deciding whether Western countries ought to, from an ethical point of view, donate these antiviral drugs to African countries, which have the most HIV-infected people on the earth, these issues are beyond science. The appeal to facts and objective knowledge cannot give us answers and thus we must turn to philosophy. In short, many of life's most important ethical and social questions can only be answered by philosophical analysis. In short, philosophy is not contrary or opposed to science but an important and necessary component of it. As we will see throughout the book, the same can be said for many other disciplines as well.

Philosophy is important and relevant to our lives; it is a necessity, not a "nice to have." Philosophy is central to who we are as humans. To understand the world in which we currently live, and where we are going in the future, we must understand the philosophical ideas and concepts that have shaped our past and, in some cases, radically changed the fabric of society. Philosophy is actually so obviously visible and relevant that all we need to do is open our eyes. The real problem with philosophy is that it is often presented in ways devoid of relevance. This book offers a contemporary perspective to traditional philosophical problems. The goal is not only to deepen understanding of philosophy but also to highlight its relevance to the real world.

The Approach of this Book

Philosophy is difficult. Not only are the ideas and concepts intellectually challenging, but also students often have no background in philosophical thinking. Philosophy is too often presented as an abstract and arcane discipline unrelated to the "real world." The goal of *An Introduction to Philosophy* is to combine classical and contemporary readings into a short introductory book, with special emphasis given to first-year students. The articles have been carefully selected to ensure they are easily accessible, well written, and of high philosophical quality.

Many anthology-based texts on the market today leave students to their own devices to decipher and interpret the readings, which can be daunting to say the least. Traditional philosophy texts may be difficult to read for students who are unfamiliar with the technical philosophical lexicon and the antiquated writing style of historical works. As a result, many students give up. My first attempt at reading Kant's *Critique of Pure Reason* ended with the book being hurled across the room in frustration. Of course, most students read primary articles as part of a philosophy course. This means that the instructor must interpret, explain, and provide context for the selections. And let us face it: some instructors will be better or worse at making the readings relevant. *An Introduction to Philosophy* tries to ease these kinds of philosophical frustrations in several ways.

First, although this introductory text contains primary readings, they have been heavily edited to ensure students have easy and clear access to the most salient philosophical points without having to read unnecessary detail.

Second, important critical perspectives have been added. In most cases, a critical essay accompanies each primary reading. In some cases, such as in the section on epistemology (study of knowledge), primary readings from Descartes and Locke offer theories that are opposite of each other. The strength of this book comes in striking a philosophical balance of arguments for and against specific issues. The aim is to facilitate a deeper understanding of the issues for students and, most important, to help students hone their critical thinking skills through the analysis of such work.

Third, to help students and instructors, *An Introduction to Philosophy* takes some of the exegetical work out of the readings by providing in-depth introductions or commentaries. These introductions are intended to provide students with a general overview of the philosophical issue within its historical context and to give an overview of each article. Most important, the introductions provide students with a critical analysis of the issue in question. The introductions may be more or less detailed, according to the difficulty of the reading. And, in some cases, the introductions explain issues or criticisms not addressed in specific readings to ensure students understand the complexities and intricacies of specific philosophical problems.

Fourth, *An Introduction to Philosophy* makes relevant connections between the classic and contemporary literature and students new to the discipline of philosophy. The introductions are written specifically to bring this relevance to life. Philosophy can be downright strange, weird, and inaccessible to new students. Compared to other academic disciplines, Berkeley's argument that a world unperceived would cease to exist and talk about zombies as an objection against functionalism, for example, are bizarre indeed. In some respects, the obscure nature of philosophy is a blessing because students are not confined to think about the world as having merely black-and-white answers, but if relevant connections are not made, key philosophical ideas and concepts may be lost. The aim has been to make such relevant connections using clear, interesting, and, in some cases, provocative examples to drive home the philosophical point.

Fifth, another goal of this book is to view philosophy from a uniquely Canadian perspective. Wherever possible, Canadian examples and cases are used to bring philosophy's relevance to bear on specific issues. For example, important moral questions can be raised about the role of Canadian troops in Afghanistan. Are the deaths of Canadian soldiers in Afghanistan justified compared to the lack of progress made in removing the Taliban from the country? Billions of dollars have been on the war in Afghanistan. Can such spending be morally right in the face of our concerns about child poverty, the environment, First Nations land claim settlements, and protection of universal health care here in Canada? Canadian examples have been used to highlight the traditional problems philosophers have wrestled with for millennia.

An Introduction to Philosophy has a number of pedagogical features. Quotations accompany each chapter as a way of stimulating thought and debate. "What Do You Think?" boxes are intended to help students formulate their own initial opinions about specific issues. It is hoped that as students study the various arguments, they will reject or accept their initial opinions through the process of philosophical discovery. Each reading has a picture of the author and a brief biographical sketch. Each subsection within a chapter has its own discussion questions. These discussion questions are designed to facilitate understanding and stimulate independent questioning. The discussion questions are meant to be fun, current, and provocative.

Each chapter ends with a listing of reading-based key terms and concepts, study questions to help prepare for exams, further readings, and Internet resources.

This book is intended exclusively for a four-month introductory course for students in their first year of university or college. It is designed for the non-philosophy major, for students who are curious about philosophy and who wish to fulfill a humanities/arts credit or those who wish to take only one or two courses. To this end, it is hoped that readers will enjoy their philosophical journey and, most important, make their search for wisdom and truth fruitful.

Note

1. Statistics Canada. *University Qualifications Awarded by Field of Study.* 7 November 2006. 24 June 2007 <http://www.statcan.ca/Daily/English/061107/d061107c.htm>.

Chapter 1 The Value of Philosophy

The philosopher is not a citizen of any community of ideas.
— Ludwig Wittgenstein

Philosophy is the eternal search of truth, a search which inevitable fails and yet is never defeated; which continually eludes us, but which always guides us.
— William James

Box 1.1 What Do You Think?

Students entering into a first-year philosophy class usually have preconceived ideas about what philosophy is. After all, most people in the Western world have heard of Socrates, one of the greatest philosophers ever, even if they don't know the details of his views. Moreover, out of the hundreds of available courses, you picked philosophy. What, in your opinion, is philosophy? Why did you pick this course? And what do you think is the value of studying philosophy?

Philosophy is like sex; everyone does it. We all, at some point in our lives, seek answers to questions that ultimately make up the discipline called philosophy. Does God exist? What is the meaning of life and happiness? Is there life after death? What is love? What is the difference between right and wrong? For the past two thousand years, philosophers have sought answers to these questions, and countless others, with varying degrees of success. What is important is that philosophy starts with an insatiable curiosity about human nature and the world, and ends with the discovery of truth and wisdom.

The search for truth and wisdom makes philosophy unlike other courses offered at university or college. In fact, students new to philosophy are often surprised by how different it is. To get to our destination, we do not take the same road as everyone else—that would be boring—we take bumpy ones filled with twists and turns, and many ups and downs. Most students enter philosophy with preconceptions of how to learn, such as by remembering facts or formulas. In philosophy, because many of the questions asked are open-ended (i.e., have more than one answer), much of our emphasis is on critical analysis. This means that, unlike other disciplines, getting to an answer is, in some respects, more important than the answer itself. These answers are better because they are supported with well-thought-out and reasoned arguments. The development and analysis of arguments are at the heart of what philosophers do.

What is an argument? In philosophical terms, an **argument** is not a verbal disagreement between people, but a claim (conclusion) that one tries to establish by supporting it with reasons (premises). Here is a brief example: Sally is out with friends for coffee when the conversation turns to ethics. In Sally's anthropology class she learned that the Inuit, historically speaking, used to commit infanticide if hunting was so poor that the survival of the family was at risk. By killing innocent offspring, the family unit was able to survive until hunting improved. Although some of Sally's friends are horrified by these murderous practices, Sally argues that morality is relative to specific cultures. Right or wrong behaviour is determined by specific societies, and other cultures have no right to frown upon such practices. Sally's argument can be put more formally as follows:

1. What is considered morally right and wrong varies from society to society so that there are no universal moral standards held by all societies.

2. Whether or not it is right for an individual to act in a certain way depends on or is relative to the society to which he or she belongs.
3. Therefore, there are no absolute or objective moral standards that apply to all people everywhere and at all times. (Pojman 20)

Sally's conclusion for relativism (3) is supported by reasons (1) and (2), which, taken together, make up an argument. In short, infanticide is morally justified.

But is Sally's argument a good one? The second important aspect of philosophy is **analysis**. Philosophy seeks to establish methods for evaluating ideas, arguments, and concepts. In short, we have to test whether the conclusions and premises are true. Hence, if we can show that Sally's argument contains a logical error, her argument will be weakened considerably. For critics of relativism, Sally's argument contains an error in premise 1. It's false that all standards of right or wrong are relative to specific societies. In fact, some moral standards *are* universal. Consider, once again, the Inuit. If the Inuit did not care for and protect their young, they would never have survived as a group. This suggests, far from being monstrous, the Inuit were as loving and caring as other societies that believe infanticide is immoral. We can put this more formally as follows:

1. Human infants are helpless and cannot survive if they are not given extensive care for a period of years.
2. Therefore, if a group did not care for its young, the young would not survive, and the older members of the group would not be replaced. After a while the group would die out.
3. Therefore, any cultural group that continues to exist must care for its young. Infants that are *not* cared for must be the exception rather than the rule. (Rachels 25)

Always love and care for infants is thus a universal moral rule. Another example that shows the falsity of relativism is language and communication. Language and communication depend on a general and implicit prohibition on lying. If no one told the truth, language and communication would be impossible, because no one would believe what people say. In other words, there would be no point in talking to people if we couldn't believe their words. And if no one believed what others said, then complex societies would not exist because communication amongst people is a necessary part of any functioning society. Therefore, telling the truth must be an objective moral principle. Our brief analysis shows that relativism is false because there are some moral rules that all societies must have in common in order to exist. Although much more needs to be said about the ethical relativism debate, my point here is to encourage you to read the articles in this book with a critical eye by pointing out incomplete arguments and contradictions, suggesting counterarguments, and putting forward alternative theories.

The formulation and analysis of arguments make philosophy's methodology unique. It is devoted, although not exclusively, to helping you sharpen your analytic skills necessary to identify, evaluate, and support arguments for and against various issues. In philosophy, like life, nothing is ever black or white, but a mixture of gray. The beauty of gray, on a personal level, means philosophy can help you understand and clarify your own beliefs and values. But a word of caution: the search for truth and wisdom is not easy. The "gray" nature of philosophy means that issues are open to debate. In this sense, one of the main goals of philosophy is to challenge commonsense opinions. Your opinions, beliefs, and values will most likely be challenged as well. This may require a level of self-reflection and questioning that makes you feel uncomfortable. Don't worry; you are merely suffering from philosophical angst. Embrace these feelings because it means that you are moving closer to real self-understanding, truth, and wisdom. The upshot is that philosophy pushes you to think about the world in a different way. It helps you see divergent points of view and helps open the mind to new ideas, different perspectives, and, hopefully, a deeper sense of tolerance and understanding about yourself and others. In other words, philosophy is also the search for **understanding self and others**.

More formally, the word **philosophy** comes from the Greek words *philos*, meaning "to love," and *sophia*, meaning "wisdom." In short, philosophy is the love of wisdom. But what is wisdom? Among other citations, dictionaries often define wisdom as the quality or state of being wise. Being wise is having the power to discern and judge what is true and right. To put it another way, to be wise is to have deep insight or understanding about what is true or false, or right or wrong, as well as the capacity to make sound judgments based on these insights. So if we expand our original definition, we can define philosophy as the use of understanding and insight to judge and discern what is true and right about human nature and the world in which we live.

Philosophy, by definition and methodology, is unique. Few other disciplines address a comparable breadth of subjects crisscrossing a multitude of academic fields. Philosophy is traditionally broken into four main areas:

1. Metaphysics: What is ultimately real?
2. Epistemology: What can we know?
3. Axiology: What do we value (aesthetics, ethics, etc.)?
4. Logic: What is the best way to argue?

However, each area can be broken down into further fields of specialized study, as listed in Box 1.2.

The breadth of subject matter highlights philosophy's fluid and changing nature. The ability to evaluate ideas and arguments and see the world from different perspectives can help us clarify and understand new issues that affect human experience and society. Consider, for example, stem cell research. Current medical research has discovered that stem cells—primary cells that can differentiate into specialized tissues (heart, liver, lung, nerve, etc.)—have significant potential for curing a variety of illnesses and diseases. The best stem cells usually come from embryos that are five to seven days old. In most cases, stem cells are harvested after a couple has gone through in-vitro fertilization and have decided not to use the remaining embryos. Scientists can extract stem

> ## Box 1.2 The Main Subject Areas of Philosophy and Its Specialized Fields
>
> **Metaphysics:** philosophy of mind, philosophy of religion
>
> **Epistemology:** philosophy of science, philosophy of biology, philosophy of language, philosophy of education, philosophy of linguistics
>
> **Axiology:** ethics, political philosophy, social philosophy, philosophy of law, medical ethics, business ethics, philosophy of art, philosophy of feminism
>
> **Logic:** philosophy of logic, inductive logic, philosophy of mathematics
>
> **Source:** Adapted from Robert Audi, "Philosophy: A Brief Guide for Undergraduates." *American Philosophical Association.* 28 August 2001. 14 July 2005 <http://www.apa.udel.edu/apa/publications/texts/briefgd.html>.

cells from these embryos for research purposes. The problem is that when stem cells are extracted, the embryo is destroyed. And for critics who believe that human life begins at conception (the fertilization of an egg by a sperm), the destruction of the embryo is akin to murder. The consequences of this ethical issue for society should not be underestimated. The ethical dilemma of stem cell research raises a number of specific philosophical questions, such as the following:

- When does an embryo become a human being? Does it become a human at conception? When does the heart or brain develop?
- Are embryos human beings at conception? If so, do they deserve our respect and moral consideration? Do they have the same rights as children or adults? Do we have an obligation to protect them?
- If embryos are not humans at conception, are they potentially human? If so, what respect and consideration, if any, should we give these potential human beings?

Box 1.3 Major Areas of Study and Related Philosophical Questions

Biology

- What is a species?
- Does rationality have a biological origin?
- How does a biological understanding of race, sexuality, and gender impact social values?
- What is natural selection and how does it work in nature?
- Is there a biological basis of consciousness?
- Is there a biological basis of morality?
- What makes humans truly unique from other species?

Business

- What is a corporation?
- Do corporations have rights and obligations similar to humans?
- Do corporations have an obligation to give money to charity?
- Is it ethical to bribe government officials?
- Is the use of insider information morally legitimate?
- Is the use of sex in advertising acceptable?
- Is corporate monitoring of employee e-mail a violation of employee privacy?
- Is it moral to use child labour in countries where such practices are acceptable?

Economics

- What is a market?
- Is economics a science similar to the natural sciences?
- Are economic generalizations similar to the laws of nature?
- How can humans make rational economic choices?
- Is it just and fair to have unequal distributions of wealth in the world?

- Do we have a moral obligation to reduce our material wealth?

Environment

- Do animals have rights?
- Should we clear-cut forests merely for the sake of human consumption?
- Do we have moral obligations to protect the environment for future generations?
- Should humans protect other species from extinction?
- Do we have a moral obligation to reduce the human population?

History

- Does history reveal consistent patterns of human behaviour?
- Is history cyclical in nature or merely random independent events lacking meaning?
- Can humans learn from the past or are we doomed to repeat the same mistakes?
- Does history have a direction or does it progress towards something?
- If human societies do progress, is our progress negative or positive?

Mathematics

- Is math a human creation or part of our natural world?
- What is a mathematical object?
- Can mathematics describe nature?
- Do numbers exist?
- How do we know mathematical statements are true?
- What is the point and purpose of mathematical inquiry?

- Is it moral for laboratories to create embryos for research purposes or must embryos only come from natural means?
- Since most reproductive clinics normally destroy unused embryos, do we have a moral obligation to use these embryos to help rid the world of illness and disease?

Until the concepts of human life, conception, and the moral status of embryos are carefully defined, and the arguments for and against such research are debated philosophically, little progress will be made regarding the stem cell debate. The stem cell debate, however, reveals an important aspect of philosophy: almost every field of study makes philosophical assumptions and raises philosophical problems. Hence, far from being antiquated, philosophy is relevant to many of today's current issues including biology, business, economics, environmental issues, history, and mathematics, just to name a few (see Box 1.3). In short, philosophy plays a crucial role in determining how current events and issues affect our lives.

In a rapidly changing technological world, you may wonder if there is any point to studying philosophy at all, let alone taking it as a major. Why study philosophy when your degree is practically useless? Why study philosophy when degree marketability is next to zero? These sentiments are nicely expressed in the cartoon in Figure 1.1.

This kind of thinking that philosophy is valueless must be debunked. Studying philosophy, either one course or a major, has practical import often not recognized by students or the general public. The American Philosophical Association article "Philosophy: A Brief Guide for Undergraduates" outlines four general purposes of philosophy; see Box 1.4.

Research reveals that studying philosophy is also excellent training for careers in business and law. For example, students interested in getting their MBA must first write the Graduate Management Admissions Test (GMAT). One would think that students with undergraduate business degrees would do the best, right? Not so—business majors did the worst. According to a review of standardized test scores of college graduates by the National Institute of Education, the top GMAT scores were from students with degrees in mathematics, philosophy, and engineering respectively (Hoekema 604). Philosophy, like math, develops the reasoning and communication skills necessary for success in the business world. As Thomas Hurka explains:

> Corporations report that, though technical skills are most important in low-level managerial jobs, they become less so in middle and top jobs, where the key traits include communications skills, the ability to formulate problems, and reasoning. Liberal arts education may be weak in the prerequisites for beginning managerial jobs, but provides just what's needed for success at the top.(A8)

Philosophy majors did equally well on the Law School Admissions Test (LSAT). They did

Figure 1.1 What Is the Purpose of Philosophy?

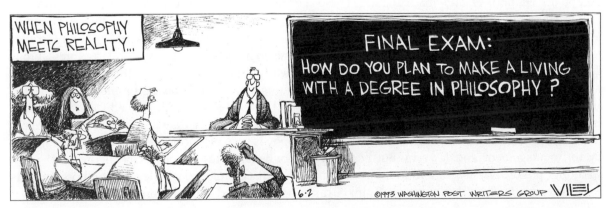

> ## Box 1.4 The General Uses of Philosophy
>
> - **General Problem Solving.** The study of philosophy enhances, in a way no other activity does, one's problem-solving capacities. It helps one to analyze concepts, definitions, arguments and problems. It contributes to one's capacity to organize ideas and issues, to deal with questions of value, and to extract what is essential from masses of information. It helps one both to distinguish fine differences between views and to discover common ground between opposing positions. And it helps one to synthesize a variety of views or perspectives into a unified whole.
>
> - **Communication Skills.** Philosophy also contributes uniquely to the development of expressive and communicative powers. It provides some of the basic tools of self-expression—for instance, skills in presenting ideas through well-constructed, systematic arguments—that other fields either do not use, or use less extensively. It helps one to express what is distinctive of one's view; enhances one's ability to explain difficult material; and helps one to eliminate ambiguities and vagueness from one's writing and speech.
>
> - **Persuasive Powers.** Philosophy provides training in the construction of clear formulations, good
>
> arguments, and apt examples. It thereby helps one develop the ability to be convincing. One learns to build and defend one's own views, to appreciate competing positions, and to indicate forcefully why one considers one's own views preferable to alternatives. These capacities can be developed not only through reading and writing in philosophy, but also through the philosophical *dialogue*, in and outside the classroom, that is so much a part of a thoroughgoing philosophical education.
>
> - **Writing Skills.** Writing is taught intensively in many philosophy courses, and many regularly assigned philosophical texts are unexcelled as literary essays. Philosophy teaches interpretive writing through its examination of challenging texts, comparative writing through emphasis on fairness to alternative positions, argumentative writing through developing students' ability to establish their own views, and descriptive writing through detailed portrayal of concrete examples: the anchors to which generalizations must be tied. . . . Originality is also encouraged, and students are generally urged to use their imagination and develop their own ideas.
>
> **Source:** Robert Audi, "Philosophy: A Brief Guide for Undergraduates." *American Philosophical Association.* 28 August 2001. 14 July 2005 <http://www.apa.udel.edu/apa/publications/texts/briefgd.html>.

better than all social science and natural science (biology, chemistry, and physics) majors except for economics and mathematics. These results were confirmed by a more recent study by Michael Nieswiadomy who collected LSAT scores for 1991–1992 and 1994–1995 from 29 different majors. The top scores on LSAT exams were from physics/math, philosophy/religion, and economics majors. The top ten disciplines are charted in Table 1.1.

Philosophy fits perfectly with the skills needed by top management and lawyers. But generally speaking, philosophy teaches you how to think. An article in the *The Times* entitled "Think On:

Philosophy Is a Quintessentially Modern Discipline" sums up the practicality of philosophy succinctly, stating, "The great virtue of philosophy is that it teaches not what to think, but how to think.… The skills it hones are the ability to analyse, to question orthodoxies and to express things clearly." Of course critical thinking, communicating clearly, and solving problems are not just for those interested in higher education but skills necessary for everyday life. In this sense, philosophy is very practical indeed, but perhaps should not be taken too seriously (see Figure 1.2).

What is philosophy's relevance for those students not interested about becoming a senior executive,

Table 1.1 Average LSAT Scores for 10 Majors, 1994–1995			
Rank	Major	Average Score	Number of Students
1	Physics/Math	157.6	689
2	Philosophy/Religion	156.0	1884
3	Economics	155.3	2916
4	International Relations	155.1	1546
5	Chemistry	154.5	893
6	Government/Service	154.4	812
7	Anthropology/Geography	154.1	898
8	History	154.0	5819
9	English	153.7	6324
10	Biology	153.6	1858

Source: Adapted from Michael Nieswiadomy. (1998). "LSAT Scores of Economics Majors." *Journal of Economic Education.* 29, 379.

Figure 1.2 Taking Philosophy Too Seriously

lawyer, or philosophy major? What is the point of spending time, money, and energy studying a subject that has little practical application in "the real world"? In short, what is the value of philosophy? Much of the value of philosophy comes from not merely dealing with arguments or advancing our cognitive skills but from discovering the meaning of life. That is, it is through philosophical contemplation and analysis that we can distill that which makes life worth living, pursue the "good life," and ultimately attain happiness.

However, the search for a meaningful life is often elusive. Consider the myth of Sisyphus. In the myth, Sisyphus is condemned to a life of pushing a heavy rock up to the top of a steep hill. He strains and pushes the rock with all of his might to the top, only to have it roll back down to the bottom. He then pushes the rock up to the top again and again only to suffer the same cruel fate of having it roll back down. What is the point of his existence? The pushing of the rock accomplishes nothing, serves no purpose, and Sisyphus gets no satisfaction or joy from doing so. His life, it is said, is meaningless. Now consider the lives most people live. Do they not resemble Sisyphus'? They are a cycle of repetitive and endless drudgery. We get up, go to work at a job we often dislike, return home, watch TV, and go to bed. We repeat this pattern year after year until we retire, utterly drained by our life's work, and then die. The next generation will repeat the same cycle and lead comparable meaningless lives.

However, I am not so convinced about life's meaninglessness. To study philosophy is, in part, to search for the meaning of life and of one's existence. To find meaning in life is to understand our role as humans in the world in which we live. This understanding is often informed by the beliefs and values that we hold. Hence, it's through the critical analysis of the relationships we have with others and the world, and the beliefs and values underling them, that meaning is derived. Consider, for example, a corporate executive. A corporate executive can find meaning if she asks questions about her role in the organization, the role of the corporation within society, and the role of the corporation within a globalized economy. This means that philosophical questions regarding the beliefs/values of corporate power, bribery, insider trading, privacy, and so forth need to be addressed. Or consider God. Many people derive meaning and purpose in life through worshiping a higher deity. But this raises important questions: Does God exist? Is God all-powerful and good? Is morality determined by God's command? Philosophical analysis can help answer these questions and ultimately our beliefs and values. And it is through such beliefs and values that life's meaning can be gleaned.

The Purpose of Philosophy

The unexamined life is not worth living.
                                        —Socrates

Discussion Questions

1. Not everyone is willing to fight or die for his or her beliefs. Henry Morgentaler is an example of someone who is. Born in Poland in 1923, Morgentaler survived the horrors of Auschwitz before studying medicine in Montreal. He later joined the Humanist Fellowship, a group devoted to rational thought and compassion for humanity (Mallick F1). As a Fellowship representative, Morgentaler argued before a 1967 government committee that the law against abortion should be overturned to ensure safe reproductive options for women. In 1968, he performed his first illegal abortion and in following years endured numerous arrests and trials, raids on his clinics, death threats, a firebombing, and ten months in jail (Mallick F1). On January 28, 1988, the Supreme Court of Canada struck down Canada's abortion law because it violated the Charter of Rights and Freedoms—specifically, a woman's right to "life, liberty, and security of person." Morgentaler's conviction, dedication, and courage to hold to his beliefs were key to this outcome. Are some beliefs worth going to jail for or even dying for? If not, why not? If so, which ones? Would you be willing to endure years of hardship in support of your beliefs and convictions?

2. Like Socrates, Bertrand Russell suggests that philosophically examining one's life makes it worth living and that if we are merely concerned with our own needs such as sex, money, and success, we will not lead very fulfilling lives. Is Russell wrong? In what ways could someone live an equally happy life full of debauchery?

3. Russell says that one of philosophy's strengths is its uncertainty. That is, the lack of demonstrable truths forces one to be open-minded and also simulates child-like wonder about the world. However, most people seem to seek concrete answers to specific questions and problems instead of engaging in endless philosophical debate. Why is philosophical questioning not a waste of time if we are unlikely to find correct answers?

The Death of Socrates

In 1994, Canadian Lieutenant General Roméo Dallaire commanded the United Nations force in Rwanda during the Rwandan genocide. Between April and July, 800,000 Tutsis and moderate Hutus were slaughtered by Hutu extremists. Before the genocide, a UN force was set up in Rwanda to monitor a peace agreement signed by the Hutu-dominated government and Tutsi-backed Rwandan Patriotic Front to end a four-year civil war. The peace agreement, however, was short-lived when the Hutu military and militia began to systematically murder Tutsis en masse. Thousands of Tutsis fled or took refuge in schools and churches only to be mercilessly killed—men, women, and children, no one was spared. Once the slaughter started, Dallaire desperately pleaded with the UN and the international community for more troops and a mandate to take aggressive action. By Dallaire's own estimates, a few thousand more UN troops could have prevented countless deaths. Instead, the UN reduced his force, was told not to intervene, and to withdraw from the area. And appeals to the international community fell on deaf ears;

the world community abandoned Rwanda to their gruesome fate. Dallaire and a small group of humanitarians and soldiers did not leave or abandon their post but stayed and frantically helped to save as many lives as possible. However, like trying to hold back a tidal wave with an umbrella, the violence that swept over Rwanda that summer was unstoppable.

Dallaire is a hero, the brave solitary voice of reason in a land that slipped into the clutches of hell. Dallaire blames himself for not pressing the international community more to intervene. In his own mind, he had failed the mission. The guilt and shame he felt afterwards took a severe toll on his psychological health. He suffered from depression and post-traumatic stress disorder. To ease his personal torment, he self-medicated by using copious amounts of alcohol, which resulted in a suicide attempt. The mission in Rwanda eventually led to his dismissal from the Canadian Forces in 2000 as he was unfit to command. Over the years, Dallaire, with the help from his family, has painstakingly picked up the pieces of his life. He studied and wrote about conflict resolution at the prestigious Carr Center at Harvard University and is currently a senator in Ottawa. Dallaire's self-sacrifice and courage to fight for what is right is a model for Canadians to emulate. As we will see, this kind of moral determination has deep roots.

On April 4, 1968, Martin Luther King Jr. was assassinated at the Lorraine Hotel in Memphis, Tennessee. The captivating leader was instrumental in the fight for civil rights where racial discrimination and segregation was commonplace, especially in the southern United States. Blacks, for example, could not go to school with whites; rent or buy a home where they wanted; eat at the same lunch counters or use the same restrooms as

Photo 1.1 The Death of Socrates

"The Death of Socrates" by Jacques-Louis David. Socrates has been described as the first philosophical martyr.

whites; and, of course, could not vote. For King, the 1950s and 1960s was a time of struggle, non-violent resistance, and ultimately legislative change. In 1964, the U.S. government passed the Civil Rights Act, prohibiting discrimination. And, in 1965, the government passed the Voting Rights Act, securing black voting rights. The struggle for civil rights did not come without costs. Blacks and whites who supported equality were often victims of assault, humiliation, and, in some cases, murder. King himself fell victim; his house was bombed; he was imprisoned, received countless death threats, and was assassinated on April 4, 1968. Dr. King's steadfast belief in justice and equality changed the course of history. He lived and died protecting the civil rights that so many of us take for granted today.

Socrates also died for his beliefs. He was unjustly sentenced to death for not believing in the Olympian gods (impiety) and for corrupting the youth. Theses charges were without foundation. Socrates was not an atheist and, in fact, much of the *Apology* is devoted to his defence of his philosophical mission set out by the god of Delphi. As for corrupting the youth, this charge was simply untrue. These charges were the backdrop of one of the most famous trials in human history portrayed in Plato's *Apology*.[1]

In the *Apology,* Socrates defends himself against his accusers by explaining why he is wrongly convicted. Socrates' troubles started when his friend Chaerephon went to the oracle of Apollo and asked the god of Delphi if there was anyone wiser than Socrates—there wasn't. Upon hearing what the oracle said, Socrates set out to prove it wrong. In doing so, he sought out the wisdom of the brightest politicians, poets, and artisans in Athens, pestering them with questions about the nature of justice, beauty, knowledge, and other topics. Socrates quickly discovered that these intellectual leaders were not very smart; they preached wisdom but, in fact, were ignorant. Socrates, on the other hand, came to the conclusion that he was wise because he recognized his own ignorance. However, Socrates' persistent questioning made many

Athenians angry. He questioned not only beauty, justice, and knowledge but the value system of Athens itself. This generated deep-seated animosity towards Socrates, which ultimately was the foundation of his conviction.

Socrates also castigated Athenians, especially his students, for showing more concern for accruing practical truth rather than philosophical truth, thanks to the **Sophists.** The Sophists (a Greek word meaning "wisest" or "wise man") were a group of itinerant professors who taught the skills of debate and rhetoric for a fee. They were, in short, the first paid teachers devoted to teaching practical skills to achieve practical ends. The skills of debate (eristics) were especially important in Athenian life since most men played an active role in politics. In order to persuade others of their opinions regarding civic affairs, men sought the skills Sophists provided. The ability to win debate was also important for business. Acquiring wealth and success is, in part, dependent on convincing others to buy your product or engage in trade. The idea of seeking truth for its own sake was lost on the Sophists; success and fortune were their main goals. They were also cynics about religion; it was considered merely an invention used to control people by instilling fear in them of some divine wrath. However, the Sophists are probably best known for espousing relativism. As Protagoras famously said, "Man is the measure of all things." Each person is his or her own standard of what is true and false. Consider, once again, ethics. In some Middle Eastern countries it's morally acceptable to cut off the hand of a thief, whereas in the West we find this morally repugnant and a violation of human rights. Morality, according to the Sophists, is relative to specific societies; no moral code is better or worse than any another, just different.[2] For many Athenians, the Sophist teachings were the road to a better life.

It is not surprising that Socrates was one of the Sophists' main critics. Socrates proclaimed that truth, not wealth or fortune, must be sought above all else. This meant that one must deeply question everything, even the traditional values held by Athenians, like democracy. This kind of deep questioning appears to be the impetus behind the charge of corrupting the youth. The charge ". . . is really a charge of infusing into the young a spirit of criticism in regard to the Athenian Democracy" (Copleston 144). Alcibiades and Critias were at one time Socrates' students who not only defected to Sparta (the enemy) but were also responsible for the overthrow of Athenian democracy leading to a brutal oligarchy. The implication is that if Socrates had not taught his students to question their beloved democracy, Athenian citizens would not have suffered under their rule. Although these crimes were not Socrates' doing, but crimes committed by some of his pupils, the jury saw differently. If it weren't for Socrates' incessant questioning, the youth of Athens would have never fallen under his corrupt spell and undermined the very democratic principles the population held in esteem.

Socrates' trial ended with a jury of his peers voting 280 for conviction and 220 for acquittal. The conviction carried a mandatory death penalty. In his defence, Socrates claimed that he provided a valuable service to Athens and, therefore, should not be put to death. Instead of convincing the jury of a lesser punishment (exile, for example), Socrates argued that he should be rewarded for his services to Athens akin to Olympic winners and military heroes. Socrates likened his services to that of a gadfly (horsefly) that pesters and arouses a great steed to life. The state is also a great steed, and equally tardy; Socrates merely awakened its citizens to the need of pursuing the truth. After all, it's only through examining one's life that makes it worth living. Disgusted by his response, the jury overwhelmingly voted for Socrates' death.

While awaiting his execution, some of Socrates' supporters encouraged him to escape and flee from Athens. Socrates refused. He argued that it is never right to do wrong intentionally. To flee Athens not only violated the laws of the state but undermined his implicit agreement to obey such laws, even at his own expense. For Socrates, he must obey the law, not because the law is right, but out of moral principle. To break the law and flee, would perhaps correct the injustice of being brought to trial in the first place, but, for Socrates, we should never correct a wrong with a wrong. In other words, two wrongs do not make a right. By breaking the law, he would be saying to others that it is okay to break the law as well. And since violating the law undermines Socrates' quest for truth, justice, and the good life, there was only one alternative; he must remain in prison and accepted his punishment. He thus dutifully drank a cup of hemlock, thereby becoming the first philosophical martyr.

Russell: Philosophy as Wonder and Liberation

The impact of science on our lives is often undervalued. From vaccinating us as children to providing lifesaving procedures, medical science has improved human life to the point where the average life expectancy in Canada is 79.3 years of age and 77 years in the United States, according to the United Nations Human Development Index (United Nations). The science of automotive engineering, to give another example, has transformed human mobility, and astrophysics has allowed space travel. In short, biology, physics, chemistry, and the medical sciences have tremendous practical importance to our lives. However, according to Bertrand Russell in his paper "The Value of Philosophy," the practical import of philosophy is notoriously difficult to find. Philosophers have been wrestling with questions about God's existence, problems of knowledge, mind–body dualism, and ethics for centuries without pinning concrete answers to the mat. And when we do find specific answers, they cease to be called philosophy and become specific sciences. After all, the sciences began as part of philosophical study, and then fragmented into different disciplines over the centuries. This means that the value of philosophy, according to Russell, rests in its uncertainty. The lack of demonstrable truth requires open-mindedness. We must be freed from custom and dogmatism in order to think "outside the box." The more we think beyond our indoctrinated beliefs and values, the more answers we will hopefully find. But, for Russell, finding concrete answers is not as important as the philosophical process itself. Philosophical uncertainty keeps a sense of child-like wonder alive by showing how old problems can be recast in new light.

Moreover, for Russell, uncertainty underscores another chief value of philosophy: contemplating the great philosophical questions of life liberates people of their narrow self-interest. An "**instinctive man**" caught up by his own immediate needs (food, drink, sex, success, money, etc.) will be unable to see the intellectual joys of philosophical questioning and fail to enlarge the "boundaries of self." A person consumed by his or her own needs will fail to grow intellectually. And for Russell, it's philosophical contemplation that is the road to intellectual growth. In this sense, philosophy is not only mind-expanding but also liberating. To philosophize is to accept freedom and impartiality, which Russell suggests, will be translated into our actions and emotions. That is, we must be careful not to presuppose knowledge before we start searching for it. Our thinking must be impartial, not filtered through our subjective beliefs and values, but a way of seeking knowledge for knowledge's sake—the not-Self. Philosophical questioning helps remove the veils of dogma and ideology as we pursue the truth dispassionately. And by taking this not-Self objective view, we will also find ourselves developing as well. The enlargement of self will be revealed in our wider interests, reflective capabilities, and deeper understanding of things. In this sense, philosophy enlarges our self by leaving behind preconceptions and prejudices and by forcing us to see ourselves as part of the greater world in which we live. Philosophical contemplation liberates us from the bondage of our narrow hopes and fears to reveal a world in which all humans are citizens.

1

Plato (427–347 B.C.)

The son of Ariston and Perictione, Plato was born in Athens in 427 B.C. Although originally named Aristocles, he was given the nickname of Plato because of his wrestler-like broad shoulders.

Plato's father died when he was young and his mother remarried Pyrilampes, in whose house Plato would grow up. His early years were devoted to receiving the best education Athens had to offer and being groomed for a life in politics. During the Peloponnesian wars with Sparta, Plato served in the military from 409 to 404 B.C. After the defeat of Athens, Plato became part of the oligarchy of the Thirty Tyrants that ruled the country by force. The violence inflicted upon the people of Athens by the oligarchy disillusioned Plato, causing him to leave politics, becoming instead a student of Socrates in search of the truth. After Socrates' death in 399 B.C., Plato travelled for the next twelve years, studying philosophy in various countries. He returned to Athens in 387 B.C. and founded the Academy, Europe's first university, where philosophy, astronomy, and mathematics were taught and studied. Plato's writings include the Apology, Crito, Euthyphro, Meno, Phaedo, *and, most famously, the* Republic. *Plato died in 347 B.C.*

Apology (Selection)

One of you might perhaps interrupt me and say: "But Socrates, what is your occupation? From where have these slanders come? For surely if you did not busy yourself with something out of the common, all these rumors and talk would not have arisen unless you did something other than most people. Tell us what it is, that we may not speak inadvisedly about you." Anyone who says that seems to be right, and I will try to show you what has caused this reputation and slander. Listen then. Perhaps some of you will think I am jesting, but be sure that all that I shall say is true. What has caused my reputation is none other than a certain kind of wisdom. What kind of wisdom? Human wisdom, perhaps. It may be that I really possess this, while those whom I mentioned just now are wise with a wisdom more than human; else I cannot explain it, for I certainly do not possess it, and whoever says I do is lying and speaks to slander me. Do not create a disturbance, gentlemen, even if you think I am boasting, for the story I shall tell does not originate with me, but I will refer you to a trustworthy source. I shall call upon the god at Delphi as witness to the existence and nature of my wisdom. If it be such.[1] You know Chaerephon. He was my friend from youth, and the friend of most of you, as he shared your exile and your return. You surely know the kind of man he was, how impulsive in any course of action. He went to Delphi at one time and ventured to ask the oracle—as I say, gentlemen, do not create a disturbance—he asked if any man was wiser than I, and the Pythian replied that no one was wiser. Chaerephon is dead, but his brother will testify to you about this.

Consider that I tell you this because I would inform you about the origin of the slander. When I heard of this reply I asked myself: "Whatever does the god mean? What is his riddle? I am very conscious that I am not wise at all; what then does he mean by saying that I am the wisest? For surely he does not lie; it is not legitimate for him to do so." For a long time I was at a loss as to his meaning; then I very reluctantly turned to some such investigation as this; I went to one of those reputed wise, thinking that there, if anywhere, I could refute the oracle and say to it: "This man is wiser than I, but you said I was." Then, when I examined this man—there is no need for me to tell you his name, he was one of our public men—my experience was something like this: I thought that he appeared wise to many people and especially to himself, but he was not. I then tried to show him that he thought himself wise, but that he was not. As a result he came to dislike me, and so did many of the bystanders. So I withdrew and thought to myself: "I am wiser than this man; it is likely that neither of us knows anything worthwhile, but he thinks he knows something when he does not, whereas when I do not know, neither do I think I know; so I am likely to be wiser than he to this small extent, that I do not think I know what I do not know." After this I approached another man, one of those thought to be wiser than he, and I thought the same thing, and so I came to be disliked both by him and by many others.

After that I proceeded systematically. I realized, to my sorrow and alarm, that I was getting unpopular, but I thought that I must attach the greatest importance to the god's oracle, so I must go to all those who had any reputation for knowledge to examine its meaning. And by the dog,[2] men of Athens—for I must tell you the truth—I experienced something like this: in my investigation in the service of the god I found that those who had the highest reputation were nearly the most deficient, while those who were thought to be inferior were more knowledgeable. I must give you an account of my journeyings as if they were labors I had undertaken to prove the oracle irrefutable. After the politicians, I went to the poets, the writers of tragedies and dithyrambs and the others, intending in their case to catch myself being more ignorant than they. So I took up those poems with which they seemed to have taken most trouble and asked them what they meant, in order that I might at the same time learn something from them. I am ashamed to tell you the truth, gentlemen, but I must. Almost all the bystanders might have explained the poems better than their authors could. I soon realized that poets do not compose their poems with knowledge, but by some inborn talent and by inspiration, like seers and prophets who also say many fine things without any understanding of what they say. The poets seemed to me to have had a similar experience. At the same time I saw that, because of their poetry, they thought themselves very wise men in other respects, which they were not. So there again I withdrew, thinking that I had the same advantage over them as I had over the politicians.

Finally I went to the craftsmen, for I was conscious of knowing practically nothing, and I knew that I would find that they had knowledge of many fine things. In this I was not mistaken, they knew things I did not know, and to that extent they were wiser than I. But, men of Athens, the good craftsmen seemed to me to have the same fault as the poets: each of them, because of his success at his craft, thought himself very wise in other most important pursuits, and this error of theirs overshadowed the wisdom they had, so that I asked myself, on behalf of the oracle, whether I should prefer to be as I am, with neither their wisdom nor their ignorance, or to have

both. The answer I gave myself and the oracle was that it was to my advantage to be as I am.

As a result of this investigation, men of Athens, I acquired much unpopularity, of a kind that is hard to deal with and is a heavy burden; many slanders came from these people and a reputation for wisdom; for in each case the bystanders thought that I myself possessed the wisdom that I proved that my interlocutor did not have. What is probable, gentlemen, is that in fact the god is wise and that his oracular response meant that human wisdom is worth little or nothing, and that when he says this man, Socrates, he is using my name as an example, as if he said: "This man among you, mortals, is wisest who, like Socrates, understands that his wisdom is worthless." So even now I continue this investigation as the god bade me—and I go around seeking out anyone, citizen or stranger, whom I think is wise. Then if I do not think he is, I come to the assistance of the god and show him that he is not wise. Because of this occupation, I do not have the leisure to engage in public affairs to any extent, nor indeed to look after my own, but I live in great poverty because of my service to the god.

Furthermore, the young men who follow me around of their own free will, those who have most leisure, the sons of the very rich, take pleasure in hearing people questioned; they themselves often imitate me and try to question others. I think that they find an abundance of men who believe they have some knowledge but do little or nothing. The result is that those whom they question are angry, not with themselves but with me. They say: "That man Socrates is a pestilential fellow who corrupts the young." If one asks them what he does and what he teaches to corrupt them, they are silent, as they do not know, but, so as not to appear at a loss, they mention those accusations that are available against all philosophers, about "things in the sky and things below the earth," about "not believing in the gods" and "making the worse the stronger argument"; they would not want to tell the truth, I'm sure, that they have been proved to lay claim to knowledge when they know nothing. These people are ambitious, violent, and numerous; they are continually and convincingly talking about me; they have been filling your ears for a long time with vehement slanders against me. From them Meletus attacked me, and Anytus and Lycon, Meletus being vexed on behalf of the poets, Anytus on behalf of the craftsmen and the politicians, Lycon on behalf of the orators, so that, as I started out by saying, I should be surprised if I could rid you of so much slander in so short a time. That, men of Athens, is the truth for you. I have hidden or disguised nothing. I know well enough that this very conduct makes me unpopular, and this is proof that what I say is true, that such is the slander against me, and that such are its causes. If you look into this either now or later, this is what you will find. [. . .]

Now if by saying this I corrupt the young, this advice must be harmful, but if anyone says that I give different advice, he is talking nonsense. On this point I would say to you, men of Athens: "Whether you believe Anytus or not, whether you acquit me or not, do so on the understanding that this is my course of action, even if I am to face death many times." Do not create a disturbance, gentlemen, but abide by my request not to cry out at what I say but to listen, for I think it will be to your advantage to listen, and I am about to say other things at which you will perhaps cry out. By no means do this. Be sure that if you kill the sort of man I say I am, you will not harm me more than yourselves.

Neither Meletus nor Anytus can harm me in any way; he could not harm me, for I do not think it is permitted that a better man be harmed by a worse; certainly he might kill me, or perhaps banish or disfranchise me, which he and maybe others think to be great harm, but I do not think so. I think he is doing himself much greater harm doing what he is doing now, attempting to have a man executed unjustly. Indeed, men of Athens, I am far from making a defence now on my own behalf, as might be thought, but on yours, to prevent you from wrongdoing by mistreating the god's gift to you by condemning me; for if you kill me you will not easily find another like me. I was attached to this city by the god—though it seems a ridiculous thing to say—as upon a great and noble horse which was somewhat sluggish because of its size and needed to be stirred up by a kind of gadfly. It is to fulfill some such function that I believe the god has placed me in the city. I never cease to rouse each and every one of you, to persuade and reproach you all day long and everywhere I find myself in your company.

Another such man will not easily come to be among you, gentlemen, and if you believe me you will spare me. You might easily be annoyed with me as people are when they are aroused from a doze, and strike out at me; if convinced by Anytus you could easily kill me, and then you could sleep on for the rest of your days, unless the god, in his care for you, sent you someone else. That I am the kind of person to be a gift of the god to the city you might realize from the fact that it does not seem like human nature for me to have neglected all my own affairs and to have tolerated this neglect now for so many years while I was always concerned with you, approaching each one of you like a father or an elder brother to persuade you to care for virtue. Now if I profited from this by charging a fee for my advice, there would be some sense to it, but you can see for yourselves that, for all their shameless accusations, my accusers have not been able in their impudence to bring forward a witness to say that I have ever received a fee or ever asked for one. I, on the other hand, have a convincing witness that I speak the truth, my poverty. [. . .]

Why then do some people enjoy spending considerable time in my company? You have heard why, men of Athens, I have told you the whole truth. They enjoy hearing those being questioned who think they are wise, but are not. And this is not unpleasant. To do this has, as I say, been enjoined upon me by the god, by means of oracles and dreams, and in every other way that a divine manifestation has ever ordered a man to do anything. This is true, gentlemen, and can easily be established.

If I corrupt some young men and have corrupted others, then surely some of them who have grown older and realized that I gave them bad advice when they were young should now themselves come up here to accuse me and avenge themselves. If they were unwilling to do so themselves, then some of their kindred, their fathers or brothers or other relations should recall it now if their family had been harmed by me. I see many of these present here, first Crito, my contemporary and fellow demesman, the father of Critobulus here; next Lysanias of Sphettus, the father of Aeschines here; also Antiphon the Cephisian, the father of Epigenes; and others whose brothers spent their time in this way; Nicostratus, the son of Theozotides, brother of Theodotus, and Theodotus has died so he could not influence him; Paralius here, son of Demodocus, whose brother was Theages; there is Adeimantus, son of Ariston, brother of Plato here; Aeantidorus, brother of Apollodorus here.

I could mention many others, some of whom surely Meletus should have brought in as witness in his own speech. If he forgot to do so, then let him do it now; I will yield time if he has anything of the kind to say. You will find quite the contrary, gentlemen. These men are all ready to come to the help of the corruptor, the man who has harmed their kindred, as Meletus and Anytus say. Now those who were corrupted might well have reason to help me, but the uncorrupted, their kindred who are older men, have no reason to help me except the right and proper one, that they know that Meletus is lying and that I am telling the truth.

Very well, gentlemen. This, and maybe other similar things, is what I have to say in my defense. [. . .]

[The jury now gives its verdict of guilty, and Meletus asks for the penalty of death.]

There are many other reasons for my not being angry with you for convicting me, men of Athens, and what happened was not unexpected. I am much more surprised at the number of votes cast on each side, for I did not think the decision would be by so few votes but by a great many. As it is, a switch of only thirty votes would have acquitted me. I think myself that I have been cleared on Meletus' charges, and not only this, but it is clear to all that, if Anytus and Lycon had not joined him in accusing me, he would have been fined a thousand drachmas for not receiving a fifth of the votes.

He assesses the penalty at death. So be it. What counter-assessment should I propose to you, men of Athens? Clearly it should be a penalty I deserve, and what do I deserve to suffer or to pay because I have deliberately not led a quiet life but have neglected what occupies most people: wealth, household affairs, the position of general or public orator or the other offices, the political clubs and factions that exist in the city? I thought myself too honest to survive if I occupied myself with those things. I did not follow that path that would have made me of no use either to you or to myself, but I went to each of you privately and conferred upon him what I say is the greatest benefit, by trying to persuade him not to care for any of his belongings before caring that he himself should be as good and as wise as possible, not to care for the city's possessions more than for the city itself, and to care for other things in the same way. What do I deserve for being such a man? Some good, men of Athens, if I must truly make an assessment according to my deserts, and something suitable. What is suitable for a poor benefactor who needs leisure to exhort you? Nothing is more suitable, gentlemen, than for such a man to be fed in the Prytaneum[3] much more suitable for him than for any one of you who has won a victory at Olympia with a pair or a team of horses. The Olympian victor makes you think yourself happy; I make you be happy. Besides, he does not need food, but I do. So if I must make a just assessment of what I deserve, I assess it as this: free meals in the Prytaneum. [. . .]

[The jury now votes again and sentences Socrates to death.]

Now I want to prophesy to those who convicted me, for I am at the point when men prophesy most, when they are about to die. I say, gentlemen, to those who voted to kill me, that vengeance will come upon you immediately after my death, a vengeance much harder to bear than that which you took in killing me. You did this in the belief that you would avoid giving an account of your life, but I maintain that quite the opposite will happen to you. There will be more people to test you, whom I know held back, but you did not notice it. They will be more difficult to deal with as they will be younger and you will resent them more. You are wrong if you believe that by killing people you will prevent anyone from reproaching you for not living in the right way. To escape such tests is neither possible nor good, but it is best and easiest not to discredit others but to prepare oneself to be as good as possible. With this prophecy to you who convicted me, I part from you. [. . .]

You too must be of good hope as regards death, gentlemen of the jury, and keep this one truth in mind, that a good man cannot be harmed either in life or in death, and that his affairs are not neglected by the gods. What has happened to me now has not happened of itself, but it is clear to me that it was better for me to die now and to escape from trouble. That is why my divine sign did not oppose me at any point. So I am certainly not angry with those who convicted me, or with my accusers. Of course that was not their purpose when they accused and convicted me, but they thought they were hurting me, and for this they deserve blame. This much I ask from them: when my sons grow up, avenge yourselves by causing them the same grief that I caused you, if you think they care for money or anything else more than they care for virtue, or if they think they are somebody when they are nobody. Reproach them as I reproach you, that they do not care for the right things and think they are worthy when they are not worthy of anything. If you do this, I shall have been justly treated by you, and my sons also.

Now the hour to part has come. I go to die, you go to live. Which of us goes to the better lot is known to no one, except god.

Notes

1. The god Apollo had a very famous shrine at Delphi, where his oracles were delivered through the mouth of a priestess, the "Pythian."

2. A curious oath, occasionally used by Socrates, it appears in a longer form in *Gorgias* (482b) as "by the dog, the god of the Egyptians."

3. The Prytaneum was the magistrates' hall or town hall of Athens in which public entertainment were given, particularly to Olympian victors on their return home.

2

Bertrand Russell

(1872–1970)

Bertrand Russell is one of the most influential philosophers of the twentieth century. He was a prolific writer, activist, and spokesman for his generation. Born May 18, 1872, into an aristocratic family, Russell's first few years of life were difficult. His mother and sister both died of diphtheria in 1874 and his father died two years later from the strain of his wife's and daughter's deaths. Raised by his grandmother and primarily schooled at home, Russell went on to study philosophy at Cambridge University, graduating in 1894. Russell was a fellow at Cambridge from 1895 to 1901 and then lecturer from 1910 to 1916, until he was dismissed for participating in anti-war protests during the First World War. Two years later he was convicted of the same offence and spent six months in prison. In 1938, he moved to the United States, teaching at a number of institutions, including the University of Chicago and University of California at Los Angeles. In 1944, he moved back to England to take up another fellowship at Cambridge. He became a member of the British Academy and received the Order of Merit in 1949. The following year, Russell won the Nobel Prize for literature. Russell was a strong advocate of women's right to vote, nuclear disarmament, and the liberation of men and women from sexual repression. This, in part, accounts for the four wives and numerous affairs he had during his life. Some of Russell's works include The Principles of Mathematics (1903), The Problems of Philosophy (1912), Our Knowledge of the External World (1914), The Conquest of Happiness (1930), An Inquiry into Meaning and Truth (1940), *and* A History of Western Philosophy (1945). *He died of influenza in 1970 at the age of 97.*

The Value of Philosophy

Having now come to the end of our brief and very incomplete review of the problems of philosophy, it will be well to consider, in conclusion, what is the value of philosophy and why it ought to be studied. It is the more necessary to consider this question, in view of the fact that many men, under the influence of science or of practical affairs, are inclined to doubt whether philosophy is anything better than innocent but useless trifling, hair-splitting distinctions, and controversies on matters concerning which knowledge is impossible.

This view of philosophy appears to result, partly from a wrong conception of the ends of life, partly from a wrong conception of the kind of goods which philosophy strives to achieve. Physical science, through the medium of inventions, is useful to innumerable people who are wholly ignorant of it; thus the study of physical science is to be recommended, not only, or primarily, because of the effect on the student, but rather because of the effect on mankind in general. Thus utility does not belong to philosophy. If the study of philosophy has any value at all for others than students of philosophy, it must be only indirectly, through its effects upon the lives of those who study it. It is in these effects, therefore, if anywhere, that the value of philosophy must be primarily sought.

But further, if we are not to fail in our endeavour to determine the value of philosophy, we must first free our minds from the prejudices of what are wrongly called 'practical' men. The 'practical' man, as this word is often used, is one who recognizes only material needs, who realizes that men must have food for the body, but is oblivious of the necessity of providing food for the mind. If all men were well off, if poverty and disease had been reduced in their lowest possible point, there would still remain much to be done to produce a valuable society; and even in the existing world the goods of the mind are at least as important as the goods of the body. It is exclusively among the goods of the mind that the value of philosophy is to be found; and only those who are not indifferent to these goods can be persuaded that the study of philosophy is not a waste of time.

Philosophy, like all other studies, aims primarily at knowledge. The knowledge it aims at is the kind of knowledge which gives entity and system to the body of sciences, and the kind which results from a critical examination of the grounds of our convictions, prejudices, and beliefs. But it cannot be maintained that philosophy has had any very great measure of success in its attempts to provide definite answers

to its questions. If you ask a mathematician, a mineralogist, a historian, or any other man of learning, what definite body of truths has been ascertained by his science, his answer will last as long as you are willing to learn. But if you put the same question to a philosopher, he will, if he is candid, have to confess that his study has not achieved positive results such as have been achieved by other sciences. It is true that this is partly accounted for by the fact that, as soon as definite knowledge concerning any subject becomes possible, this subject ceases to be called philosophy, and becomes a separate science. The whole study of the heavens, which now belongs to astronomy, was once included in philosophy; Newton's great work was called the 'mathematical principles of natural philosophy'. Similarly, the study of the human mind, which was a part of philosophy, has now been separated from philosophy and has become the science of psychology. Thus, to a great extent, the uncertainty of philosophy is more apparent than real: those questions which are already capable of definite answers are placed in the sciences, while those only to which, at present, no definite answer can be given, remain to form the residue which is called philosophy.

This is, however, only a part of the truth concerning the uncertainty of philosophy. There are many questions—and among them those that are of the profoundest interest to our spiritual life—which, so far as we can see, must remain insoluble to the human intellect unless its powers become of quite a different order from what they are now. Has the universe any unity of plan or purpose, or is it a fortuitous concourse of atoms? Is consciousness a permanent part of the universe, giving home of indefinite growth in wisdom, or is it a transitory accident on a small planet on which life must ultimately become impossible? Are good and evil of importance to the universe or only to man? Such questions are asked by philosophy, and variously answered by various philosophers. But it would seem that, whether answers be otherwise discoverable or not, the answers suggested by philosophy are none of them demonstrably true. Yet, however slight may be the hope of discovering an answer, it is part of the business of philosophy to continue the consideration of such questions, to make us aware of their importance, to examine all the approaches to them, and to keep alive that speculative interest in the universe which is apt to be killed by confining ourselves to definitely ascertainable knowledge.

Many philosophers, it is true, have held that philosophy could establish the truth of certain answers to such fundamental questions. They have supposed that what is of more importance in religious beliefs could be proved by strict demonstration to be true. In order to judge of such attempts, it is necessary to take a survey of human knowledge, and to form an opinion as to its methods and its limitations. On such a subject it would be unwise to pronounce dogmatically; but if the investigations of our previous chapters have not led us astray, we shall be compelled to renounce the hope of finding philosophical proofs of religious beliefs. We cannot, therefore, include as part of the value of philosophy any definite set of answers to such questions. Hence, once more, the value of philosophy must not depend upon any supposed body of definitely ascertainable knowledge to be acquired by those who study it.

The value of philosophy is, in fact, to be sought largely in its very uncertainty. The man who has no tincture of philosophy goes through life imprisoned in the prejudices derived from common sense, from the habitual beliefs of his age or his nation, and from convictions which have grown up in his mind without the co-operation or consent of his deliberate reason. To such a man the world tends to become definite, finite, obvious; common objects rouse no questions, and unfamiliar possibilities are contemptuously rejected. As soon as we begin to philosophize, on the contrary, we find, as we saw in our opening chapters, that even the most everyday things lead to problems to which only very incomplete answers can be given. Philosophy, though unable to tell us with certainty what is the true answer to the doubts which it raises, is able to suggest many possibilities which enlarge our thoughts and free them from the tyranny of custom. Thus, while diminishing our feeling of certainty as to what things are, it greatly increases our knowledge as to what they may be; it removes the somewhat arrogant dogmatism of those who have never travelled into the region of liberating doubt, and it keeps alive our sense of wonder by showing familiar things in an unfamiliar aspect.

Apart from its utility in showing unsuspecting possibilities, philosophy has a value—perhaps its chief value—through the greatness of the objects which it contemplates, and the freedom from narrow and personal aims resulting from this contemplation. The life of the instinctive man is shut up within the circle of his private interests: family and friends may be included, but the outer world is not regarded except as it may help or hinder what comes within the circle of instinctive wishes. In such a life there is something feverish and confined, in comparison with which the philosophic life is calm and free. The private world of instinctive interests is a small one, set in the midst of a great and powerful world which must, sooner or later, lay our private world in ruins. Unless we can so enlarge our interests as to include the whole outer world, we remain like a garrison in a beleaguered fortress, knowing that the enemy prevents escape and that ultimate surrender is inevitable. In such a life there is no peace, but a constant strife between the insistence of desire and the powerlessness of will. In one way or another, if our life is to be great and free, we must escape this prison and this strife.

One way of escape is by philosophic contemplation. Philosophic contemplation does not, in its widest survey, divide the universe into two hostile camps—friends and foes, helpful and hostile, good and bad—it views the whole impartially. Philosophic contemplation, when it is unalloyed, does not aim at proving that the rest of the universe is akin to man. All acquisition of knowledge is an enlargement of the Self, but this is enlargement in best attained when it is not directly sought. It is obtained when the desire for knowledge is alone operative, by a study which does not wish In advance that its objects should have this or that character, but adapts the Self to the characters which it finds in its objects. This enlargement of Self is not obtained when, taking the Self as it is, we try to show that the world is similar to this Self that knowledge of it is possible without any admission of what seems alien. The desire to prove this is a form of self-assertion and, like all self-assertion, it is an obstacle to the growth of Self which it desires, and of which the Self knows that it is capable. Self-assertion, in philosophic speculation as elsewhere, views the world as a means to its own ends; thus it makes the world of less account than Self, and the Self sets bounds to the greatness of its goods. In contemplation, on the contrary, we start from the not-Self, and through its greatness the boundaries of Self are enlarged; through the infinity of the universe the mind which contemplates it achieves some share in infinity.

For this reason greatness of soul is not fostered by those philosophies which assimilate the universe to Man. Knowledge is a form of union of Self and not-Self; like all union, it is impaired by dominion, and therefore by any attempt to force the universe into conformity with what we find in ourselves. There is a widespread philosophical tendency towards the view which tells us that Man is the measure of all things, that truth is man-made, that space and time and the world of universals are properties of the mind, and that, if there be anything not created by the mind, it is unknowable and of no account for us. This view, if our previous discussions were correct, is untrue; but in addition to being untrue, it has the effect of robbing philosophic contemplation of all that gives it value, since it fetters contemplation to self. What it calls knowledge is not a union with the not-Self, but a set of prejudices, habits, and desires, making an impenetrable veil between us and the world beyond. The man who finds pleasure in such a theory of knowledge is like the man who never leaves the domestic circle for fear his word might not be law.

The true philosophic contemplation, on the contrary, finds its satisfaction in every enlargement of the not-Self, in everything that magnifies the objects contemplated, and thereby the subject contemplating. Everything, in contemplation, that is personal or private, everything that depends upon habit, self-interest, or desire, distorts the object, and hence impairs the union which the intellect seeks. By thus making a barrier between subject and object, such personal and private things become a prison to the intellect. The free intellect will see as God might see, without a *here* and *now,* without hopes and fears, without the trammels of customary beliefs and traditional prejudices, calmly, dispassionately, in the sole and exclusive desire of knowledge—knowledge as impersonal, as purely contemplative, as it is possible for man to attain. Hence also the free intellect will value more the abstract and universal knowledge into which the accidents of private history do not enter, than the knowledge brought by the senses, and dependent, as such knowledge must be, upon an exclusive and personal point of view and a body whose sense-organs distort as much as they reveal.

The mind which has become accustomed to the freedom and impartiality of philosophic contemplation will preserve something of the same freedom and impartiality in the world of action and emotion. It will view its purposes and desires as part of the whole, with the absence of insistence that results from seeing them as infinitesimal fragments in a world of which all the rest is unaffected by one man's deeds. The impartiality which, in contemplation, is the unalloyed desire for truth, is the very same quality of mind which, in action, is justice, and in emotion is that universal love which can be given to all, and not only to those who are judged useful or admirable. Thus contemplation enlarges not only the object of our thoughts, but also the objects of our actions and our affections: it makes us citizens of the universe, not only of one walled city at war with all the rest. In this citizenship of the universe consists man's true freedom, and his liberation from the thraldom of narrow hopes and fears.

Thus, to sum up our discussion of the value of philosophy: Philosophy is to be studied, not for the sake of any definite answers to its questions, since no definite answers can, as a rule, be known to be true, but rather for the sake of the questions themselves; because these questions enlarge our conception of what is possible, enrich our intellectual imagination, and diminish the dogmatic assurance which closes the mind against speculation, but above all because, through the greatness of the universe which philosophy contemplates, the mind also is rendered great, and because capable of that union with the universe which constitutes its highest good.

Key Terms and Concepts

Argument
Analysis
Understanding self and others
Philosophy
Sophists
Instinctive man

Study Questions

1. What did Meletus, Anytus, and Lycon accuse Socrates of and why?
2. What did the oracle of Delphi say about Socrates?
3. Explain how Socrates tried to prove the oracle wrong. What was his discovery?
4. How does Socrates defend his course of life?
5. What, in Russell's view, is the value of philosophy?
6. Explain how the self can be enlarged through philosophical contemplation.
7. How does Russell describe the practical person?
8. What are the practical prejudices from which we must free ourselves? Why?
9. What is the chief value of philosophy?

Further Reading

Ahbel-Rappe, Sara, and Rachana Kamtekar. *A Companion to Socrates*. Malden, MA: Blackwell, 2006.

Copleston, Frederick. *A History of Philosophy Volume I: Greece and Rome*. New York: Image Books, 1946.

Ortega y Gasset, José. *What Is Philosophy?* New York: W. W. Norton & Company, Inc., 1960.

Rosenberg, Jay. *The Practice of Philosophy: A Handbook for Beginners*. 3rd ed. Upper Saddle River, NJ: Prentice Hall, 1996.

Stone, I. F. *The Trial of Socrates*. Boston: Little, Brown and Company, 1988.

Thompson, Samuel. *The Nature of Philosophy*. New York: Holt, Rienhart and Winston, Inc., 1961.

Internet Sources

Nails, Debra. "Socrates." *Stanford Encyclopaedia of Philosophy*. Ed. Edward Zalta. Stanford, CA: The Metaphysics Research Lab, 2005. 22 May 2007 <http://plato.stanford.edu/entries/epistemology>.

"The Last Days of Socrates." *Clarke College Philosophy Department*. n.d. 24 September 2007 <http://socrates.clarke.edu/index.htm>.

Notes

1. In ancient Greece, the word *apology* is translated as "defence." In the English language, *apology* means "to be sorry" or "to express regret." Socrates was not expressing regret about what he had done but merely defending himself from false accusations.

2. The Sophists were also relativists when it came to sense perception. Colour, taste, sound, texture, and smell were all relative or subjective to each individual.

Works Cited

Audi, Robert. "Philosophy: A Brief Guide for Undergraduates." *American Philosophical Association*. 28 August 2001. 14 July 2005 <http://www.apa.udel.edu/apa/publications/texts/briefgd.html>.

Copleston, Frederick. *A History of Philosophy: Greece and Rome*. Volume 1. New York: Bantam Doubleday Publishing Group, Inc., 1962.

Hoekema, David. "Issues in the Profession: Why Major in Philosophy?" *Proceedings and Addresses of the American Philosophical Association* 59 (1986): 601–607.

Hurka, Thomas. "How to Get to the Top—Study Philosophy." *Globe and Mail*, 2 January 1990: A8.

Mallick, Heather. "Why Doesn't This Man Have the Order of Canada?" *Globe and Mail*, 18 January 2003: F1.

Nieswiadomy, Michael. "LSAT Scores of Economics Majors." *Journal of Economic Education* 29 (1998): 377–379.

Pojman, Louie. *Ethics: Discovering Right and Wrong*. Belmont, CA: Wadsworth Publishing Company, 1995.

Rachels, James. *The Elements of Moral Philosophy*. 2nd ed. New York: McGraw Hill, Inc., 1993.

"Think On: Philosophy Is the Quintessentially Modern Discipline." *The Times*, 15 August 1998, Factiva. Mackimmie Lib, Calgary, AB. 29 Dec. 2005 <http://global.factiva.com.ezproxy.lib.ucalgary.ca/ha/default.aspx; http://www.cep.unt.edu/times.html>.

United Nations. *Human Development Index: 2005*. 19 July 2005 <http://hdr.undp.org/statistics/data/indic/indic_5_1_1.html>.

Webster's College Dictionary. New York: Random House, 1991.

Chapter 2 Ways of Knowing

Knowledge of what is does not open the door directly to what should be.

— Albert Einstein

Knowledge is true opinion.

— Plato

We will start our philosophical journey by looking at one of the most intriguing areas of philosophy, known as **epistemology**. The term *epistemology* comes from the Greek words *episteme*, meaning knowledge, and *logos*, meaning rational discourse. In short, epistemology is the philosophy of knowledge. Epistemologists usually focus their efforts on solving three important questions:

1. What is knowledge?
2. Can we know anything at all?
3. How do we obtain knowledge?

Before we start with the first question, consider Box 2.1.

What is knowledge? People claim to know many things often without realizing that there are different kinds of knowledge. Consider the following list:

1. I know that I had cereal for breakfast.
2. I know that my foot hurts.
3. I know that I am sitting in front of a computer screen.
4. I know how to dance.
5. I know how to speak French.
6. I know how to ride a bike.
7. I know that John A. Macdonald was Canada's first prime minister.
8. I know that the earth is approximately four billion years old.
9. I know that $2 + 3 = 5$.

How do the above knowledge statements differ from one another? Well, if you look

---

Box 2.1 Ten Things I Know *For Sure*

During your school years, you learned many things. Perhaps you know how to speak French, solve mathematical problems, play chess, or, perhaps, you won medals for track, worked part-time, and so forth. Make a list of ten things you know *for sure*, and then write down beside each item how you might *prove* that you know these things with absolute certainty.

1.

2.

3.

4.

5.

6.

7.

8.

9.

10.

closely, you will see that they can be broken into three general types. The first type is **knowledge by acquaintance**. Knowledge by acquaintance is based on direct experience (statements 1–3). I know that my foot hurts, for example, because I directly experienced stubbing my toe last night. The second type is **competence knowledge** or *knowing how* (statements 4–6). Knowing how to dance or speak French is a skill acquired over time through training. Such skills are not innate; one must train the mind/body to think/move in specific ways. **Propositional knowledge** or *knowing that*, the third type, is usually based on having information about some fact (statements 7–9). I know that the earth is approximately four billion years old because geology books say so. Philosophers are usually concerned with the first and third types of claims because they underscore some of the conditions necessary to have knowledge.

Traditionally, there are three conditions for having knowledge. The first condition for knowledge is **truth**. If S knows that P, then P must be *true*. For example, if Fred knows that John A. Macdonald was Canada's first prime minister, then it must be true that John A. Macdonald was the first prime minister of Canada. If it turns out that Fred's claim is false, it can scarcely be said that Fred *knows* that John A. Macdonald was the prime minister. In short, what is false cannot be known.

The second condition for knowledge is **belief**. If S knows that P, then P must not only be *true* but S must *believe* P to be true (see Box 2.2). It would be very odd indeed if someone were to say, "I know that 2 + 3 = 5, but I do not believe it." Of course, there are cases of disbelief where the truth is denied. For example, Londoners might exclaim, "I know terrorists killed 52 people in London on July 7, 2005, but I don't believe it!" Being thunderstruck is different from not believing that the event took place. In this sense, knowledge implies belief. However, the reverse is not true. Just because you believe something, it does not imply that it's true and, therefore, that you have knowledge. After all, people believe many things, some more suspect than others. Many people believe in God and some people believe in witches and ghosts,

> ## Box 2.2 What Do You Believe In?
>
> Give five answers to this question: What do you believe in? Do you believe that love conquers all; that family and friends are most important; that equal rights is the foundation of democracy; or that Wayne Gretzky was the best hockey player in National Hockey League history? How can you *prove* that the beliefs you list are true?
>
> 1.
> 2.
> 3.
> 4.
> 5.

but this does not mean they know these things exist. Or consider someone who believes that Elvis is alive. Most of us would consider this belief highly suspect because of the speculations (such as a wax dummy in his coffin) used to support this opinion. In this sense, the connection between belief and truth is, at times, tenuous. But even cases of true belief are not sufficient for knowledge. Consider playing the stock market. If someone believes that a specific stock will go up in price, there is no guarantee it will. If S believes X's stock will go up, and it does not, S cannot be said to have knowledge of this fact, since false belief is not part of the definition of knowledge. However, if S believes X's stock will go up, and it does (i.e., it's true), we would still be hard pressed to say that S *knew* X's stock would go up. Correctly guessing is not the same as knowledge. In other words, beliefs that turn out to be true because of luck cannot be knowledge. True belief alone does not imply knowledge.

So the third condition of knowledge, as hinted at above, is **justification**. Knowledge statements must not only be true, they must also be believed and supported or justified by evidence, data, facts, experience, and so forth. Consider some of my previous examples. I know I am in pain because I stubbed my toe. In this sense, my knowledge of pain is intimately subjective. I do not have to infer I am in pain; I know this via my experience. However, if someone were to doubt that I am in pain because I am a hypochondriac, I could appeal to the blood on my sock and scuff on the table leg as evidence to support my claim. That is, unless my friend has reason to believe I concocted the evidence, he would be remiss not to believe me. However, the claim that John A. Macdonald was Canada's first prime minister is harder to justify. Since he died in 1891, I have never met John A. Macdonald, shaken his hand, or talked to him on the phone; I have, however, seen stories about him on TV and read about him in the newspapers and history books. Would this be sufficient justification to support my claim? Yes, it would. There is no reason to suspect that the media in all its forms (TV, newspapers, Internet, etc.) has engaged in an elaborate scheme of deception to trick me into falsely believing this claim. And if someone were to ask me how I know that John A. Macdonald was Canada's first prime minister, I can produce countless books, TV programs, historical documents, and so on to justify my statement. Knowledge claims require evidence; the more evidence a person has to support a belief, the stronger the possibility that the claim will be true. Many of our propositional knowledge claims come from sources outside our immediate experience and must be assumed to be true. But we can always check knowledge claims against evidence and other forms of justification to ensure their truth.

Taking the three criteria together, we can formulate a definition of knowledge: *Knowledge is true justified belief.* Beliefs must be true and justified in order to have knowledge.

However, there are problems with the traditional account of knowledge. Let me raise two concerns. First, is belief really a condition of knowledge? Consider this counter-example showing that belief is not a necessary condition of knowledge. A student in a Canadian history class has been taught that the Dieppe raid took place on the beaches of France during the Second World War on August 19, 1942. In the next class, the same student is asked by her teacher the date

of the Battle of Dieppe. Lacking confidence that she believes this is correct, and starting to panic, the only date that comes to her mind is August 19, 1942. It seems the student knows when the Battle of Dieppe took place, since she responded correctly to the teacher's question. However, if pressed by her teacher if she *believes* the date is correct, she may deny it. If so, the student has knowledge, but does not think she does, and therefore has knowledge but not the belief. And if knowledge without belief is possible, then a person does not necessarily have to fulfill the three criteria in order to have knowledge.

Second, is it possible for someone to have a true justified belief, yet not have knowledge? Edmund Gettier, in his classic paper "Is Justified True Belief Knowledge?", thinks it is possible. Consider this example.[1] Sally is watching on TV the last stage of the Tour de France and witnesses Lance Armstrong, the American cyclist, winning the gruelling race. Sally believes justifiably: (1) I have just seen Armstrong win the Tour de France and infers (2) Armstrong is this year's Tour de France winner. However, things are not as they appear. Satellite troubles have made transmission of this year's race impossible. To keep viewers happy, the television station replays a recording of a previous Tour de France which Armstrong also won. So while Sally sits watching what she thinks is this year's race, she is witness to a repeat broadcast. But as she watches, Armstrong, in reality, is cycling to victory in Paris. So Sally's true belief that Armstrong is this year's winner of the Tour de France is surely justified, but we would be hard pressed to conclude that she knows Armstrong is this year's winner. In short, here we have a case where true justified belief does not equal knowledge. This is known as the Gettier problem. The Gettier problem is significant since the point of justifying true beliefs was to avoid beliefs being true via epistemic luck. In other words, Gettier has shown there to be a major defect in the tripartite account of knowledge.

Despite these problems, if justification is a necessary condition for any theory of knowledge, it also raises other important philosophical questions: Is experience a reliable justification for our beliefs? How much justification is sufficient for knowledge? Do beliefs have to be absolutely certain in order to count as knowledge? These are just some of the questions we will try to answer in this chapter (see Boxes 2.3 and 2.4).

Can we know anything at all? As discussed previously, justification is supposed to be a necessary condition of any knowledge claim. The problem is that if justification is the linchpin

to having knowledge, when justification is called into doubt, so too is knowledge. And the justification of true beliefs can be thrown into doubt in numerous ways. Our senses, for example, can deceive us in subtle and surprising ways. An oar placed in water looks bent, water appears on highways when travelling on hot summers days, and railway tracks appear to converge into a point when viewed at ground level.

Box 2.3 Is Creationism True Justified Belief?

In June 2007, a small Alberta town opened the Big Valley Creation Museum. The museum is devoted to debunking the traditional conflict between evolution and creationism. According to the owner, evolution is false; humans, life, the earth, and the universe did not evolve due to natural scientific process but was created by God. Contrary to geological records that show the earth to be around 4.5 billion years old, the Alberta creation museum contends the earth is only 6000 years old and, moreover, humans and dinosaurs inhabited the earth together (Harding A1). The Big Valley Creation Museum opened on the heels of the much larger Creation Museum in Petersburg, Kentucky. Costing $27 million, the Creation Museum, like the museum in Alberta, argues that the Book of Genesis is literally true and scientifically accurate (Ibbitson A1). This kind of creationism should not be confused with theistic evolution. Theist evolution supports the idea that evolution and God are compatible and that the evolutionary process is part of God's creation. Both museums hold stronger beliefs systems based on a literal interpretation of the Bible. Is belief in creationism justifiable? What evidence, scientific or otherwise, might provide justification for or against such a view? Can we consider creationism knowledge?

Box 2.4 What Do You Think?

July 20, 1969, was a monumental day for humankind. It was the day that Apollo 11 landed on the moon. Some conspiracy theorists, however, believe that the lunar landing was a hoax. Neil Armstrong's walk on the moon, the planting of the American flag, driving of the moon buggy, and so on, were all faked. The moon landing was really an elaborate Hollywood production (a bad one at that) aimed at winning the space race between the United States and Russia during the 1960s. Two examples are often used to support this hoax. The first example claims that pictures of earth taken by the astronauts do not reveal any visible stars. If astronauts were really on the moon taking pictures of the earth, say critics, then we should see stars around the earth similar to when we look at the night sky and see stars around the moon. The second example is the fluttering flag. An American flag was planted on the moon to celebrate the landing. Pictures and film reveal that it rippled and waved back and forth. Now, since the moon has no atmosphere, this should be impossible. The only explanation is that the flag was planted on the earth, not the moon. Again, for conspiracy theorists, these are just two examples justifying their beliefs (knowledge?) that the moon landing was a hoax.

Is the moon landing a hoax? Is there sufficient justification to show beliefs about the moon landing are true/false? What do you think?[2]

Although adults are usually not fooled by these examples, children can be. A more mundane example is shopping. If store lighting is poor, people can be fooled into believing they are buying black trousers when it actual fact they are dark blue. A famous example of faulty perception is the Muller-Lyer illusion below. Which of these horizontal lines is longer?

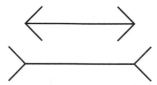

Both lines are exactly the same length but many people are fooled into thinking the bottom one is longer than the other. Or consider Wittgenstein's example below: Do you see a duck or a rabbit?

These examples raise doubts about perception as a means of justifying our beliefs. The problem is that how we perceive the world is not necessarily how the world actually *is*; appearance can differ from reality. And if our senses have deceived us even once, perhaps it is prudent not to trust them at all. This is known as **scepticism**. For the sceptic, doubt is a pervasive cancer eating away at the justification of our beliefs until all knowledge claims are suspect. No belief is beyond critique; there is always the possibility of error. Doubt is not merely a logical possibility but a genuine fact; there is always the chance that you do not know what you think you know (Lehrer, *Theory of Knowledge* 177). For

example, nestled in the bosom of common sense, most people would claim they are sitting reading this book. But are you? It's possible that you are dreaming, hallucinating, or being deceived by an evil demon into thinking that you are reading this book when, in fact, you are not. After all, our senses are imperfect. The empirical sciences are also not immune from doubt. The claim that the earth is four billion years old could turn out to be false. Scientists may discover the earth is six billion years old, two billion years older than originally thought. For sceptics, all justified true beliefs are questionable, which means there is no such thing as genuine knowledge.

But we should be careful here. It's important to make a distinction between local and global scepticism (Pojman 151). A **global sceptic** argues that knowledge is impossible; there is no indubitable knowledge at all.[3] This kind of deep scepticism permeates all forms of justification. A **local sceptic**, in contrast, argues that only certain types of knowledge are insufficiently justified and, therefore, open to doubt, such as the existence of God, knowledge of other minds, objective moral truths, and so forth. Other obvious forms of knowledge, however, such as reading this book, are insulated from doubt. The problem is that local scepticism can collapse into global scepticism. Once we start to question the justification process of specific issues, it quickly contaminates more innocuous beliefs. Defeating global scepticism will be one of the primary objectives in this chapter, since failure to do so has dire consequences for all human knowledge.

Students are usually quick to point out the self-refuting character of scepticism. The sceptic cannot claim there is no knowledge without making a knowledge claim. This lands the sceptic into a self-refuting position. But the sceptic can avoid this problem by merely claiming no more than they *strongly believe* there is no knowledge. This would put the sceptic on par with everyone else. In just the same way the sceptic forces us to accept the possibility of error regarding knowledge, he or she must also accept the possibility of error regarding scepticism itself.

However, most people are not global sceptics and, perhaps, the criterion for knowledge is too strong. An alternative to the standard definition of knowledge is **reliablism**. This type of epistemological theory suggests that a belief qualifies as true so long as the person has reason to believe it is true. It's the link between a belief and truth that is important, not its justification. So, for example, I know that John A. Macdonald was Canada's first prime minister because I believe it's true. And I believe it's true because I read it in a history book. Although there is no guarantee of truth, so long as the process by which I acquired my belief is reliable, then I am justified in my belief. For Alvin Goldman, one of the strongest proponents of reliablism, ". . . beliefs produced or preserved by perception, memory, introspection, and 'good' reasoning are justified, whereas beliefs produced by hunch, wishful thinking, or 'bad' reasoning are unjustified"("Reliablism" 693). If correct, then it's fair to say that most of our true beliefs will count as knowledge so long as the belief forming process is adequate.[4]

Our third, and last, important question to be explored in this chapter: How do humans obtain knowledge?

Traditionally, answering this question is broken into two camps: empiricism and rationalism. According to **empiricists** like John Locke, George Berkeley, and David Hume, all knowledge is derived from experience—through the five senses (*a posteriori*). For Locke, the infant mind is akin to a blank canvas or slate (*tabula rasa*) awaiting experience to paint its unique picture. All knowledge is gleaned over a lifetime and is the result of experience, nothing else. For Sally, knowing a red apple is on her desk is the product of directly seeing the red apple. The apple causes her to have the belief and also justifies her belief by virtue of this experience. Notice that the natural sciences also take an empiricist strategy. In order to know at what temperature lead melts, for example, scientists conduct experiments, directly observing and measuring various factors. However, for some sciences, like palaeontology, knowledge claims are inferential, i.e., not based on direct experience. Despite the fact that dinosaurs became extinct millions of years ago, palaeontologists know a lot about dinosaurs by making inferences based on collecting and observing remaining skeletons. Both direct and inferential knowledge claims are supported by the empiricist strategy, and any beliefs that cannot be confirmed or falsified in this way are suspect. This means empirical knowledge is contingent. It's always possible that empirical knowledge will end up false or mistaken if new evidence comes to light.

Rationalists like René Descartes, in contrast, argue that certain general propositions are known to be true or false in advance of experience or empirical verification. To put another way, reason and the intellect is the only source of knowledge (*a priori*). We can have knowledge about something without seeing, touching, hearing, tasting, or smelling it. Although rationalism for many students is counterintuitive, let's consider some examples. According to the United Nations' Declaration of Human Rights[5] all humans have fundamental rights and freedoms regardless of race, national identity, colour, sex, language, religion, property, birth, or political affiliation. Some of these rights include the following:

- Right to life, liberty, and security
- Right not to be tortured or subjected to cruel, inhuman, or degrading treatment or punishment
- Right to be treated equally under the law without discrimination
- Right not to be arbitrarily arrested, detained, or exiled
- Right to a nationality
- Right to own property
- Right to freedom of association and peaceful assembly

So how do we know all humans have these rights? It's doubtful that rights can be known through experience the same way skydiving or riding a motorcycle can be experienced. Rights can't be discovered by laboratory experiments and giving blood to the Red Cross does not drain a person of their rights. Rights are intangible, cannot be experienced, and yet they exist. We know they exist, not due to our senses, but due to the mind and reason alone—*a priori*. To be a human being is all that is necessary to have these fundamental rights. To be a human, by definition, is to have these rights.

Consider some other examples of rationalist knowledge:

• All triangles have three sides.
• All dogs are animals.
• All bachelors are unmarried males.

We can know each of these statements *a priori* without having to refer to any specific experience of triangles, dogs, or bachelors. Scientists don't have to experiment or go on a field trip to know that all triangles have three sides, dogs are animals, or bachelors are unmarried males. These knowledge claims are true by definition. A triangle by definition has three sides; a dog by definition is an animal; and a bachelor by definition is an unmarried male. In other words, so long as we know via our mind and reason what triangles, dogs, and bachelors are, then we must necessarily know that they have three sides, are animals, and are unmarried males, respectively.

At this point, students usually point out an obvious problem. Surely, they say, we must experience triangles, dogs, and bachelors in order to learn such concepts. If so, then *a priori* knowledge is mistaken; it's really based on experience.

Although it is true most children will learn about triangles, dogs, and bachelors by seeing them, touching them, or hearing them, experiencing all triangles, dogs, or bachelors is not necessary to know these things. In this sense, we can know *a priori* these claims by reason and understanding alone.

Closely tied to the idea of *a priori* is the notion of **necessary truth**. A necessary truth means that it's not logically possible that a given sentence could be false. It's not logically possible for a dog not to be an animal or a bachelor not to be an unmarried male because this would contradict their very definitions. In contrast, a proposition is a **contingent truth** if its truth depends on how the world actually is. So if someone claims that "Madonna has sold more records than Britney Spears," the truth of this statement is dependent upon whether Madonna has *actually* sold more records (Rauhut 76–77). And we can verify such a claim by checking record sales *a posteriori*. Other contingent truths include "Calgary has a current population over 1 million" and "New Delhi is the capital of India." In other words, if there is a logical possibility that a sentence could be false, it's a contingent truth. It is possible, then, given changes in circumstances and history, that both these claims could be false. So, generally speaking, where *a priori* knowledge is necessarily true, *a posteriori* knowledge is contingently true (see Box 2.5).

Box 2.5 The Distinction between Analytic and Synthetic

A distinction closely related to necessary and contingent truths is that between analytic and synthetic truths. An **analytic truth** is a sentence being true merely by definition. So, for example, the statement "all bachelors are unmarried men" is true simply by analyzing the meaning of the words. After all, *bachelor* means "unmarried man." No observation or sensory experience is necessary to know analytic statements are true; we know *a priori*—by thinking about the meaning of the words themselves. In contrast, the statement "Ottawa is the capital of Canada" is a **synthetic truth**. No mere analysis of the words will determine whether the statement is true or false. The truth of "Ottawa is the capital of Canada" is dependent upon observation and experience. In this sense, such statements are contingent. The problem with analytic statements, as outlined by the Logical Positivists in the 1930s, is that they are trivially true. Analytic statements don't give us any new information about the world with which we can acquire knowledge; they merely give us trivial information about how to use language. If true, then *a priori* reasoning may be helpful in sorting out analytic truths, but it cannot be the key to knowledge as rationalists suggest.

Having laid out some general problems and definitions, this chapter starts by looking at the problem of scepticism. Can we know anything at all?

Scepticism and Rationalism

The path of sound credence is through the thick forest of skepticism.
— George Jean Nathan

All men are born with a nose and ten fingers, but no one was born with a knowledge of God.
— Voltaire

Discussion Questions

1. How do you know that you are not a brain in a vat or in a computer network as claimed in the movie *The Matrix*? How do you know that your life and your experiences are not the result of some supercomputer tricking you into believing a reality that is entirely false?

2. Descartes instructs us to doubt all of our beliefs. What are some of the obstacles to doubting all our beliefs as he suggests?

3. Are dreams really so similar to our waking experiences that we cannot distinguish between them? How would you distinguish a dream from reality?

4. If you cannot doubt the existence of your mind, but can doubt the existence of your body, does this mean you are nothing but a mind—a thinking thing? Why or why not?

No Knowledge Please, We're Sceptics

The Matrix highlights the perennial problem of scepticism. Released in 1999, *The Matrix* instantly became a cult classic. Its status was due in part to its spectacular special effects, for which it won an Oscar, but most importantly the movie's philosophical references make it so interesting. Thomas Anderson (played by Canadian actor Keanu Reeves) leads a relatively normal life as a software programmer during the day and computer hacker at night under the alias Neo. Anderson, like many people, suffers from the daily grind of life—getting up, going to work, paying a seeming endless array of bills, and, generally, trying to be happy. But this all changes when Anderson, through a series of events, makes contact with Morpheus (Laurence Fishburne) and a small band of followers. Morpheus explains that Anderson's world—his reality, his life—is not what it appears. It's fake! Perceived reality is a dream created in an artificial world called the Matrix. Disbelieving at first, Anderson is given a choice of learning the truth about his world. In accepting the truth, he is suddenly pulled from his false reality into the real world. It turns out the year is not 1999, but two hundred years into the future. Humans are fighting a war against intelligent machines. In order to keep the human population docile, the machines created an artificial reality for them. All experiences, sensations, memories, thoughts, and so forth, are merely part of a computer program designed to make us believe (falsely) that we are living normal, productive lives. In truth, humans are connected to machines, kept subdued, and used as a power source. Leaving the details aside, the movie raises important philosophical questions: How do you know that the world you are experiencing right now is not merely the product of computer simulation? If you cannot be sure if you are experiencing the real world or a computer-simulated world, does it lay waste to knowledge generally (true justified belief)? A sceptic would argue that justifying true beliefs via experience is impossible under a *Matrix* scenario. If there is no way to distinguish between reality and a false, computer-generated world, then taken to its natural conclusion, there is not such thing as knowledge at all.

John Pollock draws a similar sceptical conclusion regarding knowledge using the now-famous "Brain in a Vat" thought experiment.[6] It's wonderfully summarized below:

> You do not know that you are not a brain, suspended in a vat full of liquid in a laboratory, and wired to a computer which is feeding your current experiences under the control of some ingenious technician/scientist (benevolent or malevolent according

to taste). For if you were such a brain, then, provided that the scientist is successful, nothing in your experience could possibly reveal that you were; for your experience is *ex hypothesi* identical with that of something which is not a brain in a vat. Since you have only your own experiences to appeal to, and that experience is the same in either situation, nothing can reveal to you which situation is the actual one. (Dancy 10)

If your experiences cannot reveal to you whether you are in the real world or a world of computer simulation, your beliefs cannot be justified, and, therefore, you cannot have knowledge. All beliefs are suspect, cannot be justified, and thus scepticism wins the day.

Descartes' Methodological Scepticism: The Road to Doubt

The roots of *The Matrix* can be traced back to the scepticism of the seventeenth-century philosopher René Descartes. However, to understand Descartes' scepticism, we must first understand the environment in which he lived. Up until the seventeenth century, the traditional view of the universe was geocentric or earth-centred. It was believed that God placed humans at the centre of the universe as part of an hierarchically ordered divine plan that could be understood only through prayer and devotion. The Scientific Revolution of the 1600s ushered in a radically different cosmology based on a heliocentric or sun-centred universe. The idea of a heliocentric universe was first proposed by Nicholas Copernicus in 1453, but it was not given significant support until Galileo Galilei, a contemporary of Descartes, discovered the moons of Jupiter in 1610. This idea sent shockwaves throughout the religious establishment of the time because it directly contradicted the Bible. Stars, planets, and the earth could be explained via mathematics/science and ceased to have spiritual meaning and purpose. The earth was merely another celestial body hurtling through space with no special significance or place in the universe. The broader implication

was that reason, science, and mathematics are the routes to knowledge, not prayer and devotion to God. And if we take heliocentric cosmology to its natural conclusion, it implies that God does not exist. Although most people during the 1600s would reject such atheistic conclusions, Galileo's scientific discoveries ushered in an important shift in thinking about the universe and our place in it. This kind of scientific thinking did not impress the seventeenth-century religious authorities; in fact, they imprisoned Galileo (house arrest) in 1633 for teaching geocentric cosmology.[7]

For Descartes, the scientific discoveries during the seventeenth century had a significant impact on him as a philosopher. Filled with doubt about universe and God, Descartes turned to philosophy for certain knowledge in hopes to build a system of knowledge based on human reason alone. A rationalistic account of knowledge, thought Descartes, would not only withstand the fiercest scepticism but also provide a foundation for his scientific claims. It was through Descartes' *Meditations on First Philosophy* that he intended to tear down the edifice of knowledge and rebuild it upon a foundation of indubitable and certain knowledge. To do this Descartes used scepticism. Descartes was not at heart a sceptic but merely used scepticism as a tool to determine which beliefs were absolutely certain. His method of doubt is known as **methodological scepticism**. Descartes didn't subjugate every belief to the rigours of scepticism, only the foundations of knowledge itself. Like a house of cards, once the foundation is disturbed, the whole edifice of knowledge would collapse. And whatever belief remained standing would be known indubitably and create a new foundation for his system of knowledge. But first, we must subject our beliefs to an acid bath of scepticism.

Cogito Ergo Sum

Descartes outlined three sceptical arguments: doubt of the senses, dream argument, and the evil demon argument. First, Descartes observes that our senses are not always trustworthy. Consider my previous examples: an oar placed in water will look bent, water appears on highways on hot summer days, and if you squat down on railway tracks, they appear to converge into a single point. Although these illusions usually don't fool adults, many of us as children were fooled. And for Descartes, if our senses have ever deceived us once (even as children), they cannot be trusted as a foundation for knowledge. Second, Descartes acknowledges that sometimes dreams are so real they cannot be distinguished from our waking experiences. For example, many of us have had the terrifying dream of falling off a building or cliff. However, once we wake up, we realize it's only a dream; but at the precise moment of terror, it's very hard to distinguish it from reality. If we cannot distinguish our waking experiences from a dream, then our current perceptual beliefs are not immune from doubt. That is, our ordinary perceptual knowledge is undermined if we cannot rule out the possibility that we are dreaming. Finally, Descartes puts forward his evil demon argument, which is comparable to the brain in a vat scenario. The creator of the universe may not be a benevolent God but an evil genius, a malevolent demon whose sole purpose is to deceive our senses and our knowledge of the simplest of mathematical judgments (e.g., $2 + 2 = 4$). If Descartes is right, then the foundation of all our beliefs is compromised, dubitable, and uncertain. In short, we cannot have any knowledge at all.

In the Second Meditation, Descartes makes an important rationalist discovery: he is a thinking thing. I think, therefore I am (*cogito ergo sum*). He comes to this conclusion through his sceptical arguments. If he tries to doubt that he doubts, then he is necessarily confirming in fact that he doubts, that he is thinking and, therefore, exists. So even if his senses deceive him, he cannot distinguish between dreams and reality, or there exists a deceptive evil demon, he knows he doubts, which can only occur if he exists. Try this yourself by saying, "I doubt that I have a mind." You cannot doubt that you have a mind without contradiction, since doubting is an activity of the mind itself (thinking). In short, "I think, therefore I am" is a necessary truth. In contrast, the statement "I doubt that I have

a body" is a contingent truth since it's a possibility that I may exist without a body (reincarnation, for example). Descartes is arguing that whenever someone asserts, doubts, or wills, for example, it entails someone doing the asserting, doubting, or willing. That is, it entails a mind and, therefore, existence (see Box 2.6).

But this leaves Descartes' philosophy suffering from what is known as *solipsism*. Solipsism is an extreme form of epistemology that refuses to acknowledge the existence of anything other than one's own mind. So how does Descartes know he is a thinking being? Descartes arrives at this conclusion via reason itself. In short, the foundation of all knowledge is *a priori*. To see this, consider an variation of Descartes' famous wax example. Wanting to impress a hot date, you make a nice dinner, buy flowers, open a bottle of wine, and light a beeswax candle. As you set the candle in place you notice that the wax still smells like the flowers from which it was gathered; it's hard and a bit sticky; and as you put it into the candleholder, it makes a sound. You and your date have a wonderful time. As you clean the dishes, you notice the candle has melted; it

---

Box 2.6 Descartes Humour

Rene Descartes walks into a restaurant and sits down for dinner. When the waiter comes over, he asks if Descartes would like an appetizer.

"No, thank you," replies Descartes, "I'd just like to order dinner."

"Would you like to hear our daily specials?" continues the waiter.

"No," says Descartes, getting impatient.

"Would you like a drink before dinner?" the waiter asks.

Descartes is insulted, since he's a teetotaller. "I think not!" he replies indignantly, and POOF! he disappears.

Source: Many variations of this joke exist, including this version found on the website of David Chalmers. 21 May 2007 <http://consc.net/misc/descartes.html>.

no longer retains its scent; it's liquid and runny, and no longer makes a sound. Despite having a few glasses of wine, you probably wouldn't deny it is the same candle. It might have changed shape, but it's the same piece of wax, isn't it? How do you know it's the same piece of wax? For Descartes, we know it's the same piece of wax, not through our senses, since the properties of the wax that we initially relied on are no longer the same or have vanished completely, but though pure mental perception. We know it's the same piece of wax with our mind alone. And if we can know that it's the same piece of wax via reason, we can surely know that we exist more clearly and distinctly through the mind, as a thinking being, than through the senses, as a physical being. Thus, Descartes concludes, knowledge is grasped by the mind, not the senses.

3

René Descartes

(1596–1650)

René Descartes was born on March 31, 1596, in the small town of La Heye en Tourain (later renamed "Le Heye-Descartes" in 1802 and renamed, once again, "Descartes" in 1967). At the age of ten, Descartes' father sent him to the Jesuit college in La Fleche, one of the leading academic schools in Europe. Descartes went on to study law at the University of Poitiers, graduating in 1616. He never practised law; instead, at the age of 22, he enlisted

in the army of Prince Nassau. It's speculated that Descartes was part of the engineering corps and unlikely saw combat. But it was during a tour of duty in Germany (1619) that Descartes had an epiphany. It occurred to him that a new system of mathematics and science could be developed based on human reason alone. After this awakening, Descartes left the army, pursuing a life of pleasure (travelling, gambling, and duelling). In 1628, he left for Holland to fulfill his vision of a rational science. His time in Holland was particularly fruitful, as he published Discourse on Method *(1637),* Meditations on First Philosophy *(1641),* Principles of Philosophy *(1644), and* The Passions of the Soul *(1649). Descartes' philosophical views made him quite famous. One admirer was Queen Christina of Sweden. In 1649, she invited Descartes to come to Sweden as her personal tutor. Feeling obligated, Descartes reluctantly accepted. However, Queen Cristina demanded that her tutorials be held at 5:00 a.m. for five hours, three days a week. Descartes, who suffered from a delicate constitution, habitually worked from bed until noon every day. Queen Christian's early hours and the cold climate of Sweden played havoc with his health. The tutoring sessions wore him down, eventually resulting in severe pneumonia. After suffering for a week, Descartes died on February 11, 1650.*

Meditations on First Philosophy

Meditation One: Concerning Those Things That Can Be Called into Doubt

Several years have now passed since I first realized how many were the false opinions that in my youth I took to be true, and thus how doubtful were all the things that I subsequently built upon those opinions. From the time I became aware of this, I realized that for once I had to raze everything in my life, down to the very bottom, so as to begin again from the first foundations, if I wanted to establish anything firm and lasting in the sciences. But the task seemed so enormous that I waited for a point in my life that was so ripe that no more suitable a time for laying hold of these disciplines would come to pass. For this reason, I have delayed so long that I would be at fault were I to waste on deliberation the time that was left for action. Therefore, now that I have freed my mind from all cares, and I have secured for myself some leisurely and carefree time, I withdraw in solitude. I will, in short, apply myself earnestly and openly to the general destruction of my former opinions.

Yet to this end it will not be necessary that I show that all my opinions are false, which perhaps I could never accomplish anyway. But because reason now persuades me that I should withhold my assent no less carefully from things which are not plainly certain and indubitable than I would to what is patently false, it will be sufficient justification for rejecting them all, if I find a reason for doubting even the least of them. Nor therefore need one survey each opinion one after the other, a task of endless proportion. Rather—because undermining the foundations will cause whatever has been built upon them to fall down of its own accord—I will at once attack those principles which supported everything that I once believed.

Whatever I had admitted until now as most true I took in either from the senses or through the senses; however, I noticed that they sometimes deceived me. And it is a mark of prudence never to trust wholly in those things which have once deceived us.

But perhaps, although the senses sometimes deceive us when it is a question of very small and distant things, still there are many other matters which one certainly cannot doubt, although they are derived from the very same senses; that I am sitting here before the fireplace wearing my dressing gown, that I feel this sheet of paper in my hands, and so on. But how could one deny that these hands and that my whole body exist? Unless perhaps I should compare myself to insane people whose brains are so impaired by a stubborn vapor from a black bile that they continually insist that they are kings when they are in utter poverty, or that they are wearing purple robes when they are naked, or that they have a head made of clay, or that they are gourds, or that they are made of glass. But they are all demented, and I would appear no less demented if I were to take their conduct as a model for myself.

All of this would be well and good, were I not a man who is accustomed to sleeping at night, and to undergoing in my sleep the very same things—or now and then even less likely ones—as do these insane people when they are awake. How often has my evening slumber persuaded me of such customary things as these: that I am here, clothed in my dressing gown, seated at the fireplace, when in fact I am lying undressed between the blankets! But right now I certainly am gazing upon this piece of paper with eyes wide awake. This head which I am moving is not heavy with sleep. I extend this hand consciously and deliberately and I feel it. These things would not be so distinct for one who is asleep. But this all seems as if I do not recall having been deceived by similar thoughts on other occasions in my dreams. As I consider these cases more intently, I see so plainly that there are no definite signs to distinguish being awake from being asleep that I am quite astonished, and this astonishment almost convinces me that I am sleeping.

Let us say, then, for the sake of argument, that we are sleeping and that such particulars as these are not true: that we open our eyes, move our heads, extend our hands. Perhaps we do not even have these hands, or any such body at all. Nevertheless, it really must be admitted that things seen in sleep, are, as it were, like painted images, which could have been produced only in the likeness of true things. Therefore at least these general things (eyes, head, hands, the whole body) are not imaginary things, but are true and exist. For indeed when painters wish to represent sirens and satyrs by means of bizarre and unusual forms, they surely cannot ascribe utterly new natures to these creatures. Rather, they simply intermingle the members of various animals. And even if they concoct something so utterly novel that its likes have never been seen before (being utterly fictitious and false), certainly at the very minimum the colors from which the painters compose the thing ought to be true. And for the same reason, although even these general things (eyes, hand, hands, and the like) can be imaginary, still one must necessarily admit that at least other things that are even more simple and universal are true, from which, as from true colors, all these things—be they true or false—which in our thought are images of things, are constructed.

To this class seems to belong corporeal nature in general, together with its extension; likewise the shape of extended things, their quantity or size, their number; as well as the place where they exist, the time of their duration, and other such things.

Hence perhaps we do not conclude improperly that physics, astronomy, medicine, and all the other disciplines that are dependent upon the consideration of composite things are all doubtful. But arithmetic, geometry, and other such disciplines—which treat of nothing but the simplest and most general things and which are indifferent as to whether these things do or do not exist—contain something certain and indubitable. For whether I be awake or asleep, two plus three makes five, and a square does not have more than five sides; nor does it seem possible that such obvious truths can fall under the suspicion of falsity.

All the same, a certain opinion of long standing has been fixed in my mind, namely that there exists a God who is able to do anything and by whom I, such as I am, have been created. How do I know that he did not bring it about that there be no earth at all, no heavens, no extended thing, no figure, no size, no place, and yet all these things should seem to me to exist precisely as they appear to do now? Moreover—as I judge that others sometimes make mistakes in matters that they believe they know most perfectly—how I do know that I am not deceived every time I add two and three or count the sides of a square or perform an even simpler operation, if such can be imagined? But perhaps God has not walked that I be thus deceived. For it is said that he is supremely good. Nonetheless, if it were repugnant to his goodness that he should have created me such that I be deceived all the time, it would seem, from this same consideration, to be foreign to him to permit me to be deceived occasionally. But we cannot make this last assertion.

Perhaps there are some who would rather deny such a powerful God, than believe that all other matters are uncertain. Let us not put these people off just yet; rather, let us grant that everything said here about God is fictitious. Now they suppose that I came to be what I am either by fate or by chance or by a continuous series of events or by some other way. But because being deceived and being mistaken seem to be imperfections, the less powerful they take the author of my being to be, the more probably it will be that I would be so imperfect as to be deceived perpetually. I have nothing to say in response to these arguments. At length I am forced to admit that there is nothing, among the things I once believed to be true, which it is not permissible to doubt—not for reasons of frivolity or a lack of forethought, but because of valid and considered arguments. Thus I must carefully withhold assent no less from these things than from the patently false, if I wish to find anything certain.

But it is not enough simply to have made a note of this; I must take care to keep it before my mind. For long-standing opinions keep coming back again and again, almost against my will; they seize upon my credulity, as if it were bound over to them by long use and the claims of intimacy. Nor will I get out of the habit of assenting to them and believing in them, so long as I take them to be exactly what they are, namely, in some respects doubtful as by now is obvious, but nevertheless highly probable, so that it is much more consonant with reason to believe them than to deny them. Hence, it seems to me, I would do well to turn my will in the opposite direction, to deceive myself and pretend for a considerable period that they are wholly false and imaginary, until finally, as if with equal weight of prejudice[1] on both sides, no bad habit should turn my judgment from the correct perception of things. For indeed I know that no danger or error will follow and that it is impossible for me to indulge in too much distrust, since I now am concentrating only on knowledge, not on action.

Thus I will suppose not a supremely good God, the source of truth, but rather an evil genius, as clever and deceitful as he is powerful, who has directed his entire effort to misleading me. I will regard the heavens, the air, the earth, colors, shapes, sounds, and all external things as nothing but the deceptive games of my dreams, with which he lays snares for my credulity. I will regard myself as having no hands, no eyes, no flesh, no blood, no senses, but as nevertheless falsely believing that I possess all these things. I will remain resolutely fixed in this meditation, and, even if it be out of my power to know anything true, certainly it is within my power to take care resolutely to withhold my assent to what is false, lest this deceiver, powerful and clever as he is, have an effect on me. But this undertaking is arduous, and laziness brings me back to my customary way of living. I am not unlike a prisoner who might enjoy an imaginary freedom in his sleep. When he later begins to suspect that he is sleeping, he fears being awakened and conspires slowly with these pleasant illusions. In just this way, I spontaneously fall back into my old beliefs, and dread being awakened, lest the toilsome wakefulness not in the light but among the inextricable shadows of the difficulties now brought forward.

Meditation Two: Concerning the Nature of the Human Mind: That the Mind Is More Known Than the Body

Yesterday's mediation filled my mind with so many doubts that I can no longer forget about them—nor yet do I see how they are to be resolved. But, as if I had suddenly fallen into a deep whirlpool, I am so disturbed that I can neither touch my foot to the bottom, nor swim up to the top. Nevertheless I will work my way up, and I will follow the same path I took yesterday, putting aside everything which admits the least doubt, as if I had discovered it to be absolutely false. I will go forward until I know something certain—or, if nothing else, until I at least know at least for certain that nothing is certain. Archimedes sought only a firm and immovable point in order to move the entire earth from one place to another. Surely great things are to be home for if I am lucky enough to find at least one thing that is certain and indubitable.

Therefore I will suppose that all I see is false. I will believe that none of those things that my deceitful memory brings before my eyes ever existed. I thus have no senses: shape, extension, movement, and place are all figments of my imagination. What then will count as true? Perhaps only this one thing: that nothing is certain.

But on what grounds do I know that there is nothing over and above all those which I have just reviewed, concerning which there is not even the lease cause for doubt? Is there not a God (or whatever name I might call him) who instills these thoughts in me? But why should I think that, since perhaps I myself could be the author of these things? Therefore am I not at least something? But I have already denied that I have any senses and any body. Still, I hesitate; for what follows from that? Am I so tied to the body to the senses that I cannot exist without them? But I have persuaded myself that there is nothing at all in the world: no heaven, no earth, no minds, no bodies. Is it not then true that I do not exist? But certainly I should exist, if I were to persuade myself of something. But there is a deceiver (I know not who he is) powerful and sly in the highest degree, who is always purposely deceiving me. Then there is no doubt that I exist, if he deceives me. And deceive me as he will, he can never bring it about that I am nothing so long as I shall think that I am something. Thus it must be granted that, after weighing everything carefully and sufficiently, one must come to the considered judgment that the statement "I am, I exist" is necessarily true every time it is uttered by me or conceived in my mind.

But I do not yet understand well enough who I am—I, who now necessarily exist. And from this point on, I must take care lest I imprudently substitute something else in place of myself; and thus be mistaken even in that knowledge which I claim to be the most certain and evident of all. To this end, I shall meditate once more on what I once believed myself to be before having embarked upon these deliberations. For this reason, then, I will set aside whatever can be refuted even to a slight degree by the arguments brought forward, so that at length there shall remain precisely nothing but what is certain and unshaken.

What therefore did I formerly think I was? A man, of course. But what is a man? Might I not say a rational animal? No, because then one would have to inquire what an "animal" is and what "rational" means. And then from only one question we slide into many more difficult ones. Nor do I now have enough free time that I want to waste it on subtleties of this sort. But rather here I pay attention to what spontaneously and at nature's lead came into my thought beforehand whenever I pondered what I was. Namely, it occurred to me first that I have a face, hands, arms, and this entire mechanism of bodily members, the very same as are discerned in a corpse—which I referred to by the name "body." It also occurred to me that I eat, walk, feel and think; these actions I used to assign to the soul as their cause. But what this soul was I either did not think about or I imagined was something terribly insubstantial—after the fashion of a wind, fire, or ether—which has been poured into my coarser parts. I truly was not in doubt regarding the body; rather I believed that I distinctly knew its nature, which, were I perhaps tempted to describe it such as I mentally conceived it, I would explain it thus; by "body," I understand all that is suitable for being bounded by some shape, for being enclosed in some place, and thus for filling up space, so that it excludes every other body from that space; for being perceived by touch, sight, hearing, taste, or smell; for being moved in several ways, not surely by itself, but by whatever else that touches it. For I judged that the power of self-motion, and likewise of sensing or of thinking, in no way pertains to the nature of the body. Nonetheless, I used to marvel especially that such faculties were found in certain bodies.

But now what am I, when I suppose that some deceiver—omnipotent and, if I may be allowed to say it, malicious—takes all the pains he can in order to deceive me? Can I not affirm that I possess at least a small measure of all those traits which I already have said pertain to the nature of the body? I pay attention, I think, I deliberate—but nothing happens. I am wearied about of repeating this in vain. But which of these am I to ascribe to the soul? How about eating or walking? These are surely nothing but illusions, because I do not have a body. How about sensing? Again, this also does not happen without a body, and I judge that I really did not sense those many things I seemed to have sensed in my dreams. How about thinking? Here I discover that thought is an attribute that really does belong to me. This alone cannot be detached from me. I am; I exist; this is certain. But for how long? For as long as I think. Because perhaps it could also come to pass that if I should cease from all thinking I would then utterly cease to exist. I now admit nothing that

is not necessarily true. I am therefore precisely only a thing that thinks; that is, a mind, or soul, or intellect, or reason—words the meaning of which I was ignorant before. Now, I am a true thing, and truly existing; but what kind of thing? I have said it already; a thing that thinks.

What then? I will set my imagination going to see if I am not something more. I am not that connection of members which is called the human body. Neither am I some subtle air infused into these members, not a wind, not a fire, not a vapor, not a breath—nothing that I imagine to myself, for I have supposed all these to be nothing. The assertion stands; the fact still remains that I am something. But perhaps is it the case that, nevertheless, these very things which I take to be nothing (because I am ignorant of them) in reality do not differ from that self which I know? This I do not know. I shall not quarrel about it right now; I can make a judgment only regarding things which are known to me. I know that I exist; I ask now who is this "I" whom I know. Most certainly the knowledge of this matter, thus precisely understood, does not depend upon things that I do not yet know to exist. Therefore, it is not dependent upon any of those things that I feign in my imagination. But this word "feign" warns me of my error. For I would be feigning if I should "imagine" that I am something, because imagining is merely the contemplation of the shape or image of corporeal thing. But I know now with certainty that I am, and at the same time it could happen that all these images—and, generally, everything that pertains to the nature of the body—are nothing but dreams. When these things are taken into account, I would speak no less foolishly were I to say: "I will imagine so that I might recognize more distinctly who I am," than were I to say: "Now I surely am awake, and I see something true, but because I do not yet see it with sufficient evidence, I will take the trouble of going to sleep so that my dreams might show this to me more truly and more evidently." Thus I know that none of what I can comprehend by means of the imagination pertains to this understanding that I have of myself. Moreover, I know that I must be diligent about withdrawing my mind from these things so that it can perceive its nature as distinctly as possible.

But what then am I? A thing that thinks. What is that? A thing that doubts, understands, affirms, denies, wills, refuses, and which also imagines and senses.

It is truly no small matter if all of these things pertain to me. But why should they not pertain to me? Is it not I who now doubt almost everything, I who nevertheless understand something, I who affirm that this one thing is true, I who deny other things, I who desire to know more things, I who wish not to be deceived, I who imagine many things against my will, I who take note of many things as if coming from the senses? Is there anything in all of this which is not just as true as it is that I am, even if I am always dreaming or even if the one who created me tries as hard as possible to delude me? Are any of these attributes distinct from my thought? What can be said to be separate from myself? For it is so obvious that it is I who doubt, I who understand, I who will, that there is nothing through which it could be more evidently explicated. But indeed I am also the same one who imagines; for, although perhaps as I supposed before, no imagined thing would be wholly true, the very power of imagining does really exist, and constitutes a part of my thought. Finally, I am the same one, who senses or who takes note of bodily things as if through the senses. For example, I now see a light, I hear a noise, I feel heat. These are false, since I am asleep. But I certainly seem to see, hear,

and feel. This cannot be false; properly speaking, this is what is called "sensing" in me. But this is, to speak precisely, nothing other than thinking.

From these considerations I begin to know a little better who I am. But it still seems that I cannot hold back from believing that bodily things—whose images are formed by thought, and which the senses themselves examine—are much more distinctly known than this unknown aspect of myself which does not come under the imagination. And yet it would be quite strange if the very things which I consider to be doubtful, unknown, and foreign to me are comprehended by me more distinctly than what is true, what is known—than, in fine, myself. But I see what is happening; my mind loves to wander and does not allow itself to be restricted to the confines of truth. Let it be that way then; let us allow it the freest rein in every respect, so that, when we pull in the reins at the right time a little later, the mind may suffer itself to be ruled more easily.

Let us consider those things which are commonly believed to be the most distinctly comprehended of all; namely the bodies which we touch and see. But not bodies in general, for these generic perceptions are often somewhat more confused; rather let us consider one body in particular. Let us take, for instance, this piece of wax. It has very recently been taken from the honeycombs; it has not as yet lost all the flavor of its honey. It retains some of the smell of the flowers from which it was collected. Its color, shape, and size are obvious. It is hard and cold. It can easily be touched, and if you rap on it with a knuckle it makes a sound. In short, everything is present in it that appears to be needed in order that a body can be known as distinctly as possible. But notice that while I am speaking, it is brought close to the fire; the remaining traces of the honey flavor are purged; the odor vanishes; the color is changed; the original shape disappears. Its magnitude increases, it becomes liquid and hot, and can hardly be touched; and now, when you knock on it, it does not emit any sound. Up to this point, does the same wax remain? One must confess that it does; no one denies it; no one thinks otherwise. What was there then in the wax that was so distinctly comprehended? Certainly none of the things that I reached by means of the senses. For whatever came under taste or smell or sight or touch or hearing by now has changed, yet the wax remains.

Perhaps the wax was what I now think it is; namely that it really never was the sweetness of the honey or the fragrance of the flowers, not this whiteness, not a figure, not a sound, but a body which a little earlier manifested itself to me in these ways, and now does so in other ways. But just what precisely is this thing which I imagine thus? Let us direct our attention to this and see what remains after we have removed everything which does not belong to the wax; only that it is something extended, flexible and subject to change. What is this flexible and mutable thing? Is it not the fact that I imagine that this wax can change from a round to a square shape, or from the latter to a rectangular shape? Not at all: for I comprehend that the wax is capable of innumerable changes, yet I cannot survey these innumerable changes by imagining them. Therefore this comprehension is not accomplished by the faculty of imagination. What is this extended thing? Is this thing's extension also unknown? For it becomes larger in wax that is beginning to liquify, greater in boiling wax, and greater still as the heat is increased. And I would not judge rightly what the wax is if I did not believe that this wax can take on even more varieties of extension than I could ever have grasped by the imagination. It remains then for

me to concede that I in no way imagine what this wax is, but perceive it by the mind only. I am speaking about this piece of wax in particular, for it is clearer in the case of wax in general. But what is this wax which is perceived only by the mind? It is the same that I see, touch, and imagine; in short it is the same as I took it to be from the very beginning. But we must take note of the fact that the perception of the wax is neither by sight, nor touch, nor imagination, nor was it ever so (although it seemed so before), but rather an inspection on the part of the mind alone. This inspection can be imperfect and confused, as it was before, or clear and distinct, as it is now, according to whether I pay greater or less attention to those things which that wax consists.

But meanwhile I marvel at how prone my mind is to errors; for although I am considering these things within myself silently and without words, nevertheless I latch onto words themselves and I am very nearly deceived by the ways in which people speak. For we say that we see the wax itself, if it is present, and that we judge it to be present from its color or shape. Whence I might conclude at once: the wax is therefore known by eyesight, and not by an inspection on the part of the mind alone, unless I perhaps now might have looked out the window at the men crossing the street whom I say I am no less wont to see than the wax. But what I do I see over and above the hats and clothing? Could not robots be concealed under these things? But I judge them to be men; thus what I believed I had seen with my eyes, I actually comprehend with nothing but the faculty of judgment which is in my mind.

But a person who seeks to know more than the common crowd should be ashamed of himself if he has come upon doubts as a result of an encounter with the forms of speech devised by the common crowd. Let us then go forward, paying attention to the following question: did I perceive more perfectly and evidently what the wax was when I first saw it and believed I had known it by the external sense—or at least by the common sense, as they say, that is, the imaginative power—than I know it now, after having examined more diligently both what the wax is and how it is known. Surely it is absurd to doubt this matter. For what was there in the first perception that was distinct? What was there that any animal could not have seemed capable of possessing? But when I distinguish the wax from its external forms, as if having taken off its clothes, as it were, I look at the naked wax, even though at this point there can be an error in my judgment; nevertheless I could not perceive it without a human mind.

But what am I to say about this mind, or about myself? For as yet I admit nothing else to be in me over and above my mind. What, I say, am I who seem to perceived this wax so distinctly? Do I not know myself not only much more truly and with more certainty, but also much more distinctly and evidently? For if I judge that the wax exists from the fact that I see it, certainly it follows much more evidently that I myself exist, from the fact that I see the wax. For it could happen that what I see is not truly wax. It could happen that I have no eyes with which to see anything. But it could not happen that, while I see or think I see (I do not now distinguish these two), I who think am not something. Likewise, if I judge that the wax exists from the fact that I touch it, the same thing will again follow: I exist. If from the fact that I imagine, or from whatever other cause, the same thing readily follows. But what I noted regarding the wax applies to all the other things that are external to me. Furthermore, if the perception of the wax seemed more distinct after it became known to me not only

from sight or touch, but from many causes, how much more distinctly I must be known to myself; for there are no considerations that can aid in the perception of the wax or any other body without these considerations demonstrating even better the nature of my mind. But there are still so many other things in my mind from which one can draw a more distinct knowledge of the mind, so that those things which emanate from a body seem hardly worth enumerating.

But lo and behold, I have arrived on my own at the place I wanted. Since I know that bodies are not, properly speaking, perceived by the senses or by the faculty of imagination, but only by the intellect, and since, moreover, I know that they are not perceived by being touched or seen, but only insofar as they are expressly understood, nothing can be more easily and more evidently perceived by me than my mind. But because an established habit of belief cannot be put aside so quickly, it is appropriate to stop here, so that by the length of my meditation this new knowledge may be more deeply impressed on my memory.

Note

1. A "prejudice" is a prejudgment, that is, an adjudication of an issue without having first reviewed the appropriate evidence.

Empiricism

The only source of knowledge is experience.
—Albert Einstein

It is beyond a doubt that all our knowledge begins with experience.

—Immanuel Kant

Discussion Questions

1. Imagine that you were born with severe physical abnormalities. You are blind and deaf; you have no taste buds and no sense of smell; and your skin consists of thick calluses restricting your sense of touch. Despite these problems, doctors have determined that you are mentally and cognitively above normal. Having no senses means that you spend much of your day consumed by your own thoughts and thinking about the world. If you were stricken by this condition, how could you come to know that tables, chairs, trees, and cars exist without experiencing them? Could you come to know the seductive sweet taste of chocolate, the smell of a rose, or feel of silk by mere thought? How important is experience to our knowledge of the world?

2. If we take modern physics seriously, then the *real* world is colourless, odourless, and tasteless. Does modern physics lend support for Locke's claim that, for example, the scent of a rose will be independent of the rose itself? Does this prove that secondary qualities have no resemblance at all to objects? Are qualities like hot and red inherent in objects, or do we merely experience them as such? Give reasons for your answers.

3. If we take Locke to the full extent of his conclusion, the real essences of objects can never be truly discovered and their underlying reality can never be truly known. How might this negate the primary assumption of empiricism?

4. Bertrand Russell explained Hume's position this way, "The mere fact that something has happened a certain number of times causes animals and men to expect that it will happen again. Thus our instincts certainly cause us to believe that the sun will rise tomorrow, but we may be in no better a position than the chicken which unexpectedly has its neck wrung" (35). Are humans, like chickens, lulled into a false sense of security through the regularities of our experiences only to find, suddenly and unexpectedly, such regularities do not hold? Why might you agree with Hume that we cannot be sure whether the sun will rise tomorrow? Alternately, why would you be justified in believing the sun *will* rise tomorrow? How does the problem of induction make life impossible to live?[8]

Locke: I'll Believe It When I See It

Most people find empiricism very appealing. Its appeal, in part, stems from the natural sciences. Over the past 300 years, chemistry, biology, and physics have immensely deepened our knowledge of the world through the use of careful observation. To get a better understanding of empiricism, try to answer the following questions using reason (rationalism) alone:

- How old is the earth?
- Did dinosaurs roam the planet?
- How many people are suffering from AIDS?
- At what temperature does lead melt?
- Are humans sexually active over the age of eighty?
- What is the cause of schizophrenia?

Using the mind alone is wholly ineffective at answering these questions. We cannot merely conjure up in our mind how many people have AIDS. We have to get out there in the real world to see (count) and hear from those affected by this horrible disease to know how many have it and how it spreads. With this knowledge at hand, social policies can help reduce the spread of AIDS (family planning, access to condoms, and so on) and science can work towards developing antiviral drugs to ease the suffering and, with luck, eventually find a cure. It is only through empiricism—the discovery of scientific facts/evidence—that questions regarding AIDS can be answered (See Box 2.7).

Another appealing aspect of empiricism is that it can give us a much more accurate objective analysis of the way the world really is. To explain why ice forms on lake surfaces during winter, many people might simply say that water solidifies when cold and floats on top. But such

Box 2.7 Inductive and Deductive Reasoning

There are two basic types of arguments in philosophy: inductive and deductive. In deductive arguments, the conclusion necessarily follows from the premises. For example:

1. All men are immortal.
2. Socrates is a man.
3. Therefore, Socrates is immortal.

Although the conclusion is obviously false—Socrates died many centuries ago—the argument is perfectly valid. It is valid, not because the premises are true, but because the conclusion directly follows from the premises. If men are immortal, and Socrates is a man (which he is), then it necessarily follows he is immortal.

Inductive arguments, in contrast, are based on probability, not necessity. That is, the premises make the conclusion more or less probable. For example:

1. The downtown is not usually very busy on Monday evenings.
2. Today is Monday.
3. Therefore, the downtown will not be very busy tonight.

Because Monday nights are usually not very busy downtown, and given today is Monday, it is reasonable to conclude that downtown will not be busy tonight. And we normally would come to such conclusions by experience. But inductive reasoning does not guarantee the truth of the conclusion. It could be true that tonight is jam-packed with shoppers and is the busiest Monday night ever. And the only way we can know this is by going downtown and seeing for ourselves. In this sense, inductive arguments are considered either strong or weak by virtue of the justification provided. Strong justification entails strong arguments.

Most of science is also based on inductive reasoning. Pharmaceutical companies, for example, spend massive amounts of money developing and testing drugs to ensure they are safe for general human consumption. Drugs are usually tested on small groups of people and it's from such tests that conclusions can be drawn about drug safety. But although manufacturers infer conclusions about the drug onto the general population, there is always the possibility that some people may experience negative health consequences not revealed during initial testing. In this sense, drug manufacturing is based on inductive reasoning. (Lawhead 39).

an explanation does not fully represent what happens. In contrast, a physics professor might explain ice forming on lakes this way: a decrease in temperature slows the movement of H_2O molecules to the point of solidification. During solidification, the H_2O molecules spread out because of a slight electrical charge, making it less dense. Less dense material is lighter than denser material. The result: ice forms on lake surfaces. In this sense, science gives us direct access to the "real world." The same can be said of our perceptual experiences. Most people do not doubt that what they see, hear, taste, smell, and touch directly reflects the way the world actually is. If I see a red cherry, then there really is a cherry with a property of red, which is causing me to have a red-seeing experience. This is known as **direct (naïve) realism.** The world is exactly as it is perceived.

But direct (naïve) realism is problematic. Try this simple experiment at home. Get three small buckets or bowls, set them in front of you. Fill the right bucket with hot water, the middle bucket with lukewarm water, and the left bucket with cold water. Place your right hand into the hot water and your left hand into the cold water. Wait about a minute. Take both hands out and plunge them into the lukewarm bucket. How do your hands feel? How can the lukewarm bucket of water feel both hot and cold at the same time? What does this tell us about our experiences? Is the world exactly as we perceive it to be? The answer is no. If our perceptions of reality can often differ from the way the world actually is, then the problem of scepticism is reintroduced.

John Locke was not only a staunch empiricist—arguing that without experience humans could not acquire knowledge—he also recognized the preceding problem with direct (naïve) realism. Since our experiences do not always represent the world exactly as it appears, for Locke, the best we can hope for is probable knowledge based on inductive reasoning. However, to avoid scepticism, Locke must explain how to reconcile empiricism with the problem of direct realism. He does this by making a distinction between primary and secondary qualities. But first, let's start with Locke's conception of simple and complex ideas.

All knowledge, according to Locke, can be decomposed into its basic building blocks called **ideas**. Now Locke's meaning of "idea" is very different than what we mean by "idea" today. Generally speaking, when we talk about an "idea" it means to have a conception, notion, or thought. For example, someone might have an idea for how to get rich, design a more fuel-efficient engine, or plan a prison escape. In contrast, Locke defined an idea as the immediate object of perception, thought, or understanding. Locke gives a number of examples of ideas including whiteness, hardness, sweetness, motion, man, drunkenness, and so forth. To see a red cherry, for example, is to have the idea of a red cherry.

But for Locke, ideas can be decomposed into more basic components known as **simple ideas**. Consider, for example, salt. Just as salt (NaCl) can be reduced to its building blocks of sodium and chloride ions, ideas can also be reduced to the building blocks of simple ideas, specifically, reflection and sensation. Ideas of reflection come from experiencing our own mental processes at work—including believing, doubting, thinking, and reasoning—as well as our emotions. In short, we can think about our thoughts, emotions, beliefs, and so on. Ideas of sensation consist of things like heat, red, white, soft, hard, round, bitter, and sweet. In this sense, the mind is passive, receiving simple ideas through our senses and experiences of the world. For example, the

idea of a red cherry is really a culmination of the simpler ideas of red, round, and sweetness. The idea of a snowball is the culmination of the simpler ideas of round, white, and cold. Our ideas of the world can be separated into their component parts based on our experiences of sight, smell, taste, hearing, and touch.

Simple ideas can be combined into what Locke calls **complex ideas**. Complex ideas are formed in one of three ways: (1) The mind *compounds* or unites one or more simple ideas. The complex idea of apple, for example, is the combination of simpler ideas of red, sweet, and hard. (2) Simple ideas can be *related* to one another by keeping them separate for comparison's sake. The simple idea of size can be gleaned by observing a golf ball and basketball, and when compared to one another, we form the complex idea of bigger or taller. The complex idea of cause and effect is merely the observed relation of two simple ideas, say of two billiard balls as one strikes the other. (3) Finally, complex ideas can be *abstracted* away from simpler ideas. We don't need to experience all dogs to acquire the general idea of "dog." By experiencing some dogs, all of which will have the same distinctive features such as four legs, barking, wet nose, and so forth, and by ignoring their specific individual characteristics, we can form the complex idea of "dog." The same can be said for humans, buildings, books, cars, etc.; we are using abstract complex ideas when we refer to such things.

As mentioned earlier, although Locke argues that experience is necessary for knowledge, he does realize that our experiences sometimes do not always represent the world exactly as it appears. Consider my earlier examples. If direct realism were true, then the lukewarm water should feel lukewarm. But it doesn't; it feels both hot and cold, which contradicts the tenets of direct realism. The only other explanation is that since the water cannot be both hot and cold, it must mean that our experiences occasionally do not accurately represent reality but instead are independent of it. To put this another way, sometimes our experiences of colour, smell, taste, etc. are dependent upon our perceptual systems and do not represent reality as it actually is. This may seem counterintuitive. You may want to believe that if you see a red cherry, then the cherry, according to direct realism, has the property red and is giving you your experience of red. But this is not necessarily the case. To understand this problem, let's look at the physics of colour.

The earth is blanketed with electromagnetic radiation. Electromagnetic radiation is a term used to identify all types of radiation including radio waves, microwaves, ultraviolet waves, x-rays, gamma rays, and radiation within the range of human visibility—light. Humans can perceive light because our eyes have evolved to detect wavelengths between the range of 380 nm (violet) and 740 nm (red); see Figure 2.1.[9]

Light hits the retinas at the back of the eyeballs stimulating photoreceptors, which then send electrical signals to the brain via the optic nerve. We perceive an object as blue, red, yellow, and other colours because light is reflected and absorbed by the object itself. A cherry looks red because the cherry's surface absorbs all visible light except red, which is reflected back to us. Snow is white because it reflects all visible light equally. Coal is black because it absorbs all light and does not reflect any. A banana looks yellow because its skin absorbs all visible light except yellow, which is reflected back to us at approximately 580 nm. But we should be careful here. It would be a mistake to conclude that the cherry, snow, coal, or the banana give off red, white, black, or yellow light, respectively. A red cherry merely absorbs and reflects various wavelengths of light such that our photoreceptors perceive it as red. A cherry is not *really red*; it's just how we see it. Colours are dependent upon humans, not the objects themselves. The implications are important. If seeing colour is dependent upon human perceptual systems, then it raises doubts about the objectivity of colour itself. It also raises sceptical doubts about the accuracy of our colour perceptions, especially when we consider other animals that may see the world radically different from humans. Bats, for example, "see" the world using echolocation, and certain kinds of rattlesnakes have built-in "night vision"

Figure 2.1 The Human Visible Light Spectrum

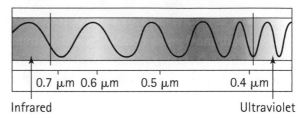

Visible Light Region of the Electromagnetic Spectrum

0.7 μm   0.6 μm   0.5 μm   0.4 μm

Infrared   Ultraviolet

Humans perceive visible light because we have evolved to detect specific wavelengths of electromagnetic radiation. Each colour has a specific wavelength with red being the longest and violet being the shortest. When all the wavelengths are reflected we see white and when all the wavelengths are absorbed we see black. Seeing colour, then, is dependent upon having eyes similar to humans.

Source: National Aeronautical Administration and Space Administration. *The Electromagnetic Spectrum.* 2007. 22 May 2007 <http://imagers.gsfc.nasa.gov/ems/visible.html>.

goggles." To further illustrate the point, imagine that aliens land on the earth and it's discovered (how it's discovered is unimportant) that they have a different physiology than humans such that their colour spectrum is inverted to ours—when humans see a red cherry, aliens see a green cherry; when humans see a blue sky, aliens see a yellow sky; and so forth. Notice, alien perceptual systems are still detecting the exact same electromagnetic radiation as humans, but given their different physiology, their coloured world is radically different from ours. In this sense, colour is only in the mind of the beholder (human or alien). Colour is not independent of us or in the objects themselves but dependent upon perceptual systems that have evolved over million of years. If correct, direct (naïve) realism fails. It's not true that cherries are really red and give us our red experiences. Red experiences are independent of cherries themselves. All colours are dependent upon perception.

Primary and Secondary Qualities

The failure of direct realism also explains why people differ regarding the taste of food, quality of music, smell of perfume, and so forth. The dependent elements within the objects we perceive (ideas) motivated Locke to make a distinction between primary and secondary qualities. It is the primary and secondary qualities of the simple ideas we perceive that produce complex ideas of objects. **Primary qualities** are qualities in the object itself independent of human perception. These qualities include size, shape, motion, rest, and number. For example, a cherry has a particular shape, size, and number independent of whether humans are perceiving it. That is, if humans never existed, a cherry would still possess these qualities. When we perceive primary qualities, our idea of shape, size, or motion exactly resembles those corresponding qualities in the object itself. Moreover, even if the cherry were broken down into its subatomic particles, these too would have a particular size, shape, motion, and number. In contrast, when we perceive secondary qualities, they do not correspond to qualities within objects. **Secondary qualities** are those qualities dependent upon human perception, including colour, smell, sound, warmth, and cold. So a red cherry looks round and is round, but whether it tastes sweet or sour will depend on the individual. To put it another way, the idea of round produced by the cherry represents the reality of the cherry itself—its roundness. But how the cherry tastes is dependent on our own preferences. For Locke, secondary qualities exist only in our mind and not in the objects themselves. Without eyes there could be no colour, without noses there could be no odour, and without minds there could be no secondary qualities at all. Locke is making an important distinction between appearance and reality. The way the world appears to us via the secondary qualities is not necessarily how the world actually is via the primary qualities. Locke is also providing us with a solution to scepticism. Primary qualities actually represent the real properties of objects, and, therefore, we can know they exist objectively. Secondary qualities, on the other hand, are dependent upon human perception and represent how the world subjectively appears to be to us.

Locke's views are often called *representative realism* because the ideas in the mind mirror or represent material objects to us in perception. In just the same way that photographs accurately represent the world, our ideas derived from experience accurately represent what we see, smell, hear, touch, and taste. This view is also known as the causal theory of perception because the material objects are the cause of our ideas that we have of them.

Locke's representationalism is problematic. At heart, Locke wants to argue that we can know something if we perceive it. But his philosophy is based on the notion that we do not experience objects or the world directly. In other words, the mind is like a camera and the only thing we can know about the world is through the ideas or photographs gleaned from our senses. But a photograph is not the real thing itself, merely a copy. And copies can be wrong or in error. A difference could remain between the idea of something and the thing itself. If so, then an empiricist must admit that the best we can do is infer that objects exist. Moreover, experience will not justify our knowledge claims since, like a malfunctioning camera, our senses can give rise to distorted ideas or pictures of the world. If so, then Locke's theory is open to scepticism of the deepest kind.

Berkeley's Idealism

George Berkeley, like Locke, was also an empiricist. He believed experience was the source of all knowledge and ideas (or what Berkeley calls "sense data"). But this is where they part company. Recall, for Locke, there are objects in the external world independent of us, which cause the primary and secondary qualities of our ideas. Berkeley emphatically rejects this distinction, claiming that the primary qualities are just as dependent upon human perception as secondary qualities. This makes perfect sense if we push Locke's analysis to its natural conclusion. Consider, once again, a red cherry. Although Locke argues that the cherry's primary and secondary qualities are independent/dependent upon us, Berkeley suggests differently. For Berkeley, the primary qualities of the cherry (roundness and size) are just as subjective or dependent upon human perception as its secondary qualities (redness and taste). Let's look at a different example to illustrate Berkeley's point. Imagine looking at the Eiffel Tower while vacationing in Paris. Locke would argue that your idea of the Eiffel Tower consists of its primary qualities (size—300 metres or 900 feet tall; shape—triangular structure; number—there's only one; and motion—stationary) independent of human perception and its secondary qualities (colour—gray/black; smell—metallic; touch—smooth/rough; taste—yuck; and sound—elevator/wind rustling through the metal trellises) dependent upon us. But are not primary qualities also dependent upon human perception? Berkeley argues they are. The colour, smell, taste, touch, and sound are not only dependent upon human perception but so too are its size, shape, motion, and number. Viewed from different perspectives, the Eiffel Tower can look tall, short, wide, or narrow, and if you have had one too many glasses of French wine, you might actually see more than one. But even if there were general agreement about the tower's primary qualities, they still wouldn't exist unless someone actually perceived it. For Berkeley, primary and secondary qualities are thus mind-dependent. The only way to know size, shape, or location of an object is by touching it, seeing it, and so forth, all of which are dependent upon human perception. In short, descriptions of primary qualities are really interpretations of secondary qualities—different ways of talking about colours, sounds, tastes, odours, and so on. Primary qualities, like secondary qualities, then exist only in the mind and are equally dependent upon human perception.

How Do I Know It's True? God

By collapsing the distinction between primary and secondary qualities, Berkeley successfully refutes Locke, but it leads to a rather shocking conclusion. Given that our ideas of the material world consist of primary and secondary qualities, which are mind-dependent, it follows that our ideas of objects themselves are mind-dependent. This means, for Berkeley, the very existence of the material world is also dependent upon the human mind. In short, if material objects are not perceived by the human mind, they do not exist. As Berkeley states, "to be is to perceived": *esse est percipi*. Therefore, if you were staring at the Eiffel Tower and then looked away from it, according to Berkeley, it would cease to exist. Material objects cannot exist unless perceived. Using a different example, Theodore Schick Jr. and Lewis Vaughn make a similar point:

> The classic philosophical conundrum—if a tree falls in the forest and no one is around to hear it, does it make a sound?—is often associated with Berkeley. It is commonly believed that Berkeley would answer no to this question. But Berkeley would not respond to this question because it is based on the assumption that he rejects, namely, that objects can exist unperceived. If there were no one around to hear a tree fall, there would be no tree in the first place. So the question makes no sense. (Schick and Vaughn 505)

Berkeley's philosophy is a version of **idealism.** The physical world does not exist independent of consciousness experience (see Figure 2.2). The only thing we can truly know to exist is the mental world. Again, Berkeley is merely drawing Locke's distinction to its logical conclusion. If we can only know the material world via sensory experience, and if sense experience is dependent solely on our minds, then the sensible world must exist solely in our mind.

Most students find Berkeley's claims downright silly. The material world exists when not perceived! Upon hearing of Berkeley's claims, the English writer Samuel Johnson supposedly kicked a rock while saying, "I refute him thus!" But we must be careful here. Berkeley is not saying that rocks, red cherries, the Eiffel Tower, tables, chairs, cars, and so forth, don't exist. He acknowledges that these things exist. What he denies is that the material world is directly responsible for our ideas of various objects. For Berkeley, objects do

Figure 2.2 Berkeley's Idealism from a Non-Human Perspective

indeed exist even when not perceived by humans, not because objects exist independent of human perception, but because God gives our world continuity and consistency. In other words, God gives us the ideas we have of the world, not raw sensory experiences. That is, things continue to exist even when no human mind perceives them because God perceives them from his perch in the sky. God has everything before his mind, and, therefore, the external world exists even if not perceived by humans. Samuel Stumpf and James Feiser put Berkeley's point nicely: "The ideas that exist in our minds are God's ideas, which He communicates to us, so that the objects or things that we perceive in daily experience are caused not by *matter* or *substance* but by God" (266). Again, Berkeley does not deny the existence of houses, books, trees, people, and so forth. However, he does deny that these things or any other physical object are directly responsible for our ideas—it's God who is responsible. Moreover, Berkeley's

argument also defeats scepticism. We no longer have to worry about whether our ideas truly represent reality. And if there is no gap between reality and appearance, then scepticism can never take root. Hence, contrary to the sceptic, we can have knowledge (ideas) of the material world thanks to God's love and good grace.

Philosophically speaking, Berkeley's arguments are open to a number of objections. The first and most obvious objection is that God does not exist. Remember, for Berkeley, God is the sole provider of our experiences and ideas; material objects are rejected as a causal force. But if we can show that God does not exist as the source of our experiences and ideas, then the very foundation of Berkeley's epistemology collapses. Although putting forward objections to God's existence requires us to move beyond present concerns, Berkeley's solution raises other significant questions. How does God choose the sensations we will have? How does God transmit these sensations to us (energy, telepathy, etc.)? Why do sensations differ in people? One would expect, if God were in charge of all human experience, our experiences would be more uniform than what they are. But people radically differ in what they consider hot and cold, good music, good food, and so on. Berkeley's solution seems to raise more questions than it answers. Second, Berkeley's appeal to God to ensure the consistency and constancy of material objects, and as the cause of our sensations, is not the best nor the most logical explanation. A simple and better explanation may be to appeal to the natural sciences. Material objects have certain internal qualities, and when they interact with our sense organs, they produce various sensations. Consider, for example, our sense of hearing. To hear something, you first need sound. From rustling leaves, traffic, to jet airplanes, sound can vary in loudness and pitch, but all sound is a wave of compressed air molecules that eventually strikes the ear. The outer ear funnels the sound into the inner eardrum, a taut membrane that vibrates in time with the sound waves. Three little bones behind the eardrum pick up these vibrations and transmit them to the cochlea. The sound wave vibrations ripple through cochlea stimulating its tiny hairs, which then converts these vibrations into electrical impulses. These impulses are then sent to the brain and we hear sound. Similar to seeing, then, hearing involves external stimuli that cause our sense experiences, and therefore material objects must exist independent of us in order to have various sensory experiences. If correct, then direct (not naïve) realism is true.

Hume's Problem of Induction

David Hume, like Locke and Berkeley, was an empiricist, but he recognized a significant philosophical problem that casts the whole empiricist enterprise into question. If all knowledge comes from experience, then knowledge is dependent upon causal relations. Objects in the external world will cause us to have various effects (experiences) and it's by virtue of such effects (experiences) that we derive knowledge. For example, my knowledge that this is an oak tree is based on experiencing the tree (seeing, touching, smelling, etc.). In other words, the oak tree causes me to have experiences of the tree from which my knowledge is derived. But what gives me the idea of causality? For Hume, the idea of causality cannot come from sensory experience because causality is not literally seen, touched, heard, tasted, or smelled. In short, we do not literally see causality at work. If our knowledge of the world depends entirely on our senses, then how do we know the future will be like the past? The answer, for Hume, is that we don't. We cannot make inferences from the existence of one object to that of another because we can never be sure of the causal connections at work. In short, knowledge derived form experience leads to scepticism.

At first glance, Hume's thesis seems highly suspect. The hammer *drives* down the nail, the rock *breaks* the window, the hockey stick *hits* the puck, and soccer player *strikes* the ball (see Photo 2.1). In each of these cases, we surely have a clear example of the necessary connection between cause and effect. Not so, says Hume.

To understand Hume's philosophical position, he first makes an important distinction between impressions and ideas. Impressions are what

Photo 2.1 Causality at Work

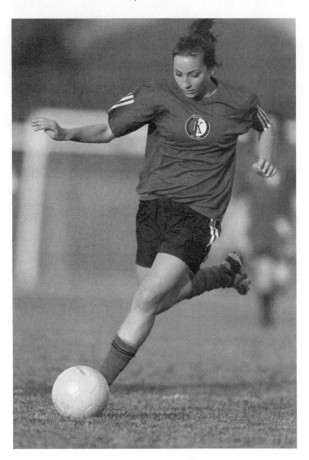

Hume's "problem of induction" attempts to dislodge our commonsense notion that the future will be like the past. For Hume, we cannot make such inductive inferences because we cannot accurately say that one event caused another.

we immediately feel or experience and ideas are what we imagine or can remember. For example, to see a red apple is to have an impression of the apple, but if later on you were to think about the same apple, this would be an idea. Impressions are vivid, colourful, and clear; ideas are not. Ideas are poor copies of the original impressions derived from the senses. Hume then makes a distinction between *relations of ideas* and *matters of fact* (see Box 2.8). Relations of ideas are those objects of human inquiry, such as mathematics and geometry, which are intuitively or demonstrably certain (*a priori*). Although seemingly contradictory, Hume's empiricism is compatible with *a priori* knowledge, since relations of ideas are less vivid impressions derived from

---

Box 2.8　Hume: Relations of Ideas Are Different Than Matters of Fact

Relations of Ideas (*a priori*)

- All triangles have three sides.
- $3 \times 5 = 15$
- All bachelors are unmarried.

Matters of Fact (*a posteriori*)

- Lead melts at 327 degrees Celsius.
- The sun will rise tomorrow.
- The hammer strikes the nail.

---

experience. We don't need to experience every triangle, for example, to know all triangles have three sides. Matters of fact, on the other hand, can only be known by experience (*a posteriori*). For example, it's by observing the melting process and recording the temperature that we know lead melts at 327 degrees Celsius.

The problem, says Hume, is that matters of fact are not evidently true and the opposite does not imply a contradiction. For example, although we may believe that the sun will rise tomorrow, because we have experienced the sun rising in the past, it would not be contradictory if the sun did not rise. Why? Because all matters of fact are based on cause and effect and causality can never be apprehended by the senses (see Box 2.9). Ask yourself the following: Do you really see the hammer *drive* down the nail; the rock *break* the window; the hockey stick *hit* the puck, and the soccer player *strike* the ball?

For Hume, you do not see any such drive, break, hit, or strike. What you really see are two separate events constantly conjoined which we take for causality. Causality, however, is never experienced itself. Or to use Hume's famous example, if you see one billiard ball hit another billiard ball, you might say that the first caused the second to move. But, as Hume points out, you assume cause and effect where none is found. All you see is one billiard ball hitting another. You assume cause and effect because the future will be like the past, but for Hume, such a connection is mistaken. You do not know what effect the first billiard ball will have on the second. Even if you have experienced a consistent causal connection between billiard balls, for all you know, the second billiard ball could have shot into space, the nail could have remained motionless, or the window could have failed to break, and so forth. Why? Again, because you do not experience cause and effect, all you experience is the motion of one object and then the motion of another. This is the problem of induction.

Box 2.9　The Relation between Cause and Effect Cannot Be Known Through Experience

Object	Causal Relation	Object	
Hammer (cause)	⟶ (drives)	Nail (effect)	
Rock (cause)	⟶ (breaks)	Window (effect)	
Stick (cause)	⟶ (hits)	Puck (effect)	
Foot (cause)	⟶ (strikes)	Ball (effect)	

Despite apparent perceived regularities observed in the part, we have no good ground for thinking the future will be the same. In short, we cannot justifiably infer knowledge claims about the world from experience.

Hume's conclusion is significant. If all of our experiences rest on faulty assumptions about the past and future, then it means we don't really know what we think we know. So why are we so confident in our knowledge claims? For Hume, it's the regulatory of our experiences that allows us to draw conclusions about nature as a whole. We assume that nature is uniform and thus allows us to make the necessary connection between cause and effect. That is, the future will be like the past. But what reason, asks Hume, do we have for making such assumptions about nature? We cannot establish the claim that nature is uniform by experience without begging the question or implying that it is so before proving it. Inductive inferences via experience are a matter of custom and habit. And it's because of custom and habit that we come to conclude that objects and events are constantly conjoined. When we experience the causal connection between two objects we develop causal expectations that it will happen again in the future. In this way, via experience and repetition, we are not surprised that hammers *drive* down nails, rocks *break* windows, hockey sticks *hit* the pucks, and soccer players *strike* balls. In short, habit and custom ensure the future will be like the past. But we must be careful here. Hume's assertion that there is no necessary connection between cause and effect to support our knowledge claims is a devastating sceptical attack against empiricism. When we say that A causes B, we are merely reporting our expectations that the future will be like the past. This is a psychological fact, not a fact about the world. If we cannot be sure of the causal relations between our experiences and objects in the external world, then we may believe that certain things exist, but there is no definitive proof. All knowledge is therefore suspect.

4

John Locke

(1632–1704)

John Locke was born in Wrington, England, in 1632. Educated at the prestigious Westminster School in London, Locke eventually was admitted into Oxford University where he earned a bachelor's degree in 1656 and master's degree in 1658. Locke had a broad range of interests, including philosophy, politics, and medicine. Although he never became a medical doctor, Locke did become the household physician and political advisor to Anthony Ashley Cooper (First Earl of Shaftesbury), eventually receiving a bachelor's of medicine in 1675. Locke's political ideas were revolutionary at the time. Locke believed that people should have religious and civil freedom. The purpose of government was not to oppress citizens but to protect their right to life, liberty, and property. If government failed to meet these obligations, then open revolt and rebellion by the citizenry was wholly justified. In seventeenth-century England, Locke's ideas directly challenged the King's absolute rule. In 1683, Locke fled to Holland for fear of reprisal. It was while in exile that Locke completed and published his most famous works: An Essay Concerning Human Understanding *(1689) and* Two Treaties of Government *(1689). In 1689, Locke returned to England. Locke's* Two Treaties *eventually became the*

foundation of the American Constitution, while his Essay on Human Understanding *became the foundation of empiricism in the United Kingdom. Locke died in 1704. He never married nor had children.*

An Essay Concerning Human Understanding

Book II: Chapter I
Of Ideas in General, and Their Original

1. Idea is the object of thinking.

Every man being conscious to himself, that he thinks, and that which his mind is applied about, whilst thinking, being the ideas, that are there, 'tis past doubt that men have in their minds several ideas, such as are those expressed by the words, *whiteness, hardness, sweetness, thinking, motion, man, elephant, army, drunkenness,* and others: it is in the first place then to be inquired, how he comes by them? I know it is a received doctrine, that men have native ideas, and original characters stamped upon their minds, in their very first being. This opinion I have at large examined already; and, I suppose, what I have said in the foregoing book, will be much more easily admitted, when I have shown, whence the understanding may get all the ideas it has, and by what ways and degrees they may come into the mind; for which I shall appeal to every one's own observation and experience.

2. All ideas come from sensation or reflection.

Let us then suppose the mind to be, as we say, white paper, void of all characters, without any ideas; how comes it to be furnished? Whence comes it by that vast store, which the busy and boundless fancy of man has painted on it, with an almost endless variety? Whence has it all the materials of reason and knowledge? To this I answer, in one word, from *experience:* in that, all our knowledge is founded; and from that it ultimately derives itself. Our observation employed either *about external sensible objects, or about the internal operations of our minds, perceived and reflected on by ourselves, is that, which supplies our understandings with all the materials of thinking.* These two are the fountains of knowledge, from whence all the ideas we have, or can naturally have, do spring.

3. The objects of sensation one source of ideas.

First, *our senses,* conversant about particular sensible objects, do *convey into the mind,* several distinct *perceptions* of things, according to those various ways, wherein those objects do affect them: and thus we come by those ideas, we have of *yellow, white, heat, cold, soft, hard, bitter, sweet,* and all those which we call sensible qualities, which when I say the senses convey into the mind, I mean, they from external objects convey into the mind what produces there those *perceptions.* This great source, of most of the ideas we have, depending wholly upon our senses, and derived by them to the understanding, I call *sensation.*

4. The operations of our minds, the other source of them.

Secondly, the other fountain, from which experience furnisheth the understanding with ideas, is the *perception of the operations of our own minds within us,* as it is employed about the ideas it has got; which operations, when the soul comes to reflect on, and consider, do furnish the understanding with another set of ideas, which could not be had from things without; and such are, *perception, thinking, doubting, believing, reasoning, knowing, willing,* and all the different actings of our own minds; which we being conscious of, and observing in ourselves, do from these receive into our understandings, as distinct ideas, as we do from bodies affecting our senses. This source of ideas, every man has wholly in himself; and though it be not sense, as having nothing to do with external objects; yet it is very like it, and might properly enough be called internal sense. But as I call the other *sensation,* so I call this *reflection,* the ideas it affords being such only, as the mind gets by reflecting on its own operations within itself. By *reflection* then, in the following part of this discourse, I would be understood to mean, that notice which the mind takes of its own operations, and the manner of them, by reason whereof, there come to be ideas of these operations in the understanding. These two, I say, *viz.* external, material things, as the objects of *sensation;* and the operations of our own minds within, as the objects of *reflection,* are, to me, the only originals, from whence all our ideas take their beginnings. The term *operations* here I use in a large sense, as comprehending not barely the actions of the mind about its ideas, but some sort of passions arising sometimes from them, such as is the satisfaction or uneasiness arising from any thought. [...]

Chapter II
Of Simple Ideas

1. Uncompounded appearances.

The better to understand the nature, manner, and extent of our knowledge, one thing is carefully to be observed, concerning the ideas we have; and that is, that *some* of them are *simple* and *some complex.*

Though the qualities that affect our senses, are, in the things themselves, so united and blended, that there is no separation, no distance between them; yet 'tis plain, the ideas they produce in the mind enter by the senses simple and unmixed. For though the sight and touch often take in from the same object, at the same time, different ideas; as a man sees at once motion and colour; the hand feels softness and warmth in the same piece of wax: yet the simple ideas thus united in the same subject, are as perfectly distinct, as those that come in by different senses. The coldness and hardness, which a man feels in a piece of *ice,* being as distinct ideas in the mind as the smell and whiteness of a lily; or as the taste of sugar, and smell of a rose: and there is nothing can be plainer to a man than the clear and distinct perception he has of those simple ideas; which being each in itself uncompounded, contains in it nothing but *one uniform appearance,* or conception in the mind, and is not distinguishable into different ideas.

2. The mind can neither make nor destroy them.

These simple ideas, the materials of all our knowledge, are suggested and furnished to the mind, only by those two ways above mentioned, *viz. sensation* and *reflection.* When the understanding is once stored with these simple ideas, it has the power to repeat, compare, and unite them, even to an almost infinite variety, and so can make at pleasure new complex ideas. But it is not in the power of the most exalted wit, or enlarged understanding, by any quickness or variety of thought, to *invent* or *frame one new simple idea* in the mind, not taken in by the ways before mentioned: nor can any force of the understanding, *destroy* those that are there. The dominion of man, in this little world of his own understanding, being muchwhat the same, as it is in the great world of visible things; wherein his power, however managed by art and skill, reaches no farther, than to compound and divide the materials, that are made to his hand; but can do nothing towards the making the least particle of new matter, or destroying one atom of what is already in being. The same inability, will every one find in himself, who shall go about to fashion in his understanding any simple idea, not received in by his senses from external objects; or by reflection from the operations of his own mind about them. I would have anyone try to fancy any taste which had never affected his palate; or frame the idea of a scent, he had never smelt: and when he can do this I will also conclude, that a blind man hath ideas of colours, and a deaf man true distinct notions of sounds. [. . .]

Chapter VIII
Some Further Considerations Concerning Our Simple Ideas of Sensation

8. Our ideas and the qualities of bodies.

Whatsoever the mind perceives in itself, or is the immediate object of perception, thought, or understanding, that I call *idea;* and the power to produce any idea in our mind, I call *quality* of the subject wherein that power is. Thus a snowball having the power to produce in us the ideas of *white, cold,* and *round,* the power to produce those ideas in us, as they are in the snowball, I call *qualities;* and as they are sensations, or perceptions, in our understandings, I call them *ideas;* which ideas, if I speak of sometimes, as in the things themselves, I would be understood to mean those qualities in the objects which produce them in us.

9. Primary qualities of bodies.

Qualities thus considered in bodies are, first, such as are utterly inseparable from the body, in what estate soever it be; such as in all the alterations and changes it suffers, all the force can be used upon it, it constantly keeps; and such as sense constantly finds in every particle of matter,

which has bulk enough to be perceived, and the mind finds inseparable from every particle of matter, though less than to make itself singly be perceived by our senses: *v.g.* take a grain of wheat, divide it into two parts, each part has still *solidity, extension, figure,* and *mobility;* divide it again, and it retains still the same qualities: and so divide it on, till the parts become insensible, they must retain still each of them all those qualities. For division (which is all that a mill, or pestle, or any other body, does upon another, in reducing it to insensible parts) can never take away either solidity, extension, figure, or mobility from any body, but only makes two, or more distinct separate masses of matter, of that which was but one before; all which distinct masses, reckoned as so many distinct bodies, after division make a certain number. These I call *original* or *primary qualities* of body, which I think we may observe to produce simple ideas in us, *viz.* solidity, extension, figure, motion or rest, and number.

10. Secondary qualities of bodies.

Secondly, such *qualities,* which in truth are nothing in the objects themselves, but power to produce various sensations in us by their *primary qualities,* i.e., by the bulk, figure, texture, and motion of their insensible parts, as colours, sounds, tastes, *etc.* These I call *secondary qualities.* To these might be added a third sort, which are allowed to be barely powers, though they are as much real qualities in the subject, as those which I, to comply with the common way of speaking, call *qualities,* but for distinction, *secondary qualities.* For the power in fire to produce a new colour, or consistency, in wax or clay by its primary qualities, is as much a quality in fire, as the power it has to produce in me a new idea or sensation of warmth or burning, which I felt not before, by the same primary qualities, *viz.* the bulk, texture and motion of its insensible parts.

11. How bodies produce ideas in us.

The next thing to be considered is, how *bodies* produce ideas in us, and that is manifestly *by impulse,* the only way which we can conceive bodies to operate in.

12. By motions, external, and in our organism.

If then external objects be not united to our minds, when they produce ideas in it; and yet we perceive *these original qualities* in such of them as singly fall under our senses, 'tis evident, that some motion must be thence continued by our nerves, or animal spirits, by some parts of our bodies, to the brains, or the seat of sensation, there to *produce in our minds the particular ideas we have of them.* And since the extension, figure, number, and motion of bodies of an observable bigness, may be perceived at a distance *by* the sight, 'tis evident some singly imperceptible bodies must come from them to the eyes, and thereby convey to the brain some *motion;* which produces these ideas which we have of them in us.

13. How secondary qualities produce their ideas.

After the same manner, that the ideas of these original qualities are produced in us, we may conceive that the ideas of *secondary* qualities are also *produced, viz. by the operation of insensible particles on our senses.* For, it being manifest, that there are bodies, and good store of bodies, each whereof are so small, that we cannot, by any of our senses, discover either their bulk, figure, or motion, as is evident in the particles of the air and water, and others extremely smaller than those, perhaps, as much smaller than the particles of air, or water, as the particles of air or water, are smaller than peas or hail-stones: Let us suppose at present, that the different motions and figures, bulk and number of such particles, affecting the several organs of our senses, produce in us those different sensations, which we have from the colours and smells of bodies, *v.g.* that a violet, by the impulse of such insensible particles of matter of peculiar figures, and bulks, and in different degrees and modifications of their motions, causes the ideas of the blue colour, and sweet scent of that flower to be produced in our minds. It being no more impossible, to conceive, that God should annex such ideas to such motions, with which they have no similitude; than that he should annex the idea of pain to the motion of a piece of steel dividing our flesh, with which that idea hath no resemblance.

14. They depend on the primary qualities.

What I have said concerning *colours* and *smells,* may be understood also of *tastes,* and *sounds, and other the like sensible qualities;* which, whatever reality we by mistake, attribute to them, are in truth nothing in the objects themselves, but powers to produce various sensations in us, and *depend on those primary qualities, viz.* bulk, figure, texture, and motion of parts as I have said.

15. Ideas of primary qualities are resemblances; of secondary, not.

From whence I think it easy to draw this observation, that the *ideas of primary qualities* of bodies, *are resemblances* of them, and their patterns do really exist in the bodies themselves, but the ideas, *produced* in us *by* these *secondary qualities, have no resemblance* of them at all. There is nothing like our ideas, existing in the bodies themselves. They are in the bodies, we denominate from them, only a power to produce those sensations in us: and what is sweet, blue, or warm in idea, is but the certain bulk, figure, and motion of the insensible parts, in the bodies themselves, which we call so.

16. Examples.

Flame is denominated *hot* and *light;* snow, *white* and *cold;* and *manna, white* and *sweet,* from the ideas they produce in us. Which qualities are commonly thought to be the same in those bodies, that those ideas are in us, the one the perfect resemblance of the other, as they are in a mirror, and it would by most men be judged very extravagant, if one should say otherwise. And yet he, that will consider, that the *same fire,* that at one distance *produces* in us the sensation of *warmth,* does at a nearer approach, produce in us the far different sensation of *pain,* ought to bethink himself what reason he has to say, that his idea of *warmth,* which was produced in him by the fire, is actually *in the fire*; and his idea of *pain,* which the same fire produced in him the same way, is *not* in the *fire.* Why are whiteness and coldness in snow, and pain not, when it produces the one and the other idea in us; and can do neither, but by the bulk, figure, number, and motion of its solid parts?

17. The ideas of the primary alone really exist.

The particular *bulk, number, figure, and motion of the parts of fire, or snow, are really in them,* whether anyone's senses perceive them or no: and therefore they may be called *real qualities,* because they really exist in those bodies. But *light, heat, whiteness,* or *coldness, are no more really in them than sickness or pain is in* manna. Take away the sensation of them; let not the eyes see light, or colours, nor the ears hear sounds; let the palate not taste, nor the nose smell, and all colours, tastes, odours, and sounds, as they are such particular ideas, vanish and cease, and are reduced to their causes, i.e., bulk, figure, and motion of parts. [. . .]

21. Explains how water felt as cold by one hand may be warm to the other.

Ideas being thus distinguished and understood, we may be able to give an account, how the same water, at the same time, may produce the idea of cold by one hand, and of heat by the other: whereas it is impossible that the same water, if those ideas were really in it, should at the same time be both hot and cold. For, if we imagine *warmth,* as it is *in our hands,* to be *nothing but a certain sort and degree of motion in the minute particles of our nerves, or animal spirits,* we may understand, how it is possible, that the same water may at the same time produce the sensation of heat in one hand, and cold in the other; which yet figure never does, that never producing the idea of a square by one hand, which has produced the idea of a globe by another. But if the sensation of heat and cold, be nothing but the increase or diminution of the motion of the minute parts of our bodies, caused by the corpuscles of any other body, it is easy to be understood, that if that motion be greater in one hand than in the other; if a body be applied to the two hands, which has in its minute particles a greater motion, than in those of one of the hands, and a less than in those of the other, it will increase the motion of the one hand, and lessen it in the other, and so cause the different sensations of heat and cold that depend thereon. [. . .]

26. Secondary qualities twofold; first, immediately perceivable; secondly, mediately perceivable.

To conclude, besides those before-mentioned *primary qualities* in bodies, *viz.* bulk, figure, extension, number, and motion of their solid parts; all the rest whereby we take notice of bodies, and distinguish them one from another, are nothing else, but several powers in them, depending on those primary qualities; whereby they are fitted, either by immediately operating on our bodies, to produce several different ideas in us; or else by operating on other bodies, so to change their primary qualities, as to render them capable of producing ideas in us, different from what before they did. The former of these,

I think, may be called *secondary qualities, immediately perceivable*: the latter, *secondary qualities, mediately perceivable*.

5

George Berkeley

(1685–1753)

Born in 1685, George Berkeley (pronounced Bark-lee) grew up near Thomastown, Ireland. Educated at Kilkenny College and Trinity College, Dublin, Berkeley completed his master's degree in 1707. He remained at Trinity College after graduation, taking up a position as tutor and lecturer. Berkeley's best-known contributions to philosophy are his A Treatise Concerning the Principles of Human Knowledge (1710) and Three Dialogues between Hylas and Philonous (1713). Although Berkeley's views were largely ridiculed at the time, he felt an obligation to counter the rise of materialism during this period. In short, Berkeley wanted to bring God back into mainstream philosophy. This shouldn't be too surprising, since Berkeley was ordained an Anglican priest in 1710 and received his doctorate in divinity in 1721. In 1725, he planned to open up a college in Bermuda for colonists and Native Americans. While he waited for financial backing, he and his new bride set sail for America in 1728, eventually settling in Newport,

Rhode Island. After three years, it became clear that no money was forthcoming to build his college. He eventually left America, returning to London, then Ireland to become Bishop of Cloyne, a post he held for eighteen years. In 1752, Berkeley and his family moved to Oxford; a year later he died. It should be noted that Berkeley, California, is named after this Irish philosopher, but its pronunciation has been Americanized (pronounced Berk-lee).

A Treatise Concerning the Principles of Human Knowledge

Part I

1. It is evident to anyone who takes a survey of the *objects* of human knowledge that they are either ideas actually imprinted on the senses, or else such as are perceived by attending to the passions and operations of the mind; or lastly, ideas formed by help of memory and imagination—either compounding, dividing, or barely representing those originally perceived in the aforesaid ways. By sight I have the ideas of light and colors, with their several degrees and variations. By touch I perceive, for example, hard and soft, heat and cold, motion and resistance, and of all these more and less either as to quantity or degree. Smelling furnishes me with odors, the palate with tastes, and hearing conveys sounds to the mind in all their variety of tone and composition. And as several of these are observed to accompany each other, they come to be marked by one name, and so to be reputed as one thing. Thus, for example,

a certain color, taste, smell, figure, and consistence having been observed to go together, are accounted one distinct thing signified by the name "apple"; other collections of ideas constitute a stone, a tree, a book, and the like sensible things—which as they are pleasing or disagreeable excite the passions of love, hatred, joy, grief, and so forth.

2. But, besides all that endless variety of ideas or objects of knowledge, there is likewise something which knows or perceives them and exercises divers operations, as willing, imagining, remembering, about them. This perceiving, active being is what I call *mind, spirit, soul,* or *myself.* By which words I do not denote any one of my ideas, but a thing entirely distinct from them, wherein they exist or, which is the same thing, whereby they are perceived—for the existence of an idea consists in being perceived.

3. That neither our thoughts, nor passions, nor ideas formed by the imagination exist without the mind is what everybody will allow. And it seems no less evident that the various sensations or ideas imprinted on the sense, however blended or combined together (that is, whatever objects they compose), cannot exist otherwise than in a mind perceiving them—I think an intuitive knowledge may be obtained of this by anyone that shall attend to what is meant by the term *exist* when applied to sensible things. The table I write on I say exists, that is, I see and feel it; and if I were out of my study I should say it existed—meaning thereby that if I was in my study I might perceive it, or that some other spirit actually does perceive it. There was an odor, that is, it was smelled; there was a sound, that is, it was heard; a color or figure, and it was perceived by sight or touch. This is all that I can understand by these and the like expressions. For as to what is said of the absolute existence of

unthinking things without any relation to their being perceived, that seems perfectly unintelligible. Their *esse* is *percepi,* nor is it possible they should have any existence out of the minds or thinking things which perceive them.

4. It is indeed an opinion strangely prevailing amongst men that houses, mountains, rivers, and, in a word, all sensible objects, have an existence, natural or real, distinct from their being perceived by the understanding. But with how great an assurance and acquiescence soever this principle may be entertained in the world, yet whoever shall find in his heart to call it in question may, if I mistake not, perceive it to involve a manifest contradiction. For, what are the forementioned objects but the things we perceive by sense? And what do we perceive besides our own ideas or sensations? And is it not plainly repugnant that any one of these, or any combination of them, should exist unperceived?

5. If we thoroughly examine this tenet it will, perhaps, be found at bottom to depend on the doctrine of *abstract ideas.* For can there be a nicer strain of abstraction than to distinguish the existence of sensible objects from their being perceived, so as to conceive them existing unperceived? Light and colors, heat and cold, extension and figures—in a word the things we see and feel—what are they but so many sensations, notions, ideas, or impressions on the sense? And is it possible to separate, even in thought, any of these from perception? For my part, I might as easily divide a thing from itself. I may, indeed, divide in my thoughts, or conceive apart from each other, those things which, perhaps, I never perceived by sense so divided. Thus I imagine the trunk of a human body without the limbs, or conceive the smell of a rose without thinking on the rose itself. So far, I will not deny, I can abstract—if that may

properly be called *abstraction* which extends only to the conceiving separately such objects as it is possible may really exist or be actually perceived asunder. But my conceiving or imagining power does not extend beyond the possibility of real existence or perception. Hence, as it is impossible for me to see or feel anything without an actual sensation of that thing, so is it impossible for me to conceive in my thoughts any sensible thing or object distinct from the sensation or perception of it.

6. Some truths there are so near and obvious to the mind that a man need only open his eyes to see them. Such I take this important one to be, to wit, that all the choir of heaven and furniture of the earth, in a word, all those bodies which compose the mighty frame of the world, have not any subsistence without a mind—that their *being* is to be perceived or known, that, consequently, so long as they are not actually perceived by me, or do not exist in my mind or that of any other created spirit, they must either have no existence at all or else subsist in the mind of some eternal spirit—it being perfectly unintelligible, and involving all the absurdity of abstraction, to attribute to any single part of them an existence independent of a spirit. To be convinced of which, the reader need only reflect, and try to separate in his own thoughts, the *being* of a sensible thing from its *being perceived.*

7. From what has been said it follows there is not any other substance than *spirit,* or that which perceives. But, for the fuller proof of this point, let it be considered the sensible qualities are color, figure, motion, smell, taste, and such the like—that is, the ideas perceived by sense. Now, for an idea to exist in an unperceiving thing is a manifest contradiction, for to have an idea is all one as to perceive; that, therefore, wherein color, figure, and the like qualities exist must perceive them; hence it is clear there can be no unthinking substance or *substratum* of those ideas.

8. But, say you, though the ideas themselves do not exist without the mind, yet there may be things like them, whereof they are copies or resemblances, which things exist without the mind in an unthinking substance. I answer, an idea can be like nothing but an idea; a color or figure can be like nothing but another color or figure. If we look but never so little into our thoughts, we shall find it impossible for us to conceive a likeness except only between our ideas. Again, I ask whether those supposed originals or external things, of which our ideas are the pictures or representations, be themselves perceivable or no? If they are, then they are ideas and we have gained our point; but if you say they are not, I appeal to anyone whether it be sense to assert a color is like something which is invisible; hard or soft, like something which is intangible; and so of the rest.

9. Some there are who make a distinction betwixt *primary* and *secondary* qualities. By the former they mean extension, figure, motion, rest, solidity or impenetrability, and number; by the latter they denote all other sensible qualities, as colors, sounds, tastes, and so forth. The ideas we have of these they acknowledge not to be the resemblances of anything existing without the mind, or unperceived, but they will have our ideas of the primary qualities to be patterns or images of things which exist without the mind, in an unthinking substance which they call "matter." By "matter," therefore, we are to understand an inert, senseless substance, in which extension, figure, and motion do actually subsist. But it is evident from what we have already shown that extension, figure, and motion are only ideas existing in the mind, and that an idea can be like nothing but another idea, and that

consequently neither they nor their archetypes can exist in an unperceiving substance. Hence, it is plain that that the very notion of what is called *matter* or *corporeal substance,* involves a contradiction in it.

10. They who assert that figure, motion, and the rest of the primary or original qualities do exist without the mind in unthinking substances do at the same time acknowledge that colors, sounds, heat, cold, and suchlike secondary qualities, do not—which they tell us are sensations existing in the mind alone, that depend on and are occasioned by the different size, texture, and motion of the minute particles of matter. This they take for an undoubted truth, which they can demonstrate beyond all exception. Now, if it be certain that those original qualities are inseparably united with the other sensible qualities, and not, even in thought, capable of being abstracted from them, it plainly follows that they exist only in the mind. But I desire anyone to reflect and try whether he can, by any abstraction of thought, conceive the extension and motion of a body without all other sensible qualities. For my own part, I see evidently that it is not in my power to frame an idea of a body extended and moved, but I must withal give it some color or other sensible quality which is acknowledged to exist only in the mind. In short, extension, figure, and motion, abstracted from all other qualities, are inconceivable. Where therefore the other sensible qualities are, there must these be also, to wit, in the mind and nowhere else.

11. Again, *great* and *small, swift* and *slow* are allowed to exist nowhere without the mind, being entirely relative, and changing as the frame or position of the organs of sense varies. The extension, therefore, which exists without the mind is neither great nor small, the motion neither swift nor slow; that is, they are nothing at all. But, say you, they are extension in general, and motion in general: thus we see how much the tenet of extended movable substances existing without the mind depends on the strange doctrine of *abstract ideas.* And here I cannot but remark how nearly the vague and indeterminate description of matter or corporeal substance, which the modern philosophers are run into by their own principles, resembles that antiquated and so much ridiculed notion of *materia prima,* to be met with in Aristotle and his followers. Without extension solidity cannot be conceived; since, therefore, it has been shown that extension exists not in an unthinking substance, the same must also be true of solidity.

12. That number is entirely the creature of the mind, even though the other qualities be allowed to exist without, will be evident to whoever considers that the same thing bears a different denomination of number as the mind views it with different respects. Thus, the same extension is one, or three, or thirty-six, according as the mind considers it with reference to a yard, a foot, or an inch. Number is so visibly relative and dependent on men's understanding that it is strange to think how any one should give it an absolute existence without the mind. We say one book, one page, one line; all these are equally units, though some contain several of the others. And in each instance it is plain the unit relates to some particular combination of ideas arbitrarily put together by the mind.

13. Unity I know some will have to be a simple or uncompounded idea accompanying all other ideas into the mind. That I have any such idea answering the word *unity* I do not find; and if I had, methinks I could not miss finding it: on the contrary, it should be the most familiar to my understanding, since it is said to accompany all other ideas and to be perceived by all the ways of

sensation and reflexion. To say no more, it is an *abstract idea.*

14. I shall farther add, that, after the same manner as modern philosophers prove certain sensible qualities to have no existence in matter, or without the mind, the same thing may be likewise proved of all other sensible qualities whatsoever. Thus, for instance, it is said that heat and cold are affections only of the mind, and not at all patterns of real beings existing in the corporeal substances which excite them, for that the same body which appears cold to one hand seems warm to another. Now, why may we not as well argue that figure and extension are not patterns or resemblances of qualities existing in matter, because to the same eye at different stations, or eyes of a different texture at the same station, they appear various and cannot, therefore, be the images of anything settled and determinate without the mind? Again, it is proved that sweetness is not really in the sapid thing, because the thing remaining unaltered, the sweetness is changed into bitter, as in case of a fever or otherwise vitiated palate. Is it not as reasonable to say that motion is not without the mind, since if the succession of ideas in the mind become swifter, the motion, it is acknowledged, shall appear slower without any alteration in any external object?

15. In short, let anyone consider those arguments which are thought manifestly to prove that colors and taste exist only in the mind, and he shall find they may with equal force be brought to prove the same thing of extension, figure, and motion. Though it must be confessed this method of arguing does not so much prove that there is no extension or color in an outward object as that we do not know by sense which is the true extension or color of the object. But the arguments foregoing plainly shew it to be

impossible that any color or extension at all, or other sensible quality whatsoever, should exist in an unthinking subject without the mind, or in truth, that there should be any such thing as an outward object.

16. But let us examine a little the received opinion.—It is said extension is a mode or accident of matter, and that matter is the *substratum* that supports it. Now I desire that you would explain to me what is meant by matter's *supporting* extension. Say you, I have no idea of matter and, therefore, cannot explain it. I answer, though you have no positive, yet, if you have any meaning at all, you must at least have a relative idea of matter; though you know not what it is, yet you must be supposed to know what relation it bears to accidents, and what is meant by its supporting them. It is evident "support" cannot here be taken in its usual or literal sense—as when we say that pillars support a building; in what sense therefore must it be taken?

17. If we inquire into what the most accurate philosophers declare themselves to mean by *material substance,* we shall find them acknowledge they have no other meaning annexed to those sounds but the idea of being in general together with the relative notion of its supporting accidents. The general idea of being appears to me the most abstract and incomprehensible of all other; and as for its supporting accidents, this, as we have just now observed, cannot be understood in the common sense of those words; it must, therefore, be taken in some other sense, but what that is they do not explain. So that when I consider the two parts or branches which make the signification of the words *material substance,* I am convinced there is no distinct meaning annexed to them. But why should we trouble ourselves any further in discussing this material substratum or support

of figure and motion and other sensible qualities? Does it not suppose they have an existence without the mind? And is not this a direct repugnancy and altogether inconceivable?

18. But, though it were possible that solid, figured, movable substances may exist without the mind, corresponding to the ideas we have of bodies, yet how is it possible for us to know this? Either we must know it by sense or by reason. As for our senses, by them we have the knowledge only of our sensations, ideas, or those things that are immediately perceived by sense, call them what you will; but they do not inform us that things exist without the mind, or unperceived, like to those which are perceived. This the materialists themselves acknowledge. It remains therefore that if we have any knowledge at all of external things, it must be by reason, inferring their existence from what is immediately perceived by sense. But what reason can induce us to believe the existence of bodies without the mind, from what we perceive, since the very patrons of matter themselves do not pretend there is any necessary connexion betwixt them and our ideas? I say it is granted on all hands (and what happens in dreams, frenzies, and the like, puts it beyond dispute) that it is possible we might be affected with all the ideas we have now, though no bodies existed without resembling them. Hence it is evident the supposition of external bodies is not necessary for the producing our ideas; since it is granted they are produced sometimes, and might possibly be produced always in the same order we see them in at present, without their concurrence.

19. But though we might possibly have all our sensations without them, yet perhaps it may be thought easier to conceive and explain the manner of their production by supposing external bodies in their likeness rather than

otherwise; and so it might be at least probable there are such things as bodies that excite their ideas in our minds. But neither can this be said, for, though we give the materialists their external bodies, they by their own confession are never the nearer knowing how our ideas are produced; since they own themselves unable to comprehend in what manner body can act upon spirit, or how it is possible it should imprint any idea in the mind. Hence it is evident the production of ideas or sensations in our minds can be no reason why we should suppose matter or corporeal substances, since that is acknowledged to remain equally inexplicable with or without this supposition. If therefore it were possible for bodies to exist without the mind, yet to hold they do so must needs be a very precarious opinion, since it is to suppose, without any reason at all, that God has created innumerable beings that are entirely useless and serve to no manner of purpose.

20. In short, if there were external bodies, it is impossible we should ever come to know it; and if there were not, we might have the very same reasons to think there were that we have now. Suppose—what no one can deny possible—an intelligence without the help of external bodies, to be affected with the same train of sensations or ideas that you are, imprinted in the same order and with like vividness in his mind. I ask whether that intelligence hath not all the reason to believe the existence of corporeal substances, represented by his ideas and exciting them in his mind, that you can possibly have for believing the same thing? Of this there can be no question—which one consideration is enough to make any reasonable person suspect the strength of whatever arguments he may think himself to have for the existence of bodies without the mind.

21. Were it necessary to add any farther proof against the existence of matter after what has

been said, I could instance several of those errors and difficulties (not to mention impieties) which have sprung from that tenet. It has occasioned numberless controversies and disputes in philosophy, and not a few of far greater moment in religion. But I shall not enter into the detail of them in this place as well because I think arguments *a posteriori* are unnecessary for confirming what has been, if I mistake not, sufficiently demonstrated *a priori,* as because I shall hereafter find occasion to speak somewhat of them.

22. I am afraid I have given cause to think I am needlessly prolix in handling this subject. For to what purpose is it to dilate on that which may be demonstrated with the utmost evidence in a line or two to anyone that is capable of the least reflection? It is but looking into your own thoughts, and so trying whether you can conceive it possible for a sound, or figure, or motion, or color to exist without the mind or unperceived. This easy trial may make you see that what you contend for is a downright contradiction. Insomuch that I am content to put the whole upon this issue: if you can but conceive it spossible for one extended movable substance, or, in general, for any one idea, or anything like an idea, to exist otherwise than in a mind perceiving it, I shall readily give up the cause. And, as for all that compages of external bodies which you contend for, I shall grant you its existence, though you cannot either give me any reason why you believe it exists, or assign any use to it when it is supposed to exist. I say, the bare possibility of your opinion's being true shall pass for an argument that it is so.

23. But, say you, surely there is nothing easier than to imagine trees, for instance, in a park, or books existing in a closet, and nobody by to perceive them. I answer, you may so, there is no difficulty in it; but what is all this, I beseech you, more than framing in your mind certain ideas which you call books and trees, and the same time omitting to frame the idea of anyone that may perceive them? But do not you yourself perceive or think of them all the while? This therefore is nothing to the purpose; it only shows you have the power of imagining or forming ideas in your mind: but it does not shew that you can conceive it possible the objects of your thought may exist without the mind. To make out this, it is necessary that you conceive them existing unconceived or unthought of, which is a manifest repugnancy. When we do our utmost to conceive the existence of external bodies, we are all the while only contemplating our own ideas. But the mind taking no notice of itself, is deluded to think it can and does conceive bodies existing unthought of or without the mind, though at the same time they are apprehended by or exist in itself. A little attention will discover to anyone the truth and evidence of what is here said, and make it unnecessary to insist on any other proofs against the existence of *material substance.*

6

David Hume

(1711–1776)

David Hume was born in Edinburgh, Scotland, in 1711. Although his family wanted him to become a lawyer, he rejected this idea. Instead, he went to the University

of Edinburgh for two years, eventually withdrawing to pursue private studies in philosophy, literature, and history. He continued his studies in philosophy in France between 1734 and 1737, during which time he wrote his Treatise on Human Nature. *After finishing his work, he returned to the U.K., spending a year and a half in London polishing and, eventually, publishing his* Treatise on Human Nature. *Disappointed with his book's reception, Hume made his way from London to Scotland, seeking positions at the University of Edinburgh and University of Glasgow, both of which he did not get. Disappointed, Hume accepted a position of librarian at the Advocates' Library in Edinburgh in 1752. It was during his time as librarian that Hume wrote the* Natural History of Religion, *which was published in 1757, and* Dialogues Concerning Natural Religion, *which was published posthumously in 1779. Hume was also an historian. He published his six-volume* History of England *between 1754 and 1762, making him very wealthy. In 1763, he accepted a position as the secretary to the British ambassador to France. He returned from France in 1766 and was appointed as an Under Secretary of State in the Home Office. Hume held the position for one year, whereupon he retired and returned to Edinburgh. He died of intestinal cancer in 1776. His other major works include* An Enquiry Concerning the Principles of Morals *(1751) and* Political Discourses *(1752).*

Enquiries Concerning Human Understanding

Section IV

Sceptical Doubts Concerning the Operations of the Understanding

Part I

All the objects of human reason or enquiry may naturally be divided into two kinds, to wit, *Relations of Ideas*, and *Matters of Fact*. Of the first kind are the sciences of Geometry, Algebra, and Arithmetic; and in short, every affirmation, which is either intuitively or demonstratively certain. *That the square of the hypothenuse is equal to the square of the two sides*, is a proposition, which expresses a relation between these figures. *That three times five is equal to the half of thirty*, expresses a relation between these numbers. Propositions of this kind are discoverable by the mere operation of thought, without dependence on what is anywhere existent in the universe. Though there never were a circle or triangle in nature, the truths demonstrated by Euclid, would for ever retain their certainty and evidence.

Matters of fact, which are the second objects of human reason, are not ascertained in the same manner; nor is our evidence of their truth, however great, of a like nature with the foregoing. The contrary of every matter of fact is still possible; because it can never imply a contradiction, and is conceived by the mind with the same facility and distinctness, as if ever so conformable to reality. *That the sun will not rise tomorrow* is no less intelligible a proposition, and implies no more contradiction, than the affirmation, *that it will rise*. We should in vain, therefore, attempt to demonstrate its falsehood. Were it demonstratively false, it would imply a contradiction, and could never be distinctly conceived by the mind.

It may, therefore, be a subject worthy of curiosity, to enquire what is the nature of that evidence which assures us of any real existence and matter of fact, beyond the present testimony of our senses, or the records of our memory. This part of philosophy, it is observable, has been little cultivated, either by the ancients or moderns; and therefore our doubts and errors, in the prosecution of so important an enquiry, may be the more excusable; while we march through such difficult paths, without any guide or direction. They may even prove useful, by exciting curiosity, and destroying that implicit faith and security, which is the bane of all reasoning and free enquiry. The discovery of defects in the common philosophy, if any such there be, will not, I presume, be a discouragement, but rather an incitement, as is usual, to attempt something more full and satisfactory, than has yet been proposed to the public.

All reasonings concerning matter of fact seem to be founded on the relation of *Cause and Effect*. By means of that relation alone we can go beyond the evidence of our memory and senses. If you were to ask a man, why he believes any matter of fact, which is absent; for instance, that his friend is in the country, or in France; he would give you a reason; and this reason would be some other fact; as a letter received from him, or the knowledge of his former resolutions and promises. A man, finding a watch or any other machine in a desert island, would conclude that there had once been men in that island. All our reasonings concerning fact are of the same nature. And here it is constantly supposed, that there is a connexion between the present fact and that which is inferred from it. Were there nothing to bind them together, the inference would be entirely precarious. The hearing of an articulate voice and rational discourse in the dark assures us of the presence of some person: Why? because these are the effects of the human make and fabric, and closely connected with it. If we anatomize all the other reasonings of this nature, we shall find, that they are founded on

the relation of cause and effect, and that this relation is either near or remote, direct or collateral. Heat and light are collateral effects of fire, and the one effect may justly be inferred from the other.

If we would satisfy ourselves, therefore, concerning the nature of that evidence, which assures us of matters of fact, we must enquire how we arrive at the knowledge of cause and effect.

I shall venture to affirm, as a general proposition, which admits of no exception, that the knowledge of this relation is not, in any instance, attained by reasonings *a priori*; but arises entirely from experience, when we find that any particular objects are constantly conjoined with each other. Let an object be presented to a man of ever so strong natural reason and abilities; if that object be entirely new to him, he will not be able, by the most accurate examination of its sensible qualities, to discover any of its causes or effects. Adam, though his rational faculties be supposed, at the very first, entirely perfect, could not have inferred from the fluidity and transparency of water that it would suffocate him, or from the light and warmth of fire that it would consume him. No object ever discovers, by the qualities which appear to the senses, either the causes which produced it, or the effects which will arise from it; nor can our reason, unassisted by experience, ever draw any inference concerning real existence and matter of fact.

This proposition, *that causes and effects are discoverable, not by reason but by experience*, will readily be admitted with regard to such objects, as we remember to have once been altogether unknown to us; since we must be conscious of the utter inability, which we then lay under, of foretelling what would arise from them. Present two smooth pieces of marble to a man who has no tincture of natural philosophy;

he will never discover that they will adhere together in such a manner as to require great force to separate them in a direct line, while they make so small a resistance to a lateral pressure. Such events, as bear little analogy to the common course of nature, are also readily confessed to be known only by experience; nor does any man imagine that the explosion of gunpowder, or the attraction of a loadstone, could ever be discovered by arguments *a priori*. In like manner, when an effect is supposed to depend upon an intricate machinery or secret structure of parts, we make no difficulty in attributing all our knowledge of it to experience. Who will assert, that he can give the ultimate reason, why milk or bread is proper nourishment for a man, not for a lion or a tiger?

But the same truth may not appear, at first sight, to have the same evidence with regard to events, which have become familiar to us from our first appearance in the world, which bear a close analogy to the whole course of nature, and which are supposed to depend on the simple qualities of objects, without any secret structure of parts. We are apt to imagine that we could discover these effects by the mere operation of our reason, without experience. We fancy, that were we brought on a sudden into this world, we could at first have inferred that one Billiard-ball would communicate motion to another upon impulse; and that we needed not to have waited for the event, in order to pronounce with certainty concerning it. Such is the influence of custom, that, where it is strongest, it not only covers our natural ignorance, but even conceals itself, and seems not to take place, merely because it is found in the highest degree.

But to convince us that all the laws of nature, and all the operations of bodies without exception, are known only by experience, the following reflections may, perhaps, suffice. Were any object presented to us, and were we required to pronounce concerning the effect, which will result from it, without consulting past observation; after what manner, I beseech you, must the mind proceed in this operation? It must invent or imagine some event, which it ascribes to the object as its effect; and it is plain that this invention must be entirely arbitrary. The mind can never possibly find the effect in the supposed cause, by the most accurate scrutiny and examination. For the effect is totally different from the cause, and consequently can never be discovered in it. Motion in the second Billiard-ball is a quite distinct event from motion in the first; nor is there anything in the one to suggest the smallest hint of the other. A stone or piece of metal raised into the air, and left without any support, immediately falls: but to consider the matter *a priori*, is there anything we discover in this situation, which can beget the idea of a downward, rather than an upward, or any other motion, in the stone or metal?

And as the first imagination or invention of a particular effect, in all natural operations, is arbitrary, where we consult not experience; so must we also esteem the supposed tie or connexion between the cause and effect, which binds them together, and renders it impossible, that any other effect could result from the operation of that cause. When I see, for instance, a Billiard-ball moving in a straight line towards another; even suppose motion in the second ball should by accident be suggested to me, as the result of their contact or impulse; may I not conceive, that a hundred different events might as well follow from that cause? May not both these balls remain at absolute rest? May not the first ball return in a straight line, or leap off from the second in any line or direction? All these suppositions are consistent and conceivable. Why then should we give the preference to one, which is no more consistent or conceivable than the rest? All our reasonings *a priori* will never be able to show us any foundation for this preference.

In a word, then, every effect is a distinct event from its cause. It could not, therefore, be discovered in the cause, and the first invention or conception of it, *a priori*, must be entirely arbitrary. And even after it is suggested, the conjunction of it with the cause must appear equally arbitrary; since there are always many other effects, which, to reason, must seem fully as consistent and natural. In vain, therefore, should we pretend to determine any single event, or infer any cause or effect, without the assistance of observation and experience. [. . .]

Part II

[. . .] I shall content myself, in this section, with an easy task, and shall pretend only to give a negative answer to the question here proposed. I say then, that, even after we have experience of the operations of cause and effect, our conclusions from that experience are *not* founded on reasoning, or any process of the understanding. This answer we must endeavour, both to explain and to defend.

It must certainly be allowed, that nature has kept us at a great distance from all her secrets, and has afforded us only the knowledge of a few superficial qualities of objects; while she conceals from us those powers and principles on which the influence of these objects entirely depends. Our senses inform us of the colour, weight, and consistence of bread; but neither sense nor reason can ever inform us of those qualities which fit it for the nourishment and support of a human body. Sight or feeling conveys an idea of the actual motion of bodies; but as to that wonderful

force or power, which would carry on a moving body for ever in a continued change of place, and which bodies never lose but by communicating it to others; of this we cannot form the most distant conception. But notwithstanding this ignorance of natural powers and principles, we always presume, when we see like sensible qualities, that they have like secret powers, and expect that effects, similar to those which we have experienced, will follow from them. If a body of like colour and consistence with that bread, which we have formerly eat, be presented to us, we make no scruple of repeating the experiment, and foresee, with certainty, like nourishment and support. Now this is a process of the mind or thought, of which I would willingly know the foundation. It is allowed on all hands, that there is no known connexion between the sensible qualities and the secret powers; and consequently, that the mind is not led to form such a conclusion concerning their constant and regular conjunction, by anything which it knows of their nature. As to past *Experience*, it can be allowed to give *direct* and *certain* information of those precise objects only, and that precise period of time, which fell under its cognizance: but why this experience should be extended to future times, and to other objects, which for aught we know, may be only in appearance similar; this is the main question on which I would insist. The bread, which I formerly eat, nourished me; that is, a body of such sensible qualities, was, at that time, endued with such secret powers: but does it follow, that other bread must also nourish me at another time, and that like sensible qualities must always be attended with like secret powers? The consequence seems nowise necessary. At least, it must be acknowledged that there is here a consequence drawn by the mind; that there is a certain step taken; a process of thought, and an inference, which wants to be explained. These two propositions are far from being the same, *I have found that such an object has always been attended with such an effect*, and *I foresee, that other objects, which are, in appearance, similar, will be attended with similar effects*. I shall allow, if you please, that the one proposition may justly be inferred from the other: I know in fact, that it always is inferred. But if you insist that the inference is made by a chain of reasoning, I desire you to produce that reasoning. [. . .]

Section V
Sceptical Solution of These Doubts
Part I

The passion for philosophy, like that for religion, seems liable to this inconvenience, that, though it aims at the correction of our manners, and extirpation of our vices, it may only serve, by imprudent management, to foster a predominant inclination, and push the mind, with more determined resolution, towards that side which already *draws* too much, by the bias and propensity of the natural temper. It is certain, that, while we aspire to the magnanimous firmness of the philosophic sage, and endeavour to confine our pleasures altogether within our own minds, we may, at last, render our philosophy like that of Epictetus, and other *Stoics*, only a more refined system of selfishness, and reason ourselves out of all virtue as well as social enjoyment. While we study with attention the vanity of human life, and turn all our thoughts towards the empty and transitory nature of riches and honours, we are, perhaps, all the while, flattering our natural indolence, which, hating the bustle of the world, and drudgery of business, seeks a pretence of reason to give itself a full and uncontrolled indulgence. There is, however, one

species of philosophy which seems little liable to this inconvenience, and that because it strikes in with no disorderly passion of the human mind, nor can mingle itself with any natural affection or propensity; and that is the Academic or Sceptical philosophy. The academics always talk of doubt and suspense of judgment, of danger in hasty determinations, of confining to very narrow bounds the enquiries of the understanding, and of renouncing all speculations which lie not within the limits of common life and practice. Nothing, therefore, can be more contrary than such a philosophy to the supine indolence of the mind, its rash arrogance, its lofty pretensions, and its superstitious credulity. Every passion is mortified by it, except the love of truth; and that passion never is, nor can be, carried to too high a degree. It is surprising, therefore, that this philosophy, which, in almost every instance, must be harmless and innocent, should be the subject of so much groundless reproach and obloquy. But, perhaps, the very circumstance which renders it so innocent is what chiefly exposes it to the public hatred and resentment. By flattering no irregular passion, it gains few partizans: By opposing so many vices and follies, it raises to itself abundance of enemies, who stigmatize it as libertine, profane, and irreligious.

Nor need we fear, that this philosophy, while it endeavours to limit our enquiries to common life, should ever undermine the reasonings of common life, and carry its doubts so far as to destroy all action, as well as speculation. Nature will always maintain her rights, and prevail in the end over any abstract reasoning whatsoever. Though we should conclude, for instance, as in the foregoing section, that, in all reasonings from experience, there is a step taken by the mind, which is not supported by any argument or process of the understanding; there is no danger that these reasonings, on which almost all knowledge depends, will ever be affected by such a discovery. If the mind be not engaged by argument to make this step, it must be induced by some other principle of equal weight and authority; and that principle will preserve its influence as long as human nature remains the same. What that principle is, may well be worth the pains of enquiry.

Suppose a person, though endowed with the strongest faculties of reason and reflection, to be brought on a sudden into this world; he would, indeed, immediately observe a continual succession of objects, and one event following another; but he would not be able to discover any thing farther. He would not, at first, by any reasoning, be able to reach the idea of cause and effect; since the particular powers, by which all natural operations are performed, never appear to the senses; nor is it reasonable to conclude, merely because one event, in one instance, precedes another, that therefore the one is the cause, the other the effect. Their conjunction may be arbitrary and casual. There may be no reason to infer the existence of one from the appearance of the other. And in a word, such a person, without more experience, could never employ his conjecture or reasoning concerning any matter of fact, or be assured of anything beyond what was immediately present to his memory and senses.

Suppose again, that he has acquired more experience, and has lived so long in the world as to have observed similar objects or events to be constantly conjoined together; what is the consequence of this experience? He immediately infers the existence of one object from the appearance of the other. Yet he has not, by all his experience, acquired any idea or knowledge of the secret power, by which the one object produces the other; nor is it, by any process of reasoning, he is engaged to draw this inference. But still he finds himself determined to draw it: And though he should be convinced that his understanding has no part in the operation, he would nevertheless continue in the same course of thinking. There is some other principle, which determines him to form such a conclusion.

This principle is Custom or Habit. For wherever the repetition of any particular act or operation produces a propensity to renew the same act or operation, without being impelled by any reasoning or process of the understanding; we always say, that this propensity is the effect of *Custom*. By employing that word, we pretend not to have given the ultimate reason of such a propensity. We only point out a principle of human nature, which is universally acknowledged, and which is well known by its effects. Perhaps we can push our enquiries no farther, or pretend to give the cause of this cause; but must rest contented with it as the ultimate principle, which we can assign, of all our conclusions from experience. It is sufficient satisfaction, that we can go so far, without repining at the narrowness of our faculties because they will carry us no farther. And it is certain we here advance a very intelligible proposition at least, if not a true one, when we assert that, after the constant conjunction of two objects—heat and flame, for instance, weight and solidity—we are determined by custom alone to expect the one from the appearance of the other. This hypothesis seems even the only one which explains the difficulty, why we draw, from a thousand instances, an inference which we are not able to draw from one instance, that is, in no respect, different from them. Reason is incapable of any such variation. The conclusions which it draws from considering one circle are the same which it would form upon surveying all the circles in the universe. But no man, having seen only one body move after being impelled by another, could infer that every other body will move after a like impulse. All inferences from experience, therefore, are effects of custom, not of reasoning.

Custom, then, is the great guide of human life. It is that principle alone, which renders our experience useful to us, and makes us expect, for the future, a similar train of events with those which have appeared in the past. Without the influence of custom, we should be entirely ignorant of every matter of fact beyond what is immediately present to the memory and senses. We should never know how to adjust means to ends, or to employ our natural powers in the production of any effect. There would be an end at once of all action, as well as of the chief part of speculation.

But here it may be proper to remark, that though our conclusions from experience carry us beyond our memory and senses, and assure us of matters of fact which happened in the most distant places and most remote ages, yet some fact must always be present to the senses or memory, from which we may first proceed in drawing these conclusions. A man, who should find in a desert country the remains of pompous buildings, would conclude that the country had, in ancient times, been cultivated by civilized inhabitants; but did nothing of this nature occur to him, he could never form such an inference. We learn the events of former ages from history; but then we must peruse the volumes in which this instruction is contained, and thence carry up our inferences from one testimony to another, till we arrive at the eyewitnesses and spectators of these distant events. In a word, if we proceed not upon some fact, present to the memory or senses, our reasonings would be merely hypothetical;

and however the particular links might be connected with each other, the whole chain of inferences would have nothing to support it, nor could we ever, by its means, arrive at the knowledge of any real existence. If I ask, why you believe any particular matter of fact, which you relate, you must tell me some reason; and this reason will be some other fact, connected with it. But as you cannot proceed after this manner, *in infinitum*, you must at last terminate in some fact, which is present to your memory or senses; or must allow that your belief is entirely without foundation.

What then is the conclusion of the whole matter? A simple one; though, it must be confessed, pretty remote from the common theories of philosophy. All belief of matter of fact or real existence is derived merely from some object, present to the memory or senses, and a customary conjunction between that and some other object. Or in other words; having found, in many instances, that any two kinds of objects—flame and heat, snow and cold— have always been conjoined together; if flame or snow be presented anew to the senses, the mind is carried by custom to expect heat or cold, and to *believe* that such a quality does exist, and will discover itself upon a nearer approach. This belief is the necessary result of placing the mind in such circumstances. It is an operation of the soul, when we are so situated, as unavoidable as to feel the passion of love, when we receive benefits; or hatred, when we meet with injuries. All these operations are a species of natural instincts, which no reasoning or process of the thought and understanding is able, either to produce, or to prevent.

On Certainty

Knowledge is in the end based on acknowledgement.
—Ludwig Wittgenstein

Discussion Questions

1. By holding up his hands and saying, "I know these are my hands," does Moore show that scepticism is false? Why or why not? Would such a commonsense approach convince you that knowledge of the external world is indubitable? What other kinds of Moore-type statements are beyond doubt?

2. Is it possible to defend scepticism? How might a sceptic answer the question, "How do you (the sceptic) know that Moore is wrong?" Is there any way a sceptic could answer this without falling victim to his or her own scepticism?

3. In what ways do you agree or disagree with Wittgenstein's claim that some human knowledge is beyond doubt? As a child, what sorts of things did you learn about the world that were absolutely certain? Discuss whether or not Wittgenstein offers a sufficient argument against the sceptic.

G. E. Moore's Hands

As we saw earlier, stalking the wild horse of scepticism is a difficult task. Although Descartes, Locke, and Berkeley each argued against scepticism differently, for the English philosopher G. E. (George Edward) Moore, a unique approach was needed, not one based on introspection, primary and secondary qualities, or God, but one based on common sense. Moore defended such a commonsense view of knowledge in two famous papers entitled "A Defence of Common-Sense" and "Proof of an External World." In "Proof of an External World," Moore offers us a very interesting commonsense argument against scepticism. It is ingenious in its subtly and simplicity. Moore states:

> I can prove now, for instance, that two hands exist. How? By holding up my two hands, and saying, as I make a certain gesture with the right hand, 'Here is one hand', and adding, as I make a certain gesture with the left, 'and here is another'. . . But did I prove just now that two hands were then in existence? I do want to insist that I did; that the proof which I gave was a perfectly rigorous one; and that it is perhaps impossible to give a better or more rigorous proof of anything whatever. (145–146)

By raising his hands to his face, according to Moore, he has established convincing proof that a real and knowable world exists external to the mind.[10] In light of Moore, raise your own hands in front of your face while make declarative statements that these are your hands. Does Moore's simplistic example show that scepticism is false?

Although Moore states in the above quotation that he is giving us a proof that his hands exist, in fact, he thought no proof or justification could be given. He writes, "How am I to prove now that 'Here's one hand, and here's another'? I do not believe I can do it" (Proof of an External World 149). For Moore, we can know some things with certainty without justification. This kind of unjustified certainty is applicable to other knowledge claims as well. In his "A Defence of Common-Sense," Moore produces a list of other propositions he knows with certainty to be true:

> There exists at present a living body, which is my body . . . Ever since it [my body] was born, it has been either in contact with or not far from the surface to the earth; and, at every moment since it was born, there have also existed many other things, having shape and size in three dimensions; . . . there have, at every moment since its birth, been large numbers of other living human bodies; . . . the earth had existed also for many years before my body was born; . . . I am a human being, and I have, at different times since my body was born, had many different experiences. . . . (33)

Folk, not bitten by scepticism, would hardly question such claims. It is this commonsense view that Moore was highlighting in his papers. The commonsense view of the world proves the truth of these propositions without the need for justification. More importantly, however, he claimed to know such propositions by virtue of other propositions. For example, the belief that I am now typing on the computer presupposes other propositions such as the belief that my body has not been far from the surface of the earth, the existence of my hands, and so forth. It's the latter type of propositions that Moore thinks lends support for his commonsense approach to knowledge without the need for proof or justification.

Avoiding the Sceptic's Challenge

This apparent lack of justification poses problems for Moore. Recall earlier, knowledge is traditionally defined as true justified belief. Without justification, it is hard to imagine how Moore, or anyone else, could have knowledge at all. However, as Georg Hendrik von Wright points out, it was important for Moore to meet the sceptical challenge on different grounds to avoid the deep kind of scepticism lurking around traditional epistemological corners. Consider, for example, how a sceptic might respond to Moore's claim, "I know that my hands exist." A sceptic might respond by asking Moore to give a proof or justification of how he knows they exist. Moore might respond by claiming, "I can see my hands and, therefore, I know they exist." But the sceptic can pull from a hat any number of challenges, including brains in a vat, evil demons, and perceptual illusions to show such a criterion is insufficient for knowledge. Moore would then be required to offer another proof, which, once again, is open to some form of sceptical challenge—and an infinite regress looms. In short, so long as sceptics can show it's logically possible that the justification for one's knowledge claim is weak, they win the day. To avoid this problem, Moore said nothing other than he knows some things with certainty.

The Nature of Doubt Wittgenstein-Style

Ludwig Wittgenstein was both perplexed and fascinated by Moore's solution to scepticism. He was perplexed because he thought Moore's defence of common sense was not really a defence at all. Moore's proposition that the earth existed long before his birth, for example, was not a paradigm example of knowledge because, in most cases, he never doubted it in the first place. Wittgenstein was also fascinated because he thought Moore's propositions were correct; they played a special foundational role regarding knowledge, generally, and also provided a significant attack against scepticism. Let me explain these points in detail.

As we saw earlier, Moore outlines a number of propositions he knows with certainty, including:

- I have two hands.
- There exists at present a living body, which is *my* body.
- My body has been either in contact with or not far from the surface to the earth.
- At every moment since it was born, there have also existed many other things, having shape and size in three dimensions.
- There have, at every moment since its birth, been large numbers of other living human bodies.
- The earth had existed for many years before my body was born.
- I am a human being.
- I have, at different times since my body was born, had many different experiences.

But Wittgenstein thinks there is something odd about these statements as a proof of certain knowledge. Imagine over cocktails someone casually mentions to you, "I know these are my hands." You would probably find this a strange thing to say, given the circumstances. We, normally speaking, don't doubt everything we see, touch, hear, smell, or taste. Although we may doubt (i.e., be unsure), under special circumstances, whether the Calgary Flames won the Stanley Cup in 1989, our doubts are usually held in check. Wittgenstein remarks that normally these kinds of propositions stated by Moore lack sense. To say, "here is my hand" is not only out of context but seems utterly wrong and misguided in the first place. To see this, consider, for example, the question, "How do you know that 2 + 2 = 4?" Giving grounds or evidence could take the form of seeing or calculating. I can know that 2 + 2 = 4 by calculating it by hand, by watching carefully, by checking my answer with a calculator, and so forth. Moreover, I can provide further evidence that my hand, eyes, and calculator are all working properly. But, for Wittgenstein, there comes an end-point where no more evidence can be given; these grounds or evidence that cannot be doubted. And, says von Wright, this was the problem with Moore's proposition; they were end-points themselves; they were never doubted in the first place but, most importantly, are the grounds upon which, say, calculating 2 + 2 depends. Ask yourself, did Moore really believe his hands did not exist and, therefore, had to prove it to himself and his students? No, he not only never doubted it but also proved his hands existed by his previous behaviour—writing, open doors, tying shoes, etc. Perhaps in the grips of psychosis you might wonder if that really is your hand, and reassure yourself by saying, "I know this is my hand," but normally such claims of certainty are meaningless or senseless. This is the point Wittgenstein wishes to make of Moore. Moore's claims of certainty are meaningless because they fall outside of normal circumstances and, most importantly, we usually do not doubt the existence of our hands. Moore's proofs are superfluous; his hands were never doubted before or after his proof. And it's this *peculiar* role of Moore's propositions, says von Wright, not whether we know the propositions themselves, which is at issue for Wittgenstein.

Language Games and the Meaning of Doubt

Languages games, put generally, are the everyday human activities, institutions, customs, and situations that define a particular practice. In Moore's examples, the use of "I know" is nonsense because it is not being used in ordinary circumstances and therefore stands outside of the language games we play. To highlight the concept of language games, consider the difference between two propositions:

- At this distance from the sun there is a planet.
- Here is a hand.

Although both look like empirical propositions, whereby evidence and proof can determine their truth or falsity, Wittgenstein thinks there is a sharp boundary between them. Although we could perhaps doubt that a planet is a particular distance from the sun, doubting the existence of one's hands loses sense. We normally do not doubt the existence or our hands—our hands are beyond doubt—not because we say we are certain of them à la Moore but because our actions and experience prove otherwise. Doubting can only be played in certain context or language games where it makes sense. Moore fails to realize that the proof of his hands falls outside the language game of doubt. Wittgenstein writes, "521. Moore's mistake lies in this—countering the assertion that one cannot know that, by saying, 'I do know it'" (68). Moore's attempt to prove that there is an external world is both misguided and unnecessary. It is misguided because the existence of one's hands is beyond doubt; and because it is beyond doubt, no proof is necessary (Stroll 123). To understand what Wittgenstein is saying, ask yourself under what circumstances you would make such pronouncements as Moore? Under what circumstances, might you doubt, say, the existence of your hands?

As von Wright mentions, Wittgenstein is trying to drive a wedge between ordinary doubt and philosophical doubt, i.e., scepticism. Moore's answer to the sceptic is to show that various propositions are true. But what Moore did not realize is that philosophical doubt makes no sense at all because doubt itself presupposes certainty (Wittgenstein 18). Philosophical sceptics would not only have to doubt that their hands existed but also the very words they used to make such claims against knowledge; this would make language itself meaningless. That is, in order to say, "I doubt my hands exist," a person must understand the words "I," "doubt," "my," "hands," and "exist." True sceptics would not only have to doubt their hands but also the words they use to express such doubts. But sceptics do not doubt their words; therefore, philosophical scepticism is doomed from the start because it presupposes some level of certainty, in this case, language. Children growing up in a culture that doubted its words would never learn language; they would never be sure of their own names. Not only is universal doubt impossible but also doubt presupposes certainty—the very words we use. Ordinary doubt, in contrast, depends on the language game played; it depends on the context in which such utterances are stated. So I might doubt that Pluto is 2.7 billion kilometres from Earth because such distances are beyond ordinary comprehension; however, I cannot doubt that I live in Calgary. At some point ordinary doubt comes to an end, a bedrock of certainty is reached, says von Wright. We do not doubt the words we use, that our hands exist, the earth has existed long before our birth, or that we live in a particular place. Consider historical knowledge, asks von Wright. If the truth of the position "the earth has existed many years in the past" were seriously doubted, all historical claims would cease to exist. However, we don't usually doubt historical knowledge and, more importantly, it presupposes that the earth has existed in the past; for without such a claim, acting as a bedrock or foundation, no historical investigation could take place. Moore's propositions are beyond doubt and, as such, act as the foundation upon which ordinary doubts are based. Outside of appropriate situations to say "I know . . . X" is senseless.

Moore was not wrong in stating the propositions he did, only in using "I know" to establish certainty. Doubting such Moore-type propositions is senseless because some propositions are exempt for justification and act as hinges upon which our questions and doubts turn. Granted, says von Wright, there are circumstances where such doubts might be justified. Consider a hor-rible car accident whereby two people each have a hand ripped off and coincidently the hands end up lying side by side. Each person might point to a hand lying in the gutter and say, "I know that is my hand," to ensure doctors reattach the right one. In this extraordinary situation, doubt comes into play and, therefore, such statements are meaningful because they are played in context, or what Wittgenstein calls language games. But, for Moore, it is unnecessary to prove that he has two hands because these propositions are not only beyond doubt but necessary for doubt itself (Wittgenstein 44). Moore's propositions need no justification; they are the field upon which our doubting language games are played.

Knowledge: It's Child's Play

The heart of Wittgenstein's argument against scepticism is based on the notion that humans have certain knowledge (von Wright calls this pre-knowledge) beyond propositions we can consciously or intellectually conceive. This is known as epistemic **foundationalism.** Foundationalism is the idea that some knowledge claims are beyond doubt and act as a foundation for other beliefs. Descartes, for example, was also a foundationalist; his *cogito ergo sum* (I think, therefore, I am) was the base upon which his rationalist philosophy was built. Wittgenstein's foundationalism is non-intellectual; it's the ground, bedrock, or base upon which our language games are played. For Wittgenstein, the concept of knowledge does not apply to Moore-type propositions because they cannot be doubted themselves. People generally accept the reliability of their senses, memory, and that objects don't vanish or transmogrify whenever not perceived. Moreover, much of history and science would be unavailable to humans if we did not believe that the earth has existed long before our birth. The activities we carry out in our daily lives are too deeply rooted in our thoughts and behaviour to warrant doubt.

To fully appreciate what Wittgenstein is arguing, consider how children develop (see Photo 2.2). Infants quickly develop from total dependency in the first weeks of birth

Photo 2.2 Child's Play

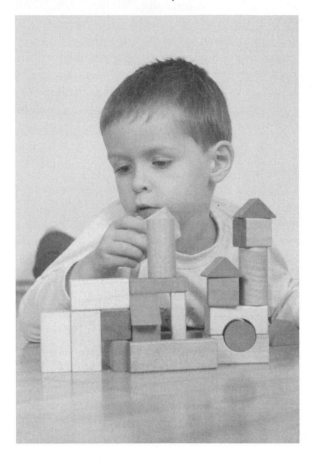

Wittgenstein says that Moore's claim to know "he has two hands" is senseless because it is beyond doubt. Such knowledge is not taught but comes through acting, much like the knowledge children acquire through play.

to independent exploration of their environment within months. Infants have an insatiable curiosity to touch, taste, and feel everything in sight. This is an essential part of learning about one's environment. Some of the things learned would include that objects have shape, size, hardness, and exist when not seen; their legs, and most furniture, will support their weight; other humans exist in the world; and they have two hands. It's this background certainty that allows us to act and do what we do in life. We learn that our legs will support our weight, and under normal circumstances (unless injured or sick) we don't question their solidity or stability (Wittgenstein 22). Children learn about chairs,

trees, and hands by acting. It is through this kind of active exploration that children come to know about their world, which ultimately forms a bedrock of certainty. Children learn how to fetch books and sit in chairs; they are not taught that these things exist. The existence of books and chairs is presupposed by their actions. And over time, a system of unshakable beliefs is developed. Children simply act and trust the language games of adults. In this sense, the problem of the existence of the external world is in fact solved before it can be raised. Children must know a great deal about the world before they can question its existence. It is this bedrock of certainty, for Wittgenstein, which is indubitable and ultimately undermines the very idea of scepticism itself.

7

Georg Henrik von Wright

(1916–2003)

Born in Helsinki, Finland, on June 14, 1916, Georg Henrik von Wright made significant contributions to logic, philosophy of science, and ethics. At eighteen, von Wright enrolled in the University of Helsinki, where he studied philosophy and mathematics. After his graduation in 1937, he went to the University of Cambridge to continue his studies under the tutelage of C. D. Broad. While at Cambridge,

von Wright also met Ludwig Wittgenstein. Although they would eventually become friends, von Wright was very disappointed with their initial meeting. Wittgenstein supposedly was very angry that von Wright was attending his course so late in the term. Wittgenstein, however, calmed down and invited von Wright to attend the next day. On May 3, 1941, the day his doctoral thesis was published, he married Marie Elizabeth von Troil. Two years later, he was appointed as a lecturer at the University of Helsinki and full Professor of Philosophy in 1946 at the age of 29. In 1948, he succeeded Wittgenstein at the University of Cambridge and stayed there until Wittgenstein's death in 1951, at which time he moved back to Finland. Von Wright was appointed the Academy of Finland in 1961, which freed him up from his teaching duties. He took this opportunity to write and travel. He took up a visiting professorship at Cornell University from 1965 to 1977, amongst other institutions. In conjunction with his many awards, von Wright was a prolific writing publishing works in English, Finnish, and German. Some of his English works include Problems of Induction *(1941),* An Essay on Model Logic *(1951),* Norm and Action *(1963),* Causality and Determinism *(1974),* Wittgenstein *(1982), and* In the Shadows of Descartes *(1998). He died on June 16, 2003, at the age of 87.*

Wittgenstein on Certainty

1

During the last year and a half of his life Wittgenstein wrote almost exclusively about knowledge and certainty, commenting on some of G.E. Moore's views.[1] These writings possess a thematic unity which makes them almost unique in Wittgenstein's whole literary output. One can speculate about the reasons for this. Does it signify a change in Wittgenstein's philosophical style? Or does it only show that the author was losing his power of keeping a thousand threads of thought in his hand at once? There is no indication, however, that the quality of the thoughts was declining. Considering that the remarks constitute a first, unrevised manuscript they seem to me remarkably accomplished both in form and content.

Wittgenstein's treatise on certainty can be said to summarize some of the essential novelties of his thinking. But it does this in a way which is rather different from any which, to the best of my knowledge, Wittgenstein's numerous commentators have tried. The book opens new vistas on his philosophical achievement.

I shall here try to give a brief presentation of its main ideas. I shall not make any attempt to evaluate it critically—nor try to indicate the extent to which I can agree myself with what Wittgenstein has to say. But I shall at the end sketch a few of its implications, as I see them, for further research.

2

A main problem of epistemology since Descartes has been whether any single contingent proposition can be known for certain to be true. Moore claimed that *he knew* a great number of such propositions. He gave as examples, among others, that he was a human being, that the object he was now pointing to was his hand, or that the earth has existed for many years past. Since he knew such things, he could also prove that there existed a world external to his mind—and thereby settle, so he thought, a problem long under dispute. Moore further claimed that such items as those just mentioned were by no means known exclusively by him, but that they wee specimens of what most human beings under normal circumstances can rightly claim to know.

Moore thought, moreover, that our knowledge of most of these 'common sense' propositions, as he called them, is founded on some *evidence* for their truth.[2] But what this evidence is we often cannot tell. We are all, Moore said, 'in this strange position that we do *know* many things, with regard to which we *know* further that we must have had evidence for them, and yet we do not know *how* we know them, that is, we do not know what the evidence was.'[3]

In order to appreciate both Moore's position and Wittgenstein's criticism of it, it is important to keep the distinction clear between the 'common sense' proposition which Moore claimed he knew and the philosophical proposition which he thought provable[4] on the basis of them. Moore thought of the members of both classes of propositions as being *contingent* truths.[5] This opinion may seem very natural as far as the various propositions of the first category are concerned. With regard to the propositions of the second category this view seems much less natural or even quite dubious. Yet Moore was of the opinion that it is a contingent truth that there is an external world, that time is real, or that there exist selves. To deny these things is not to maintain anything which is logically impossible, that is, self-contradictory.

Suppose somebody wanted to dispute some of the things Moore claimed to know for certain, for example, that he, Moore, was a human being or was pointing to his right hand. This critic would then have to adduce some evidence showing that Moore was mistaken. Moore again would have to accept this evidence, if he was going to give up his claim to knowledge. But what could this evidence be, other than some contingent propositions which contradicted the first ones and which Moore, 'on second thought,' would have to admit as true? And then it would still be the case that there existed a great many 'common sense' propositions which he would claim to know for certain—and which could be used to prove the sort of philosophical propositions which Moore was anxious to defend, for example, that time is real or that there exists an external world.

Moore's philosophical position would therefore not be touched by justified doubts about this or that proposition of the first group. For the justification of the doubts would entail accepting that very position. In order to prove the philosophical propositions on the basis of 'common sense' propositions all that is required is that at any time *some* such 'common sense' propositions should be accepted as certain. Moore did not say this. He, on the contrary, was anxious to claim that he knew for certain a number of specific things (propositions), of which he had enumerated a great many in his classic paper. But when in his paper called 'Certainty' which was not published until after his death Moore was fighting the sceptic's argument from dreaming, then—so it seems to me—he unsuccessfully tried to articulate thoughts which point to a more 'relaxed' relationship between the two groups of propositions. How this is to be done in order to be successful can, I think, be seen more clearly on the basis of Wittgenstein's comments on Moore's views.

3

So much then for certain things which Moore has said. Wittgenstein thought Moore's rebuttal of scepticism most interesting and original. But he would not have been the philosopher he was, had he declared himself in agreement with Moore. On the contrary, he was anxious to refute Moore's *explicit* philosophical position at practically every point. Moore's claim that he knew this or that was philosophically worthless, Wittgenstein thought; most of the 'common sense' things Moore said he knew are things which nobody can, in fact, be correctly said to *know*. Moore, moreover, was mistaken in thinking that there was *evidence* for the truth of the propositions in question; mistaken also in thinking that they could be used for *proving* such things as the existence of the external world; and mistaken finally in holding the allegedly proved theses to be *contingent* truths. But, while disagreeing with what Moore had said, Wittgenstein was at the same time in sympathy with the tendency implicit in Moore's efforts. I think we can say that what Wittgenstein did was to give to this tendency a clearer and truer expression.

Let us look briefly at some of the reasons Wittgenstein gave for disagreeing with Moore.

An assurance, however sincere, that one knows something cannot by itself establish that this is so (§§13, 14). Moore, therefore, cannot attack the sceptics 'by assuring them that *he* knows this and that. For one need not believe him. If his opponents had asserted that one could not *believe* this and that, then he could have replied: "I believe it"' (§520). Wittgenstein is here pointing to an important conceptual difference between belief and knowledge. In order to establish that I believe that *p,* I need not give grounds for thinking *p* true. But in order to vindicate a claim to knowledge, grounds must normally be provided, that is, we must be able to tell, *how* we know this. And it must be open to others to accept or to remain unconvinced by our grounds. '"I know" often means: I have the proper grounds for my statement. So if the other person is acquainted with the language-game, he would admit that I know. The other,

if he is acquainted with the language-game, must be able to imagine *how* one may know something of the kind' (§18). Wittgenstein says that the situation is *often* of this kind when a claim to knowledge is being raised. Perhaps one could even say that it is always or typically of this kind, when it is open to argument whether a person knows something or not, that is, when the situation is as envisaged in §§13 and 14. And this is the situation which Wittgenstein opposes to the Moorean one. One could call the one 'genuine' and the other 'spurious' and say that in a genuine knowledge situation there must be grounds for knowing—and that where grounds are lacking the situation is 'spurious'.

An answer to the question 'How do you know?' could be, for example, 'I saw it myself', 'I calculated it', or 'He told me so'. These grounds on which one *can* know things and therefore types of 'proper grounds' for my statement that I know. A person who is given these grounds in support of a knowledge-claim will, 'if he is acquainted with the language-game', realize that they are grounds of the proper *type*—but it does not follow from this that he will accept them. He may voice doubts in the form of a rejoinder 'Did you watch it carefully?' or 'Let's check your calculation' (cf. §50), or 'Is he a trustworthy person?'

To answer the question 'How do you know?' is not the same thing as to produce evidence for the truth of the known proposition. But when we remove doubts about the answer, we produce such evidence. If I watched something carefully, I should be able to tell that I saw this and this and . . ., which, if true, should establish that it is also true what I claim to know—say that a man was stabbed in the street. To check the calculation is to check the truth of a number of statements which jointly entail that the result was what I claimed it to be. To show that a person is trust-worthy, finally, is to point to a number of state-ments which are accepted as true and which speak in favour of the truth of what we said we knew on the basis of what he had told us.

The evidence which we produce for the truth of a proposition which we claim to know con-sists of propositions which we accept as true. If the question is raised, how we know these latter propositions, further grounds may be offered to show how we know them and further evidence given for the truth of the propositions thus claimed to be known. But the chain of grounds (evidence) has an end, a point beyond which no further grounds can be given. This is a thing which Wittgenstein often stressed.[6] The reason, why Moore was mistaken in thinking that his knowledge of the 'common sense' truths was founded on evidence, Wittgenstein would have said, was that they were themselves such 'end-points' in chains of grounds. They might serve as evidence for other propositions which some-body claimed to know. But nothing would count as evidence for them.

Consider for example the proposition that I have two hands. It would sometimes be said, I think, that it is based on the evidence of my senses.[7] But this is not, as a general statement, correct. Sometimes, however, it is correct. I have undergone an operation and been unconscious. I wake up and am not quite clear what has hap-pened to me. Was it that one of my hands was amputated? I look and see them both. Then my knowledge that I *still* have two hands can be said to rest on 'the evidence of my senses'. But I did not learn that I have two hands by looking at them and counting. If under quite normal circumstances I happened to look at my hands—holding them up before my eyes—and, to my amazement, saw only one, then I should doubt

my senses and not that I have two hands. And this shows that the implicit trust which under normal circumstances I have that I have two hands is *not* founded on 'the evidence of my senses.' (Cf. §125.)

Let it be granted that the proposition 'I have two hands' entails the proposition 'there are material objects'. *One* way of showing that the second is *not* contingent would then be to show that the first is necessary. (For a neces-sary proposition can entail only other neces-sary propositions.) But is it not obvious that the first is contingent? For all I know I could have only one hand, or none. Perhaps I can imagine myself having more than two. And yet the truth, as known to me, of the proposition that I have two hands, is peculiar. It is not like the many truths which I have learnt from reading or by being instructed or because I have made inves-tigations. Surely the propositions which Moore claimed are indubitable have 'a peculiar logical role in the system of our empirical propositions' (§136). It is this *peculiar* role, not the question whether we really can be said to 'know' these propositions, which Wittgenstein investigates in his book.

4

The core of Wittgenstein's thoughts on these matters could perhaps be paraphrased as follows. In every situation where a claim to knowledge is being established, or a doubt settled, or an item of linguistic communication (information, order, question) understood, a bulk of proposi-tions already stand fast, are taken for granted. They form a kind of 'system'. If this were not so, knowledge and doubt, judging and under-standing, error and truth would not 'exist', that is, we should not have and handle those concepts in the way we do. 'All testing, all confirmation and disconfirmation of a hypothesis takes place already within a system. And this system is not a more or less arbitrary and doubtful point of departure for all our arguments; no, it belongs to the essence of what we call an argument. The system is not so much the point of departure, as the element in which arguments have their life' (§105).

The concept of knowledge does not itself apply to that which is presupposed in its use, that is, to the propositions which 'stand fast' in any given situation. This is one reason, why Moore's use of 'I know' was out of place. But perhaps one could call the 'common sense' things to which Moore was referring a pre-knowledge (*Vor-Wissen*). (Wittgenstein himself does not use this term.) It is better, however, to speak of *certainty* here (§511), with the addition perhaps that it is a certainty in our *practice* of judging rather than in our *intellection* of the content of our judgements. (See section 8 below.)

Thus, for example, the truth of the proposition that the earth has existed for many years past can be said to be presupposed in all so-called historical knowledge. But it is not itself an item of historical knowledge, that is, it is not anything which one has come to know on the basis of investigations about the past. Through geophysical investigations we may come to know that the earth has existed, say, for at least 300 billion years—or that it could not have existed for more than 500 billion years. These are possible items of genuine (scientific) knowledge. But in all the ground which we could give for, or against, these scientific propositions it would be presupposed—though not in the form of a geophysical hypotheses—that the earth has existed for many, that is, '*for a good many,*' years past. (Cf. §138.)

The problem of the existence of the external world, one could say, *is* in fact solved before it can be raised.—In order to raise the question we must know what ('sort of thing') an external world is—or else we do not know what our question is about. But in order to acquire the notion of an external world we must first acknowledge a huge number of facts, all of which 'entail' (in that Moorean sense) the existence of material objects, that is, of a world external to my mind. I can inquire whether this or that object is in the external world, or is perhaps only an illusion. But whether the result in the individual case is positive or negative, the grounds for the decision will be some facts which stand fast and which entail the existence of an external world. This also explains why there is no procedure for investigating whether or not the external world itself exists. Its existence is, so to speak, '*the logical receptacle*' within which all investigations concerning the mind-dependent existence of various objects are conducted.—'Material object' is a logical—in the *Tractatus* Wittgenstein would have said formal—concept (§36).

5

The propositions belonging to the system of our pre-knowledge cannot be enumerated and 'laid down' once and for all. Many of the items can—temporarily or permanently—be removed and treated as propositions which are supported, or contradicted, by the propositions of the bulk. 'What I hold fast to is not *one* proposition but a nest of propositions,' Wittgenstein says (§225). (Cf. also §§140–142.)

Imagine the following case. I am the victim of an accident and one of my hands is torn off. Someone comes along and finds it lying in the street. 'Whose hand is that?' he cries horrified. 'It is mine,' I say. Then I presumably know this and have evidence for it. But when set in such circumstances, my knowledge that this is my hand seems quite irrelevant to the philosophical purposes which Moore was pursuing when he said he knew certain things. Here I could initially also have doubted what then I knew. Perhaps a hand was torn from someone else too in the disaster. When I establish that this is *my* hand and settle my doubts, if I have any, *then* part of my evidence are things 'I know for certain' in that other and 'deeper' sense which Moore had been thinking of.

Moore's 'common sense' propositions, one could say, have the form of experiential propositions but perform the function of logical propositions or rules (cf. §§56, 82, 308). Their truth 'is fused into the foundations of our language-game' (§558)—like the truth of mathematical propositions.[8] But the fact that we can, at least for a good many of them, imagine circumstances which turn their use into a *move* (as distinct from a *rule*) of one of our language-games (§622) shows that there is no hard and fast distinction between 'analytic' and 'synthetic,' between logical necessity and contingent truth or falsehood. (Cf. §§308, 319, 401.)

Moore's famous gesture, when he wanted to prove the existence of an external world, was no 'proof' of a contingent conclusion from contingent premises. It was rather an attempt to say (show) that with our *notion* of an external world we take many *truths* (*facts*) for granted (cf. §§83, 617). We *cannot* question these truths, since they go with the possession of the notion. Therefore it is not a contingent proposition that *there is an external world*—as it is contingent that there are, or are not, lions or unicorns. But it is a contingent fact about us, a fact of 'the natural history of man', that *we have the notion* of an external world.

I should like to call attention here to two features which can be said to pervade the whole of Wittgenstein's philosophy. The one could be called, using pre-*Tractatus* terminology, the idea of Bi-polarity.[9] In the *Tractatus* this idea is reflected above all in the alliance between a proposition's having a *meaning* and it's being contingent(ly true or false). Necessary propositions are 'senseless' (but not 'nonsensical')[10] and therefore not strictly speaking true. They are, to use an expression which Wittgenstein employed later in his writings on the foundations of mathematics, senseless expressions 'on the side of truth.'[11] Epistemic attitudes such as knowing and believing apply in the first instance to contingent matters. That which cannot conceivably be doubted, cannot be known or certain either—except under some 'eccentric' use of the words.[12] In his writings from the years when he was working on the *Investigations*, Wittgenstein sometimes expressed himself with a certain dogmatic flavour on questions relating to this topic. It may look as though he wanted to deny, for example, that a man can know that he is in pain or is seeing a red flash—the very things which so many other philosophers have regarded as the prototype of what *can be known*, if anything can be. But Wittgenstein did not wish to deny this—if by 'deny' one here means that he was casting doubts on things which are regarded as certain by others. He only wanted to draw attention to 'the peculiar logical role' of indubitable propositions in connection with our epistemic attitudes. In *On Certainty* Wittgenstein can be said to extend to the whole field of epistemology things which he had before mainly been discussing in connection with, at the one extreme, our immediate experience and, at the other extreme, the necessary truths of logic and mathematics. This extension should help us to see more clearly also the connection and relatedness of the two extremes.

The idea of bi-polarity is related to another *Leitmotiv* which runs through all Wittgenstein's work. This is his preoccupation with the question of the *limits of the world* (and of what can be said and what can be thought). In the preface to the *Tractatus* he said: 'The book will, therefore, draw a limit to thinking, or rather—not to thinking but to the expression of thoughts; for in order to draw a limit to thinking we should have to be able to think both sides of this limit (we should therefore have to be able to think what cannot be thought).' Very much the same thing he could have said in a preface, had he ever written one, to his last writings, those published under the title *On Certainty*. Beyond everything we know or conjecture or think of as true there is a foundation of accepted truth without which there would be no such thing as knowing or conjecturing or thinking things true. But to think of the things, whereof this foundation is made, as known to us or as true is to place them among the things which stand on this very foundation, is to view the receptacle as another object *within*. This clearly cannot be done. If the foundation is what we have to accept before we say of anything that it is known or true, then it cannot itself be known or true. Moore's common sense propositions can indeed be regarded as proof that certain things can be known, namely all those things which commonly are said to be known on the basis of grounds which we do not question. What Moore called 'common sense'—using this phrase in a rather queer sense[13]—is very much the same thing as that which Wittgenstein in the *Tractatus* would have referred to as 'the limits of the world'. Wittgenstein's high appreciation of Moore's article must partly have stemmed from the fact that he recognized in Moore's efforts a strong similarity with his own. And his criticism of Moore in *On Certainty* we could, in the language of the *Tractatus*, characterize as a criticism of an attempt to say the unsayable.

6

The bulk of propositions belonging to our pre-knowledge can also be said to constitute a world-picture, *Weltbild*. This latter expression is used frequently by Wittgenstein himself. It does not mean a view of the world in the esoteric sense of a philosopher's *Weltanschauung*. It is not a private possession, but bound up with the notion of a 'culture' and with the fact 'that we belong to a community which is bound together by science and education' (§298). One could also say that it is the common ground which we must share with other people in order to *understand* their actions and words and in order to come to an understanding with them in our judgements. It is, in fact, Moore's 'common sense', *Tractatus*' world-boundary. I know no better way to describe its nature and role than to quote Wittgenstein's own words:

> 94. But I did not get my picture of the world by satisfying myself of its correctness; nor do I have it because I am satisfied of its correctness. No: it is the inherited background against which I distinguish between true and false.

> 95. The propositions describing the world-picture might be part of a kind of mythology. And their role is like that of rules of a game; and the game can be learned purely practically, without learning any explicit rules.

> 96. It might be imagined that some propositions, of the form of empirical propositions, were hardened and functioned

as channels for such empirical prop-ositions as were not hardened but fluid; and that this relation altered with time, in that fluid propositions hardened, and hard ones became fluid.

97. The mythology may change back to a state of flux, the river-bed of thoughts may shift. But I distinguish between the movements of the waters of the river-bed and the shift of the bed itself; though there is not a sharp division of the one from the other.

98. But is someone were to say 'So logic too is an empirical science' he would be wrong. Yet this is right: the same proposition may get treated at one time as something to test by experience, at another as a rule of testing.

99. And the bank of the river consists partly of hard rock, subject to no alteration or only to an imperceptible one, partly of sand, which now in one place now in another gets washed away, or deposited.

7

The system of propositions which constitute a world-picture not only has no fixed boundaries. It also has a very inhomogenous composition. It is an agglomeration of a huge number of sub-systems, each with a fluctuating boundary and a 'mixed' content. These sub-systems are related to what Wittgenstein calls language-games. One could say that every language-game has a foundation which is a fragment of the players' pre-knowledge. (Cf. §§519, 560.)

There is no *rigid* order among the language-games, neither logically nor from the point of view of genetic development. But there certainly is *some* order among them in both these respects.

The games are of different age in the develop-ment of the individual as well as in the history of the language community ('culture'). Some could not have been learned, until others were already mastered. Among the relatively late ones are the language-games with words like 'know', believe', or 'be certain'. (Cf. §538.) For this reason alone, the fragments of a world-picture which underlie the language-games from the beginning repre-sent only a 'pre-knowledge'. If this is subsequently honoured by the name 'knowledge', as Moore and some other philosophers have wanted to do, its conceptual character still is very different from those items to which we apply this name in the ordinary language-games with the epistemic words. Wittgenstein's 'builders' cannot *say they know* these are building-stones (slabs, columns, etc.); yet this is nevertheless what they can *be said to know* in knowing how to play the game (§396). Wittgenstein asks: 'Does a child believe that milk exists? Or does it know that milk exists? Does a cat know that a mouse exists?' (§478) and 'Are we to say that the knowledge that there are physical objects comes very early or very late?' (§479). Each of these questions could be answered both Yes and No—depending upon how we understand them.

8

Considering the way language is taught and learned, the fragments of a world-picture under-lying the uses of language are not originally and strictly *propositions* at all. The pre-knowledge is not propositional knowledge. But if this founda-tion is not propositional, what then *is* it? It is, one could say, a *praxis*. 'Giving grounds, how-ever, justifying evidence, comes to an end;—but the end is not certain propositions striking us immediately as true, i.e., it is not a kind of *seeing* on our part; it is our *acting*, which lies at the bottom of the language-game' (§204, cf. also §§110 and 229). And Wittgenstein quotes *Faust:* 'Im Anfang war die Tat' (§402).

How does it show, for example, that I do not doubt that I have a body, that this is something I, in Moore's sense, know for certain? Not in that I say *this* or reflect upon it. But in innumerable things I say, and do, and refrain from doing. Such as complaining of headache or of pain in my leg, avoiding collision with other bodies, not putting my hand in the fire or throwing myself out of the window as if nothing was going to hurt me. It is within this framework of certainties in my behaviour that I learn the names of the parts of my body and of various bodily sensations and also the word 'body'. Within it I acquire the notions which the various words in the language-game symbolize. But in order that my behaviour should be describable as actions of a certain kind, it must be interpreted in terms of the notions of the language-game itself. So, to this extent the *praxis* at the basis of the language-game is a *pre-praxis*, one could say, and not yet full-fledged *action.*

9

The world-picture in its 'practical,' pre-propositional stage could also be called a *form of life.* 'My life shews that I know or am certain that there is a chair over there, or a door, and so on' (§7). 'Now I would like to regard this certainty, not as something akin to hastiness or superficiality, but as a form of life,' Wittgenstein says (§358).

A world-picture, therefore, is neither true nor false (cf. §§162, 205). Disputes about truth are possible only inside its frame. The presupposition then is that the disputants share the same culture or form of life, play *the same* language-games. They must, for example, *mean* the same by the words they use. But sameness or difference of meaning is possible only if there is already a certain amount of agreement about facts. (Cf. §§114, 126, 306, 456, 486, 506, 507, 523, 624.)

There are some typical cases when this presupposition breaks down or is not fulfilled. One case is when one person denies or doubts that which is part of the world-picture of most other persons in the community. Then it would often be said that the person is mentally deranged rather than that he is in error. (Cf. §§71–73, 155, 156.) What should we, for example, say of somebody who earnestly doubts that the world has existed before he was born and manifests his doubt in everything he does and says? Perhaps we should say that his lunacy consists in that we cannot teach him history. (See §206.) He is not capable of participating in all forms of our life. But we can imagine circumstances under which we should admit that this is not really a 'mental defect', but is due to a difference in 'culture.' 'Why should not a king be brought up in the belief that the world began with him? And if Moore and this king were to meet and discuss, could Moore really prove his belief to be the right one?' (§92). Moore could perhaps convert the king to his view, bring him to look at the world in a different way. This would happen through a kind of *persuasion* (§262) and would not be to convince the king of error. (Cf. also §§608–612.) We should then not be correcting his opinions, but combatting his world-picture.

When we look back on a defeated world-picture we easily do it injustice. We regard it as 'primitive' or 'superstitious'. We think of the change as a transition from darkness to light. This is often an unfair judgement.[14] But we must on the other hand also acknowledge that there are various *reasons* why world-pictures change in the course of history. Simplicity and symmetry are such reasons, Wittgenstein says (§92).

Another type of reasons, I would suggest, is diverging interests in the uses of knowledge.

10

Wittgenstein's investigations into the role of the concept of a world-picture have, I think, interesting applications to the sociology of knowledge.

In his influential and justly praised book *The Structure of Scientific Revolutions,*[15] T.S. Kuhn holds that normal science is conducted within the framework of what Kuhn calls *paradigms.* The accepted paradigms set the frame of questions for scientific inquiry and determine the range of possible answers. Partly as a result of the growth of the body of scientific knowledge, these patterns tend to 'wear out', to become unsuited for their role. 'Revolutions' in science consist in an overthrow of established paradigms and the acceptance of new ones. This is a good illustration for Wittgenstein's idea about the role of world-pictures. But the illustration stands in need of much more elaboration than given to it by Kuhn.[16] One line of elaboration leads us to consider the differences between the natural sciences and the sciences of man.

Even if natural science is not the uniformly growing body of knowledge which sometimes (and traditionally) has been thought, it still is, it seems, at any one time basically *one* body of paradigms. It is only during protracted periods of crisis, such as the transition from Aristotelian to Galilean physics during the late Renaissance and the Baroque, that the unity temporarily gets lost. But does this apply also to the social sciences and to the so-called *Geisteswissenschaften*? Perhaps their history is too short to allow a definite judgement. Kuhn seems to think[17] that the social sciences have not yet reached a stage, when paradigms

have been articulated with sufficient clarity to make a confrontation of paradigms possible. I am not sure, however, that he is right—and that he is not looking for the paradigms in the wrong direction, so to speak. The paradigms of social science, I would suggest, are set in the last resort by political and social *ideologies.* Sometimes ideologies try to extend their influence into the paradigmatic background of the natural sciences too. But here the effects of ideology never penetrate deep. Lenin's attack on Mach notwithstanding, there is no serious Marxist alternative to relativity theory. Nor is there a respectable Marxist alternative to Mendelean genetics. But there *are* bourgeois and Marxist economics or sociology in their own rights, I would say. To say that they differ in valuations would not be quite correct. Valuations do not belong *within* the body of a social science, whether 'bourgeois' or 'Marxist'. This is the truth contained in Max Weber's famous postulate of *Wertfreiheit* (value-freedom). But types of social science may differ in paradigmatic conceptions as to what constitutes the social reality and conditions social change. These differences in paradigms may be traced back to differences in interests (valuations) and the articulation of interests to form ideologies. The fight between the interests is therefore a factor which matters to the conversion of men from the world-picture of one type of social science to that of another type, or which makes them anxious to defend the one against the other.

Notes

1. These writings were published, with the German text alongside the English translation, as *Über Gewissheit – On Certainty,* Basil Blackwell, Oxford, 1969, edited by

G.E.M. Anscombe and G.H. von Wright; see the Editors' Preface. See also the brief but excellent account of conversations with Wittgenstein in the summer of 1949 in Norman Malcolm, *Ludwig Wittgenstein, A Memoir*, Oxford University Press, London, 1958, pp. 87–92.

2. 'A Defence of Common Sense', p. 44. References are to G.E. Moore, *Philosophical Papers*, Allen & Unwin, London, 1959.

3. Ibid.

4. The idea of a proof does not appear until the paper 'Proof of an External World'. But it is implicit already in 'A Defence of Common Sense.' The known 'common sense' propositions *imply*, Moore says there (p. 38), the reality of material things, etc.

5. Neither in 'A Defence of Common Sense' nor in 'Proof of an External World' does Moore use the term 'contingent (proposition)'. In the first paper he says (p. 42) that 'it seems to me quite clear that it *might* have been the case that Time was not real, material things not real, Space not real, selves not real'. In his later paper called 'Certainty,' however, Moore employs the term 'contingent proposition' for 'proposition which is not self-contradictory and of which the contradictory is not self-contradictory' (p. 230). He also says that 'from the fact that a given proposition might have been true it always follows that the proposition in question is not self-contradictory' (ibid.). From this we can conclude that, according to Moore, a proposition affirming or denying the reality of time or of material things is contingent. But Moore also says that propositions which he thinks he knows for certain, such as that he is now standing up, are contingent (ibid.). It is therefore safe to attribute to Moore the view that propositions of both the classes which we have here distinguished are contingent.

6. *Philosophical Investigations,* Part 1, §§326, 485. Cf. also *On Certainty,* §471.

7. Cf. Moore, 'Certainty', p. 243.

8. Cf. Malcolm, *Memoir*, p. 88.

9. See 'Notes on Logic' (September 1913), printed as an Appendix to Ludwig Wittgenstein, *Notebooks 1914–1916*, Basil Blackwell, Oxford, 1961.

10. Cf. *Tractatus Logico-Philosophicus,* 4.461 and 4.4611.

11. *Remarks on the Foundations of Mathematics*, Basil Blackwell, Oxford, 3rd edition, 1978, Pt. III, §33.

12. Cf. *Philosophical Investigations,* Part 1, §246.

13. What Moore was referring to with the phrase 'common sense' is certainly not what is commonly and naturally called this. The oddity of Moore's usage is exposed and commented on in Norman Malcolm, 'George Edward Moore', in Malcolm, *Knowledge and Certainty,* Prentice-Hall, Englewood Cliffs, N.J., 1963.

14. In his *Remarks on Frazer's Golden Bough,* ed. by Rush Rhees, Brynmill, Retford, 1979, Wittgenstein wanted to show how shallow and stupid the judgements by 'civilized' men about 'primitive' cultures are when no account is taken of the basic differences in world-pictures and forms of life.

15. T.S. Kuhn, *The Structure of Scientific Revolutions,* The University of Chicago Press, Chicago, 1962.

16. There are pertinent references to Wittgenstein in Kuhn's book, though not, for obvious reasons, to the late writings which we are considering here.

17. Ibid., p. 15.

Feminist Epistemology

For Feminists, the purpose of epistemology is not only to satisfy intellectual curiosity, but also to contribute to an emancipatory goal: the expansion of democracy in the production of knowledge.
—Linda Alcoff and Elizabeth Potter

Discussion Questions

1. In the 1982 movie *Tootsie,* Dustin Hoffman plays a young aspiring actor with a reputation for being difficult. Unable to find work, in desperation, he dresses up as a woman to audition for a role on a popular soap opera. Amazingly, he gets the part and becomes a huge star on the show. Unfortunately, no one knows he is a man, and events get rather humorously complicated. Of a similar genre is the 1999 movie *Boys Don't Cry,* based on the life of Brandon Teena. Hilary Swank plays a transsexual who identifies with being male but who is actually born female. Swank's character is murdered after falling in

love with a woman who thinks Teena is male. Each movie highlights the unique opportunity of experiencing the world from the perspective of the opposite sex. Imagine yourself as a member of the opposite sex. What epistemological advantages would you have being the opposite sex? What unique attributes or features might affect your epistemic standpoint? In what ways would you agree or disagree with Code that who the knower *is* is important to epistemic justification?

2. Code argues that traditional epistemological theories have failed to consider the subjective perspective of the knower, especially women. Why might you agree or disagree that traditional epistemological theories are sexist? What knowledge claims are objective regardless of one's perspective or gender?

3. If all knowledge is relative to the knower, then according to Code, we are to evaluate each claim in light of the empirical adequacy of such claims. In other words, we seem to fall back to the traditional definition of knowledge: true justified belief. If so, does the feminist perspective merely collapse into traditional epistemological criteria for knowledge? Does this justify the male-dominated tradition in epistemology? Why or why not?

4. Traditional epistemologies argue that "S knows that P" only if P is true, believed, and justifiable. How would changing "S" affect "P"? Consider, for example, same-sex marriage. Canada passed its same-sex marriage law in 2005. How would changing the gender, social class, or race of "S" affect the moral justification of same-sex marriage?

Men Are from Mars, Women from Venus

The Western epistemological tradition has historically disregarded the perspective of women as a counterpoint to traditional ways of knowing. From a feminist perspective, traditional epistemological claims have failed to take into consideration the role gender plays in shaping what and how we know. Over centuries of oppression and discrimination, women have been prevented from attaining the intellectual and political power necessary to make their voices heard. The subjugation of women has led to male-biased institutions with male-dominated points of view. According to feminists, however, we must recognize that it's through women's role as the oppressed that they have developed an understanding of reality and the world that is much truer and more accurate that those of the insulated oppressor. Women have different perspectives and different points of view from males developed within the larger social context in which women find themselves. The result is a unique feminist epistemology not recognized in traditional philosophical circles.

The desire to develop a feminine epistemology should not be surprising, especially if one looks at the history of philosophy. A quick survey of historical readings will reveal virtually no notable women philosophers. This is not because there weren't any, there were but their voices were not heard above the din of male bias. Feminists claim male bias also dominates most traditional theories of knowledge. Traditional epistemological theories tend to focus on establishing true justified belief using the physical sciences as the paradigm case of knowledge because it supposedly is uncluttered by emotions, culture, and other forms of subjective contamination. As Andrea Nye explains, "Science is the canonical, propositional core of justified true belief—hypotheses or propositions in logical order along with experimental evidence—a core that stands as truth regardless of its use, the emotions it arouses, the reasons anyone has to believe or disbelieve it, or the social interests it might serve" (88). But as feminists pointed out, science, as the paradigm of true justified belief, is often male biased, has social and environmental implications often not recognized, and can lead to unwarranted conclusions. An example of such male-biased scientific research comes from Harvard psychologist *Carol Gilligan.* Her 1982 book, *In a Different Voice: Psychological Theory and Women's Development,* outlined how much of the research on moral development by Lawrence Kohlberg is male-biased. This should not be surprising since Kohlberg's experiments on moral development used young boys as the primary subject. Although Kohlberg's stages of moral development are supposed to be universal, when women are compared to the criteria set out, they appear to be morally deficient. For Gillian, we ought to cautious about science that uses the male point of view as the norm. The psychology of women is distinctive with a greater orientation towards relationships and interdependence between people, which implies a contextual mode of understanding devoid in the traditional scientific enterprise.

Traditional epistemological theories, as outlined in the reading by Loraine Code, must also recognize that science is not value free. It's not obvious that science is the paradigm of knowledge if it is not ideally objective. We must understand that in order to say "S knows that P" we must have some understanding of their sex, interests, and values. As Nye states, "What is needed . . . is attention to the anonymous genderless 'S' in the analytical formula 'S knows that P,' attention to the 'speaker,' to his or her sex, interests, community standards and values that shape views of what that knowledge is" (94). For Code, there are good reasons for trying to determine who the knower *is.* The history of philosophy is concerned, if not obsessed, with determining the necessary and sufficient conditions for justifying knowledge claims. The problem is that the justification of such propositions as "S knows that P" uses criteria devoid of the subjective, historical, and circumstantial framework in which S is situated. The question of *who* the knower is as a person and the circumstances from which he or she originates never arises or is never questioned in traditional epistemology. After all, there may be unique attributes or features that

affect epistemic standpoints including gender, race, religion, family background, education level, and so forth. The problem is that the ideal observer—view from nowhere—mindset blinds philosophers to the fact that knowledge claims are always a view from somewhere. Once such a perspective is recognized, Codes thinks, we can debunk much of the traditional assumptions of traditional epistemology.

One such mistaken assumption is a hangover from Descartes' question for epistemic certainty. For Descartes, the quest for knowledge is a solitary affair conducted in a private, introspective way using reason and abstract thought as a guide. But clearly, such assumptions do not hold. Why should we think that knowledge is always a solitary, private, or introspective enterprise? Knowledge is, in many respects, a communal activity. The discoveries of diabetes, cancer, and AIDS, to name a few, were the results of scientists working collectively within the empiricist tradition.[11] But the solitary and introspective rationalist tradition of Descartes did lead to another important assumption that has played a central role in epistemology— namely, that all knowers are alike in their cognitive abilities and methods to achieve knowledge. So, for example, in science the notion that everyone will be able to observe and see the data implies that perception is invariant from person to person. Who the person *is* is irrelevant. To use Code's example, everyone can ascertain the truth of the claim "John knows that the book is red" by seeing the book themselves. But Code says that the epistemic status of the knower is relevant. We must question not only the justification of the criteria of knowledge but also the nature of the knower him or herself. Why? Because by looking at the status of the knower we can decide whether the knower is credible. The claim "John knows that the book is red" may be contingent upon whether he is colour blind or is a drug addict. Or consider the claim that "I know it's right to send Canadian troops to Afghanistan." The truth of this knowledge claim will depend upon the knower, specifically, political ideology, education level, or if a soldier or a wife, sister, or daughter of a soldier is overseas. Although the decision by the Canadian government to send troops to Afghanistan is highly contestable, the sex of the knower, says Code, is relevant to such epistemic claims. As Code states in her paper "Taking Subjectivity into Account":

> My contention that subjectivity has to be taken into account takes issue with the belief that epistemologists need only to understand the conditions of propositional, observationally derived knowledge, and all the rest will follow. It challenges the concomitant belief that epistemologists need only to understand how such knowledge claims are made and justified by individual, autonomous, self-reliant reasoners to understand all the rest. Such beliefs derive from conceptions of detached and faceless cognitive agency that mask the variability of the experiences and practices from which knowledge is constructed. (26)

These experiences and practices, says Code, include a person's material, historical, and cultural circumstances; their knowledge and power; their ethical and aesthetic judgments; and their political agendas. These, says Code, are epistemologically significant in understanding knowledge claims.

Consider abortion, for example. Arguments for and against abortion usually revolve the key questions, such as the following: Is the fetus of a person with a right to life comparable to that of children or adults? Is the body of woman her own property to do with as she sees fit? Although these are important questions in and of themselves, from a feminist perspective, the question of abortion can be recast, not focusing on personhood or autonomy, but on the knowledge that women have of oppression, especially in male-dominated societies.[12] In such cases, women ought to control abortion decisions, especially in societies where women bear the majority of responsibility for pregnancy, birth, and child rearing (Markowitz 145). A woman's right to abortion, so the argu-

ment goes, rests on her relationship with society and other social variables. In societies where men sexually oppress women, for example, women are in a better position, because of their suffering, to *know* whether anti-abortion polices are morally justified. In non-egalitarian societies, abortion would be permissible for a woman if not doing so would exacerbate or perpetuate the oppression (Markowitz 146). In other words, abortion is morally justified due to the knowledge women have of oppression and how male-dominated societies can make their lives worse off. Leaving the details to one side, the point is that from a feminist perspective women are best to know and decide the moral status of abortion.

Another assumption we ought not to make is that the knower is male, white, adult, affluent, educated, and a man of standing. Whether this assumption is derived from coincidence or a manifestation of philosophical convictions, history has shown that in order to count as a knower one has to be male. Aristotle, Rousseau, Kierkegaard, and Nietzsche have all made disparaging remarks about women's cognitive abilities to varying degrees, but the implication is that women's knowledge is subjective, while men's knowledge is objective. A woman's perspective thus disqualifies her as having full epistemic status. But if her sex does indeed disqualify her as an objective knower then, for Code, her subjective perspective is still epistemologically significant. So although a 55-year-old male philosophy professor may have a fundamentally different epistemic standpoint than a 35-year-old Asian female peasant farmer, it's surely wrong to conclude that this female point of view is less epistemologically significant. What feminist philosophers have recognized is that a woman's culture, socioeconomic status, family relations, and history all have a bearing on what and how she knows.

Of course, one does not need to be a woman to have been in an unique epistemic position. According to what are known as **standpoint epistemologies,** groups that are marginalized from mainstream society and politics can be in unique epistemic positions to see how society functions in ways dominant groups are unable to see or know. Marginalized groups have epistemic privileges to see problems and solutions that mainstream society does or cannot see. First Nations ecological knowledge is a case in point. Traditional ecological knowledge is often discounted or discredited because it does not fit into ideological frameworks of non-Native people. Deborah McGregor explains:

> Because the already established (and stereotyped-based) frame of reference held by researchers is so different from that of Native people . . . the aboriginal voice is frequently discredited, distorted, or ignored. Since information provided by aboriginal voices often does not fit into the stenotype-based ideological frameworks of non-Native researchers, aboriginal people are routinely seen as less valid sources of information than other non-Native researchers. (327)

However, traditional First Nations knowledge offers non-Native people valuable lessons in sustainable development. The Vuntut Gwitchin First Nation in the Yukon is case in point (Sherry and Myers 2002). From forestry to hunting caribou, their knowledge of the environment has allowed them to coexist with nature for thousands of years. Ideologically, First Nation cultures have traditionally viewed the environment very differently than that of non-Native people. For many non-Native people, especially in Western countries, the environment is to be controlled, dominated, and used for self-interested ends. The Vuntut Gwitchin, however, see the land as sacred and, as such, use of the land is a privilege, not a right. Everyone is to use resources wisely, without compromising use for future generations. Vuntut Gwitchin believe that all living things are alive and, therefore, there is no metaphysical distinction between the animate and inanimate. The excessive consumption of resources beyond one's own personal needs, for example, inevitably harms oneself and family in the long run. This kind of traditional knowledge is extremely

valuable and Western countries (or is it merely Western leaders) have much to learn from indigenous populations. In short, such standpoint epistemologies ought not be discounted but recognized as ways of constructing alternative solutions to our environmental problems.

However, in traditional epistemology, the knowledge sought entails an objective perspective free from the confines of culture, history, or personal interests—a view from nowhere. The problem, as feminist epistemologists point out, is that such objectivity is impossible—a view is always from somewhere. But if the view from somewhere is always to some degree relative to the community in which one lives, this raises the problem of relativism—one view is as true/right as another. In short, female ways of knowing will be no better or worse than male ways of knowing. And if we push the idea further, relativism states that all opinions have equal value including racist, sexist, and feminist opinions.

These unacceptable consequences have pushed feminists to respond the problem of relativism by trying to find some middle ground between accepting certain relative factors that impact ways of knowing and objectivity. Code, for example, developed a middle ground called mitigated relativism. For Code, we must recognize the relativist nature of our knowledge claims, but this does not mean that all knowledge claims are valid. We must evaluate such claims while being committed to empirical adequacy. Code states:

> . . . although the ideal objectivity of the universal knower is neither possible or desirable, a realistic commitment to achieving empirical adequacy that engages in situated analysis of the subjectivities of both the knower and . . . the known is both desirable and possible. . . . Objectivity *requires* taking subjectivity into account. (31–32)

In short, the sex of the knower and his or her history, interests, and so forth, are important but not the end all and be all of epistemic evaluation. Epistemic relativism makes our evaluation more discerning without sliding to a strong form of relativism. Code thinks that although subjectivity and agent specificities are important, it does not commit an inquirer to outright subjectivism. The cannons of science must still come to bear on the relativist nature of our epistemological claims.

8

Lorraine Code

(1937–)

Lorraine Code is Distinguished Research Professor of Philosophy at York University in Toronto, Canada, and a Fellow of the Royal Society of Canada. In addition to numerous articles and chapters in books, and four co-edited books, she is the author of Epistemic Responsibility *(1987),* What Can She Know? Feminist Theory and the Construction of Knowledge *(1991),* Rhetorical Spaces: Essays on (Gendered) Locations *(1995), and* Ecological Thinking: The Politics of Epistemic Location *(2006). She is General Editor of the Routledge* Encyclopedia of Feminist Theories *(2000), editor of* Feminist Interpretations of Hans-Georg Gadamer *(2003), and co-translator with Kathryn Hamer of Michèle Le Dœuff's [1998]* Le Sexe du savoir *as* The Sex of Knowing *(2003). She is currently developing a moral epistemology sensitive to vulnerability and working*

on questions generated by the new epistemologies of ignorance, on knowing across differences, and on the contestability of "natural kinds."

Is the Sex of the Knower Epistemologically Significant?

The Question

A question that focuses on the knower, at the title of this chapter does, claims that there are good reasons for asking who that knower is.[1] Uncontroversial as such a suggestion would be in ordinarily conversations about knowledge, academic philosophers commonly treat 'the knower' as a featureless abstraction. Sometimes, indeed, she or he is merely a place holder in the proposition 'S knows that p.' Epistemological analysis of the proposition tend to focus on the 'knowing that', to determine conditions under which a knowledge claim can legitimately be made. Once discerned, it is believed, such conditions will hold across all possible utterances of the proposition. Indeed, throughout the history of modern philosophy the central 'problem of knowledge' has been to determine necessary and sufficient conditions for the possibility and justification of knowledge claims. Philosophers have sought ways of establishing a relation of correspondence between knowledge and 'reality' and/or ways of establishing the coherence of particular knowledge claims within systems of already-established truths. They have proposed methodologies for arriving at truth, and criteria for determining the validity of claims to the effect that 'S knows that p'. Such endeavors are guided by the putatively self-evident principle that truth once discerned, knowledge once established, claim their status *as* truth and knowledge by virtue of a grounding in or coherence within a permanent, objective, ahistorical, and circumstantially neutral framework or set of standards.

The question 'Who is S?' is regarded neither as legitimate nor as relevant in these endeavors. As inquirers into the nature and conditions of human knowledge, epistemologists commonly work from the assumption that they need concern themselves only with knowledge claims that meet certain standards of *purity*. Questions about the circumstances of knowledge acquisitions serve merely to clutter and confuse the issue with contingencies and other impurities. The question 'Who is S?' is undoubtedly such a question. If it matters who S is, then it must follow that something peculiar to S's character or nature could bear on the validity of the knowledge she or he claims; that S's *identity* might count among the conditions that make that knowledge claim possible. For many philosophers, such a suggestion would undermine the cherished assumption that knowledge can—and should—be evaluated on its own merits. More seriously still, a proposal that it matters who the knower is looks suspiciously like a move in the direction of epistemological relativism. For many philosophers, and endorsement of relativism signals the end of knowledge and of epistemology. [. . .]

The only thing that is clear about S from the standard proposition 'S know that p' is that S is a (would-be) knower. Although the question 'Who is S?' rarely arises, certain assumptions about S as knower permeate epistemological inquiry. Of special importance for my argument is the assumption that knowers are self-sufficient

and solitary individuals, at least in their knowledge-seeking activities. This belief derives from a long and venerable heritage, with its roots in Descartes's quest for a basis of perfect certainty on which to establish his knowledge. The central aim of Descartes's endeavors is captured in this claim: "I shall have the right to conceive high hopes if I am happy enough to discover one thing only which is certain and indubitable."[2] That "one thing," Descartes believed, would stand as the fixed, pivotal, Archimedean point on which all the rest of his knowledge would turn. Because of its systematic relation to that point, his knowledge would be certain and indubitable.

Most significant for this discussion is Descartes's conviction that his quest will be conducted in a private, introspective examination of the contents of his own mind. It is true that, in the last section of the *Discourse on the Method*, Descartes acknowledges the benefit "others may receive from the communication of [his] reflection," and he states his belief that combining "the lives and labours of many"[3] is essential to progress in scientific knowledge. It is also true that this individualistically described act of knowing exercises the aspect of the soul that is common to and alike in all knowers: namely, the faculty of reason. Yet his claim that knowledge seeking is an introspective activity of an individual mind accords no relevance either to a knower's embodiment or to his (or her) intersubjective relations. For each knower, the Cartesian route to knowledge is through private, abstract thought, through the efforts of reason unaided either by the senses or by consultation with other knowers. It is this individualistic, self-reliant, private aspect of Descartes's philosophy that has been influential in shaping subsequent epistemological ideals.

Reason is conceived as autonomous in the Cartesian project in two ways, then. Not only is the quest for certain knowledge an independent one, undertaken separately by each rational being, but it is a journey of reason alone, unassisted by the senses. Descartes believed that sensory experiences had the effect of distracting reason from its proper course.

The custom of formulating knowledge claims in the 'S knows that p' formula is not itself of Cartesian origin. The point of claiming Cartesian inspiration for an assumption implicit in the formulation is that the knower who is commonly presumed to be the subject of that proposition is modeled, in significant respects, on the Cartesian pure inquirer. For epistemological purposes, all knowers are believed to be alike with respect both to their cognitive capacities and to their methods of achieving knowledge. In the empiricist tradition this assumption is apparent in the belief that simple, basic observational data can provide the foundation of knowledge just because perception is invariant from observer to observer, in standard observation conditions. In fact, a common way of filling the places in the 'S knows the p' proposition in with substitutions such as "Peter knows that the door is open" or "John knows that the book is red." It does not matter who John or Peter is.

Such knowledge claims carry implicit beliefs not only about would-be knowers but also about the knowledge that is amenable to philosophical analysis. Although (Cartesian) rationalists and empiricists differ with respect to what kinds of claim count as foundational, they endorse similar assumptions about the relation of foundational claims to the rest of a body of knowledge. With 'S knows that p' propositions, the belief is that such propositions stand as paradigms for knowledge in general. Epistemologists assume that knowledge is analyzable into propositional 'simples' whose truth can be demonstrated by establishing relations of correspondence to reality, or coherence within a system of known truths. These relatively simple knowledge claims (i.e., John knows that the book is red) could indeed be made by most 'normal' people who know the language and are familiar with the objects named. Knowers would seem to be quite self-sufficient in acquiring such knowledge. Moreover, no one would claim to know "a little" that the book is red or to be in the process of acquiring knowledge about the openness of the door. Nor would anyone be likely to maintain that S knows better than W does that the door is open or that the book is red. Granting such examples paradigmatic status creates the mistaken assumption that all knowledge worthy of the name will be like this. [. . .]

In proposing that the sex of the knower is epistemologically significant, I am claiming that the scope of epistemological inquiry has been too narrowly defined. My point is not to denigrate projects of establishing the best foundations possible or of developing workable criteria of coherence. I am proposing that even if it is not possible (or not *yet* possible) to establish an unassailable foundationalist or coherentist position, there are numerous questions to be asked about knowledge whose answers matter to people who are concerned to know well. Among them are questions that bear not just on criteria of evidence, justification, and warrantability, but on the 'nature' of cognitive agents: questions about their character; their material, historical, cultural circumstances; their interests in the inquiry at issue. These are questions about how credibility is established, about connections between knowledge and power, about the place of knowledge in ethical and aesthetic judgments, and about political agendas and the responsibilities of knowers. I am claiming that all of these questions are epistemological significant. [. . .]

Although it has rarely been spelled out prior to the development of feminist critiques, it has long been tacitly assumed that S is male. Nor could S be just any man, the apparently infinite substitutability of the 'S' term notwithstanding. The S who could count as a model, paradigmatic knower has most commonly—if always tacitly—been an adult (but not *old*), white, reasonably affluent (latterly middle-class) educated man of status, property, and publicly acceptable accomplishments. In theory of knowledge he has been allowed to stand for all men.[4] This assumption does not merely derive from habit or coincidence, but is a manifestation of engrained philosophical convictions. Not only has it been taken for granted that knowers properly so-called are male, but when male philosophers have paused to note this fact, as some indeed have done, they have argued that things are as they should be. Reason may be alike in all men, but it would be a mistake to believe that 'man', in this respect, 'embraces woman'. Women have been judged incapable, for many reasons, of achieving knowledge worthy of the name. It is no exaggeration to say that anyone who wanted to *count* as a knower has commonly had to be male.

In the *Politics*, Aristotle observes: "The freeman rules over the slave after another manner from that in which the male rules over the female, or the man over the child; although the parts of the soul are present in all of them, they are present in different degrees. For the slave has no deliberative faculty at all; the woman has, but it is without authority, and the child has, but it is immature."[5] Aristotle's assumption that a woman will naturally be ruled by a man connects directly with his contention that a woman's

deliberative faculty is "without authority." Even if a women could, in her sequestered, domestic position, acquire deliberative skills, she would remain reliant on her husband for her sources of knowledge and information. She must be ruled by a man because, in the social structure of the *polis*, she enjoys neither the autonomy nor the freedom to put into visible practice the results of the deliberations she may engage in, in private. If she can claim no authority for her rational, deliberative endeavors, then her chances of gaining recognition as a knowledgeable citizen are seriously limited, whatever she may do.[6]

Aristotle is just one of a long line of western thinkers to declare the limitations of women's cognitive capacities.[7] Rousseau maintains that young men and women should be educated quite differently because of women's inferiority in reason and their propensity to be dragged down by their sensual natures. For Kierkegaard, women are merely aesthetic beings: men alone can attain the (higher) ethical and religious levels of existence. And for Nietzsche, the Apollian (intellectual) domain is the male preserve, whereas women are Dionysian (sensuous) creatures. Nineteenth-century philosopher and linguist Wilhelm von Humboldt, who writes at length about women's knowledge, sums up the central features of this line of thought as follows: "A sense of truth exists in [women] quite literally as a sense: . . . their nature also contains a lack or a failing of analytical capacity which draws a strict line of demarcation between ego and world; therefore, they will not come as close to the ultimate investigation of truth as man."[8] The implication is that women's knowledge, if ever the products of their projects deserve that label, is inherently and inevitably *subjective*—in the most idiosyncratic sense—by contrast with the best of men's knowledge.

Objectivity, quite precisely construed, is commonly regarded as a defining feature of knowledge per se.[9] So if women's knowledge is declared to be *naturally* subjective, then a clear answer emerges to my question. The answer is that if the would-be knower is female, then her sex is indeed epistemologically significant, for it disqualifies her as a knower in the fullest sense of that term. Such disqualifications will operate differently for women of different classes, races, ages, and allegiances, but in every circumstance they will operate asymmetrically for women and for men. Just what is to be made of these points—how their epistemological significances is to be construed—is the subject of this book.

The presuppositions I have just cited claim more than the rather simple fact that many kinds of knowledge and skill have, historically, been inaccessible to women on a purely practical level. It is true, historically speaking, that even women who were the racial and social 'equals' of standard male knowers were only rarely able to become learned. The thinkers I have cited (and others like them) claim to find a rationale for this state of affairs through appeals to dubious 'facts' about women's natural incapacity for rational thought. Yet deeper questions still need to be asked: Is there knowledge that is, quite simply, inaccessible to members of the female, or the male, sex? Are there kinds of knowledge that only men, or only women, can acquire? Is the sex of the knower crucially determining in this respect, across all other specificities? The answers to these questions should not address only the *practical* possibilities that have existed for members of either sex. Such practical possibilities are the constructs of complex social arrangements that are themselves constructed out of historically specific choices, and are, open to challenge and change.

Knowledge, as it achieves credence and authoritative states at any point in the history of the male-dominated mainstream, is commonly held to be a product of the individual efforts of human knowers. References to Phythagoras's theorem, Copernicus's revolution, and Newtonian and Einsteinian physics signal an epistemic community's attribution of pathbreaking contributions to certain of its individual members. The implication is that *that* person, singlehandedly, has effected a leap of progress in a particular field of inquiry. In less publicly spectacular ways, other cognitive agents are represented as contributors to the growth and stability of public knowledge.

Now any contention that such contributions are the results of independent endeavor is highly contestable. As I argue elsewhere,[10] a complex of historical and other sociocultural factors produces the conditions that make 'individual' achievement possible, and 'individuals' themselves are socially constituted.[11] The claim that individual *men* are the creators of the authoritative (often Kuhn-paradigm-establishing) landmarks of western intellectual life is particularly interesting for the fact that the contributions—both practical and substantive—of their lovers, wives, children, servants, neighbors, friends, and colleagues rarely figure in analyses of their work.[12]

The historical attribution of such achievements to specific cognitive agents does, nonetheless, accord a significance to individual efforts which raises questions pertinent to my project. It poses the problem, in another guise, of whether aspects of human specifically could, in fact, constitute conditions for the existence of knowledge or determine the kinds of knowledge that a knower can achieve. It would seem that such incidental physical attributes as height, weight, or hair color would not count among factors that would determine a person's capacities to know (though the arguments that skin color *does* count are too familiar). It is not necessary to consider how much Archimedes weighed when he made his famous discovery, nor is there any doubt that a thinner or fatter person could have reached the same conclusion. But in cultures in which sex differences figure prominently in virtually every mode of human interaction,[13] being female or male is far more fundamental to the construction of subjectivity than are such attributes as size or hair color. So the question is whether femaleness or maleness are the kinds of subjective factor (i.e., factors about the circumstances of a knowing subject) that are constitutive of the form and content of knowledge. Attempts to answer this question are complicated by the fact that sex/gender does not function uniformly and universally, even in western societies. Its implications vary across class, race, age, ability, and numerous other interwoven specificities. A separated analysis of sex/gender, then, always risks abstraction and is limited in its scope by abstracting process. Further, the question seems to imply that sex and gender are themselves constants, thus obscuring the processes of *their* sociocultural construction. Hence the formulation of adequately nuanced answers is problematic and necessarily partial.

Even if it should emerge that gender-related factors play a crucial role in the construction of knowledge, then, the inquiry into the epistemological significance of the sex of the knower would not be complete. The task would remain of considering whether a distinction between 'natural' and socialized capacity can retain any validity. The equally pressing question as to know the hitherto devalued products of *women's* cognitive projects can gain acknowl-

edgment as 'knowledge' would need to be addressed so as to uproot entrenched prejudices about knowledge, epistemology, and women. 'The epistemology project' will look quite different once its tacit underpinnings are revealed. [. . .]

Feminist philosophy simply did not exist until philosophers learned to perceive the near-total absence of women in philosophical writings from the very beginning of western philosophy, to stop assuming that 'man' could be read as a generic term. Explicit denigrations of women, which became the focus of philosophical writing in its early years of the contemporary women's movement, were more readily perceptible. The authors of derogatory views about women in classical texts clearly needed power to be able to utter their pronouncements with impunity: a power they claimed from a 'received' discourse that represented women's nature in such a way that women undoubtedly merited the negative judgments that Aristotle or Nietzsche made about them. Women are now in a position to recognize and refuse these overt manifestations of contempt.

Notes

1. This question is the title of my paper published in *Metaphilosophy* 12 (July–October 1981): 267–276. In this early essay an essentialism with respect to masculinity and femininity, and convey the impression that 'positive thinking' can bring an end to gender imbalances. I would no longer make these claims.

2. René Descartes, *Meditations*, in *The Philosophical Works of Descartes*, trans. Elizabeth S. Haldane and G. R. T. Ross (Cambridge: Cambridge University Press, 1969), 1:149.

3. René Descartes, *Discourse on the Method of Rightly Conducting the Reason and Seeking for Truth in the Sciences,* in ibid., pp. 124, 120.

4. To cite just one example: in *The Theory of Epistemic Rationality* (Cambridge: Harvard University Press, 1987), Richard Foley appeals repeatedly to the epistemic judgments of people who are "like the rest of us" (p. 108). He contrasts their beliefs with beliefs that seem "crazy or bizarre out outlandish . . . beliefs to most of the rest of us" (p. 114), and argues that an account of rational belief is plausible only if it can be presented from "some nonweird perspective" (p. 140). Foley contends that "an individual has to be at least minimally like us in order for charges of irrationally even to make sense" (p. 240). Nowhere does he address the question of who 'we' are. (I take this point up again in Chapter 7.)

5. Aristotle, *Politics*, trans. Benjamin Jowett, in *The Basic Works of Aristotle*, ed. Richard McKeon (New York: Random House, 1941), 1260b.

6. I discuss the implications of this lack of authority more fully in Chapters 5 and 6. See Elizabeth V. Spelman, *Inessential Women: Problems of Exclusion of Feminist Thought* (Boston: Beacon, 1988), for an interesting discussion of some more complex exclusions effected by Aristotle's analysis.

7. It would be inaccurate, however, to argue that this line is unbroken. Londa Schiebinger demonstrates that in the history of science—and, by implication, the history of the achievement of epistemic authority—there were many periods when women's intellectual achievements were not only recognized but respected. The "long line" I refer it is the dominant, historically most visible one. Schiebinger, *The Mind Has No Sex? Women in the Origins of Modern Science* (Cambridge: Harvard University Press, 1989).

8. *Humanist without Portfolio: An Anthology of the Writings of Wilhelm von Humboldt,* trans. with intro. by Marianne Cowan (Detroit: Wayne State University Press, 1963), p. 349.

9. I analyze this precise construal of objectivity in Chapter 2.

10. See Chapter 7, "Epistemic Community," of my *Epistemic Responsibility.*

11. I discuss the implications of these points for analyses of subjectivity in Chapter 3.

12. I owe this point—and the list—to Polly Young-Eisendrath, "The Female Person and How We Talk about Her," in Mary M. Gergen, ed., *Feminist Thought and the Structure of Knowledge* (New York: New York University Press, 1988).

13. Marilyn Frye points out: "Sex-identification intrudes into every moment of our lives and discourse, no matter what the supposedly primary focus or topic of the moment is. Elaborate, systematic, ubiquitous and redundant marking of a distinction between two sexes of humans and most animals is customary and obligatory. One *never* can ignore it." Frye, *The Political of Reality: Essay in Feminist Theory* (Trumansburg, N.Y.: Crossing Press, 1983), p.19.

Key Terms and Concepts

Epistemology
Knowledge by acquaintance
Competence knowledge
Propositional knowledge
Truth
Belief
Justification
Scepticism
Global scepticism
Local scepticism
Reliablism
Empiricists
A posteriori
Tabula rasa
Rationalists
A priori
Necessary truth
Contingent truth
Analytic truth
Synthetic truth
Methodological scepticism
Direct (naïve) realism
Ideas
Simple ideas
Complex ideas
Primary qualities
Secondary qualities
Idealism
Foundationalism
Standpoint epistemologies

Study Questions

1. What is the difference between *a priori* and *a posteriori* knowledge?
2. What are the major differences between rationalism, empiricism, and scepticism?
3. What are Descartes' three arguments in the First Meditation?
4. How does scepticism plays a crucial role in Descartes' search for knowledge?
5. What is Descartes' conclusion at the end of the Second Meditation?
6. How does the wax example prove rationalism is true?
7. Why does Locke think there are no innate ideas?
8. What is the difference between simple and complex ideas?
9. What are primary and secondary qualities and how do they relate to our knowledge of objects, people, cars, and the world generally?
10. How does Locke defeat scepticism?
11. What is Berkeley's objection against Locke?
12. Why does Berkeley believe that material objects don't give rise to our experiences?
13. What role does God play in Berkeley's epistemology?
14. What is G. E. Moore's argument against scepticism?
15. Why does Moore think no proof is necessary to defeat scepticism? Does he succeed?
16. What is Wittgenstein's response to Moore's argument against scepticism?
17. Why does Wittgenstein argue that doubt entails certainty?
18. How does the circumstance of the knower impact the knowledge claims, according to Code?
19. Does Code think the justification of such knowledge claims fall outside of who the knower is?
20. Why does Code's position lead to relativism? What is her solution?

Further Reading

Alcoft, Linda, and Elizabeth Potter, eds. *Feminist Epistemologies*. London: Routledge, 1993.

Audi, Robert. *Belief, Justification, and Knowledge*. Belmont, CA: Wadsworth, 1988.

Ayer, A. J. *The Problem of Knowledge*. Harmondsworth, Middlesex: Penguin Books, Ltd., 1956.

Greco, John, and Ernest Sosa, eds. *The Blackwell Guide to Epistemology*. Malden, MA: Blackwell, 1999.

Heil, John. *Perception and Cognition*. Berkeley: University of California Press, 1983.

Hookway, Christopher. *Scepticism*. London: Routledge, 1990.

Klein, Peter. *Certainty: A Refutation of Scepticism*. Brighton, Sussex: The Harvester Press, 1981.

Lehrer, Keith. *Theory of Knowledge*. Boulder, CO: Westview Press, 1990.

Nye, Andrea. *Philosophy and Feminism: At the Boarder.* New York: Twayne Publishers, 1995.

Tanesine, Alessandra. *An Introduction to Feminist Epistemologies*. Oxford: Blackwell, 1999.

Internet Resources

Grasswick, Heidi. "Feminist Social Epistemology." *Stanford Encyclopaedia of Philosophy*. Ed. Edward Zalta. Stanford, CA: The Metaphysics Research Lab, 9 November 2006. 12 June 2007 <http://plato.stanford.edu/entries/feminist-social-epistemology/>.

Janack, Marianne. "Feminist Epistemology." *The Internet Encyclopaedia of Philosophy*. Eds. James Fieser and Bradley Dowden. n.d. 12 June 2007 <http://www.iep.utm.edu/f/fem-epis.htm>.

Klein, Peter. "Epistemology." *Routledge Encyclopaedia of Philosophy*. Ed. F. Craig. London: Routledge, 1998, 2005. 22 May 2007 <http://www.rep.routledge.com/article/P059>.

Korcz, Keith. *The Epistemology Research Guide*. 12 July 2007. 22 May 2007 <http://www.ucs.louisiana.edu/~kak7409/EpistemologicalResearch.htm>.

Steup, Matthias. "Epistemology." *Stanford Encyclopaedia of Philosophy*. Ed. Edward Zalta. Stanford, CA: The Metaphysics Research Lab, 14 December 2005. 22 May 2007 <http://plato.stanford.edu/entries/epistemology/>.

Notes

1. I have adapted this from Jonathan Dancy (25).
2. According to a 1999 Gallup poll, 6 percent of Americans believe the moon landing was faked. Although this

may appear insignificant, it translates into millions of people. However, the two examples given in Box 2.3 can be explained. According to NASA, the reason why there are no stars in the photos taken by the astronauts is simply because starlight is too dim to be picked up by photographic film. The second example is more interesting. On earth, a flag stops waving because air slows it down. When the astronauts twisted and pushed the flagpole into the ground, the energy of these motions was transferred to the flag itself, and because the moon has no atmosphere, there is no air to stop the motion and, therefore, appears to be waving. For more general information which debunks the lunar moon hoax, see NASA at http://liftoff.msfc.nasa.gov/News/2001/News-MoonLanding.asp. For a more in-depth analysis of the hoax and its criticisms, see http://www.badastronomy.com/bad/tv/foxapollo.html.

3. For a defence of deep scepticism, see Keith Lehrer, "Why Not Scepticism?".

4. See Alvin Goldman, "A Causal Theory of Knowing," for an explicit account of reliablism.

5. To access the Declaration of Human Rights online, go to http://www.un.org/Overview/rights.html.

6. Hillary Putnam originally developed the "brain in a vat" thought experiment.

7. It was during this time that Descartes finished his first major work, *The World*, on the laws of falling bodies (Galileo was studying the same problem). When it came to Descartes' attention that Galileo had been imprisoned, he supposedly ran to the publisher to withdraw his manuscript.

8. For Hume, knowledge that the future will be like the past is unjustifiable because the future is beyond observation. No empirical observation will allow us to infer the future will be like the past. But what about laws of nature? Laws of nature are supposed to be general rules with no exceptions. Consider, for example, Newton's laws of motion, stated as follows: 1) A body remains at rest, or moves in a constant straight line, unless acted upon by an outside force. 2) The acceleration of an object is proportional to the force acting on the object. 3) Whenever one body exerts a force on a second body, the second body excerpts an equal and opposite force on the first body (Kaufmann 38–40). Newton's laws, taken collectively, could be used to justify observations that if one billiard ball hit another billiard ball, the second will regularly and consistently act in a predictable manner. Could Newton's laws of motion, amongst other laws, be used to refute the problem of induction?

9. nm = nanometres or one billionth of a metre.

10. It is reputed that Moore originally gave this proof in front of his students at Cambridge.

11. Code points out another erroneous assumption: epistemological leaps forward are individual endeavours that are done single-handedly. This, argues Code, is highly contestable. Such intellectual efforts are always a complex history of factors that make individual achievements possible including wives, lovers, children, family members, and so forth.

12. According to the Center for Reproductive Rights, 69 countries worldwide, primarily in South America, South East Asia, and the Middle East, have laws either prohibiting abortion altogether or only permitting it to save a woman's life.

Works Cited

Center for Reproductive Rights. "The World's Abortion Laws." n.d. 12 June 2007 <http://www.reproductiverights.org/pub_fac_abortion_laws.html>.

Code, Lorraine. "Taking Subjectivity into Account." *Feminist Epistemologies*. Ed. Linda Alcoff and Elizabeth Potter. London: Routledge, 1993.

Dancy, Jonathan. *Introduction to Contemporary Epistemology*. New York: Basil Blackwell Ltd., 1985.

Gettier, Edmund. "Is Justified True Belief Knowledge?" *Analysis* 23 (1963): 121–123.

Gilligan, Carol. *In a Different Voice: Psychological Theory and Women's Development*. Cambridge, MA: Harvard University Press, 1982.

Goldman, Alvin. "Reliablism." *The Cambridge Dictionary of Philosophy*. Ed. Robert Audi. New York: Cambridge University Press, 1995.

—. "A Causal Theory of Knowing." *Journal of Philosophy* 64 (1967): 357–372.

Harding, Katherine. "Debunking Evolution in Dinosaur Land." *Globe and Mail,* 6 June 2007: A1+.

Ibbitson, John. "Genesis of a Theory Evolves into Museum." *Globe and Mail,* 28 May 2007: A1+.

Kaufmann, William J. *Discovering the Universe*. New York: W. H. Freeman and Company, 1987.

Lawhead, William F. *The Philosophical Journey: An Interactive Approach*. 2nd ed. New York: McGraw Hill, 2003.

Lehrer, Keith. *Theory of Knowledge*. London: Routledge, 1990.

—. "Why Not Scepticism?" *Philosophical Forum* 2 (1971): 283–298.

Markowitz, Sally. "A Feminist Defense of Abortion." *Morality in Practice*. 5th ed. Ed. James Sterba. Belmont, CA: Wadsworth Publishing Company, 1997.

McGregor, Deborah. "Exploring Aboriginal Environmental Ethics." *Canadian Issues in Environmental Ethics*. Ed. Alex Wellington, Allan Greenbaum, and Wesley Cragg. Peterborough, ON: Broadview Press, 1997.

Moore, David. "Three in Four Americans Believe in Paranormal." *The Gallup Poll*. 16 June 2005. 20 August 2006 <http://poll.gallup.com/content/default.aspx?ci=16915&pg-1>.

Moore, G. E. "A Defence of Common-Sense." *Philosophical Papers*. London: George Allen and Unwin Ltd., 1959.

—. "Proof of an External World." *Philosophical Papers*. London: George Allen and Unwin Ltd., 1959.

Nye, Andrea. *Philosophy and Feminism at the Boarder*. New York: Twayne Publishers, 1995.

Pojman, Louis. *Philosophy: The Pursuit of Wisdom*. 4th ed. Belmont, CA: Wadsworth/Thomson Learning, 2004.

Putnam, Hilary. *Reason, Truth and History*. New York: Cambridge University Press, 1981.

Rauhut, Nils. *Ultimate Questions: Thinking about Philosophy*. New York: Pearson/Longman, 2004.

Russell, Bertrand. *Problems of Philosophy*. New York: Oxford University Press, 1980.

Schick, Theodore, Jr., and Lewis Vaughn. *Doing Philosophy: An Introduction through Thought Experiments*. New York: McGraw Hill, 2003.

Sherry, Erin, and Heather Myers. "Traditional Environmental Knowledge in Practice." *Society and Natural Resources* 15 (2002): 345–358.

Stroll, Avrum. *Moore and Wittgenstein on Certainty*. New York: Oxford University Press, 1994.

Stumpf, Samuel, and James Fieser. *Philosophy: History and Problems*. 6th ed. New York: McGraw Hill, 2003.

United Nations. "Universal Declaration of Human Rights." n.d. September 1, 2007 <http://www.un.org/Overview/rights.html>.

Wittgenstein, Ludwig. *On Certainty*. Ed. G. E. M. Anscombe and G. H. von Wright. Trans. Denis Paul and G. E. M Anscombe. Oxford: Basil Blackwell, 1969.

Chapter 3 The Existence of God

If there were no God, it would be necessary to invent him.
          —Voltaire

Is man one of God's blunders? Or is God one of man's blunders?
          —Friedrich Nietzsche

Does God exist? Is belief in God central to religious faith? Trying to find answers to these questions, amongst others, has been central to the human condition. For centuries, philosophers and theologians have attempted to prove God's existence in a variety of ways and understand the purpose of religious faith. Belief in God **(theism)** can give meaning, purpose, and inspiration to people's lives; can deepen their understanding of the world and their place in it (God created the earth and humans as part of a divine plan); can provide moral guidance (e.g., the Ten Commandments; Upanishad); and can give people a sense of internal peace (e.g., one's soul will go to heaven when one dies; reincarnation). Moreover, religious faith can influence day-to-day activities, including prayer times, what to eat, and what clothes to wear. For billions of people across the world, God's centrality in religious faith explains where humans have come from and where we are going in the future.

For people who do not believe in God **(atheism)**[1] or lack religious faith, they can think of the world very differently. It's human beings, not God, Allah, or Brahman, who ultimately give meaning, purpose, and inspiration to people's lives. Their understanding of the world and their place in it is the result of evolution and the sciences or, perhaps, the universe has always existed without the need of some divine creator. What is right and wrong is a human creation or based on *karma*. And when one dies, a soul doesn't go to heaven; the body simply decomposes as part of the natural lifecycle. Moreover, religious determinants of prayer, food, and clothing can be explained by social convention rather than religious fact.

The famous psychologist, Sigmund Freud, for example, believed that religion was a human creation (see Box 3.1). We construct the illusion

Box 3.1 Religion as Illusion

Many people, such as Freud, argue that religion is an illusion and gives us a false sense of hope, especially in times of crisis. Is this necessarily a bad thing? Why or why not? List five ways in which religion can help people overcome difficulties in their lives.

1.

2.

3.

4.

5.

of God because we need to have a fatherly (motherly) figure in our lives. Children, generally speaking, look to their parents for meaning, security, love, and happiness. But parents, unlike God, are real. Belief in God, Freud argued, gives us no deep meaning and purpose in our lives, a false sense of protection, fleeting feelings of love, and unrealistic expectations of eternal happiness. Although it might appear that God give us all of these things, it is merely wishful thinking; and once we realize this we will come to know that God does not exist. In short, religion is a myth.

Regardless of who is right, trying to prove or disprove the existence of God is fraught with problems. One significant problem is that there is no concrete objective evidence to confirm one's belief or disbelief in a higher being. Unlike a detective who uses physical evidence (murder weapon, fibre analysis, DNA, and so forth) to confirm or

---

Box 3.2 Religion and Personal Identity

The philosophical question "Does God exist?" is often challenging for students, especially if they have been raised in a religious household and espouse a particular faith. Arguments against God's existence and discussing other secular and cultural views can leave students feeling unnerved and threatened, not only religiously but also personally. Try to answer the questions below as truthfully as possible to determine how religious or nonreligious beliefs might affect you.

1. How does your belief or non-belief affect your identity?

2. Are there any significant symbols that would identify you with your faith? How do these symbols reflect an aspect of your faith?

3. If you were to find out that God does not exist, would that matter? Would it affect you personally?

4. What do you hope to gain from a belief in God?

5. Does gender influence someone's belief or non-belief in God?

---

reject that a suspect has committed a crime, no such concrete evidence is available when discussing religion. Any evidence is circumstantial. But for many of the world's population, evidence is irrelevant. Faith, and faith alone, is all that is needed to know God exists (fideism). **Fideism** makes it very difficult to engage people in a philosophical discourse of God's existence because faith is given precedence over reason (see Box 3.2). From a philosophical perspective, however, faith alone is insufficient proof. Theists (and atheists) need well-thought-out, logical arguments to support their beliefs. Much of this chapter is devoted to determining if there is objective evidence of God's existence and whether this evidence is philosophically valid.

However, one thing is certain, atheists are the minority. The majority of the world's population believe in some form of higher being. The cultural universality of religious belief is impressive. Consider the results of the 2005 survey of world religions in Figure 3.1.

Figure 3.1 Major Religions of the World

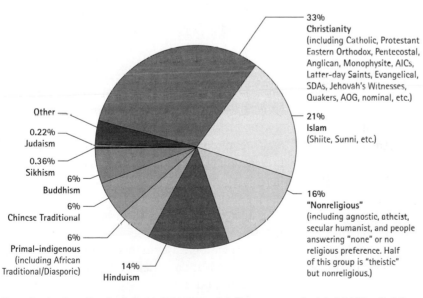

33%
Christianity
(including Catholic, Protestant Eastern Orthodox, Pentecostal, Anglican, Monophysite, AICs, Latter-day Saints, Evangelical, SDAs, Jehovah's Witnesses, Quakers, AOG, nominal, etc.)

21%
Islam
(Shiite, Sunni, etc.)

16%
"Nonreligious"
(including agnostic, atheist, secular humanist, and people answering "none" or no religious preference. Half of this group is "theistic" but nonreligious.)

14%
Hinduism

Other
0.22% **Judaism**
0.36% **Sikhism**
6% **Buddhism**
6% **Chinese Traditional**
6% **Primal–indigenous**
(including African Traditional/Diasporic)

The cultural universality of religious belief is impressive. There are approximately 2.1 billion Christians, 1.5 billion Muslims, and 900 million Hindus in the world today. However, Islam is the fastest growing religion, partly due to the high birth rates in Muslim countries, which are almost double that of Christian countries.

Source: © 2005 www.adherents.com. *Major Religions of the World Ranked by Adherents.* 19 April 2007. 12 June 2007 <http://www.adherents.com/Religions_By_Adherents.html>.

Table 3.1 Top 10 Religious Denominations, Canada, 2001

Religion	Numbers	Percentage
Roman Catholic	12,793,125	43.2%
Protestant	8,654,845	29.2%
Christian Orthodox	479,620	1.6%
Christian*	780,450	2.6%
Muslim	579,640	2.0%
Jewish	329,995	1.1%
Buddhist	300,345	1.0%
Hindu	297,200	1.0%
Sikh	278,415	0.9%
No religion	4,796,325	16.2%

*(Includes persons who report "Christian," as well as those who report "Apostolic," "Born-again Christian," and "Evangelical.")

Source: Statistics Canada. *Overview: Canada Still Predominantly Roman Catholic and Protestant.* 2001. 23 May 2007 <http://www12.statcan.ca/english/census01/Products/Analytic/companion/rel/canada.cfm>.

Christianity is the largest religion with 33 percent of the world's population, Islam the second largest religion at 21 percent, and Hinduism the third largest religion at 14 percent. Similar statistics are reflected in North America. The breakdown of religious affiliation in Canada, according to the 2001 census conducted by Statistics Canada, is shown in Table 3.1.

Although the U.S. government cannot officially ask its citizens about religious affiliation, the most comprehensive study to date on religious affiliation comes from the Graduate Center of the City University of New York. According to the *American Religious Identity Survey* (ARIS) conducted in 2001, the vast majority of Americans are Christian (including Roman Catholics, Protestants, and so on); see Table 3.2.

However, we should be careful here. People with no religion or who are not religious are not necessarily atheists. The *American Religious Identity Survey* found that only 0.4 percent of Americans are atheist (0.5 percent are agnostic), while 13.2 percent consider themselves theists but not associated with any religious group. In Canada, approximately 3 percent of the population consider themselves atheist and another 3 percent agnostic (Vilar).

This sociological evidence is important if we think of it within a wider philosophical context. If we can find rational arguments to demonstrate God's existence, then the small percentage of atheists in the world will, rightly, be seen as intransigent—unwilling to accept what is universally believed across most human societies. However, if we can find rational arguments to

Table 3.2	Major Religions of the United States, 2001

Religion	Percentage
Christian	76.5%
Muslim	0.5%
Jewish	1.3%
Buddhist	0.5%
Hindu	0.4%
Sikh	0.03%
Nonreligious	13.2%

Source: Adapted from Kosmin, Barry, Mayer, Egon, and Ariela Keysar. (2001). *American Religious Identity Survey, 2001.* The Graduate Center of the City University of New York, 12–13. 23 May 2007 <http://www.gc.cuny.edu/faculty/research_studies/aris.pdf>.

earliest human remains—religious funeral artifacts—to the most recent wars in the Mideast, religion—belief in God or gods—has been the mainspring of the whole watch that is human history. (11)

Rewriting the annals of history would be arduous, if not impossible, if God does not exist, because some of the most important events in human history were justified in God's name. The first Christian Crusade in Europe against Islam in 1097; the conversion of Spanish Jews and Muslims to Christianity during the fifteenth-century Spanish Inquisition; Michelangelo's Sistine Chapel; the American Constitution; and the bombing of the World Trade Center on September 11, 2001, to name a few, have all been inspired by God according to one traditional belief system or another. God's non-existence would have significant implications indeed.

Whether you consider yourself a theist or atheist, the debate surrounding God's existence is one of the most interesting and controversial issues in philosophy. This chapter is devoted to outlining the main philosophical positions for and against the existence of God. We will critically assess five traditional arguments: ontological, cosmological, teleological, problem of evil, and belief and faith. These arguments deal exclusively with the monotheistic conception of God found in Christianity, Islam, and Judaism. **Monotheism** is the claim that there is only one God who created the world, its processes, and with whom we can have intimate contact.[2] Moreover, these arguments also, generally speaking, define God as a being who is omnipotent (all-powerful), omniscient (all-knowing), omnibenevolent (all-good), eternal, compassionate, creator of the universe, and perfect. Although these concepts of God are debatable (see Box 3.3), it would not be mere speculation to suggest that these concepts still define much of people's belief and perspective of God. This said, before we begin, let's find out what you think (Box 3.4).

demonstrate God's non-existence, then the majority of the world's population is, perhaps, mistaken about believing in something that does not exist. This would mean the justification of much of human history would be suspect. As Peter Kreeft explains:

> The idea of God has guided or deluded more lives, changed more history, inspired more music and poetry and philosophy than anything else, real or imagined. It has made more of a difference to human life on this planet, both individually and collectively, than anything else ever has. To see this clearly for yourself, just try this thought experiment: suppose no one in history had ever conceived the idea of God. Now, rewrite history following that premise. The task daunts and staggers the imagination. From the

Box 3.3 A Feminist Conception of God

As we saw in the last chapter, feminist philosophy makes connections between women's role in society and the social institutions that keep women in subordinate positions. And no other institution in human history has had such importance than that of religion and the church. Over the years, feminist theologians (see Chopp; Daly; Ruether, *Sexism*) have argued that traditional religious institutions and concept of God are inherently gender biased and have systematically kept women in a state of oppression. As Carol Christ states, "Religions centered on the worship of a male God creates 'moods' and 'motivations' that keep women in a state of psychological dependence on men and male authority, while at the same [time] legitimating the *political* and *social* authority of fathers and sons in the institutions of society" (312).

After all, both Christianity and Judaism suggest that Eve was "born" from Adam's rib, not the other way around; it was Eve who tempted Adam to commit the first original sin; and it was Jesus, God's son—not daughter—who came to the earth as our saviour. Moreover, the Roman Catholic Church still refuses to allow women to become ordained priests. Collectively, the concept of God is considered masculine and, as such, males not only engender these masculine characteristics of power and domination but they are also instilled in religious institutions. God is, therefore, envisioned as a "supreme, ruling, judging, and loving male...a single, absolute subject, is named Father [the son, and Holy Spirit], and is conceived as standing in a relation of hierarchical domination over the world" (Frankenberry). Implicitly and explicitly, this masculine conception of God reinforces the social institution of patriarchy. This means women, children, and others, such as non-white middle class males, are marginalized and kept in subordinate roles.

In response, some feminist theologians like Mary Daly argue that the very concept of God must be deconstructed so that feminine characteristics and points of view are taken into consideration. One option is to redefine God as a Goddess. This concept would reaffirm female power by focusing on her ability to give birth; the interconnectedness and dependency between nature and humans; and the importance of relationships and family (compassion and caring) (Christ). Another option is to use a plurality of images to be drawn from both women's and men's experiences (Ruether, *Twenty Questions*). God can be strong and powerful but also healing, nurturing, and loving. However, both options have the same goal: to conceptualize God differently. Unlike the traditional male view that associates power with domination, force, or coercion, a feminist point of view sees power as empowering, healing, reconciling, and transforming (Ruether, *Twenty Questions* 34). Although the details are beyond this introductory text, what is important is that by redefining the concept of God we can avoid the inherent male biased found in Western religions and the dominative and oppressive consequences of patriarchy.

Box 3.4 What Do You Think?

Does God exist? Before answering this question consider this quotation from Peter Kreeft:

> The idea of God is a fact, like sand, or a fantasy, like Santa.
>
> If it is a fantasy, a human invention, it is the greatest invention in all of human history. Measure it against all the other inventions, mental or physical. Put on the one side of the scale the control of fire, the domestication of animals, and the cultivation of wheat; the wheel, the ship, and the rocket ship; baseball, the symphony orchestra, and anesthetics—and a million other similarly great and wonderful things. Then put on the other side of the scale a single idea: the idea of a being that is actual, absolute, perfect, eternal, one, and personal; all-knowing, all loving, all-just, all-merciful, and all powerful; undying, impervious, unbribeable, uncompromising, and unchangeable; a cosmic creator, designer, redeemer, and provider; cosmic artist, musician, scientist, and sage; the infinite abyss of pure Being who is yet a person, a self, an "I." It is disputable whether such a being is in a fact or a fantasy, but it is indisputable that if it is a fantasy, it is by far the greatest fantasy in history. If it is humanity's invention, it is humanity's masterpiece. (11)

Interestingly, most Western children (usually between the ages of 3–7 years), unlike adults, believe Santa Claus is a fact rather than fantasy. As a child, my sister and I would sneak down stairs early on Christmas morning to see if Santa had visited our house. Much to our delight, he came every year. However, as my sister and I got older, we slowly came to disbelieve in Santa. At some point we came to realize that it was our parents, not Santa, who delivered the presents each Christmas morning. Although the idea of Santa is logically possible,[3] scientists claim that it would be physically (causally) impossible[4] for Santa to deliver presents to all the children in world in one night without violating the laws of physics. For non-believers, the burden of proof is on those who make claims concerning the existence of Santa (or vampires, leprechauns, etc.) to provide some hard evidence. But since hard evidence is lacking in this case, a simpler explanation is found by appealing to one's parents. In short, Santa is a fantasy.

Some atheists take a certain amount of ironic pleasure in pointing out that while most adults don't believe in Santa, many adults believe in God. And if God is omniscient, omnipotent, omnibenevolent, and the creator of the universe, this suggests that God, like Santa, has powers beyond the physical realm. But why accept the existence of God while dismissing the existence of Santa? In response, many theists point out God's non-existence is a logical impossibility. The very notion that God is all-powerful, all-knowing, and all-good necessarily entails his or her existence. That is, it would be impossible for a being to possess all these qualities and not exist. However, for some atheists, proving God's existence by definition is insufficient; what is needed is hard objective evidence uncontaminated by bias or evidence that already presupposes belief in God. And since none such evidence is forthcoming, God does not exist. In short, perhaps God, like Santa, is a fantasy. Do you agree? Is there a difference between Santa and God that would justify belief in one but not the other? Can you know God exists with more certainty than knowing Santa does not exist? Is there proof (scientific) that God exists? What do you think?

The Ontological Argument

I'm an atheist and I thank God for it.
— George Bernard Shaw

Discussion Questions

1. Generally speaking, to conceive of a perfect thing does not entail its existence. Imagine the most perfect spouse, cook, athlete, car, computer, and so on. From the mere fact you can conceive of these things it does not necessarily entail they exist. However, God is considered by many religious traditions as a perfect being; a being that is knowledgeable, powerful, good, eternal, the creator of life, and so forth. How would God's perfection convince or dissuade you that God exists? Discuss whether or not Anselm's ontological proof is right.

2. As Yeager Hudson points out, Anselm's ontological proof can be used to show that Satan exists. How is this a valid or invalid argument? In what ways would you agree or disagree that if the most perfectly good being (God) can exist, then the most perfectly evil being (Satan) could exist as well?

3. The very concept of a unicorn contains within it an idea of a single-horned creature. Hence, if unicorn exists, then a single-horned creature would exist. But this is not a necessary condition. After all, even if humans can conceive of a single-horned creature, it is a contingent truth whether such creatures actually exist. And no unicorns do exist. Hence, can we not say the same thing about God? Although the very concept of God contains within it the idea of a perfect being, does it follow that God must necessarily exist because of God's perfection? Perhaps the ontological argument is merely demonstrating that the idea of God possesses certain perfections, but whether they exist in reality is another matter. Would you agree that perfection entails God's existence (Lawhead 343)? Why or why not?

God Exists.... All You Have to Do Is Think about It

St. Anselm's ontological argument is unique among traditional arguments for God's existence because it is *a priori* in nature. As we saw in the previous chapter, *a priori* in Latin literally means "from the previous." Knowledge is independent of sensory experience; we can come to know things simply by reason and the mind alone. For Anselm, proof of God's existence rests on thinking about God rationally and logically. Anselm is convinced of his faith in God; even a fool (atheist) who disbelieves in God will come to see the error of his or her ways.

Anselm argues that God exists because nothing greater can be conceived. But not everyone is a believer. The fool in the *Book of Psalms* believes in his heart that God does not exist. For Anselm, the fool is in a contradiction. In order for the fool to deny God's existence, the fool must be able to understand that God is a being *than which nothing greater can be conceived*—a being that is omniscient, omnipotent, omnibenevolent, creator of the universe, eternal, etc. In short, God is perfect. But if God is the greatest possible being, then this being must also exist in reality. Why? Because existing in reality, according to Anselm, makes something better or more perfect than existing in the intellect alone. If the fool were to merely conceive of God only in his understanding, then God would not be greatest being, since he could always conceive a greater being who exists in reality. But this is absurd and contradictory, according to Anselm, because the fool is saying that the greatest possible being isn't the greatest. He cannot conceive God not to exist, otherwise it's not God. The fool who understands what he is denying cannot do this without contradiction. To deny God's existence is to suggest that God is not perfect. But if God were not perfect, then this would not be God but something else. God, by definition, entails existence as part of perfection. Hence, if God is truly the greatest (most perfect) being we can conceive of, and if a truly great being must exist not only in one's mind but also in reality, then God must exist in reality. Anselm's argument can be summarized as follows:

1. I have, within my understanding, an idea of God.
2. This idea of God is the idea of the greatest possible being.
3. A being is greater if it exists in reality than if it exists only in the understanding.
4. If God exists in the understanding alone, then a greater being can be conceived, namely, one that also exists in reality.
5. But premise 4 is a contradiction, for it says I can conceive of a greater being than the greatest possible being.
6. So if I have an idea of the greatest conceivable being, such a being must exist both in my understanding and in reality.
7. Therefore, God exists in reality. (Lawhead 340)

To gain a better understanding of the ontological argument, consider the comic book hero Superman (Rauhut 193). Superman is an imaginary hero created by Canadian Joe Shuster in 1933. His impact on popular culture has been enormous. He has spawned comic books, action figures, games, movies, and television programs. The cultural phenomenon of Superman has spanned generations, in part, because he possesses properties many of us wish we had. These properties include:

- Faster than a speeding bullet
- Leap tall building in a single bound
- Fly
- Incredible strength
- X-ray vision
- Super-hearing
- Super-breath (can produce gale force winds by blowing)

Despite the fact that Superman has powers far greater than any human, he lacks one important property—existence. Superman does not exist. But what if there were another Superman—let's call him Superman 2—existing not only in our imagination but also in reality? Would Superman 2 be greater than non-existent Superman? Yes, Superman 2 would be greater because he *really*

could rescue people in distress, save lives, catch criminals, and maybe even prevent natural disasters. In other words, if Superman 2 existed, he would possess one property that Superman does not, namely, existence. It's the property of existence that makes Superman 2 superior. Superman 2's properties could be listed as follows:

- Faster than a speeding bullet
- Leap tall building in a single bound
- Fly
- Incredible strength
- X-ray vision
- Super-hearing
- Super-breath (can produce gale force winds by blowing)
- EXISTENCE

If Superman 2 existed not only in our imagination but also in reality, then Superman wouldn't be super after all, since existing in reality, following Anselm, makes something greater. In short, Superman 2 is greater than the idea of Superman because Superman 2 exists in both the imagination and reality.

I am not suggesting that Superman 2 does, in fact, exist, but merely drawing an analogy between Anselm's argument for God's existence and the existence of Superman 2. For something to be the greatest or most perfect, it must exist in the imagination and reality, since existing in reality is a property that makes the thing itself great. In other words, for a being to instantiate the perfections of omniscience, omnipotence, and omnibeneficence, it must exist. In just the same way that existence defines the greatness of Superman 2, existence also defines the greatness of God. To conceive of the most perfect being, and yet not exist in reality, means that God lacks perfection. But lacking perfection is contradictory to the very idea of God. Therefore, God must exist.

However, as Yeager Hudson explains, Gaunilo, a Benedictine monk and contemporary of Anselm, objected to the ontological argument. Being a monk, Gaunilo obviously believed in God, but thought Anselm's proof was inadequate. Just because we can bring God into existence by merely conceiving of the greatest possible being, says Gaunilo, does not follow that God exists. Anselm seems to be guilty of conjuring up material things out of the blue. To see this, go over the argument again and replace "God" with "a perfect island" (or a perfect hockey player, a perfect spouse, a perfect car, and so on). The result is that Anselm's argument for God's existence also seems to prove the existence of a perfect island. And this is surely too much. No one would affirm that a perfect island exists just because one can conceive of it. Likewise, just because the property of existence makes God the greatest conceivable being, it does not follow God exists.

But isn't there a vast difference between conceiving of a perfect island and conceiving of God? The problem with Gaunilo's reply to Anselm is that it is inconsistent; it cannot equally be applied to God. No matter how perfectly conceived an island is, it is always possible to conceive of another island more perfect than the first. So if white sandy beaches and palm trees are perfect-making properties, it is always possible to imagine a greater island with, say, fresh water and bananas. There are no limits to the perfections a person can think of regarding a perfect island. In other words, there are no properties that make an island maximally perfect. But, as Hudson explains in his article, this is not true for the concept of God. To conceive of God is to conceive of the ultimate or maximal limits of perfection. Nothing is more knowledgeable, powerful, or good as God. We cannot conceive of a being greater than God because God is the embodiment of perfection itself. As Hudson explains, Gaunilo's reply is not a serious attack against the ontological argument.

Kant's Ontological Disproof

Hudson next outlines one of the most damaging objections against Anselm from the German philosopher Immanuel Kant. Kant objects to the notion of "existence" as a perfection-making property (premise 3). Recall for Anselm, a being is greater if it exists in reality than if it exists only in the mind alone. The implication is two-fold: (1) existence is considered an actual property, and (2) existence makes something greater or more perfect. To

understand the force of Kant's objection, let's look at an example. Imagine two single women, Sally and Samantha, are having coffee when the conversation turns to men. Having been on numerous dates with various men over the years, they have yet to find their perfect partners. Disillusioned, they are convinced that they will never find the men of their dreams, never get married, and never have children. In a moment of reflection, they consider the possibility that they are being too picky when it comes to the qualities and properties they are looking for in a partner. To test this possibility, they each decide to write down the qualities they are looking for in a perfect mate. Here are their lists:

Sally's perfect partner	Samantha's perfect partner
Good sense of humour	Good sense of humour
Physically fit	Physically fit
Handsome	Handsome
Does not smoke	Does not smoke
Unselfish	Unselfish
Kind and generous	Kind and generous
Good job	Good job
	EXISTS

The two lists are identical *except* that Samantha's list includes the property of existence. Does the inclusion of "existence" as a property add anything important to Samantha's list? For Kant, the answer is no. "Existence" is not a property of something the same way that handsome or kind is a property of a man. Existence is a precondition of having a specific property, not a property itself. In other words, to say a man is handsome and kind presupposes his existence. Existence does not add anything to the concept of Samantha's perfect partner because existence can only be exemplified or instantiated by virtue of the properties themselves. As Hudson explains in his article, to say that something exists does not add an addition characteristic of existence, but rather says that the subject exists in the real world. To use a different example, it would be like telling someone that my newborn son weighs 7 pounds and 15 ounces, has blond hair, is

22 inches long, and also *exists*. Odd indeed! Existence is a precondition of weighing 7 pounds and 15 ounces, having blond hair, and being 22 inches long. In short, existence is not a property.

Moreover, if existence adds nothing to the concept of a being, we are now in a position to reject the claim that existence adds to a being's greatness. Remember, given Anselm's argument, if existence is a property, and existence makes something better or more perfect, then Samantha's partner will be more perfect than Sally's partner and, therefore, must exist. Does existence make something better or more perfect? Does perfection entail existence? For Kant, the answer is no. Samantha has listed qualities and characteristics that her potential husband would have, but it's another matter altogether whether these qualities are actually exemplified in a real male. Likewise, even if we define God as being omniscient, omnipotent, and omnibenevolent, these properties are logically independent of the question of whether God exists. In other words, if existence is not a property, then existence does not make something great, and therefore it does not necessarily follow that God or Samantha's perfect partner exists. The problem is that if existence is perfection, then we can will anything we want into existence by definition. But willing something into existence by definition is very different from whether it actually does. For Kant, this is the fatal flaw with the ontological argument.

Necessary Beings and Possible Worlds

Contemporary philosophers have tried to salvage the ontological argument by developing various model versions. These model versions are based on necessary truths and possible worlds. The general idea, as Hudson outlines, is that certain things are going to hold true in all possible worlds, such as "unicorns have one horn" and "it's false that 2 + 2 = 7." In this sense, it's logically impossible for unicorns to have two horns or for 2 + 2 = 7. Likewise, if we define God as the most (maximally) perfect being, then such a being would

have to exist in every possible world. And if God exists in every possible world, then God must exist in the actual world. In short, God exists.

The problem, says Hudson, with model arguments is that they are based on the premise that existence of a maximally perfect being is possible. But this is controversial. If it can be shown that there is no such thing as a maximally perfect being, then its existence is called into question. For example, as we will see later in this chapter, it might be argued that if God were a perfect being then evil would not exist. A perfect being who is omniscient, omnipotent, and omnibenevolent would know when evil happens, be powerful enough to stop it, and prevent evil as a manifestation of his or her goodness. If evil in the world shows that God is not maximally perfect, then God's existence is suspect. In other words, if we cannot know that God is maximally perfect, then we cannot draw conclusions about God's existence.

Does Satan Exist?

Hudson next explains how Anselm's ontological argument can be used to show that the devil exists. Although it's a radical response, it does present problems for ontological supporters. Consider the following:

1. I have, within my understanding, an idea of the devil.
2. This idea of the devil is the idea of the greatest possible evil being.
3. A being is greater if it exists in reality than if it exists only in the understanding.
4. If the devil exists in the understanding alone, then a greater evil being can be conceived, namely, one that also exists in reality.
5. But premise 4 is a contradiction, for it says I can conceive of a greater evil being than the greatest possible evil being.
6. So if I have an idea of the greatest conceivable evil being, such a being must exist both in my understanding and in reality.
7. Therefore, the devil exists in reality.

The problem is that the ontological argument can be used to prove the existence of God and

Satan. But in order to make the ontological argument work we must assume that God is good. The argument is question begging, since we would then have to figure out whether God or Satan is the greater of the two. In short, a supremely perfect being could be either good or evil.

Theists, of course, might respond to the existence of Satan argument by bolstering, somehow, the necessary existence of God. After all, if necessary beings have existential import, God's existence has not been disproved. The question, says Hudson, is whether God's existence can be demonstrated by ontological proofs. This, however, is still a matter of debate.

9

St. Anselm (1033–1109)

Anselm was born in 1033 in Aosta, Italy. He joined the Benedictine order in Normandy, France, in 1060, despite his father's demands he go into politics. By 1063, Anselm had become head (prior) of the Bec monastery, and by

1078, he was elected abbot. It was during his tenure as abbot that Anselm made many influential friends while travelling to England to inspect land given to the monastery by William the Conqueror. One such friend was William Rufus (son of William the Conqueror), who appointed Anselm archbishop of Canterbury in 1093. Anselm died in 1109 and was canonized in 1494. His most influential work is the Proslogium, *from which this reading is taken.*

Proslogium

Chapter II

Truly there is a God, although the fool has said in his heart, There is no God.

AND so, Lord, do you, who do give understanding to faith, give me, so far as you knowest it to be profitable, to understand that you are as we believe; and that you are that which we believe. And indeed, we believe that you are a being than which nothing greater can be conceived. Or is there no such nature, since the fool has said in his heart, there is no God? (Psalms xiv. 1). But, at any rate, this very fool, when he hears of this being of which I speak—a being than which nothing greater can be conceived—understands what he hears, and what he understands is in his understanding; although he does not understand it to exist.

For, it is one thing for an object to be in the understanding, and another to understand that the object exists. When a painter first conceives of what he will afterwards perform, he has it in his understanding, but he does not yet understand it to be, because he has not yet performed it. But after he has made the painting, he both has it in his understanding, and he understands that it exists, because he has made it.

Hence, even the fool is convinced that something exists in the understanding, at least, than which nothing greater can be conceived. For, when he hears of this, he understands it. And whatever is understood, exists in the understanding. And assuredly that, than which nothing greater can be conceived, cannot exist in the understanding alone. For, suppose it exists in the understanding alone: then it can be conceived to exist in reality; which is greater.

Therefore, if that, than which nothing greater can be conceived, exists in the understanding alone, the very being, than which nothing greater can be conceived, is one, than which a greater can be conceived. But obviously this is impossible. Hence, there is doubt that there exists a being, than which nothing greater can be conceived, and it exists both in the understanding and in reality.

Chapter III

God cannot be conceived not to exist.—God is that, than which nothing greater can be conceived.—That which can be conceived not to exist is not God.

AND it assuredly exists so truly, that it cannot be conceived not to exist. For, it is possible to conceive of a being which cannot be conceived not to exist; and this is greater than one which can be conceived not to exist. Hence, if that, than which nothing greater can be conceived, can be conceived not to exist, it is not that, than which nothing greater can be conceived. But this is an irreconcilable contradiction. There is, then, so truly a being than which nothing greater can be conceived to exist, that it cannot even be conceived not to exist; and this being you are, O Lord, our God.

So truly, therefore, do you exist, O Lord, my God, that you cannot be conceived not to exist; and rightly. For, if a mind could conceive of a being better than you, the creature would rise above the Creator; and this is most absurd. And, indeed, whatever else there is, except you alone, can be conceived not to exist. To you alone, therefore, it belongs to exist more truly than all other beings, and hence in a higher degree than all others. For, whatever else exists does not exist so truly, and hence in a less degree it belongs to it to exist. Why, then, has the fool said in his heart, there is no God (Psalms xiv. 1), since it is so

evident, to a rational mind, that you do exist in the highest degree of all? Why, except that he is dull and a fool?

Chapter IV

[...] BUT how has the fool said in his heart what he could not conceive; or how is it that he could not conceive what he said in his heart? since it is the same to say in the heart, and to conceive.

But, if really, nay, since really, he both conceived, because he said in his heart; and did not say in his heart, because he could not conceive; there is more than one way in which a thing is said in the heart or conceived. For, in one sense, an object is conceived, when the word signifying it is conceived; and in another, when the very entity, which the object is, is understood.

In the former sense, then, God can be conceived not to exist; but in the latter, not at all. For no one who understands what fire and water are can conceive fire to be water, in accordance with the nature of the facts themselves, although this is possible according to the words. So, then, no one who understands what God is can conceive that God does not exist; although he says these words in his heart, either without any or with some foreign, signification. For, God is that than which a greater cannot be conceived. And he who thoroughly understands this, assuredly understands that this being so truly exists, that not even in concept can it be non-existent. Therefore, he who understands that God so exists, cannot conceive that he does not exist.

I thank you, gracious Lord, I thank you; because what I formerly believed by your bounty, I now so understand by your illumination, that if I were unwilling to believe that you do exist, I should not be able not to understand this to be true.

10

Yeager Hudson

(1931–2007)

Born in Mississippi in 1931, Yeager Hudson earned his undergraduate degree from Millsaps College, graduating with honours in 1954. It was while attending Millsaps College he met and married his wife of 53 years, Louise. Upon completion of his undergraduate studies, he attended Boston University where he earned a Masters in Sacred Theology and a Ph.D. in Philosophy. While completing his doctoral work, he accepted a temporary teaching position in 1959 at Colby College in Waterville, Maine. This temporary position would eventually result in a teaching career at Colby College of 40 years as Charles A. Dana Professor of Philosophy. During his studies at Boston University, Hudson developed an affinity for South Asian philosophy, culminating in many trips to South East Asia including, in 1967–68, as a Fulbright visiting lecturer at Poona University and Ahmednagar College in India. In addition to his teaching position, Hudson was also an ordained minister of the United Methodist Church. He was named full professor in 1977 and served as department chair for almost 20 years. He retired in 1998. Some of his books include The Philosophy of Religion *(1991),* The Power of Social Ideas *(1995), and* Globalism and the Obsolescence of the State *(1999). After a long battle*

with cancer, Hudson died on April 22, 2007, and is survived by his wife, two sons, and five grandchildren.

The Ontological Argument

The ontological argument for the existence of God attempts to demonstrate that the existence of God is a necessary truth on grounds that the denial of God's existence is self-contradictory. What is perhaps most distinctive about the ontological argument is that it is alleged to be an *a priori* argument. That means that the properties of the argument claim that it does not depend in any way on empirical evidence. Since many philosophers, especially those before the twentieth century, have shown considerable suspicion about sense impressions and the evidence they provide, the fact that this argument does not depend on such evidence has been regarded as a very great advantage. The ontological argument is also supposed to be deductive, the kind of argument that, if it is valid and its premises are true, provides conclusive evidence for the truth of its conclusion. Thus it would appear to be the ideal kind of argument for the theist. Yet, as we will see, it has been one of the most controversial.

The Claim That God Does Not Exist Is Self-Contradictory

The ontological argument has been formulated in a variety of ways. Indeed, it might be better to say that a cluster of arguments with certain similarities are collectively referred to as the ontological argument. Some thinkers, Descartes for example, have said that the argument amounts to pointing out that the claim that God does not exist is contradictory. God means "the supremely perfect being."

But to deny that such a being exists is like saying, "The supremely perfect being lacks a perfection." Stated in this way, the contradiction becomes blatant. Another way of putting it is to say that God is a being who essence includes existence; to deny the existence of such a being is to contradict oneself. God allegedly is the kind of being who could not exist—whose nonexistence is inconceivable. We know that there are some kinds of things whose existence is inconceivable and that therefore do not exist because it is impossible for them to exist. For example, no square circles exist because there could not be any; the very concept is contradictory, the nature of such a thing is inconceivable, and its existence is impossible. Conversely, so the argument goes, God is the sort of thing that could not fail to exist. The very concept of God include the notion of existence as the concept of square circle includes nonexistence. Thus the nonexistence of God is inconceivable and God's actual nonexistence is impossible.

Existence Is Inseparable from God's Existence

René Descartes (1596–1650) argues that existence is an inseparable part of the essence of God and for this reason God must exist.

> I find it manifest that we can no more separate the existence of God from his essence than we can separate from the essence of a triangle the fact that the size of its three angles equals two right angles . . . It is no less self-contradictory to conceive of a God, a supremely perfect Being who lacks existence—that is, who lacks some perfection—than it is to conceive of a mountain for which there is no valley.[1]

This argument does not prove that triangles or mountains must exist, but only that they must have all the features that are parts of their existence. It does, so it is claimed, prove that God must exist, because existence is a part of God's essence. To be a triangle means to have the some of internal angles add up to 180 degrees; similarly to be Gods means to exist. Thus "God does not exist" is a much a self-contradiction as "A triangle has internal angles that add up to more than two right angles," or "There is a mountain with no valley."

Anselm's "Something Than Which No Greater Can Be Conceived"

The classic statement of the ontological argument comes from St. Anselm (1033–1109), although it was Immanuel Kant who gave the argument its name. Anselm tells us that God means that than which nothing greater can be conceived. We understand something by that expression, and thus that being exists in our thought. But a being that exists only in thought is less great than a being that exists in thought and in reality. To deny that this being exists in reality is to say, in effect, that the being than which no greater can be conceived is not as great as another that can be conceived (the one existing in both in thought and reality). That is clearly a contradiction. Thus God must exist not only in thought but also in reality.

Anselm argues further that a being than which no greater can be conceived cannot be conceived as nonexistent. This means that God is a necessary being, one that could not possibly fail to exist—or, in the parlance of contemporary philosophy, one that exists in every possible world. Clearly a being that only happens to exist but that might not have existed—that is, a being that is contingent or that exists in some but not all possible worlds—is less great or less perfect than one that exists necessarily in every possible world. So the existence of

God is not contingent like that of a human or a horse; rather, God's existence is necessary. Indeed, as some theologians expressed it, God *is* his existence just as God *is* his goodness, his power, and all of the other aspects of his essence.

Criticisms of the Ontological Argument

The ontological argument has had a checkered career. Some have regarded it as the decisive argument that succeeds in proving conclusively the existence of God. Others have thought it a little better than sophistry. But there is something intriguing about this position, and philosophers have returned to it again and again to see whether it might not be made to do what it is supposed to do—or to see whether it might be turned against itself to prove that God does not, or even could not, exist. It is the traditional argument to which scholars in the twentieth century have probably devoted most attention.

St. Thomas Aquinas (1225–1275) held that it was a valid argument but that only God could realize that it is a proof in the strict sense, for only an omniscient being could possess the knowledge necessary to know that the premises of the argument are true. Finite humans cannot know the essence of God; the ontological argument turns on claims about God's essence; thus only God and not humans can know the truths that make the ontological argument a conclusive proof. Aquinas elected as a consequence to rely on other arguments than the ontological.

One of the most formidable critics of the ontological argument was Immanuel Kant (1724–1804). One of the objections that Kant pressed against Anselm's version had already been raised by Gaunilo, a contemporary of Anselm. Gaunilo argued that if Anselm's argument was valid, it could be used to prove the existence of any conceivable excellent thing. For example, we

can conceive of an island idyllic in every way, an island paradise "than which no greater could be conceived." Because we understand the description, the island exists in our minds. But the island "than which no greater could be conceived" must also exist in reality; otherwise, we could conceive of a greater one existing both in thought and in reality, an obvious contradiction. Thus this most excellent island—or anything else conceived along similar lines—must exist. But an argument that proves the existence of all sorts of absurd things is not a sound argument. Thus Gaunilo insisted that the ontological argument fails.

A possible reply to Guanilo, one that Anselm himself attempted in part, is to insist that God is the only being to whom the title "that than which nothing greater can be conceived" applies. It is a mistake to suppose that we could conceive an island that is supremely idyllic in every way. No matter how many varieties of luscious fruit it might have, we could always imagine adding one more or improving the flavor slightly. But God is the supremely perfect being in the sense that every perfection is actualized fully and harmonized completely in God's essence. God is not merely a being than whom feeble human intellect cannot think of a better; God is *the* being than which a greater is inconceivable. Thus God is the only being for which the ontological argument works.

Kant was not impressed by this response. He raises two objections to the ontological argument. One, which resembles Gaunilo's, is that Anselm mistakenly assumes that existence is a real predicate. A *predicate* is a word that attributes some property or characteristic to a subject. When we say that God is powerful, we predicate the property of power to God. But when we say that God exists, we do not attribute a property, for existence is not a property a subject can or cannot have. We would make a similar error if we think that in saying, "American eagles are rare," we are attributing a property to eagles. What we are actually saying is that there are not very many American eagles. Descartes makes the same error when he argues that God must exist because to deny that God exists is to say that the supremely perfect being lacks a perfection. But existence is not a perfection that can be added to or subtracted from the other perfections on properties that something may have. To say that something exists is not to say that it has some additional characteristic, existence, but rather to say that there is such a thing, that the subject named or described is present in the real world.

Kant puts it this way: "A hundred real dollars does not contain one penny more than a hundred imaginary dollars."[2] No doubt we prefer the real to the imaginary dollars, but that is beside the point; the essential nature of the two is no way different. And this, according to Kant, is the error of the ontological argument. If existence is not an attribute that the subject can either have or fail to have, then it cannot be argued that God must exist because existence is an inseparable aspect or perfection of God's essence. Given the coherence of the *notion* of a supremely perfect being (a point not everyone would grant), like that of an idyllic island or a hundred dollars, the question remains whether or not any of them exists. The existence of God can no more be inferred from God's definition as the supremely perfect being than one that of the island from its definition as the island than which no greater can be imagined.

Kant's other major objection to this argument is grounded in the claim that no existential proposition is logically necessary. The ontological argument attempts to derive the existence of God from the definition of God, by way of the claim that a being so defined is a necessary being, but Kant is convinced that no such derivation is possible. Necessity applies to propositions

and not to beings. Every existential proposition—that is, every proposition that asserts the existence of something—must be grounded on empirical evidence. Thus Kant rejects the whole notion of necessary being as incoherent.

It seems, however, that the nonexistence of some things can be derived from their definition and thus that some sense can be given to the notion of necessary nonbeing. The nonexistence of four-sided triangles can be derived from their definition as four-sided plane figures that have three sides, because such a definition is incoherent. Thus we say not just that such things do not exist, as we claim that unicorns do not exist; rather, we say that they *necessarily* do not exist. The proposition "Four-sided triangles do not exist," seems to be an existential proposition that is logically necessary. Richard Swinburne claims that there are also affirmative existential propositions that are logically necessary or, in other words, that there are some things that necessarily exist. "There exists a number greater than one million—and it is a logically necessary truth that there does."[3] We might say that a plain figure with more sides than anyone has counted exists or that the ratio between two numbers larger than anyone has ever calculated exists, and so on. Thus it seems to be too much to claim that no essential proposition can be logically necessary or that the concept of necessary existence is incoherent.

It might be claimed that an eternal being is a necessary being because such a being could not begin to exist or cease to exist. Such a beginning or ending is inconsistent with the meaning of "eternal being." But this necessity is not quite like the kind of necessity we have been discussing. Even if we admit that it is proper to designate such a being as necessary, we are still justified in asking whether or not any such being exists. The statement, "Eternal beings are necessary beings," can thus be understood to mean not, "There are eternal beings that are necessary beings," but rather, "If anything is an eternal being, then it is a necessary being." Similarly, the ontological argument may be taken to mean not "God exists," but rather, "If anything is God, then it exists." Granted, if there is an eternal being, it is a necessary being, but to call it necessary does not prove that it exists. Likewise, we may grant that if there is a God, that is, a supremely perfect being—if anything answers to that description—then it exists. The question is whether or not there is anything that answers to the description. We will look more closely at the concept of necessary being when we examine the so-called ontological disproof later in this chapter.

The Model Version of the Ontological Argument

The most popular formulation of the ontological argument among contemporary philosophers, advanced by such thinkers as Charles Hartshorne,[4] Norman Malcolm,[5] and Alvin Plantinga,[6] is grounded in modal logic, the logic of necessity, possibility, and impossibility, and is usually stated in possible world language. Its various advocates state it in slightly different ways, but all versions seem to have essentially the same strengths and weaknesses.

The modal version of the ontological argument attempts to infer God's existence from the claim that God's existence is logically possible, together with certain allegedly necessary truths about God's nature and the laws of modal logic. It is the assertion of the possibility of God's existence that sharply differentiates this from the classic versions of the ontological argument, which argued from the definition or from certain allegedly necessary traits of God without explicitly asserting that a being with those traits was possible.

It is a principle of modal logic that contingent truths vary from one possible world to another, but that necessary truths obtain in every possible world. This means that contingent truths such as "Horses exist" and "Logicians are fond of verbal puzzles" could not be necessary truths in any possible world, but that necessary truths such as "Unicorns have one horn" and "It is false that $2 + 2 = 7$" are necessarily true in every possible world. This is another way of saying that the modal status—whether something is necessary or possible—is a universal fact and not one that applies to specific worlds. Unicorns may exist in one world and not in another, but in every possible world they have a single horn, that is, their existence is contingent, but their nature is not contingent. If we can say of anything that its existence is necessary, then it must exist in every possible world.

The argument begins, then with the claim that if it is possible that God's existence is necessary, then God exists in every possible world, including the actual world. But is it possible? That it is allegedly follows from the nature of God. God is defined by certain contemporary philosophers of religion as a maximally great or maximally perfect being. It seems to be possible that such a being exists; that is, it seems that there is a possible world in which a maximally perfect being exists, even if we think this being does not exist in the actual world. But a being that exists in every possible world is more perfect than a being that exists in only one or some possible worlds. Indeed, to be maximally perfect means to exist in every possible world or, in other words, to be a necessary being. Thus if it is possible for a maximally perfect being to exist—that is, God exists in some possible world—then it is necessarily true that God exists—that is, that God exists in every possible world. But we have already remarked that the existence of a maximally perfect being seems to be possible. There is nothing contradictory in the notion and no absurdity seems to follow from it. The conclusion is that "God exists" is necessarily true, that is, true not just in some possible world but in every possible world. But the actual world is one possible world. From all this it follows that "God exists" is true of the actual world, or in other words, that God actually does exist.

The modal argument is more complex than the earlier versions of the ontological argument. It can be stated in several different ways, and some constructions of the argument are more intuitively appealing than others. There is a fairly widespread agreement among contemporary modal logicians that at least some versions of the argument are valid. But considerable disagreement remains concerning what the agreement, even if it is valid, proves. One of the most serious problems lies in the premise that asserts that the existence of the maximally perfect being is possible. Some philosophers believe that perfection or greatness is like numbers; there is no such thing as maximum. Just as there is no highest number than which not higher is possible; just as there is no island so perfect that some alteration cannot improve it; so there may be no coherent concept of a being than which no greater can be conceived. Thus if there is no such conceivable thing as a maximally perfect being, the existence of such a being is not possible. In that case, since the modal argument depends on the assumption that the existence of God is possible, it fails to establish its conclusion not because it is invalid, but because one of its premises is false.

Even if the situation is not quite this bad for argument, we may still not be justified in claiming that the argument proves that God exists, because even if it is valid and even if all its premises are true, it may not be possible for any humans to know that the premises are true. This was St. Thomas's point about the ontology

argument. He maintained that the argument is valid and that its premises are true, and thus God can recognize that it establishes its conclusion, but we humans cannot have sufficient knowledge of the characteristics of God to justify our making any confident use of the argument. Even Alvin Plantinga, one of the most able contemporary defenders of the argument, is unwilling to claim that it proves the existence of God. "What I claim for this argument, therefore, is that it establishes, not the *truth* of theism, but its rational acceptability."[7] Even that is a lot to claim, and a great many contemporary philosophers would insist that it is too much.

The So-Called Ontological Disproof

We have examined briefly the argument by which Gaunilo attempted by a reductio ad absurdum to refute the ontological argument by showing that, taken to its logical conclusion, it implied an absurdity. Gaunilo and Kant both tried to discredit the argument by demonstrating that parallel reasoning could establish the existence of anything that we wish to conceive of as perfect, such as the perfect island. In recent times even more radical responses to this argument have appeared. We will briefly examine just one,[8] by David and Marjorie Haight,[9] that purports to use the ontological argument to prove the existence of a devil.

The Haight argument is similar to Gaunilo's except that it parodies the ontological argument by arguing for the existence of a supremely evil being rather than an idyllic island. We have a concept of a being than which no worse can be conceived. If this being did not actually exist, it would not be that than which no worse could be conceived, since we could conceive such a being as existing, and this being would clearly be worse. Now this being than which a worse is inconceivable is called the devil. Therefore the devil exists.

The Haights point out that this argument is exactly parallel to the ontological argument. If the ontological argument is valid, so must this one be; if it establishes the existence of God, this one must establish the existence of the devil. They suggest that what the argument really proves, if it proves anything at all, is the existence of one greatest thing that might be called either God or devil. The argument, as stated by Anselm, does not prove that the being than which no greater can be conceived is a good being, unless an implicit assumption has been made identifying greatness with goodness or including goodness in greatness. But such an assumption would be question begging. And if the argument is formulated in such a way that the conception on which it turns is of a supremely perfect being, the counterargument might be made to hinge on the concept of a supremely imperfect being and the parallel would still obtain.

If the ontological argument is to work and also avoid criticisms like those of Gaunilo and the Haights, it must be supplemented somehow to show that God is the only being to which such argument can apply. This Anselm attempted to do in his reply to Gaunilo. He first argued that any being that can be conceived to exist but does not exist can be conceived as having a beginning. But any being that can be conceived as having a beginning or an end is not that being than which a greater is inconceivable. Now an island, however perfect, or anything else whose nonexistence is conceivable, can be conceived as having a beginning. Thus the argument does not prove the existence of imagined perfect things such as island or hundred dollars, but does prove the existence of the one thing than which no greater is conceivable, namely, God.

But this response will not work against the Haight argument. For the devil, as the supremely evil being, is a being that need not be conceived

as having a beginning or an end. Indeed, his chief difference from God is only that he is evil and God is good. Anselm maintains that his argument can apply only to one thing than which any greater is inconceivable. If God is conceived as the greatest good being and the devil as the greatest evil being, the question would still need to be raised of which is the greater of these two, that is, the single being than which no greater is conceivable. Perhaps, a case could be made for the claim that to be good is greater than to be evil, but it would require an additional argument, one that Anselm does not supply and one that does not readily present itself. Wanting such an argument, the claim that to be good is greater than to be evil becomes question begging, assuming without supplying grounds a point that need not be accepted unless grounds are supplied.

The upshot of the dispute between Anselm and the Haights seems to be that the ontological argument might establish the existence of some supreme being but leave us uncertain whether it is God or the devil. This is what the Haights themselves suggest. Many theists would be pleased to welcome this concession and would regard this outcome of the Haights' argument as friendly rather than hostile to theism. These theists would then resort to empirical arguments, such as the argument from design and beauty in the world, to support their further contention that the being whose existence the ontological argument has been conceded to establish is God and not the devil. They would have to face, however, a potentially formidable counterargument based on the existence of evil in the world.

What seems really to be at issue with the ontological argument and its counterarguments, the so-called ontological disproofs, is the question of whether the concept of a necessary being or a maximally great being is intelligible and whether any proposition asserting the existence of such a being can be necessarily, and not merely contingently, true. The conventional view of necessity follows Hume and Kant in the assumption that no existential statement can be necessary. All existential propositions are regard as contingent, empirical claims, and all necessary propositions as nonexistential. If "God exists" were a necessary proposition, then it could not be about existence—a patent absurdity. And if it is to be about existences, then it will be contingent or nonnecessary.

We have already questioned the claim that no necessity proposition can make an assertion about what exists. We noted that propositions such as "No four-sided triangles exist" seem to be both necessary and existential. If these are indeed examples of propositions that are both existential and necessary, they would seem to be just the kind of proposition one could need to formulate an ontological proof or disproof successfully. An ontological disproof claims to be an analogue of the ontological proof that attempts to establish the existence of God on the basis of an analysis of the concept's meaning. An ontological disproof therefore would proceed by analyzing the concept of God and showing that it is incoherent— from which the disproof would infer that no such being could exist. If, for example, an analysis of the attributes of God like what we undertook in the previous chapter turned up convincing reasons to believe that these attributes are mutually inconsistent, and if no consistent set of modified or attenuated attributes still compatible with the notion of deity could be discovered, we could have to conclude the concept of God is incoherent.

Now if the concept of a necessary being or a supremely perfect being really is incoherent— like the concept of a seven-sided square—the ontological disproof would seem to be successful. We believe that when we show that the

concept of a seven-sided square is self contradictory, we demonstrate not only that the concept is incoherent but also that no seven-sided squares could possibly exist. In other words, we acknowledge that such statements are both necessary and existential. An appropriate proposition of this sort about God is just what an advocate of an ontological disproof needs. If we recognize that there can be necessary existential propositions, this opens up the possibility of an ontological disproof. But we must notice that such a recognition cuts both ways: It also opens up the possibility of an ontological proof. This is the possibility that such contemporary supports of the ontological argument as Swinburne seek to exploit.

Are we in a position to draw any conclusions about the ontological argument? One seems to be that the advocates of the ontological argument have not been able by means of the argument to demonstrate the existence of God. Another is that its critics have equally failed to demonstrate God's nonexistence and have not even been able to show decisively that the ontological argument itself completely fails. Indeed, the Haights interpret the argument in a way that amounts to a substantial concession to the theist. Many would say that theirs is much too much of a concession.

Perhaps one of the most important things we have discovered in examining the ontological argument is the plausibility of the claim that necessary judgments can have existential import. If such necessary propositions as the basic laws of logic and mathematics are admitted to have implications about what cannot exist, why may not certain necessary propositions have implications about what can or must exist? But if this point clears the way for either an ontological proof or an ontological disproof, at the same time a fully satisfactory formulation of either of these arguments remain to be discovered. The ontological argument continues to exert great powers of fascination, however. There can be little doubt that philosophers will continue to refine it and to attempt to fine new ways to formulate it in hope of making it work. Up to this time, however, it seems not yet to have contributed in any substantial way to settling the question whether or not God exists. [...]

Notes

1. René Descartes, *Meditations on First Philosophy*, in *Discourse on Method and Meditations*, trans. by Laurence J. Lafleur (Indianapolis: Bobbs-Merrill, 1960), p. 121.

2. Immanuel Kant, *Critique of Pure Reason*, trans. by N. K. Smith (London: Random House, 1964), p. 503.

3. Richard Swinburne, *The Coherence of Theism* (Oxford: Clarendon Press, 1977), p. 27.

4. See Charles Hartshorne, *Anselm's Discovery* (La Salle, Ill.: Open Court, 1965) and *The Logic of Perfection* (La Salle, Ill.: Open Court, 1962).

5. Norman Malcolm, "Anselm's Ontological Arguments," *The Philosophical Review* (January 1960), reprinted in John Hick, ed., *The Existence of God* (New York: Macmillan, 1964).

6. Alvin Plantinga, *The Nature of Necessity* (Oxford: Clarendon Press, 1974).

7. Alvin Plantinga, *God, Freedom, and Evil* (New York: Harper & Row, 1974).

8. A celebrated argument, put forward by J. N. Findlay, attempted to turn the ontological argument on its head and prove the nonexistence of God. Although the argument enjoyed great currency for a while, it is now regarded as seriously faulty (some would say simple a piece of sophistry) and decisively refuted. See Findlay's presentation of the argument: "Can God's Existence Be Disproved?" in Antony Flew and Alasdair MacIntrye, eds., *New Essays in Philosophical Theology* (London: SCM Press, 1955), p. 48. This book also contains some of the counterarguments that finally convinced Findlay that his argument does not work.

9. David and Marjorie Haight, "An Ontological Argument for the Devil," *The Monist* 54 (1970): p. 218–20.

The Cosmological Argument

If everything must have a cause, then God must have a cause.
　　　　　—Bertrand Russell

Discussion Questions

1. Historically, magicians used sleight-of-hand to wow audiences by pulling rabbits out of hats, making coins disappear, and sawing people in half. Today, magicians (illusionists) like David Copperfield and David Blane shock audiences by making the Statue of Liberty disappear, walking through the Great Wall of China, levitating, and performing other Houdini-like stunts. However, the fascinating part about magic is that we are not usually surprised by *what* magicians do but by *how* they do it. That is, we usually are not fooled into believing that a rabbit pops into existence out of a hat or that the Stature of Liberty really disappears. In a similar vein, according to Aquinas, the world did not simply pop into existence and we would be fools to think otherwise. The most pressing problem is explaining *how* it came about. The world came about, says Aquinas, through the "sleight-of-hand" of God. If the world could not simply pop into existence, does this entail a creator? Why or why not? How does the very existence of our world prove or disprove that God exists?

2. According to the Hindu religion, the universe is cyclical in nature. The universe, like humans, is born, dies, and then reborn again in a perpetual cycle. For Hindus, our rebirth and status in the next life is determined by our good or bad actions in this life—*karma*. In this sense, our existence is eternal. Likewise, for the universe, there is no finite beginning or end, just an infinite cycle of creation and destruction. Put simply, there is no first cause. This is

comparable to what Schick calls the "bounce theory." Could something other than God have caused our universe to come into existence? Is it reasonable to believe the universe came into existence without a cause? Could the "bounce theory" of the universe account for its existence? Give reasons for your answer.

If There Is No God, Then There Is No World

The next argument we will look at in favour of God's existence is known as the cosmological argument. The most famous of which comes from Thomas Aquinas. In *Summa Theologiae*, Aquinas argues for God's existence through as series of arguments. The first three arguments from motion, efficient cause, and necessity have come to be known collectively as the cosmological arguments. For Aquinas, the cosmological arguments are based on experience or, in philosophical terms, *a posteriori* reasoning. As noted earlier, *a posteriori* in Latin literally means "from the latter." In this sense, knowledge of God's existence comes from experience—the five senses.

Aquinas' first argument is based on motion. We experience some objects in the world that are in motion, which presupposes that something caused the object to move in the first place. After all, things don't move without some cause. Trees, for example, don't move without another moving thing affecting them, namely, wind. The wind, at least based on medieval science, moves because of the motion of the moon, while the moon moves because of the motion of the planets (Stumpf and Fieser 169). The problem is that if every motion has a mover, we end up with an infinite regress. If every moving thing is moved by another moving thing indefinitely, nothing would exist because there would be no first mover to get things moving in the first place. That is, trees would not move unless there was a first mover to set the planets, moon, and wind in motion. And for Aquinas, because the world contains motion, the first mover must, therefore, be God.

Aquinas' second argument is similar to the first. In our world of efficient causes (i.e., causes that bring something into existence), there must be a first cause in order to bring everything into existence in the first place. And for Aquinas, God is the ultimate first cause or creator (unmoved mover) of the universe and our world. Let me illustrate Aquinas' point. Look up from reading this book and glance around your room. What do you see (chair, desk, pens, computer, window, dog, or cat)? Now ask yourself: What is the cause of each of these things? We can trace the existence of, say, a book via a causal chain to an author, publishing company, paper producer, trees, etc. In the same way we can trace the existence of a chair to a manufacturer, plastics maker, oil producer, and so forth. Generally speaking, we experience (*a posteriori*) things in our environment that are contingent upon something else for their existence. Now consider your own existence. What is the cause of you? Well, as much as you may not want to admit it, the cause of you is your parents. Go back further, who caused your parents to exist? Your grandparents, of course, and what caused them to exist? Your great-grandparents . . . and so on. Now consider everything else in this world that has a cause (flowers, animals, cups, rockets, etc.). Keep following this cause/effect chain through human history, natural selection, and the creation of the earth and universe. You eventually reach a point where you have to ask: What caused the universe to come into being? And the answer, for Aquinas, is God. There cannot be an infinite causal chain because if there were nothing would exist. God is the ultimate cause of everything on the earth and in the universe. To put another way, if God did not exist, there would be no world. But since the world exists, God must also exist.

The third argument, for Aquinas, is based on the idea that God is a necessary being. To see this, consider again Aquinas' two previous arguments. If they are right, then everything that exists is contingent or dependent upon something else for its existence. As we saw earlier, contingency is based on the idea that it's logically possible for things in nature not to have existed. Again, consider yourself. It is possible you would not exist today if the genetic combinations, which make you up, had been different. Similarly, it's possible the Canadian Rockies would not exist if geological forces had been different. Everything you can touch, see, smell, taste, and hear could have been very different from what they actually are. They need not have existed at all. But because things do exist, and we also know that things would have never existed without some cause, then every contingent thing must have an ultimate first cause, namely, God.

However, this is an obvious objection to Aquinas' argument. If it's true that everything is contingent or dependent upon something else for its existence, then why couldn't God's existence also be contingent upon something else? In other words, if God caused the universe to exist, what caused God to exist? As Theodore Schick explains in his article, if everything has a cause, then God must have a cause as well. This means that God could not be the first cause and does not exist. But for Aquinas, such an objection is flawed. If God were dependent upon something else for his existence, it would undermine his omnipotence. God would not be very powerful if he needed to be caused by something else. God's existence is necessary, not contingent. A necessary being is one who does not depend on anything for its existence and nothing can prevent it from existing. If so, then God is the sole author of our contingent world, therefore, he must exist.

Taking these three arguments together, Aquinas' first-cause argument can be summarized more formally as follows:

1. The world contains things that are brought into existence by some cause.
2. Everything that exists is either caused by something else (contingent) or uncaused (necessary).
3. There cannot be an infinite regress of causes—no infinite cause/effect chain.
4. So, there must exist an uncaused first cause or unmoved mover.
5. The word *God* means, in part, uncaused first cause.
6. Therefore, God exists. (Lawhead 320)

The "Big Bang" and the Uncaused Universe

There are a number of objections against the cosmological argument; one of the most important comes from David Hume. Hume argues that there is no reason to suppose a finite causal chain starting with God. In fact, the universe may have existed forever uncaused. For Hume, an infinite causal chain is perfectly reasonable to accept. To see this, as Theodore Schick points out in his article, consider a stack of children's building blocks. In a finite stack of blocks, with each one stacked on top of the other, there must be a first block resting on the table to start the column. No first block, no stack. However, we don't need to posit some first mover or a first cause to explain an infinite causal chain. In an infinite causal chain, every event will have a cause, despite not having a first cause. The individual links in a causal chain find their cause in their immediate predecessor, which is enough to explain or account for the chain itself. In other words, if Hume is right, there is no need to posit some first mover or a first cause to explain the causal chain. And if there is no first cause, based on Aquinas' argument, then God does not exist.

However, contrary to Hume, the causal chain appears to be finite. The universe has a beginning. In the 1920s, the astronomer Edwin Hubble made a remarkable discovery: the universe was expanding. Hubble noticed that remote galaxies were moving away from us at speeds proportional to their distances. The greater a galaxy is from the earth, the greater its speed (Kaufmann 342). The most likely theory that accounts for the expanding galaxy is known as the Big Bang. The **Big Bang**, according to most physicists, is a massive explosion that caused the universe to come into existence some 20 billion years ago (Kaufmann 344). But what caused the Big Bang? According to some theists, the Big Bang is scientific proof of God's ultimate handiwork. It's God—the uncaused first cause—who created the Big Bang and started the finite causal chain in motion (see Figure 3.2).

Figure 3.2 God Starts the Universe

Even if the Big Bang theory is correct, does it really prove that there is a God who created the universe? For Schick, there are good reasons for thinking that the universe does not have a cause. First, modern physics claims that sub-atomic particles (the building blocks of the universe) can spontaneously come into existence in the vacuum of space without a cause; these are known as vacuum fluctuations. For physicists, the Big Bang is the result of a vacuum fluctuation and, therefore, happened spontaneously without a cause. Second, even if the universe has a cause, it need not be God. Some scientists speculate that the expanding universe will one day stop and collapse upon itself, known as the **Big Crunch** (Kaufmann 349). This means the Big Bang may be the result of a prior Big Crunch bouncing back and forth between the two. In other words, the universe may be in a perpetual state of oscillation between periods of expansion and contraction in an endless cycle of creation and destruction. There would be no beginning or end; it would just exist without a first cause. Although the "bounce theory" of the universe has fallen out of favour, Schick correctly points out, that when faced with an inexplicable event, like the creation of the universe, it's more rational to look for a natural—opposed to supernatural—cause. The evidence, says Schick, does not support appealing to God as the first cause of the universe.

11

St. Thomas Aquinas (1225–1274)

St. Thomas Aquinas was born in Roccasicca, Italy, in 1225. The son of a nobleman, he ran away from home at the age of 14 to join the Dominican order where he studied philosophy and theology in Paris and Cologne, Germany. After four years of study, Aquinas was ordained as a priest and quickly set off to the University of Paris for advanced study with Albertus Magnus (Albert the Great), receiving his degree in 1256. He went on to teach at the University of Paris and at various Dominican schools in Italy. Aquinas eventually created a new Dominican house at the University of Naples in 1272. He died in 1274 while on route to Lyons where he was to meet with Pope Gregory X. Aquinas was a prolific writer; his two

major contributions to philosophy and theology are Summa Contra Gentiles (*Comprehensive Treatise Against the Gentiles*) and Summa Theologiae (*Comprehensive Treatise on Theology*).

Summa Theologiae

The Five Ways
Whether God Exists?

Objection 1. It seems that God does not exist; because if one of two contraries be infinite, the other would be altogether destroyed. But the word "God" means that He is infinite goodness. If, therefore, God existed, there would be no evil discoverable; but there is evil in the world. Therefore God does not exist.

Objection 2. Further, it is superfluous to suppose that what can be accounted for by a few principles has been produced by many. But it seems that everything we see in the world can be accounted for by other principles, supposing God did not exist. For all natural things can be reduced to one principle which is nature; and all voluntary things can be reduced to one principle which is human reason, or will. Therefore there is no need to suppose God's existence.

On the contrary, It is said in the person of God: "I am Who am." (Exodus 3:14)

I answer that, The existence of God can be proved in five ways.

The first and more manifest way is the argument from motion. It is certain, and evident to our senses, that in the world some things are in motion. Now whatever is in motion is put in motion by another, for nothing can be in motion except it is in potentiality to that towards which it is in motion; whereas a thing moves inasmuch as it is in act. For motion is nothing else than the reduction of something from potentiality to actuality. But nothing can be reduced from potentiality to actuality, except by something in a state of actuality. Thus that which is actually hot, as fire, makes wood, which is potentially hot, to be actually hot, and thereby moves and changes it. Now it is not possible that the same thing should be at once in actuality and potentiality in the same respect, but only in different respects. For what is actually hot cannot simultaneously be potentially hot; but it is simultaneously potentially cold. It is therefore impossible that in the same respect and in the same way a thing should be both mover and moved, i.e., that it should move itself. Therefore, whatever is in motion must be put in motion by another. If that by which it is put in motion be itself put in motion, then this also must needs be put in motion by another, and that by another again. But this cannot go on to infinity, because then there would be no first mover, and, consequently, no other mover; seeing that subsequent movers move only inasmuch as they are put in motion by the first mover; as the staff moves only because it is put in motion by the hand. Therefore it is necessary to arrive at a first mover, put in motion by no other; and this everyone understands to be God.

The second way is from the nature of the efficient cause. In the world of sense we find there is an order of efficient causes. There is no case known (neither is it, indeed, possible) in which a thing is found to be the efficient cause of itself; for so it would be prior to itself, which is impossible. Now in efficient causes it is not possible to go on to infinity, because in all efficient causes following in order, the first is the cause of the intermediate cause, and the intermediate is the cause of the ultimate cause, whether the intermediate cause be several, or only one. Now to take away the cause is to take away the effect.

Therefore, if there be no first cause among efficient causes, there will be no ultimate, nor any intermediate cause. But if in efficient causes it is possible to go on to infinity, there will be no first efficient cause, neither will there be an ultimate effect, nor any intermediate efficient causes; all of which is plainly false. Therefore it is necessary to admit a first efficient cause, to which everyone gives the name of God.

The third way is taken from possibility and necessity, and runs thus. We find in nature things that are possible to be and not to be, since they are found to be generated, and to corrupt, and consequently, they are possible to be and not to be. But it is impossible for these always to exist, for that which is possible not to be at some time is not. Therefore, if everything is possible not to be, then at one time there could have been nothing in existence. Now if this were true, even now there would be nothing in existence, because that which does not exist only begins to exist by something already existing. Therefore, if at one time nothing was in existence, it would have been impossible for anything to have begun to exist; and thus even now nothing would be in existence—which is absurd. Therefore, not all beings are merely possible, but there must exist something the existence of which is necessary. But every necessary thing either has its necessity caused by another, or not. Now it is impossible to go on to infinity in necessary things which have their necessity caused by another, as has been already proved in regard to efficient causes. Therefore we cannot but postulate the existence of some being having of itself its own necessity, and not receiving it from another, but rather causing in others their necessity. This all men speak of as God.

The fourth way is taken from the gradation to be found in things. Among beings there are some more and some less good, true, noble and the like. But "more" and "less" are predicated of different things, according as they resemble in their different ways something which is the maximum, as a thing is said to be hotter according as it more nearly resembles that which is hottest; so that there is something which is truest, something best, something noblest and, consequently, something which is uttermost being; for those things that are greatest in truth are greatest in being, as it is written in Metaph. ii. Now the maximum in any genus is the cause of all in that genus; as fire, which is the maximum heat, is the cause of all hot things. Therefore there must also be something which is to all beings the cause of their being, goodness, and every other perfection; and this we call God.

The fifth way is taken from the governance of the world. We see that things which lack intelligence, such as natural bodies, act for an end, and this is evident from their acting always, or nearly always, in the same way, so as to obtain the best result. Hence it is plain that not fortuitously, but designedly, do they achieve their end. Now whatever lacks intelligence cannot move towards an end, unless it be directed by some being endowed with knowledge and intelligence; as the arrow is shot to its mark by the archer. Therefore some intelligent being exists by whom all natural things are directed to their end; and this being we call God.

Reply to Objection 1. As Augustine says (Enchiridion xi): "Since God is the highest good, He would not allow any evil to exist in His works, unless His omnipotence and goodness were such as to bring good even out of evil." This is part of the infinite goodness of God, that He should allow evil to exist, and out of it produce good.

Reply to Objection 2. Since nature works for a determinate end under the direction of a higher agent, whatever is done by nature must needs be traced back to God, as to its first cause. So also whatever is done voluntarily must also be traced back to some higher cause other than human reason or will, since these can change or fail; for all things that are changeable and capable of defect must be traced back to an immovable and self-necessary first principle, as was shown in the body of the Article.

12

Theodore Schick Jr. (1952–)

Theodore Schick is Professor of Philosophy and Director of the Muhlenberg Scholars Program at Muhlenberg College. Born in Davenport, Iowa, on March 12, 1952, he received his B.A. from Harvard University and his Ph.D. from Brown University. He is the author (with Lewis Vaughn) of How to Think about Weird Things: Critical Thinking for a New Age *(1995), editor of* Readings in the Philosophy of Science: From Positivism to Postmodernism *(2000), and author (with Lewis Vaughn) of* Doing Philosophy: An Introduction Through Though Experiments *(2002). He serves on the editorial board of* Philo *and has published numerous articles on the nature of knowledge, reality, and value. His work also appears in a number of volumes of*

Open Court's Philosophy and Popular Culture series including Seinfeld and Philosophy, The Matrix and Philosophy, *and* The Lord of the Rings and Philosophy.

The 'Big Bang' Argument for the Existence of God

The evidence is in. There is now little doubt that our universe was brought into existence by a "big bang" that occurred some 15 billion years ago. The existence of such a creation event explains a number of phenomena including the expansion of the universe, the existence of the cosmic background radiation, and the relative proportions of various sorts of matter. As the theory has been refined, more specific predictions have been derived from it. A number of these predictions have recently been confirmed. Although this is a major scientific achievement, many believe that it has theological implications as well. Specifically, they believe that it provides scientific evidence for the existence of god. Astronomer George Smoot suggested as much when he exclaimed at a press conference reporting the findings of the Cosmic Background Explorer (COBE) satellite, "If you're religious, it's like looking at the face of god."[1] Why? Because something must have caused the big bang, and who else but god could have done such a thing? Astronomer Hugh Ross in his book, *The Creator and the Cosmos*, puts the argument this way: "If the universe arose out of a big bang, it must have had a beginning. If it had a beginning, it must have a beginner."[2] So beguiling is this argument that astronomer Geoffrey Burbridge has lamented that his fellow scientists are rushing off to join the "First Church of Christ of the Big Bang."[3] In what follows, I will attempt to determine whether such a conversion is the most rational response to the evidence.

The Traditional First-Cause Argument

The problems with the traditional first-cause or cosmological argument for the existence of god are legion. Before we examine the merits of the big bang argument, it will be helpful to have them before us.

The traditional first-cause argument rests on the assumption that everything has a cause. Since nothing can cause itself, and since the string of causes can't be infinitely long, there must be a first cause, namely, god. This argument received its classic formulation at the hands of the great Roman Catholic philosopher, Thomas Aquinas. He writes:

> In the world of sensible things, we find there is an order of efficient causes. There is no case known…in which a thing is found to be the efficient cause of itself; for so it would be prior to itself, which is impossible. Now in efficient causes it is not possible to go to infinity, because…the first is the cause of the intermediate cause, and the intermediate is the cause of the ultimate cause…Now to take away the cause is to take away the effect. Therefore, if there be no first cause among efficient causes, there will be no ultimate, nor any intermediate, cause…therefore it is necessary to admit a first efficient cause, to which everyone gives the name god.[4]

Saint Thomas's argument is this:

1. Everything is caused by something other than itself.

2. Therefore the universe was caused by something other than itself.

3. The string of causes cannot be infinitely long.

4. If the string of causes cannot be infinitely long, there must be a first cause.

5. Therefore, there must be a first cause, namely god.

The most telling criticism of this argument is that it is self-refuting. If everything has a cause other than itself, then god must have a cause other than himself. But if god has a cause other than himself, he cannot be the first cause. So if the first premise is true, the conclusion must be false.

To save the argument, the first premise could be amended to read:

1'. Everything except god has a cause other than itself.

But if we're willing to admit the existence of uncaused things, why not just admit that the universe is uncaused and cut out the middleman? David Hume wondered the same thing:

> But if we stop, and go no farther, why go so far? Why not stop at the material world?…By supposing It to contain the principle of its order within itself, we really assert it to be god; and the sooner we arrive at that Divine Being, so much the better. When you go one step beyond the mundane system, you only excite an inquisitive humor, which it is impossible ever to satisfy.[5]

The simplest way to avoid an infinite regress is to stop it before it starts. If we assume that the universe has always existed, we don't need to identify its cause.

Even if the universe is not eternal (as the big bang suggests), 1' is still unacceptable because modern physics has shown that some things are uncaused. According to quantum mechanics, subatomic particles like electrons, photons, and positrons come into and go out of existence randomly (but in accord with the Heisenberg uncertainty principles). As Edward Tryon reports:

> …quantum electrodynamics reveals that an electron, positron, and photon occasionally emerge spontaneously in a perfect vacuum. When this happens, the three particles exist for a brief time, and then annihilate each other, leaving no trace behind. (Energy conservation is violated, but only for a particle lifetime Δt permitted by the uncertainty $\Delta t \Delta E \sim h$ where ΔE is the net energy of the particles and h is Planck's constant.) The spontaneous, temporary emergence of particles from a vacuum is called a vacuum fluctuation, and is utterly commonplace in quantum field theory.[6]

A particle produced by a vacuum fluctuation has no cause. Since vacuum fluctuations are commonplace, god cannot be the only thing that is uncaused.

Premise 1, in either its original or its amended version, is unacceptable. But even if it could be salvaged, the argument would still not go through because premise 3 is false. An infinitely long causal chain is not a logical impossibility. Most of us have no trouble conceiving of the universe existing infinitely into the future. Similarly we should have no trouble conceiving of it existing infinitely into the past. Aquinas's view that there must be a first cause rests on the mistaken notion that an infinite series of causes is just a very long finite one.

Consider a single-column stack of children's blocks resting on a table. Each block rests on the block below it except for the block that rests on the table. If the bottom block were taken away, the whole stack would fall down. In a finite stack of blocks, there must be a first block.

In an infinite causal chain, however, there is no first cause. Aquinas took this to mean that an infinite causal chain is missing something. But it is a mistake to think that anything is missing from an infinite causal chain. Even though an infinite causal chain has no first cause, there is no event that doesn't have a cause. Similarly, even though the set of real numbers has no first member, there is no number that doesn't have a predecessor. Logic doesn't demand a first cause anymore than it demands a first number.

Finally, even if this argument did succeed in proving the existence of a first cause, it wouldn't succeed in proving the existence of god because there is no reason to believe that the cause of the universe has any of the properties traditionally associated with god. Aquinas took god to be all-powerful, all-knowing, and all-good. But from the existence of the universe, we cannot conclude that its creator had any of these properties.

An all-powerful being should be able to create an infinite number of different universes. But we are acquainted with only one. Maybe our universe is the only one the creator had the power to create. In the absence of any knowledge of other universes, we are not justified in believing that the creator is all-powerful.

Similarly, an all-knowing being should know everything there is to know about every possible universe. But our universe gives us no reason to think that the creator has this kind of knowledge. Maybe our universe is the only universe he knew how to make. Without further information about the cognitive capacity of the creator, we can't conclude that the creator is all-knowing.

Finally, a universe created by an all-powerful, all-knowing, all-good being should be perfect.

But the universe as we know it seems flawed. It certainly doesn't seem particularly hospitable to humans. Clarence Darrow explains:

> Even a human being of very limited capacity could think of countless ways in which the earth could be improved as the home of man, and from the earliest time the race has been using all sorts of efforts and resources to make it more suitable for its abode. Admitting that the earth is a fit place for life, and certainly every place in the universe where life exists is fitted for life, then what sort of life was this planet designed to support? There are some millions of different species of animals on this earth, and one-half of these are insects. In numbers, and perhaps in other ways, man is in a great minority. If the land of the earth was made for life, it seems as if it was intended for insect life, which can exist almost anywhere. If no other available place can be found they can live by the million on man, and inside of him. They generally succeed in destroying his life, and, if they have a chance, wind up by eating his body.[7]

Every place on Earth is subject to natural disasters, and there are many places where humans cannot live. Insects, on the other hand, seem to thrive most everywhere. When the great biologist G. B. S. Haldane was asked what his study of living things revealed about god, he is reported to have said, "An inordinate fondness for beetles." If the Earth was created for us (as many theists, including Ross, believe), it certainly leaves something to be desired.

Not only might the first cause be something less than perfect, it might be something less than human. David Hume provides the following example:

> The Brahmins assert, that the world arose from an infinite spider, who spun this whole complicated mass from his bowels, and annihilates afterwards the whole or any part of it, by absorbing it again, and resolving it into his own essence.[8]

This is a coherent account of the creation of the world. It is logically possible that everything in the universe came from the belly of an infinite spider. So even if there was a first cause, it need not have been god.

The Big Bang Argument

The big bang argument for the existence of god is supposed to succeed where the traditional first-cause argument fails. Let's see if it does. Ross's version of the argument goes like this:

6. Everything that had a beginning in time has a cause.
7. The universe had a beginning in time.
8. Therefore the universe had a cause.
9. The only thing that could have caused the universe is god.
10. Therefore, god exists.

Unlike the traditional first-cause argument, this argument is not self-refuting because it does not imply that god has a cause. If god had no beginning in time, he need not have a cause. Moreover, this argument doesn't deny the possibility of an infinite causal chain. It simply denies that the actual chain of causes is infinite. While this represents an improvement over the traditional first-cause argument, the big bang argument runs into difficulties of its own.

Premise 6 conflicts with quantum mechanics because, as we have seen, quantum electrodynamics claims that subatomic particles can come into existence through a vacuum fluctuation. These particles have a beginning in time, but they have no cause because vacuum fluctuations are purely random events. Such particles, then, serve as a counterexample to premise 6.

Premise 7 conflicts with relativity theory because the general theory of relativity claims that there was no time before there was a universe. Time and the universe are coterminous—they came into existence together. This finding of Einstein's was anticipated by Augustine who proclaimed, "The world and time had both one beginning. The world was made, not in time, but simultaneously with time."[9] If there was no time before there was a universe, the universe can't have a beginning in time.

Ross tries to avoid this conclusion by claiming that although the universe did not have a beginning in time as we know it, it had a beginning in another time dimension. He writes:

> By definition, time is that dimension in which cause-and-effect phenomena take place. No time, no cause and effect. If time's beginning is concurrent with the beginning of the universe, as the space-time theorem says, then the cause of the universe must be some entity operating in a time dimension completely independent of and preexistent to the time dimension of the cosmos. This conclusion is powerfully important to our understanding of who god is and who or what god isn't. It tells us that the Creator is transcendent, operating beyond the dimensional limits of the universe.[10]

Ross needs the premise that the universe has a beginning in time to arrive at the conclusion that the universe has a cause. But the general theory of relativity prohibits the universe from having a beginning in its own time dimension. So he postulates a higher time dimension that is independent of and preexistent to the time dimension of the universe.

As confirming evidence for the existence of this higher time dimension, Ross cites the Bible:

> Again, by definition, time is that realm or dimension in which cause-and-effect phenomena take place. According to the space-time theorem of general relativity, such effects as matter, energy, length, width, height, and time were caused independent of the time dimension of the universe. According to the New Testament (2 Timothy 1:9, Titus 1:2), such effects as grace and hope were caused independent of the time dimension of the universe. So both the Bible and general relativity speak of at least one additional time dimension for god.[11]

Whether the Bible speaks of an additional time dimension for god, the general theory of relativity does not. It makes no mention of an agent that exists outside of the space-time continuum. God is not written into the general theory of relativity.

Ross's argument here is a transcendental one, in both the logical and the theological senses of the word. It goes like this:

11. There can be no cause and effect unless there is time.
12. The universe has a cause.
13. Therefore the universe has a beginning in time.
14. The universe cannot have a beginning in its own time dimension.
15. Therefore the universe has a beginning in a time dimension independent of and preexistent to its own time dimension.

This argument arrives at the conclusion that the universe has a beginning in time by assuming that the universe has a cause. But the big bang argument uses the premise that the universe has a beginning in time to arrive at the conclusion that the universe has a cause. So Ross is arguing in a circle. He is assuming that the universe has a cause to prove that the universe has a cause. Because Ross begs the question about whether the universe has a cause, he does not succeed in proving the existence of a higher dimensional time, let alone the existence of a transcendental god.

Even if Ross's argument were not circular, it would still be equivocal because it uses the words "time" and "cause" in two different senses. Ordinary time is one-dimensional because it flows in only one direction. Ross's hypothetical time is two-dimensional because it flows in an infinite number of directions, just as the lines on a plane point in an infinite number of directions.[12] Cause, as ordinarily understood, requires a one-dimensional time because a cause must always precede its effects. (An effect cannot precede its cause.) In a two-dimensional time, however, the notion of precession or succession (before or after) makes no sense. So from the fact that the universe has a beginning in a higher time dimension, it doesn't follow that it has a cause (in the ordinary sense), and that is what must be shown in order for the argument to succeed.

Furthermore, Ross's appeal to the Bible is unwarranted. Before we can accept the Bible as a source of data, we need some reason for believing it to be true. Traditionally, the truth of the Bible has been justified on the grounds that god wrote it. But this approach is not available to Ross because the existence of god is what he is trying to prove. He cannot assume the existence of god to prove the existence of god. So he can't appeal to the Bible for evidential support.

The claim that the universe has a cause is essential to the big bang argument. Premises 6 and 7 do not justify this claim, for neither of them is true. But the failure of these premises to justify that claim does not necessarily mean that it is false.

There are good reasons for believing that the universe does not have a cause, however. Edward Tryon and others have suggested that the universe is the result of a vacuum fluctuation. Ross considers this theory but rejects it on the grounds that a vacuum fluctuation the size of the universe could only exist for 10^{-103} seconds, "a moment a bit briefer than the age of the universe."[13] But this follows only if we consider mass-energy to be the only type of energy in the world. Tryon suggests, however, that there is "another form of energy which is important for cosmology, namely gravitational potential energy."[14] If the total amount of gravitational potential energy in the universe is equivalent to the total amount of mass-energy, then the universe may have a zero net value for all conserved quantities. But if it does, then a vacuum fluctuation the size of the universe could exist for a very long time. Tryon summarizes his reasoning as follows:

> If it is true that our Universe has a zero net value for all conserved quantities, then it may simply be a fluctuation of a vacuum, the vacuum of some larger space in which our universe is imbedded. In answer to the question of why it happened, I offer the modest proposal that our Universe is simply one of those things which happen from time to time.[15]

So not only can subatomic particles be uncaused, so can the universe.

Premise 9 is also suspect because even if the universe has a cause, it need not be god.

Like the traditional first-cause argument, the big bang argument tells us nothing about the nature of the creator. Specifically, it doesn't tell us whether he (she, it?) is all-powerful, all-knowing, or all-good. And the universe itself gives us no reason to believe that the creator has any of those qualities.

Ross's argument, if successful, would give us reason to believe that the creator is transcendent, at least in the sense that he exists outside of the normal time dimension. On the basis of scripture, Ross makes the further claim that God is a person.[16] But if God is transcendent in Ross's sense, it's hard to see how he can also be a person. Paul Davies explains:

> The problem about postulating a god who transcends time is that, though it may bring him into the "here and now," many of the qualities which most people attribute to god only make sense within the context of time. Surely god can plan, answer prayers, express pleasure or anxiety about the course of human progress, and sit in judgement afterwards? Is he not continually active in the world, doing work "oiling the cogs of the cosmic machine" and so on? All of these activities are meaningless except in a temporal context. How can god *plan* and *act* except *in time*? Why, if god transcends time and so knows the future, is he concerned about human progress or the fight against evil. The outcome is already perceived by god.[17]

Ross's god exists in a two-dimensional time—like a plane—in which he can travel an infinite number or directions.[18] Thus Ross's god knows the future as well as the past. How such a being can plan, act, hope, or even think is a mystery. In the absence of an explanation of how such a being can be a person, Ross's claim is incoherent.

Not only does the cause of the universe not have to be god, it does not have to be supernatural. It has long been known that if the amount of matter in the universe is great enough, then the universe will someday stop expanding and start contracting. Eventually, all the matter in the universe will be drawn back to a single point in what has come to be known as "the big crunch." Since matter supposedly cannot be crushed out of existence, the contraction cannot go on indefinitely. At some point the compressed matter may rebound in another big bang. If so, the big bang would have been caused by a prior state of the universe rather than some external agency.

This bounce theory of the universe has fallen on hard times, however. In a paper entitled "The Impossibility of a Bouncing Universe," Marc Sher and Alan Guth argued that the universe is not mechanically efficient enough to bounce.[19] In terms of mechanical efficiency, the universe appears to be more like a snowball than a super-ball. Moreover, recent estimates indicate that there is not enough mass in the universe to stop its expansion. So it is doubtful that the big bang was the result of a prior big crunch.

Although the universe as a whole may never contract, we know that certain parts of it do. When a star has used up its fuel, the force of gravity causes it to contract. If the star is massive enough, this contraction results in a black hole. The matter in a black hole is compressed toward a point of infinite density known as a "singularity." Before it reaches the singularity, however, some physicists, most notably Lee Smolin, believe that it may start expanding again and give rise to another universe. In a sense, then, according to Smolin, our universe may reproduce itself by budding off. He writes:

> A collapsing star forms a black hole, within which it is compressed to a very dense state. The universe began in a similarly very dense state from which it expands. Is it possible that these are one and the same dense state? That is, is it possible that what is beyond the horizon of a black hole is the beginning of another universe?
>
> This could happen if the collapsing star exploded once it reached a very dense state, but after the black hole horizon had formed around it....
>
> What we are doing is applying this bounce hypothesis, not to the universe as a whole, but to every black hole in it. If this is true, then we live not in a single universe, which is eternally passing through the same recurring cycle of collapse and rebirth. We live instead in a continually growing community of "universes," each of which is born from an explosion following the collapse of a star to a black hole.[20]

Smolin's vision is an appealing one. It suggests that the universe is more like a living thing than an artifact and thus that its coming into being doesn't require an external agent.

Smolin's theory has the advantage of simplicity over Ross's. Because it does not postulate the existence of any supernatural entities, it has less ontological baggage than Ross's. It also has the advantage of conservatism over Ross's theory. Because it doesn't contradict any laws of science, such as the conservation laws (which must be rejected by anyone who believes in creation ex nihilo), it fits better with existing theory. Other things being equal, the simpler and more con-

servative a theory, the better. The fewer independent assumptions made by a theory and the less damage it does to existing theory, the more it systematizes and unifies our knowledge. And the more it systematizes and unifies our knowledge, the more understanding it produces. Since Smolin's theory is simpler and more conservative than Ross's, it is the better theory.

Smolin's theory is also potentially more fruitful than Ross's because it is possible to draw testable predictions from it. But what if these predictions are not born out? Does that mean that we must embrace the god hypothesis? No, because our inability to explain a phenomenon may simply be due to our ignorance of the operative laws. Augustine concurs. "A miracle," he tells us, "is not contrary to nature but contrary to our knowledge of nature."[21]

We would be justified in believing that an inexplicable event is the work of god only if we were justified in believing that a natural explanation of it would never be found. But we can never be justified in believing that, because we can't predict what the future will bring. We can't rule out the possibility that a natural explanation will be found, no matter how incredible the event. When faced with an inexplicable event, it is always more rational to look for a natural cause than to attribute it to something supernatural. Appealing to the supernatural does not increase our understanding. It simply masks the fact that we do not yet understand.

What's more, any supposed miracle could be the result of a superadvanced technology rather than a supernatural being. Arthur C. Clarke once said that any sufficiently advanced technology is indistinguishable from magic. So the seemingly inexplicable events that many attribute to god could simply be the work of advanced aliens. Erik von Däniken argues as much in his book *Chariots of the Gods,* where he claims that the wheel that Ezekiel saw in the sky was really a UFO. Explanations that appeal to advanced aliens are actually superior to explanations that appeal to supernatural beings because they are simpler and more conservative—they do not postulate any nonphysical substances and they do not presuppose the falsity of any natural laws. If astronomers feel the need to join a church, they would do better to join the First Church of Space Aliens than the First Church of Christ of the Big Bang.

Notes

1. Thomas H. Maugh, "Relics of 'Big Bang' Seen for First Tillie," *Los Angeles Times* April 24, 1992, p. A30.

2. Hugh Ross, *The Creator and the Cosmos* (Colorado Springs: Navpress, 1995), p. 14.

3. Stephen Strauss, "An Innocent's Guide to the Big Bang Theory: Fingerprint in Space Left by the Universe as a Baby Still Has Doubters Hurling Stones," *Globe and Mail* (Toronto), April 25, 1992, p. 1.

4. Thomas Aquinas, *Summa Theologica* (New York: Benziger Bros., Inc., 1947).

5. David Hume, *Dialogues Concerning Natural Religion,* ed. Norman Kemp Smith (Indianapolis: Bobbs-Merril, 1947), pp. 161–62.

6. Edward Tryon, *Nature* 246, December 14, 1973.

7. Clarence Darrow, *The Story of My Life* (New York: Charles Scribner's Sons, 1932), pp. 419–20.

8. Hume, *Dialogues Concerning Natural Religion,* p. 180.

9. Augustine, *The City of God* (trans. Dods) 11.6.

10. Ross, *The Creator and the Cosmos,* p. 76.

11. Ibid., p. 80.

12. Ibid., P. 81.

13. Ibid., p. 96.

14. Edward Tryon, "Is the Universe a Vacuum Fluctuation?"

15. Ibid.

16. Ross, *The Creator and the Cosmos,* pp. 77f.

17. Paul Davies, *God and the New Physics* (New York: Simon and Schuster, 1983), pp. 38–39.

18. Ross, *The Creator of the Cosmos,* p. 81.

19. Alan H. Guth and Marc Sher, "The Impossibility of a Bouncing Universe," *Nature* 302 (1983): 505–507.

20. Lee Smolin, *The Life of the Cosmos* (New York: Oxford University Press, 1997), pp. 87–88.

21. Augustine, *The City of God* (trans. Dods) 21.8.

The Teleological (Design) Argument

God does not play dice with the universe.
—Albert Einstein

Discussion Questions

1. Imagine that while walking in a field you come across a watch. What features of the watch might lead you infer from its function that it had a watchmaker?

2. If Paley's teleological argument is correct, the sheer complexity of the universe entails an intelligent designer. This seems to suggest God designed the universe for some purpose. After all, if humans design watches and ships to achieve the goals of time and transportation, then God must have created the universe to achieve some goal. Although we can only speculate about the goal(s) achieved by creating a universe, it is important to notice that if the designer *needs* a universe to achieve some goal, then this seems to go against the omnipotent, omniscient, and omnibenevolent nature of God. Such a being should be able to accomplish goals without having to create a medium through which to do so. The existence of the universe, therefore, casts doubt on the existence of an all-powerful designer. If humans, the earth, and the universe are the result of some divine grand design, what do you think God's goal is? In what ways does the fact that God needed to create the

universe to achieve some goal count against God's existence?

3. Dawkins argues that natural selection and the laws of physics can fully explain the apparent order in the universe. Discuss your reasons for the probability or improbability that eyes, stomach, brains, and other complex entities could come about by chance as Dawkins suggests. If one accepted that nature is too complex to have come about by chance, would the process of evolution imply an intelligent designer? Why or why not?

Intelligent Design in God's Creation

In *Natural Theology*, William Paley outlines what has come to be known as the argument from design or the teleological argument.[5] The design argument, like the cosmological argument, argues for God's existence upon *a posteriori* reasoning. Put simply, Paley intends to show that the world we experience exhibits design (order) and the most likely (probable) author of this design (order) is God. To see how Paley arrives at his conclusion, image crossing a field when you suddenly stub your toe on a rock. Aside from a few choice curses, you probably wouldn't question how the stone came to be there. For all you know, the stone has probably been there forever. But if you stumbled across a watch, this is quite different. Why? Because once you inspect the watch, unlike the rock, you will see it's a human creation; it doesn't just pop into existence. Watches, generally speaking, have various components such as silicon chips, springs, and teethed wheels, which when carefully put together are designed for the sole purpose of telling time. And once we understand its function or purpose, for Paley, the inference is inevitable; some intelligent maker must have made the watch for this particular purpose.[6]

Of course, we can draw similar inferences regarding other human inventions. Look, once again, around the room in which you sit. What do you see (pens, paper, computer, books, cup,

scissors, etc.)? Notice that each of these items has been designed for a particular purpose in mind. A pen, for example, is designed to write; a cup to hold liquids; scissors to cut things, and so forth. In fact, we could say that all human inventions have a function or goal. A car, for example, is designed for the purpose of travel; a house is designed for the purpose of keeping us warm and dry; the space shuttle is designed for the purpose of travelling into space. Remember, for Paley, purpose or function entails an intelligent creator. After all, it takes very smart, if not brilliant, scientists and engineers to build cars, houses, and rocket ships capable of achieving speed, comfort, and space exploration.

The next step in Paley's argument is the analogy he draws between human inventions and creationism.[7] An argument from analogy is based on the idea that from similarities in X and Y, we can infer that Z will be the same. So, for Paley, if we look at nature we see things that appear to have been designed for a specific purpose or function, which is analogous to purpose-built human creations. Eyes, for example, are designed for the purpose of sight; stomachs are designed for the purpose of digesting food; and cheetahs are designed for the purpose of speed. If the purpose within human inventions entails intelligent design, then we make similar claims about what we see in nature. Anyone who has been awed by the wonder and complexity of nature will surely find Paley's argument appealing. The sheer complexity of the universe must entail an intelligent designer because it could not have come about by chance. So, if the watch is the manifestation of design by a watchmaker, the universe is probably the manifestation of design by a universe maker, i.e., God. More formally, the argument can be put as follows:

1. Human artefacts are products of human design (purpose).
2. The universe resembles these artefacts.
3. Therefore, the universe is (probability) a product of intelligent design (purpose).
4. But the universe is vastly more complex and gigantic than a human artefact.
5. Therefore, there probability is a powerful and vastly intelligent designer who designed the universe.

6. This intelligent designer is God.

7. Therefore, God probably exists. (Pojman 79)

In support of the design argument, the astronomer Fred Hoyle once compared the existence of life on earth as the result of chance to a whirlwind passing through an airplane parts factory and producing a functioning plane. And the physicist Paul Davies stated that the odds of DNA occurring randomly are $10^{40,000}$ to one. This would be equivalent to tossing a coin in the air 130,000 times in a row and getting heads each time (28). The probability of our intricate and immensely complex world and universe coming about by chance is so miniscule it's unintelligible. For Hoyle and Davis, like Paley, these examples are sufficient to show that the complexity of our world necessitates an intelligent designer—God exists.

Hume's Religious Scepticism

In his *Dialogues Concerning Natural Religion*, David Hume puts forward three main arguments against Paley. As the name implies, the *Dialogues* are based on a series of conversations between Cleanthes, who is representing Paley as the natural theologian; Philo, who is representing Hume as the religious sceptic; and Demea, who is representing the orthodox believer who uses both faith and rational arguments to support God's existence.

First, Hume argues that the analogy between the creation of watches, houses, ships, etc. and the creation of the universe is weak. Comparing the design of human artefacts to the design of the universe is like comparing apples to oranges. Houses, watches, and cars are not similar enough to the universe to support Paley's analogy. If we see a house, says Hume, we would be justified in inferring a builder because houses are designed for a specific purpose and past experience tells us houses don't simply pop into existence. For every house (effect), there must be a builder (cause). But we cannot make similar inferences about the design of the universe to the probability of an all-mighty maker. The problem is that human creations like houses, watches, and cars are not sufficiently *like* the universe to draw inferences regarding its cause. In other words, the differences between the builder of a house and the builder of a universe are so great, the fact that the first had an intelligent designer does not allow us to infer that the universe does as well. We are just too unfamiliar with the creation of universes to draw any inferences at all about how it came into existence. For Hume, the analogy is so weak we are left only to guess, presume, and conjecture about the causes of the universe and, subsequently, God's existence.

Second, Hume argues we cannot reason from parts to the whole. His argument is based on the idea that we can only infer similar causes from what we actually experience. And since our experience of the universe is limited to parts of this world, we cannot infer an intelligent designer of the universe as a whole. For example, a house is evidence of an intelligent designer because we have made the association between houses and builders by our past experiences. After all, most of us have seen houses being built. Therefore, when we see a house, we infer the existence of a builder. The problem is that we cannot make a similar inference regarding the universe because the creation of the universe is something that we cannot experience. If we were to apply Paley's analogy between human creations and the universe, we would need past experiences of universe making in order to infer a designer. But since no human has experienced a universe being made by an intelligent designer, nothing can justify this inference that God is its creator. In the same way we cannot make inferences about the origins of humans or trees from a single hair or leaf, we cannot make inferences about the origins of the universe from our limited experiences of this world. For Hume, Paley's argument from analogy is weak and so the probability of God's existence.

Third, Hume argues that Paley's analogy shows God is much more human than what we think. First, God is finite, not infinite. Hume argues that causes ought only to be proportional to their effects. To see what Hume is driving at (no pun intended), let's use automobiles as an example. Cars are, by nature, finite. From conception and design, to manufacturing and consumer use, they have a limited life span. All cars eventually wear out and die. Cars are the effect of the creative forces of humans; we are the cause. For Hume, if causes are proportional of their effects, then humans are finite as well; we eventually wear out and die. Now consider God. If God created the universe this means the universe is finite. That is, the universe is depended upon God for its coming into existence—it has not existed forever. This means the universe is the finite effect of God (the cause). And if cause and effect are proportional, as Hume suggests, then this means that God, like the universe, is also finite. Secondly, God is imperfect, not perfect. To see the force of Hume's objection, let's start by considering human artefacts. Human artefacts are imperfect. For example, computers can "crash" and cars can breakdown. Nature is imperfect as well. Animals and humans are often born with deformities and diseases. So if God is the creator of nature and our universe, then drawing the analogy with human artefacts, God must also be imperfect. Third, God is not omniscience. If we survey a ship, says Hume, we may think this complicated, purposeful, and beautiful machine is perfect. But upon closer inspection we would find flaws. In many cases, things are built from trial and error. Humans are not omniscient; we often don't have perfect knowledge of our creations before we build, and it's only once we begin building, that we realize the best-laid plans are wrong and so we have to try something else until it works. In this way, humans often refine their knowledge during the building process. Likewise, from analogy, we shouldn't be surprised to find the universe the result of trial and error as well. For all we know, God could have made numerous errors during the creation process until he got it right. This hardly makes God omniscient. An omniscient deity would be able to clearly know what needs to be done to create the universe, humans, animals, and so on.

Fourth, why must we think there is only one deity who created the universe? A crew of builders and designers make ships and houses, and so the universe might also be the result of a crew of designers (many gods). Finally, if the cause of the universe is similar to the cause of human artefacts, then the designer is mortal, comes in two genders, and is physical. Surely something no theist would accept. Therefore, God's existence, says Hume, is highly suspect.

The Blind Watchmaker

At 22 years old, Charles Darwin (1809–1882) had an important decision to make: either set sail on a five-year voyage as the HMS *Beagle's* naturalist or continue on with his studies to become a doctor, as his father wanted. Considering the sight of blood made him squeamish, Darwin decided to embark on the sea voyage. Good thing he did so because his discoveries would radically change human thinking regarding intelligent design.

The HMS *Beagle* set sail in 1831 with the purpose of mapping the coast of South America. And like all voyages at the time, the ship needed a captain, doctor, artist, and naturalist. As a naturalist, Darwin's job was to document, collect, and record the flora and fauna, geological features, fossils, minerals, native persons, and the weather. It was during these observations that Darwin developed his theory of evolution based on natural selection.

Natural selection is based on the idea that the seemingly "intelligent" design of our world and universe is really the result of blind, dumb, natural, not supernatural, forces at work. All living creatures have evolved from simpler life forms through the random variation of genes passed on from one generation to the next. These random variations manifest themselves in physical traits. These physical traits aid organisms to better adapt to their environment and, therefore, pass on those genes to subsequent generations. Those organisms not well adapted to their environment will eventually die out. In short, the random process of natural selection helps organisms achieve better reproductive success. The basic tenants of natural selection can be outlined as follows:

1. Species are comprised of individuals that vary ever so slightly from each other with respect to their many traits.

2. Species have a tendency to increase in size over generations at an exponential rate.

3. This tendency, given limited resources, disease, predation, and so on, creates a constant condition of struggle for survival among the members of a species.

4. Some individuals will have variations that give them a slight advantage in this struggle, variations that allow more efficient or better access to resources, greater resistance to disease, greater success at avoiding predation, and so on.

5. These individuals will tend to survive better and leave more offspring.

6. Offspring tend to inherit the variations of their parents.

7. Therefore favourable variations will tend to be passed on more frequently than others, a tendency Darwin labelled "Natural Selection."

8. Over time, especially in a slowly changing environment, this process will cause the character of species to change.

9. Given a long enough period of time, the descendant populations of an ancestor species will differ enough to be classified as a different species, a process capable of indefinite iteration. There are, in addition, forces that encourage divergence among descendant populations, and the elimination of intermediate varieties. (Lennox)

One of Darwin's most important observations, which provided support for his theory of natural selection, came when Darwin and crew sailed to the Galapagos Islands in 1835. Darwin discovered 13 species of finches, which differed significantly from the finch species in South America. For example, some finches had strong beaks for cracking nuts and seeds, others had fine beaks for feeding on insects, and others had beaks designed for grasping twigs to extract insects and larvae out from under tree bark (see Figure 3.3).

How can these differences be explained? Darwin theorized that the Galapagos finches (later renamed Darwin's finches) must have adapted to their new environmental conditions from an ancestral species that had travelled from South America years earlier. Each new environmental condition would bring

Figure 3.3   Darwin's Finches as an Example of Evolution

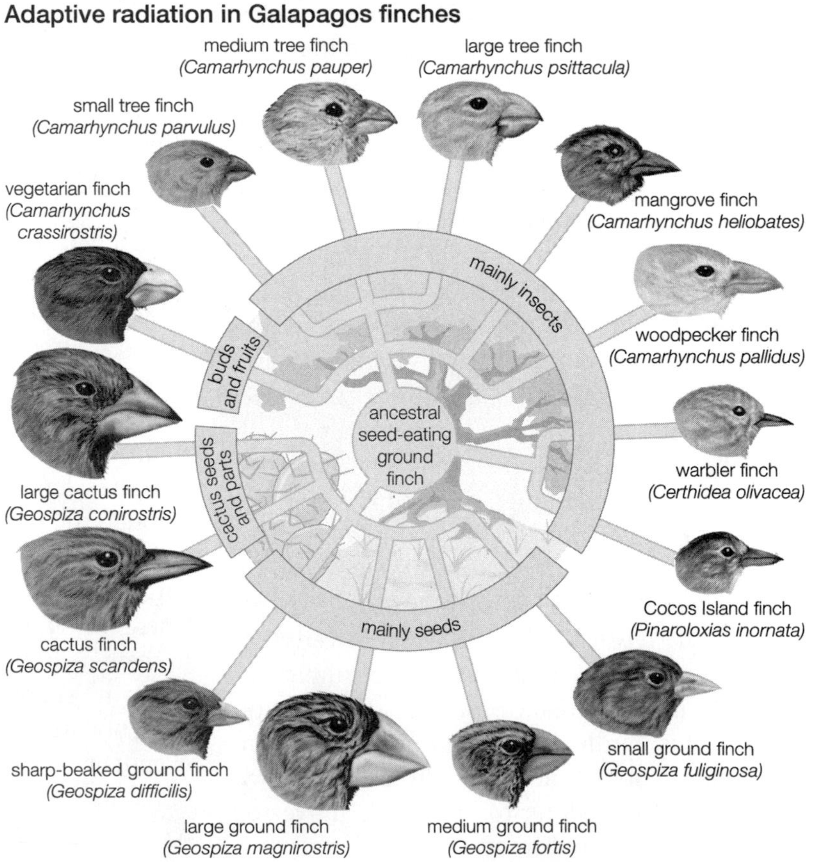

Adaptive radiation in Galapagos finches

Darwin collected and observed many different species on the Galapagos Islands in 1835, including small finches. He discovered that each bird species was slightly different, filling specific niches on the islands. This realization led Darwin to develop the theory of natural selection and, thereby, radically change the world of science.

about new adaptations. The struggle for survival ensures that some individuals are better adapted to their environmental niche due to random genetically determined differences. These differences increase the likelihood of individual finches surviving and passing on their genes. Over time, each species adapted to their new habitat and new way of life.[8] In short, each species evolved by having specific traits selected for by their natural environments.

After returning to England from his five-year voyage in 1837, Darwin spent his time thinking and writing about his theory of evolution via natural selection. For more than 25 years, he carefully collected evidence to support his theory, which culminated in his *The Origin of Species* being published in 1859. Darwin argued that gradual physical changes over time allowed organisms to best adapt to their environment. For Darwin, the evidence gathered during his five-year voyage convinced him that there is no intelligent design within nature, just random blind forces acting on species to create specific functional traits and abilities.[9]

Darwin's theory of evolution has been taught in biology classes for years as the best theory to explain the complexity of life on the earth. However, for most scientists, evolution is no mere theory; it's a fact. But evolution is increasingly coming under attack from religious groups[10] claiming that evolution, far from disproving God's intelligent design, actually proves it. Advocates of **intelligent design creationism** want biology classes to teach evolution in conjunction with intelligent design. Critics argue there are gaps in evolutionary theory and, given it's just a theory, students ought to have chance to hear other alternative explanations of how life evolved. This means, for some theists, the selection of one gene over the other is not a random occurrence, but the work of God. In this sense, natural selection is purposeful; intelligent design is behind the idea of evolution itself. The important of intelligent design creationism cannot be overstated, for if it is correct, by looking at the complexity of nature, we can get a glimpse into the mind of God.

There are three main arguments put forward to support intelligent design creationism. First, if evolution is correct, then all life evolved from simpler forms to more complex forms. But how did the first DNA molecule or protein come into existence? Could it have just popped into existence by chance? Not likely, say intelligent design creationists. The odds of random processes creating the first strand of DNA or first simple protein, from which all life evolved, are slim to nil. The only reasonable explanation is that God plays an important role in the evolutionary process.

Although this line of reasoning is tempting, it's not persuasive, says Richard Dawkins, in his article "The Improbability of God." He argues that DNA could have spontaneously sprung into existence, without the aid of God. Although our modern DNA code is too complicated to have come about by a single chance event, it must have evolved from an earlier hereditary system, no longer in existence. This DNA structure, says Dawkins, was simple enough that could have arisen by chance via the laws of chemistry. Moreover, no matter how unlikely DNA came about by chance, for Dawkins, we cannot rule out this possibility.

The second argument in support of intelligent design creationism comes from the lack of fossil evidence. If evolution is a gradual process, biologists should have a more detailed account of transitional creatures—they don't. This lack of transitional creatures is especially apparent during the Cambrian period (600 million years ago) when lots of organisms came into existence all of a sudden. The only reasonable explanation of this explosion of life is intelligent design.

But for neo-Darwinists, like Kathleen Hunt, we shouldn't be surprised there are gaps in the fossil record. First, only a very small percentage of organisms actually get fossilized. Terrestrial, small, fragile, and forest dwelling animals rarely get fossilized because they decompose so rapidly. Hence, the explosion of new species during the Cambrian period proves nothing except that many more species became fossilized during this time. Secondly, gaps in the fossil record can be explained because they have simply not been found. Europe and North America are the only two continents in the world that have been systematically surveyed for fossils. As other continents are surveyed, these gaps will likely be filled. Thirdly, biologists have a good, albeit incomplete, transitional fossil record. For example, biologists know that primitive jawless fish evolved into bony fish; bony fish evolved into amphibians, amphibians evolved into amniotes (first reptiles); reptiles evolved into birds; and early apes evolved into humans. In short, there is an abundance of transitional fossils that shows natural selection at work, not intelligent design.

The third, and most popular, argument for intelligent design creationism is that living bodies are too complex to have come about by chance. Michael Behe, the author of *Darwin's Black Box: The Biochemical Challenge to Evolution,* claims that some systems are so complex they cannot be reduced along Darwinian lines. Consider the human eye. It is unreasonable to believe that the cornea, iris, lens, pupil, retina, and all of its other components could have come about by chance. For Behe, the eye could not have been the product of accidental mutations. The eye resembles a camera, and if the camera is a product of intelligent design, then the eye must also be the product of intelligent design by God. Other examples by Behe include bacterial flagella, blood clotting, protein transportation in cells, the immune system, and metabolic pathways. All of these examples, says Behe, are irreducibly complex and can only be explained by intelligent design. As Behe states:

> The result of these cumulative efforts to investigate the cell—to investigate life at the molecular level—is a loud, clear, piercing cry of "design!" The result is so unambiguous and so significant that it must be ranked as one of the greatest achievements of the history of science.... The observation of intelligent design in life is as momentous as the observation that the earth goes around the sun or that disease is caused by bacteria.... This triumph of science

should evoke cries of "Eureka!" from ten thousand throats, should occasion much hand-slapping and high-fiving, and perhaps even be an excuse to take a day off.

But no bottles have been uncorked, no hands slapped. Instead, a curious, embarrassed silence surrounds the stark complexity of the cell. When the subject comes up in public, feet start to shuffle, and breathing gets a bit labored. In private people are a bit more relaxed; many explicitly admit the obvious but then stare at the ground, shake their heads, and let it go at that.

Why does the scientific community not greedily embrace its startling discovery? Why is the observation of design handled with intellectual gloves? The dilemma is that while one side of the elephant is labeled intelligent design, the other side might be labeled God. (232–33)

Although Dawkins' article does not address Behe directly, he emphatically disagrees with the notion of intelligent design. We can explain the complexity of life, says Dawkins, by random genetic mutations, not God. Although Dawkins would agree with Behe (and Paley) that the world is incredibly complex, this complexity is the result of gradual evolutionary processes at work. Evolution is the step-by-step process of transforming simple organisms into more complex ones. The process of evolution starts with chance and accumulates into non-random arrangements explained by physical forces. For example, if you walk along a beach you will notice that the pebbles are not randomly scattered across the beach. The smaller and lighter pebbles are on top, and the medium sized and heavier in the middle, and the larger and heaviest on the bottom. Although this appears to be the produce of some intelligent design, the laws of physics best explain this non-random arrangement. There is no mind or intentionality at work creating non-randomness and order; it can simply be explained by physical forces at work in the world. Likewise for evolution, small-accumulated changes via natural selection create non-random order in the most complex of organs. It is possible, says Dawkins, for an eye to spring into being from bare skin; not instantaneously, of course, but over millions of years of small differences that accumulate at each evolutionary stage into something more complex. These changes, caused by chance genetic mutations, eventually give rise to physical characteristics that help organisms survive and reproduce. But such forces are not the result of God's intentional design, but are blind natural forces at work.[11]

13

William Paley

(1743–1805)

Born in Peterborough, England, in 1743, William Paley came to be known as a strong supporter of natural theology—the idea that all life is the result of intelligent

design and creation. Paley entered Christ College, Cambridge University as an undergraduate in 1759. He was an excellent student, excelling at mathematics and debating, eventually graduating in 1763. Paley was elected fellow of Christ College in 1766 and lectured on metaphysics, morality, and Locke. Ordained as Anglican priest in 1767, he left academia and took up various ecclesiastical positions, working his way up the ranks in the Anglican Church. His two most famous works are Evidences of Christianity *(1794) and* Natural Theology *(1801). He died in 1805.*

Natural Theology

Chapter One: "The State of the Argument"

In crossing a heath, suppose I pitched my foot against a *stone* and were asked how the stone came to be there, I might possibly answer that for anything I knew to the contrary it had lain there forever; nor would it, perhaps, be very easy to show the absurdity of this answer. But suppose I had found a *watch* upon the ground, and it should be inquired how the watch happened to be in that place, I should hardly think of the answer which I had before given, that for anything I knew the watch might have always been there. Yet why should not this answer serve for the watch as well as for the stone? Why is it not as admissible in the second case as in the first? For this reason, and for no other, namely, that when we come to inspect the watch, we perceive—what we could not discover in the stone—that its several parts are framed and put together for a purpose, e.g., that they are so formed and adjusted as to produce motion, and that motion so regulated as to point out the hour of the day; that if the different parts had been differently shaped from what they are, of a different size from what they are, or placed after any other manner or in any other order than that in which they are placed, either no motion at all would have been carried on in the machine, or none which would have answered the use that is now served by it. To reckon up a few of the plainest of these parts and of their offices, all tending to one result; we see a cylindrical box containing a coiled elastic spring, which, by its endeavor to relax itself, turns round the box. We next observe a flexible chain—artificially wrought for the sake of flexure—communicating the action of the spring from the box to the fusee. We then find a series of wheels, the teeth of which catch in and apply to each other, conducting the motion from the fusee to the balance and from the balance to the pointer, and at the same time, by the size and shape of those wheels, so regulating that motion as to terminate in causing an index, by an equable and measured progression, to pass over a given space in a given time. We take notice that the wheels are made of brass, in order to keep them from rust; the springs of steel, no other metal being so elastic; that over the face of the watch there is placed a glass, a material employed in no other part of the work, but in the room of which, if there had been any other than a transparent substance, the hour could not be seen without opening the case. This mechanism being observed—it requires indeed an examination of the instrument, and perhaps some previous knowledge of the subject, to perceive and understand it; but being once, as we have said, observed and understood—the inference we think is inevitable, that the watch must have had a maker—that there must have existed, at some time and at some place or other, an artificer or artificers who formed it for the purpose which we find it actually to answer, who comprehended its construction and designed its use.

I. Nor would it, I apprehend, weaken the conclusion, that we had never seen a watch made—that we had never known an artist capable of making one—that we were altogether incapable of executing such a piece of workmanship ourselves, or of understanding in what manner it was performed; all this being no more than what is true of some exquisite remains of ancient art, of some lost arts, and, to the generality of mankind, of the more curious productions of modern manufacture. Does one man in a million know how oval frames are turned? Ignorance

of this kind exalts our opinion of the unseen and unknown artist's skiff, if he be unseen and unknown, but raises no doubt in our minds of the existence and agency of such an artist, at some former time and in some place or other. Nor can I perceive that it varies at all the inference, whether the question arise concerning a human agent or concerning an agent of a different species, or an agent possessing in some respects a different nature.

II. Neither, secondly, would it invalidate our conclusion, that the watch sometimes went wrong or that it seldom went exactly right. The purpose of the machinery, the design, and the designer might be evident, and in the case supposed, would be evident, in whatever way we accounted for the irregularity of the movement, or whether we could account for it or not. It is not necessary that a machine be perfect in order to show with what design it was made: still less necessary, where the only question is whether it were made with any design at all.

III. Nor, thirdly, would it bring any uncertainty into the argument, if there were a few parts of the watch, concerning which we could not discover or had not yet discovered in what manner they conduced to the general effect; or even some parts, concerning which we could not ascertain whether they conduced to that effect in any manner whatever. For, as to the first branch of the case, if by the loss, or disorder, or decay of the parts in question, the movement of the watch were found in fact to be stopped, or disturbed, or retarded, no doubt would remain in our minds as to the utility or intention of these parts, although we should be unable to investigate the manner according to which, or the connection by which, the ultimate effect depended upon their action or assistance; and the more complex is the machine, the more likely is this obscurity to arise. Then, as to the second thing supposed, namely, that there were parts which might be spared without prejudice to the movement of the watch, and that we had proved this by experiment, these superfluous parts, even if we were completely assured that they were such, would not vacate the reasoning which we had instituted concerning other parts. The indication of contrivance remained, with respect to them, nearly as it was before.

IV. Nor, fourthly, would any man in his senses think the existence of the watch with its various machinery accounted for, by being told that it was one out of possible combinations of material forms; that whatever he had found in the place where he found the watch, must have contained some internal configuration or other; and that this configuration might be the structure now exhibited, namely, of the works of a watch, as well as a different structure.

V. Nor, fifthly, would it yield his inquiry more satisfaction, to be answered that there existed in things a principle of order, which had disposed the parts of the watch into their present form and situation. He never knew a watch made by the principle of order; nor can he even form to himself an idea of what is meant by a principle of order distinct from the intelligence of the watchmaker.

VI. Sixthly, he would be surprised to hear that the mechanism of the watch was no proof of contrivance, only a motive to induce the mind to think so.

VII. And not less surprised to be informed that the watch in his hand was nothing more than the result of the laws of *metallic* nature. It is a perversion of language to assign any law as the efficient, operative cause of any thing. A law presupposes an agent, for it is only the mode according to which an agent proceeds: it implies a power, for it is the order according to which that power acts. Without this agent, without

this power, which are both distinct from itself, the *law* does nothing, is nothing. The expression, "the law of metallic nature," may sound strange and harsh to a philosophic ear; but it seems quite as justifiable as some others which are more familiar to him, such as "the law of vegetable nature," "the law of animal nature," or, indeed, as "the law of nature" in general, when assigned as the cause of phenomena, in exclusion of agency and power, or when it is substituted into the place of these.

VIII. Neither, lastly, would our observer be driven out of his conclusion or from his confidence in its truth by being told that he knew nothing at all about the matter. He knows enough for his argument; he knows the utility of the end; he knows the subserviency and adaptation of the means to the end. These points being known, his ignorance of other points, his doubts concerning other points affect not the certainty of his reasoning. The consciousness of knowing little need not beget a distrust of that which he does know. [...]

Chapter Five: "Application of the Argument Continued"

Every observation which was made in our first chapter concerning the watch may be repeated with strict propriety concerning the eye, concerning animals, concerning plants, concerning, indeed, all the organized parts of the works of nature. As,

I. When we are inquiring simply after the *existence* of an intelligent Creator, imperfection, inaccuracy, liability to disorder, occasional irregularities may subsist in a considerable degree without inducing any doubt into the question; just as a watch may frequently go wrong, seldom perhaps exactly right, may be faulty in some parts, defective in some, without the smallest ground of suspicion from thence arising that it was not a watch, not made, or not made for the purpose ascribed to it. When faults are pointed out, and when a question is started concerning the skill of the artist or dexterity with which the work is executed, then, indeed, in order to defend these qualities from accusation, we must be able either to expose some intractableness and imperfection in the materials or point out some invincible difficulty in the execution, into which imperfection and difficulty the matter of complaint may be resolved; or, if we cannot do this, we must adduce such specimens of consummate art and contrivance proceeding from the same hand as may convince the inquirer of the existence, in the case before him, of impediments like those which we have mentioned, although, what from the nature of the case is very likely to happen, they be unknown and unperceived by him. This we must do in order to vindicate the artist's skill, or at least the perfection of it; as we must also judge of his intention and of the provisions employed in fulfilling that intention, not from an instance in which they fail but from the great plurality of instances in which they succeed. But, after all, these are different questions from the question of the artist's existence; or, which is the same, whether the thing before us be a work of art or not; and the questions ought always to be kept separate in the mind. So likewise it is in the works of nature. Irregularities and imperfections are of little or no weight in the consideration when that consideration relates simply to the existence of a Creator. When the argument respects His attributes, they are of weight; but are then to be taken in conjunction—the attention is not to rest upon them, but they are to be taken in conjunction with the unexceptionable evidence which we possess of skill, power, and benevolence displayed in other instances;

which evidences may, in strength, number, and variety, be such and may so overpower apparent blemishes as to induce us, upon the most reasonable ground, to believe that these last ought to be referred to some cause, though we be ignorant of it, other than defect of knowledge or of benevolence in the author.

14

David Hume (1711–1776)

David Hume was born in Edinburgh, Scotland, in 1711. Although his family wanted him to become a lawyer, he rejected this idea. Instead, he went to the University of Edinburgh for two years, eventually withdrawing to pursue private studies in philosophy, literature, and history. He continued his studies in philosophy in France between 1734 and 1737, during which time he wrote his Treatise on Human Nature. *After finishing his work, he returned to the U.K., spending a year and a half in London polishing and, eventually, publishing his* Treatise on Human Nature. *Disappointed with his books reception, Hume made his way from London to Scotland, seeking positions at the University of Edinburgh and University of Glasgow, both of which he did not get. Disappointed, Hume accepted a position of librarian at the Advocates' Library in Edinburgh in 1752. It was during his time as librarian that Hume wrote the*

Natural History of Religion, *which was published in 1757, and* Dialogues Concerning Natural Religion, *which was published posthumously in 1779. Hume was also an historian. He published his six-volume* History of England *between 1754 and 1762, making him very wealthy. In 1763, he accepted a position as the secretary to the British ambassador to France. He returned from France in 1766 and was appointed as an Under Secretary of State in the Home Office. Hume held the position for one year, whereupon he retired and returned to Edinburgh. He died of intestinal cancer in 1776. His other major works include* An Enquiry Concerning the Principles of Morals *(1751) and* Political Discourses *(1752).*

Dialogues Concerning Natural Religion

[The Weak Analogy Argument]

[...] Look round the world: Contemplate the whole and every part of it: You will find it to be nothing but one great machine, subdivided into an infinite number of lesser machines, which again admit of subdivisions to a degree beyond what human senses and faculties can trace and explain. All these various machines, and even their most minute parts, are adjusted to each other with an accuracy which ravishes into admiration all men who have ever contemplated them. The curious adapting of means to ends, throughout all nature, resembles exactly, though it much exceeds, the productions of human contrivance—of human designs, thought, wisdom, and intelligence. Since, therefore, the effects resemble each other, we are

led to infer, by all the rules of analogy, that the causes also resemble, and that the Author of Nature is somewhat similar to the mind of man, though possessed of much larger faculties, proportioned to the grandeur of the work which he has executed. By this argument *a posteriori,* and by this argument alone, do we prove at once the existence of a Deity and his similarity to human mind and intelligence.

I shall be so free, Cleanthes, said Demea, as to tell you, that from the beginning, I could not approve of your conclusion concerning the similarity of the Deity to men; still less can I approve of the mediums by which you endeavour to establish it. What! No demonstration of the Being of God! No abstract arguments! No proofs *a priori!* Are these, which have hitherto been so much insisted on by philosophers, all fallacy, all sophism? Can we reach no further in this subject than experience and probability? I will not say that this is betraying the cause of a Deity; but surely, by this affected candour, you give advantages to atheists which they never could obtain by the mere dint of argument and reasoning.

What I chiefly scruple in this subject, said Philo, is not so much that all religious arguments are by Cleanthes reduced to experience, as that they appear not to be even the most certain and irrefragable of that inferior kind. That a stone will fall, that fire will burn, that the earth has solidity, we have observed a thousand and a thousand times; and when any new instance of this nature is presented, we draw without hesitation the accustomed inference. The exact similarity of the cases gives us a perfect assurance of a similar event, and a stronger evidence is never desired nor sought after. But wherever you depart, in the least, from the similarity of the cases, you diminish proportionably the evidence; and may at last bring it to a very weak analogy, which is confessedly liable to error and uncertainty. After having experienced the circulation of the blood in human creatures, we make no doubt that it takes place in Titius and Maevius, but from its circulation in frogs and fishes, it is only a presumption, though a strong one, from analogy that it takes place in men and other animals. The analogical reasoning is much weaker when we infer the circulation of the sap in vegetables from our experience that the blood circulates in animals; and those who hastily followed that imperfect analogy are found, by more accurate experiments, to have been mistaken.

If we see a house, Cleanthes, we conclude, with the greatest certainty, that it had an architect or builder because this is precisely that species of effect which we have experienced to proceed from that species of cause. But surely you will not affirm, that the universe bears such a resemblance to a house that we can with the same certainty infer a similar cause, or that the analogy is here entire and perfect. The dissimilitude is so striking that the utmost you can here pretend to is a guess, a conjecture, a presumption concerning a similar cause; and how that pretension will be received in the world, I leave you to consider.

It would surely be very ill received, replied Cleanthes; and I should be deservedly blamed and detested did I allow that the proofs of a Deity amounted to no more than a guess or conjecture. But is the whole adjustment of means to ends in a house and in the universe so slight a resemblance? The economy of final causes? The order, proportion, and arrangement of every part? Steps of a stair are plainly contrived that human legs may use them in mounting; and this inference is certain and infallible. Human legs are also contrived for walking and mounting; and this inference, I allow, is not altogether so certain because of the dissimilarity which you

remark; but does it, therefore, deserve the name only of presumption or conjecture? [...]

[Cannot Reason from the Parts to the Whole]

That all inferences, Cleanthes, concerning fact, are founded on experience and that all experimental reasonings are founded on the supposition that similar causes prove similar effects, and similar effects similar causes, I shall not at present much dispute with you. But observe, I entreat you, with what extreme caution all just reasoners proceed in the transferring of experiments to similar cases. Unless the cases be exactly similar, they repose no perfect confidence in applying their past observation to any particular phenomenon. Every alteration of circumstances occasions a doubt concerning the event; and it requires new experiments to prove certainly that the new circumstances are of no moment or importance. A change in bulk, situation, arrangement, age, disposition of the air, or surrounding bodies—any of these particulars may be attended with the most unexpected consequences. And unless the objects be quite familiar to us, it is the highest temerity to expect with assurance, after any of these changes, an event similar to that which before fell under our observation. The slow and deliberate steps of philosophers here, if anywhere, are distinguished from the precipitate march of the vulgar, who, hurried on by the smallest similitude, are incapable of all discernment or consideration.

But can you think, Cleanthes, that your usual phlegm and philosophy have been preserved in so wide a step as you have taken when you compared to the universe houses, ships, furniture, machines; and, from their similarity in some circumstances, inferred a similarity in their causes? Thought, design, intelligence, such as we discover in men and other animals, is no more than one of the springs and principles of the universe, as well as heat or cold, attraction or repulsion, and a hundred others which fall under daily observation. It is an active cause by which some particular parts of nature, we find, produce alterations on other parts. But can a conclusion, with any propriety, be transferred from parts to the whole? Does not the great disproportion bar all comparison and inference? From observing the growth of a hair, can we learn any thing concerning the generation of a man? Would the manner of a leaf's blowing, even though perfectly known, afford us any instruction concerning the vegetation of a tree?

But, allowing that we were to take the *operations of* one part of nature upon another, for the foundation of our judgment concerning the *origin of* the whole (which never can be admitted), yet why select so minute, so weak, so bounded a principle, as the reason and design of animals is found to be upon this planet? What peculiar privilege has this little agitation of the brain which we call *thought,* that we must thus make it the model of the whole universe? Our partiality in our own favor does indeed present it on all occasions; but sound philosophy ought carefully to guard against so natural an illusion.

So far from admitting, continued Philo, that the operations of a part can afford us any just conclusion concerning the origin of the whole, I will not allow any one part to form a rule for another part if the latter be very remote from the former. Is there any reasonable ground to conclude that the inhabitants of other planets possess thought, intelligence, reason, or anything similar to these faculties in men? When nature has so extremely diversified her manner of operation in this small globe, can we imagine that she incessantly copies herself throughout so immense a universe? And if thought, as we may

well suppose, be confined merely to this narrow corner and has even there so limited a sphere of action, with what propriety can we assign it for the original cause of all things? The narrow views of a peasant who makes his domestic economy the rule for the government of kingdoms is in comparison a pardonable sophism.

But were we ever so much assured that a thought and reason resembling the human were to be found throughout the whole universe, and were its activity elsewhere vastly greater and more commanding than it appears in this globe; yet I cannot see why the operations of a world constituted, arranged, adjusted, can with any propriety be extended to a world which is in its embryo-state, and is advancing towards that constitution and arrangement. By observation, we know somewhat of the economy, action, and nourishment of a finished animal; but we must transfer with great caution that observation to the growth of a foetus in the womb, and still more in the formation of an animalcule in the loins of its male parent. Nature, we find, even from our limited experience, possesses an infinite number of springs and principles which incessantly discover themselves on every change of her position and situation. And what new and unknown principles would actuate her in so new and unknown a situation as that of the formation of a universe, we cannot, without the utmost temerity, pretend to determine. [...]

[God Is All Too Human]

Now, Cleanthes, said Philo, with an air of alacrity and triumph, mark the consequences. *First,* by this method of reasoning you renounce all claim to infinity in any of the attributes of the Deity. For, as the cause ought only to be proportioned to the effect, and the effect, so far as it falls under our cognizance, is not infinite; what pretensions have we, upon your suppositions, to ascribe that attribute to the divine Being? You will still insist that, by removing him so much from all similarity to human creatures, we give in to the most arbitrary hypothesis, and at the same time weaken all proofs of his existence.

Secondly, you have no reason, on your theory, for ascribing perfection to the Deity, even in his finite capacity, or for supposing him free from every error, mistake, or incoherence, in his undertakings. There are many inexplicable difficulties in the works of nature which, if we allow a perfect author to be proved *a priori,* are easily solved, and become only seeming difficulties, from the narrow capacity of man, who cannot trace infinite relations. But according to your method of reasoning, these difficulties become all real; and, perhaps, will be insisted on as new instances of likeness to human art and contrivance. At least, you must acknowledge that it is impossible for us to tell, from our limited views, whether this system contains any great faults, or deserves any considerable praise if compared to other possible and even real systems. Could a peasant, if the *Aeneid* were read to him, pronounce that poem to be absolutely faultless, or even assign to it its proper rank among the productions of human wit, he who had never seen any other production?

But were this world ever so perfect a production, it must still remain uncertain whether all the excellences of the work can justly be ascribed to the workman. If we survey a ship, what an exalted idea must we form of the ingenuity of the carpenter who framed so complicated, useful, and beautiful a machine? And what surprise must we feel, when we find him a stupid mechanic who imitated others, and copied an art which, through a long succession of ages, after multiplied trials, mistakes, corrections, deliberations, and controversies, had been

gradually improving? Many worlds might have been botched and bungled, throughout an eternity, ere this system was struck out; much labor lost, many fruitless trials made; and a slow, but continued improvement carried on during infinite ages in the art of world-making. In such subjects, who can determine, where the truth, nay, who can conjecture where the probability lies, amidst a great number of hypotheses which may be proposed, and a still greater which may be imagined?

And what shadow of an argument, continued Philo, can you produce from your hypothesis to prove the unity of the Deity? A great number of men join in building a house or ship, in rearing a city, in framing a commonwealth; why may not several deities combine in contriving and framing a world? This is only so much greater similarity to human affairs. By sharing the work among several, we may so much further limit the attributes of each, and get rid of that extensive power and knowledge, which must be supposed in one deity, and which, according to you, can only serve to weaken the proof of his existence. And if such foolish, such vicious creatures as man can yet often unite in framing and executing one plan, how much more those deities or demons, whom we may suppose several degrees more perfect?

To multiply causes without necessity is indeed contrary to true philosophy: but this principle applies not to the present case. Were one deity antecedently proved by your theory who were possessed of every attribute requisite to the production of the universe, it would be needless, I own (though not absurd), to suppose any other deity existent. But while it is still a question whether all these attributes are united in one subject, or dispersed among several independent beings, by what phenomena in nature can we pretend to decide the controversy?

Where we see a body raised in a scale, we are sure that there is in the opposite scale, however concealed from sight, some counterpoising weight equal to it; but it is still allowed to doubt whether that weight be an aggregate of several distinct bodies or one uniform united mass. And if the weight requisite very much exceeds any thing which we have ever seen conjoined in any single body, the former supposition becomes still more probable and natural. An intelligent being of such vast power and capacity as is necessary to produce the universe—or, to speak in the language of ancient philosophy, so prodigious an animal—exceeds all analogy, and even comprehension.

But further, Cleanthes, men are mortal, and renew their species by generation; and this is common to all living creatures. The two great sexes of male and female, says Milton, animate the world. Why must this circumstance, so universal, so essential, be excluded from those numerous and limited deities? Behold, then, the theogeny of ancient times brought back upon us.

And why not become a perfect anthropomorphite? Why not assert the deity or deities to be corporeal, and to have eyes, a nose, mouth, ears, etc.? Epicurus maintained that no man had ever seen reason but in a human figure; therefore the gods must have a human figure. And this argument, which is deservedly so much ridiculed by Cicero, becomes, according to you, solid and philosophical.

In a word, Cleanthes, a man who follows your hypothesis is able perhaps to assert or conjecture that the universe sometime arose from something like design; but beyond that position he cannot ascertain one single circumstance, and is left afterwards to fix every point of his theology by the utmost license of fancy and hypothesis. This world, for aught he knows, is very faulty and imperfect, compared to a superior standard; and was only the first rude essay of some infant deity who afterwards abandoned it, ashamed of his lame performance; it is the work only of some dependent, inferior deity, and is the object of derision to his superiors; it is the production of old age and dotage in some superannuated deity; and ever since his death has run on at adventures, from the first impulse and active force which it received from him. [...]

15

Richard Dawkins

(1941–)

Richard Dawkins' father moved to Kenya from England during the Second World War to join the Allied Forces. It was in Kenya that Dawkins was born in 1941 and raised until his family moved back to England in 1948. Between 1959 and 1962, Dawkins was an undergraduate of zoology at Balliol College, Oxford University. After graduating, Dawkins began his doctoral studies under the influential Dutch biologist Niko Tinbergen, who won a Nobel Prize in 1973 for his work on animal behaviour. Dawkins graduated with his Ph.D. from Oxford University in 1966, eventually taking up a teaching position at the University of California, Berkeley. He is currently Charles Simonyi Professor of the Public Understanding of Science at Oxford University, a

position he has held since 1995. He is married to actress and artist Lalla Ward. His books include The Selfish Gene *(1976),* The Blind Watchmaker: Why Evolution Reveals a Universe Without Design *(1986),* River Out of Eden: A Darwinian View of Life *(1995), and* The God Delusion *(2006).*

The Improbability of God

Much of what people do is done in the name of God. Irishmen blow each other up in his name. Arabs blow themselves up in his name. Imams and ayatollahs oppress women in his name. Celibate popes and priests mess up people's sex lives in his name. Jewish *shohets* cut live animals' throats in his name. The achievements of religion in past history—bloody crusades, torturing inquisitions, mass-murdering conquistadors, culture-destroying missionaries, legally enforced resistance to each new piece of scientific truth until the last possible moment—are even more impressive. And what has it all been in aid of? I believe it is becoming increasingly clear that the answer is absolutely nothing at all. There is no reason for believing that any sort of gods exist and quite good reason for believing that they do not exist and never have. It has all been a gigantic waste of time and a waste of life. It would be a joke of cosmic proportions if it weren't so tragic.

Why do people believe in God? For most people the answer is still some version of the ancient Argument from Design. We look about us at the beauty and intricacy of the world—at the aerodynamic sweep of a swallow's wing, at the delicacy of flowers and of the butterflies that fertilize them, through a microscope at the teeming life in every drop of pond water, through a telescope at the crown of a giant redwood tree. We reflect on the electronic complexity and optical perfection of our own eyes that do the looking. If we have any imagination, these things drive us to a sense of awe and reverence. Moreover, we cannot fail to be struck by the obvious resemblance of living organs to the carefully planned designs of human engineers. The argument was most famously expressed in the watchmaker analogy of the eighteenth-century priest William Paley. Even if you didn't know what a watch was, the obviously designed character of its cogs and springs and of how they mesh together for a purpose would force you to conclude "that the watch must have had a maker: that there must have existed, at some time, and at some place or other, an artificer or artificers, who formed it for the purpose which we find it actually to answer; who comprehended its construction, and designed its use." If this is true of a comparatively simple watch, how much the more so is it true of the eye, ear, kidney, elbow joint, brain? These beautiful, complex, intricate, and obviously purpose-built structures must have had their own designer, their own watchmaker—God.

So ran Paley's argument, and it is an argument that nearly all thoughtful and sensitive people discover for themselves at some stage in their childhood. Throughout most of history it must have seemed utterly convincing, self-evidently true. And yet, as the result of one of the most astonishing intellectual revolutions in history, we now know that it is wrong, or at least superfluous. We now know that the order and apparent purposefulness of the living world has come about through an entirely different process, a process that works without the need for any designer and one that is a consequence of basically very simple laws of physics. This is the process of evolution by natural selection, discovered by Charles Darwin and, independently, by Alfred Russel Wallace.

What do all objects that look as if they must have had a designer have in common? The answer is statistical improbability. If we find a transparent pebble washed into the shape of a crude lens by the sea, we do not conclude that it must have been designed by an optician: the unaided laws of physics are capable of achieving this result; it is not too improbable to have just "happened." But if we find an elaborate compound lens, carefully corrected against spherical and chromatic aberration, coated against glare, and with "Carl Zeiss" engraved on the rim, we know that it could not have just happened by chance. If you take all the atoms of such a compound lens and throw them together at random under the jostling influence of the ordinary laws of physics in nature, it is *theoretically* possible that, by sheer luck, the atoms would just happen to fall into the pattern of a Zeiss compound lens, and even that the atoms round the rim should happen to fall in such a way that the name Carl Zeiss is etched out. But the number of other ways in which the atoms could, with equal likelihood, have fallen, is so hugely, vastly, immeasurably greater that we can completely discount the chance hypothesis. Chance is out of the question as an explanation.

This is not a circular argument, by the way. It might seem to be circular because, it could be said, *any* particular arrangement of atoms is, with hindsight, very improbable. As has been said before, when a ball lands on a particular blade of grass on the golf course, it would be foolish to exclaim: "Out of all the billions of blades of grass that it *could* have fallen on, the ball actually fell on this one. How amazingly, miraculously improbable!" The fallacy here, of course, is that the ball had to land somewhere. We can

only stand amazed at the improbability of the actual event if we specify it *a priori:* for example, if a blindfolded man spins himself round on the tee, hits the ball at random, and achieves a hole in one. That would be truly amazing, because the target destination of the ball is specified in advance.

Of all the trillions of different ways of putting together the atoms of a telescope, only a minority would actually work in some useful way. Only a tiny minority would have Carl Zeiss engraved on them, or, indeed, *any* recognizable words of any human language. The same goes for the parts of a watch: of all the billions of possible ways of putting them together, only a tiny minority will tell the time or do anything useful. And of course the same goes, *a fortiori,* for the parts of a living body. Of all the trillions of trillions of ways of putting together the parts of a body, only an infinitesimal minority would live, seek food, eat, and reproduce. True, there are many different ways of being alive—at least ten million different ways if we count the number of distinct species alive today—but, however many ways there may be of being alive, it is certain that there are vastly more ways of being dead!

We can safely conclude that living bodies are billions of times too complicated—too statistically improbable—to have come into being by sheer chance. How, then, did they come into being? The answer is that chance enters into the story, but not a single, monolithic act of chance. Instead, a whole series of tiny chance steps, each one small enough to be a believable product of its predecessor, occurred one after the other in sequence. These small steps of chance are caused by genetic mutations, random changes—mistakes really—in the genetic material. They give rise to changes in the existing bodily structure. Most of these changes are deleterious and lead to death. A minority of them turn out to be slight improvements, leading to increased survival and reproduction. By this process of natural selection, those random changes that turn out to be beneficial eventually spread through the species and become the norm. The stage is now set for the next small change in the evolutionary process. After, say, a thousand of these small changes in series, each change providing the basis for the next, the end result has become, by a process of accumulation, far too complex to have come about in a single act of chance.

For instance, it is theoretically possible for an eye to spring into being, in a single lucky step, from nothing: from bare skin, let's say. It is theoretically possible in the sense that a recipe could be written out in the form of a large number of mutations. If all these mutations happened simultaneously, a complete eye could, indeed, spring from nothing. But although it is theoretically possible, it is in practice inconceivable. The quantity of luck involved is much too large. The "correct" recipe involves changes in a huge number of genes simultaneously. The correct recipe is one particular combination of changes out of trillions of equally probable combinations of chances. We can certainly rule out such a miraculous coincidence. But it *is* perfectly plausible that the modern eye could have sprung from something almost the same as the modern eye but not quite: a very slightly less elaborate eye. By the same argument, this slightly less elaborate eye sprang from a slightly less elaborate eye still, and so on. If you assume a *sufficiently large number of sufficiently small differences* between each evolutionary stage and its predecessor, you are bound to be able to derive a full, complex, working eye from bare skin. How many intermediate stages are we allowed to

postulate? That depends on how much time we have to play with. Has there been enough time for eyes to evolve by little steps from nothing?

The fossils tell us that life has been evolving on Earth for more than 3,000 million years. It is almost impossible for the human mind to grasp such an immensity of time. We, naturally and mercifully, tend to see our own expected lifetime as a fairly long time, but we can't expect to live even one century. It is 2,000 years since Jesus lived, a time span long enough to blur the distinction between history and myth. Can you imagine a million such periods laid end to end? Suppose we wanted to write the whole history on a single long scroll. If we crammed all of Common Era history into one metre of scroll, how long would the pre-Common Era part of the scroll, back to the start of evolution, be? The answer is that the pre-Common Era part of the scroll would stretch from Milan to Moscow. Think of the implications of this for the quantity of evolutionary change that can be accommodated. All the domestic breeds of dogs—Pekingeses, poodles, spaniels, Saint Bernards, and Chihuahuas—have come from wolves in a time span measured in hundreds or at the most thousands of years: no more than two meters along the road from Milan to Moscow. Think of the quantity of change involved in going from a wolf to a Pekingese; now multiply that quantity of change by a million. When you look at it like that, it becomes easy to believe that an eye could have evolved from no eye by small degrees.

It remains necessary to satisfy ourselves that every one of the intermediates on the evolutionary route, say from bare skin to a modern eye, would have been favored by natural selection; would have been an improvement over its predecessor in the sequence or at least would have survived. It is no good proving to ourselves that there is theoretically a chain of almost perceptibly different intermediates leading to an eye if many of those intermediates would have died. It is sometimes argued that the parts of an eye have to be all there together or the eye won't work at all. Half an eye, the argument runs, is no better than no eye at all. You can't fly with half a wing; you can't hear with half an ear. Therefore there can't have been a series of step-by-step intermediates leading up to a modern eye, wing, or ear.

This type of argument is so naive that one can only wonder at the subconscious motives for wanting to believe it. It is obviously not true that half an eye is useless. Cataract sufferers who have had their lenses surgically removed cannot see very well without glasses, but they are still much better off than people with no eyes at all. Without a lens you can't focus a detailed image, but you can avoid bumping into obstacles and you could detect the looming shadow of a predator.

As for the argument that you can't fly with only half a wing, it is disproved by large numbers of very successful gliding animals, including mammals of many different kinds, lizards, frogs, snakes, and squids. Many different kinds of tree-dwelling animals have flaps of skin between their joints that really are fractional wings. If you fall out of a tree, any skin flap or flattening of the body that increases your surface area can save your life. And, however small or large your flaps may be, there must always be a critical height such that, if you fall from a tree of that height, your life would have been saved by just a little bit more surface area. Then, when your descendants have evolved that extra surface area, their lives would be saved by just a bit more still if they fell from trees of a slightly greater height. And so on by insensibly graded

steps until, hundreds of generations later, we arrive at full wings.

Eyes and wings cannot spring into existence in a single step. That would be like having the almost infinite luck to hit upon the combination number that opens a large bank vault. But if you spun the dials of the lock at random, and every time you got a little bit closer to the lucky number the vault door creaked open another chink, you would soon have the door open! Essentially, that is the secret of how evolution by natural selection achieves what once seemed impossible. Things that cannot plausibly be derived from very different predecessors *can* plausibly be derived from only slightly different predecessors. Provided only that there is a sufficiently long series of such slightly different predecessors, you can derive anything from anything else.

Evolution, then, is theoretically *capable* of doing the job that, once upon a time, seemed to be the prerogative of God. But is there any evidence that evolution actually has happened? The answer is yes; the evidence is overwhelming. Millions of fossils are found in exactly the places and at exactly the depths that we should expect if evolution had happened. Not a single fossil has ever been found in any place where the evolution theory would not have expected it, although this *could* very easily have happened: a fossil mammal in rocks so old that fishes have not yet arrived, for instance, would be enough to disprove the evolution theory.

The patterns of distribution of living animals and plants on the continents and islands of the world is exactly what would be expected if they had evolved from common ancestors by slow, gradual degrees. The patterns of resemblance among animals and plants is exactly what we should expect if some were close cousins, and others more distant cousins to each other. The fact that the genetic code is the same in all living creatures overwhelmingly suggests that all are descended from one single ancestor. The evidence for evolution is so compelling that the only way to save the creation theory is to assume that God deliberately planted enormous quantities of evidence to make it *look* as if evolution had happened. In other words, the fossils, the geographical distribution of animals, and so on, are all one gigantic confidence trick. Does anybody want to worship a God capable of such trickery? It is surely far more reverent, as well as more scientifically sensible, to take the evidence at face value. All living creatures are cousins of one another, descended from one remote ancestor that lived more than 3,000 million years ago.

The Argument from Design, then, has been destroyed as a reason for believing in a God. Are there any other arguments? Some people believe in God because of what appears to them to be an inner revelation. Such revelations are not always edifying but they undoubtedly feel real to the individual concerned. Many inhabitants of lunatic asylums have an unshakable inner faith that they are Napoleon or, indeed, God himself. There is no doubting the power of such convictions for those that have them, but this is no reason for the rest of us to believe them. Indeed, since such beliefs are mutually contradictory, we can't believe them all.

There is a little more that needs to be said. Evolution by natural selection explains a lot, but it couldn't start from nothing. It couldn't have started until there was some kind of rudimentary reproduction and heredity. Modern heredity is based on the DNA code, which is itself too complicated to have sprung spontaneously into being by a single act of chance. This seems

to mean that there must have been some earlier hereditary system, now disappeared, which was simple enough to have arisen by chance and the laws of chemistry and which provided the medium in which a primitive form of cumulative natural selection could get started. DNA was a later product of this earlier cumulative selection. Before this original kind of natural selection, there was a period when complex chemical compounds were built up from simpler ones and before that a period when the chemical elements were built up from simpler elements, following the well-understood laws of physics. Before that, everything was ultimately built up from pure hydrogen in the immediate aftermath of the big bang, which initiated the universe.

There is a temptation to argue that, although God may not be needed to explain the evolution of complex order once the universe, with its fundamental laws of physics, had begun, we do need a God to explain the origin of all things. This idea doesn't leave God with very much to do: just set off the big bang, then sit back and wait for everything to happen. The physical chemist Peter Atkins, in his beautifully written book *The Creation,* postulates a lazy God who strove to do as little as possible in order to initiate everything. Atkins explains how each step in the history of the universe followed, by simple physical law, from its predecessor. He thus pares down the amount of work that the lazy creator would need to do and eventually concludes that he would in fact have needed to do nothing at all!

The details of the early phase of the universe belong to the realm of physics, whereas I am a biologist, more concerned with the later phases of the evolution of complexity. For me, the important point is that, even if the physicist needs to postulate an irreducible minimum that had to be present in the beginning, in order for the universe to get started, that irreducible minimum is certainly extremely simple. By definition, explanations that build on simple premises are more plausible and more satisfying than explanations that have to postulate complex and statistically improbable beginnings. And you can't get much more complex than an Almighty God!

The Problem of Evil

The evil that is in the world almost always comes of ignorance, and good intentions may do as much harm as malevolence if they lack understanding.
— Albert Camus

Evil is, good or truth misplaced.
— Mohandas Gandhi

Discussion Questions

1. First-year students are often quick to defend evil in the world. They point out that we live in a world of opposites and dichotomies—day and night; hot and cold; pleasure and pain; good and evil. Evil, for most students, is not only a necessary counterpart for goodness to exist but also necessary to come to know goodness. In what ways is evil a necessary counterpart to goodness? Discuss whether goodness would cease to exist in a world without evil. How might you know goodness without evil?

2. July 1, 2006, marked the 90th anniversary of the Battle of the Somme, one of the bloodiest battles of the First World War. Britain and her allies (including four Canadian divisions) staged a massive attack to penetrate German trenches. British loses at the end of the first day of fighting, from the 100,000 troops who advanced, totalled 60,000 casualties, including 20,000 dead or missing (Keegan 295). The 1st Newfoundland Regiment was virtually wiped out, with 710 of its 801 officers and men killed or wounded (Berton 63). The battle went on for five months, pushing the Germans back 10 kilometres at a horrific cost to human life: the combined dead, wounded, or missing Allied and German soldiers exceeded 1 million men, including 24,029 Canadians (Veterans Affairs Canada). Why might one argue that the Battle of the Somme was necessary to achieve good ends? Is there always a "silver lining" when evil events happen? Why or why not? What are your reasons for agreeing or disagreeing that the Battle of the Somme, amongst other wars, shows that God does not exist?

3. Does the free will defence undermine God's omnipotence? If God made humans with free will, this must mean that God cannot, or will not, intervene when people willing choose evil. According to atheists, there is no reason why God could not intervene when humans start to make evil, opposed to good, choices. Consider, once again, the Battle of the Somme. How could God have stepped in to prevent the mass slaughter during the First World War? Should God have stepped in to prevent people (Hitler, Pol Pot, Stalin, and so on) from fulfilling their evil intentions? Why or why not? Does lack of prevention make God powerless or callously indifferent to the plight of human suffering? Why or why not? In what ways does the free will problem show that God has limited power, knowledge, and goodness?

What Are Good and Evil?

Before start discussing the problem of evil, it's important to understand and clarify our terms. Although difficult to specifically define, the concepts of "good" and "evil" usually cover a broad range of things, including what are right/wrong, just/unjust, moral/immoral, pleasurable/painful, and so forth. Starting with evil, we can say that an event or act is evil if it falls under one of the following conditions (Trakakis):

a) Harm to a sentient being either physical or psychological which causes pain or suffering such as breaking a leg, having a miscarriage, or being held captive. b) Unjust treatment or some injustice occurs. The refusal to allow minorities or women the right to vote, for example, would be considered unjust. c) The loss of opportunity due to premature death not caused by natural causes or aging such as murder, car accident, earthquake, and so forth. d) Anything that prevents someone from leading a fulfilling and virtuous life. Living in severe poverty, for example, can deprive people of attaining their full potential and, subsequently, they may commit questionable acts such as stealing or prostituting themselves. e) Immoral choices or actions including murder, rape, genocide, theft, and so forth. f) The deprivation of good; absence of good in life such that a person fails to functional optimally as a person with inherent value and dignity.

Conversely, we can say that event or act is good if falls under one of the following conditions (Trakakis):

a) Improves the physical or psychological well being of a sentient being. So, for example, giving money to the homeless to buy food, rescuing a cat from a burning house, or giving sincere praise to others for some accomplishment. b) Just treatment of a sentience creature, which may include awarding promotions based on merit, financial compensation for wrongful imprisonment, an apology, or protecting species habitat to prevent extinction. c) Preventing premature death not due to natural causes or aging. For example, developing vaccinations or other medications to prevent life threatening diseases such as small pox or

diabetes. d) The improving or advancing of sentient creatures' lives so they can live a fulfilling and virtuous life. Setting minimal incomes to prevent poverty, access to education, and protecting habitat would be such examples. d) A person doing what is morally right such as not lying, cheating, stealing, and so forth. e) The bestowal of good such that a person can fulfill their full potential while maintaining their value and dignity.

Although this is by no means a complete analysis, it should be sufficient to give you a better understanding of how you could define good and evil. However, it is perhaps best to concentrate on some examples of evil to help drive home the previous definitions.

Examples of Evil

It's unfortunate, but true, that bad things happen to good people. Every day, somewhere in the world, people fall victim to murder, robbery, or sexual assault, to name only a few crimes. In Canada, according to government statistics, there were 302,000 incidences of violent crimes nationally in 2004, including 622 murders (1.9 homicides per 100,000 people), 26,000 robberies (86 robberies per 100,000 people), and 23,000 sexual assaults (74 sexual assaults per 100,000 people) (Sauve 6–7). In the United States, according to the Federal Bureau of Investigation (FBI), there were 16,137 homicides (5.5 homicides per 100,000 people), 401,326 robberies (136.7 robberies per 100,000 people), and 9,463,512[12] forcible rapes (32.2 rapes per 100,000 people) in 2004 (Federal Bureau of Investigation). These crimes are horrendous, but there are some criminal actions so unspeakably cruel and evil that they receive international media attention.

One of the most sensational murder trials in Canadian history is that of Paul Bernardo and his wife/accomplice Karla Homolka. In 1987, the couple met at a hotel restaurant in Scarborough, Ontario. Romance blossomed and they became engaged in 1989; however, their relationship was marked by an escalation in sexual fantasies each more perverted than the other. One such fantasy involved Karla's 15-year-old sister Tammy. On December 23, 1990, after a family dinner at Mr. and Mrs. Holmolka's home, Paul and Karla laced Tammy's drinks with a sedative. After the rest of the family went to bed, they took turns sexually assaulting an unconscious Tammy while the other videotaped the act. Unfortunately, complications arose and Tammy began choking on her own vomit. Attempts to revive her failed and she died. The police, in conjunction with the coroner, deemed Tammy's death an accident (Jenish, "Horror Stories").

Their sexual fantasies escalated to murder when, on June 14, 1991, Bernardo kidnapped 14-year-old Leslie Mahaffy at knifepoint and brought her back to their home in St. Catherines. For the next 24 hours, Bernardo and Homolka repeatedly raped and beat Mahaffy before finally strangling her with an electrical cord. Although Bernardo and Homolka videotaped the molestation, they did not record the murder. Her dismembered body was eventually found in a nearby lake. Police quickly identified Mahaffy as the victim, and a fruitless manhunt ensued (Jenish, "Horror Stories.").

Bernardo and Homolka's second murder victim was 15-year-old Kristen French. The teen was abducted from a church parking lot under the pretence that the couple was lost and looking for directions. After forcing French into their car, they once again took her back to their home. For three days the couple repeatedly molested and raped French, all of which was caught on videotape. Bernardo eventually strangled her with the same electrical cord used to kill Mahaffy. French's body was then dumped in a ditch (Jenish, "Horror Stories").

After French's murder, a task force was set up to investigate the murders and tips from the public. Meanwhile, the relationship between Bernardo and Homolka became strained. Bernardo began physically abusing Homolka to the point where she was hospitalized in early 1993. She filed charges against him, which peaked police interest, since they were also investing a number of unsolved rapes in the Scarborough area where Bernardo lived between 1987 and 1991. In 1990, Bernardo was a suspect in these attacks and gave blood and saliva samples to

police investigating the rapes, but, incredibly, his samples were not tested until 1993—a 26-month interval in which Mahaffy, French, and Tammy Homolka were killed (Jenish, "Heart of Darkness"). The forensic testing revealed conclusively that Bernardo had raped three women from the Scarborough area. (Bernardo was later admitted to police he was responsible for at least 14 rapes in Southern Ontario.) With this evidence in hand, police arrested Bernardo on February 13, 1993.

A few days after Bernard's arrest a warrant was issued to search his home, but police were unable to find the most damning evidence of all: the videotapes the pair had made of their crimes. Meanwhile, Homolka pleaded with police that she was an abused wife forced to engage in Bernardo's sick fantasies. To save her own skin, Homolka pleaded guilty to two counts of manslaughter and also made a deal with the Crown to testify against Bernardo in exchange for a reduced sentence of 12 years. However, the videotapes revealed Homolka as an eager and willing participant in much of the sexual crimes committed. Her allegations of abuse were highly exaggerated, and, subsequently, many critics have argued that the Crown should have reneged on the deal and charged her with the murders as well. The Crown refused. Homolka was released in 2005.

Bernardo's trial started in the summer of 1995. Over four months the jury of eight men and four women listened to 86 witnesses and, most importantly, watched the deeply disturbing videos of sexual degradation shot by Bernardo and Homolka. On September 1, the jury took just eight hours to reach a verdict of guilty, including the first-degree murders of Mahaffy and French. Bernardo was sentenced to 25 years in prison, and with the addition of being declared a dangerous offender, he will spend the rest of his life in jail (Jenish, "Heart of Darkness").

The impact of the rapes and murders on the Mahaffy, French, and Homolka families cannot be overstated. Their lives forever changed by the acts of two sadistic people bent on fulfilling their deprived fantasies. Victim impact statements were read out loud during Bernardo's sentencing, and one in particular, as described by D'Arcy Jenish in his article "Locked Up for Life," sums up what many Canadians were thinking at the time:

> Ryan Mahaffy is only 11 years old, but already the handsome, blond youngster understands the horror of rape and murder. He has grotesque nightmares. He receives psychological counselling. He has seen his parents lose their sense of humor, their lives consumed with sorrow and anger. Last week, the Grade 6 student from Burlington, Ont., spoke eloquently, and often tearfully, about his family's ordeal as part of a sentencing hearing for 31-year-old Paul Bernardo, who raped and murdered Ryan's 14-year-old sister, Leslie, and 15-year-old Kristen French. "You have changed my life in so many ways—some of them too personal to talk about," Ryan Mahaffy said, as Bernardo stared at him impassively from the prisoner's box. "Some people have called you a monster and evil, and I agree." (68)

Unfortunately, Bernardo is one of many sadistic murderers including Ted Bundy, Jeffrey Dahmer, Clifford Olson, Gary Ridgeway, and Charles Manson, to name a few. But they all have one thing in common: they inflicted evil upon the world that resulted in needless suffering.

Of course, if we look back through history, the sheer amount of human misery and suffering is mind boggling: 6 million Jews killed during the Second World War (see Box 3.5), 7 million people killed by Stalin, 2 million civilians murdered by Pol Pot in Cambodia, 800,000 lives lost in Rwanda—and the list goes on and on.

Nature also wreaks havoc on our world. At 7 a.m. (GMT) on December 26, 2004, an earthquake with a magnitude of 9.0 struck 100 miles off the Indonesian coast. According to the U.S. Geological Society, the energy released by the earthquake was equivalent to 23,000 Hiroshima-type bombs dropped at the end of the Second World War. The earthquake resulted in a gigantic wave some 10 metres high, known as a tsunami, inundating 11 countries in Asian and East Africa. The tsunami destroyed homes, schools, and medical facilities; it washed away roads, bridges, and power lines; it contaminated drinking water and destroyed crops. Given the magnitude of this disaster, we will perhaps never know how many people have actually been killed, but estimates put the death toll at 280,000, with 27,000 more missing and 1.2 million people displaced. The risk of death and sickness due to disease poses long-term challenges for these countries affected by the tsunami, which may regrettably take many more lives. There are other natural disasters that cause death and destruction: floods, mudslides, volcanic eruptions, tornadoes, and hurricanes result in thousands of deaths per year. And a trip to the local children's hospital will reveal nature's worst: cancer, leukemia, genetic disorders, and other deformities inflicted upon the most innocent.

These cases highlight a distinction usually made between moral and natural evils. **Moral evils** are regarded as morally culpable behaviour. That is, humans are held morally responsible for their actions. Moral evils include murder, theft, rape, torture, and so forth, because one's actions are freely chosen—one knowingly could have acted otherwise and, therefore, ought to be held accountable for one's behaviour. In contrast, **natural evils** include diseases, earthquakes, floods, tornadoes, tidal waves, and other natural phenomena. Natural evils are not the fault of human action, but the fault of various natural processes. This, of course, is controversial, since natural evil is often the result of human error or ignorance (Trakakis). Building houses and cities, like San Francisco, on unstable geological terrain is no fault of nature but of humans. Generally speaking, however, it can be said that nature is responsible for the evil inflicted upon thousands of people every year.

These examples also highlight what has come to be known as the **problem of evil**; one of the main arguments atheists use against God's existence. As William Rowe points out in his article, the problem of evil comes in two forms: the **logical problem** and the **evidential problem**. Let's start with the logical problem of evil.

Box 3.5 A Grim History of Concentration Camps

Auschwitz-Berkenau, where more than one million men, women, and children were killed between 1940 and 1945, mostly Jews from countries in Europe, was one of nearly 6,000 concentration camps set up by the Nazis in Poland during the Second World War.

Out of the 7.5 million prisoners of Nazi camps on Polish soil, some 6.7 million went to their deaths in gas chambers or died of hunger, illness, exhaustion from forced labour, or torture and other acts of brutality.

Six million Jews from Poland and other European countries were killed during the war, many of them perishing in specially built death camps, which played a key role in carrying out Adolf Hitler's gruesome "final solution"—the extermination of some 11 million Jews who lived in Europe.

Some 750,000 mainly Jewish men, women, and children were herded to their deaths in the gas chamber at Treblinka, which lies 80 kilometres northwest of Warsaw.

From June to December of 1942, the Nazis killed 600,000 people—550,000 of them Jewish—at Belzec camp, set up in the heart of the Jewish communities of southeastern Poland. Belzec's victims were killed by carbon-monoxide suffocation.

Of the 500,000 prisoners held at Majdanek, near the southeastern city of Lublin, 360,000 died in the gas chamber or were shot dead by the Nazis. Two hundred thousand were Jews, and 120,000 were Poles of other faiths and Soviet prisoners of war.

In a particularly twisted form of ingenuity, the Nazis transformed trucks into gas chambers at the death camp at Kulmhof—the German name given to the Polish town of Chelmno on the Ner, in central Poland—where 310,000 people were killed between 1941 and 1945.

Most of the victims of Kulmhof were Jews from Lodz, 70 kilometres from the camp.

The grim list continues. At Sobibor, near the eastern border with Ukraine, around 250,000 Jews from Poland and other Nazi-occupied European countries were killed. Stutthof, the German name for the Polish town of Sztutowo, which lies near the northern port of Gdansk, held 110,000 prisoners from 25 countries, of whom 65,000 died during captivity.

Stutthof also has the ignominy of being the first concentration camp to be set up by the Nazis outside Germany and the last to be liberated by the Allies. Its sinister operations began on Sept. 2, 1939, one day after the Nazi invasion of Poland that sparked the Second World War, and was liberated on May 10, 1945, two days after Victory in Europe day, which marked the end of the war.

Source: Agence France-Presse

Evil and the Logical Inconsistency of God

Evil is a problem because if God is omnibenevolent, omniscient, and omnipotent, then God ought to be able to prevent evil from happening in the first place. And since God does not prevent the unnecessary pain and suffering of innocent people, then God is not all knowing, all powerful, or all good. In short, evil undermines the very predicates that make God's existence necessary and worthy of worship.

Let me put the problem of evil another way. As a parent, I try to do everything in my power to prevent my child from unnecessary pain and suffering, and, thankfully, I am successful most of the time. Similarly, if there were an all-knowing and all-powerful God, then God would also do everything in his power to prevent needless suffering of his children (humans). But since there is needless suffering in the world, there cannot be a loving and powerful God. In other words, we would expect that an all-powerful, all-knowing, and all-good being could and would create a world free from evil. After all, an omniscient being would *know* what evil was to occur; an omnipotent being would *be able* to prevent evil; and an omnibenevolent being would *want* to prevent evil (Schick and Vaughn 445). In other words, if God has enough power to create and sustain our universe, then surely God can prevent evil. A being that does nothing is powerless, ignorant, or not good. Hence, a logical inconsistency entails. It's from the very fact that evil exists that God does not.

Philosophers and theologians have put forward a number of classic responses to justify God's existence in the face of evil in our world. Such theories are known as **theodicies**. Let's briefly look some of the key theodicies, as outlined by Rowe.

Evil Is Necessary for Good

As Rowe points out, it is sometimes said that evil is necessary to achieve good ends. This is not to say that God could not prevent evil—God could—it's just that there is no other way to achieve various goods without allowing evil to occur. For example, a general may knowingly sacrifice a few of his soldiers to protect a town besieged by the enemy. After all, if the general lets the enemy capture the town, then death, misery, and suffering of innocent lives would occur. We must not think, however, that the general is evil by sending his troop to fight and die for the town; it's merely a matter of fact that in order to save lives in the future and protect the town from the enemy, soldiers must be sacrificed (death = evil). As Rowe explains, perhaps some evils are connected to good in such a way that we cannot achieve the one without the other. Again, this is not to say that God was powerless to save the town—God could have—but evil is sometimes necessary to achieve good. In short, there is a logical relationship between good and evil that prevents excluding evil without excluding good.

The problem with this argument, say critics, is that, unlike the general, God is supposed to be omnipotent. And if God is omnipotent, then no matter how closely connected good and evil are, God will always be able to prevent evil and promote the good. Hence, such a being, by virtue of the fact that he does not prevent evil, does not exist.

However, as Rowe explains, what these critics fail to realize is that the relationship between good and evil is one of logical necessity. In just the same way it is logically impossible for God to make a round square or 2 + 2 = 5, it is logically impossible for God to achieve good ends while preventing evil from occurring. Therefore, since God cannot only do what is logically impossible, and it is logically impossible for God to prevent evil from occurring while achieving good ends, then it's not necessarily true that an omniscient, omnipotent, and good being would prevent any evil whatsoever. What Rowe argues is that God's power, knowledge, and goodness is not in contradiction with the fact that evil exists. Hence, it is by virtue of evil being a logical necessity of good that God exists.

The Free Will Defence

One of the most controversial objections against the problem of evil is the free will defence. The idea is that God created humans with free will; hence, we are responsible for evil, not God. Now it should be noted that God is often defined as omnipotent, but under this defence, God's power again is restricted to what is logically possible. In other words, it would be impossible for God to create humans with free will who are programmed to only do what is good. In short, if we only did good things, we would be like robots, which would contradict the supposition that we are free. So God had a choice to either: a) create a world in which there is no free will and no moral evil; or b) create a world with free agents and the possibility of humans doing evil (Lawhead 363). Free will, in other words, comes at a price: the price of humans making evil choices. And although Rowe does not go through detailed arguments against the free will defence, he does think that because evil is the sole responsibility of humans, there is no logical inconsistency between: (1) God exists and is all-knowing, all-powerful, and all-good; and (2) evil exists. This lack of inconsistency, says Rowe, poses problems for atheists, even if it turns out the free will defence is inadequate.

For the sake of clarity, let me raise one controversial objection against the free will defence not discussed by Rowe.

If God created humans with free will, why couldn't God make humans such that we always freely choose good over evil? In this way, God wouldn't be in a dilemma of choosing between making human-like robots with no free will and humans with free will with the potential of causing evil in the world. If God is all-powerful, then humans could be created such that we always choose the non-evil action. Clearly, this inability of God to make humans capable of only choosing good undermines his power and benevolence.

However, Daniel Howard-Snyder is quick to point out that if humans only made good—opposed to evil—choices, our freedom would be compromised. That is, being restricted to only good options is no freedom at all. The ability to make good/evil choices is a necessary condition for freedom. For example, if God gave us free will, then it is up to each individual to freely decide whether to go for a walk. Suppose you do, indeed, decide to go for a walk. Now suppose that God tried to make a world in which you *freely refrain* from going for a walk. Can He do it? No, because if God restricted your choice, and you refrain from going for a walk, then it cannot be said that you have free will. For if you had free will, you would go for a walk. Similarly, if God tried to make a world in which you freely refrain from robbery, murder, embezzlement, and other evils, then you would not have free will because God would be making your decisions for you. In short, free will requires evil.

But this theist response seems too strong. They claim that if God restricted our choices we would not have free will, but this is based on

the notion that our decisions necessarily entail a choice between good *or* evil. There is no reason to presume this. If we define free will as the ability to choose, then there will be many options open to us, and for most people, this does not mean choosing evil. In short, God could have created humans so that we only choose good options without undermining our free will. For example, imagine Fred discovers his wife of 20 years is having an extramarital affair behind his back. Fred's wife does not know that he knows. Distraught and angry, Fred sits in a local pub drowning his sorrows contemplating what to do. Free will dictates there are many viable options from which Fred could choose, including:

- Getting a divorce
- Forgiving his wife and rebuilding the relationship
- Murdering his wife and/or her lover
- Physically assaulting his wife and/or her lover
- Pretending it never happened
- Staying in the relationship, never letting on he knows about his wife's adultery, for the sake of the children
- Writing a note to his wife, demanding separation and then slipping away with the kids in the middle of the night
- Taking on a lover himself and stay in the marriage

Now what Fred ought to do in this situation is something he will have to freely decide for himself, but it's a mistake to assume that God could not restrict his choice to avoid evil. Fred could freely choose between a variety of good (or perhaps neutral) options like getting a divorce, forgiving his wife, or pretending it never happened, without having the option of inflicting pain and suffering, such as murder or physical assault, on others. Fred's options are not merely a choice between good *or* evil but a combination of both. If God restricted choice, it would not undermine free will. In fact, an omnipotent, omniscient, and omnibenevolent being could easily do so without compromising our ability to freely choose. Free will, in other words, does not justify evil.[13]

The Evidential Problem of Evil

The evidential problem of evil, says Rowe, is a more serious objection against God's existence. The evidential problem of evil is based on the idea that the amount of evil in the world provides rational justification, not logical necessity, for atheism. As I have pointed out earlier, there is unfortunately tremendous suffering in the world. Or consider Rowe's example. Suppose lightning strikes a tree and starts a forest fire. The fire traps a fawn resulting in horrific burns. The fawn eventually dies after a few days of excruciating pain. The pointless suffering of the animal (and humans) seems to suggest that an omniscient, omnipotent, and omnibenevolent being does not exist.

Evil Leads to Unknown Greater Goods

One of the main theodicies against the evidential problem of evil is known as the greater good defence. Similar to our earlier argument, it's based on the notion that evil is necessary to achieving some good. As Rowe states, there may be good consequences that arise from the fawn's pain and suffering. What kind of good consequences? Well, to name one, the fawn's death becomes an important food source for other animals and organisms, and without such food, some animals and organisms may suffer and die. Other examples of greater goods include immunization against various childhood diseases including diphtheria, tetanus, polio, measles, mumps, and rubella; the deaths of Tammy Homolka, Leslie Mahaffy, and Kristen French led to the capture of the Scarborough rapist and increased the speed at which DNA is tested; the Holocaust directly resulted in the development of the state of Israel and increased awareness about horrors of genocide; and the most significant good to come out of the Asian tidal wave has been tsunami awareness. The idea should be clear: without evil there would not be good in the world. The good that is achieved through various evils outweighs the negative consequences. A comparable or greater amount of good could not have been produced without evil.

Admittedly, however, knowing or recognizing these greater good is often difficult or impossible. After all, humans don't have God-like omniscience. But, for **sceptical theists**, despite these epistemological challenges, we have to put our faith in God that evil has a purpose. In the same way children are often ignorant of the good consequences produced by evil (e.g., vaccinations, surgery, etc.), which is allowed by good (loving) parents, humans may be ignorant of the good consequences of evil, which is allowed by a loving God. After all, given that God is infinitely more powerful and knowledgeable than humans, our minds may be unable to comprehend the goods that are a necessary outcome of evil.

But for Rowe, there is little reason to think evil justifies the good. The problem is that the good-parent analogy is weak. First, the parent, unlike the theistic God, has finite power. Although the parent might be unable to prevent evil from being inflicted upon their child, it's hard to believe an infinitely powerful, knowledgeable, and good God could not prevent pain and suffering in the world. Second, even if a child cannot comprehend the good produced by some evil (e.g., chemotherapy), parents usually make every effort to reassure their child is loved, cared for, and that the suffering will not last. On the basis of this good-parent analogy, says Rowe, God ought to be present consciously to humans when permissible suffering is to occur. Unfortunately, this is profoundly lacking. Humans fall victim to countless acts of evil every day without any awareness of God's presence or assurances that they are loved and cared for. So either God does not exist, says Rowe, or the analogy is inadequate as a defence of evil.[14]

Evil and Soul-Making

The last argument in support of God's existence, as outlined by Rowe, is the soul-making theodicy.

Theists can respond to the previous argument by asserting that the universe is better with some evil in it than if there were no evil in it. One way of supporting this defence is that without evil in the world, humans would not strive to become better people.[15] Without evil we would not develop good moral traits such as courage, forgiveness, compassion, sympathy, heroism, and so forth. According to John Hick, a leading proponent of the greater good defence, God's purpose for humans is to lead us beyond our biological needs to a personal life of eternal worth. And we can only achieve this eternal worth by alleviating, resisting, and overcoming evil. Just as parents must foster in their children quality and strength of character, which only comes through adversity, God allows evil in the world to build human souls. As Hick states,

> If, then, there is any true analogy between God's purpose for his human creatures, and the purpose of loving and wise parents for their children, we have to recognize that the present of pleasure and the absence of pain cannot be the supreme and overriding end for which the world exists. Rather, this world must be a place of soul-making. And its value is to be judged, not primarily by the quantity of pleasure and pain occurring in it at any particular moment, but by its fitness for its primary purpose, the purpose of soul-making. (171)

That is, by alleviating, resisting, and overcoming evil, not only do we help those around us, but we become better people as well. God can't create the ideal human, but by allowing evil to exist, we can learn from our own mistakes and work towards our utmost potential as spiritual beings. Moreover, it's by virtue of soul-making that humans can create the best world possible, perhaps a world filled with peace and harmony.

However, problems arise. As Rowe explains, if an innocent child is brutally beaten and murdered by an adult, it's unreasonable to think that the adult's moral development would be in jeopardy if God were to prevent this evil from occurring. Moreover, if evil is crucial to soul-building,

then we have a moral obligation not to reduce suffering in the world. If spiritual growth is the result of facing challenges (evil, suffering) and learning how to create a better world, then reducing suffering eliminates the opportunity for spiritual growth and develop virtues in accord with God's plan. In short, the more misery people go through, the better people they become. For example, independent researchers have estimated that approximately 38,000 to 42,000 Iraqi citizens have been killed by military operations since the United States–led invasion (Iraq Body Count). Given Hick's reasoning, we ought not work towards peace because in doing so we would be depriving the Iraqi citizenry a chance to become better people. From a moral point of view, this is absurd (Schick and Vaughn 454).

Adding to Rowe's article, let me raise two other problems with Hick's theodicy. First, if God is all-powerful and good, why couldn't He simply give us fully developed virtues without making us struggle against evil? To put another way, if benevolence, heroism, and sympathy are merely a means to happiness, safety, and well-being, then an omnipotent, omniscient, omnibenevolent being could make these virtues possible without evil. Or perhaps God could help us develop such character traits without the need of *real* evil in the world. For example, God could have created humans with superior imaginations or with the ability to create computer programs, drugs, or other kinds of machines to simulate evil. Simulated evil, opposed to real evil, would surely have the same effect and, yet, no one would suffer.

Second, the necessity of evil raises problems about how much suffering one has to go through in order to develop these moral characteristics? Everyone endures some amount of misery, but some people turn out to be decent and compassionate people, while enduring a gross amount of suffering, and others endure a minimal amount of suffering and turn out to be mean and uncaring people. As Edward H. Madden and Peter H. Hare explain in their book *Evil and the Concept of God*, the sheer magnitude of unnecessary evil in the world does not seem to justify the soul-building theodicy. Surely a minimal amount of unnecessary suffering would have equal effect on our character. Hick seems to be committing the "all or nothing fallacy." God either creates a world with no evil in it or creates a world just like ours with all of its pain and suffering. But the sheer amount of misery is not necessary; God's omnipotence suggests that God could have made a world with considerably less evil, which would be sufficient in developing our moral virtues. Moreover, what kind of suffering does one have to go through in order to become a decent human? If someone is a victim of sexual or physical abuse as a child, should we say their souls are better developed because they have suffered more? But notice the opposite might be true; victims of sexual assault may turn violent or sexual predators themselves. Psychological research seems to indicate a correlation between sex offenders and sexual victimization in childhood.[16] A study by Sonia Dhawan and W. L. Marshall revealed that of 29 rapists interviewed, 18 or 62 percent were victims of sexual abuse themselves. The same study showed 50 percent of child molesters were also victims of sexual abuse. This history of abuse, say Ray Coxe and William Holmes, seems to be an important factor in the backgrounds of sexual offenders and may even lead to a cycle of abuse. In another study, Dominique Simons, Sandy Wurtele, and Peggy Heil indicated that male childhood sexual abuse undermines the ability to empathize with others, and therefore, male victims are more likely to abuse women and children. Suffering can lead to people being defeated, resentful, demoralized, humiliated, helpless, dehumanized, and filled with hate. If evil can build souls, evil can also break souls, leading to more pain and suffering in the world.

So what are we to make of the problem of evil? Well, as Rowe explains, the logical problem of evil seems to provide convincing support for theists, while the evidential problem of evil seems to support atheism. Although both atheism and theism cannot both be true, clearly each of us must judge for ourselves whether there is rational support for believing in God or not.

16

William Rowe (1931–)

William L. Rowe, who received a Ph.D. in philosophy from the University of Michigan, is Professor Emeritus of Philosophy at Purdue University. He has published numerous articles on the philosophy of religion and metaphysics. His books include Philosophy of Religion: Selected Reading *(edited with William J. Wainwright), third edition (1998);* The Cosmological Argument *(1998);* Can God Be Free? *(2004); and* Philosophy of Religion: An Introduction, *fourth edition (2007), from which this reading is taken.*

The Problem of Evil

Thus far we have been engaged in acquainting ourselves with the major ideas of God that has emerged in western civilization—the theistic idea of God as a supremely good being, creator of but separate from and independent of world, omnipotent, omniscient, eternal, and self-existent (chapter 1)—and in examining some of the major attempts to justify belief in the existence of the theistic God (chapters 2 through 5). In chapters 2 through 4 we considered the three major arguments for the existence of God (Cosmological, Ontological, and Design), arguments which appeal to facts supposedly available to any rational person, whether religious or not. And in chapter 5 we examined religious and mystical experience as a source and justification for belief in God. In chapter 6 we considered the rule of faith in forming and sustaining religious beliefs, reflecting on the legitimate role of pragmatic reasons, as opposed to truth-conclusive reasons, in justifying religious belief. We also considered the important issue of whether belief in God might be rationally justified as a properly basic belief, without justification in terms of evidence derived from other beliefs. It is now time to turn to some of the difficulties for theistic belief—some of the sources which have been thought to provide grounds for atheism, the belief that the theistic God does not exist. The most formidable of these difficulties is the problem of evil.

The existence of evil in the world has been felt for centuries to be a problem for theism. It seems difficult to believe that a world with such a vast amount of evil as our world contains could be the creation of, and under the sovereign control of, a supremely good, omnipotent, omniscient being. The problem has confronted the human intellect for centuries and every major theologian has attempted to offer a solution to it.

There are two important forms of the problem of evil which we must be careful to distinguish. I shall call these two forms to the *logical* form of the problem of evil and the *evidential* form of the problem of evil. Although the important difference between these two forms of the problem will become fully clear only as they are discussed in detail, it will be useful to have a brief statement of each form of the problem set before us at the beginning of our inquiry. The logical form of the problem of evil is the view that the existence of evil in our world is *logically inconsistent* with the existence of the the-

istic God. The evidential form of the problem of evil is the view that the variety and profusion of evil in our world, although perhaps not logically inconsistent with the existence of the theistic God, provides, nevertheless, *rational support* for the atheism, for the belief that the theistic God does not exist. We must now examine each of these forms of the problem in some detail.

The Logical Problem

The logical form of the problem implies that theism is internally inconsistent, for the theist accepts each of the two statements which are logically inconsistent. The two statements in question are:

1. God exists and is omnipotent, omniscient, and wholly good.
2. Evil exists.

These two statements, so the logical form of the problem exists, are logically inconsistent in the same way as

3. This object is red.

is inconsistent with

4. This object is not colored.

Suppose, for the moment, that the proponent of the logical form of the problem of evil were to succeed in proving to us that statements 1 and 2 are logically inconsistent. We would then be in the position of having to reject either 1 or 2, for if two statements are logically inconsistent, it is impossible for both of them to be true. If one of them is true, then the other *must* be false. Moreover, since we could hardly deny the reality of evil in our world, it seems we would have to reject belief in the theistic God; we would be driven to the conclusion that atheism is true. Indeed, even if we should be tempted to reject 2, leaving us to the option of believing 1, this temptation is not one to which most theists could easily yield. For most theists adhere to religious traditions which emphasize the reality of evil in our world. In the Judeo-Christian tradition, for example, murder is held to be an evil, sinful act, and it can hardly be denied that murder occurs in our world. So, since theists generally accept and emphasize the reality of evil in our world, it would be something of a disaster for theism if the central claim in the logical form of the problem of evil were established; that 1 is logically inconsistent with 2.

Establishing Inconsistency

How can we establish that two statements are inconsistent? Sometimes nothing needs to be established because the two statements are *explicitly* contradictory, as, for example, the statements "Elizabeth is over five feet tall" and "Elizabeth is not over five feet tall." Often, however, two inconsistent statements are not explicitly contradictory. In such cases we can establish that they are inconsistent by deriving from them two statements that are explicitly contradictory. Consider statements 3 and 4, for example. It's clear that these two statements are logically inconsistent; they cannot both be true. But they are not explicitly contradictory. If asked to prove that 3 and 4 are inconsistent, we can do this by deriving explicitly contradictory statements we need to add another statements to 3 and 4.

5. Whatever is red is colored.

From 3, 4, and 5 we can then easily derive the explicitly contradictory pair of statements, "This object is colored" (from 3 and 5) and "This object is not colored" (repetition of 4). This, then, is the procedure we may follow if we are asked to establish our claim that two statements are logically inconsistent.

Before we consider whether the proponent of the logical form of the problem of evil can *establish* the claim that statements 1 and 2 are logically inconsistent, one very important point about the procedure for establishing that two statements are logically inconsistent needs to be clearly understood. When we have two statements which are not explicitly contradictory, and we want to establish that they are logically inconsistent, we do this by adding some further statement or statements to them and then deriving from the entire group (the original pair and the additional statement or statements) a pair of statements that are explicitly contradictory. Now the point that needs very careful attention is this: in order for this procedure to work, the statement or statements we add must be not just true but *necessarily true*. Notice, for example, that the statement we added to 3 and 4 in order to establish that they are inconsistent is a necessary truth—it is logically impossible for something to be red but not colored. If, however, the additional statement or statements used in order to deduce the explicitly contradictory statements are true, but not necessarily true, then although we may succeed in deducing explicitly contradictory statements, we will *not* have succeeded in showing that the original pair of statements are logically inconsistent.

To see that this is so let's consider the following pair of statements:

6. The object in my right hand is a coin.
7. The object in my right hand is not a dime.

Clearly, 6 and 7 are *not* logically inconsistent, for both of them might be, or might have been, true. They aren't logically inconsistent because there is nothing logically impossible in the idea that the coin in my right hand should be a quarter or a nickel. (Contrast 6 and 7 with 3 and 4. Clearly there is something logically impossible in the idea that this object be red and yet not colored.) But notice that we can add a statement to 6 and 7 such that from the three of them explicitly contradictory statements can be derived.

8. Every coin in my right hand is a dime.

From 6, 7, and 8 we can derive the explicitly contradictory pair of statements. "The object in my right hand is a dime" (from 6 and 8) and "The object in my right hand is not a dime" (repetition of 7). Now suppose 8 is true, that in fact every coin in my right hand is a dime. We will have succeeded, then, in deducing explicitly contradictory statements from our original pair, 6 and 7, with the help of the *true* statement 8. But, of course, by this procedure we won't have established that 6 and 7 are logically inconsistent. Why not? Because 8—the additional statement—although true, is not necessarily true. Statement 8 is not a necessary truth because I might (logically) have had a quarter or a nickel in my right hand. Statement 8 is in fact true, but since it logically could have been false, it is not a necessary truth. We must, then, keep clearly in mind that to *establish* two statements to be logically inconsistent by adding a statement and then driving explicitly contradictory statements, the additional statement must be not just true, but necessarily true.

Application to the Logical Problem of Evil

Since (1) "God exists and is omnipotent, omniscient, and wholly good" and (2) "Evil exists" are not explicitly contradictory, those who hold that 1 and 2 are logically inconsistent need to make good this claim by adding a necessarily true statement to 1 and 2 and deducing explicitly contradictory statements. But what statement might we add? Suppose we begin with

9. An omnipotent, omniscient, good being will prevent the occurrence of any evil whatsoever.

From 1, 2, and 9 we can derive the explicitly contradictory statements, "No evil exists" (from 1 and 9) and "Evil exists" (repetition of 2). So if we can show that statement 9 is necessarily true, we will have succeeded in establishing the thesis of the logical form of the problem of evil; that 1 and 2 are logically inconsistent. But is 9 necessarily true? Well, recalling our discussion of omnipotence, it would seem that God would have the power to prevent any evil whatever, for "preventing the occurrence of an evil" does not appear to be a logically contradictory task like "making a round square." But it is no easy matter to establish that 9 is necessarily true. For in our own experience we know that evil is sometimes connected with good in such a way that we are powerless to achieve the good without permitting the evil. Moreover, in such instances, the good sometimes outweighs the evil, so that a good being might intentionally permit the evil to occur in order to realize the good which outweighs it.

Gottfried Leibniz gives the example of a general who knows that in order to achieve the good of saving the town from being destroyed by an attacking army he must order his men to defend the town, with the result that some of his men will suffer and die. The good of saving the women and children of the town outweighs the evil of the suffering and death of a few of the town defenders. Although he could have prevented their suffering and death by ordering a hasty retreat of his forces, the general cannot do so without losing the good of saving the town and its inhabitants. It certainly does not count against the general's goodness that he permits the evil to occur in order to achieve the good which outweighs it. Perhaps, then, some evils in our world are connected to goods which outweigh them in such a way that even God cannot achieve the goods in question without permitting the evils to occur that are connected to those goods. If this is so, statement 9 is not necessarily true.

Of course, unlike the general's, God's power is unlimited, and it might be thought that no matter how closely evil and good may be connected, God could always achieve the good and prevent evil. But this overlooks the possibility that the occurrence of some evils in our world is *logically necessary* for the achievement of goods which outweigh them so that the task of bringing about those goods without permitting the evils that are connected to them is as impossible a task as making a round square. If so, then, again, while being omnipotent God could prevent the evils in question from occurring, he could not, even though omnipotent, achieve the outweighing goods while preventing the evils from occuring.[1] Therefore, since (i) omnipotence is not the power to do what is logically impossible and (ii) it may be logically impossible to prevent the occurrence of certain evils in our world and yet achieve some very great goods that outweigh those evils, we cannot be sure that statement 9 is necessarily true; we can be sure that an omnipotent,

wholly good being will prevent the occurrence of any evil whatever.

What we have just seen is that the attempt to establish that 1 and 2 are inconsistent by deducing explicitly contradictory statements from 1, 2, and 9 is a failure. For although 1, 2, and 9 do yield explicitly contradictory statements, we are not in a position to know that 9 is necessarily true.

The suggestion that emerges from the proceeding discussion is that we replace 9 with

10. A good omnipotent, omniscient being prevents the occurrence of any evil that is not logically necessary for the occurrence of a good which outweighs it.

Statement 10, unlike 9, takes into account the possibility that certain evils might be so connected to goods which outweigh them that even God cannot realize those goods without permitting the evils to occur. Statement 10, then, appears to be not only true but necessarily true. The problem now, however, is that from 1, 2, and 10, explicitly contradictory statements cannot be derived. All that we can conclude from 1, 2, and 10 is that the evils which do exist in our world are logically necessary for the occurrence of goods which outweigh them, and that statement is not an explicit contradiction.

The general difficulty affecting attempts to establish that 1 and 2 are logically inconsistent is now apparent. When we add a statement, such as 9, which allows us to derive explicitly contradictory statements, we cannot be sure that the additional statement is necessarily true. On the other hand, when we add a statement, such as 10, which does seem to be necessarily true, it turns out that explicitly contradictory statements cannot be derived. No one has succeeded in producing a statement which is known to be necessarily true *and* which, when added to 1 and 2, enables us to derive explicitly contradictory statements. In view of this, it is reasonable to conclude that the logical form of the problem of evil is not much of a problem for theism. Its central thesis, that 1 and 2 are logically inconsistent, is a thesis that no one has been able to establish by a convincing argument.

The "Free Will Defense"

Before turning to the evidential form of the problem of evil, it is important to understand the bearing of one traditional theistic defense on the logical form of the problem of evil. According to this defense—the "Free Will Defense"—God, even though omnipotent, *may not have been able* to create a world in which there are free human creatures without, thereby, permitting the occurrence of considerable evil. The basic assumption in this defense is that it is logically impossible for a person both to perform some act *freely* and to have been *caused* to perform that act. Without this assumption, the Free Will Defense collapses. For if it is possible for a person to be caused to do an act and yet to perform that act freely, then clearly God could have created a world in which there are free human creatures who only do what is right, who never do evil—for he, being omnipotent, could simply create the creatures and cause them to do only what is right.

Let's suppose that the basic assumption of the Free Will Defense is true, that it is logically impossible to be caused to do an act and yet to do that act freely. What this assumption means is that although God can cause there to be creatures and cause them to be free with respect to a certain act, he *cannot* cause them

freely to perform the act, and he cannot cause them freely to refrain from performing the act, whether the person performs the act or refrains from performing it will be up to that person, and not up to God, if the performing or refraining is to be freely done. Now suppose God creates a world with free human creatures, creatures who are free to do various things, including good and evil. Whether the free human creatures he creates will exercise their freedom to do good or evil will be up to them. And it is logically possible that no matter what free creatures God causes to exist, each of them will use his freedom on some occasion to do evil. Since this is so, it is *possible* that God could not have created a world with free creatures who do only what is right; it is possible that any world that God can create containing creatures free to do good or evil is a world in which these creatures sometimes do evil.

What the above line of argument endeavors to establish is that it is logically possible that the following statement is true.

11. God, although omnipotent, cannot create a world in which there are free human creatures and no evil.

But if it is possible that 11 is true, and also possible that a world with free human creatures is a better world than a world without free human creatures, then it follows that 1 and 2 are not inconsistent at all. For consider the following group of statements:

1. God exists and is omnipotent, omniscient, and wholly good.
11. God, although omnipotent, cannot create a world in which there are free human creatures and no evil.

12. A world with free human creatures and some evil is a better world than a world with no free human creatures.
13. God creates the best world he can.

From 1, 11, 12, and 13 it follows that 2 "Evil exists." But if 1, 11, 12, and 13 imply 2 and there is no inconsistency in 1, 11, 12, and 13, then there can be no inconsistency between 1 and 2. If a group of statements is not inconsistent, then no statement that follows from that group can be inconsistent with any or all statements in the group.

We can now see the relevance of the Free Will Defense to the logical form of the problem of evil. We objected to the logical form of the problem of evil because no one has succeeded in establishing its central thesis, that (1) "God is omnipotent, omniscient, and wholly good" is inconsistent with (2) "Evil exists." But, of course, from the fact that no one has *proved* that 1 and 2 are inconsistent, it doesn't follow that they aren't inconsistent. What the Free Will Defense endeavors to do is to go to the final step, to *prove* that 1 and 2 are really consistent. It does this by trying to establish that it is *possible* (logically) that both 11 and 12 are true and that there is no logical inconsistency in the group of statements 1, 11, 12, and 13. Whether the Free Will Defense is successful in its aim of showing that 1 and 2 are logically consistent is a matter too complicated and controversial for us to pursue here.[2] Even if it is unsuccessful, however, the theist need not be unduly troubled by the logical form of the problem of evil, for, as we've seen, no one has established 1 and 2 are inconsistent.

The Evidential Problem

I turn now to the evidential form of the problem of evil—the form of the problem which holds that the variety and profusion of evil in our world, although perhaps not logically inconsistent with the existence of God, nevertheless provides *rational support* for the belief that the theistic God does not exist. In developing this form of the problem of evil, it will be useful to focus on some particular evil that our world contains in considerable abundance. Intense human and animal suffering, for example, occurs daily and in great plenitude in our world. Such intense suffering is a clear case of evil. Of course, if the intense suffering leads to some greater good, a good we could not have obtained without undergoing to the suffering in question, we might conclude that the suffering is justified, but it remains an evil nevertheless. For we must not confuse the intense suffering in and of itself with the good things to which it sometimes leads or of which it may be a necessary part. Intense human or animal suffering is *in itself* bad, an evil, even though it may sometimes be justified by virtue of being a part of, or leading to, some good which is unobtainable without it. What is evil in itself may sometimes be good as a *means* because it leads to something which is good in itself. In such a case, while remaining an evil in itself, the intense human or animal suffering is, nevertheless, an evil which someone might be morally justified in permitting.

Taking intense human or animal suffering as an intrinsic evil, however, does not mean that the capacity to experience intense suffering is itself bad or evil. For as we've seen, there are times when experiencing intense suffering is very helpful in that it may cause us to act quickly to remove ourselves from extremely harmful situations. So, the capacity to experience intense suffering is helpful to us. Moreover, something that is bad in itself (intense pain or suffering) may sometimes serve a good purpose. The evidential form of the problem of evil is based on instances of intense human or animal suffering that apparently serve no good purpose at all. Here we develop the argument focusing on an example of animal suffering: a fawn's being horribly burned in a fire caused by lightning, and suffering terribly for five days before death ends its life. Unlike humans, fawns are not credited with free will, and so the fawn's terrible suffering cannot be attributed to its misuse of free will. Why then would God permit it to happen when, if he exists, he could have so easily prevented it? It is generally admitted that we are simply unable to imagine any greater good whose realization can reasonably be thought to require God to permit that fawn's terrible suffering. And it hardly seems reasonable to suppose there is some greater evil that God would have been unable to prevent had he not permitted that fawn's five days of suffering. Suppose that by a "pointless evil" we mean *an evil that God (if he exists) could have presented without thereby losing an outweighing good or hating to permit an evil equally bad or worse.* Is the fawn's suffering a pointless evil? Clearly, the fawn's terrible suffering over five days certainly *seems* to us to be pointless. On that point there appears to be near universal agreement. For given God's omniscience and absolute power it would be child's play for him to have prevented either the fire or the fawn's being caught in fire. Moreover, as we've noted, it is extraordinarily difficult to think of a greater good whose realization can sensibly be thought to require God to permit the fawn's suffering. And it is just as difficult to imagine an equal or even worse evil that God would be required to permit were he to have prevented the fawn's suffering. It therefore seems altogether reasonable to think that the

fawn's suffering is a pointless evil, an evil that God (if he exists) could have prevented without thereby losing some outweighing good or having to permit some other evil just as bad or worse.

In light of such examples of horrendous evils, the evidential argument can be started as follows:

1. Probably there are pointless evils (e.g., the fawn's suffering).
2. If God exists, there are no pointless evils.

Therefore,

3. Probably, God does not exist.

This argument grows out of the not uncommon view that terrible evils occur daily in our world, evils we have reason to believe an all-powerful, all-knowing, perfectly good being would prevent. And it appears to provide us with a good reason to think it likely that God does not exist.

Responses to the Evidential Problem

Of course the two forms of evil we've considered, the first (the *logical* form) seems not to be a serious difficulty for theistic belief. The second (the *evidential* form) does seem to be a significant difficulty, for its basic thesis — that the profusion of terrible evil in our world provides reason to think that God does not exist—appears to be plausible. We must now consider two important responses to the challenge posed by the evidential problem of evil.

Skeptical Theism

Within the field of philosophy there has emerged a position known as *skeptical theism*. Skeptical theism can be roughly described as the position which holds that arguments against the truth of theism suffer from the defect of presupposing certain claims to be true that are either false or not shown to be true. The skeptical theist's response to the evidential argument from evil is that the crucial premise in the argument (Probably, there are pointless evils) has not been shown to be true; for, according to the skeptical theist, we have no adequate reason to think it is even likely that there is no good that would justify God in permitting either the fawn's terrible suffering or any other case of terrible suffering of which we are aware. Why are we disposed to think that the fawn's suffering is very likely pointless? It is because we cannot think of or even imagine a good that would both outweigh the fawn's suffering and be such that an all-powerful, all-knowing being could not find some way of bringing about that good, or some equal or better good, without having to permit the fawn's terrible suffering. Think again of the fawn's suffering. It is not only terribly burned, but it lives for five days on the forest floor in agony, before death finally ends its life. Is there some great good that an all-powerful, all-knowing being could bring about only by allowing that fawn to suffer for five full days, rather than, say, four, three, two, one, or even not at all—say, by mercifully bringing it about that its death is instantaneous with its being horribly burned? It baffles the human mind to think that an all-power, all-knowing being would find itself in such a predicament. But the skeptical theist's response is that, *for all we know,* the reason why the human mind is baffled by this state of affairs is simply because it doesn't know enough. The suggestion is that if God exists and we were to know what God knows, then we might know that God really had no choice at all. For, according to the skeptical theist, God might very well know that if he prevented that fawn's being terribly burned, or prevented even

one day of the fawn's five days of terrible suffering, he either would have to permit some other evil equally bad or worse or forfeit some great good, with the result that the world as a whole would be worse than it is by virtue of his permitting that fawn to suffer intensely for five days. Furthermore, the fact that we can't imagine what that good might be is not at all surprising given to disparity between the goods knowable by our minds and the goods knowable by a perfectly good, all-knowing creator of the world. So, according to the skeptical theist, we simply are in no position to *reasonably judge* that God could have prevented the fawn's five days of terrible suffering without losing some outweighing good or having to permit some equally bad or worse evil. Our limited minds are simply unable to think of the goods that the mind of God would know. And since we are simply unable to know many of the goods God would know, the fact that no good *we know* of can reasonably be thought to justify an infinitely good, all-powerful being in permitting the fawn's terrible suffering is not really surprising. In fact, given the enormous gulf between God's knowledge and our knowledge, that no good we know of appears to in any way justify God in permitting the fawn's terrible suffering is perhaps just what we should expect if such a being as God actually exists.[3]

Stephen Wykstra, a proponent of skeptical theism, has argued that to reasonably believe that the fawn's suffering is likely to have been pointless we must have a *positive reason* to think that if some good should justify God in permitting the fawn's suffering it is likely that we would know of that good. But goods knowable to God, he claims, are quite likely not going to be knowable to us. To illustrate his claim Wykstra points out that upon looking in his garage and seeing no dog, we would be entitled to conclude that there is no dog in the garage. But upon looking in his garage and seeing no fleas, we would not be entitled to conclude that there are no fleas in his garage. For we have reason to think that if there were any fleas in his garage it would not be likely that we would see them. And similarly, our not being able to think of a good that might justify God in permitting the fawn's suffering does not entitle us to think there isn't such a good. For, on Wykstra's view, were there such a God-purposed good for permitting the fawn's suffering it is altogether likely that we would not know of it. So, the fact that we cannot even imagine what such a good would be, far from being a reason to think it unlikely that God exists, is just what we should expect to be true if God does exist.

Wykstra acknowledges that a wholly good God would allow suffering such as the fawn's terrible suffering, only if "there is an outweighing good served by so doing." He also notes "that such goods are, in many cases, nowhere within our ken." But he then says:

> The linchpin of my critique has been that if theism is true, this is just what one would expect: for if we think carefully about the sort of being theism proposes for our belief, it is entirely expectable—given what we know of our cognitive limits— that the goods by virtue of which this Being allows known suffering should very often be beyond our ken. Since this state of affairs is just what one should expect if theism were true, how can its obtaining be evidence *against* theism? (p. 91)

In his essay Wykstra points out that, among believers as well as nonbelievers, there is a "persistent intuition that the inscrutable suf-

fering in our world in some sense disconfirms theism." Believers too, he notes, have a strong, natural tendency to see inscrutable suffering, especially as it affects those they dearly love, as an intellectual difficulty or obstacle to belief, something that in the absence of a sensible explanation tends to count against theism. He, nevertheless, thinks that this persistent intuition of believers and nonbelievers is a mistake. For given our cognitive limitations and God's omniscience and omnipotence, he believes that it should be expected that much of the suffering in our world will be inscrutable to us. So, he concludes that believers and nonbelievers simply fail to see what is really contained in the theistic hypothesis.

An analogy to which Wykstra appeals in defending the reasonableness of supposing that the goods justifying the horrendous evils in our world are unknowable by us is the *good-parent analogy*. The idea is that God, being perfectly loving, is to us humans as good parents are to their children whom they love. And just as their children often cannot comprehend the goods for which their loving parents permit things to happen to them, so too we humans cannot comprehend the goods for which God permits us, his created children, to endure the evils that happen to us. There is, however, genuine disagreement over whether this analogy proposed by Wykstra is as favourable to theism as Wykstra supposes. It is true that good, loving parents may have to permit their ailing child to be separated from them, confined to a hospital, forced to swallow evil-tasting medicines, and put in the care of strangers in order to cure the child of some illness. The very young child, of course, may not understand why his parents have removed him from his home and left him in the care of strangers. So too, the theist may say, our sin or something beyond our comprehension may have separated us from God. But the good-parent analogy is in other respects a failure. When children are ill and confined to a hospital, the loving parents by any means possible seek to comfort their child, giving special assurances of their love while he is separated from them and suffering for a reason he does not understand. No loving parents use their child's stay in the hospital as an occasion to take a holiday, saying to themselves that the doctors and nurses will surely look after little Johnny while they are away. But countless human beings, including many believers, have endured horrendous suffering without any awareness of God's assurances of his love and concern during their period of suffering. Evidence for this claim can be found in the literature concerning the holocaust victims. Indeed, contrary to Wykstra's view, some who consider the issue of divine silence and hiddenness conclude that given the horrendous evils in our world, the absence of God is decisive evidence that there is no God.[4] For surely, it is claimed, if there were a loving god he would wish to make his presence known to us, given that the horrendous evils in our world seem to provide us with reason to doubt his existence. The evil and suffering in our world, as Wykstra acknowledges, are judged by many people to be grounds for concluding that no such being as God exists. And the apparent hiddenness of God seems only to provide further grounds to conclude that no such being exists. The skeptical theists, however, make a good point in arguing that if God does not exist, then since his knowledge would far exceed ours, it would not be unlikely that there would be goods beyond our ken that he would know, goods whose realization, for all we know, may justify God both in being hidden from us

and in permitting all the human and animal suffering not due to a misuse of human free will. Clearly, this problem will continue to be a serious issue for human thought and controversy for some time to come.

Theodicies

The second response consists in presenting a theodicy—an attempt to explain what God's purposes might be permitting the profusion of evil in our world. Unlike the response of skeptical theism, which consists in questioning whether the sufficient reasons have been given to show that premise 1 in the evidential argument is true, a theodicy endeavors to provide some positive reasons to think that premise 1 may well be false. Rather than providing very brief comments about various theodicies—evil is punishment for sin, evil is due to free will, evil is necessary for us to appreciate good, etc.—it will be more helpful for us to look in some depth at one of the more promising theodicies, a theodicy for "soul-making," developed and defended by the prominent contemporary philosopher and theologian John Hick.[5]

Before giving a synopsis of the soul-making theodicy, it will be useful to reflect on the general bearing of theodicies on the evidential problem of evil. Just what does a theodicy endeavor to do? Does it propose to tell us in some detail just what good it is that justifies God in permitting the fawn's suffering? No. Such an account would presume a knowledge of God's specific purposes, a knowledge that it would be unreasonable to expect we would have without some detailed revelation from God. What a theodicy does endeavor to do is to fasten on some good (real or imaginary) and argue that achieving that good would justify an omnipotent being in permitting evil like the fawn's suffering. Whether obtaining the good in question is God's actual reason for permitting evils like the fawn's suffering is really part of what a theodicy tries to establish. It only hopes to show that *if* obtaining the good in question were God's aim in permitting evils like the fawn's suffering, then (given what we know) it would be reasonable to believe that an omnipotent being would be justified in permitting such evils. In that, then, a theodicy endeavors to cast doubt on premise 1 in our argument from evil.

The fawn's suffering is an instance of *natural* evil—evil that results from natural forces. When a person tortures and kills an innocent, the suffering of the child is an instance of *moral* evil—evil that results from the conscious decision of some personal agent. What goods does Hick think are served by the profusion of natural and moral evil in our world? There are two goods that figure in Hick's theodicy. The first is in the state in which all human beings develop themselves through their free choices into moral and spiritual beings. The second is the state in which such beings enter into an eternal life of bliss and joy in fellowship with God. Let's begin our synopsis by considering the first of those states, the state in which all human beings develop themselves through their free choices into moral and spiritual beings. How might the obtaining of such a good justify an omnipotent, omniscient being in permitting evils like the fawn's suffering and the suffering of the innocent child who is brutally tortured and killed?

Since the fawn's suffering and the child's suffering are instances of natural and moral evil, respectively, different answers may be required. Let's begin with horrendous moral evils like the child's suffering while being tortured. Hick's first step is to argue that if moral and spiritual

development through free choices is the good in question, then an environment in which there is no significant suffering, no occasion for significant moral choices, would not be one in which moral and spiritual growth would be possible. In particular, a world in which no one can harm another, in which no pain or suffering results from any action, would not be a world in which such moral and spiritual growth could occur.

I think we can concede to Hick that a pain-free paradise, a world in which no one could be injured and no one could do harm, would be a world devoid of significant moral and spiritual development. But what are we to make of the fact that the world we live in is so often inimical to such moral and spiritual development? For clearly, as Hick is careful to note, much of the pain and suffering in our world frustrates such development.

> The overall situation is thus that, so far as we can tell, suffering occurs haphazardly, uselessly, and therefore unjustly. It appears to be only randomly related either to past desert or to future soul-making. Instead of serving a constructive purpose, pain and misery seem to fall upon men patternlessly and meaningfully, with the result that suffering in often underserved and often occurs in amounts exceeding anything that could have been morally planned.[6]

Hick's response to this point is to ask us what would happen were our world one in which suffering occurred "not haphazardly and therefore unjustly, but on the contrary justly and therefore non-haphazardly."[7] In such a world, Hick reasons that people would avoid wrongdoing out of fear rather than from a sense of duty. Moreover, once we saw that suffering was always for the good of the sufferer, human misery would no longer "evoke deep personal sympathy or call forth organized relief and sacrificed help and service. For it is presupposed in those compassionate reactions both that the suffering is not deserved and that is *bad* for the sufferer."[8] Hick then concludes:

> It seems, then, that in a world that is to be the scene of compassionate love and self-giving for others, suffering must fall upon mankind with something of the haphazardness and inequity that we now experience. It must be apparently unmerited, pointless, and incapable of being morally rationalized. For it is precisely this feature of our common human lot that creates sympathy between man and man and evokes the unselfishness, kindness and goodwill which are among the highest values of personal life.[9]

Let's assume with Hick that an environment fit for human beings to develop the highest qualities of moral and spiritual life must be one that include real suffering, hardships, disappointments, failure, and defeat. For moral and spiritual growth, presuppose these. Let's also assume that such an environment must operate, at least for the most part, according to general dependable laws; for only on the basis of such general laws can a person engage in the purposeful decision-making essential to rational and moral life. And given these two assumptions it is, I think, understandable how an omniscient, omnipotent being may be morally justified in permitting the occurrence of evils, both moral and natural. Moreover, it is important, as Hick stresses, that it not be apparent to us that all the instances of suffering that

occur are required for and result in the good of moral and spiritual growth. For then we would cease to strive to eliminate these evils and thereby diminish the very human struggles that so often bring about moral and spiritual development.

Our excursion into Hick's theodicy has shown us, perhaps, how a theodicy may succeed in justifying God's permission of both natural and moral evil. But so far we haven't been given any justification for the permission of the fawn's awful suffering, nor have we a justification for the intense suffering of the innocent child who is brutally tortured and killed by an adult human being. In the case of the fawn's suffering we can say that given the existence of the animals in our world and the operation of the world according to natural laws, it is unavoidable that instances of intense and prolonged animal suffering would occur. In the case of the suffering that particular innocent child we can say that on their way toward moral and spiritual development, it is perhaps unavoidable that human beings will sometimes seriously harm others through a bad use of freedom. But neither of these points will morally justify an omnipotent, omniscient being in permitting the suffering of that particular fawn or the suffering of that particular innocent child. It is simply unreasonable to believe that if the adult acted freely in brutally beating and killing that innocent child, his moral and spiritual development would have been permanently frustrated had he been prevented from doing what he did. And it is also unreasonable to believe that permitting such an act is morally justified even if preventing it would somehow diminish the perpetrator's moral and spiritual odyssey. And in the case of the fawn, it is simply unreasonable to believe that preventing its being severely burned, or mercifully ending its life so that it does not suffer intensely for several days, would so shake our confidence in the orderliness of nature that we would forsake our moral and spiritual development. Hick seems not unaware of this limitation to his theodicy, at least with respect to natural evils. With respect to human pain due to sources independent of the human will, he remarks:

> In response to it, theodicy, if it is wisely conducted, follows a negative path. It is not possible to show positively that each item of human pain serves God's purpose of good: on the other hand, it does seem possible to show that the divine purpose . . . could not be forwarded in a world that was designed as a permanent hedonistic paradise.[10]

What we've seen is that Hick's theodicy fails if it is intended to provide a good that would justify an omnipotent, omniscient being in permitting the fawn's intense suffering or the innocent child's intense suffering. The best that Hick can do is to argue that a world *utterly devoid* of natural and moral evil would preclude the realization of the goods he postulates as justifying an omnipotent, omniscient being in permitting evil. However, since the prevention of the fawn's suffering or the innocent child's suffering would not leave our world utterly devoid of natural or moral evil, his all-or-nothing argument provides no answer to our question. Now will it do to say that if an omnipotent, omniscient being were to prevent the suffering of the fawn or the innocent child it would thereby be obligated to prevent all such evils. For were it to do so it may well be, as Hick has argued, that we would cease to engage

in very significant soul-making. The problem Hick's theodicy leaves us is that it is altogether reasonable to believe that some of the evils that occur could have been prevented without either diminishing our moral and spiritual development or undermining our confidence that the world operates according to natural laws. Hick's theodicy, therefore, does not succeed in providing a reason to reject premise 1, that there exist pointless evils, instances of suffering that an omnipotent, omniscient being could have prevented without thereby preventing the occurrence of any greater good. [...]

Argument and Response: An Assessment

It is now time to assess the relative merits of the basic argument for atheism as well as the theist's best response to it. Suppose that someone is in the best position of having no rational grounds for thinking that the theistic God exists. Either this person has not heard of the arguments for the existence of God or has considered them but finds them altogether unconvincing. Perhaps, too, he has not had any visions of God and is rationally convinced that the religious experiences of others fail to provide any good grounds for theistic belief. Contemplating the variety and scale of human and animal suffering in our world, however, this individual concludes that it is altogether reasonable to accept premise 1 as true. It must be admitted, I think, that such a person is rationally justified in accepting atheism. Suppose, however, that another person has had religious experiences which justify him in believing that the theistic God exists. Perhaps, too, this person has carefully examined the Ontological Argument and found it rationally coercive. It must be admitted, I think, that such a person has some rational grounds for accepting theism. But what if this individual is aware of the basic argument for atheism and the considerations advanced in support of its first premise? In that case he will have some rational grounds for believing that theism is true and some rational grounds for believing 1 is true, and, therefore, that theism is false. This person must then weigh the relative strength of his grounds for theism against his grounds for 1 and atheism. If the grounds for theism seems rationally stronger than the grounds for 1, this individual may reasonably reject 1, since its denial is implied by theism and 2. Of course, assessing, the relative merit of competing rational grounds is no easy matter, but it seems clear that someone may be rationally justified in accepting theism and concluding that 1 and the basic argument for atheism are mistaken.

In terms of our own response to the basic argument for atheism and the theist's counterargument against 1, each of us must judge in the light of personal experience and knowledge whether our grounds for believing 1 are stronger or weaker than our grounds for believing that the theistic God exists. What we have seen is that since our experience and knowledge may differ it is possible, indeed likely, that some of us may be justified in accepting 1 and atheism, while others of us may be rationally justified in accepting theism and rejecting 1.

The conclusion to which we have come is that the evidential form of the problem of evil is a serious but not insurmountable problem for theism. To the extent that she has stronger grounds for believing that the theistic God exists than for accepting 1, the theist, on balance, may have more reason to reject 1 than she has for accepting it. However, in the absence of good reasons for believing that the theistic God exists, our study of the evidential form of the problem of evil has led us to the view that we are rationally justified in concluding that probably God does not exist.

We must not confuse the view that someone may be rationally justified in accepting theism, while someone else is rationally justified in accepting atheism, with the *incoherent* view that both theism and atheism may be true. Since theism (in the narrow sense) and atheism (in the narrow sense) express contradictory claims, one must be true and the other false. But since the evidence one possesses may justify one in believing a statement which, in the light of the total evidence, is a false statement, it is possible for different people to be rationally justified in believing statements which cannot both be true. Suppose, for example, a friend of your takes a flight to Hawaii. Hours after takeoff you learn that the plane has gone down at sea. After a twenty-four-house search, no survivors have been found. Under these circumstances it is rational for you to believe that your friend has perished. But it is hardly rational for your friend to believe that while she is bobbing up and down in a life vest and wondering why the search planes have failed to spot her. Theism and atheism cannot both be true. But because of differing experience and knowledge, someone may be rationally justified in accepting theism while someone else is rationally justified in believing atheism.

Earlier we characterized a theist as someone who believes that the theistic God exists, and an atheist as someone who believes that the theistic God does not exist. In the light of our study of the problem of evil, perhaps we should introduce further distinctions. A *friendly atheist* is an atheist who believes that someone may well be rational justified in believing that the theistic God exists. An unfriendly atheist is an atheist who believes that no one is rationally justified in believing that the theistic God exists. Similar distinctions are to be made with respect to theism and agnosticism. An *unfriendly agnostic,* for example, is an agnostic who thinks that no one is rationally justified in believing that the theistic God exists and no one is rationally justified in believing that the theistic God does not exist. Again, we must note that the friendly atheist (theist) does not believe that the theist (atheist) has a true belief, only that he may well be rationally justified in holding that belief. Perhaps the final lesson to be drawn from our study of the problem of evil is that the *friendly* versions of theism, agnosticism, and atheism are each preferable to their respective unfriendly versions.

Notes

1. Suppose, for example, that there are occasions when the act of *forgiving someone for an evil deed* is a good that outweighs the evil deed that is forgiven. Clearly, even an omnipotent being could not bring about this good without permitting the evil deed it outweighs. Again, *courageously bearing pain* might be a good that on occasion outweigh the evil of the pain that is courageously borne. But it is logically impossible for someone to bear courageously an evil pain, without the occurrence of an evil pain.

2. A more elaborate account of the Free Will Defense can be found in Alvin Plantinga, *God, Freedom, and Evil* (New York: Harper & Row Publishers, 1974).

3. See Stephen J. Wykstra, "The Human Obstacle to Evidential Arguments from Suffering: On Avoiding the Evils

of Appearance," *International Journal for the Philosophy of Religion* 16 (1984) 73–93. Also see William L. Rowe, "Evil and the Theistic Hypothesis: A Response to Wykstra," *International Journal for the Philosophy of Religion* 16 (1984): 95–100.

4. See J. L. Schellenberg, *Divine Hiddenness and Human Reason* (Ithaca and London: Cornell University Press, 1993).

5. See Hick's *Evil and the God of Love* (New York: Harper and Row, 1966), particularly chapter XVII of the revised edition, published in 1978, *God and the Universe of Faiths* (New York: St. Martin's Press, 1973), and chapter 4 of *Philosophy of Religion,* 4th ed. (Englewood Cliffs, NJ: Prentice-Hall, 1990).

6. Hick, *God and the Universe of Faiths,* p. 58.

7. Ibid.

8. Ibid, p. 60.

9. Ibid.

10. Hick, *Philosophy of Religion,* p. 46.

11. See, for example, the two chapters on Hume in G. E. Moore, *Some Main Problems of Philosophy* (London: George Allen & Unwin Ltd., 1953).

Belief and Faith

But for my faith in God, I should have been a raving maniac.
—Mohandas Gandhi

Discussion Questions

1. In "The Ethics of Belief," William Clifford argues that it is wrong to believe in something without sufficient evidence. To illustrate his point, Clifford gets us to imagine a ship owner who sends to sea an emigrant ship full of men, women, and children, knowing the vessel is old, in need of repair, and generally unseaworthy. The ship owner believes, contrary to the evidence, that the ship will make the voyage safely because she has

weathered so many past storms. The ship sinks at mid-ocean, killing everyone on board. For Clifford, the ship owner had no right to believe the ship was safe when he had evidence to the contrary. Clifford's premise that it is always wrong to form beliefs upon insufficient evidence (84) poses problems for Pascal's wager. If we merely believe in God's existence because of the possibility of eternal life and happiness, despite insufficient evidence to support such a belief, are we unjustified in our faith? Why or why not?

2. Natalie Angier suggests that religious faith has usurped the voice of reason. In our world of increasing religious intransigence, we are losing the objectivity that science brings to society. Discuss whether or not science is any more objective than religious belief. Is science merely another form of religious faith filled with its own subjective biases? Why or why not?

3. In a classic rejoinder to Clifford, the American philosopher William James argues in "The Will to Believe" that when evidence is lacking we must have faith or cease to act. That is, when we are faced with making a momentous and forced decision, such as whether to believe in God, sometimes the risks of error are insignificant when compared to the benefits that are gained by believing. In other words, sometimes we are forced to make decisions (will to believe) when we lack sufficient evidence. This is not to suggest that we ignore objective evidence when we are confronted with it. In the case of God's existence, however, such objective evidence is lacking. For William James, Clifford's claim that it is always wrong to believe something upon insufficient evidence seems too strong a criterion, and since there is no definitive evidence against God's existence, it is better to believe in God than not to believe. In what ways do you agree or disagree with James? Is religious belief a matter of being willing to believe that something exists regardless of whether there is sufficient evidence? Is blind faith justified? (See Figure 3.4.)

Figure 3.4   Is There Life Beyond Earth?

Is belief in aliens or other extraterrestrial beings justified?

It's Better to Believe in God, Than Not to Believe in God

This chapter has been devoted to find rational proof of God's existence. But, as you have probably figured out, finding rational proof is difficult. For every argument for God's existence, there is an argument against it. So what are we to do? Well, perhaps reason is insufficient to determine whether God exists. Maybe we don't need reason and rational arguments to show God exists; maybe all we need is faith.

In Simon Blackburn's article, he outlines how the mathematician, physicist, and philosopher Blaise Pascal thought that reason could not be used to make religious decisions. It's easy to see why. Reason leads us down philosophical dead ends. Theists say one thing, which is then countered by atheists. It's a never-ending game of tug-of-war with no clear winner or loser. But we ought not to give up. We must decide one way or the other whether God exists. And for Pascal, the only way we can decide is if we look deep within ourselves to our own subjective considerations. In short, we must ask ourselves if we are justified in believing in God even if there is no sound proof?

For Pascal, the answer is yes. If we weigh the pros and cons of believing or not believing in

God, we'll see it's better to believe than not to believe. Here's why. Notice we have four options and outcomes:

1. If you believe in God, and God exists, then you will gain eternal life and happiness in heaven. This surely is a great reward. All of your time praying, reading the Bible (or Koran), behaving as the scriptures say, and so forth, have been worth it and given meaning and purpose to your life.
2. If you believe in God, and God does not exist, then your loss is minimal. You have wasted some time praying, reading the Bible (or Koran), behaving as the scriptures say, and so forth, but you have probably lived a life full of meaning and purpose.
3. If you do not believe in God, and God exists, then your loss is maximal. You will never attain an eternal life and happiness in heaven; in fact, you may end up going to hell.
4. If you do not believe in God, and God does not exist, then your loss is minimal. There is no eternal life or happiness and no sense of meaning and purpose.

In other words, you have nothing to lose and everything to gain by believing in God. To believe in God, even if the probability is very slim, **Pascal's wager** suggests we ought to believe in God because the potential gain of eternal life and happiness give us significant overall benefits. For Pascal, this argument does not show that God exists but that it is rational to believe in God, since the benefits of believing outweigh the negatives of not believing. In short, no matter what your religion, it's better to believe than not to believe.

The problem with Pascal's wager, says Blackburn, is that it starts with metaphysical premises it has no right to assume. For Pascal, we are supposed to know in advance the rewards and punishments of belief or non-belief in God. But why assume this? We are metaphysically ignorant of such rewards and punishments. After all, it could turn out that God rewards those who use reason and avoid religious conviction.

Pascal's wages assumes too much to be a plausible reason for believing in God. To what, then, shall we turn?

In Atheism We Trust

Natalie Angier argues that we ought to put our faith in science, not God. Instead of turning to God in trying to find answers to life's questions, we ought to look to evolution through natural selection. Reason and rationality ought to be our guide, not blind faith. The problem is that to be an atheist is to swim upstream—against the grain—of contemporary society. Current right-wing political trends, in both Canada and the United States, undermine the separation of church and state. The atheist's voice in secular society is stifled under the din of religious fervour. And some of these religious beliefs ought to be held to the fire of scepticism. Religious beliefs ought to be questioned and criticized but rarely are. In some cases, belief in God is held blindly to one's bosom like a child desperately grasping a security blanket, unable or unwilling to let it go, even for a few moments, so the dirt can be washed out. But we need to question, to find sound reasons for our beliefs, whatever they are. And, as we will see later on, when theists make the link between religion and ethics, atheists are considered immoral, amoral, or haters of humankind. Angier emphatically disagrees. Atheism can give us a profound appreciation for the wonders of the world from a purely scientific point of view. One doesn't need to soften the cold hard facts of natural selection by bringing in some kind of supreme deity. All we need to do is appreciate that the world in which we live is miraculous and can be explained by science. We don't need God to give us answers to life's questions; all we need is faith in ourselves.

What Conclusions Can Be Drawn Regarding God's Existence?

The debate over God's existence will, no doubt, continue for decades, if not centuries, to come. One of the concerns about the debate over God's existence is that devoted theists and atheists will unlikely be moved by either arguments for or against. Such intransigence is not easily overcome. But for theists, atheists, and those who are not wholly convinced either way, according to Peter Kreeft, there are three things everyone can do to decide for him or herself about what is true (287–290).

First, a person must be honest and pure in their motives. Deciding whether God exists can have a profound impact on one's life, and if you are merely trying to reinforce what you already believe, you are bound to fail. Being truthful requires being honest with yourself and to accept the consequences regardless of what they are. You must step back from our well-worn convictions and check and recheck the evidence.

Second, the evidence must be looked at from all sides and not "cherry picked" to suit personal ends. If the evidence supports one side over the other, then that's the more probable conclusion. No yelling, screaming, or crying.

Third, you must not only read and learn the various arguments for and against the existence of God but you must also perform active experiments. What kinds of experiments? Well, first, it's important to seek out theists and atheists. Ask and observe how their views make a difference in their lives. Second, go for a test drive. Spend one day being a Christian (Muslim, Buddhist, Hindu, etc.) and another day being an atheist. Granted this may be easier said than done, but to know the truth is to take each philosophical position seriously. Third, take Pascal's wager. Despite being problematic, try believing God exists and see what happens. And finally, pray. Pray to God that you are seeking the truth and asking for help in your quest. If theism is true, God will hear your prayer and guide you—in, perhaps, subtle ways—to the answers.

Although Kreeft acknowledges that his approach is not perfect, he does suggest we open our hearts and minds to the question of God's existence. If we start from the hypothesis of "all who seek, shall find," we have nothing to lose and everything to gain. So go out and start testing this hypothesis. As Kreeft states,

"I can think of only two reasons for hesitating: the fear that your will find nothing, and the fear that your will find something. Honesty, like love, casts out fear" (290). The choice is up to you.

17

Simon Blackburn

(1944–)

Simon Blackburn was born in 1944 near Bristol, England. After a formal education in the moral sciences at Clifton College and Trinity College, Cambridge, he was appointed Junior Research Fellow, Churchill College, Cambridge from 1967 to 1969 and then Fellow and Tutor in Philosophy, Pembroke College, Oxford from 1969 to 1990. In 1990, he travelled to the United States to become Edna J. Koury Distinguished Professor of Philosophy, University of North Carolina, Chapel Hill, where he stayed until 2001. He is currently the Professor of Philosophy at the University of Cambridge and Fellow of Trinity College, Cambridge. He has also held numerous visiting appointments at the University of Melbourne, University of British Columbia, Oberlin College, Princeton University, Ohio State University, the Universidad Autonomia da Mexico, and was for ten years Adjunct Professor at the Research School

of Social Sciences, Australian National University, Canberra. From 1984 until 1990 he was the editor of the renowned journal Mind. *He was elected Fellow of the British Academy in 2001. Blackburn's books include* Reason and Prediction *(1973),* Spreading the Word *(1984),* Essays in Quasi-Realism *(1993),* The Oxford Dictionary of Philosophy *(1994),* Ruling Passions *(1998),* Think *(1999),* Being Good *(2001),* Lust *(2004), and* Truth: A Guide *(2005).*

Infiniti—Rien

None of the metaphysical arguments we have considered do much to confirm the hypothesis that the universe is the creation of a traditional God. And Hume's analysis of testimony from miracles destroys their value as evidence. Faced with these blanks, religious faith may try to find other arguments.

An interesting and ingenious one is due to the French mathematician and theologian, Blaise Pascal (1632–62), and is known as Pascal's wager. Unlike the arguments we have been considering, it is not presented as an argument for the *truth* of religious belief, but for the *utility* of believing in some version of a monotheistic, Judaic, Christian, or Islamic God.

The argument is this, First, Pascal confesses to metaphysical ignorance:

> Let us now speak according to natural lights.
>
> If there is a God, he is infinitely incomprehensible, since, having neither parts, nor limits, He has no affinity to us. We are therefore incapable of knowing either what He is, or if He is…Who then will blame the Christians for not being able

to give a reason for their belief, since they profess a religion for which they cannot give a reason?

It is not too clear why this excuse is offered for the Christians, as opposed to those of other faiths, as well as believers in fairies, ghosts, the living Elvis, and L. Ron Hubbard. Still, suppose the choice is between religious belief and a life of religious doubt or denial:

> You must wager. It is not optional. Which will you choose then?…Let us weigh the gain and the loss in wagering that God is. Let us estimate these two chances. If you gain, you gain all, if you lose, you lose nothing. Wager, then, without hesitation that He is.

With great clarity Pascal realizes that this is rather an odd reason for choosing a belief. But he also says, perceptively, that

> your inability to believe in the result of your passions, since reason brings you to this, and yet you cannot believe…Learn of those who have been bound like you, and who now stake all their possessions… Follow the way by which they began; by acting as if they believe, taking the holy water, having masses said, etc. Even this will naturally make you believe, and deaden your acuteness.

After you have 'stupefied' yourself, you have become a believer. And then you will reap the rewards of belief: infinite rewards, if the kind of God you believe in exists. And if it does not? Well, you have lost very little, in comparison with infinity: only what Pascal calls the 'poisonous pleasures' of things like playing golf on Sundays instead of going to mass.

The standard way to present this argument is in terms of a two-by-two box of the options:

	God Exists	God Does Not Exist
I believe in God	+ infinitely!	0
I do not believe in God	– infinitely!	0

The zeros on the right correspond to the thought that not much goes better or worse in this life, whether or not we believe. This life is of vanishingly little account compared to what is promised to believers. The plus-infinitely figure corresponds to infinite bliss. The minus-infinity figure in the bottom left corresponds to the traditional jealous God, who sends to Hell those who do not believe in him, and of course encourages his followers to give them a hard time, here, as well. But the minus-infinity figure can be soft-pedalled. Even if we put 0 in the bottom left-hand box, the wager looks good. It would be good even if God does not punish disbelief, because there is still that terrific payoff of ' + infinity' cranking up the choice. In decision-theory terms, the option of belief 'dominates,' because it can win, and cannot lose. So—go for it!

Unfortunately, the lethal problem with this argument is simple, once it is pointed out.

Pascal starts from a position of metaphysical ignorance. We just know nothing about the realm beyond experience. But the set-up of the wager presumes that we do know something. We are supposed to know the rewards and penalties attached to belief in a Christian God. This is a God who will be pleasured and reward us for our attendance at mass, and will either be indifferent or, in the minus-infinity option, seriously discombobulated by our non-attendance. But this is a case of false options. For consider that if we are really ignorant metaphysically, then it is at least as likely that the options pan out like this:

> There is indeed a very powerful, very benevolent deity. He (or she or they or it) has determined as follows. The good human beings are those who follow the natural like of reason, which is given to them to control their beliefs. These good humans follow the arguments, and hence avoid religious convictions. These ones with strength of mind not to believe in such things go to Heaven. The rest go to Hell.

This is not such a familiar deity as the traditional jealous God, who cares above all that people believe in him. (Why is God so jealous? Alas, might his jealousy be a projection of human sectarian ambitions and emotions? Either you are with us or against us! The French sceptic Voltaire said that God created mankind in his image, and mankind returned the compliment.) But the problem for Pascal is that if we really know nothing, then we do not know whether the scenario just described is any less likely than the Christian one he presented. In fact, for my money, a God that punishes belief is just as likely, and a lot more reasonable, than one that punishes disbelief.

And of course, we could add the Humean point that whilst for Pascal it was a simple two-way question of mass versus disbelief, in the wider world it also a question of the Koran versus mass, or L. Ron Hubbard versus the Swami Maharishi, or the Aquarian Concepts Community Divine New Order Government versus the First Internet Church of All. The wager has to be silent about those choices.

18

Natalie Angier

(1958–)

Natalie Angier was born in 1958 and was raised in the Bronx, New York, and Michigan. She studied English literature, physics, and astronomy at Barnard College, graduating in 1978. Angier was a founding writer for the upstart magazine Discover, *launched in 1980. She has also written for* Time, Atlantic, Parade, Reader's Digest, Fox Television Network, *the Canadian Broadcasting Corporation, and numerous other magazines. She joined the* New York Times *as a science writer in 1990 and the following year she won the Pulitzer Prize for beat reporting. Her books include* Natural Obsessions: The Search for the Oncogene *(1988),* The Beauty of the Beastly: New Views of the Nature of Life *(1996),* Woman: An Intimate Geography *(1999), and* The Best American Science and Nature Writing *(2002). Her latest book is entitled* The Canon: A Whirligig Tour of the Beautiful Basics of Science *(2007).*

Sorry . . . I'm No Believer

The vapid calls to prayer made by George W. Bush exclude those of us who prefer to put our faith in life's real miracles.

In the beginning—or rather, at the end of a very lo-o-ng beginning—George W. Bush made an earnest acceptance speech and urged our nation to "rise above a house divided." He knows, he said, that "America wants reconciliation and unity," and that we all "share hopes and goals and values." After his speech he reached out, up, down and across aisles, to embrace Republicans, Democrats, Naderites, Palm Beach Buchananites, the disaffected, the disinclined.

The only problem was what President-elect Bush wanted from me and "every American." "I ask you to pray for this great nation," he said. "I ask your prayers for leaders from both parties," and for their families too, while we're at it.

Whatever else I might have been inclined to think of Bush's call for comity, with his simple little request, his assumption that prayer is some sort of miracle Vicks VapoRub, it was clear that his hands were reaching for any hands but mine.

Again and again the polls proclaim the United States to be a profoundly and persistently religious nation, one in which faith remains a powerful force despite the temptations of secularism and the decline of religion's influence in most other countries of the developed world.

Every year, pollsters such as Gallup and the National Opinion Research Center ask Americans whether they believe in God, and every year the same overwhelming majority, anywhere from 92 per cent to 97 per cent, say yes. In one survey, 80 per cent professed belief in life after death. When asked how often they attend church, at least 60 per cent say once a month or more, and have said as much for the past 40 years.

So who in her right mind would want to be an atheist in America today, a place where presidential candidates compete for the honour of divining "what Jesus would do," and where

Senator Joseph Lieberman can declare that we shouldn't deceive ourselves into thinking that our constitutional "freedom of religion" means "freedom from religion" or "indulge the supposition that morality can be maintained without religion"?

I'll out myself. I'm an atheist. I don't believe in God, gods, godlets or any sort of higher power beyond the universe itself, which seems quite high and powerful enough to me. I don't believe in life after death, channelled chat rooms with the dead, reincarnation, telekinesis or any miracles but the miracle of life and consciousness, which again strike me as miracles in nearly obscene abundance.

I believe that the universe abides by the laws of physics, some of which are known, others of which will surely be discovered, but even if they are not, that will simply be a result, as my colleague George Johnson put it, of our brains having evolved for life on this one little planet and thus being inevitably limited. I'm convinced that the world as we see it was shaped by the again genuinely miraculous, let's even say transcendent, hand of evolution through natural selection.

I'm in the minority, even among friends and family. When I sent out a casual and non-scientific poll of my own to a wide cast of acquaintances, friends and colleagues, I was surprised, but not really, to learn that maybe 60 per cent claimed a belief in a god of some sort, including people I would have bet were unregenerate sceptics. Others just shrugged. They don't think about this stuff. It doesn't matter to them. They can't know, they won't beat themselves up trying to know and for that matter they don't care if their kids believe or not.

Rare were the respondents who considered atheism to be a significant part of their self-identities. Most called themselves "passive"

atheists and said they had stopped doing battle with the big questions of life and death, meaning and eternity, pretty much when they stopped using Clearasil. To be an active atheist seems almost silly and beside the point. After all, the most famous group devoted to atheism, the American Atheists, was founded by Madalyn Murray O'Hair, an eccentric megalomaniac whose greatest claim to fame is that she and her son were kidnapped several years ago and are presumed dead.

Other atheistic groups, such as the Freedom From Religion Foundation or the Council for Secular Humanism, are more concerned with maintaining an unshakeable separation between church and state than they are with spreading any gospel of godlessness. And yet there is something to be said for a revival of pagan peevishness and outspokenness. It's not that I would presume to do something as foolish and insulting as try to convert a believer. Arguments over the question of whether God exists are ancient, recurring, sometimes stimulating but more often tedious. Arrogance and righteousness are nondenominational vices that entice the churched and unchurched alike.

Still, the current climate of religiosity can be stifling to non-believers, and it helps now and then to cry foul. For one thing, some of the numbers surrounding the deep religiousness of America, and the rarity of non-belief, should be held to the fire of scepticism, as should sweeping statistics of any sort. Yes, Americans are comparatively more religious than Europeans, but while the vast majority of them may say generically that they believe in God, when asked what their religion is, a sizable fraction, 11 per cent, report "no religion".

What's more, in some quarters, atheism, far from being rare, is the norm. When researchers targeted members of the National Academy of Sciences, an elite coterie if ever there was one, belief in a personal god was 7 per cent, the flip of the American public at large.

Among the more irritating consequences of our flagrantly religious society is the special dispensation that mainstream religions receive. We all may talk about religion as a powerful social force, but unlike other similarly powerful institutions, religion is not to be questioned, criticized or mocked. When the singer-songwriter Sinead O'Connor ripped apart a photograph of John Paul II to protest at what she saw as his overweening power, even the most secular humanists were outraged by her iconoclasm, and her career has never really recovered.

When conspicuous true believers such as Lieberman make the claim that religion and ethical behaviour are inextricably linked, the corollary premise is that atheists are, if not immoral, then amoral, or nihilistic misanthropes, or, worst of all, moral relativists. Believers and doubters will always be with us—and it's just possible that they need each other.

From my godless perspective, the devout remind me that it is human nature to thirst after meaning and to desire an expansion of purpose beyond the cramped Manhattan studio of self and its immediate relations.

In her brief and beautiful book *The Sacred Depths of Nature,* Ursula Goodenough, a cell biologist, articulates a sensibility that she calls "religious naturalism," a profound appreciation of the genuine workings of nature, conjoined with a commitment to preserving that natural world in all its staggering, interdependent splendour. Call it transcendent atheism: I may not believe in life after death, but what a gift it is to be alive now.

Key Terms and Concepts

Theism
Atheism
Fideism
Monotheism
Big Bang
Big Crunch
Intelligent design creationism
Moral evils
Natural evils
Problem of evil
Logical problem of evil
Evidential problem of evil
Theodicies
Sceptical theism
Pascal's wager

Study Questions

1. What does Anselm mean when he says that God is *a being than which nothing greater can be conceived*? Why does this definition of God entail existence?
2. What is Guanilo's objection against the ontological argument? How might Anselm respond?
3. Why does Kant argue that "existence" is not a property and, therefore, undermines Anselm's claim that God is the greatest conceivable being?
4. What is the "model version" of the ontological argument? Why do critics object to this proof?
5. Does the ontological argument prove the existence of Satan?
6. Why did Aquinas argue that the universe must have a "first cause" or "unmoved mover"?
7. How do the arguments from "efficient causes" and "necessity" show that God exists?
8. How would you defend the cosmological argument if someone asked you, "Who caused God?"
9. What is the "big bang"? Why does Schick argue the first-cause argument is false?

10. What is the teleological argument, as outlined by Paley? What sorts of evidence might support his argument and, thereby, God's existence?

11. Why does Hume think Paley's argument from analogy is weak?

12. If you see houses being built, then you infer a builder. Does this argument support the claim that God is the ultimate "builder" of our universe?

13. Why does Hume argue that God is "all too human"?

14. Does evolution pose problems for theists? How might theists explain evolution?

15. Why does Dawkins argue that we can explain the natural world by evolution, not God?

16. What is the difference between the "logical" and "evidential" problems of evil?

17. What is the difference between natural and moral evils?

18. What is the free will defence? Would you agree that it offers sufficient support for God's existence?

19. Does the greater good defence justify evil?

20. According to John Hick, why did God create a world in which there is suffering?

21. Why does Pascal think we ought to believe in God? What is his reasoning?

22. Would Clifford's claim that it is wrong to hold beliefs in the absence of sufficient evidence prevent you from believing in God?

23. Why does Angier think it's more rational and reasonable to believe in science than God?

Further Readings

Adams, Marilyn, and Robert Adams, eds. *The Problem of Evil*. New York: Oxford University Press, 1990.

Hicks, John. *Philosophy of Religion*. Englewood Cliffs, NJ: Prentice Hall, 1973.

Mackie, John. *The Miracle of Theism*. Oxford: Oxford University Press, 1971.

Madden, Edward H., and Peter H. Hare, eds. *Evil and the Concept of God*. Springfield, IL.: Charles C. Thomas, 1968.

Martin, Michael. *Atheism*. Philadelphia: Temple University Press, 1990.

Moreland, J. P., and Kai Nielsen. *Does God Exist: The Great Debate*. Nashville: Thomas Nelson, Inc., 1990.

Peterson, Michael, Hasker, William, Reichenbach, Bruce, and David Basinger, eds. *Philosophy of Religion: Selected Readings*. 2nd ed. New York: Oxford University Press, 2001.

Plantinga, Alvin. *God, Freedom, and Evil*. New York: Harper & Row, 1974.

Swinburne, Richard. *The Existence of God*. Oxford: Oxford University Press, 1979.

Internet Resources

Center for Science and Culture. n.d. Discover Institute. 17 June 2007 <http://www.crsc.org/>.

C.S. Lewis Society. n.d. 17 June 2007 <http://www.apologetics.org/>.

Himma, Kenneth. "The Ontological Argument." *The Internet Encyclopedia of Philosophy*. Ed. James Fieser and Bradley Dowden. 2006. 17 June 2007 <http://www.utm.edu/research/iep/o/ont-arg.htm>.

Leader U. Apologetics. n.d. 16 June 2007 <http://www.leaderu.com/menus/theo-apol.html>.

Ratzch, Del. "Teleological Argument for God's Existence" *The Stanford Encyclopedia of Philosophy*. Ed. Edward N. Zalta. Stanford University, 10 June 2005. 17 June 2007 <http://plato.stanford.edu/entries/teleological-arguments/>.

Tooley, Michael. "The Problem of Evil." *The Stanford Encyclopedia of Philosophy*. Ed. Edward N. Zalta. Stanford University, 16 September 2002. 20 August 2006 <http://plato.stanford.edu/archives/win2004/entries/evil/>.

Welsh, Stephen, ed. "Cosmological Arguments." 24 April 2007. 17 June 2007 <http://www.infidels.org/library/modern/theism/cosmological.html>.

Notes

1. A campaign is underway to rename atheists "Brights." The Brights movement was started in 2003 by Paul Geisert and Mynga Futrell in order to find a term that would have positive connotations for non-believers. According to Geisert and Futrell, a Bright is someone who takes a naturalistic worldview free of supernatural or mystical elements (gods, deities, or other entities) and is the foundation of action and ethics. Brights believe

that a worldview based on science and reason will offer hope in solving many of the world's problems. The term Bright, however, has been criticized because it suggests that a naturalist worldview is more intelligent that those with other non-naturalistic views.

2. A polytheist believes there is more than one god (e.g., Hinduism).

3. Something is logically possible if it does not entail a contradiction.

4. Something is not causally possible if it violates the laws of nature.

5. The word *teleological* comes from the Greek word *telos* which means "end" or "goal."

6. Everyone will arrive at the same conclusion that the watch must have had a creator, says Paley, for the following reasons: 1) Even if we had never seen a watch being made, or are unfamiliar with the artisan who created it, we would still have to conclude that function = design = creator. 2) Sometimes watches are faulty and give us the incorrect time. Imperfection, says Paley, does not exclude design. 3) Even if we only saw parts of the watch we would still draw the conclusion that it was designed. For example, if the watch had been smashed to pieces, it would not imply there are no function to the parts themselves and no designer. 4) If told that the watch came about by chance, we would never believe this because design cannot result from chance alone. 5) Similarly, if we were told that the watch was the result of some natural law that caused parts of the watch to form a specific way, it would not be believed because natural laws presuppose a lawmaker or designer. 6) Others may try to convince us the designer of the watch is a figment of our imagination. This is absurd, says Paley, since everyone will see that the evidence of design is impartial and objective. 7) Again, if we were told that the watch was the result of some metallic law that caused the watch to form, we would not believe them because such a law would presuppose a lawmaker or designer. 8) Lastly, critics might argue that we cannot infer from the function of the parts of the watch to intelligent design. But, for Paley, if we know that the purpose or goal of the watch is to tell time, then we must correctly presuppose a watchmaker or creator because without one the watch wouldn't achieve the goal of telling time.

7. Traditional creationism holds that the story of Genesis is true, that God created the earth, humans, and other creatures in six days.

8. Peter Grant, along with his wife Rosemary (also see Weiner), has accumulated an impressive array of research supporting Darwin's theory of natural selec-

tion. Since 1973, the Grants have engaged in a long-term research program studying Darwin's finches at the Galapagos Islands. To see natural selection at work, they have painstakingly spent countless hours catching, measuring, weighting, and identifying finches and their diet. Their research reveals that if body size and beak size enable different species of finches to adapt to their environment, then if environmental changes occur, we should see changes in body and beak size. This is exactly what happened after a drought hit the islands in 1977. The drought had a devastating impact on the total amount of vegetation. Lower vegetation yields meant the small soft seeds that some finches usually ate were exhausted quickly. Finches were left trying to eat larger hard seeds that they usually ignored. But given the struggle to survive, the Grants discovered that only those birds with individual random adaptations for stronger and deeper beaks could open the harder seeds. Over time, the finches with weaker beaks perished, while those with stronger beaks survived to reproduce.

9. Another classic case of evolution comes from the peppered moth. In nineteenth-century England, many people collected moths and butterflies, especially if they were rare. Biologists looked at the collections of moths between 1850 and 1950 and discovered that the peppered moth, which lives in all parts of England, became increasingly black in colour through subsequent decades. At first, this didn't make sense. The peppered moth hunts at night and during the day rests on tree trucks were they are camouflaged from predators. But if the moths were black, instead of their usually peppered grey, they would be prime targets for hungry predators. What biologists discovered is that as cities became more industrialized and pollution blackened tree trunks in and around cities, the moths needed to adapt to ensure their usually grey colour would not stand in contrast to the blackened trees. Failure to adapt would have meant death. Hence, over the decades of industrial growth, moths evolved from peppered grey to black to ensure their survival and reproductive success.

10. As Claudia Wallis points out in her article "The Evolution Wars," evolution has always been a hard sell for many Americans. According to a recent poll of 1,000 adults surveyed, 54 percent of respondents did not believe humans evolved from earlier species, and 55 percent of Americans want intelligent design creationism taught alongside evolution. In fact, according to Wallis, 45 percent of Americans believe God created the world and all of its inhabitants in six days.

11. For criticisms of Michael Behe's *Darwin's Black Box,* see Robert Dorit's "Molecular Evolution and Scientific Inquiry Misperceived"; Jerry Coyne's "God in the Details"; David Ussery's "A Biochemist's Response to 'The Biochemical Challenge to Evolution'"; and H. Allen Orr's "Darwin and Intelligent Design (Again)".

12. According to the Bureau of Justice Statistics, the incident of rape is much higher. Shannon Catalano, author of "The Criminal Victimization Report, 2004," puts the total number of rapes at approximately 209,880, or 90 per 100,000 people.

13. Second, the free will defence leads to the paradox of omnipotence (Mackie). Traditionally the paradox can be stated as follows: Could God create a stone so heavy that he cannot lift it? If the answer is yes, then God is not omnipotent because he lacks the power to lift the stone. If the answer is no, then God is not omnipotent because he lacks the ability to create such a stone. Similarly, we can ask: Could God create things he cannot control? If the answer is yes—God can create humans with free will and cannot control them—then God is not omnipotent. If the answer is no—God cannot create humans with free will and cannot control them—then God is not omnipotent as well. In this sense, God is equally powerless. In short, free will does not solve the problem of evil.

14. Moreover, the greater good theodicy implies severe restrictions on God's power. If God must introduce evil as a means of achieving some good, then God seems much less powerful than traditional definitions suggest. After all, if God is all-powerful, he ought to be able to create good in the world without having to resort to evil as a way of achieving good ends. Humans, on the other hand, are finite. Humans often have to use painful means to achieving good ends, such as when a child is vaccinated or when a surgeon performs surgery to repair a diseased organ. But if God cannot achieve good without evil, God's power is undermined and existence is thus called into question.

15. This idea can also be supported by an aesthetic analogy whereby contrasts enhance the beauty of a piece of work such as when discords heighten a piece of music. Or to put another way, after suffering through some of my niece's rap and hip-hop music, Bach and Tchaikovsky take on heightened qualities of beauty and taste.

16. Michael Tooley, in his article "The Problem of Evil," argues that childhood sexual abuse is also a problem for Hick. If the purpose of evil is soul-making, it's hard to see how children can become better people by being innocent victims of such horrors. The same can be said of animals. Hick's soul-building theodicy cannot justify the amount of pain in the animal world. The predator and prey relationship is inherently filled with pain for most animals and yet it's laughable to think the very concept of soul-building applies to the animal world.

Works Cited

Behe, Michael. *Darwin's Black Box: The Biochemical Challenge to Evolution.* New York: The Free Press, 1996.

Berton, Pierre. *Vimy.* Markham, ON: Penguin Books, 1986.

Catalano, Shannon. "Criminal Victimization, 2004." *Bureau of Justice Statistics.* n.d. 14 August 2006 <http://www.ojp.usdoj.gov/bjs/pub/pdf/cv04.pdf>.

Chopp, Rebecca. *The Power to Speak: Feminism, Language, God.* New York: The Cross Publishing Company, 1989.

Christ, Carol. "Why Women Need the Goddess: Phenomenological, Psychological, and Political Reflections." *Philosophy and Choice: Selected Reading from Around the World.* 2nd ed. Ed. Kit Christensen. New York: McGraw Hill, 2002.

Clifford, William. "The Ethics of Belief." *Philosophy of Religion: Selected Readings.* 2nd ed. Ed. Michael Peterson, William Hasker, Bruce Reichenbach, and David Basinger. New York: Oxford University Press, 2001.

Coxe, Ray, and William Holmes. "A Study of the Cycle of Abuse among Child Molesters." *Journal of Child Sexual Abuse* 10 (2001): 111–118.

Coyne, Jerry. "God in the Details." *Nature* 383 (1996): 227–228.

Daly, Mary. *Beyond God the Father.* Boston: Beacon Press, 1973.

Davies, Paul. *Are We Alone?* New York: Harper Collins, Basic Books, 1995.

Dhawan, Sonia, and W. L. Marshall. "Sexual Abuse Histories of Sexual Offenders." *Sexual Abuse: Journal of Research and Treatment* 8 (1996): 7–15.

Dorit, Robert. "Molecular Evolution and Scientific Inquiry Misperceived." *American Scientist* 85.5 (1997): 474.

Federal Bureau of Investigation. *Crime in the United States 2004*. n.d. 5 July 2006 <http://www.fbi.gov/ucr/cius_04/documents/CIUS2004.pdf>.

Flesher, Paul. "Hinduism." *Exploring Religions*. University of Wyoming, n.d. 13 June 2007 <http://uwacadweb.uwyo.edu/religionet/er/hinduism/index.htm>.

Frankenberry, Nancy. "Feminist Philosophy of Religion." *The Stanford Encyclopaedia of Philosophy*. Ed. Edward N. Zalta. Stanford University, 14 March 2005. 17 June 2007 <http://plato.stanford.edu/entries/feminist-religion/>.

Freud, Sigmund. *The Future of an Illusion*. Trans. James Starchey. New York: W. W. Norton, 1961.

Grant, Peter R. *Ecology and Evolution of Darwin's Finches*. Princeton: Princeton University Press, 1986.

Hick, John. "Soul-Making and Suffering." *The Problem of Evil*. Ed. Marilyn Adams and Robert Adams. New York: Oxford University Press, 1990.

Howard-Snyder, Daniel. "God, Evil, and Suffering." *Reason for the Hope Within*. Ed. Michael Murray. Grand Rapids, MI: Eerdmans Publishing Company, 1999.

Hunt, Kathleen. "Transitional Vertebrate Fossils FAQ." *The Talk.Origins Archive: Exploring the Creation/Evolution Controversy*. 17 March 1997. 8 November 2005 <http//www.talkorgins.org/faqs/faq-transitional.html>.

Iraq Body Count. n.d. 15 September 2007 <http://www.iraqbodycount.org>.

James, William. "The Will to Believe." *Philosophy of Religion: Selected Readings*. Ed. Michael Peterson, William Hasker, Bruce Reichenbach, and David Basinger. 2nd ed. New York: Oxford University Press, 2001.

Jenish, D'Arcy. "Horror Stories." *Maclean's* 22 (1995): 14–18. Academic Search Primer. EBSCO. MacKimmie Lib., Calgary, AB. 20 August 2006 <http://plinks.ebscohost.com.ezproxy.lib.ucalgary.ca/ehost/detail?vid=7&hid=102&sid=b9015b7c-9cab-4fe7-b5bf-34b36c7b762f%40sessionmgr4>.

—. "Heart of Darkness." *Maclean's* 37 (1995): 18–19. Academic Search Primer. EBSCO. MacKimmie Lib., Calgary, AB. 20 August 2006 <http://plinks.ebscohost.com.ezproxy.lib.ucalgary.ca/ehost/detail?vid=17&hid=102&sid=b9015b7c-9cab-4fe7-b5bf-34b36c7b762f%40sessionmgr4>.

—. "Locked Up for Life." *Maclean's* 46 (1995): 68. Academic Search Primer. EBSCO. MacKimmie Lib., Calgary, AB. 20 August 2006 <http://plinks.ebscohost.com.ezproxy.lib.ucalgary.ca/ehost/detail?vid=8&hid=102&sid=64e8e138-12b5-45d1-a2b1-3795a44b3d85%40sessionmgr4>.

Kaufmann, William J. *Discovering the Universe*. New York: W. H. Freeman and Company, 1987.

Keegan, John. *A History of Warfare*. New York: Vintage Books, 1993.

Kreeft, Peter. "Introduction." *Does God Exist: The Great Debate*. Nashville: Thomas Nelson, 1990.

Lawhead, William F. *The Philosophical Journey: An Interactive Approach*. 2nd ed. New York: McGraw Hill, 2003.

Lennox, James. "Darwinism." *The Stanford Encyclopaedia of Philosophy Online*. Ed. Edward N. Zalta. 14 August 2004. Stanford University, 7 November 2005 <http://plato.stanford.edu/archives/fall2004/entries/darwinism/>.

Mackie, John. "Evil and Omnipotence." *Mind* 64 (1955): 200–212.

Madden, Edward H., and Peter H. Hare. *Evil and the Concept of God*. Springfield, IL.: Charles C. Thomas, 1968.

Pojman, Louis. *Philosophy: The Pursuit of Wisdom*. 4th ed. Belmont, CA: Wadsworth/Thomson Learning, 2004.

Orr, H. Allen. "Darwin and Intelligent Design (Again)." *Boston Review* Dec/Jan. 1996/1997: 28–31.

Rauhut, Nils. *Ultimate Questions: Thinking about Philosophy*. New York: Pearson/Longman, 2004.

Ruether, Rosemary Radford. "The Image of God's Goodness." *Twenty Questions: An Introduction to Philosophy*. 5th ed. Ed. G. Lee Bowie, Meredith Michaels, and Robert Solomon. Belmont, CA: Wadsworth, 2004.

—. *Sexism and God-talk: Toward a Feminist Theology*. Boston: Beacon Press, 1983.

Sauve, Julie. "Crime Statistics in Canada, 2004." *Juristat: Canadian Centre for Justice Statistics*. 2004. 18 August 2006 <http://www.statcan.ca/english/freepub/85-002-XIE/0050585-002-XIE.pdf>.

Schick, Theodore, Jr., and Lewis Vaughn. *Doing Philosophy: An Introduction through Thought Experiments*. New York: McGraw Hill, 2003.

Simons, Dominique, Wurtele, Sandy, and Peggy Heil. "Childhood Victimization and Lack of Empathy as Predictors of Sexual Offending Against Women and Children." *Journal of Interpersonal Violence* 17 (2002): 1291–1307.

Stumpf, Samuel, and James Fieser. *Philosophy: History and Problems*. 6th ed. New York: McGraw Hill, 2003.

Tooley, Michael. "The Problem of Evil." *The Stanford Encyclopaedia of Philosophy*. Ed. Edward N. Zalta. Stanford University. 16 September 2002. 20 August 2006 <http://plato.stanford.edu/archives/win2004/entries/evil/>.

Trakakis, Nick. "The Evidential Problem of Evil." *The Internet Encyclopaedia of Philosophy*. Ed. James Fieser and Bradley Dowden. 2006. 15 June 2007 <http://www.iep.utm.edu/e/evil-evi.htm>.

Veterans Affairs Canada. *Canadians on the Somme*. 29 July 2004. 20 August 2006 <http://www.vac-acc .gc.ca/remembers/sub.cfm?source=history/firstwar/canada/Canada8>.

Vilar, Carles. *Real International Statistics on Religion.* 12 June 2005. 15 September 2007 <http://www .religionstatistics.net/statamer1.htm>.

Wallis, Claudia. "The Evolution Wars." *Time* August 15, 2005: 9–15.

Weiner, Jonathan. *The Beak of the Finch: The Story of Evolution in Our Time*. New York: Knopf, 1994.

Ussery, David. "A Biochemist's Response to 'The Biochemical Challenge to Evolution.'" *Bios* 70 (1999): 40–45.

Chapter 4 The Mind–Body Problem

We know that brains are the de facto causal basis of consciousness, but we have, it seems, no understanding whatever of how this can be so. It strikes us as miraculous, eerie, even faintly comic. Somehow, we feel, the water of the physical brain is turned into the wine of consciousness, but we draw a total blank on the nature of this conversion.

—Colin McGinn

We know a lot about our world and how it works. In fact, if we didn't have knowledge of how things worked, physicians wouldn't be able to perform medical procedures that save countless lives, nor could we build things that make our lives so comfortable such as houses, computers, and cell phones. Consider, for example, the ubiquitous automobile. According to the Worldwatch Institute, there are approximately 539 million cars worldwide and growing fast (Prugh, Flavin, and Sawin 103). And let's face it, cars are wonderful: they give us mobility and freedom; they can bring us excitement and fun; they can be driven for sport or to make a living. Despite their benefits, cars produce noxious fumes like hydrocarbons and nitrogen oxides that are harmful to humans and the environment. To eliminate these emissions, scientists developed catalytic converters. Without a detailed knowledge of the science behind car pollutants, catalytic converters could never have been developed in the first place. Here is how a physicist could explain how catalytic converters work:

> A catalytic converter transforms the noxious hydrocarbons and nitrogen oxides in hot automobile exhaust into water, carbon dioxide, and nitrogen gas. It does this through the use of tiny platinum and rhodium particles that are deposited on the highly porous surface of a ceramic honeycomb. When hot hydrocarbon and oxygen molecules in the exhaust encounter a platinum particle in this honeycomb, they dissociate into molecular fragments on the particle's surface. These fragments then recombine into water and carbon dioxide molecules, which then return to the exhaust gas. (Bloomfield)

If you don't quite understand the physics behind catalytic converters, don't worry. The point to be gleaned is that humans have physical knowledge of how they work and without this knowledge the world would be a much dirtier place. This example, amongst countless others, clearly demonstrates that the sciences (biology, chemistry, and physics) have provided detailed physical knowledge of world in which we live.

What about the mind? Do we have detailed physical knowledge of the mind and its relationship with the body? Can we explain the mind in physical terms the same way we can explain catalytic converters? Before we answer these questions, it's prudent to first figure out what we mean by the *mind*. Or to put another way, let's determine what would count as *having a mind*. The list of what counts as having a mind in Box 4.1 is not exhaustive, but if we look closely it can be broken down into three general categories of mental activities: experiencing (pain, love, pleasure), attitudinizing (believing, desiring, deciding), and acting (building a home, painting a picture) (Guttenplan, *Mind's Landscape* 9). In short, to have a mind is to experience, have attitudes (also known as propositional attitudes[1]), and to act—i.e., actions are an indication of having a mind.[2] Having a mind, then, is to have various mental states.

With this general definition in tow, let's go back to our earlier question: Do humans have detailed physical knowledge of the mind the same way we have physical knowledge of catalytic converters? Well, yes and no. Scientists have discovered that neurons in the brain, along with various biochemicals, are a necessary condition to think, believe, want, desire, remember, and to have mental states generally. We also know

> ## Box 4.1 What Counts as Having a Mind?
>
> | | | |
> |---|---|---|
> | Ability to learn | Acting intentionally | Believing |
> | Choosing | Deciding | Feeling |
> | Remembering | Reflecting on a problem | Consciousness |
> | Dreaming | Happiness | Imagining |
> | Loving | Perceiving | Building a home |
> | Desiring a holiday | Experiencing pain | Hearing a violin |
> | Painting a picture | Pleasure | Thinking |
>
> **Source:** Adapted from Samuel Guttenplan. (2000). *The Mind's Landscape: An Introduction to the Philosophy of Mind.* Oxford: Blackwell Publisher, Ltd., 7–8.

mental states causally affect our physical bodies. For example:

- Fred believes he is driving too fast and steps on the brake.
- Sally desires another beer and waves over the waitress.
- Bob wants a promotion and buys his boss a bottle of Scotch whiskey.

The mind (beliefs, desires, and wants), in these cases, caused the body or a physical event to occur (step on brake, wave hand, and buy Scotch). However, the body or a physical event can also affect the mind. Consider the following:

- Fred has a car accident and is in pain.
- Sally drank too much beer and is feeling sick.
- Bob is laid off and is sad.

In these examples, a physical event (car accident, drinking beer, being laid off) caused a mental state to occur (pain, feeling sick, sad). It's rather obvious that the mind and body interact with one another. But the interaction between mind and body quickly becomes mysterious when we reflect on the different properties of each. If neuroscientists were to crack open a person's skull, they would not find beliefs, desires, or memories sitting alongside the 100 billion neurons making up the brain. In fact, the mind seems to have properties unlike the brain or physical body,

which makes it potentially unsuitable for scientific investigation and explanation. In this sense, scientists have little knowledge of how the brain works and ultimately cause mental states.

To see the problem, consider one of the previous examples: Fred believes he is driving too fast and steps on the brake. A scientist could dissect (metaphorically and literally) Fred's behaviour to explain why he stepped on the brake by investigating the physical properties of the act itself: the weight of the car and its velocity in relation to city speed limits; the physiology and biomechanics of Fred's leg; Fred's vision and his perception of the speedometer; and so forth. But how would a scientist investigate and describe Fred's belief? Beliefs, desires, hopes, fears, and mental states have non-physical properties—they do not have size, shape, mass, or extension; they cannot be seen, touched, smelled, tasted, or heard. Describing the mind is very different than describing the body (see Box 4.2). If we were to ask Fred the weight of his belief, its taste, its smell, or its texture, he would not be remiss in calling us crazy. But here's the problem. If mental states have non-physical properties and the body has physical properties, then causal interaction between the two should be impossible.

Of course, I do not want to suggest that humans cannot describe the mind. Humans do describe mind and emotions with great clarity and passion. But the mind, unlike physical bodies, is not directly

Box 4.2 What Do You Think?

Do the mind and body have different properties or characteristics? List below the properties of body and mind.

Properties of the Body

Properties of the Mind

If the mind and body have different properties, would this convince you that the interaction between mind and body is impossible?

observable and has no size or spatial location; we only have intimate first-person access to our own thoughts, feelings, beliefs, desires, and emotions. On the other hand, bodies are solid chunks of material stuff, extend in three-dimensional space, and are publicly observable and measurable. So is the mind physical or non-physical? If the mind has no space, size, or mass—if it's non-physical—how does it causally affect our bodies, and vice versa? How can the non-physical mind—a massless, weightless, unextended thing—push against my nerves, muscles, and bones to cause me to act? If the mind has space, size, and mass—if it is physical—then it needs to be explained how mental states can be physical and in what way. This is the **mind–body problem.**

Initially, many students are not perplexed by the mind–body problem because scientific research has shown that humans have a mind and body that causally interact via neurons and biochemicals (the brain). Like reducing car emissions, science has amassed mounds of knowledge thereby erasing the mystery of how the mind and body interact. In other words, there is no mind–body problem at all. However, it would be a mistake to assume that science has unlocked

all the biological details of the mind. In fact, the scientific investigation of mind–brain is only in its infancy. Thus, in order to solve this problem we must turn to **metaphysics**.

Metaphysics, broadly defined, is the philosophical investigation into the constitution, structure, and nature of reality. It tends to be broader in scope than the sciences (e.g., physics) since, as we saw earlier, it traditionally was concerned with the existence of non-physical entities such as God's existence (Butchvarov 489). More specifically, the mind–body problem is part of a branch of metaphysics called ontology. **Ontology** is the study of being or existence. Typical questions include What things exists? Are there basic things out of which other things are composed? How are things related to one another? (Martin 166). These definitions, for our purposes, are fitting because this chapter will investigate the ultimate structure, constitution, and nature of the mind and how it relates to the body. And to do this, we must move beyond the sciences to find potential answers. As I mentioned before, scientists are still behoved to find a scientific explanation of mental states and, yet, we know thinking, believing, desiring, wanting, and so forth, are fundamental to us as conscious beings. In short, if scientists cannot explain the mind, perhaps we should turn to philosophers. This is not to suggest that philosophy is superior; philosophy is continuous with science. However, what is necessary is philosophical analysis to determine whether minds exist, and if so, in what way? There are two general answers to this question: 1) Metaphysical **materialists (physicalists)** argue all reality is physical in nature. The mind is nothing but biochemical and neurological happening in the brain; it's not mysterious, ghostly, or unexplainable. 2) Metaphysical **dualists** argue that one part of reality is physical (boats, houses, cars, etc.), the other is non-physical (mind, God,[3] etc.). The mind and body are two different substances that, somehow, interact.

The philosophy of mind is one of the most intriguing areas of philosophy because it bridges other disciplines including psychology, neuroscience, cognitive science, artificial intelligence, chemistry, and biology. It is also where contemporary philosophers are conducting some of the

Figure 4.1 Overview of the Philosophy of Mind

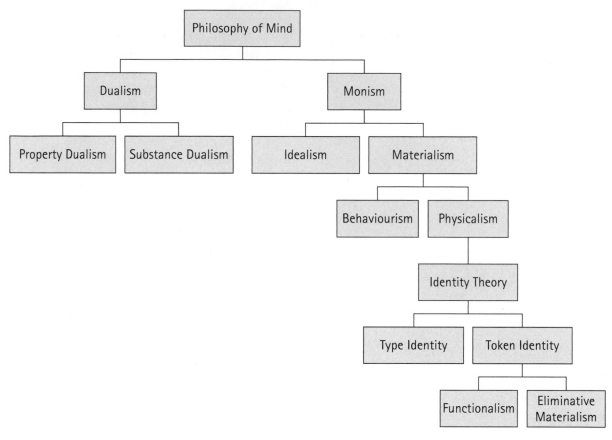

Philosophy of mind has three main categories: dualism, idealism, and materialism, also known as physicalism. However, most contemporary philosophers reject substance dualism and idealism as coherent philosophical doctrines, instead adhering to some form of physicalism. Physicalism is the metaphysical thesis that everything is physical or supervenes on the physical. Although physicalists do not deny that some things *appear* to be non-physical, such as beliefs, hopes, fears, thoughts, emotions, and so on, they nevertheless believe that *in reality* these things are physical in nature.

Source: Adapted from John Searle. (2004). *Mind: A Brief Introduction.* New York: Oxford University Press, 52.

most cutting-edge research. The mind–body problem can be challenging due to the conceptual nature of some of the ideas; however, it is important to our modern understanding of who we are and who we might become in the future; see Figure 4.1. I encourage students to approach this chapter with an open mind (no pun intended) and not to dismiss the mind–body problem as a relic of the past. How the mind and body relate to one another is one of the most pressing and difficult problems in philosophy today. To understand the history of the mind–body problem, we must, once again, start with Descartes.

Dualism

I was thrown out of N.Y.U. my freshman year…for cheating on my metaphysics final. You know, I looked within the soul of the boy sitting next to me.
—Woody Allen

If you die you're completely happy and your soul somewhere lives on. I'm not afraid of dying. Total peace after death, becoming someone else is the best hope I've got.
—Kurt Cobain

Discussion Questions

1. Talk of souls is commonplace in our society. Some people are soulless, others are soulful; finding true love is akin to finding a soul mate; some people like soul music, while others spend their life soul searching. Poetry, music, books,[4] and evangelical preachers often refer to souls as a way of giving inspiration, meaning, and purpose to our lives. Our modern concept of soul dates back to the Hebrews (eleventh and twelfth centuries B.C.E.) and ancient Greeks.[5] Throughout Christian history, the soul has been thought of as the source of thinking, consciousness, and free will. It was also considered, and still is, that part of a person that survives death, something not part of the physical world and outside the laws of physics. The soul is a *spiritual reality*, not a physical reality (Elbert 29–30). Inconsistently, although souls are supposed to be immaterial, it is commonly believed they can produce physical effects such as being visible or even audible. Do souls exist? Can souls affect our physical world? If souls exist, does it mean there is a physical and non-physical reality? Discuss how the existence of souls might show that dualism is true.

2. One of Descartes' arguments for dualism is based on the notion that minds can exist without a body. To have a mind, or to be conscious, is to be a thinking thing. In this sense, one's body will have no causal effects on one's mind. A body can exist independent of a mind because it's an extended thing and is not a necessary component to having thoughts, beliefs, emotions, and so forth. If so, then destruction of the body will not destroy the mind because, according to Descartes, they are two distinct substances. Is Descartes' conclusion correct? Is it possible for one to exist without a body? Is there life after death? Give reasons for your answers.

3. Other arguments for dualism use the paranormal—such as telepathy (mind reading), precognition (seeing the future), telekinesis (thought control), and clairvoyance (knowledge of distance objects)—as evidence. Such paranormal activity is difficult to explain using scientific laws and physics (Churchland, *Matter and Consciousness* 14). Do such paranormal activities show that dualism is true? Are there physical causes to such phenomena? Why or why not?

The Mind and Body Don't Mix

As we saw earlier, Descartes wrote the *Meditations* in a time when the natural sciences were taking on secular overtones. Prior to Descartes, the science of the day was based on Aristotle. For Aristotle, the natural world is goal-directed or **teleological**. This means that the behaviour of things could be explained and predicted by appealing to their various goals and ends or what Aristotle calls **final causes**. For example, the final cause of a caterpillar is a butterfly; the final cause of a tadpole is a frog; and the final cause of the human eye is sight. Being a butterfly, frog, and giving sight are goals to which each individual thing strives. This is not to say that they consciously reach their goals, but they do each seek their own natural ends. However, the new science of Copernicus, Galileo, and Newton was a direct attack against Aristotle's teleological theory. We can explain and predict the world, not by referring to final causes as Aristotle suggests, but by appealing to laws of nature and other physical processes. For example, the transformation of a tadpole to a frog is explained not because the tadpole is trying to achieve some natural end but due to thyroxine, a hormone produced by the thyroid gland, which causes the animal to reabsorb its tail and grow legs (Postlethwait and Hopson 569). Similarly, we can explain the human eye not by appealing to the final cause of sight but by appealing to the cornea, pupil, iris, lens, retina, photoreceptor cells, and the optic nerve. In short, light energy is converted into electrical energy that creates a visual image of the object in the brain (Postlethwait and Hopson 596). In other words, there is no need to appeal to Aristotelian final causes because there is no goal, design, or purpose in nature except mechanical laws and biological processes.

However, the shift from Aristotelian final causes to mechanical laws often fails to apply to human behaviour. Much of human behaviour is explained by talking about mental states, which involves goals, intentions, or purposes—final causes. As Neil Campbell explains, "It became a mistake to talk about the natural world as though it were goal-directed. However, human behaviour continued to be explained in terms of mental states like goals and purposes. Thus, human beings began to seem very different from ordinary physical things…" (15). For example, we can explain that Sally is putting on her raincoat because she believes it's raining and desires not to get wet. Staying dry is the goal or purpose of her putting on the raincoat and we can explain this purpose by referring to her mental states. Explaining human behaviour in mechanical terms, however, becomes problematic, if not impossible, because the mind can only be explained by referring to final causes. Descartes sought to solve this problem by arguing that humans are composed of two kinds of things: a material body and an immaterial mind. Thus mind–body dualism was born.

To understand Descartes' dualism, we must look back to his earlier arguments on knowledge. Recall that Descartes used methodological scepticism as a way of producing a suitable foundation upon which he could build his edifice of knowledge. After submersing his beliefs in an acid bath of doubt, Descartes found one thing of which he is absolutely certain, namely, that he is a thinking thing. And if he is a thinking thing, then by extension he must also necessarily exist. Why? Because he cannot doubt that he doubts. That is, it's by virtue of doubting that proves to Descartes clearly and distinctly that he is a conscious being and, therefore, must exist (*cogito ergo sum*).

At the end of the *Second Meditation,* Descartes' *cogito* only applies to his mind, since Descartes is less certain about the physical world. However, it's rekindled in the *Sixth Meditation* and is one of the main arguments for dualism known as the **argument from doubt**. Descartes argues that he clearly and distinctly has an idea of himself as a thinking,

non-extended thing. He also has a distinct idea of his body as a non-thinking and extended thing. Moreover, because his mind is distinct from his body, he can exist without it. What Descartes means is that the mind and body are independent of one another. For Descartes, he cannot doubt that he has a mind because so long as he doubts, or is conscious, it means he is a thinking being and therefore exists. But he can doubt that he has a body because his body is not necessary for him to exist. That is, a body can exist independently of a mind because it's merely an extended thing and not a necessary component to defining who he is as a conscious being. So the destruction of the body will not destroy the mind. Hence, the mind and body are two distinct substances.

Still, we ought not to dismiss the existence of the physical world altogether. The bridge or connection that Descartes sought between the physical world and mental world was based on the existence of God. Put simply, God would not allow people to be so massively deceived by their conscious experiences of the physical world because what is clear and distinct to one's consciousness is always true. And since God would never create humans in such a way that our clearest beliefs are false, then our beliefs about the external world will also be true. To allow humans to believe that their perceptions are deceitful implies that God himself is deceitful. And this implies that God is imperfect, something Descartes thinks is impossible. But we ought to be careful here. Descartes is not suggesting that material objects exactly represent their specific shape, size, motion, location, and so forth. After all, says Descartes, they may not exist in the way that exactly corresponds to how they are perceived by the senses. In short, we are still in the grip of doubt.

What emerges, for Descartes, is that humans are made up of two distinct realities or substances: a mind and a body, which are somehow linked together. We have bodies, which are part of the physical world, and minds, which are not part of the physical world, but something else. The argument can be put as follows:

1. Anything that I can clearly and distinctly understand can be created by God exactly

as I understand it. So if I can clearly and distinctly understand one thing a part from another, this is enough to make me certain that the two things are distinct.

2. I can form a clear and distinct understanding of my own existence as depending on nothing more than the fact that I think, and hence (from Premise 1) it follows that nothing belongs to my essence except thought.

3. I also have a clear and distinct understanding of physical bodies (including my own) simply as extended matter, without possessing any thought.

> Hence, I (or my soul) am distinct from my physical body, and can exist without it. (Morton 89–90)

The world thus consists of two different realties: mental substances and physical substances. To make his argument stick, Descartes uses what is now known as the **Principle of the Nonidentity of Discernibles** or **Leibniz's Law**. Although Descartes precedes Leibniz, the argument is similar: if two distinct things have identical properties, then they must be the same thing. Or, put in other words, if two things do not have the same identical properties, then they are not identical. Minds have the properties of being non-spatial, immaterial, and can only be known privately; bodies, on the other hand, have the properties of being spatial, material, and can be known publicly. In fact, Descartes thought the body was akin to a machine, like a clock. The mind is a ghost in a machine. Hence, given that minds and bodies do not share the exact same properties, then they cannot be identical or the same thing.

An interesting corollary of Descartes' conclusions seems to be that one's body does not define one's concept of self. If you draw your attention to your own thoughts, sensations, and emotions, you do not apprehend the physical working of the brain. The only thing you can know with certainty is what is going on within your head. Introspection reveals not only that the mind is vastly different from the body (Churchland, *Matter and Consciousness* 14) but also that the body does not play a role in who we are as persons. As David

Cockburn explains:

> Descartes' argument for the conclusion that he—that is, his mind—is entirely and truly distinct from his body is, then, this. I can form a conception of myself—conjure up a picture of myself—as a being that doubts, imagines, desires and so on without including anything bodily in that picture.…We can conclude, Descartes suggests, that the relation between him—that is, his mind—and his body is not like that between, for example, a smile and the face that the smile is on. The smile is not 'entirely and truly distinct' from the face… we do not know what it would be for there to be a smile without a face. By contrast, Descartes insists, he is quite clear what it would be like for him to exist without a body. In that sense the real person is quite distinct from his or her body. (5–6)

But is it true that our concepts of self is independent of our bodies? For Cockburn, we cannot separate ourselves from either our physical or mental qualities and activities because both are crucial in making up who we are as human beings (143). Consider, for example, Rick Hansen. It's been over 20 years since Rick Hansen started his wheelchair marathon around the world. His *Man in Motion* tour covered 40,000 kilometres and raised over $26 million for spinal cord research. Today, almost 50, Hansen is married with two children and CEO of the Rick Hansen Foundation. The foundation has raised over $178 million to aid research and improve the quality of life for those suffering from spinal cord injuries. Hansen, a native of Williams Lake, B.C., was 15 years old when he lost the use of his legs in a car accident. The first two years after the accident Hansen says he was filled with anger, depression, and denial. However, Hansen states, "I believe my accident defined me as a person. It forced me to persevere over so many difficult challenges…I would never trade that for the use of my legs. I feel like I'm one of the luckiest guys on the planet" (Mickleburgh A6). Hansen seems to prove that Descartes is wrong regarding how we define ourselves. We define ourselves, in part, by our body. If so, physicalism looks like it's incorrect.

Descartes' second argument for dualism, which occurs much later in the *Sixth Meditation*, is known as the **argument from divisibility**. Put simply, the argument is as follows:

1. The mind is indivisible.
2. The body is divisible.
3. Therefore, the mind and body are not identical.

On the one hand, if we consider our thoughts, beliefs, emotions, etc., we will see that they are indivisible, in a literal way. For example, I cannot separate or divide my belief that John A. Macdonald was Canada's first prime minister. Equally, I cannot cut into parts my love for my wife and children. For Descartes, mental states like beliefs, love, and countless others, make up a unified conscious self, and, by their very nature, are indivisible.[6] On the other hand, the body is divisible. I can have surgery to remove my gall bladder or lose a limb in a car accident, for example. However, losing parts of the body takes nothing away from the mind; it remains intact. This is another way in which the body is divisible and the mind indivisible. Given this difference between minds and bodies, says Descartes, we have to conclude they are two different substances. In short, dualism is true.

Although the idea of dualism is fundamentally flawed, as we will see shortly, perhaps we ought not to dismiss it right away. In some respects, common sense supports dualism, as William Lyons explains:

> When the neurosurgeon operates, he operates on the brain not the mind. When the mad axeman attacks the lonely hiker, he dismembers the body not the mind. On the other hand, even if our body is rendered more or less totally inactive, the mind might remain healthy and active, thinking, imagining, regretting, hoping, planning, dreaming and day-dreaming. When the psychoanalyst treats his or her patients, eschewing the psychiatrist's application of surgery or chemicals to the body, he or she seeks a cure by contacting the mind directly. In short, we do seem to live two parallel lives such that it comes naturally to speak of ourselves as having both mental powers and physical skills, as having *a* mind and *a* body. (10)

Moreover, as Patricia Churchland points out in her article, Descartes was also suitably impressed with the human ability to reason and use language. If humans were merely mechanical things (bits of clockwork), it's hard to see how we could follow the rules of logic or use language in a creative way. In fact, Descartes thought animals were mechanical objects incapable of thought, emotion, or consciousness; they were like bits of clockwork. The human mind, however, is not bound by the laws of physics and allows us to produce unique thought. Hence, isn't dualism true?

However, common sense also tells us that the mind and body must also interact. For example, if you believe you're late for work and you start to run to make it on time, your belief (mental state) is causing your body to move (physical state). If you have a stomachache and don't feel like eating, your stomach (physical state) is causing you to not desire (mental state) food. But this raises a serious problem for Descartes. If dualism is true, Descartes must explain how the immaterial mind can interact with the material body. And unless we truly believe that the mind is literally a ghost in a machine, the wispy nature of mind would be unable to act on our body. In other words, if humans are composed of two substances—a material body and an immaterial mind—how can an immaterial mind move a material body, and vice versa?

Descartes certainly recognized this problem, and despite the fact that the mind and body are separate, he was convinced that they interact (see Figure 4.2). How? For Descartes, they interact by what is called the pineal gland, located at the base of the brain. Although scientists at the time didn't actually know what the gland did, Descartes surmised that it facilitated the interaction between mind and body. The interaction between mind and body worked via animal spirits, or what we know today as

Figure 4.2 The Mechanical Philosophy

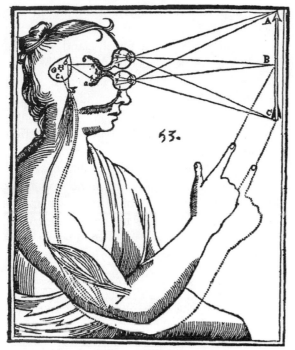

A diagram from a 1664 work on physiology by Descartes showing how inputs by the sensory organs are passed on to the pineal gland and then to the immaterial spirit.

Source: Descartes' *Treatise of Man* (1664).

cerebrospinal fluid, which permeates the body. Although detailed discussion of Descartes' interactionism is beyond present purposes, he clearly had a well thought out theory of mind–body interaction that supported his dualist position. But what's crucial for Descartes' argument, as explained in Churchland's article, is that reason and consciousness were thought to be beyond physical explanation.

Descartes' dualism, also known as Cartesian dualism (Descartes = Cartesian), was one of the most influential theories between the seventeenth and twentieth centuries. Although other philosophers put forward their own theories of mind,[7] none had the staying power of dualism. Why did dualism persist for so long? It persisted because of two important reasons. First, the very idea of consciousness—the ability to use the mind's eye to survey the seemingly never-ending thoughts,

emotions, and sensations that parade across one's mental stage—seems to be central to who we are as humans. The idea of consciousness, also known as **introspection**, shows that we have intellectual powers to think about our thoughts in a contemplative way not found in other animals (Lyons 13–14).[8] Second, a scientific/mechanical point of view threatens to make us less human; machine-like and soulless creatures subservient to universal laws and striped of divine creation and the freedom and dignity that goes along with it (Leahey 109). In other words, a purely scientific view of consciousness would render the mind merely another physical object, removed from God's providence.

Problems with Dualism

But is dualism an acceptable theory of mind? There are numerous problems with Cartesian dualism. The first, says Patricia Churchland, is the interaction problem. If Descartes is right that the mind and body are two separate substances, one material and the other non-material—interaction will be impossible. There is no way a ghost-like mind will be able to affect the physical world, including our body. And notice, the pineal gland doesn't solve this problem, since Descartes is just making reference to another physical object. That is, Descartes must now explain how the pineal gland, which is physical, can effect mental events, and vice versa (Guttenplan, *The Mind's Landscape* 184). Moreover, Descartes was wrong about what the pineal gland does. The pineal gland is not the centre of interaction between the mind and body; it secretes a hormone called melatonin which regulates sleep and may influence mood, reproduction, and puberty (Postlethwait and Hopson 569). In short, Descartes has yet to explain how the mind and body interact.

Second, Descartes cannot explain where this interaction between mind and body is to take place. From a purely physical perspective, we can trace human movement from muscles and bones, to electrical impulse in the brain, each having a specific spatial position. But if the

Box 4.3 Descartes' Category-Mistake

This objection comes from the English philosopher Gilbert Ryle. Ryle's ordinary language argument rests on the idea that Descartes' ghost in the machine dogma rests on a category-mistake (17–18). The mistake results when we represent certain things belonging to one logical type or category, when in fact they belong to another logical type or category. Imagine, for example, a close friend visits you at school. She asks to be shown around. You oblige and show her the library, lecture halls, sports facilities, administrative offices, and so forth. After the tour, she asks, "That is all well and good but where is the university?" Although you might think her mad, in reality, she has made a category-mistake. The "university" is not something separate or beyond its constitutive parts. Its individual parts make up the university. Descartes is making a similar mistake. Minds are not something separate or above and beyond the body. Descartes is wrong in thinking that human movements are the result of some immaterial mind or non-mechanical causes. The "mental" world belongs to the "physical" world; there is no ghost in the machine. Instead, Ryle argues that many mentalistic terms are merely dispositions to behave in certain ways. In other words, he is a behaviourist. For example, to describe someone as intelligent does not imply some occult or mysterious process going on in that person's head, but a disposition to behave in intelligent ways. To put another way, to say that "Sally believes it is raining" is to say that Sally is behaving in ways consistent with her belief: putting on a raincoat, picking up an umbrella, etc. Ryle's point is that the very idea of a non-material mind is myth. In this sense, the mind–body problem simply disappears. There is no interaction problem because human mind just is part of a very complicated physical process within the body.

mind is non-physical, then there will be no physical space where mind–body interaction can take place. And, again, bringing in the pineal gland does not solve the issue. If the mind is non-physical, the pineal gland, which is physical, cannot be locus of interaction because there will be no physical location in which the mind will be able to push and pull on the pineal gland, its animal spirits, and muscles and bones. The very idea of mind–body interaction is incoherent (see Box 4.3).

Third, if dualism cannot explain how and where interaction between the mind and body takes place, Ockham's Razor[9] dictates we appeal to the most simple of explanations, namely, that the mind and body are not two separate substances but the same substance. That is, we appeal to materialism (physicalism). The explanatory impotence of dualism, compared to materialism, suggests that physicalism is the best, and most simple, explanation (Churchland, *Matter and Consciousness* 18). Although we do not have perfect knowledge of how the mind and brain work, says Churchland, we have sophisticated knowledge of the brain and how it works, including how neurons are organized and its various biochemicals. The story is complex and beyond the scope of this text, but support for physicalism is most striking when we consider cases of neural impairment and damage. Consider the classic case of Phineas Gage. Gage was a highly intelligent, efficient, and competent 26-year-old railway foreman working near Cavandish, Vermont, on September 14, 1848. He and his crew were preparing the way for the railway line by removing debris and clearing rock. This meant that large sections of rock had to be blasted apart in order to clear them. To do this, they would drill a hole in the rock, put down explosive powder, put in a fuse, and then fill with the rest of the hole with sand, which was then tamped using a 3-foot, 7-inch steel rod. In the late afternoon on this summer day, Gage became distracted and tamped down the explosive power instead of the sand. A spark resulted and the subsequent explosion sent the steel rod through his left cheek and ripped through the frontal cortex of his brain.

Box 4.4 Does Psychiatry Prove Descartes Wrong?

Another example in support of physicalism comes from psychiatry. Although most of us have felt depressed or "blue" sometime in our lives, major depressive disorder is significantly more severe. Symptoms include weight loss or gain, sleeping problems, fatigue, inability to think clearly, loss of pleasure in life, frequent thoughts about death and feelings of worthlessness (Price and Lynn 186). Research tends to support a biochemical cause for major depressive disorder, including low levels of chemical neurotransmitters, such as dopamine and norepinephrine, resulting in reduced neural activation in the brain. Antidepressant drugs can change the brain's biochemical levels and thereby increase neural activity and elevate a person's mood (Price and Lynn 196). Psychiatrists have also found a biochemical cause for schizophrenia. Schizophrenia is a debilitating disease marked by symptoms such as delusions, hallucinations, listlessness, catatonic behaviour, or inappropriate emotion. Excess dopamine at certain synapses of the brain is associated with the disorder and can be blocked with antipsychotic drugs, thereby alleviating schizophrenic symptoms (Price and Lynn 238–239). Does depression and schizophrenia offer convincing proof that dualism is false? Now consider disorders like anorexia nervosa and phobias. There is little evident linking anorexia nervosa and phobias to biological or neurological causes. How could a physicalist explain such disorders? Do these disorders suggest that dualism is true?

Amazingly, Gage survived the accident despite massive injury to his head and extensive bleeding. But what is most remarkable about this story is the effect this accident had on his personality. Although physically the accident had no lasting

consequences, Gage was never the same person. Gage changed from being a loving, caring, responsible, polite, and thoughtful person, to a selfish, uncaring, irresponsible, and offensive person spewing profanity. This change in character eventually cost him his job with the railway company (Schaffhausen). But, if Descartes' dualism were true, then he needs to explain how the steel rod, and the resulting brain damage, could affect the non-physical mind. From Descartes' perspective, the accident should not have changed Gage's personality. In short, the brain damage ought not to have had any mental effect. But it did. Likewise, alcohol, drugs, and the degeneration of neurons can also profoundly impair, cripple, or destroy rational thought. This clearly demonstrates that dualism is false; that the mind and brain are the same substance (see Box 4.4).

A fourth problem for dualism, says Churchland, is taken from evolutionary biology. If we assume that humans are the product of natural selection sharing a common ancestor from chimpanzees, a question is raised about where this "soul stuff" could come from. If it's unlikely that minds could have evolved, the only other explanation is to espouse some supernatural force. However, this is not only contrary to evolutionary biology but rules out the possibility of higher mammals, like chimps and monkeys, having minds. Research clearly demonstrates chimps, monkeys, and other higher animals have minds; they can think, have emotions, and solve problems.[10] Dualism, from an evolutionary perspective, is false.

However, as Churchland points out, dualists might argue that materialism cannot explain the unity of consciousness (or self). The problem is that the physicalists must explain how unconscious brain processes can relate to our conscious experiences in such a way to form a united whole. This is difficult from a physicalist point of view because in giving a neurological explanation they risk eliminating the very thing they are trying to explain—consciousness. Unity of consciousness or self is not problematic for dualism because who we are—our consciousness or self—is clearly and distinctly known through introspection and self-awareness. However, as Churchland observes, consciousness is not a single type of brain process that is either on or off. The brain has numerous mechanisms responsible for this apparent unity of consciousness. But, most importantly, dualism must explain how the non-physical mind unifies our experiences in consciousness. It cannot do this without begging the question—that is, dualism presupposes the very thing (unity of consciousness) that it is trying to explain.

Another problem for physicalists is free will. Explaining our ability to freely choose between actions has been problematic because free will had never been captured in a reductionist approach to mind. If humans are nothing but physical creatures governed by physical laws, then our behaviour must also be governed by physical laws. This would mean we could not willfully change our behaviour. In short, we don't have free will. Recently, however, Daniel Dennett, in his book *Freedom Evolves*, has tackled the problem of free will head on, arguing that there is nothing non-physical about it. Having free will is congruent with our long evolutionary history. Even though free will is determined by our biology, humans have evolved with the ability to freely make decisions. But notice, says Churchland, free will is also problematic for dualism. To say our ability to freely choose is congruent with a non-physical mind is no explanation of why this is so. Descartes must explain how the non-physical mind can freely choose and cause us to behave in willful ways. And dualists cannot do this without taking us back to the interaction problem discussed earlier. Although both issues are complex, says Churchland, the arguments presented make dualism highly suspect.

However, the dualist's focus on the qualitative properties of mind is not lost on philosophers. The mind does seem to have qualities or properties different than the body. This is known as **property dualism**. But as Churchland points out, for some philosophers property dualism is an insuperable problem that cannot be reduced to scientific explanations, while other philosophers envision a future where scientific explanation will eliminate the problem altogether. These ideas will be taken up in subsequent sections.

19

René Descartes

(1596–1650)

René Descartes was born March 31, 1596, in the small town of La Heye en Tourain (later renamed "Le Heye-Descartes" in 1802 and renamed, once again, "Descartes" in 1967). At the age of ten, Descartes' father sent him to the Jesuit college in La Fleche, one of the leading academic schools in Europe. Descartes went on to study law at the University of Poitiers, graduating in 1616. He never practised law; instead, at the age to 22, he enlisted in the army of Prince Nassau. It's speculated that Descartes was part of the engineering corps and unlikely saw combat, but it was during a tour of duty in Germany (1619) that Descartes had an epiphany. It occurred to him that a new system of mathematics and science could be developed based on human reason alone. After this awakening, Descartes left the army, pursuing a life of pleasure (travelling, gambling, and duelling). In 1628, he left for Holland to fulfill his vision of a rational science. His time in Holland was particularly fruitful, as he published Discourse on Method *(1637),*

Meditations on First Philosophy (1641), Principles of Philosophy (1644), and The Passions of the Soul (1649). Descartes' philosophical views made him quite famous. One admirer was Queen Christina of Sweden. In 1649, she invited Descartes to come to Sweden as her personal tutor. Feeling obligated, Descartes reluctantly accepted. However, Queen Cristina demanded that her tutorials be held at 5:00 a.m. for five hours, three days a week. Descartes, who suffered from a delicate constitution, habitually worked from bed until noon every day. Queen Christian's early hours, and the cold climate of Sweden, played havoc with his health. The tutoring sessions wore him down, eventually resulting in severe pneumonia. After suffering for a week, Descartes died on February 11, 1650.

Sixth Meditation

However, now, after having begun to know better the cause of my coming to be, I believe that I must not rashly admit everything that I seem to derive from the senses. But, then, neither should I call everything into doubt.

First, because I know that all the things that I clearly and distinctly understand can be made by God exactly as I understand them, it is enough that I can clearly and distinctly understand one thing without the other in order for me to be certain that the one thing is different from the other, because at least God can establish them separately. The question of the power by which this takes place is not relevant to their being thought to be different. For this reason, from the fact that I know that I exist, and that meanwhile I judge that nothing else clearly belongs to my nature or essence except that I am a thing that thinks, I rightly conclude that my essence consists

in this alone: that I am only a thing that thinks. Although perhaps (or rather, as I shall soon say, to be sure) I have a body that is very closely joined to me, nevertheless, because on the one hand I have a clear and distinct idea of myself—insofar as I am a thing that thinks and not an extended thing—and because on the other hand I have a distinct idea of a body—insofar as it is merely an extended thing, and not a thing that thinks—it is therefore certain that I am truly distinct from my body, and that I can exist without it.

Moreover, I find in myself faculties endowed with certain special modes of thinking—namely the faculties of imagining and sensing—without which I can clearly and distinctly understand myself in my entirety, but not vice versa: I cannot understand them clearly and distinctly without me, that is, without the knowing substance to which they are attached. For in their formal concept they include an act of understanding; thus I perceive that they are distinguished from me just as modes are to be distinguished from the thing of which they are modes. I also recognize certain other faculties—like those of moving from one place to another, of taking on various shapes, and so on—that surely no more can be understood without the substance to which they are attached than those preceding faculties; for that reason they cannot exist without the substance to which they are attached. But it is clear that these faculties, if in fact they exist, must be attached to corporeal to extended substances, but not a knowing substance, because extension—but certainly not understanding—is contained in a clear and distinct concept of them. But now there surely is in me a passive faculty of sensing, that is, of receiving and knowing the ideas of sensible things; but I cannot use it unless there also exists, either in me or in something else, a certain active faculty of producing or bring about these ideas. This faculty surely cannot be in me, since it clearly presupposes no intellection, and these ideas are produced without my cooperation and often against my will. Because this faculty is in a substance other than myself, in which ought to be contained—formally or eminently—all the reality that is objectively in the ideas produced by this faculty (as I have just now taken notice), it thus remains that either this substance is a body (or corporeal nature) in which is contained formally all that is contained in ideas of objectively or it is God—or some other creature more noble than a body—in which it is all contained eminently. But, since God is not a deceiver, it is absolutely clear that he sends me these ideas neither directly and immediately—nor even through the mediation of any creature, in which the objective reality of these ideas is contained not formally but only eminently. Since he plainly gave me no faculty for making this discrimination—rather, he gave me a great inclination to believe that these ideas proceeded from corporeal things—I fail to see why God cannot be understood to be a deceiver, if they proceeded from a source other than corporeal things. For this reason, corporeal things exist. Be that as it may, perhaps not all bodies exist exactly as I grasp them by sense, because this grasp by the senses is in many cases very obscure and confused. But at least everything is in these bodies that I clearly and distinctly understand—that is, everything, considered in a general sense, that is encompassed in the object of pure mathematics.

But as to how this point relates to the other remaining matters that are either merely particular—as, for example, that the sun is of such and such a size or shape, and so on—or less clearly understood—as, for example, light, sound, pain, and so on—although they are very doubtful and uncertain, still, because God is not a deceiver, and no falsity can be found in my opinions, unless there is also in me a faculty given me by God for the purpose of rectifying this falsity, these features provide me with a certain hope of reaching the truth in them. And plainly it cannot be doubted that whatever I am taught by nature has some truth to it; for by "nature," taken generally, I understand only God himself or the coordination, instituted by God, of created things. I understand nothing else by my nature in particular than the totality of all the things bestowed on me by God.

There is nothing that this nature teaches me in a more clear-cut way than that I have a body that is ill-disposed when I feel pain, that it needs food and drink when I suffer hunger or thirst, and so on. Therefore, I ought not to doubt that there is some truth in this.

By means of these feelings of pain, hunger, thirst and so on, nature also teaches that I am present to my body not merely in the way a seaman is present to his ship, but that I am tightly joined and, so to speak, mingled together with it, so much so that I make up one single thing with it. For otherwise, when the body is wounded, I, who am nothing but a thing that thinks, would not then sense the pain. Rather, I would perceive the wound by means of the pure intellect, just as a seaman perceives by means of sight whether anything in the ship is broken. When the body lacks food or drink, I would understand this in a clear-cut fashion; I would not have confused feelings of hunger and thirst. For certainly these feelings of thirst, hunger, pain, and so on are nothing but confused modes of thinking arising from the union and, as it were, the mingling of the mind with the body.

Moreover, I am also taught by nature that many other bodies exist around my body; some of them are to be pursued, and others are to be avoided. And to be sure, from the fact that I sense widely different colors, sounds, odors, tastes, heat, roughness, and so on, I rightly conclude that in the bodies from which these different perceptions of the senses proceed, there are differences corresponding to the different perceptions—although perhaps the former are not similar to the latter. But from the fact that some of these perceptions are pleasant and others unpleasant, it is plainly certain that my body—or rather my whole self, insofar as I am composed of a body and a mind—can be affected by various benefits and harms from the surrounding bodies.

But I have accepted many other things, and, although I seem to have been taught them by nature, still it was not really nature that taught them to me, but a certain habit of making unconsidered judgments. And thus it could easily happen that they are false, as, for example, the belief that any space where there is nothing that moves my senses is empty; or, for example, the belief that in a hot body there is something plainly similar to the idea of heat which is in me; or that in a white or green body there is the same whiteness or greenness that I sense; or in a bitter or sweet thing the same taste, and so on; or the belief that stars and towers, and any other distant bodies have only the same size and shape that they present to the senses—and other examples of the same sort. But lest I not perceive distinctly enough something about this matter, I ought to define more carefully what I properly understand when I say that I am "taught something by nature." For I am using "nature" here in a stricter sense than the totality of everything bestowed on me by God. For in this totality there are contained many things that pertain only to my mind, as, for example, that I perceive that

what has been done cannot be undone, and everything else that is known by the light of nature. At the moment the discussion does not center on these matters. There are also many things that pertain only to the body, as, for example, that it tends downward, and so on. I am not dealing with these either, but only with what has been bestowed on me by God, insofar as I am composed of mind and body. Therefore it is nature, thus understood, that teaches me to flee what brings a sense of pain and to pursue what brings a sense of pleasure, and the like. But it does not appear that nature, so conceived, teaches that we conclude from these perceptions of the senses anything in addition to this regarding things external to us unless there previously be an inquiry by the intellect; for it pertains to the mind alone, and not to the composite, to know the truth in these matters. Thus, although a star affects my eye no more than the flame from a small torch, still there is no real or positive tendency in my eye toward believing that the star if any bigger than the flame; rather, ever since my youth, I have made this judgment without reason. Although I feel heat upon drawing closer to the fire, and I feel pain upon drawing even closer to it, there is indeed no argument that convinces me that there is something in the fire that is similar either to the heat or to the pain, but only that there is something in the fire that causes in us these feelings of heat or pain. Although there be nothing in a given space that moves the sense, it does not therefore follow that there is no body in it. I use the perceptions of the senses that properly have been given by nature only for the purpose of signifying to the mind what is agreeable and disagreeable to the composite, of which the mind is a part; within those limits these perceptions are sufficiently clear and distinct. However, I see that I have been in the habit of subverting the order of nature in these and many other matters, because I use the perceptions of the senses as certain rules for immediately discerning what the essence is of the bodies external to us; yet, in respect of this essence, these perceptions still show me nothing but obscurity and confusion.

I have already examined in sufficient detail how it could happen that my judgments are false, the goodness of God notwithstanding. But a new difficulty now comes on the scene concerning those very things that are shown to me by nature as things to be either sought or avoided, as well as concerning the internal senses in which I seem to have detected errors: for example, when a person, deluded by the pleasant taste of food, ingests a poison hidden inside it. But in this case he is impelled by nature only toward desiring the thing in which the pleasant taste is located, but not toward the poison, of which he obviously is unaware. Nothing else can be concluded here except that this nature is not all-knowing. This is not remarkable, since man is a limited being; thus only limited perfection is appropriate to man.

But we often err even in those things to which nature impels us; for example, when those who are ill desire food or drink that will soon be injurious to them. Perhaps it could have been said here that they erred because their nature was corrupt. But this does not remove our difficulty, because a sickly man is no less a creature of God than a healthy one; for that reason it does not seem any less repugnant that the sickly man got a deceiving nature from God. And just as a clock made of wheels and counter-weights follows all the laws of nature no less closely when it has been badly constructed and does not tell time accurately than when it satisfies on all scores the wishes of its maker, just so, if I should consider the body of a man—insofar as it is a kind of mecha-

nism composed of and outfitted with bones, nerves, muscles, veins, blood and skin—even if no mind existed in it, the man's body would still have all the same motions that are in it now except for those motions that proceed either from a command of the will or, consequently, from the mind. I readily recognize that it would be natural for this body, were it, say, suffering from dropsy, to suffer dryness of the throat, which commonly brings a feeling of thirst to the mind, and thus too its nerves and other parts are so disposed by the mind to take a drink with the result that the sickness is increased. It would be no more natural for this body, when there is no such infirmity in it and it is moved by the same dryness, to drink something useful to it. And, from the point of view of the intended purpose of the watch, I could say that it turns away from its nature when it does not tell the right time. Similarly, considering the mechanism of the human body as equipped for the motions that typically occur in it, I might think that it too turns away from its nature, if its throat were dry, when taking a drink would not be beneficial to its continued existence. Nevertheless, I realize well enough that this latter usage of the term "nature" differs greatly from the former. For this latter "nature" is only an arbitrary denomination, extrinsic to the things on which it is predicated and dependent upon my thought, because it compares a man in poor health and a poorly constructed clock with the idea of a man in good health and a well-made clock. But by "nature" taken in the former sense, I understand something that really is in things, and thus it is not without some truth.

When it is said, in the case of the dropsical body, that its "nature" is corrupt—from the fact that this body has a parched throat, and yet does not need a drink—it certainly is only an extrinsic denomination of nature. But be that as it may, in the case of the composite, that is, of a mind joined to such a body, it is not a pure denomination, but a true error of nature that this body should thirst when a drink would be harmful to it. Therefore it remains here to inquire how the goodness of God does not stand in the way of "nature," thus considered, being deceptive.

Now, first, I realize at this point that there is a great difference between a mind and a body, because the body, by its very nature, is something divisible, whereas the mind is plainly indivisible. Obviously, when I consider the mind, that is, myself insofar as I am only a thing that thinks, I cannot distinguish any parts in me; rather, I take myself to be one complete thing. Although the whole mind seems to be united to the whole body, nevertheless, were a foot or an arm or any other bodily part amputated, I know that nothing would be taken away from the mind; nor can the faculties of willing, sensing, understanding, and so on be called its "parts," because it is one and the same mind that wills, senses, and understands. On the other hand, no corporeal or extended thing can be thought by me that I did not easily in thought divide into parts; in this way I know that it is divisible. If I did not yet know it from any other source, this consideration alone would suffice to teach me that the mind is wholly different from the body.

Next, I observe that my mind is not immediately affected by all the parts of the body, but merely by the brain, or perhaps even by just one small part of the brain—namely, by that part in which the "common sense" is said to be found. As often as it is disposed in the same manner, it presents the same thing to the mind, although the other parts of the body can meanwhile orient themselves now this way, now that way, as countless experiments show—none of which need to be reviewed here.

I also notice that the nature of the body is such that none of its parts can be moved by another part a short distance away, unless it is also moved in the same direction by any of the parts that stand between them, even though this more distant part does nothing. For example, in the core ABCD, if the final part D is pulled, the first part A would be moved in exactly the same direction as it could be moved if one of the intermediate parts, B or C, were pulled and the last part D remained motionless. Just so, when I sense pain in the foot, physics teaches me that this feeling took place because the nerves scattered throughout the foot. These nerves, like cords, are extended from that point all the way to the brain; when they are pulled in the foot, they also pull on the inner parts of the brain to which they are stretched, and produce a certain motion in these parts of the brain. This motion has been constituted by nature so as to affect the mind with a feeling of pain, as if it existed in the foot. But because these nerves need to pass through the tibia, thigh, loins, back, and neck, with the result that they extend from the foot to the brain, it can happen that the part that is in the foot is not stretched; rather, one of the intermediate parts is thus stretched, and obviously the same movement will occur in the brain that happens when the foot was badly affected. The necessary result is that the mind feels the same pain. And we must believe that same regarding any other sense.

Finally, I observe that, since each of the motions occurring in that part of the brain that immediately affects the mind occasions only one sensation in it, there is no better way to think about this than that it occasions the sensation that, of all that could be occasioned by it, is most especially and most often conducive to the maintenance of a healthy man. Moreover, experience shows that such are all the senses bestowed on us by nature; therefore, clearly nothing is to be found in them that does not bear witness to God's power and goodness. Thus, for example, when the nerves in the foot are violently and unusually agitated, their motion, which extends through the marrow of the spine to the inner reaches of the brain, gives the mind at that point a sign to feel something—namely, the pain as if existing in the foot. This pain provokes it to do its utmost to move away from the cause, since it is harmful to the foot. But the nature of man could have been so constituted by God that this same motion in the brain might have displayed something else to the mind: either the motion itself as it is in the brain, or as it is in the foot, or in some place in between—or somewhere else entirely different. But nothing else serves so well the maintenance of the body. Similarly, when we need a drink, a certain dryness arises in the throat that moves its nerves, and, by means of them, the inner recesses of the brain. This motion affects the mind with a feeling of thirst, because in this situation nothing is more useful for us to know than that we need a drink to sustain our health; the same holds for the other matters.

From these considerations it is totally clear that, notwithstanding the immense goodness of God, the nature of man—insofar as it is composed of mind and body, cannot help but sometimes be deceived. For if some cause, not in the foot but in some other part through which the nerves are stretched from the foot to the brain—or perhaps even in the brain itself—were to produce the same motion that would normally be produced by a badly affected foot, then the pain will be felt as if it were in the foot, and the senses will naturally be deceived, because it is reasonable that the motion should always show the pain to the mind as something belonging to the foot rather than to some other part, since an identical motion in the brain can bring about only the identical effect

and this motion more frequently is wont to arise from a cause that harms the foot than from something existing elsewhere. And if the dryness of the throat does not, as is the custom, arise from the fact that drink aids in the health of the body, but from a contrary cause—as happens in the case of the person with dropsy—then it is far better that it should deceive, than if, on the contrary, it were always deceptive when the body is well constituted. The same goes for the other cases.

This consideration is most helpful, not only for noticing all the errors to which my nature is liable, but also for easily being able to correct or avoid them. To be sure, I know that every sense more frequently indicates what is true than what is false regarding those things that concern the advantage of the body, and I can almost always use more than one sense in order to examine the same thing. Furthermore, I can use memory, which connects present things with preceding ones, plus the intellect, which now has examined all the causes of error. I should no longer fear lest those things that are daily shown me by the senses, are false; rather, the hyperbolic doubts of the last few days ought to be rejected as worthy of derision—especially the principal doubt regarding sleep, which I did not distinguish from being awake. For I now notice that a very great difference exists between these two; dreams are never joined with all the other actions of life by the memory, as is the case with those actions that occur when one is awake. For surely, if someone, while I am awake, suddenly appears to me, and then immediately disappears, as happens in dreams, so that I see neither where he came from or where he went, it is not without reason that I would judge him to be a ghost or a phantom conjured up in my brain, rather than a true man. But when these things happen, regarding which I notice distinctly where they come from, where they are now, and when they come to me, and I connect the perception of them without any interruption with the rest of my life, obviously I am certain that these perceptions have occurred not in sleep but in a waking state. Nor ought I to have even a little doubt regarding the truth of these things, if, having mustered all the senses, memory, and intellect in order to examine them, nothing is announced to me by one of these sources that conflicts with the others. For from the fact that God is no deceiver, it follows that I am in no way deceived in these matters. But because the need to get things done does not always give us the leisure time for such a careful inquiry, one must believe that the life of man is vulnerable to errors regarding particular things, and we must acknowledge the infirmity of our nature.

20

Patricia Churchland (1943–)

Patricia Churchland was born in British Columbia on July 16, 1943. She received her B.A. from the University of British Columbia in 1965 and received her M.A. from the University of Pittsburgh in 1966. She went on to study for her B.Phil. at Oxford University, completing it in 1969. From 1969 to 1984, she taught at the

University of Manitoba until she was appointed professor at the University of California in 1984. In 1991, Churchland was awarded the prestigious MacArthur Fellowship, an award granted to researchers that show exceptional promise so they can continue their creative work. She has also been an adjunct professor at the Salk Institute since 1989. Churchland is currently chair of the University of California, San Diego philosophy department. She is married to her colleague Paul Churchland. Her books include Neurophilosophy: Toward a Unified Science of the Mind-Brain *(1986),* The Computational Brain *(with T. J. Sejnowski) (1992),* On the Contrary: Critical Essays 1987–1997 *(with Paul Churchland) (1998), and* Brain-Wise: Studies in Neurophilosophy *(2002).*

Substance Dualism

One line of resistance to a program aimed at reducing psychological theory to neuroscience is taken by those who deny that the mind is identical with the brain and who conceive of the mind instead as a nonphysical substance. Their hypothesis is that mental states such as perceptions, thoughts, feelings, and sensations are states, not of the brain, but of a different substance altogether. This substance is characterized as independent of the body inasmuch as it allegedly survives the brain's disintegration, though it is considered to interact causally with the brain when the latter is intact.

On this hypothesis, no reduction of psychological theory to neuroscientific theory is forthcoming because the former is a theory about the states and processes of mind-substance, whereas the latter is a theory about the states and processes of a material substance, the brain. Each substance is thought to have its own laws and its own range of properties, hence research on the brain is not going to yield knowledge of the mind and its dynamics, nor, by parity of reasoning, will research on the mind tell us anything much about how the brain works.

What is the evidence for the hypothesis that minds are nonphysical substances in which mental states such as beliefs, desires, and sensations inhere? Descartes was particularly impressed by the human capacity for reasoning and for language, and though he was a keen mechanist, he simply could not imagine how a mechanical device could be designed so as to follow rules of reasoning and to use language creatively. What sort of mechanical devices were the paradigm that inspired Descartes's imagination? Clockwork machines and fountains. And though some were intricate indeed, by our standards even the most elaborate clockwork devices of the seventeenth century do not have a patch on modern symbol-manipulating machines that can perform such tasks as guiding the flight path of a cruise missile or regulating the activities of a spacecraft on Mars. The advent of the modern computer has stolen much of the thunder of Descartes's argument that reasoning betokens a nonphysical substance (Dennett 1978b, 1986). Nevertheless, [...] the theme that reasoning, the *meaningfulness* of sentences in reasoning, and the *logical* relations between sentences used in reasoning eludes an explanation in physicalist terms is taken up by contemporary philosophers as the basis for antireductionist arguments. The outward form of the contemporary arguments is new and clever, but the motivating intuitions are discernibly Cartesian.

An intractable problem confronting substance dualism concerns the nature of the interaction between the two radically different kinds of substance. Soul-stuff allegedly has none of the properties of material-stuff and is not spatially extended, and the question therefore concerns how and where the two substances interact. This problem stymied Descartes, and his completely inadequate solution was to suggest that the "animal spirits" functioned to mediate between the two types of substance and that the subtle interaction took place in the pineal gland. But his animal spirits were composed of material stuff, albeit very fine material stuff, so the problem stood its ground. Can the mind be affected by, say, electrical or magnetic fields? For Descartes, apparently not, for then it would have properties in common with matter, and its status as a radically different substance would be imperiled.

On the classical picture, essentially two types of items were exchanged at the station where mind and brain interacted, wherever it was, and these were sensations and volitions. The brain was thought to send sensations to the mind, which could then use them in perception. The mind, on the other hand, was thought to send volitions to the brain, which could then translate the volitions into motor effects. The higher functions of the mind, including reasoning, consciousness, moral feelings, and the emotions, were assumed to function independently of the brain, save for the extent to which perceptions might figure in these functions. Perceptions were excepted because they were to some extent dependent on sensations. This independence of the higher mental operations from the physical business of the brain was really the raison d'être of the substance dualist hypothesis, for it was these mental functions that seemed utterly inexplicable in material terms. Given a life of their own in the nonphysical mind, reasoning and consciousness and their kind should be amenable to nonmaterial explanations, and getting these seemed far easier than getting brain-based explanations. We shall see this theme concerning reasoning and consciousness reappear in assorted guises in virtually every antireductionist argument, including those most recently minted.

The hypothesized independence of reasoning and consciousness that makes substance dualism attractive is at the same time a chronic and aggravating problem that costs it credibility. The difficulty is straightforward: reasoning, consciousness, moral feelings, religious feelings, political convictions, aesthetic judgments, moods, even one's deep-seated personality traits—all can be affected if the brain is affected by drugs or by lesions, for example. The more we know about neurology and about neuropharmacology, the more evident it is that the functions in question are not remotely as independent as the classical hypothesis asserts. On the materialist hypothesis, the observed interdependence is precisely what would be expected, but it is distinctly embarrassing to the dualist hypothesis.

Recent hypotheses meant to explain the nature of the interaction between the nonphysical mind and the physical brain are not significant improvements upon Descartes's proposal. Although Eccles (1977, Eccles and Robinson 1984) has energetically addressed the problem, his theory of the interaction remains metaphorical. His explanatory flow diagram consists essentially of many arrows connecting the "mind" box to the box for the language areas of the human brain. The question that persists after study of the array of arrows is this: what is the manner of interaction, and how does the nonphysical mind bring about changes of state in the brain, and vice versa? The inescapable conclusion is that the arrow-array is after all as much an explanatory surd as the notion of

Descartes's animal spirits finely but mysteriously "affecting" the nonmaterial substance in the confines of the pineal gland.

The unavailability of a solution to the manner of interaction between two radically different substances does not entail that substance dualism is false. For all we know now, further research may yet discover a solution. But with no leads at all and not even any serious plans for finding a solution, it does mean that the hypothesis has diminished appeal. This failure invites the conjecture that the problems the hypothesis was designed to solve might in fact be pseudoproblems, and in this respect they might be similar to the now-discarded problems of how the heart concocts vital spirits or how the tiny homunculi in sperm can themselves contain tinier homunculi containing even tinier sperm containing yet more tiny homunculi. The phenomena, as we now know for these cases, were radically misdescribed, and the corresponding problems, therefore, did not exist to be solved.

Additional difficulties further diminish the plausibility of substance dualism, and one such problem is drawn from evolutionary biology. Assuming that humans evolved from earlier mammalian species, that we and the chimpanzees share a common ancestor, and that we can trace out lineage back to single-celled organisms, then a question arises about where the soul-stuff came from. Do all organisms have it? If some organisms do not have such a substance, how did the others come to have it? Could it have evolved from physical stuff? If humans alone have minds, where did these substances come from? A theologically based answer is that nonphysical minds, unlike physical brains, are not an evolutionary product but were for the first time placed in contact with brains by divine intervention some 80,000 years (or in some calculations merely 6,000 years) ago. Since then, apparently, there has been continual intervention by a supernatural being to invest each human brain with its own non-physical mind.

The price of espousing substance dualism begins to look too high, for among other things it entails arbitrary and unmotivated exceptions to the plausible and unified story of the development of intelligence provided by modern evolutionary biology. On the other side of the ledger, the compensatory explanatory payoff from the hypothesis seems meager. If chimpanzees or monkeys do not have minds, then presumably their learning, perception, feeling, and problem solving are explained in terms of brain function. But if theirs, then why not ours? In the absence of solid evidence for the separate existence of the mind, the appeal of substance dualism fades.

The hypothesis of substance dualism is also supposed to explain the unity of consciousness (the unity of the self), and it is alleged that such unity cannot be explained on a materialist hypothesis (Eccles 1977). The reasoning here is less than convincing, both because it is far from clear what the phenomenon is that the hypothesis is meant to explain and because it is far from clear how the hypothesis succeeds in explaining this ill-specified phenomenon.

Consider first the phenomenon. Certain questions immediately arise: How do nonconscious mental states comport with alleged unity of consciousness? How does all that nonconscious processing postulated in cognitive science fit into the picture? How do the split-brain results fit? Or the blindsight results? Or the cases of split

personality? What about when the brain is in slow-wave sleep or in REM sleep? The questions are far too numerous for unity of consciousness to be a phenomenon in clear and unproblematic focus.

In a previous publication (1983) I argued that consciousness, as it is circumscribed in folk psychology, probably is not a natural kind, in much the way that impetus is not a natural kind. Nor, for example, do the categories "gems" or "dirt" delimit a natural kind. That is to say, *something* is going on all right, but it is doubtful that the generalizations and categories of folk psychology either do justice to that phenomenon or carve Nature at her joints. The evidence already indicates that consciousness is not a single type of brain process, and that if we think of consciousness as a kind of light that is either on or off, and that when an illuminates the contents of mental life, we are hopelessly mistaken. We already know that so-called subliminal experiences can affect "conscious" problem solving. We know that one can engage in a number of highly complex activities that once, even though not "paying attention" to them all. We know that brain activity as measured on the EEG during some REM sleep looks more like brain activity during fully awake periods than during other sleep periods. We know that some subjects who are in fact blind apparently fail to be aware that they are blind. We know that some patients with temporal lobe damage can learn complex cognitive skills and yet be completely unaware that they have done so—even while engaged in one of those very skills. And so on and on.[1] The brain undoubtedly has a number of mechanisms for monitoring brain processes, and the folk psychological categories of "awareness" and "consciousness" indifferently lump together an assortment of the mechanisms. As neurobiology and neuropsychology probe the mechanisms and functions of the brain, a reconfiguring of categories can be predicted.

The second question to be asked of the substance dualist concerns how his hypothesis explains the phenomenon, whatever that phenomenon is. How is it that the nonphysical mind yields unity of consciousness? How does it unify experiences occurring at different times? If the answer is that the nonphysical mind unifies because the experiences are experiences of *one* substance, then that answer is also available to the materialist, who can say that the experiences are experiences of *one* brain. If the answer is that it is simply in the nature of the nonphysical mind to be unified and to provide unity, then the sense that an *explanation* has been provided loses its hold. It is like saying, "It just does." Moreover, the materialist is entitled to make the same futile move: it is simply in the nature of the brain to provide unity to experiences. This is a standoff, and neither hypothesis advances our understanding. Therefore, the dualist cannot claim that his cases is supported by his being able, and the materialist's being unable, to explain the unity of consciousness.

A parallel discussion can be constructed concerning nonphysical minds and free will. Here the dualist credits his hypothesis with the ability to explain how humans have free will. In this instance too, it is farm from clear what the phenomenon is or how dualism explains anything about it. A dualist hypothesis claiming that the nonphysical mind acts freely because it is the nature of the mind to do so leaves us without explanatory nuts and bolts. And as before, for every move the dualist makes here, the physicalist has a counterpart move. Again the result is

a standoff, and the dualist can claim no advantage. (For the best recent discussion of the free will issue, see Dennett 1984b.)

The two primary foci for the dualist's conviction are the logical-meaningful dimension of cognition and the qualities of consciousness. The importance of these matters has struck dualist philosophers in different ways, with the consequence that some have gravitated to one focus and some to the other. One group has taken the nature of felt experience as *the* difficulty of paramount importance and hence has tended to side with materialists on the other question. That is, they expect that eventually the logical-meaningful dimension will ultimately have a causal neurobiological explanation. For these philosophers reasoning is not the stumbling block, partly because the idea that the logical-meaningful dimension of cognition is fundamentally noncausal is found objectionable. The second group has just the converse set of intuitions. Like reductionists, they think that ultimately consciousness and the qualities of felt experience will be explained in neurobiological terms. But for them, *the* difficulty of paramount importance lies in the logical-meaningful dimension of cognition. Here, they argue, are insurmountable problems for a reductionist strategy.[2] The reductionist has been useful to both camps by providing reductionist arguments for each to use against the other.

These dualist intuitions can be respectably sustained despite the hopeless problems of substance dualism in finding a coherent fit for the mind-substance in modern physics and biology. The general strategy in support of these intuitions has been to abandon the albatross idea of a distinct *substance* but to retain the idea of irreducibility. Thus, philosophers concerned with subjective experience have argued that subjective experience is an irreducible *property,* and philosophers concerned with the logical-meaningful dimension have argued for the irreducibility of cognitive *theory.* It is among these two, albeit inharmonious, groups that the most sophisticated antireductionist arguments are to be found, and characteristically they are not to be removed by a few casual rejoinders. [...]

Notes

1. I explore these and other examples in considerable detail in the aforementioned paper (1983).

2. One argument for substance dualism (see Eccles 1977) derives from certain neurophysiological results obtained by Benjamin Libet et al. (1979). The argument is particularly interesting because it is perhaps the only argument based solely on objective emperical data. According to Eccles and Libet, the data show that a mental event *precedes in time* the brain states causally responsible for it. In their judgement this can best be explained in terms of the nonphysical mind antedating the experience in time. As Eccles and Libet see it, if the mental event and the physical counterpart are not cotemporaneous, they cannot be identical.

After analyzing Libet's papers, I came to the conclusion that the interpretation of the data was unwarranted and that other simpler and more straightforward interpretations were readily available. In brief, I could not find any grounds for concluding that mental states are distinct from brain states. The experimental setup and the interpretation of the data are too complex to present here, and for an account of the disagreement between Libet and me on this question I refer the reader to Patricia S. Churchland 1981a, 1981b, and Libet 1981.

References

Churchland, Patricia Smith (1983). Consciousness: The transmutation of a concept. *Pacific Philosophical Quarterly* 64:80–95.

Dennett, Daniel C. (1978b. *Brainstorms: Philosophical essays on mind and psychology.* Montgomery, Vt.: Bradford Books. (Reprinted (1984). Cambridge, Mass.: MIT Press.)

Dennett, Daniel C. (1984b). *Elbow room: The varieties of free will worth wanting.* Cambridge, Mass.: MIT Press.

Dennett, Daniel C. (1986). Can machines think? In *How we know,* ed. M. Shafto, 1–26. San Francisco: Harper and Row.

Eccles, John C. (1977). Part II of *The self and its brain* (Popper and Eccles 1977), 225–406.

Eccles, John C. and Daniel N. Robinson (1984). *The wonder of being human.* New York: Free Press.

Identity Theory (Physicalism)

The brain is a wonderful organ; it starts working the moment you get up in the morning and does not stop until you get into the office.
—Robert Frost

Discussion Questions

1. Identity theories argue that mental states are brain states. The theory is attractive because it avoids the problems of dualism while appealing to physicalist instincts. One objection to an identity relationship between mind and brain comes from John Searle's book *The Rediscovery of Mind* in the form of a thought experiment. Imagine that you are slowly going blind. Unable to find a traditional cure to prevent your sight from deteriorating further, physicians try a radical procedure. Doctors plug silicon chips into your visual cortex, and to their surprise, this restores your vision. Unfortunately, your brain continues to deteriorate. In desperation, physicians insert more silicon chips until your brain is entirely replaced by microprocessors (66). Despite having a brain composed of silicon chips, your mental life (beliefs, desires, memories, emotions, and so

forth) is unaffected by the replacement of your biological brain. If having mental states is identical to brain states, as identity theory suggests, does Searle's thought experiment convince you that a brain is unnecessary to having a mind? Would replacement of your brain with silicon chips mean, given identity theory, you would cease to have thoughts, hopes, fears, and so on? Give reasons for your answer.

2. Push Searle's thought experiment further and replace, not only your brain, but also your body with silicon chips. In other words, you are a robot. Would you still be a thinking thing? Could we still draw an identity relationship between your mind and brain? Would this show that identity is false? Are identity theorists carbon chauvinists?

3. Identity theory is a reductionist theory—to have a mental state is to have a brain state. This reduction tendency suggests that when we talk about the mind we are really talking about neurophysiology; but it is a scientific hypothesis. That is, scientists will one day verify whether identity theory is true. However, for critics, identity is not a realistic scientific discovery. No empirical observations would prove the identity of consciousness with brain processes. In other words, consciousness is not the sort of thing that can be discovered by empirical observation (Priest 111). After all, cracking open someone's skull will not reveal anything but the gray twisted mass we call the brain. Is there anything that could be observed to prove identity theory is true? If identity theory is difficult to verify, does it make it a meaningless or nonsensical theory (Priest 112)? Why or why not?

The Mind Is Identical to the Brain

As we have seen, dualism is very troubling. It is very difficult, if not impossible, with Descartes' view to understand how a non-material mind can affect a material body, and vice versa. The conclusion that must be drawn is that substance dualism is not an acceptable theory of mind. The mind is really nothing more than physical and chemical processes of the brain, which, contrary to dualism, explains the interaction between mind and body. This is often called **reductionism**. Historically, reductionists argue that we can reduce human nature to the observable world of matter. Drawing an analogy, consider a compact disc (CD) recording from Avril Lavigne, Nelly Furtado, John Mayer, Beyonce, or whoever your favourite artist is (Lawhead 218). Examining the surface of a music CD will reveal nothing of its sound. Sounds produced by a CD can be melodic, lively, haunting, and so on. Now, these properties are not part of the physical description of the disc's surface; however, every sound produced by the CD is caused by the physical makeup of the disc that is acted upon by the CD player (Lawhead 219). In this sense, we can reduce the properties of sound to the physical disc itself. Or consider H_2O. Although we know H_2O can take different forms—gas (vapour), solid (ice), and liquid (water)—it is always composed of the same hydrogen and oxygen molecules. The same can be said about the mind. In just the same way that sounds are nothing but physical events of a CD, and gas, ice, and water are nothing but various properties of H_2O, mental activities are nothing but biological processes of the brain. Identity theorists take a similar stand but, more specifically, argue that to have a mental state is to have a particular brain state. That is, we can identify specific mental states with specific neurological states of the brain.

Brain research over the past 150 years not only refutes dualism but also supports the development of identity theory. Throughout much of the nineteenth century, the human brain and central nervous system were the objects of much scientific study. For example, it was discovered that damage to the brain stem can affect breathing; the central nervous system works by sending electric impulses to the body and vice versa; and the cerebellum is necessary for balance and movement (Lyons 80–81). It was also discovered that speech is associated with the lower frontal lobe, known as "Broca's brain," and understanding speech is associated with the temporal lobe of the left hemisphere of the brain, know as "Wernicke's area" (Lyons 82–84). In the twentieth century, scientists began to map the structure of individual neurons; they discovered the automatic nervous system, which transmits electrical signals immediately and automatically to muscles in the body, as when a person withdraws a hand from a hot stove; and they found that various biochemicals are necessary for neurons to transmit electrical signals from one to another (Lyons 85–88). The most remarkable work occurred between the 1930s and 1960s by Wilder Penfield and Roger Sperry. Penfield, while trying to cure patients of their epileptic seizures, was one of the first scientists to probe the brain with an electrode. What he discovered was that if the cerebral cortex were touched, it would elicit a meaningful response from the conscious patient including a memory, sound, colour, and so forth. He eventually mapped the brain into what is called the motor homunculus (Lyons 89–91) (see Figure 4.3).

Roger Sperry experimented on the *corpus callosum*. The corpus callosum is a thick bundle of nerve fibre that connects the two hemispheres of the brain. Generally speaking, the two hemispheres of the brain are each responsible for the opposite side of the body. So, for example, moving my right hand will be caused by neural activity in the left side of the brain and tapping my left foot will be caused by neural activity in the right side of the brain. What Sperry discovered was that if the *corpus callosum* was cut so that the hemispheres could no longer communicate with each other, consciousness became fragmented. For example, in split-brain patients (whose *corpus callosum* was cut), if a cup was visible in only their left visual field (governed by the right hemisphere), they couldn't say anything about their visual experiences because the power of speech is limited to the left hemisphere. It's not that they couldn't see the cup—they could—it's just they couldn't say anything about what they saw. In this sense, according to Sperry, their consciousness was split (Lyons 92–94).[11]

Lyons, in his article, explains nicely how, from a philosophical point of view, these experiments wooed many philosophers to give up dualism

Figure 4.3   The Motor Homunculus

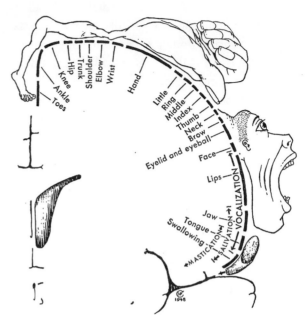

Wilder Penfield's experiments stimulating the brain allowed him to map the motor cortex into what is known as the motor homunculus. Areas of the brain assigned to various body parts are proportional to their complexity. The areas for the hand and face, for example, are large compared to, say, the elbows or toes because our ability to use language and tools are almost exclusively human traits and, therefore, large areas of the cortex are devoted to these tasks.

and take up physicalism in the form of an identity relation between the mind and brain. The mind (sensations and mental images) is not something above and beyond physiological process of the brain itself. For many philosophers working in Australia at the time, the direct offshoot of this early brain research was identity theory. Ullin T. Place conceived identity theory in the early 1950s with the help from J. J. C. (Jack) Smart, and C. B. (Charlie) Martin (Professor Emeritus at the University of Calgary). The idea behind Place's famous paper, "Is Consciousness a Brain Process?", is that the mind is a process of the brain. This, of course, is a materialist theory at heart. For Place, he does not mean that our thoughts and experiences are merely caused by events in the brain but that they are exactly the same as events in the brain (neurological happenings or firings). In this sense, when we talk about beliefs, hopes, fears, love, and so on, we are really talking about brain states. But it's no mere causal correlation at work here, since Descartes' theory also correlated the mind with brain via the pineal gland. For Place, the mind *is* the brain. In this sense, identity theory is a reductionist theory. However, it should be noted that Place's idea is merely a hypothesis. That is, the truth and falsity of identity theory is open to question by advancements in the natural sciences and neurophysiology.

To prove identity theory, Place first makes a distinction between three senses or meanings of "is." The first distinction is the **"is" of definition** (45). For example:

- Red *is* a colour.
- A square *is* an equilateral rectangle.
- A bachelor *is* an unmarried man.

Here the "is" means to express the meaning of a term. A square, by definition, *is* a rectangle with sides of equal length. A bachelor, by definition, *is* a male who is not married. To deny the meaning of these terms is contradictory; they are necessary truths.

The second distinction is the **"is" of composition.** For example:

- Her hat *is* a bundle of straw held together by string.
- His table *is* an old packing crate.
- A cloud *is* a mass of water droplets or other particles in suspension.

The "is" in these cases describes what something is made or composed of. In this sense, the "straw" is not part of the definition of a hat and "packing crate" is not part of the definition of a table. That is, to deny that a bundle of straw is a hat is not self-contradictory since the "is" in this case explains what is contingently true, namely, the composition of the hat.

The third distinction is the **"is" of predication.** For example:

- Toby *is* 80 years of age.
- Her hat *is* red.
- A giraffe *is* tall.

The meaning "is" in these cases merely expresses that something possesses certain properties or characteristics. To say that Toby is 80 years old is to express a property of Toby; red is the property of the hat; and tallness is property of a giraffe.

With this distinction in tow, Place then goes on to argue that when he says that consciousness is a brain process, it is to be taken in the second sense. To say "John loves Sally" is to express what the emotion is made or composed of, namely, brain processes. In this sense, for Place, materialism is true. In just the same way that lightning is nothing but an electrical discharge, heat is nothing but kinetic molecular energy, and a rainbow is nothing but the refraction of light through water droplets, consciousness is nothing but a brain process. And with additional support coming from Jack Smart and David Armstrong, the last nail on substance dualism was hammered home. The mind is a brain process, nothing else.[12]

In what sense is consciousness a brain process? There are two kinds of identity relation between mental states and brain states: types and tokens. Philosophically speaking, a *type* is a kind of thing, while a *token* is a specific particular member of that type. Consider, for example, cars. There are numerous types of car manufacturers including Honda, Dodge, Ford, and Subaru, for example. Each manufacturer makes various tokens of these types including the Accord, Viper, Taurus, and Forester. Or consider mammals: mammals are a type of animal and a dog is a token of that type. For type-identity theory, certain types of mental states are identical with certain types of brain states. In this case, beliefs, desires, hopes, fears, love, and hate are all types of mental states. For instance, the belief that John A. Macdonald was Canada's first prime minister is a kind or type of mental state. So in cases where Fred, Sally, and Sam all believe John A. Macdonald was Canada's first prime minister, in each instance, we have a particular type of mental states. However, if I belief that John A. Macdonald was Canada's first prime minister today and then again tomorrow, I have two tokens of the same type of belief. According to type-identity theory, for anyone who believes that John A. Macdonald was Canada's first prime minister, neuroscientists will discover that everyone is in the exact same belief-type of brain state. Likewise for anyone who desires a job promotion, each individual will be in the same desire-type of brain state. In other words, to have certain types of mental states is to be in certain types of brain states for all people. So it doesn't matter if my Russian counterpart and I both believe John A. Macdonald was Canada's first prime minister or desire a sausage for lunch; we will both be in the same neurological state for each type of mental state. Hence, if the mind is a brain process, then there ought to be an identity relation between specific beliefs, desires, pains, and so on, and particular brain states (neurological happenings). To have mental states is to be in specific brain states.

Problems with Identity Theory

First, as Lyons explains, if identity is correct, then we ought to see similar correlation between mental states and brain states for everyone. But is there any reason to believe this? Imagine neurology has advanced to the point where scientists invent a machine called a brain-o-scope to discover the connection between specific mental states and brain states. Unfortunately, researchers quickly discover that type-identity theory is elusive. They realize that people may have the same mental states realized in different brain states, or two people may have the same brain state but have different mental states. For example, my Russian counterpart and I might both desire a beer and yet have this mental state realized in different areas of the brain. Hence, if correct, it would be unrealistic to argue that there will be a strict identity between mental states and specific brain states.

Scientists are slowly piecing together how exactly brains work and it looks as if type-identity theory is false. The brain is an endless symphony of firing neurons, cascading neurotransmitters, and racing hormones that give rise to our conscious experiences and mental states. But it's not merely genetics at play; our environment and experiences as young infants play a role in determining unique neural networks within our brains. Neuroscientist Susan Greenfield states, "Certain configurations of neuronal connections, then, imperceptibly personalize the brain, and it is this personalized aspect of the physical brain that actually is the mind. This individual mind continues to respond and react by shifting neuron allegiances as we live out our lives" (64). Such neural networks are not individuated into specific type-identity areas of the brain and mental states but involve the firings of millions upon millions of neurons at a multitude of locations. Moreover, brains are malleable in nature. This is known as **neural plasticity.** When a part of the brain is damaged, say due to a birth defect or a car accident, other areas of the brain will take over the function of the damaged part (Campbell 72–73). This means that it's highly unlikely that people will have type-identical mental state and physical states. It's too much to expect that everyone who believes that Edmonton is the capital of Alberta must have an identical neurophysiologial configuration. In short, we cannot assume that mental states are identical to brain states.

One way around this objection, as Lyons explains, is to argue for token-token identity. Token identity theory is the idea that every mental state is identical with some brain states for that individual. This means that all particular mental states will have a particular identical brain state. So, for example, if Mary believes that Edmonton is the capital of Alberta, then she will be in brain state N 765 and, if Sally believes that Edmonton is the capital of Alberta, then she will be in brain state N 545. Mary's and Sally's beliefs are the same, but each belief, and every other mental state, will be identical with a specific neurological state at a specific location of the brain for that person. This avoids the type-type identity problem discussed above but it also leads to another concern. If Mary and Sally both believe that Edmonton is the capital of Alberta, how could scientists discover that N 765 and N 545 are the same mental state? Notice that identity theorists cannot identify each neurological state as similar by referring to their mental features (or propositional attitudes) because they espouse a reductionist theory. If mental states are identical to brain states, then appealing to mentalist features of the mind is a fall back to dualism, not materialism. The point, as Lyons argues, is that it's highly unlikely that brain science will develop to the point that researchers will be able to isolate specific beliefs in relation to specific brain states. But, as we saw earlier, brains don't seem to work that way; brains are holistic in nature.

There is one other problem, not addressed by Lyons. This is known as the species problem. Let's imagine that researchers, using the brain-o-scope, discover that mental states are identical with specific neurological brain states. Even if this were true, we ought not exclude the possibility of other species, with perhaps very different physiology, having identical mental states. This would pose a problem for identity theory since identity is strictly associated with biological brains like humans. As Hilary Putnam states, "Thus if we can find even one psychological predicate which can clearly be applied to both mammal and an octopus (say 'hungry'), but whose physical-chemical 'correlate' is different in the two cases, the brain-state theory has collapsed" (201). Octopi brains are radically different in size and shape than human brains; therefore, it's unreasonable to assume that if we do share the same mental states, such as "I'm hungry," we will be in the identical brain states. And given the differences in neurological structure, it's quite possible that other animals, such as dogs, cats, or even dolphins, may have beliefs, desires, or pains and not be in the same brain state as humans. And this makes sense given the difference in physiology between species. Moreover, identity theory doesn't take into consideration the possibility of other non-human life forms having radically different physiology than humans and yet similar mental states. For example, if something like the character C3P0 of the *Star Wars* franchise exists, with silicon chips in its head instead of carbon-based brains like humans, then identity theory is false. Why? Because the character C3P0 is physiologically different from humans and yet has similar thoughts, emotions, and sensations to us (see Figure 4.4). Identity theory is guilty of being **carbon chauvinists**.

As we will see, functionalism avoids these problems by arguing that having a mind does not depend on its physical makeup. On this account, an alien could have a completely different biochemical composition than a human, and still be psychologically similar. Take pain, for example. If we stumble across a creature with a different physiology than humans, according to identity theory, we would have to conclude that it would not feel pain despite the fact that it might engage in similar pain-type behaviour (jump around, scream obscenities, cry, etc.). And there is no reason to make such an assumption. It is perfectly reasonable to assume that a creature with a different physiology would be able to

Figure 4.4 Identity Theory Proves Elusive

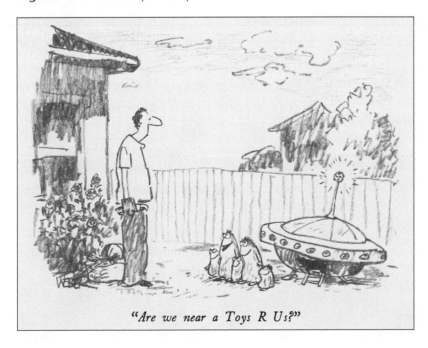

"Are we near a Toys R Us?"

feel pain just like us. If so, identity theory fails to establish identity between the mind and body.

21
William Lyons
(1939–)

William Lyons was an undergraduate student at the Australian National University, and gained graduate degrees from the

University of Calgary, Canada, and the University of Dundee, Scotland. He was a Lecturer, then Senior Lecturer in Philosophy at the University of Glasgow, Scotland (1973–1985), and then Professor of Moral Philosophy (1985–2004) in the School of Mental and Moral Science at Trinity College Dublin. He is now an Emeritus Fellow of Trinity College Dublin and a Member of the Royal Irish Academy. Lyons' areas of interest are mainly philosophy of mind and philosophical psychology. He also has an interest in philosophical drama and his award-winning play about Wittgenstein, The Crooked Roads of Genius, *was recently published (STAC, 2005). His most recent play,* The Fir Tree and the Ivy, *about Heidegger and Hannah Arendt, won the 2006 Eamon Keane Full Length Play Competition run in conjunction with the annual Listowel Writers' Week in Co Kerry, Ireland. Some of his publications include* Gilbert Ryle *(1980),*

Emotion *(1980),* The Disappearance of Introspection *(1986),* Approaches to Intentionality *(1995),* Modern Philosophy of Mind *(1995), and* Matters of the Mind *(2001).*

Nothing but the Brain

The 'Identity Theory' of Mind

By any standards, the advances in our knowledge of the brain and its functions from roughly 1800 to 1950 were quite extraordinary. At the end of each decade the brain sciences seemed to have revealed still more not merely about the human brain, but also about the human mind. By the middle of the twentieth century it seemed clear that even the most secret processes of our mental life, which lay hidden in the stream of consciousness, were related intimately to identifiable brain processes. It was increasingly tempting to think that, in the process of laying bare the workings of the brain and the central nervous system, one would learn all there was to know about a human's mental life as well. While brain scientists themselves were often remarkably conservative in their views about the nature of mind—for example, Sherrington, Penfield and Sir John Eccles were all either classical Cartesians or something very close to it—philosophers of mind felt that these remarkable advances in our knowledge of the brain and its functions pushed them towards a completely materialist and 'centralist' (or 'everything that is mental is totally inside the head') view of the mind.

Psychologists remained comparatively indifferent to these advances in neuroscience because, being still either behaviourists or deeply influenced by its ethos, they had come to think of neurophysiology as more or less irrelevant to the science of behaviour. Advances in neuroscience, they believed, were just that, advances in neuroscience, and had little or no positive consequences for psychology, except, perhaps, to reinforce its implicit and rather general commitment to materialism. Even Watson's friend and early colleague in advancing the behaviourist cause, the neurologist Karl Lashley (1890–1958), made little connection between his neurological work on animal intelligence and vision, and his behaviourist psychology. Lashley's major research work, on studying the effects of brain lesions in monkeys and rats on their vision and ability to learn, culminated in his famous monograph, *Brain Mechanisms and Intelligence*, 1929. His most famous behaviourist paper is his two-part article 'The Behaviorisitc Interpretation of Consciousness' (Lashley, 1923). In that latter article, he did not, as one might expect, identify consciousness with specific brain functions, but simply repeated Watson's review, saying that "Conscious States" have outlived their usefulness to science and with Watson we may say that, "the behaviorist does not concern himself with them because as the stream of his science broadens and deepens such older concepts are sucked under, never to reappear".[1]

More importantly it was very much in the interests of psychology, as a profession, to keep neurophysiology at a distance, otherwise it would be out of a job. Physiology, psychologists said, was the science that dealt with the 'central' aspects of human life, what went on inside humans' bodies, including inside their heads. Psychology, on the other hand, was the science that dealt with the 'peripheral' or external aspects of human life. Psychology was the science of human behaviour. So there was no obvious overlap between these two sciences. Each had its own territory clearly marked out.

Behaviourism had also come to be associated with an outright refusal to be in any way associated with the dubious practice of theory-building. Both Watson and Skinner always said that the goal of psychology was limited to the prediction and control of behaviour, and that they were not interested in hypotheses, theorems or theories, especially theories about the nature of mind. In his address in Philadelphia, in April 1955, as President of the Eastern Psychological Association, Skinner said that

> I never attacked a problem by constructing a Hypothesis. I never deduced Theorems or submitted them to Experimental Check. So far as I can see, I had no preconceived Model of behavior—certainly not a physiological or mentalistic one, and, I believe, not a conceptual one . . . [My own one attempt at conceptual work] lived up to my opinion of theories in general by proving utterly worthless in suggesting further experiments.[2]

There was one notable exception to this reluctance, on the part of psychologists of that time, to knit the new knowledge obtained from the brain sciences into their psychology. This was Edwin G. Boring (1886–1968).[3] In 1933 he published *The Physical Dimensions of Consciousness*.[4] In the first chapter of that book, Boring wrote:

> While there is no possibility of disproving or proving dualism, the exposition of the present book is based on the assumption that it is scientifically more useful to consider that all psychological data are of the same kind and that consciousness is a physiological event.[5]

The bulk of the book was spent in attempting to show that all the aspects of consciousness which the introspectionists (such as his teacher, Titchner) had discerned could be given a physiological interpretation.

From our point of view, the most remarkable thing about Boring's book was that, for a very long time, it made little or no impact, either in psychology or philosophy. The more or less complete indifferences which greeted this book, which Boring himself considered to be his major original contribution to psychology, led in part to his neurotic depression which developed around that time.[6] One can only speculate that it was the behaviourists' iron grip on psychology for most of the first half of the twentieth century, and their veto on theorising, that made psychologists neglect it. And one can only speculate that it was the, by that time, quite wide gap between psychology and philosophy that made most philosophers ignorant of the book.

It took almost twenty years for anyone to take any notice of Boring's *The Philosophy Dimensions of Consciousness.* Herbert Feigl, a member of the Vienna Circel who had migrated to America in the 1930s, introduced Boring's idea to the philosophical world in a paper entitled, 'The Mind–Body Problem in the Development of Logical Empiricism', which appeared first in the *Revue Internationale de Philosphie* in 1950.[7] However it was the English psychologist turned philosopher Ullin T. Place (1925–2000), who became the route to the full fruition of Boring's original idea. Having read *The Physical Dimensions of Consciousness* while still an undergraduate at Oxford in the 1940s reading psychology and philosophy, Place gradually became impressed by Boring's programme of giving a physiological interpretation of consciousness and, in so doing, of producing a 'physiological solution'

to 'the problem of privacy'. Place's version of an 'identity theory', a 'brain-consciousness identity theory', was given its first clear formulation after his appointment as Lecturer in Psychology in the Philosophy Department at the University of Adelaide in 1951. It had been refined through a series of discussions with the philosophers J. J. Smart and, especially, C. B. Martin, in and around 1954. Ironically, it could be said that it was only when it fell among the philosophers that Boring's idea found fertile soil. For, as we shall see, it was the philosophers Smart and David Armstrong who fully exploited Boring's initial move, via Feigl's and Place's revival of it, by developing an identity theory not merely of consciousness but of the mind itself.

Philosophers, certainly, had no reason to ignore the remarkable advances in neuroscience that had taken place over the last hundred years. Since philosophy was not an empirical science of any sort, nor had any ambitions to be one, philosophers were able to view advances in neuroscience as neither threatening nor foreign to their interests. Besides, behaviourism never did have the hold over philosophy that it had over psychology, and was only in the ascendancy in philosophy for a very short period. In addition, there was never any explicit, nor even implicit, veto on theorising in philosophy as there was in psychology. Generally speaking, for more philosophers, at least after the influence of positivism began to wane, theorism was what philosophy of mind was about.

Place's 'identity theory', or theory that consciousness is to be identified with certain brain processes, was published as 'Is Consciousness a Brain Process?', in the *British Journal of Psychology,* in 1956. Near the beginning of that article he gives the bald outline of his solution to the 'problem of privacy'.

In the case of cognitive concepts like 'knowing', 'believing', 'understanding', 'remembering', and volitional concepts like 'wanting' and intending', there can be little doubt, I think, that an analysis in terms of dispositions to behave is fundamentally sound. [Here Place refers the reader to Wittgenstein's *Philosophical Investigations* and Ryle's *The Concept of Mind*.] On the other hand, there would seem to be an intractable residue of concepts clustering around the notions of consciousness, experience, sensation, and mental imagery [i.e. what *Le Penseur* is or might be doing], where some sort of inner process story is unavoidable. It is possible, of course, that a satisfactory behaviouristic account of this conceptual residuum will ultimately be found. For our present purposes, however, I shall assume that this cannot be done and that statements about pains and twinges, about how things look, sound, and feel, about things dreamed of or pictured in the mind's eyes, are statements referring to events and processes which are in some senses private or internal to the individual of whom they are predicated.... I shall argue that an acceptance of inner processes does not entail dualism and that the thesis that consciousness is a process in the brain cannot be dismissed on logical grounds.[8]

While Place made no secret of the fact that he remained a behaviourist in regard to the analysis of most mental concepts, the chief purpose of his article was to make progress on the task of making clear *the logic* of his claim that consciousness, that is, consciousness experiences, is identical to brain processes.

Place began on this task by distinguishing between what he called 'The "Is" of Predication', 'The "Is" of Definition' and 'The "Is" of Composition'. 'The "Is" of Predication' occurs in such sentences as 'Helen is twelve years old', for 'is twelve years old', like 'has red hair', is a description of some property that is attributed to or predicated of the subject of the sentence, Helen. 'The "Is" of Definition' occurs in such sentences as 'A bachelor is an unmarried man.' Here the 'is so and so' phrase is not attributing a property to bachelors but telling us exactly what the term 'bachelors' means. It is defining 'bachelors' for us.

Now, according to Place, both of these senses of 'is' are to be contrasted with, and should not be confused with, 'The "Is" of Composition'. This latter use of 'is' occurs in such sentences 'His table is an old packing case' or, when writing in the year 2000, 'The current president of the United States is Bill Clinton.' For a start, such sentences are talking about what is really the case, not about mere word definitions or linguistic predications. In such sentences, we are being informed that what is referred to by the phrase that comes before the 'is' *is, as a matter of fact,* identical with (and so composed of) what is referred so by the phrase that comes after the 'is'. To put this another way, the phrases either side of the 'is' are really just two different descriptions for one and the same thing. They are a way of *identifying* what someone is talking about in two different ways. His table *is in fact* just that old packing case. From the view point of the year 2000, the current president of the United States *is* Bill Clinton from Arkansas.

In providing us with this taxonomy of our uses of the verb 'is' (or, in an old-fashioned grammarian's terminology, 'the copula'), Place's aim was to say that the hypothesis that consciousness is a brain process was an example of the third sort of 'is', namely 'The "Is" of Composition'. In saying that consciousness is a brain process, Place is claiming (however superficially implausibly) that the term 'consciousness' and the term 'brain process' pick out (or refer to) one and the same thing. This one thing, Place adds, is the scientific, neurophysiological truth of the matter, namely some particular sort of brain process. Thus his thesis about the core of our mental life, our consciousness, is a strongly materialist thesis.

An important aspect of this hypothesis, Place emphasises, is that the claimed identity is a 'contingent' one. What this means is that the identity in question is just a result of the way things have 'panned out'. Things could have happened otherwise, but in fact they did not. In the year 2000 Bob Dole could have been the current president of the United States but, as it turned out, Bill Clinton was elected for a second term. Consciousness could have turned out to be a spiritual substance but, in fact, the evidence suggest that it is nothing but a certain sort of brain process. Just as there was nothing necessary about Bill Clinton's being elected to a second term, for it was not a Law of Nature nor a Law of Logic that he be so, so there is nothing necessary about the fact that consciousness turns out to be nothing but a sort of brain process. Humans could have evolved differently, or God could have made things differently. However, as a simple matter of fact, it is claimed, consciousness turns out to be a sort of brain process.

Since the 'The "Is" of Composition' operates by using two different sorts of description for one and the same thing, then there is a danger, Place points out, of failing to realise the distinctiveness of these distinct descriptions. Just because we can say 'Being president of the United States is the most prestigious political office in the world', we cannot then say, in the year 2000, 'Being Bill Clinton is the most prestigious political office in the world.' For a start, most Republicans might want to be president on account of its prestige, but none of them, most probably, would have wanted to be Bill Clinton. In similar fashion, while we might speak of some of our conscious experiences as vivid or frightening, we should not thereby think that we can say that any of our brain processes was vivid and frightening.

One of Place's 'sparring partners' in Adelaide had been the Professor of Philosophy there, J. J. C. (Jack) Smart (1920–). Smart was born and went to school in Cambridge, England, but became an undergraduate at the University of Glasgow when his father moved from the Cambridge Observatory to take up the Regius Professorship of Astronomy at Glasgow. Either side of war service with the army in India, Jack Smart read mathematics and physics, with a 'minor' in philosophy, at Glasgow. However it was philosophy that came to interest him most, though he always thereafter imbued his work in philosophy with a strong scientific flavour. He believes with deep conviction the philosophers should be conversant with current science and that philosophical theories should always be constrained by the relevant scientific facts.

After Glasgow, Smart became a graduate student, reading for the newly invented B.Phil. in philosophy at Oxford. Here he fell under the spell of Rylean behaviourism, though, as he himself admits, he gave his logical behaviourism a much more openly materialist flavour than Ryle himself ever did. At Oxford he also imbibed some of the ethos of logical positivism and gained some acquaintance with Wittgenstein's views through his contact with Friedrich Waismann, who had been a member of the Vienna Circle, and George Paul, who had attended some of Wittgenstein's lectures at Cambridge.

After a brief period as a Junior Research Fellow at Corpus Christi College, Oxford, Smart was appointed in 1950 to the Hughes Chair of Philosophy at the University of Adelaide. Since then, he has lived in Australia, eventually taking out Australian citizenship. Soon after his appointment in Adelaide, Ullin Place joined his department as a junior colleague to teach the psychology segment of the curriculum. Smart saw the force of Place's grafting of a consciousness–brain theory on to regular behaviourism, and, together with his fellow Australian David Armstrong, and others, Smart eventually extended the theory into a comprehensive mind-brain identity theory. This theory became known as 'Australian materialism' or, to some of its Oxford critics, 'the Australian heresy'. For such a theory, besides flourishing on the Australian subcontinent, seemed to reflect the blunt no-nonsense realism of the Australian character itself.

Smart set himself the task of finding additional grounds for holding the identity theory. These grounds are to be found especially in his article, 'Sensations and Brain Processes' (1959) and his major work *Philosophy and Scientific Realism* (1963). The first of these grounds, namely that we should not be bewitched by our ordinary mental vocabulary, might be called Wittgensteinian. Smart argued that when we speak of beliefs and hopes, feelings and emotions, mental images and so on, this language is strictly speaking 'topic neutral' or 'reference neutral'. That is to say, it is neutral as regards what is being referred to by these mental vocabulary expressions, and so we cannot argue from these expressions to the existence of mental events or, indeed, to the existence of *any particular* sort of events. If someone says that she is imagining an orange, then, strictly speaking, this only commits the speaker

to holding that something similar to *whatever it is that goes on* in her when she actually sees an orange, with normal vision and in good light, is now going in her. This leaves open that *whatever it is that is going on in her* could be just a brain process (thought equally, as far as this argument is concerned, it leaves open the possibility that it could also be a Cartesian episode of some sort).

Smart was also keen to point out that the identity theory was supported by a very basic piece of well-grounded scientific advice called 'The Principle of Parsimony'. This principle, sometimes called 'Ockham's Razor' because of its association with the medieval English logician William of Ockham (1285–1347), is about how to proceed when forming scientific or philosophical theories or hypotheses. It advocates the greatest possible simplicity or parsimony when constructing a theory, so that one should not multiply the basic axioms or the basic entities, or, in general, the basic 'bits' of one's theory, beyond absolute necessity. This being so, then, Smart argues,

> If it be agreed that there are no cogent philosophical arguments which force us into accepting dualism, and if the brain process theory [the mind–brain identity theory] and dualism are equally consistent with the facts, then the principles of parsimony and simplicity seem to me to decide overwhelmingly in favour of the brain-process theory.[9]

Smart usually added that, in fact, while there may not be cogent reasons of a purely philosophical sort, there are cogent reasons from evolutionary biology and the brain sciences that push us towards a materialist view of the mind.

> It seems to me that science in particular is increasingly giving us a viewpoint whereby organisms are able to be seen as

physicochemical mechanisms: so it seems that even the behaviour of man himself will one day be explicable in mechanistic terms.[10]

Perhaps the most important addition to Place's initial statement of the identity theory came from another Australian philosopher, David Armstrong (1926–). He was born in Melbourne, though he received much of his early schooling in England. At the outbreak of the Second World War, his parents sent him back to Australia to finish his secondary schooling. After some war service in the Australian navy, he read philosophy as his major (or main subject) for his BA at the University of Sydney. There he came in contact with that remarkable teacher and iconoclast John Anderson (1893–1962). Like so many of his generation of philosophers, he then went to Oxford to obtain is B.Phil. After a brief period as an assistant at Birkbeck College, he returned to Australia on being appointed to a lectureship at Melbourne University. In 1964 he was appointed to the Challis Professorship of Philosophy at Sydney University, the chair which, during his undergraduate years, had been held by his esteemed teacher, John Anderson. His best-known work is the aptly, if bluntly, named, *A Materialist Theory of the Mind* (1968).[11] Armstrong could be said to have finally exorcised any trace of behaviourism from the identity theory. For, in a brilliant *coup de théâtre,* Armstrong took the behaviourists' own weapon, dispositions, which they had used with such devastating effect against the Cartesian view of mind, and turned it against the behaviourists themselves.

For what Armstrong did was to point out that a full account of dispositions involved making clear that a disposition always involved some inner physical 'something', which had a crucial causal role in producing the actions or reactions associated with the disposition in question. The behaviourists claimed that the correct account, of, say, brittleness would go as follows: 'Brittleness is the disposition of, say, this glass to break very easily when let fall from even a moderate height or when tapped even lightly with a hard object.' Armstrong suggested that the correct account must go like this: 'Brittleness is *the physiochemical crystalline structure* of the glass which causes it to break very easily when let fall from even a moderate height or when tapped even lightly with a hard object.' Indeed, Armstrong argued, that is the correct model for all dispositional analyses.

Dispositions, he said, strictly speaking *are* their inner physical structures which cause the behaviour (actions or reactions) typically associated with the dispositions. Behaviour only comes into dispositions, if at all, when this inner structure (sometimes called, in the academic papers, the 'structural basis' or 'categorical basis' of the disposition) interacts causally with the environment. This can be seen more clearly by taking another example, namely that of being a haemophiliac. A haemophiliac is some human (or animal) that lacks the usual clotting agent in the blood which makes it congeal when there is bleeding. Being a haemophiliac is a dispositional state definable as 'a person (or animal) having blood which lacks the usual clotting agent such that when that person (or animal) is cut or otherwise wounded, the blood flow is not staunched in the usual way'. The important thing to note is that a person can be a haemophiliac even if he has ever been cut or wounded and so has never exhibited the unstoppable bleeding associated with haemophilia. A medical doctor or physiologist or veterinary doctor can attribute the disposition, being a haemophiliac, to someone or some animal, even though no haemophiliac behaviour has ever been exhibited. For the doctor or scientist or vet can spot the disposition simply by spotting that the person or animal's blood lacks the usual clotting agent. A scientific or true account of a disposition is all about *finding the inner cause* of the behaviour in question. In certain cases, such as medical conditions like haemophilia, it is important to find the inner cause before it actually causes anything to happen. So a doctor might tell a mother, soon after she has given birth, that her son is a haemophiliac, in order to that appropriate measures can be taken.

It follows from this account of dispositions that if mental states are indeed dispositions (as Armstrong agrees with both Place, Smart and the behaviourists that most of them are), then mental states are to be identified with 'inner physical structures' of some sort. Thus Armstrong writes:

> According to this view, the concept of a mental state essentially involves, and is exhausted by, the concept of a state that is *apt to be the cause of certain effects or apt to be the effect of certain causes.*[12]

The obvious candidates in the case of mental dispositions, for being the relevant 'inner physical structures', are brain states or processes. So, Armstrong adds:

> But suppose that the physico-chemical view of the working of the brain is correct, as I take it to be. It will be very natural to conclude that mental states are not simply *determined* by corresponding states of the brain, but that they actually *identical* with these brain-states, brain-states the involve nothing but physical properties.[13]

Thus Armstrong often went on to call his version of the identity theory, which had completely jettisoned any remnants of behaviourism, 'central state materialism'. The pendulum had swung back again for the 'peripheralism' or externalism of behaviourism to a hard-core non-Cartesian 'centralism'. Once more minds were things wholly inside heads, but this time they were also wholly physical and to be wholly identified with brains.

Identities Prove Elusive

Smart himself realised that the mind-brain identity theory was especially vulnerable to one particular sort of objection. He aired a version of this objection, in his own book *Philosophy and Scientific Realism*, in the following way:

> It will be remembered that I suggested that in a reporting sensations we are in fact reporting likenesses and unlikenesses of brain processes. Not it may be objected (as has been done by K.E.M. Baier[14]): 'Suppose that you had some electro-encephalograph fixed to your brain, and you observed that, according to the electro-encephalograph, you did *not* have the sort of brain process that normally goes on when you have a yellow sense datum [an experience of seeing a patch of yellow]. Nevertheless, if you had a yellow sense datum you would not give up the proposition that you hade such a sense datum, no matter *what* the encephalograph said.' This part of the objection can be easily answered. I simply reply that the brain-process theory [identity theory] was put forward as a factual identification, not as a logically necessary one. I can therefore agree that it is a logically possible that the electro-encephalograph

experiment should turn out as envisaged in the objection, but I can still believe *that this will never in fact happen.* If it did happen I should doubtless give up on the brain-process theory (though later I might come to doubt the correctness of my memory of the experiment and thus reinstate the theory!)[15]

I know of no experiment whereby a person, who regularly has experiences of seeing yellow only when he or she is in brain state A, suddenly has an experience of seeing yellow when not in brain state A. However the crucial evidence, in regard to the claims of the identity theory, should be concerned with whether or not an experience of seeing yellow will be identifiable with the same brain process A *in all people.* The identity theory is an interpersonal theory. It is a theory that claims that any person whatsoever who merits *a particular type of mental description,* say, having a pang of anxiety or believing in God or seeing a patch of yellow, will be discovered to be in *exactly the same type of brain state* or undergoing exactly the same type of brain process as any other person who merits the same mental description. That is why the identity theory is called by philosophers a type–type identity theory.

To put this another way, a type–type identity claim is a very strong sort of identity claim. It is usually contrasted, in the philosophical literature, with a much weaker sort of identity claim, a token–token identity claim. In order to make this contrast clearer, let me introduce the terms 'type' and 'token'. A *type* is a class or sort of thing, for example, the class of Irish pound (or strictly *punt*) coins. A *token* is an actual example or specimen of that class. For example, the pound coin in my pocket today, which is slightly

defaced on the side with the intaglio depiction of the Irish elk, is a token of the class or type called Irish pound coins. So the pound coin in your purse, which, say, is not defaced but has damage to its rim.

To claim that there is a type–type identity between mental states and brain processes is to make the very strong claim that the true referent of (what is really referred to by), say, the mental description 'a thought that I will have a sausage for lunch' (that is, a type of thought) will be discovered, *on all occasions,* to be, say, the brain process described by the neurophysiologist's description 'brain process$_{289c}$ on the International Society of Neurophysiologists chart of brain processes' (a type of brain process). On the other hand, if one were to make merely a token–token identity claim about mental states being identical with brain processes, then the referent of the mental description 'a thought that I will have a sausage for lunch' will be discovered on Monday, when thought by Fred (a token, in Fred, of the thinking-I-will-have-a-sausage-for-lunch type of thought), to be 'brain process289c' (a token of the type of brain process called 'brain process$_{289c}$'). However, on Tuesday, when Fred again thinks that he will have a sausage for lunch (another token of the same type of thought), it will, say, turn out to be 'brain process$_{342a}$' (a token of a different type of thought). And, on the same day, when the same thought is entertained by Mary (another token of the same type of thought), it will, say, turn out to be 'brain process$_{456d}$' (a token of yet another different type of brain process).[16]

Nowadays, many neurologists would suggest that there are good grounds for saying that the mind–brain identity theory should be abandoned precisely because the predicted interpersonal, type–type identities have failed to appear. In turn, speaking more generally, this world suggest that our mental vocabulary 'does not carve the brain at its neurophysiological joints'. That is to say, it does not make neurophysiological sense even to expect that the appropriate use of a particular mental description would be an indicator of the presence of a quite particular sort or type of brain process on each and every occasion.

In more detail, there are no good reasons of a neurophysiological sort for supposing that every time someone has a particular type of belief (say, for example, a belief that it is not now raining), then, on each occasion that such a belief is attributable to any person, his or her brain will be discovered to be undergoing a particular type of process (say, brain process$_{296b}$ on the completed map of brain processing). Or, to take another example, there are no good reasons of a neurophysiological sort for supposing that each time a person is experiencing momentarily a particular type of conscious state (say, a visual image of a red hat), then that person or any other person meriting the same psychological description will be discovered on each such occasion, at just that moment, to be undergoing a particular type of brain process (say, a brain process$_{782c}$).

By the 1950s and 1960s what was most remarkable was the lack of headway that had been made by neurophysiologists in identifying mental events with brain states or processes. In 1952, for example, in a synoptic article entitled 'Neurology and the Mind–Brain Problem,' Roger Sperry was pointing out that

> Neurological science thus far has been quite unable to furnish an adequate description of the neural processes involved even the very simplest forms of mental activity.[17]

Such a conclusion probably did not worry Jack Smart or any other mind–brain identity theorist. For an identity theorist could simply reply that failure to find something does not imply its non-existence. You cannot argue from the failure to find any neural counterparts for our mental states to the non-existence of those counterparts. At this point, the identity theorist would usually invoke that most famous of all allies of the identity theory, 'future science'. Future science, with its greater sophistication and superior instrumentation, he would suggest, will supply what cannot at present be supplied, namely the awaited type type identities between types of our mental states as described by our ordinary commonsense psychology and types of brain processes picked out by latter-day neurophysiologists.

However, in that same 1952 article, Sperry recorded a long history of failure on the part of would-be identifiers. For, in that same article, Sperry gave details of the various attempts that had been made over the years to identify mental states with various aspects of brain processing. Scientists had tried to identify mental states (usually, specific sorts of conscious experiences) with *levels* of electrical activity in the brain, with the *distribution* of patterns of electrical activity in the brain, and through treating the electrical impulses of the brain as if they amounted to a *code* or system of representations. All those attempts failed dismally. His conclusion was to reiterate a comment of Sherrington's, namely that, 'We have to regard the relation of mind to brain as still not merely unsolved, but still devoid of a basis for its very beginning.'[18] By this he meant not only that science has not got very far in the experimental investigation of the possibility of identifying mental states with brain processes, but that it had made exhaustive investigations and failed to obtain any positive result. In recent years, neurophysiological knowledge has advanced. But this advance has not helped the cause of the mind–brain identity theorists. It has merely reinforced Sperry's pessimistic conclusion that, from the point of view of neurophysiology, a type–type identity between mental states and brain processes is most unlikely.

By the 1970s and 1980s the case against type–type identities between mind and brain had been strengthened. Gerold Edelman is a contemporary brain scientist who has been Vincent Astor Distinguished Professor at the Rockefeller University since 1974, and Director and Scientific Chairman of the Neurosciences Research Program at the same university since 1981. He received the Nobel Prize in Physiology or Medicine in 1972 for his research in biochemistry of the human immune system. Edelman has argued that a type–type identity between mind and brain is most unlikely for the simple reason that brain processing, in even a single brain, is very labile (unstable) and variable in regard to its incarnation of one and the same mental state. In 'Neural Darwinism: Population Thinking and Higher Brain Function', a paper delivered at the twentieth Nobel Conference at Gustavus Adolphus College in Minnesota, Edelman suggested that we should look upon the formation of each individual human brain as the product of two levels of evolution. First, there is the evolution of humans, and so the evolution of their brains, from such prior species as *Homo Erectus, Homo Habilis,* and, in the far distance, *Australopitbecus.* Second, there is an evolution of each individual's brain, an evolution that is part of individual development and takes place from

the foetal stage to childhood. It is this second sort of evolution, Edelman argues, that makes any type–type of identity between mind and brain so unlikely. Edelman puts it thus:

> The network of the brain is made during development by cellular movements, extensions, and connections of increasing numbers of neurons. It is an example of a self-organizing system. An examination of such a system during its development and at its most microscopic ramifications after development indicates that precise point-to-point wiring cannot occur. Therefore, uniquely specific connections cannot, in general, exist. If one numbered the branches of a neuron and correspondingly numbered the neurons it touched, the numbers would not correspond in any two individuals of a species (even in identical twins or in genetically identical animals).[19]

In effect, each human is an individual species as regards the formation of his or her brain. This is so because major factors in the development of human brains are the formation of individual neurones into groups, the selection of certain neuronal connections rather than others within a group, and finally the selection of one group rather than another for particular tasks. Each of these processes is evolutionary in nature. In each, there is selection, of neurone or neuronal pathway or of a whole group of neurones, according to the immediate pressure of the immediate environment and so in an *ad hoc* way. The upshot is that the 'wiring diagram' for any particular human is therefore unique. The clear implication is that this 'constitutes a crisis for those who believe that the nervous system is precise and "hard-wired" (like a computer)'.[20] He might have added that it also presents a crisis for anyone who thinks that the brains of humans are sufficiently uniform and precise in their wiring such that the electro-chemical activity that constitutes brain processing is the same in any two individuals, even when we might describe those same two individuals as being in the same mental state.[21]

This objection, that the identity of mental events with brain processing has proved not merely elusive but dubious, is unlikely to convince the 24-carat identity theorist. Smart himself, in the quotation with which I began this section, admitted as much. He indicated that, even after clear experimental proof, he would probably be moved to reinstate the identity theory at a later date. The usual moves to reinstate the theory are of two main sorts. The first is simply to doubt that the evidence from contemporary brain science is clear enough or sophisticated enough or sufficiently damning as to overthrow the identity theory. But this can look to those who do not support the identity theory as just a case of putting off the evil day when the theory has to be set aside.

The second move, a more interesting and important one, is to dilute the requirements for the identity in question. It is to move away from the strong type–type identity claim in the direction of a token–token identity claim, but without going all the way. All that we need to show, argue these more liberal identity theorists, is that some mental event, such as a sensation or an experience of some afterimage or a conscious thought, can be identified on any particular occasion with some brain process drawn from a list of possible brain processes which could be said to be 'of the same time' in a looser or more accommodating sense. Thus my current experi-

ence of toothache may be identical with brain process$_{234a}$, but last week the same sort of pain might have been identical with the brain process$_{248b}$, and the week before the same sort of pain might have been identical with brain process$_{291c}$. However, as long as these brain processes all share some (but not all) properties, say, they share some similarities of structure or function or both, then we could still say that these brain processes are all 'of the same type'. Perhaps that is why they are all to be marked, on our future comprehensive map of human brain processes, with a similar subscript number, say, some subscript number between 200 and 299.

After all, by parity of reasoning, say the identity theorists, we can and do say that all these trees over there are cypresses, even though some are small, some are tall, some broad, some thing, some dried up, some healthy, some dark green in colour, and some light green. They are all cypresses because they are all of the same arboreal type even though they do not share all their properties in common. Indeed they differ quite a lot among themselves. What makes these threes over there 'all of the same type' is their being all botanically the same. They share certain botanical properties. They can all be said to be botanically sufficiently the same because they have the same shape of leaves, the same angle at which their branches grow out from their trunk, and, say, the same taste and scent to their sap.

However, at this point, we need to look more closely at the analogy. For the analogy seems to highlight the deeper, underlying problem for the identity theory. The term 'cypress' can be analysed as a term which is shorthand for 'tree with x shape leaf, y type of branches, and z type of sap'. We learn to use the word 'cypress' by having our primary school teacher or mother or uncle show us the continuity of the particular shape of leaf, and the particular type of branch and trunk formation, and the peculiar smell and taste of the sap, over a number of specimens of cypress tree. Or else we try and teach ourselves about the characteristics of cypress trees from the text and illustrations of *The So-and-So Book of Trees*. In other words, the order is first the noticing of botanical similarities in a number of trees (similarities of leaf, of branch configuration, and of colour and odour of sap), then the bestowing of a generic or 'type' label, namely the name 'cypress'.

In regard to how our mental terms were generated, the ordering must have been completely different. Our mental terms or descriptions, such as 'the thought that I'll have a sausage for lunch' or 'mental image of a completely bare white room with no windows' or 'toothache', could not have been generated as a post-investigation-of-brains bestowal of a type-term upon perceived similarities of properties of brain processes. For we have at no time first noted neurophysiological similarities in a number of brain processes and then bestowed on such processes a generic or 'type' label or description such as 'the thought that I'll have a sausage for lunch' or 'toothache'. The reason for this is simply that our mental terms and descriptions have, and must have, arisen in complete ignorance of human neurophysiology. Such mental or psychological descriptions have long pre-existed what knowledge we do now have of human neurophysiology. They certainly date from the time of Plato and Aristotle, and most of them probably go back far beyond their time. That the generation of most of our mental vocabulary and of our mental descriptions, aeons ago by our ancestors, perhaps in part by *old Homo Habilis,* could

ipso facto have generated a way of picking our types of brain process would be scientific serendipity of a stupendous sort. It would be simply incredible.

To put this point another way. That 'cypress' names a type of tree is not a speculative assumption. It is simply the steady, assured and uncontroversial process of first finding similarities of leaf, branch, sap, and so on in a number of trees, and of then linguistically marking that noted similarity with a generic term, 'cypress'. On the other hand, saying that 'the thought that I'll have a sausage for lunch' or 'consciousness of my *faux* pas this evening' is the name of a particular identifiable brain process in highly speculative and very controversial. For it is not the culmination of a simple and straightforward process of first observing similarities in brain processes and then agreeing a description or label for that type of process defined in terms of just those similarities. It is a shot in the dark. Arguably, given current knowledge in the brain sciences, it is increasingly looking like a shot in the dark that has continually failed to hit any target. For the more we learn about human neurophysiology and about how we generate our mental terminology, the more the two drift apart, and the more controversial such an identification becomes.

Notes

1. Lashley, 1923, II, p. 343.
2. Skinner, 1956, p. 227.
3. E.G, Boring, at the time, was Edgar Pierce Professor of Psychology at Harvard University. Boring, who was the introspectionist psychologist Titchner's most famous pupil, had already won distinction with the publication of his *History of Experimental Psychology* in 1929. Though it should be pointed out that, in recent years, Boring's history (Boring, 1929) has come under critical fire for

being historically inaccurate. See, for example, Danziger, 1980.

4. While acknowledging in that book his debt to the work of the neurologist and behaviourist Karl Lashley, Boring accused him of, ultimately, being 'cautious and conservative'. The implication was that Lashley was conservative because he did not, in the light of the remarkable recent advances in neuroscience, embrace 'an identity hypothesis of the relation of "mind" to "body"'. (Boring, 1933, pp. vi and viii.)

5. Boring, 1933, p. 14.

6. Place, 1990, p. 20.

7. The most accessible version of this is Feigl, 1953.

8. Place, 1995, pp. 106–7.

9. Smart, 1995, p. 130.

10. Smart, 1995, p. 118.

11. A more accessible introduction to Armstrong's views is Armstrong, 1995.

12. Armstrong, 1995, p. 179.

13. Armstrong, 1995, p. 178.

14. Kurt Baier, an American, was for a time the Professor of Philosophy in the School of General Studies at the Australian National University. Subsequently he took up a senior post in the Philosophy Department at the University of Pittsburgh in Pennsylvania.

15. Smart, 1963, p. 99.

16. In short, as the philosophical jargon has it, with a weaker, token–token identity claim there is only a claim of 'multiple realisability' (or 'multiple forms of incarnation') of a particular mental state as brain states or processes. With a type–type identity claim there is a claim of 'single realisability' (or 'a single form if incarnation'). As we shall see, in the next chapter, functionalism claims only a token–token identity and 'multiple realisability'.

17. Sperry 1952, p. 292.

18. Sperry, 1952, p. 296. The reference to Sherrington is to Sherrington, 1933. Sperry himself suggested, towards the end of his 1952 article, that the brain of humans, as well as animals, might better be conceived as primarily a machine for coordinating 'perceptual input' (or information received through one of the senses) and 'motor output' (or behaviour). If the relation between our mental life and our brains was to be explained, it would need to be explained in that context. However, he did not go much further than the bare expression of this enigmatic suggestion.

19. Edelman, 1985, p. 4.

20. Edelman, 1985, pp. 4–5.

21. I should make it clear that there are still plenty of neurophysiologists who would not go as far as Edelman in dismissing the identity theory of mind and brain. Many would still see it as 'an open question' (see, for example, Fischbach, 1992). I admit, however, to finding Eldelman's arguments very cogent.

References

Armstrong, David (1995), 'The Causal Theory of Mind' [1977], in Lyons (1995).

Boring, Edwin G. (1933), *The Physical Dimension of Consciousness,* The Century Psychology Series, ed. Richard M. Elliot (New York, Century, and London, Appleton).

Boring, Edwin G. (1929), *A History of Experimental Psychology* (New York, Appleton-Century).

Danziger, Kurt (1980), 'The History of Introspection Reconsidered', *Journal of the History of the Behavioural Sciences,* 16.

Edelman, Gerald (1985), 'Neural Darwinism: Population Thinking and Higher Brain Function', In Michael Shafto (ed.), *How We Know* (San Francisco: Harper and Row).

Feigl, Herbert (1953), 'The Mind-Body Problem in the Development of Logical Empiricism', in Herbert Feigl and May Brodbeck (eds), *Readings in the Philosophy of Science* (New York, Appleton-Century-Crofts).

Fischbach, Gerald D. (1992), 'Mind and Brain', *Scientific America,* 267/3.

Lashley, Karl (1923), 'The Behaviouristic Interpretation of Consciousness', I and II, *Psychological Review,* 30/4 and 5.

Lyons, William (ed.) (1995), *Modern Philosophy of Mind* (Everyman-London, J.M. Dent; Vermont, Charles E. Tuttle).

Place, U. T. (1995), 'Is Consciousness a Brain Process?' [1956], in Lyons (1995)

Place, U. T. (1990), 'E. G. Boring and the Mind-Brain Identity Theory', *The British Psychological Society, History, and Philosophy of Science Section: Newsletter,* 11.

Sherrington, C. S. (1933), *The Brain and its Mechanisms* (Cambridge, Cambridge University Press).

Skinner, B. F. (1956), 'A Case History in Scientific Method', *American Psychologist,* 11.

Smart, J. J. C. (1995), 'Sensations and Brain Processes' [1959], in Lyons (1995).

Smart, J. J. C. (1963), *Philosophy and Scientific Realism*, International Library of Philosophy and Scientific Method, ed. A J. Ayer (London, Routledge & Kegan Paul).

Sperry, R. W. (1952), 'Neurology and the Mind-Brain Problem', *American Scientist*, 40.

Functionalism

Think? Why think! We have computers to do that for us.

—Jean Rostand

Discussion Questions

1. In 1997, world chess champion Garry Kasparov was defeated by the supercomputer Deep Blue in a fierce and gruelling chess match. Deep Blue won by the slimiest of margins. But the defeat of Kasparov was important; it proved to many observers that computers were smarter and, in some respects, more intelligent than humans. After all, Deep Blue could calculate approximately 200 million possible moves per second. Kasparov's defeat also raises interesting questions about what defines a mind. Imagine a chess-playing Turing test. You are playing chess in front of a computer monitor but you don't know if the moves being made by your opponent are from a computer or human. If Turing is right, and you could not tell which moves were being made by a human or by a computer, would you have to conclude that both had a mind? Would this mean that the chess-playing computer can think? Is artificial intelligence a potential reality? Give reasons for your answers.

2. Searle's Chinese room argument is intended to show that having a mind is more than just merely acting as *if* one does. A computer may act as *if* it understands Chinese but, in reality, it does not. Although it might be true the person in the Chinese room cannot understand Chinese, it must be remembered she is part of a larger system. Given the rules, symbols, and other necessary components in the room, the system as a whole might understand Chinese, not the specific individual. In short, perhaps Searle has misplaced understanding at the individual level, when, in fact, at the system level, the computer can be seen as a thinking entity. In what ways would you agree or disagree with this objection against Searle? What might Searle's reply be?

3. The notion of qualia is one of the main objections against functionalism. Certain qualitative aspects of our mental states make them feel like something to us and are essential to having a mind. For critics, it is this qualitative aspect that cannot be captured by functionalist explanations of mind. However, it's debatable whether qualia really makes a difference when it comes to classifying mental states. Not only do some of our mental states have no qualitative aspect but also some mental states can be classified only by their functional role (Campbell 94). Consider some kinds of pain: a stubbed toe; a broken bone; a headache; a burn from the stove; and a lost love. All are qualitatively different, and yet we classify them all as pain because of their functional role (Campbell 95). If that is correct, the idea of qualia is irrelevant to how we view the mind and is not a serious problem for functionalism. Would you agree? How important is qualia to your beliefs, hopes, emotions, pains, and so forth? Does qualia show that functionalism is false? Why or why not?

The Mind Is What the Mind Does

The demise of identity theory motivated philosophers such as Jerry Fodor to take up functionalism. Functionalists argue that mental states play a causal role or function in our behaviour. More specifically, mental states can be explained by their input and output relationship. The inputs to the mind are things that we can see, hear, taste, touch, and smell. The outputs are subsequent behaviour such as running, walking, sitting, and eating. Imagine you and your friend Sally are hiking in the Rocky Mountains, enjoying the beautiful scenery, when suddenly she stops, turns around, and starts running in the opposite direction. You are confused at first, but then see something off in the distance—a bear and her cubs. In other words, Sally saw the bears (seeing = input) and then ran in the opposite direction (action = output). How would we explain her behaviour? We would probably explain her behaviour by saying something like, "she *believes* the bears will attack" or "she is *afraid* of bears." In this case, it is her belief and fear that caused her to run away. In this sense, say functionalists, all mental states are shorthand terms for the causal connections between sensory inputs and behavioural outputs. This applies to other creatures as well. A rabbit might also exhibit the same bear-avoidance behaviour as Sally. In doing so, we could also attribute to the rabbit similar mental states as causally relevant to its behaviour. Here is another example: consider your belief that next week is the first mid-term exam. Given this belief, you will likely engage in certain types of behaviour including reading, studying, taking notes, etc. Your behaviour can be explained by virtue of the role these beliefs have in doing these things. As Samuel Guttenplan explains:

> There is a story to be told about the ways in which my seeing, hearing and remembering various things together account for the fact that I have this belief in the first place. If we describe how the belief affects my behaviour and other mental states as 'output' and the sources of its formation as 'input', then we can say that the functional role of the belief is some specific set of complex inputs and outputs…But this complexity should not prevent one seeing the core idea of functionalism: a mental phenomenon will be defined by its inputs and outputs, its functional role. ("Essay on Mind" 99)

Notice, there will likely be other mental states that make your propositional attitude about the pending exam rather complex. Your belief about the exam might be accompanied by a desire to do well and worry about having enough time to prepare. Although these other mental states may never be explicitly verbalized, they certainly play a part in your belief about the exam and cause you to engage in specific action. Mental states, in this sense, are defined by what they do—that is, your beliefs, desires, hopes, and fears can cause you to behave in certain ways. After all, if you didn't believe that the exam is next week, then you probably would not study. In this sense, mental states play a role or function in your actions.

The notion of "function" is important here because two things can have the same function or "do the same job" and yet be made of different materials. This is known as **multiple realizability**. The function of a hammer is to drive in nails. But, notice, if you don't have a hammer handy, a rock will serve the same purpose. Or consider the game of chess. The individual pieces of chess (rook, pawn, bishop, knight, queen, and king) each play a specific role or function within the game itself. More specifically, each chess piece is distinguished from another by virtue of how it moves. The rook moves horizontally and vertically; the bishop moves diagonally; and so forth. But their function or purpose is not determined by what they are made of. Chess pieces can be made of wood, stone, bone, metal, and a wide range of other material. In fact, you don't even need chess pieces to play because numbers and letters represent each square on the board and chess piece. Similarly, mental states are not defined by what they are made of but by the role they play in behaviour. Thus, a human, rabbit, or alien may all engage in similar bear-avoidance behaviour, despite the fact that their physiology is different, because similar mental states "do the same job" regardless of what they are made of (see Figure 4.5). This is one of the primary advantages functionalism has over identity theory.

Identity theorists argue mental states are brain states. A pain, for example, will be identical to some physical state in the brain or central nervous system. One of the main problems with

Figure 4.5   Mouse Trap

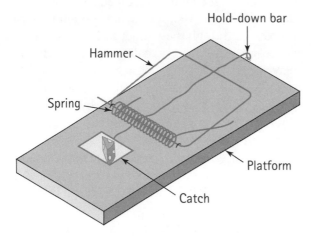

What makes a mousetrap a mousetrap? If functionalists are correct, it is not its physical composition but its purpose or function, which is to catch mice. So, what makes a mind a mind? For functionalists, it is not its physical makeup, that is, having a human-like brain, but the causal role it plays in our behaviour and actions. That is what minds do.

identity theory is that it doesn't take into consideration that other creatures may have a radically different physiology and yet have similar beliefs, hopes, fears, and so forth. As mentioned last section, it's possible for two people to have similar mental states realized in different brain states, or two people may have the same brain state but think different things. My Russian counterpart and I, for example, might both desire a beer and yet have this psychological state realized in different brain states. Hence, because of such cases, it's unrealistic to argue that there will be a one-to-one identity relationship between mind and brain. As Fodor argues in his article, the problem with identity theory and other attempts at physiological psychology is that they try to "look inside" to see if physiological processes are causally responsible for the actions in question. But given the problems with identity theory, strict identity is an unlikely candidate to explain the mind. This is not to say physiological processes are irrelevant to having a mind; it's just that there is no reason to think that various sub-parts correspond to specific mental states. To see this,

Fodor uses the examples of a carburettor, camshaft, and mousetrap to highlight his point. Let me illustrate using some different examples.

Consider the heart. The circulatory system of humans is closed, meaning that blood is contained in vessels. The job or function of a heart is to pump blood. The human heart, for example, has four chambers and is divided into two parts: the right and left atrium and the right and left ventricle. Each atrium and ventricle plays a specific role in the functioning of our circulatory system by pumping deoxygenated blood into the lungs then pushing the oxygenated blood back through the body (Postlethwait and Hopson 468). The details are unimportant for my purposes, but what is important is that the heart possesses this functional blood-pumping property because of its causal role in our circulatory system (Heil 98). To put another way, the property of being a heart is due to its material constitution or makeup; a material constitution that makes it what is: a blood pumper. But notice, and this is crucial to functionalism, other species have hearts that do the same job or function (pump blood) but have very different physiology. In open circulatory systems, found in arthropods (spiders, crabs, scorpions, etc.), the heart pumps blood partly into vessels but mostly the blood can freely slosh around the body, eventually working its way through the organism's organs. In other closed circulatory systems, for example, fish have only two chambered hearts and frogs only have three chambers (Postlethwait and Hopson 465). In fact, hearts do not need to be biological; they can be made out of plastic and metal. In 1982, Barney Clark, a dentist with severe heart disease, became the first person to receive an artificial heart. Developed by Robert Jarvik, the heart pumped Clark's heart for 112 days until other complications, not the functioning of the heart, took his life (Postlethwait and Hopson 469). Since the initial revolutionary surgery, other artificial hearts have been developed like the AbrioCor replacement heart that was implanted in a patient in Louisville, Kentucky in 2001. From a functionalist perspective, however, the property of a heart is not strictly determined by its physical constitution but by its functional role. Although a heart may be physically constituted of biological tissue or plastic, giving it the property of a heart, it is not reducible to or identical with the biological tissue or plastic itself. The lower level material properties of a heart do not make it what it is. What makes a heart a heart is its functional role in circulating blood, not its lower level microscopic configuration (Heil 98).

Another example of functionalism is antibiotics. There are countless antibiotics on the market today including penicillin, streptomycin, bacitracin, Polymyxin, and tetracycline, with all the same purpose: to kill disease-causing bacteria without causing harm to the patient (Ravenscroft 51). Each antibiotic has a different chemical makeup, but this does not affect its functional role in killing unwanted bacteria. In short, the physical chemical composition of antibiotics does not exclusively define their functional role. *Being* an antibiotic is not reducible to being a specific kind of chemical composition. So by talking about hearts as "blood pumpers" or antibiotics as "bacteria killers" does not mean we are identifying its microphysical composition. It makes no sense, says Fodor, in asking what a "blood pumper" or "bacteria killer" is made of because both are defined functionally and functions do not have microanalyzable parts.

Likewise, functionalism avoids the kinds of problems with identity theory mentioned earlier by suggesting that minds do not depend on what they are made of. Again, if we discovered aliens with a completely different biochemical composition than humans, they still may be psychologically similar. Identity theories would, of course, disagree. Take pain for an example. If we stumble across a creature with a different physiology than humans, assuming identity theory is correct, then we must conclude that it would not feel pain because it is not in the same brain state, despite the fact it may engage in comparable pain-type behaviour (cry, scream obscenities, hold wounds, etc.). This is the beauty of functionalism. It allows for creatures to be physiologically different than humans and yet, given

certain inputs and outputs, still feel pain or have mental states regardless of their microanalyzable physical constitution. But even if a microanalysis could be given, it would not by itself explain the point and purpose of, say, artificial hearts, or antibiotics. Given the wide variation of materials that each can be made from, its functional role is crucial to explaining what it does and in bringing newer models of artificial hearts and antibiotics into the larger functional domain. Likewise, even if a microanalysis could be given of mental states, it would not by itself explain the point and purpose of beliefs, desires, and so on, within our lives. We cannot reduce psychological states to an organism's neurophysiology anymore than we can reduce mousetraps to wood and metal. To explain the mind is to understand the functional role it plays in our behaviour. For Fodor, functionalism is the way of liberating us from previous outdated and faulty psychological theories of mind.

Can Computers Think?

If the physical constitution of something is irrelevant for something to have a mind, then this raises the possibility of artificial intelligence. In fact, most functionalists tend to make important analogies between human psychology and computers. According to functionalists, the hardware of a computer (wires, chips, etc.) is like the brain and the software is like the mind. In fact, the human brain might be thought of as a kind of computer that processes inputs (sensory perceptions) and generates outputs (behaviour). It's argued that once computers can process inputs and outputs like humans, they will have intelligence just like us. This idea has played heavily into the hands of contemporary cognitive scientists. If minds are not determined by their physiological makeup, but rather their input/output relationships, then computers might also have mental states by virtue of computational processes. The idea of the brain as a computational device is intriguing and has, no doubt, sparked the imaginations of many Hollywood producers. Consider, for example, *Artificial Intelligence* by Steven Spielberg. Set in the future, it's about a boy named David, the first robot ever programmed to feel love, in search of meaning, understanding, and emotional attachment after being abandoned by his adopted "mother." Another example is the new *Battlestar Galactica* television series. In the television show, technology has advanced to the point where the robotic Cylons are indistinguishable from humans in every way including emotions. Despite the technical difficulties of creating a thinking, feeling, and perceiving robot, if the brain is a computational device, then it makes sense we could build a computer to think like humans do (see Figure 4.6).

Before I explain John Searle's well-worn parable, let me explain two key terms: syntax and semantics. Let's start with **syntax**. Write the word *dog* on a piece of paper. What do you see? You should see three letters or symbols d-o-g. The word d-o-g, in other words, contains three syntactic properties or symbols. Now, if you were not a speaker or reader of English, these symbols would probably look like squiggles with no meaningful reference. That is, d-o-g would be meaningless or have no **semantics**. We know that dog means a mammal that barks, has a wet nose, and four legs, but if you didn't know English you would never understand this by merely staring at the individual letters. Travelling to a foreign country is often confusing because the syntactic properties or symbols on the signs are meaningless; they are just a bunch of lines and squiggles. Put roughly, syntax = symbols and semantics = meaning. Why is this important? Because, generally speaking, computers recognize and manipulate symbols on the basis of their syntactic properties; syntactic properties are just another name for a computer language or program, which are represented by 1s and 0s. Computers, it is said, are syntactic engines manipulating various syntactic properties encoded in a program language. And it's this program language that allows computers to play chess, check spelling, calculate numbers, and so forth. The philosophical question is whether a computer can be considered intelligent merely by the manipulation of syntax without having to understand the semantics or meaning behind the symbols themselves.

The very idea of computer or machine intelligence comes from Alan Turing, who, in 1950, developed what he called a Turing machine. Now this machine was not like a washing machine or calculator but was merely an imagined device to see if a computer could be programmed to fool someone into believing it was thinking. How does this machine work? It works by taking inputs and transforming them into outputs. So, for example, if a machine can take a series of numbers and subsequently print out new numbers, based on a set of step-by-step operations such as addition,

Figure 4.6   Strong Artificial Intelligence

subtraction, multiplication, or division, then we can say that some form of thinking is taking place. Take multiplication. I can do multiplication in my head by using a step-by-step process to solve a specific problem such as 100 × 5. I can also implement this same step-by-step process in a computer via a program and get the same answer of 500. In this way, according to functionalist dogma, the computer and I are using the same multiplication process, and if no one can tell the difference between the answer generated by me and the answer generated by the computer, we have to conclude that both can think. Or imagine you are sitting in front of a computer screen typing in questions such as "What colour are your eyes?", "What is your favourite food?", and "When did you graduate from high school?" If you cannot tell whether answers are coming from a human or a computer, then, according to Turing, you would have to conclude that both are intelligent. Why? Because only a machine that knew it was taking the test could answer and

it would have to lie since obviously computers don't have eyes, don't eat, or go to high school. But it should be pointed out that the brain is not a Turing machine. In fact, there are no Turing machines anywhere because computers did not exist at this time. Turing's point is that the arrangement of hardware or machinery could function as an intelligent system.

In his article, John Searle argues that the very idea of artificial intelligence rests upon a fundamental mistake: the mind being similar to a computer program. To illustrate, Searle's well-worn parable goes as follows: Imagine that a non-Chinese speaker is locked inside a room with a box full of Chinese symbols. She is given an instruction book (program) in English about how the Chinese symbols are to be matched. From a slot in the room a symbol is inserted, she looks in the instruction book to find the symbol that matches it, then she pushes it back through a slot leading to the outside world. Now, suppose that the symbols given to the person in the room are questions and the symbols produced answers. Let us assume that the person gets exceptionally quick at matching symbols in such a way that the answers given are indistinguishable from those of a native Chinese speaker (see Figure 4.7). The question is: Does the person in the room really understand Chinese by virtue of the instruction manual? An independent observer might be convinced that the person in the room understands Chinese. But, for Searle, this is a mistake. Even though the person in the room appears to understand Chinese, neither the person nor any part of the system literally understands Chinese the way a native speaker would. Why?

Figure 4.7 Searle's Chinese Room

Because a computer program is nothing but purely formal syntactical operations; it lacks the ability to understand what the symbols mean and represent and, unless the symbols being manipulated mean something to the system itself, their meaning is irrelevant. Understanding Chinese is not just a matter of manipulating symbols in an appropriate way. More generally, for Searle, the manipulation of computational symbols is not the same as having thoughts. To put this more formally:

> Programs are entirely syntactical.
> Minds have semantics.
> Syntax is not the same as, nor by itself sufficient for, semantics.
> Therefore, programs are not minds.
> (Guttenplan, *Mind's Landscape* 297)

For Searle, implementing a computer program cannot itself produce real understanding (or thoughts, beliefs, desires, hate, envy, etc.)—computers can simulate understanding but can't duplicate it. A computer may have syntax (symbols) but it has no semantics. The meaning of the symbols by *themselves* is irrelevant to the computer, but derivative from the people who have programmed or who use the system. Hence, a computer program is nothing like a mind because *its* states are fundamentally different than *our* mental states. Human mental states have **intentionality**, defined not only by their content (what they are about or refer to in the world) but also by what they mean to us as humans. However, we should be careful about what Searle is saying. He does suggest human thinking is, in some sense, computer-like; what Searle rejects is the claim that something can think solely by carrying out the manipulation of symbols as input and output. That is, the Chinese symbols or syntax itself has no meaning; they don't refer to anything. In short, intentionality is wholly lacking. In contrast, human intentional mental states are what they are because they mean or represent something to us. Mental processes are driven by semantic content, not syntactic computation.[13]

Furthermore, computers may be said to do all sorts of computational tasks but not in the same way that I can add two plus two: they merely manipulate 1s and 0s, and, at the electromechanical level, they do not even do that (Searle, "Searle, John. R.," 546). Humans describe computers as *computing* because that's exactly what we want them to do. Computation, like bathtubs, stop signs, and picnic tables (amongst others) are relative to the purposes of those who use or make them. If there were no people in the world, there would still be lakes, mountains, and so forth; however, there would not be picnic tables, stop signs, or bathtubs. The same can be said of the computational features of a computer—they are observer-relative. The electrical circuitry of a computer does not really multiply 4×5; it is only the manipulation of 1s and 0s, and these don't add up to computation. As Searle states, "*notions such as computation, algorithm, and program do not name intrinsic physical features of systems*. Computational states are not *discovered within* the physics, they are *assigned* to the physics" (Searle, *Rediscovery of the Mind* 210). Syntax manipulation, computation, and the computer itself are dependent upon the users and purposes of a human designer or engineer. In other words, computational features of machines are derived from us, its users. We are the ones who attribute computational abilities to such entities; computers themselves don't compute any more than nails can compute how far to sink into a piece of wood, or a visual system can compute the distance of objects (Searle, *Rediscovery of the Mind* 214). Functionalism, on Searle's account, is false.

If Searle is right, then one of the major problems with artificial intelligence is that computer programs merely manipulate symbols in accord with rules (computer program). Hence, the problem with the Turing test is that the computer doesn't know the meaning (semantics) of the questions "What colour are your eyes?", "What is your favourite food?", and "When did you graduate from high school?" Perhaps if we could build-in syntax and semantics, computers would have intelligence. In short, maybe what computers need is common sense.

Much of our ability to cope with the world is based on presuppositions and assumptions, or if you like, commonsense knowledge. The problem is trying to program computers with enough common sense to allow them to adapt and adjust their behaviour to changing situations and environments. One way to solve the problem is to program facts and information into the computer, like Doug Lenat's CYC project. Lenat has been working on programming different types of commonsense information into his computer, named Cyc (named after encyclopedia), for almost two decades. To do this, a list of commonsense information, made up of everyday banalities, is pumped (programmed) into a computer. The goal, it's hoped, is that Cyc will take over its own programming and function as an autonomous being. As Lenat explains:

> You can think of Cyc as a big repository of knowledge—knowledge that is so obvious that it's confusing or insulting to ever say it to someone else. Knowledge like if you're holding a glass of water you should hold it with the open end up. Knowledge like most people sleep at night, and so if you call people in the middle of the night, they will probably be at home sleeping and you'll wake them up. So it's that kind of knowledge—knowledge we usually don't tell our children because it's so obvious. But that's knowledge computer programs don't have. (Moody)

At first glance, this approach to solving the Turing test seems plausible. For example, if we can build-in information about eye colour, food, and graduating from high school, perhaps the computer could respond that it does not have eyes, doesn't eat, and didn't graduate from high school. But this requires commonsense information about eyes, food, and school. Consider the statements: the Canada is a big country, water is wet, and when people die they stay dead. These are such obvious commonsense facts they barely need mentioning (Thompson 30). So far, more than a 1.5 million rules and facts have been programmed into Cyc. It's these kinds of facts that Lenat thinks will solve the Turing test and artificial intelligence generally.

However, critics like Herbert Dreyfus are not impressed. Dreyfus argues that Lenat can build-in all the facts he wants into Cyc but this still won't be enough to get computer intelligence off the ground (262). There are two main problems, says Dreyfus. The first is that common sense is developed not through explicit learning but through bodily learning (skills). You cannot learn how to ride a bike, for example, by reading a book; you have to get on the bike and learn how to handle it in such a way that you develop bike-riding skills. Leaning that water is wet doesn't come from knowing its chemical composition (H_2O) but from splashing, pouring, and handling it (water skills). Much of our commonsense knowledge, thinks Dreyfus, is based on bodily skills not explicit knowledge. And since a computer doesn't have a body to develop such skills, and subsequent knowledge, it might know stuff, but not know how to use it. Knowing how to use something requires knowing how to use it in context and in different circumstances. Second, knowing how to use something in context requires the ability to determine which piece of information is relevant and irrelevant. For humans, as the world changes or situations change, we can update our beliefs and determine the appropriate action almost instantaneously. Humans can store an enormous amount of information ad infinitum and, most importantly, access this information in limited real-time situations. Humans can sort out what information is relevant and irrelevant quickly and easily. And perhaps most importantly, relevant information varies from year to year and culture to culture. In Western cultures, the sex of a person is irrelevant to whether he or she has a right to vote, but historically this wasn't always the case (Crane 122). Computers, at least to date, have had no such luck giving meaning and relevance to their syntactic-based programs (Dreyfus 43), and, therefore, it is questionable that they have intelligence. I will leave it up to students to decide whether artificial intelligence will one day come to fruition (see Box 4.5).

Box 4.5 Does Creativity Determine Intelligence?

The defeat of world chess champion Garry Kasparov by the supercomputer Deep Blue in 1997 has raised fundamental questions about what makes humans human. What separates or makes human unique and different from other non-human species and other inanimate artefacts? Traditionally, intelligence, rationality, and problem solving were considered utterly unique to humans, something no other species or object possessed. Although this view has softened over the years (chimps and dolphins are pretty smart), the advent of supercomputers like Deep Blue has thrown these traditional human features into doubt. Deep Blue, one could argue, is more intelligent, rational, and better at solving problems than humans—at least chess-playing humans. Should the success of Deep Blue make us question our human intelligence and uniqueness? Are we really that different from other species and chess-playing computers? What defines intelligence?

Perhaps we need to define intelligence outside the traditional parameters of rationality and problems solving. One alternative is to define intelligence in light of creativity. It's an obvious fact that humans are creative. From building and car designs to revolutionary ideas and concepts, human creativity and ingenuity is unique to us; no other animal species is as creative as humans. But does human creativity set us apart from computers? Could creativity define the meaning of intelligence? At first glance, the answer is yes. In the case of Kasparov's defeat by Deep Blue, Deep Blue was merely following programmed rules of chess. Deep Blue never approached the game or developed opening moves in an utterly unique way. Likewise, even if we could download every novel ever written into a computer database, it's highly doubtful a computer could come up with an original and unique novel paralleling human creativity. In short, if creativity determines intelligence, then we could say that Deep Blue does not possess it.

But even the idea of creativity is being called into question as a uniquely human characteristic of intelligence. In 2005, a museum in San Diego had an art exhibit. The exhibit got rave reviews from visitors and one art critic. Although impressed with the art, according to the art critic, it wasn't *real art* because a computer did it. The computer is known as AARON, developed by Harold Cohen, an artist and former director of the Center for Research in Computing and the Arts at the University of California San Diego. Since 1973, AARON has produced works of art, which have been displayed at London's Tate Gallery, the Brooklyn Museum, and the Ontario Science Centre, amongst other prestigious galleries. The important question is whether "creativity" is something that computers can have. Can computers produce something that is new and original and, thereby, have intelligence?

Well, if producing something *new* defines creativity, then this definition will not work. After all, a fast-flowing river can create new and original rock structures over centuries, but this doesn't mean the river is creative. Likewise, AARON can generate 50 to 60 *new* and original pieces of art in one night, but it doesn't mean the computer is creative. Part of the problem stems from the fact that AARON is merely following programmed rules from which it cannot deviate. The computer is a slave to its program, that is, the instructions that Cohen programs into it. Perhaps if AARON were to "throw out the rules" or "act" beyond the rules, then it could be considered creative. If AARON could change its perspective or outlook of art and change its approach to the process of being an artist, then maybe, just maybe, we might get close to human-like creativity. But in order to do that, AARON would have to possess, what philosophers call, phenomenal conscious. That is, have an awareness of itself and the rules it follows. It would have to be able to think about its thoughts and understand *what it is like* to be AARON as an artist. And this seems too much to ask from a machine. Imagine, one day, computers could write novels or works of act comparable to human writers and artists. Would this mean they are intelligent? Would this lessen the value of human artists and writers? How would it make you feel?

Source: Adapted from Dan Falk. "Is It Art?" *Globe and Mail* 15 Oct. 2005: F9.

Inverted Spectrums and Zombies

There are other problems with functionalism not discussed by Searle. One of the most interesting problems is based on the notion of **qualia**. Qualia are the *what it feels like* or qualitative aspect of our mental states, emotions, and sensations. Have you ever been in love? Have you ever tasted rattlesnake meat? Have you ever been so scared that you were lost for words? Each of these mental states is associated with different subjective qualia. The problem with functionalism, say critics, is that it cannot take into account this qualitative—or what does it feel like—aspect of our mind. Remember, for functionalists, a mental state is what it is by virtue of its role or function in our behaviour. Going back to our earlier example, if Sally sees a bear (input) and runs away (output), how do we explain her behaviour? Again, we would probably explain her behaviour by saying something like, "because she believes she sees a bear and is afraid it will attack." Sally's belief/fear is something in the brain that links the sensory input with the behavioural output. So consider:

- The function of her belief/fear is to cause her to run or move away from bears.
- The function of thirst is to cause us to get something to drink.
- The function of love is to cause us to act in compassionate and caring ways.
- The function of pain causes us to engage in pain-behaviour (yelling, cursing, etc.) and also to avoid things like pointy sticks, sharks, and so on.

The problem with functionalism is that it cannot account for the subjective quality of fear, thirst, love, pain, and other mental states. One of the most famous thought experiments to demonstrate this point is known as the inverted spectrum. Imagine my colour spectrum is inverted relative to yours so that when you see green, I see red (Block 221–222). Hence, we can go about our world buying apples and tomatoes, despite the fact that they look green to you and red to me. According to functionalism, your visual sensation upon viewing a tomato will be functionally identical to mine based on the fact its function or role allows us to buy, cook, and eat apples and tomatoes. So imagine that I bump into you in the produce section of a grocery store. I look at the tomatoes and say, "Those look red and delicious." And you reply, "Yes, I can tell by their redness they are ripe to eat." Now although our linguistic usage of "red" is congruent with mine, and we both functionally behave similarly by placing the tomatoes into a bag, what is left out or omitted from such a functionalist account of mind is the "what it feels like" or the qualitative nature of our sensations or perceptions. Your experience of green will be very different than my experience of red, despite the fact that we engage in the same behaviour. The problem with functionalism is that it leaves out the felt quality that makes mental states what they are. Therefore, there must be something wrong with functionalism.

Perhaps a stronger example is love. To be in love, according to functionalists, is to engage in love type behaviour. So, if you are in love, you will, at least based on North American standards, hold hands, kiss, hug, have sex, and so on. Love, generally speaking, is associated with warm and fuzzy feelings, excitement, genuine concern for others, and deep emotional attachment. Now imagine two people have their emotional spectrums inverted. That is, when Mary feels love, Barb feels hate. Mary, Barb, and their spouses go out together for dinner. Over the course of dinner we see the couples hold hands, kiss each other occasionally, and communicate their love by saying, "I love you." Now if functionalism were true, we would have to assume, given their love-type behaviour, that they are both in love. But given their emotional spectrums are inverted, can we say that Barb, like Mary, is *in love* with her spouse? No we cannot. Why? Because despite the fact that they engage in the same loving-type behaviour and talk about love, Barb's emotional state is radically different than Mary's. Functionalist explanations of mind would have to conclude that the qualitative aspect of Mary's and

Figure 4.8   Calvin and Hobbes on Zombies

Barb's emotion don't matter to being in love; all that matters is that they behave in similar ways. But surely the qualitative aspect is crucial to what love *really is*. Functionalists cannot explain this, and thus, the theory is false.

Another problem with functionalism, and related to the inverted spectrum, is the absent qualia problem (Block 216–217), which is best illustrated by current philosophers using zombies. Before the argument is presented, a distinction must be made between Hollywood zombies and philosophical zombies (Chalmers 94–95). Hollywood zombies are the living dead (see Figure 4.8). They have limited cognitive and reasoning ability; they crave human flesh and will kill for it; and their communication skills are limited. They are fundamental to horror movies such as *Army of Darkness*, *Dawn of the Dead*, *Night of the Living Dead*, and the satirical *Shaun of the Dead*. Philosophical zombies are, however, different from their Hollywood cousins. Philosophical zombies are identical to humans in everyway except they lack consciousness. That is, their behaviour is functionally identical to us, but they have no conscious experiences at all. Imagine you have a zombie twin. Your zombie will function behaviourally identical to you including reading this book, turning pages, etc. Or imagine you are chopping vegetables for dinner and you accidentally cut your finger and say, "Ouch!" in the process. Notice your zombie will also say, "Ouch!"

If functionalism is true we would have to conclude that both you and your zombie feel pain. But this is not the case. As Chalmers explains, "[your zombie] will certainly be identical to [you] *functionally*: he will be processing the same sort of information, reacting in a similar way to inputs, with his internal configurations being modified appropriately and with indistinguishable behavior resulting. . . . It is just that none of this functioning will be accompanied by any real conscious experience. There will be no phenomenal feel. There is nothing it is like to be a zombie" (95). In other words, you and your zombie twin, although functionally identical, are radically different regarding the qualitative experiences each of you will have: you actually are in pain, whereas your zombie twin is not in pain—in fact, it doesn't even have a mind. The problem with functionalism, like the inverted spectrum example, is that it's the qualitative aspect of our mental states, not just their functional role, which makes them what they are. Unfortunately, functionalism is not a viable theory because it leaves out this crucial aspect of mind.

But on the other hand, identity theory is problematic in another important way. Identity theory is a materialist theory, but according to its critics, it doesn't go far enough. Science has shown that the brain and mind are one and the same, and, yet, identity theorists still talk of the mind as being important to explaining and predicting behaviour. That is, we attribute mental states as way of making sense of what other people do. This is known as folk psychology, which we'll discuss in the next section. However, for Paul Churchland, mental state attributions are misguided because folk psychology often fails and is confused. If the mind really *is* the brain, given the importance of science in our lives, then, one day, we ought to be able to eliminate the mind altogether. This is known as eliminative materialism.

22

Jerry Fodor (1935–)

Jerry Fodor is arguably the most important and influential philosopher of mind today. Born in 1935, he was educated at Columbia University and earned his Ph.D. from Princeton University in 1960 under the guidance of Hilary Putnam. He taught at the famous Massachusetts Institute of Technology (MIT) from 1959 to 1986, when he took up a position at City University of New York. In 1988, he was appointed Professor of Philosophy at Rutgers University in New Jersey where he remains today. Fodor is said to be gentle man but has a fierce and supple philosophical style that quickly disarms even the most prepared attacker. Fodor is not only passionate about philosophy but also opera and his beloved cats. Some of his work include The Language of Thought *(1975),* The Modularity of Mind *(1983), and* The Mind Doesn't Work That Way *(2000).*

Materialism

It is frequently in philosophical discussions of the mind-body problem that it might be reasonable to regard mind states and brain states as contingently identical. How plausible one considers this suggestion to be depends on one's view of an extremely complicated tangle of philosophical problems to which the materialist doctrine is closely connected. Among these are problems that must clearly be faced during the course of providing an account of explanation in psychology.

For example, determining whether or not materialism can be true is part of understanding the relation between theories in psychology and theories in neurology—a relation that many philosophers believe poses a stumbling block for the doctrine of the unity of science. In particular, it is sometimes maintained that the unity of science requires that it prove possible to "reduce" psychological theories to neurological theories, the model of reduction being provided by the relation between constructs in chemistry and those in physics. This is usually taken to mean that, for each theoretical term that appears in psychology, there must be a true statement that articulates a psychophysical identity and that such statements are to be understood on the analogy of statements that identify hydrogen atoms with certain configurations of subatomic particles. On this view, neurological entitles are to the denotata of psychological terms, just as physical entitles are the denotata of chemical terms.[1]

This sort of issue suggests that rather more is at stake when the question of materialism is raised than may initially meet the eye. In this chapter, I shall therefore attempt to bring out some of the logical links between the controversy about materialism and some other problems in philosophical psychology, as well as to survey a number of arguments in which the truth of materialism is directly involved. [...]

Materialism and the Relation between Psychology and Neurology

For purposes of the present investigation, we are primarily interested in materialism as it bears upon problems about psychological explanation. We need, therefore, to clarify the implications of the materialist view for an account of the relations between psychological and neurological theories. I shall argue that while it is by no means evident that materialism must be regarded as conceptually incoherent, it is equally unclear that the truth of materialism would entail the views of the relation between psychology and neurology that have often been held in conjunction with it. In particular, to claim that mind states and brain states are contingently identical need not be to hold that psychological theories are reducible to neurological theories. Nor would the truth of materialism entail that the relevant relation between psychological and neurological constructs is that the latter provide "microanalyses" of the former. It is to these issues that we now proceed.

Let us commence by trying to form some picture of how the problem of the relation between psychology and neurology emerges during the course of attempts to provide systematic scientific explanation of behavior.

Such attempts have characteristically exhibited two phrases that, although they may be simultaneous in point of history, are nevertheless distinguishable in point of logic. In the first phase, the psychologist attempts to arrive at theories that provide what are often referred to as "functional" characterizations of the mechanisms responsible for the production of behavior. To say that the psy-

chologist is seeking functional characterization of psychological constructs is at least to say that, in this phase of explanation, the criteria employed for individuating such constructs are based primarily upon hypotheses about the role they play in the etiology of behavior. Such hypotheses are constrained by two general considerations. On the one hand, by the principle that the psychological states, processes, and so on hypothesized to be responsible for the production of behavior must be supposed to be sufficiently complex to account for whatever behavioral capacities the organism can be demonstrated to posses; on the other, by the principle that specific aspects of the character of the organism's behavior must be explicable by reference to specific features of the hypothesized underlying states and processes or of their interactions.

Thus, for example, a psychologist might seek to explain failures of memory by reference to the decay of a hypothetical memory "trace," an attempt being made to attribute to the trace properties that will account for such observed features of memory as selectivity, stereotyping, and so forth. As more is discovered about memory—for example, about the effects of pathology upon memory, or about differences between "short-" and "long-term" memory—the properties attributed to the trace, and to whatever other psychological systems are supposed to interact with it, must be correspondingly elaborated. It is, of course, the theorist's expectation that, at some point, speculations about the character of the trace will lead to confirmable experimental predictions about previously unnoticed aspects of memory, thus providing independent evidence for the claim that the trace does in fact have the properties it is alleged to have.

To say that, in the first phase of psychological explanation, the primary concern is with determining the functional character of the states and processes involved in the etiology of behavior is thus to say that, at that stage, the hypothesized psychological constructs are individual primarily or solely by reference to their alleged casual consequences. What one knows (or claims to know) about such constructs is the effects their activity has upon behavior. It follows that phase-one psychological theories postulate functionally equivalent mechanisms when and only when they postulate constructs of which the behavioral consequences are, in theoretically relevant respects, identical.

This sort of point has sometimes been made by comparing first-phase psychological theories with description of a "machine-table"— that is, of the sets of directions of a forming computations—of a digital computer. Neurological theories, correspondingly, are likened to descriptions of the "hardware"; that is, of the physical machinery into which such tables are programmed.[2] Since two physical realizations of the same table—that is, two computers capable of performing the mathematically identical set of computations in mathematically identical ways—may differ arbitrarily in their physical structure: two machines may, in this sense, share functionally equivalent "psychological" mechanisms even though they have neither parts nor configuration of parts in common.

The second phase of psychological explanation has to do with the specification of those biochemical systems that do, in fact, exhibit the functional characteristics enumerated by phase-one theories. The image that suggests itself to many psychologists is that of opening a "black box": having arrived at a phase-one theory of the kinds of operations performed by the mechanisms that are casually responsible for behavior, one then "looks inside" to see whether or not the nervous system does in fact contain parts capable of performing the alleged func-

tions. The situation is more complicated, however, than this image suggests since the notion of a "part," when applied to the nervous systems of organisms, is less than clear. The physiological psychologist's task of determining what, if any, organization into subsystems the nervous system of an organism exhibits is precisely the problem of determining whether the nervous system has subsystems whose functional characteristics correspond with those required by antecedently plausible psychological theories.

The two phases of psychological explanation thus condition one another. On the one hand, it is clear that a psychological theory that attributes to an organism a state or process that the organism has no physiological mechanisms capable of realizing is ipso facto incorrect. If memory is a matter of forming traces, then there must be subsystems of the nervous system that are capable of going from one steady state to another and that are capable of remaining in the relevant states for periods that are at least comparable to known retention periods. If no such mechanisms exist, then the trace is the wrong model for the functional organization of memory.

On the other hand, the relevant notion of a neurological subsystem is that of a biochemical mechanism whose operation can correspond to some state or process that is postulated by a satisfactory psychological theory. To say that the goals of physiological psychology are set by the attempt to find mechanisms that correspond to certain functions is to say that it is the psychological theory that articulates these functions that determines the principle of individuation for neurological mechanisms. Once again, analogies to the analysis of less complicated systems may be helpful. What makes a carburetor part of an engine is not the spatial contiguity of its own parts (the parts of fuel injectors exhibit no such contiguity) nor is it the homogeneity of the materials of which it is composed. It is rather the fact that its operation correspond to a function that is detailed in the theory of internal-combustion engines and that there is no sub- or superpart of the carburetor whose operation corresponds to that function.

The problem, then, is one of fit and mutual adjustment; on the one hand there is a presumed psychological theory, which requires possibly quite specific, complex, and detained operations on the part of the neurological mechanisms that underlie behavior; on the other hand, there is a putative articulation of the nervous system into subsystems that must be matched to these functional characteristics and that must also attempt to maximize functional characteristics and that must also attempt to maximize anatomical, morphological, and biochemical plausibility. This extremely complex situation is sometimes abbreviated by materialist philosophers into the claim that identification between psychological and neurological states is established on the basis of constant correlation and simplicity. We have seen that it is an open question whether the relevant relation is identification. Our present point is that the evidence required to justify postulating the relation is something considerably more complex than mere correlation. It is rather a nice adjustment of the psychological characterization of function to considerations of neurological plausibility and vice versa.

Microanalysis and Functional Analysis

This discussion of the way in which psychological and neurological theories integrate during the course of the development of scientific explanations of behavior is, to be sure, no more than the barest sketch. But, insofar as the sketch is at all plausible, it suggests that the reductivist view of the relation between psychological and neurological theories is seriously misleading, even if one accepts a materialistic account of the relation between psychological and neurological constructs. The suggestion is that if materialism is true, a completed account of behavior would contain statements that identify certain neural mechanisms as having functions detailed during the course of phase-one theory construction and that some such statements would hold for each psychological construct. But such statements, clearly, are quite different in kind from those that articulate paradigmastic cases of reductive analysis.

This distinction seems to have been pretty widely misused by materialists, particularly in the literature that relates discussions of materialism to problems about the unity of science. Oppenheim and Putnam, for example, are explicit in referring to neurological theories, such as those of Hebb, as constituting "micro-reductions" of the corresponding psychological theories of memory, learning, motivation, and so on. On the Oppenheim-Putnam account, "the essential feature of micro-reduction is that the branch [of science] B_1 [which provides the micro-reduction of B_2] deals with the parts of the objects dealt with by B_2."[3]

Our present point is that it is difficult to understand how this could be the correct model of the relation between psychological and neurological theories. Psychological entitles (sensations, for example) are not readily thought of as capable of being microanalyzed into *anything*, least of all neurons or states of neurons. Pains do not have parts, so brain cells are not parts of pains.

It is, in short, conceivable that there my be true psychophysical identity statements, but it seems inconceivable that such statements are properly analyzed as expressing what Place (1956) has called identities of composition, that is, as expressing relations between wholes and their parts. It should be emphasized that not all statements of identities *are* identities of composition. Compare "Here hat is a bundle of straw" with "He is the boy I knew in Chicago."

It is worth pursuing at some length the difference between the present view of the relation between psychological and neurological constructs and the view typical of reductivist materialism. In reductive analysis (mircoanalysis), one asks: "What does *X* consist of?" and the answer has the forms of the microstructure of Xs. Thus: "What does water consist of?" "Two atoms of hydrogen linked with one atom of oxygen." "What does lightning consist of?" "A stream of electrons." And so on. In typical cases of functional analysis, by contrast, one asks about a part of a mechanism *what role it plays* in the activities that are characteristic of the mechanism as a whole: "What does the camshaft do?" "It opens the valves, permitting the entry into the cylinder of fuel, which will then be detonated to drive the prison." Successful microanalysis is thus often contingent upon the development of powerful instruments of observation or precise methods of dissection. Successful functional analysis, on the other hand, requires an appreciation of the sorts of activity that are characteristic of a mechanism and of the contribution made by the functioning of each part of the mechanism to the economy of the whole.

Since microanalysis and functional analysis are very different ways of establishing relations between scientific theories, or between ordinary-language descriptions, conceptual difficulties may result when the vocabulary of one kind of analysis is confounded with the vocabulary of the other.

If I speak of a device as a "camshaft," I am implicitly identifying it by reference to its physical structure, and so I am committed to the view that is exhibits a characteristic and specifiable decompositions into physical parts. But if I speak of the device as a "valve lifter," I am identifying it by reference to its function and I therefore undertake no such commitment. There is, in particular, no sense to the question. "What does a valve lifter consist of?" if this is understood as a request for microanalysis—that is, an analogous to such questions as "What does water consist of?" (There *is*, of course, sense to the question "What does *this* valve lifter consist of?" but the generic valve lifter must be *functionally* defined, and functions do not have parts.) One might put it that being a valve lifter is not reducible to (is not a matter of) being a collection of rods, spring, and atoms, in the sense in which being a camshaft is. The kinds of questions that it makes sense to ask about camshafts need not make sense, and are often impertinent, when asked about valve lifters.

It is, then, conceivable that serious confusions could be avoided if we interpreted statements that relate psychological and neurological constructs not as articulating microanalyses but as attributing certain psychological functions to corresponding neurological systems. For example, philosophers and psychologists who have complained that it is possible to trace an input from afferent to central to efferent neurological systems without once encountering motives, strategies, drives, needs, hopes, along with the rest of the paraphernalia of psychological theories, have been right in one sense but wrong in another, just as one would be if one argued that a complete mechanical account of the operation of an internal-combustion engine never encounters such a thing as a valve lifter. In both cases, the confusion occurs when a term that properly figures in functional accounts of mechanisms is confounded with terms that properly appear in mechanistic accounts, so that term is tempted to think of the function of a part as though it were itself one part among others.

From a function point of view, a camshaft is a valve lifter and *this* valve lifter (i.e. this particular mechanism for lifting valves) may be "nothing but" a camshaft. But a mechanistic account of the operations of internal-combustion engines does not seek to replace the concept of a valve lifter with the concept of a camshaft, not dies it see to "reduce" the former to the latter. What it does do to explain *how* the valves get lifted: that is, what mechanical transactions are involved when the camshaft lifts the valves. In the same way, presumably, neurological theories seek to explain what biochemical transactions are involved when drives are reduced, motives entertained, objects perceived, and so on.

In short, drives, motives, strategies, and such are, on the present view, internal states postulated in attempts to account for behavior, perception, memory, and other phenomena in the domain of psychological theories. In completed accounts, they could presumably serve to characterize the function aspects of neurological mechanisms; that is, they would figure in explanations of how such mechanisms operate to determine the molar behavior of an organism, its perceptual capacities, and so on. But this does not entail that drives, motives, and strategies have microanalyses in terms of neurological systems any more than valve lifters can be microanalyzed into camshafts.

There are still further philosophical pertinent differences between the suggestion that psychophysical identity statements should be understood as articulating functional analyses and the suggestions that they should be analyzed as micro-reductions.

When, in paradigmatic cases, entitles in one theory are reduced to entities in another, it is presupposed that both theories have available conceptual mechanisms for saying what the entities have in common. For example, give that water can be "reduced" to H_2O, it is possible to say what all samples of water have in common either in the language of viscosity, specific gravity, and so on at the macrolevel, or in chemical language at the microlevel. It is patent that functional analysis need not share this property of reductive analysis. When we identify a certain mousetrap with a certain mechanism, we do not thereby commit ourselves to the possibility of saying in mechanistic terms what all members of the set of mousetraps have in common. Because it is (roughly) a sufficient condition for being a mousetrap that a mechanism be customarily *used* in a certain way, there is nothing in principle that requires that a pair of mousetraps *have* any shared mechanical properties. It is, indeed, because "mousetrap" is functionally rather than mechanically defined that "building a better mousetrap"—that is, building a mechanically novel mousetrap, which functions better than conventional mousetraps do—is a reasonable goal to set oneself.

It is a consequence of this consideration that the present interpretation of the relation between neurological and psychological constructs is compatible with very strong claims about the ineliminability of mental language from behavioral theories. Let us suppose that there are true psychological statements that identify certain neurological mechanisms as the ones that possess certain psychologically relevant functional properties. It still remains quite conceivable that identical psychological functions could sometimes be ascribed to anatomically heterogeneous neural mechanisms. In that case, mental language will be required to state the conditions upon such ascriptions of functional equivalence. It is, in short, quite conceivable that a parsing of the nervous system by reference to anatomical or morphological similarities may often fail to correspond in any uniform way to its parsing in terms of psychological function. Whenever this occurs, explicit reference to the character of such functions will be required if we are to be able to say what we take the brain states that we classify together to have in common.

Every mousetrap can be identified with some mechanism, and being a mousetrap can therefore be identified with being a member of some (indefinite) set of possible mechanisms. But enumerating the set is not a way of dispensing with the notion of a mousetrap; that notion is required to say what all the members of the set have in common and, in particular, what credentials would be required to certify a putative new member as belonging to the set.

Such considerations may be extended to suggest not only that a *plausible* version of materialism will need to view psychological theories as articulating the functional characteristics of neural mechanisms, but also that that is the *only* version of materialism that is likely to prove coherent. Consider the following argument, which Sellars has offered as a refutation of materialism:

> Suppose I am experiencing a circular red raw feel . . . (in certain cases) the most careful and sophistical introspection will fail to refute the following statement: There is a finite subregion ΔR of the raw feel patch Ψr, and a finite time interval Δt, such that during Δt no property of ΔR changes."

The refutation may now proceed by appeal to Leibniz' Law. Suppose there is a brain state Φr which is held to be identical with the psychological state Ψr, that one is in when one senses something red (i.e., with the "red raw feel"). Then substitution of Φr for Ψr permits the inference: there is a finite region ΔR of the brain state Φr and the finite time interval Δt, and such that during Δt no property of ΔR changes.

> But this, as even pre-Utopian neurophysiology shows us, is factually false… Thus, during say, 500 milliseconds, the 5° region at the center of my phenomenal circle does not change any property, whereas no region of the physical brain event can be taken small enough such that *none* of its properties change during a 500-millisecond period.[1]

The point of this argument is, I think, entirely independent of its appeal to such dubious psychological entities as "red raw feels." For it seems pretty clear that the principles we employ for individuating neurological states are in general different from, and logically independent of, those that we employ for individuating psychological states. Since what counts as one sensation, one wish, one desire, one drive, and so on is not specified by reference to the organism's neurophysiology, it seems hardly surprising that an organism may persist in a given psychological condition while undergoing neurological change. If a materialist theory is so construed as to deny this, then materialism in certain to prove *contingently* false.

Nor does Sellars' argument depend solely upon the possibility of there being differences in "grain" between neurological and psychological variation. The problem is not just that slight changes in neurophysiology may be compatible with continuity of psychological state. It is rather that we have no right to assume a priori that the nervous system may not sometimes produce indistinguishable psychological effects by *radically* different physiological means. How much redundancy there may be in the nervous system is surely an open empirical question. It would be extraordinarily unwise if the claims for materialism or for the unity of science were to be formulated in such fashion as to require that for each distinguishable psychological state there must be one and only one corresponding brain state.

I see no way to accommodate such considerations that does not involve a wholesale employment of the notion of functional equivalence. For the point on which Sellars' argument turns is precisely that there may very well be sets of neurologically distinct brain states, whose members are nevertheless psychologically indistinguishable. In such cases, identification of the psychological state with any member of such a set produces problems with the substitutivity of identity.

It seems clear that a materialist can avoid these difficulties only at the price of assuming that the objects appropriate for identification with psychological states are sets of *functionally equivalent* neurological states. In particular, it must be true of any two members of such a set that an organism may alternate between them without thereby undergoing psychological change.

This is tantamount to saying that a materialist must recognize as scientifically relevant a taxonomy of neurological states according to their psychological functions. Such a taxonomy defines a "natural kind" (although very likely not the same natural kind as emerges from purely anatomical and biochemical considerations). Thus, a reasonable version of materialism might hold that psychological theories and neurological theories both involve taxonomies defined over the same objects (brain states), but according to different principles. What we require of the members of a set of anatomically similar brain states is *not* what we require of the members of a set of functionally equivalent brain states. Yet in neither case need the classification be arbitrary. The psychological consequences of being in one or another brain state are either distinguishable or they are not. If they are distinguishable, it is a question of fact whether or not the distinction is of the kind that psychological theories recognize as systematic and significant.

It is tempting to suppose that there must be only one principle of sorting (taxonomy be physical similarity), on pain of there otherwise being chaos, that either there is *one* kind of scientifically relevant similarity or there is *every* kind. It is, however, unnecessary to succumb to any such temptation. What justifies a taxonomy, what makes a kind "natural," is the power and generality of the theories that we are enabled to formulate when we taxonomize in that way. Classifying together all the entities that are made up of the same kinds of parts is one way of taxonomizing fruitfully, but if we can find other principles for sorting brain states, principles that permit simple and powerful accounts of etiology of behavior, then that is itself an adequate justification for sorting according to those principles.

It would seem, then, that both the traditional approach to materialism and the traditional approach to the unity of science are in need of libertization. In the first case, if he is to accommodate the sort of problem that Sellars has raised, the materialist will have to settle the identifications of psychological states with sets of functionally equivalent brain states, and this means that the materialist thesis is at best no clearer than the notoriously unclear notion of functional equivalence. In the second case, it appears that if the doctrine of the unity of science is to be preserved, it will have to require something less (or other) than reducibility as the relation between constructs in neurology and those in psychology. It seems, then, that scientific theories can fit together in more than one way, perhaps in many ways. If this is correct, then reduction is only one kind of example of a relation between scientific theories that satisfies reasonable constraints on the unity of science. It would be interesting to know what other kinds of examples there are.

Notes

1. Cf. Oppenheim and Putnam (1958).
2. Cf. Putnam (1960).
3. Cf. Oppenheim and Putnam (1958), p. 6.
4. Meehl (1965), where the argument is attributed to Sellars.

References

Meehl, P. E. (1965). "The Compleat Autocerebroscopist: A Thought Experiment on Professor Feigl's Mind-Body Identity Thesis," in P. Feyerabend and G. Maxwell (eds), *Mind, Matter and Method: Essays in Philosophy and Science in Honor of Herbert Feigl*. Minneapolis: University of Minnesota Press. Pp. 103–180.

Oppenheim, P., and H. Putnam (1958). "Unity of Science as a Working Hypothesis," in H. Feigl, G. Maxwell, and M. Scriven (eds), *Concepts, Theories and the Mind-Body Problem*. Minnesota Studies in the Philosophy of Science. Minneapolis: University of Minnesota Press. Vol. II, 3–36.

Putnam, H. (1960). "Minds and Machines," in S. Hook (ed.), *Dimensions of Mind*. New York: New York University Press. Pp. 138–164. (a)

23

John Searle (1932–)

John Searle is considered one of the most influential contemporary philosophers of mind. Born in Denver, Colorado in 1932, Searle first attended the University of Wisconsin from 1949 until 1952. He went on to attend Oxford University on a Rhodes scholarship, graduating with a B.A. in 1955 and then an M.A. and Ph.D. in 1959. Searle has been teaching at the University of California, Berkeley, since 1959 and is currently Slusser Professor of Philosophy. In 2004, he received the National Humanities Medal for shaping modern thought on the nature of mind. Searle is the author of sixteen books including Intentionality *(1983),* Rediscovery of the Mind *(1992),* The Mystery of Consciousness *(1997),* Rationality in Action *(2001), and* Mind: A Brief Introduction *(2004).*

Can Computers Think?

In the previous chapter, I provided at least the outlines of a solution to the so-called 'mind-body problem'. Though we do not know in detail how the brain functions, we do know enough to have an idea of the general relationships between brain processes and mental processes. Mental processes are caused by the behavior of elements of the brain. At the same time, they are realized in the structure that is made up of those elements. I think this answer is consistent with the standard biological approaches to biological phenomena. Indeed, it is a kind of commonsense answer to the question, given what we know about how the world works. However, it is very much a minority point if view. The prevailing view in philosophy, psychology, and artificial intelligence is one which emphasises the analogies between the functioning of the human brain and the functioning of digital computers. According to the most extreme version of this view, the brain is just a digital computer and time mind is just a computer program. One could summarise this view—I call it 'strong artificial intelligence,' or 'strong AI'—by saying that the mind is to the brain, as the program is to the computer hardware.

This view has the consequence that there is nothing essentially biological about the human mind. The brain just happens to be one of an indefinitely large number of different kinds of hardware computers that could sustain the programs which make up human intelligence. On this view, any physical system whatever that had the right program with the right inputs and outputs would have a mind in exactly the same sense that you and I have minds. So, for example, if you made a computer out of old beer cans powered by windmills; if it had the right program, it would have to have a mind. And the point is not that for all we know it might have thoughts and feelings, but rather that it must have thoughts and feelings, because that is all there is to having thoughts and feeling: implementing the right program.

Most people who hold this view think we have not yet designed programs which are minds. But there is pretty much general agreement among them that it's only a matter of time until computer scientists and workers in artificial intelligence design the appropriate hardware and programs which will be the equivalent of human brains and minds. These will be artificial brains and minds which are in every way the equivalent of human brains and minds.

Many people outside of the field of artificial intelligence are quite amazed to discover that anybody could believe such a view as this. So, before criticising it, let me give you a few examples of the things that people in this field have actually said. Herbert Simon of Carnegie-Mellon University says that we already have machines that can literally think. There is no question of waiting for some future machine, because existing digital computers already have thoughts in exactly the same sense that you and I do. Well, fancy that! Philosophers have been worried for centuries about whether or not a machine could think, and now we discover that they already have such machines at Carnegie-Mellon. Simon's colleague Alan Newell claims that we have now discovered (and notice that Newell says 'discovered' and not 'hypothesized' or 'considered the possibility', but we have *discovered*) that intelligence is just a matter of physical symbol manipulation; it has no essential connection with any specific kind of biological or physical wetware or hardware. Rather, any system whatever that is capable of manipulating physical symbols in the right way is capable of intelligence in the same literal sense as human intelligence of human beings. Both Simon and Newell, to their credit, emphasise that there is nothing metaphorical about these claims; they mean them quite literally. Freeman Dyson is quoted as having said that computers have an advantage over the rest of us when it comes to evolution. Since consciousness is just a matter of formal processes, in computers these formal processes can go on in substances that are much better able to survive in a universe that is cooling off than being like themselves made of our wet and messy materials. Marvin Minsky of MIT says that the next generation of computers will be so intelligent that we will 'be lucky if they are willing to keep us around the house as household pets'. My all-time favourite in the literature of exaggerated claims on behalf of the digital computer is from John McCarthy, the inventor of the term 'artificial intelligence'. McCarthy says even 'machines as simple as thermostats can be said to have beliefs'. And indeed, according to him, almost any machine capable of problem-solving can be said to have beliefs. I admire McCarthy's courage. I once asked him: 'What beliefs does your thermostat have?' And he said: 'My thermostat has three beliefs—it's too hot in here, it's too cold in here, and it's just right here.' As a philosopher, I like all these claims for a simple reason. Unlike most philosophical theses, they are reasonably clear, and they admit of a simple and decisive refutation. It is this refutation that I am going to undertake in this chapter.

The nature of the refutation has nothing whatever to do with any particular stage of computer technology. It is important to emphasise this point because the temptation is always to think that the solution to our problems must wait on some as yet uncreated technological wonder. But in fact, the nature of the refutation is completely independent of any state of technology. It has to do with the very definition of a digital computer, with what a digital computer is.

It is essential to our conception of a digital computer that its operations can be specified purely formally; that is, we specify the steps in the operation of the computer in terms of

abstract symbols—sequences of zeros and ones printed on a tape, for example. A typical computer 'rule' will determine that when a machine is in a certain state and it has a certain symbol on its tape, then it will perform a certain operation such as erasing the symbol or printing another symbol and then enter another state such as moving the tape one square to the left. But the symbols have no meaning; they have no semantic content; they are not about anything. They have to be specified purely in terms of their formal and syntactical structure. The zeroes and ones, for example, are just numerals; they don't even stand for numbers. Indeed, it is the feature of digital computers that makes them so powerful. One and the same type of hardware, if it is appropriately designed, can be used to run an indefinite range of different programs. And one and the same program can be run on an indefinite range of different types of hardwares.

But this feature of programs, that they are defined purely formally or syntactically, is fatal to the view that mental process and program processes are identical. And the reason can be stated quite simply. There is more to having a mind than having formal or syntactical processes. Our internal mental states, by definition, have certain sorts of contents. If I am thinking about Kansas City or wishing that I had a cold beer to drink or wondering if there will be a fall in interest rates, in each case my mental state has a certain mental content in addition to whatever formal features it might have. That is, even if my thoughts occur to me in strings of symbols, there must be more to the thought than the abstract strings, because strings by themselves can't have any meaning. If my thoughts are to be *about* anything, then the strings must have a *meaning* which makes the thoughts about those things. In a word, the mind has more than a syntax, it has a semantics. The reason that no computer program can ever be a mind is simply that a computer program can ever be a mind is simply that a computer program is only syntactical, and minds are more than syntactical. Minds are semantical, in the sense that they have more than a formal structure, they have a content.

To illustrate this point I have designed a certain thought-experiment. Imagine that a bunch of computer programmers have written a program that will enable a computer to simulate the understanding of Chinese. So, for example, if the computer is given a question in Chinese, it will match the question against its memory, or data base, and produce appropriate answers to the questions in Chinese. Suppose for the sake of argument that the computer's answers are as good as those of a native Chinese speaker. Now then, does the computer, on the basis of this, understand Chinese, does it literally understand Chinese, in the way that Chinese speakers understand Chinese? Well, imagine that you are locked in a room, and in this room are several baskets full of Chinese symbols. Imagine that you (like me) do not understand a word of Chinese, but that you are given a rule book in English for manipulating these Chinese symbols. The rules specify the manipulations of the symbols purely formally, in terms of their syntax, not their semantics. So the rule might say: 'Take a squiggle-squiggle sign out of basket number one and put it next to a squoggle-squoggle sign for basket number two.' Now suppose that some other Chinese symbols are passed into the room, and that you are given further rules for passing back out of the room. Suppose that unknown to you the symbols passed into the room are called 'questions' by the people outside the room, and the symbols you pass back out of the room are called 'answers to the questions'. Suppose, fur-

thermore, that the programmers are so good at designing the programs that you are so good at manipulating the symbols, that very soon your answers are indistinguishable from those of a native Chinese speaker. There you are locked in your room shuffling your Chinese symbols and passing out Chinese symbols in response to incoming Chinese symbols. On the basis of the situation as I have described it, there is no way you could learn any Chinese simply by manipulating these formal symbols.

Now the point of the story is simply this: by virtue if implementing a formal computer program from the point of view of an outside observer, you behave exactly as if you understood Chinese, but all the same you don't understand a word of Chinese. But if going through the appropriate computer program for understanding Chinese is not enough to give *you* an understanding of Chinese, then it is not enough to *give any other digital computer* an understanding of Chinese. And again, the reason for this can be stated quite simply. If you don't understand Chinese, then no other computer could understand Chinese because no digital computer, just by virtue of running a program, has anything that you don't have. All that a computer has, as you have, is a formal program for manipulating uninterpreted Chinese symbols. To repeat, a computer has a syntax, but no semantics. The whole point of the parable of the Chinese room is to remind us of a fact that we know all along. Understanding a language, or indeed, having mental states at all, involves more than just having a bunch of formal symbols. It involves having an interpretation, or a meaning attached to those symbols. And a digital computer, as defined, cannot have more than just formal symbols because the operation of the computer, as I said earlier, is defined in terms of its ability to implement programs. And these programs are purely formally specifiable—that is, they have no semantic content.

We can see the force of this argument if we contrast what it is like to be asked and to answer questions in English, and to be asked and to answer questions in some language where we have no knowledge of any of the meanings of the words. Imagine that in the Chinese room you are also given questions in English about such things as your age or your life history, and that you answer those questions. What is the difference between the Chinese case and the English case? Well again, if like me you understand no Chinese and you do understand English, then the difference is obvious. You understand the questions in English because they are expressed in symbols whose meanings are known to you. Similarly, when you give the answers in English you are producing symbols which are meaningful to you. But in the case of the Chinese, you have none of that. In the case of the Chinese, you simply manipulate formal symbols according to a computer program, and you attach no meaning to any of the elements.

Various replies have been suggested on this argument by workers in artificial intelligence and in psychology, as well as philosophy. They all have something in common; they are all inadequate. And there is an obvious reason why they have to be inadequate, since the argument rests on a very simple logical truth, namely, syntax alone is not sufficient for semantics, and digital computers insofar as they are computers have, by definition, a syntax alone.

I want to make this clear by considering a couple of the arguments that are often presented against me.

Some people attempt to answer the Chinese room example by saying that the whole system understands Chinese. The idea here is that though I, the person in the room manipulating the symbols do not understand Chinese, I am just the central processing unit of the computer system. They argue that it is the whole system, including the room, the baskets full of symbols and the ledgers containing the program and perhaps other items as well, taken as a totality, that understands Chinese. But this is subject to exactly the same objection I made before. There is no way that the system can get from the syntax to the semantics. I, as the central processing unit have no way of figuring out what any of these symbols means; but then neither does the whole system.

Another common response is to imagine that we put the Chinese understanding program inside a robot. If the robot moved around and interacted casually with the world, wouldn't that be enough to guarantee that it understood Chinese? Once again the inexorability of the semantics-syntax distinction overcomes this manoeuvre. As long as we suppose that the robot has only a computer for a brain then, even though it might behave exactly as if it understood Chinese, it would still have no way of getting from the syntax to the semantics of Chinese. You can see this if you imagine that I am the computer. Inside a room in the robot's skull I shuffle symbols without knowing that some of them come in to me from television cameras attached to the robot's head and others go out to move the robot's arms and legs. As long as all I have is a formal computer program, I have no way of attaching any meaning to any of the symbols. And the fact that the robot is engaged in causal interactions with the outside world won't help me to attach any meaning to the symbols unless I have some way of finding out about the fact. Suppose the robot picks up a hamburger and this triggers the symbol for hamburger to come into the room. As long as all I have is the symbol with no knowledge of its causes or how it got there, I have no way of knowing what it means. The causal interactions between the robot and the rest of the world are irrelevant unless those causal interactions are represented in some mind or other. But there is no way they can be if all that the so-called mind consists of is a set of purely formal, syntactical operations.

It is important to see exactly what is claimed and what is not claimed by my argument. Suppose we ask the question that I mentioned at the beginning: 'Could a machine think?' Well, in one sense, of course, we are all machines. We can construe the stuff inside our heads as a meat machine. And of course, we can all think. So in one sense of 'machine', namely that sense in which a machine is just a physical system which is capable of performing certain kinds of operations, in that sense, we are all machines, and we can think. So, trivially, there are machines that can think. But that wasn't the question that bothered us. So let's try a different formulation of it. Could an artefact think? Could a man-made machine think? Well, once again, it depends on the kind of artefact. Suppose designed a machine that was molecule-for-molecule indistinguishable from a human being. Well then, if you can duplicate the causes, you can presumably duplicate the effects. So once again, the answer to that question is, in principle at least, trivially yet. If you could build a machine that had the same structure as a human being, then presumably that machine would be able to think. Indeed, it would be a surrogate human being. Well, let's try again.

The question isn't: 'Can a machine think?' or: 'Can an artefact think?' The question is: 'Can a digital computer think?' But once again we have to be very careful in how we interpret the question. From a mathematical point of view, anything whatever can be described as *if* it were a digital computer. And that's because it can be described as instantiating or implementing a computer program. In an utterly trivial sense, the pen that is on the desk in front of me can be described as a digital computer. It just happens to have a very boring computer program. The program says: 'Stay there.' Now since in this sense, anything whatever is a digital computer, because anything whatever can be described as implementing a computer program, then once again, our question gets a trivial answer. Of course our brains are digital computers, since they implement any number of computer programs. And of course our brains can think. So once again, there is a trivial answer to the question. But that wasn't really the question we were trying to ask. The question we wanted to ask is this: 'Can a digital computer, as defined, think?' That is to say: 'Is instantiating or implementing the right computer program with the right inputs and outputs, sufficient for, or constitutive of, thinking?' And to this question, unlike its predecessors, the answer is clearly 'no'. And it is 'no' for the reason that we have spelled out, namely, the computer program is defined purely syntactically. But thinking is more than just a matter of manipulating meaningless symbols; it involves meaningful semantic contents. These semantic contents are what we mean by 'meaning'.

It is important to emphasise again that we are not talking about a particular stage of computer technology. The argument has nothing to do with the forthcoming, amazing advances in computer science. It has nothing to do with the distinction between serial and parallel processes, or with the size of programs, or the speed of computer operations, or with computers that can interact causally with their environment, or even with the invention of robots. Technological progress is always grossly exaggerated, but even subtracting the exaggeration, the development of computers has been quite remarkable, and we can reasonably expect that even more remarkable progress will be made in the future. No doubt we will be much better able to simulate human behaviour on computers than we can at present, and certainly much better than we have been able to in the past. The point I am making is that if we are talking about having mental states, having a mind, all of these simulations are simply irrelevant. It doesn't matter how good the technology is, or how rapid the calculations made by the computer are. If it really is a computer, its operations have been defined syntactically, whereas consciousness, thoughts, feelings, emotions, and all the rest of it involve more than a syntax. Those features, by definition, the computer is unable to *duplicate* however powerful may be its ability to *simulate*. The key distinction here is between duplication and simulation. An no simulation by itself ever constitutes duplication.

What I have done so far is give a basis to the sense that those citations I began this talk with are really as preposterous as they seem. There is a puzzling question in this discussion though, and that is: 'Why would anybody ever have thought the computers could think or have feelings and emotions and all the rest of it?' After all, we can do computer simulations of any process whatever that can be given a formal description. So, we can do a computer simulation of the flow of money in the British economy, or the pattern of power distribution in the Labour party. We can do computer simulation of rain storms in the home counties, or warehouse fires in East

London. Now, in each of these cases, nobody supposes that the computer simulation is actually the real thing; no one supposes that a computer simulation of a storm will leave us all wet, or a computer simulation of a fire is likely to burn the house down. Why on earth would anyone in his right mind suppose a computer simulation of mental processes actually had mental processes? I don't really know the answer to that, since the idea seems to me, to put it frankly, quite crazy from the start. But I can make a couple of speculations.

First of all, where the mind is concerned, a lot of people are still tempted to some sort of behaviourism. They think if a system behaves as if it understood Chinese, then it really must understand Chinese. But we have already refuted this form of behaviourism with the Chinese room argument. Another assumption made by many people is that the mind is not part of the biological world, it is not a part of the world of nature. The strong artificial intelligence view relies on that in its conception that the mind is purely formal; that somehow or other, it cannot be treated as a concrete product of biological processes like any other biological product. There is in these discussions, in short, a kind of resident dualism. AI partisans believe that the mind is more than a part of the natural biological world; they believe that the mind is purely formally specifiable. The paradox of this is the AI literature is filled with fulminations against some view called 'dualism', but in fact, the whole thesis of strong AI rests on a kind of dualism. It rests on a rejection of the idea that the mind is just a natural biological phenomenon in the world like any other.

Eliminative Materialism

Reality is merely an illusion, albeit a very persistent one.
—Albert Einstein

Discussion Questions

1. One concern regarding the eliminativist argument is that eliminativists cannot assert the truth of their doctrine without refuting it. Eliminativists must *believe* their theory is correct. However, in the same breath, they deny there are beliefs, and if there are no beliefs, they cannot consistently espouse their beliefs about eliminativism. It is comparable to saying, "I believe there are no beliefs." Eliminative materialism seems to be self-defeating. Eliminativists must rely on mental states, whose very existence they deny, to make their case. Would you agree that eliminativism is self-defeating? Why or why not? How might Paul Churchland respond to this objection?

2. Paul Churchland argues that we will, one day, be able to give a more robust physiological and neurological account of mind to the point where we can eliminate the mind altogether. Imagine Simone is born colour-blind[14] (Guttenplan, *Mind's Landscape* 70–71) and lives her life as if she was watching a perpetual black-and-white movie. Colour-blindness requires no surgery or medication, and people who are colour-blind can live normal lives. However, in certain situations, colour blindness is potentially very dangerous. A mistake in distinguishing red and green traffic lights, for example, could be fatal. Simone decides to study the physical and psychological bases of colour perception by reading all she can on cognition and physics. In time, using equipment to measure wavelengths of light and other psychological techniques, she devises a way to successfully distinguish the colour of most objects and live like colour-sighted people. Would this example show that Churchland is correct? Could a neuroscientific account of mind be able to capture everything including our phenomenal experience of colour? Despite the fact that Simone can describe colour in objective physiological terms, is her qualitative experience of colour the same as that of colour-sighted people?[15] Give reasons for your answers.

3. In a perfect neuroscience of mind, says Churchland, beliefs, hopes, fears, and so on, would be replaced by a better scientific explanation. Our folk psychological concepts would be eliminated for not even remotely matching the taxonomy of a perfect science. The problem, according to Searle, is that eliminative materialism rests on the false premise that any empirical theory can better explain a particular entity means that entity does not exist (*Rediscovery of the Mind* 47). Consider a parallel from physics. Current theoretical physics can explain reality better than commonsense theories. This book could be explained by giving a purely scientific account (microphysical structure of wood fibres, chemicals, and other subatomic particles). If so, according to Churchland, the book does not exist. But this is absurd, says Searle. A theoretical physical explanation may better explain the book, but it would not eliminate the book's existence. Likewise for mental states: a neuroscientific account of mind would better explain thoughts, hopes, fears, and so forth, but not eliminate them. Is Searle right? Do mental states exist in the same way that books and other physical objects exist? Would a complete neurophysical account of mind eliminate mental states (beliefs, desires, hopes, fears, love, hate, etc.)? Why or why not?

No Minds Please, We're Physicalists

Scientific discoveries over the centuries are the foundation upon which materialist theories of mind are based. To say that such discoveries had a profound effect on how philosophers thought about the mind is an understatement. Applying Ockham's razor, it's logical to conclude that all aspects of humans, including the mind, can be reduced to and explained more accurately by appealing to material scientific causes. More specifically, human nature can be reduced to the world of observable matter and its physical, chemical, and biological processes. This is known as **inter-theoretic reduction:** the process of explaining some entity in terms of more basic properties or elements. Dismayed by dualism, philosophers like Paul Churchland hope that as our knowledge of the brain increases, a similar form of inter-theoretic reduction will take place regarding the mind. Not only will every kind of psychological state be reduced to some physiological process, but the mind will also be explained in terms of lower-level physiological processes. If successful, our current theories of mind will be usurped by a more accurate scientific explanation. But it's not mere reduction Churchland espouses, but outright extermination. No beliefs, no desires, and no hopes: no mind at all.

In order to make sense of our actions, some have put forward folk psychology as a solution. **Folk psychology** is the commonsense way we as lay people explain and predict human behaviour. In explaining and predicting human behaviour, we make reference to mental states in a systematic law-like way, using such terms as "beliefs," "desires," etc. We develop "universal laws" about human behaviour based on our collective experience: babies cry when they need attention, hungry people desire food, and someone with a nasty cut feels pain. It's from these law-like connections between the mental world and behaviour that we can determine regularities; hence, we can explain what other people are doing. In this sense, our folk psychological explanations can be similar to scientific explanations. But Paul Churchland argues that folk psychology is really just another theory of mind, rather than implicit information of our

mental states.[16] "Beliefs" and "desires" are inaccurate terms because they don't actually exist—they are not mental states but physiological processes—and this will eventually be proven by future scientific discoveries. Thus, folk psychology, says Churchland, is a mistaken theory which will one day be replaced by a proper neuroscientific account of the mind.

To understand what Churchland is driving at consider contemporary paradigms for theories including those in physics, biology, chemistry, and medicine. Under such paradigms, theories seek to explain regularities in phenomena that are assumed to be governed by laws. Consider, for example, a physical explanation of a rainbow. Rainbows occur when light rays are reflected and refracted by atmospheric water droplets. As a drop of water intercepts sunlight, some light refracts into the drop and some light refracts out of it. The relationship between the angle at which light enters and leaves is known as the law of refraction. The first refraction separates sunlight into its component parts, and the second refraction increases this separation even further, resulting in a rainbow. By referring to refraction laws, a rainbow can be predicted and explained whenever a strong light illuminates a mist of water. Thus, if someone has never seen a rainbow, but had some knowledge of the underlying physics and conditions necessary to produce this phenomenon, he or she could predict (deduce) that a rainbow will appear. An empirically minded person might even test this phenomenon by using a light and a prism as Isaac Newton did. For a more pragmatic test, a person might watch the sun as it shines through the mist of a lawn sprinkler or watch waves break over rocks on a sunny day. A person might also appeal to the fact that if light had not reflected and refracted in atmospheric water, a rainbow would not occur.

Can this scientific paradigm be applied to human behaviour? There is considerable support emerging from philosophers and psychologists to suggest that a law-like connection does in fact exist.[17] For Churchland, human behaviour

> ### Box 4.6 Is Folk Psychology Universal?
>
> Paul Churchland argues we can successfully explain and predict people's behaviour because we generally know how others will feel and act in certain circumstances. Is this true? Is there a "law-like" connection between mental states (hopes, fear, beliefs, etc.), behaviour, and situations? Under each description below, write down how you would act or feel, and determine if other people would act or feel the same way.
>
> 1. Have not eaten in 8 hours.
> 2. Smell fresh baked bread or cookies.
> 3. Eat a lemon.
> 4. A friend is late picking you up for an important meeting.
> 5. Someone cuts you off while driving.
> 6. Step on a nail.
> 7. Receive a bad mark on a school essay.
> 8. Lying on a beach in the hot sun.
> 9. Smell smoke.
> 10. Win a lottery.

conforms to general causal laws, which allows us to predict and explain the actions of others by attributing to them mental states (see Box 4.6).[18] He notes that one of the remarkable features of human beings is that the average person can explain and predict behaviour with remarkable success. This is no accident, says Churchland; humans share a tacit command of law-like relations between circumstances, internal states, and behaviour. Folk psychology is imbued with thousands of transparent causal law-like connections which give it predictive power (Churchland, "Eliminative Materialism" 69–70).

But, of course, Churchland wants to say much more than this. Eliminative materialists are sceptical of claims that suggest folk psychology will be smoothly reduced to a scientific account of the mind. The reason: our folk psychological terms are pathetically inadequate at accounting for internal happenings within our brain. They are too confused and defective, says Churchland, to survive inter-theoretic reduction; hence, they will simply be displaced or eliminated. So despite the fact that folk psychology is a theory, it's a radically false theory, a theory so fundamentally defective it will eventually be displaced. Folk psychology misrepresents the true ultimate scientific reality of the mind. Now, one might be easily confused in thinking folk psychology is already on its way out of the door. Not so! Whether folk psychology gets eliminated is an empirical question that will be answered as neuroscience makes the necessary discoveries. The elimination of our belief/desire psychology might take hundreds or even thousands of years.

What support does Churchland give for eliminativism? Well, he does consider folk psychology a theory, but it's a mistaken theory that needs to be replaced because of massive failures at the explanatory level. Historical examples include the following: in the eighteenth and nineteen century the concept of caloric (a fluid held in bodies) was replaced by kinetic energy; phlogiston was replaced by the gaining of oxygen; the heavens as a rotating starry sphere was replaced by the notion of the expanding universe; and the idea of witches as being possessed by demons was replaced by current research on the biochemical causes of schizophrenia and psychosis. In all of these examples, caloric, phlogiston, starry sphere, and demon possession are the victims of inter-theoretical reduction and elimination.

For Churchland, folk psychology will receive a similar fate for three reasons. First, it cannot explain phenomena such as perception, learning, mental illness, memory, and sleep. When we consider how utterly ignorant we are of the true nature and psychological functions of sleep, belief/desire psychology offers hopelessly inadequate insight. Most people explain the need for sleep, says Churchland, by flippant answers such as "for rest." But if we want a true physicalist/materialist picture of mind, then these types of answers will be insufficient. Second, the history of our explanatory failures suggests that it would be a miracle if we got folk psychology right. The only reason why folk psychology has survived is because it's difficult to integrate the phenomena of consciousness into the scientific picture. But this doesn't mean *won't,* it might just take longer than expected. Third, eliminative materialism is more probable than identity theory or functionalism. Folk psychology will not be vindicated by a mature neuroscience because the mind and brain are not type-identical or functionally equivalent, especially across species.

For these reasons, Churchland concludes folk psychology is a prime candidate for elimination. And if we think about it, it seems to make sense. Over thousands of years, humans have developed folk-medical theories to alleviate illness and disease. Some such theories include sucking snake bites extracts poison, lying in cold water alleviates fevers, extracting objects from one's skin reduces pain, and overeating and drinking cause discomfort. Although there is a certain primitiveness to these theories, they no doubt aided in our survival as a species. But over the last two hundred years or so, folk-medicines have been replaced by more sophisticated and accurate explanatory schemes via modern medicine and medical research. Modern medicine gives us a better explanation of illnesses, which allows us to treat and predict various types of pathology more successfully. Modern medicine has supplanted folk-medicine and, in some cases, revealed why our folk theories were wrong or right. Churchland thinks the same kind of replacement will happen to folk psychology. Mental states will be replaced by neuroscience because our current explanations of behaviour via beliefs and desires are inadequate. Folk psychology will turn out to be a good first attempt at understanding human action; however, in the end, science will reveal the real nature of mental states. And, once a more accurate account of the mind is found in science, we can simply eliminate beliefs, desires, intentions, and pains altogether. But this would not mean we would learn the language of neuroscience, it merely means that when we could

deploy talk of hope, fears, and beliefs as a way of explaining and understanding human behaviour, but strictly speaking, you don't have any mental states at all.

Eliminating Eliminative Materialism

Let me raise some problems with eliminative materialism, not discussed by Churchland. First, if we can show folk psychology is not a theory comparable to the sciences, then the heart of the eliminativist program is undermined. How can we do this? By showing that human behaviour is not universal or law-like. Imagine Sally is leaving for work, and before she steps out the door she puts on her raincoat and picks up an umbrella. How would we explain her behaviour? According to Churchland, we would attribute to her various mental states as reasons for her behaviour such as her *belief* it is raining and *desire* not to get wet. This explanation, says Churchland, holds consistently or in law-like (nomological) ways for humans. That is, most people, if they believe it's raining and desire to stay dry, will take the necessary precautions of wearing a raincoat or holding an umbrella (newspaper, palm leaf, etc.). The problem is that these generalizations are supposed to be normative. They are to tell us how we ought to behave. But there is no reason to think this is true. People behave in often inconsistent and contradictory ways. Sally, for example, might be wearing her raincoat because she has no other coat and she might be taking her umbrella to kept the sun off her skin. Or consider Churchland's claim that "A thirsty person will desire a drink" (Churchland, "Folk Psychology" 53). Although trivially true, people drink for reasons other than being thirsty. At cocktail parties people often drink to be sociable or to ease stress. It's too difficult to make such law-like generalization regarding the reasons why people behave as they do. In contrast, folk psychological generalizations, unlike the sciences, appeal to how we should behave. That is in appealing to mental states to explain Sally's actions; we are really appealing to how most people would *rationally* behave within this specific context (Campbell 139). After all if you believe its raining and desire not to get wet, it's perfectly rational to wear a raincoat and take an umbrella. But to say that everyone must behave this way is too strong. In this sense, folk psychology is unlike traditional scientific nomological theories and is, therefore, not susceptible to elimination, contrary to Churchland.

Here is a second, and more powerful, objection against eliminativism. Eliminativists argue that folk psychology is poor at explaining and predicting human behaviour such as memory, learning, and sleep. But why should we think this? Even if it were true that folk psychology is not a theory, this wouldn't mean our use of mental states, as means of understanding behaviour, has no explanatory punch. Why? Because folk psychology is not in the business of explaining deeper issues that fall outside its realm. Explaining mental illness is the business of neurology and psychiatry, not commonsense psychology. Folk psychology is used to explain normal, not abnormal behaviour. We ought not then fault folk psychology for its poor explanatory power since this is not what it's meant to do. Lack of explanatory power should not be taken as evidence that folk psychology is false or it should be replaced.

To see the power of this argument, let's look at two examples from Churchland: sleep and mental illness. For Churchland, when we consider how utterly ignorant we are of the true nature and psychological functions of sleep, belief/desire psychology offers hopelessly inadequate insight. Most people explain the need for sleep, says Churchland, by flippant answers such as "for rest." But if we want a true physicalist/materialist picture of mind, then these types of answers will be insufficient. What Churchland fails to understand is that this is not how people explain the importance of sleep. Generally speaking, people are not interested in *why* they sleep because this is just an obvious and mundane sort of affair. After all, almost all animals sleep. People explain the need for sleep by what happens when they *don't get enough*. Again, it's usually when failure

occurs, in this case sleep failure, that we seek explicit explanations. So even though folk psychology may not be able to explain the deeper physiological or psychological reasons for sleep, it is much too strong to suggest that we have absolutely no idea. Here are some examples: if Fred doesn't sleep, he will be *grumpy* with his children, *snap* at his wife, be *irritable* during tomorrow's department meeting, or may dose off while driving down the highway. Put simply, it's common knowledge sleep-deprived people are not as mentally sharp, or don't think as clearly, as those who are rested—this is what matters to people on the street. Again, perhaps we need to make a distinction between the reasons people sleep or *why* questions, and deeper scientific causes of sleep or *how* questions. For example, if you interrupt a friend's afternoon nap, you might ask something like "Why are you sleeping?" In response, you may get some kind of explanations such as "I was studying all night," "I was out partying," or "I was up with my sick child." These are perfectly legitimate reasons for taking a nap; no deeper explanation is warranted. There are, however, deeper scientific questions about sleep that go beyond common purposes. These are causal or how questions regarding sleep. Asking your friend, "How are you sleeping?" is a fundamentally different question from asking, "Why are you sleeping?" Put broadly, scientists are interested in *how* people sleep; common folk are interested in *why* people sleep. Scientists can explain the *causes* of sleep by citing a decrease in bodily temperature and changes in brainwave patterns (alpha waves, theta waves, sleep spindles and K complexes, delta sleep, and REM sleep) (Wortman and Loftus 319). Common folk offer explanations of *why* people sleep by citing *desires* about being well rested, *wanting* to get up early the next day, and so forth. Although such commonsense reasons may have acted as a springboard to deeper scientific investigation regarding the physiological and psychological causes of sleep, our folk explanations of why people sleep have a different purpose altogether.

Churchland also says mental states fail miserably at explaining mental illness. I think he is right. But again, Churchland doesn't realize that it's not because our folk psychological theories are wrong *per se*. Extreme abnormal behaviour is not something we have to explain and predict. Hence, our folk psychological explanations fall hopelessly short of the target. Moreover, it's really only in the past hundred of years or so that mental illness explanations have really taken off under a scientific guise. So yes, commonsense psychology does a poor job of explaining mental illness, but the reason is that it is not designed to explain such phenomena in the first place. Using folk psychology to explain mental illness is like using a car to do the work of a 4 × 4 truck—it's bound to breakdown and fail because it can't take the punishment. There are bound to be gaps in our folk theories because there are limits to what they concern themselves with. But a failure to explain is different from explanatory failure.

24

Paul Churchland

(1942–)

Born in British Columbia, Paul Churchland received his B.A. from the University of British Columbia and his Ph.D. from the University of Pittsburgh, under the tutelage of Willfred Sellars.

Churchland spent the next 15 years at the University of Manitoba, refining his views on eliminative materialism. In 1984, he and his wife Patricia moved to the University of California, San Diego, where he continues to teach and do research. Some of his books include Scientific

Realism and the Plasticity of Mind *(1979),* Matter and Consciousness *(1984),* A Neurocomputational Perspective: The Nature of Mind and the Structure of Science *(1989), and* The Engine of Reason, The Seat of the Soul: A Philosophical Journey into the Brain *(1995).*

Eliminative Materialism

The identity theory was called into doubt not because the prospects for a materialist account of our mental capacities were thought to be poor, but because it seemed unlikely that the arrival of an adequate materialist theory would bring with it the nice one-to-one match-ups, between the concepts of folk psychology and the concepts of theoretical neuroscience, that intertheoretic reduction requires. The reason for that doubt was the great variety of quite different physical systems that could instantiate the required functional organization. *Eliminative materialism* also doubts that the correct neuroscientific account of human capacities will produce a neat reduction of our common-sense framework, but here the doubts arise from a quite different source.

As the eliminative materialists see it, the one-to-one match-ups will not be found, and our common-sense psychological framework will not enjoy an intertheoretic reduction, *because our common-sense psychological framework is a false and radically misleading conception of the causes of human behavior and the nature of cognitive activity.* On this view, folk psychology is not just an incomplete representation of our inner natures; it is an outright *mis*representation of our internal states and activities. Consequently, we cannot expect a truly adequate neuroscientific account of our inner lives to provide theoretical categories that match up nicely with the categories of our common-sense framework. Accordingly, we must expect that the older framework will simply be eliminated, rather than be reduced, by a matured neuroscience.

Historical Parallels

As the identity theorist can point to historical cases of successful intertheoretic reduction, so the eliminative materialist can point to historical cases of the outright elimination of the ontology of an older theory in favor of the ontology of a new and superior theory. For most of the eighteenth and nineteenth centuries, learned people believed that heat was a subtle *fluid* held in bodies, much in the way water is held in a sponge. A fair body of moderately successful theory described the way this fluid substance—called "caloric"—flowed within a body, or from one body to another, and how it produced thermal expansion, melting, boiling, and so forth. But by the end of the last century it had become abundantly clear that heat was not a substance at all, but just the energy of motion of the trillions of jostling molecules that make up the heated body itself. The new theory—the "corpuscular/kinetic theory of matter and heat"—was much more successful than the old in explaining and predicting the thermal behavior of bodies. And since we were unable to *identify* caloric fluid with kinetic energy (according to the old theory, caloric is a material *substance*; according to the new theory, kinetic energy is a form of *motion*), it was finally agreed that there is *no such thing* as caloric. Caloric was simply eliminated from our accepted ontology.

A second example. It used to be thought that when a piece of wood burns, or a piece of metal rusts, a spiritlike substance called "phlogiston"

was being released: briskly, in the former case, slowly in the latter. Once gone, that 'noble' substance left only a base pile of ash or rust. It later came to be appreciated that both processes involve, not the loss of something, but the *gaining* of a substance taken form the atmosphere: oxygen. Phlogiston emerged, not as an incomplete description of what was going in, but as a radical misdescription. Phlogiston was therefore not suitable for reduction to or identification with some notion from within new oxygen chemistry, and it was simply eliminated from science.

Admittedly, both of these examples concern the elimination of something nonobservable, but our history also includes the elimination of certain widely accepted 'observables'. Before Copernicus' views became available, almost any human who ventured out at night could look up at *the starry sphere of the heavens,* and if he stayed for more than a few minutes he could also see that it *turned*, around on axis through Polaris. What the sphere was made of (crystal?) and what made it turn (the gods?) were theoretical questions that exercised us for over two millennia. But hardly anyone doubted the existence of what everyone could observe with their own eyes. In the end, however, we learned to reinterpret our visual experience of the night sky within a very different conceptual framework, and the turning sphere evaporated.

Witches provide another example. Psychosis is a fairly common affliction among humans, and in earlier centuries its victims were standardly seen as cases of demonic possession, as instances of Satan's spirit itself, glaring malevolently out at us from behind the victims' eyes. That witches exist was not a matter of any controversy. One would occasionally see them, in any city or hamlet, engaged in incoherent, paranoid, or even murderous behavior. But observable or not, we eventually decided that witches simply do not exist. We concluded that the concept of a witch is an element in a conceptual framework that misrepresents so badly the phenomena to which it standardly applied that literal application of the notion should be permanently withdrawn. Modern theories of mental dysfunction led to the elimination of witches from our serious ontology.

The concepts of folk psychology—belief, desire, fear, sensation, pain, joy, and so on—await a similar fate, according to the view at issue. And when neuroscience has matured to the point where the poverty of our current conceptions is apparent to everyone, and the superiority of the new framework is established, we shall then be able to set about reconceiving our internal states and activities, within a truly adequate conceptual framework at last. Our explanations of one another's behavior will appeal to such things as our neuropharmocological states, the neural activity in specialized anatomical areas, and whatever other states are deemed relevant by the new theory. Our private introspection will also be transformed, and may be profoundly enhanced by reason of the more accurate and penetrating framework it will have to work with—just as the astronomer's perception of the night sky is much enhanced by the detailed knowledge of modern astronomical theory that he or she possesses.

The magnitude of the conceptual revolution have suggested should not be minimized: it would be enormous. And the benefits to humanity might be equally great. If each of us possessed an accurate neuroscientific understanding of (what we know conceive dimly as) the varieties and causes of mental illness, the factors in learning, the neural basis of emotions,

intelligence, and socialization, then the sum total of human misery might be much reduced. The simple increase in mutual understanding that the new framework made possible could contribute substantially toward a more peaceful and humane society. Of course, there would be dangers as well: increased knowledge means increased power, and power can always be misused.

Arguments for Eliminative Materialism

The arguments for eliminative materialism are diffuse and less than decisive, but they are stronger than is widely supposed. The distinguishing feature of this position is its denial that a smooth intertheoretic reduction is to be expected—even a species-specific reduction—of the framework of folk psychology to the framework of a matured neuroscience. The reason for this denial is the eliminative materialist's conviction that folk psychology is a hopelessly primitive and deeply confused conception of our internal activities. But why this low opinion of our common-sense conceptions?

There are at least three reasons. First, the eliminative materialist will point to the widespread explanatory, predictive, and manipulative failures of folk psychology. So much of what is central and familiar to us remains a complete mystery from within folk psychology. We do not know what *sleep* is, or why we have to have it, despite spending a full third of our lives in that condition. (The answer, "For rest," is mistaken. Even if people are allowed to rest continuously, their need for sleep is undiminished. Apparently, sleep serves some deeper functions, but we do not yet know what they are.) We do not understand how *learning* transforms each of us from a gaping infant to a cunning adult, or how differences in *intelligence* are grounded. We have not the slightest idea how *memory* works, or how we manage to retrieve relevant bits of information instantly from the awesome mass we have stored. We do not know what *mental illness* is, nor how to cure it.

In sum, the most central things about us remain almost entirely mysterious from within folk psychology. And the defects noted cannot be blamed on inadequate time allowed for their correction, for folk psychology has enjoyed no significant changes or advances in well over 2,000 years, despite its manifest failure. Truly successful theories may be expected to reduce, but significantly unsuccessful theories merit no such expectation.

This argument from explanatory poverty has a further aspect. So long as one sticks to normal brains, the poverty of folk psychology is perhaps not strikingly evident. But as soon as one examines the many perplexing behavioral and cognitive deficits suffered by people with *damaged* brains, one's descriptive and explanatory resources start to claw the air (see, for example Chapter 7.3, p. 143). As with other humble theories asked to operate successfully in unexplored extensions of their old domain (for example, Newtonian mechanics in the domain of velocities close to the velocity of light, and the classical gas law in the domain of high pressures or temperatures), the descriptive and explanatory inadequacies of folk psychology become starkly evident.

The second argument tries to draw an inductive lesson from our conceptual history. Our early folk theories of motion were profoundly confused, and were eventually displaced entirely by more sophisticated theories. Our early folk theories of the structure and activity of the heavens were wildly off the mark, and survive only as historical lessons in how wrong we can be. Our folk theories of the nature of fire, and the nature of life, were similarly cockeyed. And one could go

on, since the vast majority of our past folk conceptions have been similarly exploded. All except folk psychology, which survives to this day and has only recently begun to feel pressure. But the phenomenon of conscious intelligence is surely a more complex and difficult phenomenon than any of those just listed. So far as accurate understanding is concerned, it would be a *miracle* if we had got *that* one right the very first time, when we fell down so badly on all the others. Folk psychology has survived for so very long, presumably, not because it basically correct in its representations, but because the phenomena addressed are so surpassingly difficult that any useful handle on them, no matter how feeble, is unlikely to be displaced in a hurry.

A third argument attempts to find an a priori advantage for eliminative materialism over the identity theory and functionalism. It attempts to counter the common intuition that eliminative materialism is distantly possible, perhaps, but is much less probably than either the identity theory or functionalism. The focus again on whether the concepts of folk psychology will find vindicating match-ups in a matured neuroscience. The eliminativist bets no; the other two bet yes. (Even the functionalist bets yet, but expects the match-ups to be only species-specific, or only person-specific. Functionalism, recall, denies the existence only of *universal* type/type identities.)

The eliminativist will point out that the requirements on a reduction are rather demanding. The new theory must entail a set of principles and embedded concepts that mirrors very closely the specific conceptual structure to be reduced. And the fact is, there are vastly many more ways of being an explanatorily successful neuroscience while *not* mirroring the structure of folk psychology, than there are ways of being an explanatorily successful neuroscience while also *mirroring* the very specific structure of folk psychology. Accordingly, the a priori probability of eliminative materialism is not lower, but substantially *higher* than that of either of its competitors. One's initial intuitions here are simply mistaken.

Granted, this initial a priori advantage could be reduced if there were a very strong presumption in favor of the truth of folk psychology— true theories are better bets to win reduction. But according to the first two arguments, the presumptions on this point should run in precisely the opposite direction.

Arguments against Eliminative Materialism

The initial plausibility of this rather radical view is low for almost everyone, since it denies deeply entrenched assumptions. That is at best a question-begging complaint, of course, since those assumptions are precisely what is at issue. But the following line of thought does attempt to mount a real argument.

Eliminative materialism is false, runs the argument, because one's introspection reveals directly the existence of pains, beliefs, desires, fears, and so forth. Their existence is as obvious as anything could be.

The eliminative materialist will reply that this argument makes the same mistake that an ancient or medieval person would be making if he insisted that he could just see with his own eyes that the heavens form a turning sphere, or that witches exist. The fact is, all observation occurs within some system of concepts, and our observation judgments are only as good as the conceptual framework in which they are expressed. In all three cases—the starry sphere, witches, and the familiar mental states—precisely what is challenged is the integrity of the background conceptual frame-works in which the observation judgments are expressed. To insist on the validity of one's experiences, *traditionally interpreted,* is therefore to beg the very question at issue. For in all three cases, the question is whether we should *reconceive* the nature of some familiar observational domain.

A second criticism attempts to find an incoherence in the eliminative materialist's position. The bald statement of eliminative materialism is that the familiar mental states do not really exist. But that statement is meaningful, runs the argument, only if it is the expression of a certain *belief,* and an *intention* to communicate, and a *knowledge* of the language, and so forth. But if the statement is true, then no such mental states exist, and the statement is therefore a meaningless string of marks or noises, and cannot be true. Evidently, the assumption that eliminative materialism is true entails that it cannot be true.

The hole in this argument is the premise concerning the conditions necessary for a statement to be meaningful. It begs the question. If eliminative materialism is true, then meaningfulness must have some different source. To insist on the 'old' source is to insist on the validity of the very framework at issue. Again, an historical parallel may be helpful here. Consider the medieval theory that being biologically *alive* is a matter of being ensouled by an immaterial *vital spirit.* And consider the following response to someone who has expressed disbelief in that theory.

> My learned friend has stated that there is no such thing as vital spirit. But this statement is incoherent. For if it is true, then my friend does not have vital spirit, and must therefore be *dead.* But if he is dead, then his statement is just a string of noises, devoid of meaning or truth. Evidently, the

assumption that antivitalism is true entails that it cannot be true!   Q.E.D.

This second argument is now a joke, but the first argument begs the question in exactly the same way.

A final criticism draw a much weaker conclusion, but makes a rather stronger case. Eliminative materialism, it has been said, is making mountains out of molehills. It exaggerates the defects in folk psychology, and underplays its real successes. Perhaps the arrival of a matured neuroscience will require the elimination of the occasional folk-psychological concept, continues the criticism, and a minor adjustment in certain folk-psychological principles may have to be endured. But the large-scale elimination forecast by the eliminative materialist is just an alarmist worry or a romantic enthusiasm.

Perhaps this complaint is correct. And perhaps it is merely complacent. Whichever, it does bring out the important point that we do not confront two simple and mutually exclusive possibilities here: pure reduction versus pure elimination. Rather, there are the end points of a smooth spectrum of possible outcomes, between which there are mixed cases of partial elimination, and partial reduction. Only empirical research (see chapter 7) can tell us where on that spectrum our own case will fall. Perhaps we should speak here, more liberally, of "revisionary materialism", instead of concentrating on the more radical possibility of an across-the-board elimination. Perhaps we should. But it has been my aim in this section to make it at least intelligible to you that our collective conceptual destiny lies substantially toward the revolutionary end of the spectrum.

Key Terms and Concepts

Mind–body problem
Metaphysics
Ontology
Materialism (physicalism)
Dualism
Teleological
Final causes
Argument from doubt
Principle of the Nonidentity of Discernables
Leibniz's law
Argument from divisibility
Introspection
Property dualism
Reductionism
"Is" of definition
"Is" of composition
"Is" of predication
Neural plasticity
Carbon chauvinists
Multiple realizability
Syntax
Semantics
Intentionality
Qualia
Inter-theoretic reduction
Folk psychology

Study Questions

1. What is the mind–body problem?
2. Dualists argue that mind and body are separate and distinct substances. Why does Descartes think the mind and body are different substances?
3. What is the argument from doubt and how does this show dualism is true?
4. What is Leibniz's law?
5. What is the argument from divisibility and how does this show dualism is true?
6. What is Descartes' solution to the mind–body problem? How does he explain interaction between mind and body?

7. Why does Descartes have trouble explaining *where* and *how* interaction occurs?
8. What does the example of Phineas Gage prove?
9. How does Ryle's category-mistake show that dualism is mistaken?
10. Why does Place think identity theory is a hypothesis?
11. What are Place's three meanings of "is"?
12. What is the difference between tokens and types?
13. Why do other species or alien life pose problems for identity theory?
14. Functionalism has certain advantages over identity theory; what are they?
15. How does functionalism relate to artificial intelligence?
16. What is the difference between syntax and semantics?
17. What is John Searle's Chinese Room argument and how does this show that functionalism is wrong?
18. What is qualia?
19. What is the inverted spectrum example? How does this show functionalism is mistaken?
20. Why are zombies problematic for functionalists?
21. Why does Churchland think that folk psychology is a theory?
22. Why does folk psychology warrant elimination?
23. Is folk psychology comparable to scientific theories? Why or why not?
24. Is folk psychology really as bad at explaining learning and sleep as he suggests?
25. Is eliminative materialism self-defeating?

Further Reading

Cockburn, David. *An Introduction to the Philosophy of Mind.* Houndmills, Basingstoke, Hampshire, England: Palgrave Macmillan, 2001.

Crane, Tim. *The Mechanical Mind: A Philosophical Introduction to Minds, Machines, and Mental Representation.* 2nd ed. London: Routledge, 2003.

Churchland, Patricia. *Brain-Wise: Studies in Neurophilosophy.* Cambridge, MA: MIT Press, 2002.

Jaegwon, Kim. *Philosophy of Mind.* Boulder, CO: Westview Press, 1998.

Guttenplan, Samuel. *Mind's Landscape: An Introduction to the Philosophy of Mind.* Oxford: Blackwell Publishers, Inc., 2000.

Heil, John. *Philosophy of Mind: A Contemporary Introduction.* 2nd ed. New York: Routledge, 2004.

Hirstein, William. *On the Churchlands.* Toronto: Wadsworth, 2003.

Lyons, William. *Matters of the Mind.* New York: Routledge, 2001.

Morton, Peter. *A Historical Introduction to the Philosophy of Mind.* Peterborough, ON: Broadview Press, 1997.

Priest, Stephen. *Theories of Mind.* London: Penguin Books, 1991.

Searle, John. *The Rediscovery of the Mind.* Cambridge, MA: MIT Press, 1992.

Internet Resources

Chalmers, David. *Contemporary Philosophy of Mind: An Annotated Bibliography.* n.d. 25 May 2007 <http://consc.net/biblio.html>.

Eliasmith, Chris, ed. *Dictionary of Philosophy of Mind.* n.d. 25 May 2007 <http://philosophy.uwaterloo.ca/MindDict/>.

Fieser, James, and Bradley Dowden, eds. *The Internet Encyclopaedia of Philosophy.* n.d. 28 May 2007 <http://www.iep.utm.edu/>.

Nani, Marco, and Massimo Marraffa, eds. *A Field Guide to the Philosophy of Mind.* Rome: The University of Rome. n.d. 25 May 2007 <http://host.uniroma3.it/progetti/kant/field/>.

Zalta, Edward, ed. *Stanford Encyclopaedia of Philosophy.* Stanford, CA: The Metaphysics Research Lab, Stanford University, n.d. 25 May 2007 <http://plato.stanford.edu/entries/>.

Notes

1. Some mental states are called *proposition attitudes* because they express some proposition. A proposition is a statement in which something is affirmed or denied. For example, to say "I believe that aliens exist" states a proposition (that aliens exist) in relation to a mental state or attitude (belief).

2. The claim that behaviour implies mental states is controversial. Zombies are a prime example. A zombie is

someone who is behaviourally identical to you or I, but lacks mental states. If true, then behaviour would not be a good indicator of mental states. In fact, behaviour may be a sign of no mental life at all.

3. Most students are metaphysical materialists. Perhaps it's because we live in a science-dominated culture, but many students find the mind–body problem a no-brainer; the mind is physically instantiated in our brains (somehow), end of story. However, students who are materialists cannot believe in God without contradiction. Since God is traditionally defined as a non-physical, spiritual entity, the only solution for theistic materialists is dualism. But, as we will see, dualism is not a tenable theory at all. The only solution, it appears, is to become an atheist or idealist. And since idealism is fraught with its own problems, as discussed in the last chapter, the conclusion is painfully obvious.

4. The *Chicken Soup for the Soul* franchise has sold 100 million copies in 54 different languages.

5. The root of our Western conception of soul dates back to Plato, a student of Socrates, and is most vividly expressed in the *Phaedo*. Plato's *Phaedo* is written against the backdrop of Socrates' death. In the story, Socrates explains to his friends Cebes and Simmias that one should not be afraid of death, since the soul or mind is immortal—it will live forever. This makes Plato a dualist. The mind is immaterial or non-physical, while the body is physical or material. Upon death, says Socrates, the soul is released from the body whereby it will be reborn in someone else. In short, Plato believed in reincarnation.

6. This may not be strictly true; consider multiple personality disorders in which some people have very distinct and separate mental states depending on their current personality. In this sense, the mind might be divisible into separate and distinct sets of beliefs and desires culminating into senses of self. We also talk at times about being "of two minds" about something. I am, for example, of two minds about the war in Afghanistan. Although I agree that Canadian troops ought to fight against the oppressive theocracy of the Taliban, I disagree that the high death toll of Canadian troops justifies this end goal. Perhaps the sharp distinction between mind and body is not as clear as Descartes suggests.

7. Thomas Hobbes, for example, argues for materialism. The activities of the mind are really nothing more than physical processes of the body. Baruch de Spinoza thought the mind and body were not distinct substances but had distinct properties or attributes of one divine sub-

stance. And, as we saw earlier, George Berkeley argued that there were no material substances at all—God causes our perceptions of the world.

8. This idea is known as second-order intentionality. It is fairly obvious that humans definitely have second-order intentional states about what they themselves and others want, desire, envy, and so forth. Fred thinks that Sally wants a computer for Christmas. In this case, Fred is the agent of a second-order intentional relation which is directed at or about the first-order relation, "Sally wants a computer for Christmas." Fred can also have second-order intentional relations about his own first-order intentional relations (beliefs about his own beliefs). For example, Fred believes that his beliefs on abortion and capital punishment are coherent.

9. Ockham's razor is called the principle of parsimony. It's a methodological principle, developed by William Ockham (1285–1347), an English philosopher, stating that we ought to value simplicity over complexity. Born near London, Ockham entered the Franciscan order and studied at Oxford University. Some of his writings were considered very controversial and he spent much of his life in exile.

10. Higher primates (chimps and gorillas) have a mind similar to that of humans and can be characterized as having knowledge, beliefs, and desires. By extension I think it is also possible to apply these results to other animals, such as monkeys, dogs, dolphins, and so on. Now, how far down the animal world do we want to go? The point is that some animals have minds similar to the human mind and, hence, have beliefs and desires (first-order intentional states). For research in this area of study, see J. C. Gomez and Peter Smith, in *Theories of Theories of Mind*.

11. Roger Sperry won the Nobel Prize in 1981 for his research on the functions of each of the brain's hemispheres.

12. Although Place's theory is clearly reductionist, he is not suggesting that we will one day be able to merely talk about brain processes. That is, we can reduce talk about the mind to talk about brain states but it doesn't mean we eliminate talk about mind. What we have to acknowledge is that mental states are really brain states. Why? Because the mind is nothing above and beyond what is going on at the neural level. In this sense, we can describe sensations like pain, for example, without knowing about how the brain works. In other words, the meaning of words such as *pain, image,* or *sensation* can be known regardless whether we know anything

about their underlying neurological causes. The mind is not part of the meaning of synapses, ganglions, or other parts of the central nervous system. Place denies that mental state concepts can be translated or reduced to statements about brain processes. Moreover, sensations and mental imagery are also verified in a different way by common folk than how a scientist might verify them. We verify our thoughts and emotions via introspection. No amount of introspection will verify brain processes. Brain processes can only be discovered empirically. In this sense, consciousness as a process of the brain is a scientific hypothesis that could be true or false, in just the same way that lightning is a motion of electrical charges could be true of false. Place does think that the sciences will one day succeed in verifying identity theory. In the say way scientists have discovered that lightning is an electrical discharge and water is H_2O, consciousness will be discovered to be identical with electrical activity of the brain.

13 There has been an enormous amount written about Searle's Chinese Room, the majority of which is beyond my present intentions. However, for those who wish to review the literature, see the commentaries to Searle's original article, "Minds, Brains, and Programs."

14. This is a revision of Frank Jackson's classic example, "What Mary Didn't Know."

15. The problem of *qualia* is also a problem for eliminativists. The problem is that no matter how well folk psychology is integrated into neuroscience, a physical explanation of the mental, no matter how complete, will never capture the *what is it likeness* of our experiences. If we reflect on this example for a minute, there still seems to be something defective about Simone's colour judgment. Despite her ability to describe the colours of objects using objective information, the enjoyment that people with normal sight get from colours is very different from Simone's enjoyment of colours. Seeing a sunset or fireworks is very different than describing the physiological facts of them. Often it's the sheer brilliance of the colours that give us so much joy. But Simone's perceptual experience, despite her knowledge of the physics of colours, cannot equal that of non-colour-blind people. There is an experiential quality of seeing sunsets and fireworks that cannot be described. Guttenplan highlights this point nicely by inviting us to image that Simone's colour vision was surgically returned to her (*Mind's Landscape* 71). Simone might say, "I knew sunsets were red, orange, yellow, and purple, but I didn't think they were like *that*." It's the *that* which is not cap-

tured by purely physiological descriptions. What Simone comes to know after the operation, are not the facts that sunsets are red and yellow, but facts about her experience of them. If Churchland's theory is to be defended then he must concede that the phenomenological features of our experiences must also be given a physical account, something that does not seem possible. As Thomas Nagel explains in his famous article "What Is It Like to Be a Bat," "every subjective phenomenon is essentially connected with a single point of view, and it seems inevitable that an objective, physical theory will abandon that point of view" (393). Eliminative materialists seem to be under the illusion that what can be identified as physical via chemistry, biology, and physics can be described physically. Hence, whatever *qualia* or immediate awareness of experience is to the physicalist, it must be able to be physically describable. But one's immediate subjective experiences, in many respects, cannot be captured by objective physical descriptions. Why? Because third-person physicalist explanations fail to take into account the unique phenomenological quality, and highly context-dependent nature, of mental states. I am not suggesting that mental states don't have neurological underpinning. Surely they do, but such underpinnings are not essential to the elucidation of how mental states feel to us. Churchland's notion that mental states can be reduced to neurological underpinnings is very odd indeed.

16. Although Patricia and Paul Churchland have both written extensively on eliminative materialism, my discussion will focus, perhaps unfairly, on Paul Churchland's work in this area. There is, however, considerable overlap between their views.

17. Alison Gopnik's child development research also supports the idea of folk psychology as a theory.

18. As I understand Churchland, the idea of theoretical explanation would also apply to oneself. That is, in order to explain why I went to the fridge to get a beer I would have to deploy a nomological theory. This can't be right. We normally don't explain our own behaviour via law-like mental states attributions, but merely experience mental states as motivating forces. John Searle makes similar remarks. We often don't postulate beliefs and desires to explain behaviour; we simply experience them. To use Searle's example, imagine driving through a scorching hot desert with no air conditioning. The heat is unbearable and you can't remember the last time you have been so thirsty. You could scream for a cold beer. We often know what we want or desire, not by

postulating theories, but by experiencing them. In short, many of our beliefs and desires are experienced as part of our mental life, not theoretical entities (*Rediscovery of the Mind* 59).

Works Cited

Block, Ned. "Troubles with Functionalism." 1978. *The Nature of Mind.* Ed. David Rosenthal. New York: Oxford University Press, 1991.

Bloomfield, Lou. "How Does a Catalytic Converter Work?" *Physics Central.* American Physical Association, 2006. 1 October 2006 <http://www.physicscentral.com/lou/2001/converters.html>.

Butchvarov, Panayot. "Metaphysics." *The Cambridge Dictionary of Philosophy.* Ed. Robert Audi. New York: Cambridge University Press, 1995.

Campbell, Neil. *A Brief Introduction to the Philosophy of Mind.* Peterborough, ON: Broadview Press, 2005.

Chalmers, David. *The Conscious Mind.* New York: Oxford University Press, 1996.

Churchland, Paul. "Folk Psychology and Explaining Human Behavior." *The Future of Folk Psychology: Intentionality and Cognitive Science.* Ed. John. D. Greenwood. New York: Cambridge University Press, 1991.

—. *Matter and Consciousness: A Contemporary Introduction to the Philosophy of Mind.* Cambridge, MA: MIT Press, 1984.

—. "Eliminative Materialism and the Propositional Attitudes." *Journal of Philosophy* (1981): 67–90.

Cockburn, David. *An Introduction to the Philosophy of Mind.* Houndsmills, Hampshire: Palgrave, 2001.

Crane, Tim. *The Mechanical Mind: A Philosophical Introduction to Minds, Machines, and Mental Representation.* 2nd ed. London: Routledge, 2003.

Dennett, Daniel. *Freedom Evolves.* Toronto, ON: Penguin Books, Ltd., 2004.

Dreyfus, Hubert. *What Computers Still Can't Do: A Critique of Artificial Intelligence.* Cambridge, MA: MIT Press, 1993.

Elbert, Jerome W. *Are Souls Real?* New York: Prometheus Books, 2000.

Gomez, J. C. "Non-Human Primate Theories of (Non-Human Primate) Minds: Some Issues Concerning the Origins of Mind Reading." *Theories of Theories of Mind.* Ed. Peter Carruthers and Peter Smith. Cambridge: Cambridge University Press, 1996.

Gopnik, Alison. "Developing the Idea of Intentionality: Children's Theories of Mind." *Canadian Journal of Philosophy* 20 (1990): 89–114.

Greenfield, Susan. *The Private Life of the Brain: Emotions, Consciousness and the Secret of the Self.* New York: John Wiley & Sons, Inc., 2000.

Guttenplan, Samuel. *The Mind's Landscape: An Introduction to Philosophy of Mind.* Oxford: Blackwell Publishers Ltd., 2000.

—. "An Essay on Mind." *A Companion to the Philosophy of Mind.* Ed. Samuel Guttenplan. Oxford: Basil Blackwell Ltd., 1994.

Heil, John. *Philosophy of Mind: A Contemporary Introduction.* 2nd ed. New York: Routledge, 2004.

Jackson, Frank. "What Mary Didn't Know." *The Journal of Philosophy* 5 (1980): 291–295.

Lawhead, William F. *The Philosophical Journey: An Interactive Approach.* 2nd ed. New York: McGraw Hill, 2003.

Leahey, Thomas. *A History of Psychology: Main Currents in Psychological Thought.* 3rd ed. Englewood Cliffs, NJ: Prentice Hall, Inc., 1992.

Lyons, William. *Matters of the Mind.* New York: Routledge, 2001.

Martin, Robert. "Ontology." *The Philosopher's Dictionary.* 2nd ed. Peterborough, Ontario: Broadview Press, 1994.

Micklebough, Rod. "Two Decades Later, Hansen Is Still a Man in Motion." *Globe and Mail,* 23 Aug. 2006: A1+.

Moody, Sid. "The Brains Behind Cyc." *The Austin Chronicle on the Web.* 28 December 1999. 19 June 2007 <http://weeklywire.com/ww/12-28-99/austin_screens_feature.html>.

Morton, Peter. *A Historical Introduction to the Philosophy of Mind.* Peterborough, ON: Broadview Press, 1997.

Nagel, Thomas. "What Is It Like to Be a Bat." *The Mind's I: Fantasies and Reflections on Self and Soul.* 1974. Ed. D. Dennett and D. Hofstadter. New York: Basic Books, Inc., 1981.

Place, U. T. "Is Consciousness a Brain Process?" *The British Journal of Psychology* 47 (1956): 44–50.

Postlethwait, John, and Janet L. Hopson. *The Nature of Life.* New York: McGraw-Hill, Inc., 1989.

Price, Richard, and Steven Lynn. *Abnormal Psychology.* 2nd ed. Chicago, IL: The Dorsey Press, 1986.

Priest, Stephen. *Theories of Mind.* London: Penguin Books, 1991.

Prugh, Thomas, et al. "Changing the Oil Economy." *State of the World 2005: A Worldwatch Institute Report on Progress Toward a Sustainable Society.* New York: W. W. Norton & Company, 2005.

Putnam, Hilary. "The Nature of Mental States." *The Nature of Mind*. 1967. Ed. David Rosenthal. New York: Oxford University Press, 1991.

Ravenscroft, Ian. *Philosophy of Mind: A Beginner's Guide*. New York: Oxford University Press, 2005.

Ryle, Gilbert. *The Concept of Mind*. London: Penguin Books, 1949.

Schaffhausen, Joanna. "The Strange Tale of Phineas Gage." *Scientific Learning*. n.d. 11 September 2006 <http://www.brainconnection.com/topics/?main=fa/phineas-gage>.

Searle, John. "Searle, John R." *A Companion to the Philosophy of Mind*. Ed. Samuel Guttenplan. Oxford: Blackwell Publishers, 1995.

—. *The Rediscovery of Mind*. Cambridge, MA: MIT Press, 1992.

—. "Minds, Brains, and Programs." *Behavioral and Brain Sciences* 3 (1980): 417–424.

Smith, Peter. "Language and the Evolution of Mind-Reading." *Theories of Theories of Mind*. Ed. Peter Carruthers and Peter Smith. Cambridge: Cambridge University Press, 1996.

Thompson, Clive. "The Knowing It: An Audacious Quest to Teach a Computer." *Lingua Franca* Sept. 2005: 26–35.

Wortman, Camille, and Elizabeth Loftus. Psychology. 3rd ed. New York: Alfred Knopf, 1988.

Chapter 5   Morality: Searching for Right and Wrong

A man without ethics is a wild beast loosed upon this world.

—Albert Camus

wrong with it. Is there any way we can support our moral intuitions regarding this case? One way of doing this is to study ethics. Studying ethics can give us explicit reasons as to why we deem certain behaviours, such as torturing cats, cold-blooded murder, stealing, incest, and infidelity, as morally wrong. Moreover, studying ethics can also give us reasons as to why helping others, keeping promises, and being honest are morally right. But notice, depending on the circumstances and situations, we may find murder (self-defence), stealing (to give to the poor), or even torturing cats (if one's life is at stake) as morally acceptable. So how can an act be morally right and wrong at the same time? Or can it? Are some actions always right or wrong? These questions, amongst others, will be addressed in this chapter. This chapter is devoted to helping you make the right ethical choices in life. To do this, we will look at five classic and contemporary ethical theories: god and morality, ethical relativism, utilitarianism, deontological ethics, and feminist ethics. Each theory is unique and gives very different reasons for being moral. However, each theory also has pros and cons. It will be up to you to determine which ethical perspective is the most reasonable in aiding your moral decision-making. First, however, let's try to answer the question: What is ethics?

What Is Ethics?

At first glance, the need to define and understand the concept of morality may appear misplaced. After all, morality is second nature for most of us. We are raised as moral beings and know, generally speaking, right from wrong. Unfortunately, there is considerable confusion regarding the concept

The challenge in the example in Box 5.1 is to explain to the boys what they did was wrong. The problem is that most people take burning and killing the cat to be obviously wrong. But why? The boys clearly don't see anything of morality because it is often used synonymously with ethics. To say that "Fred believes that capital punishment is moral" and "Sally believes abortion is ethical" are just two ways in which ethics and morality are used interchangeably. Although I will also use ethics and morality synonymously throughout this chapter, the difference should be noted. Formally speaking, **ethics** is derived from the Greek word *ethos* meaning "character or custom." More specifically, ethics is concerned with understanding moral concepts, the character of what makes someone a good person, and the social rules that regulate behaviour in society. In other words, ethics (moral philosophy) "is the systematic endeavor to understand moral concepts and justify moral principles and theories" (Pojman 2). **Morality** is derived from the Latin word *mores* which means "custom or actual practice." Morality, in other words, is the actual standards or rules (norms) that we believe to be right and wrong that govern specific behaviours. Taken together, ethics is the philosophical analysis of morality and moral concepts such as right, wrong, good, and evil (see Box 5.2). Ethics seeks guiding principles for individual and groups to

live by and, ultimately, investigates the values and virtues that make life worth living and society worthwhile to live in. Most importantly, it seeks to discover valid universal moral standards for everyone to follow (Pojman 2).

To get a better understanding of morality we can contrast these standards with the standards of etiquette, language, and grammar. Moral standards seem to have certain characteristics that separate it from other non-moral standards. For example, etiquette standards can be used to judge whether a person's manners are good; language standards can be used to judge whether a sentence is grammatical; and legal standards can be used to judge whether actions break the law. When making such judgments we are basing them on some standard of right or wrong, but we usually aren't making moral judgments. Belching in public, for example, might be rude, but we usually don't consider this act morally offensive. Dangling modifiers might be ungrammatical, but no serious wrong has been committed. So what separates moral standards from non-moral standards? Here are five distinct ways moral standards differ from non-moral standards (Velasquez, *Business Ethics* 10–11):

1. Moral standards tend to deal with matters that can cause serious injury/harm or benefit to human beings, either physical or psychological. For example, most societies have moral standards against murder, rape, incest, slander, abuse, and so on, because they cause pain and suffering (physical or psychological) to innocent people.
2. Moral standards are not established or changed by authoritative bodies. Laws and legal standards are established and changed by the authority of a legislature; moral standards are not. Moral standards are established or changed by the *reasons* given to support and justify them. The power of a legislative body cannot establish or change the moral standards in society unless good reasons are given. But it's the reasons themselves, not the legislative body, that make or change moral standards.

> ### Box 5.2 A Definition of Ethics and Morality
>
> *Ethics:* A systematic, critical study of the moral standards that an individual or society holds; asking how these standards apply to life; and analyzing if these standards are reasonable or unreasonable to hold. It is the study and analysis of moral principles, problems, concepts, and moral decision-making.
> *Morality:* The standards that an individual or group has about what is right or wrong usually developed from family, friends, church, television, and so forth.
>
> **Source:** Adapted from Manuel Velasquez. (1998). *Business Ethics: Concepts and Cases.* 4th ed. Upper Saddle River, NJ: 8–11.

3. The most striking feature of moral standards is that they are supposed to take precedence over self-interest. People are morally obligated to do the right thing, even though they may have to sacrifice their wants or desires. So, for example, keeping a promise to your child may mean missing your favourite TV show or being financially poorer. But such self-interest is supposed to be irrelevant to doing the moral thing: keeping promises. But, as we will see, such claims are controversial.

4. Moral standards are based on impartial considerations. That is, we are not supposed to take sides or play favourites. An act is right or wrong regardless of who will benefit or gain. Some philosophers have expressed this by saying that we ought to take a "moral point of view." A moral point of view does not evaluate the rightness or wrongness of an action according to whether the interests of a particular individual or group are advanced but on whether everyone's interests can be considered fairly and objectively.

5. Moral standards are associated with special emotions and vocabulary. If, for example, you act immorally, then you may feel shame or guilt. Likewise, if you act morally, then you may feel pride or satisfaction.

Despite these differences between moral and non-moral standards, both have to be learnt. We are not born with the knowledge of morality, anymore than we are born with the knowledge of etiquette; both have to be learnt, so to speak, on our parent's knee. Our moral standards, like non-moral standards, are influenced and learned, explicitly and implicitly, through the interactions with family, friends, school, church, television, and, generally speaking, the society in which we live. But unlike non-moral standards, the moral standards we accept can have profound consequences including death, injury, and psychological harm. After all, people's lives often "hang in the balance" depending on the moral code accepted. This makes the enterprise of morality very serious indeed, requiring careful thinking and analysis to determine if our moral standards are correct. And we can only determine the correctness of morality

by engaging in critical reflection and analysis. This is the point and purpose of ethics. We start to do ethics when we critically evaluate the moral standards and values of ourselves, others, and those of society, in order to determine what we ought or ought not accept (Poff and Waluchow 4). In fact, ethics can be broken down into two kinds: normative and descriptive.

If the ultimate aim of ethics is to develop a body of moral standards that we reasonably *ought* to hold and apply to our everyday lives, then, in this sense, ethics is normative (Velasquez, *Business Ethics* 12–13). **Normative ethics** is the process of critically evaluating and discovering those moral standards we ought to hold. In contrast, **descriptive ethics** merely describes or explains those moral standards already held by an individual or society. Sociologists and anthropologists, for example, have discovered that different cultures have different moral codes. For example, female infanticide is common in some cultures, such as China, but is morally unacceptable in Canadian society. In describing these very different moral codes, anthropologists and sociologists will not pass judgment; they will not try to determine whether these moral codes are right or wrong but merely describe or report the differences. This chapter will focus on normative ethics. Normative ethics is not easy because it often requires you to step back and critically evaluate your deeply held moral standards and values. And for many this can be uncomfortable, to say the least. But it is important to take a normative perspective, because without this kind of critical analysis, individual and societal moral codes would not progress. Here is a more detailed example.

In 2002, the Canadian Senate released a special report entitled *Cannabis: Our Position for a Canadian Public Policy*. Although marijuana has been considered illegal since 1923, the special senate committee argued that marijuana ought to be decriminalized for numerous reasons, including:

- It is less harmful than alcohol.
- It does not lead to the use of harder drugs (heroine, cocaine, etc.).
- Anecdotal evidence indicates it has positive medical benefits for people suffering from

multiple sclerosis, epilepsy, and various forms of cancer.

- Enforcement of drug laws is costly (between $700 million and $1 billion annually) and has little to no impact on cannabis usage. By decriminalizing cannabis this money could be better spent on drug education and prevention programs.

Given these reasons, the report outlines a number of key recommendations, including:

- Licensing of retail outlets to produce and sell cannabis.
- Trafficking of cannabis remains illegal.
- Amnesty for anyone convicted of cannabis possession under current or past laws. To date there are 1.5 million Canadians with a criminal record for cannabis possession.
- Licensing of the production and distribution of cannabis for medical purposes.

To argue for the decriminalization of cannabis is to take a normative perspective. That is, the Senate is not merely reporting/describing what

the current laws and moral codes are in Canada, but arguing against those who believe that cannabis should remain illegal and immoral. In other words, for those that decide to smoke marijuana, their behaviour ought not be condemned as illegal and immoral. In short, the decriminalization of cannabis *ought* to be legal and moral.[1]

This chapter looks specifically at five main normative theories (see Figure 5.1). Although you may find these theories abstract, be patient; they have concrete application to help you live a better life and be a better person. Each normative perspective offers a different point of view, enabling you to make prescriptions about what values and behaviour ought to be considered morally acceptable. That is, by applying normative theories you can find practical solutions to life's moral problems.

The practical application of ethical theory is known as **applied ethics**. As mentioned earlier, although our focus in this chapter is on normative theories, they can be applied to specific moral problems, such as business (business ethics), medicine (bioethics), environment (environmental ethics),

Figure 5.1 The Dimensions of Ethics

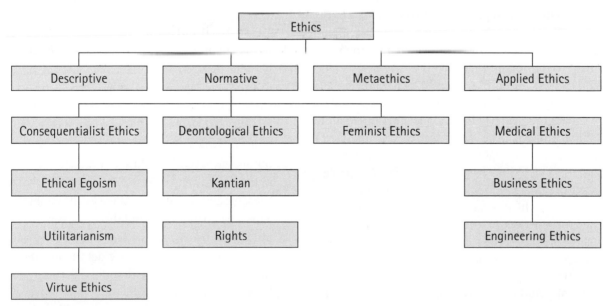

This diagram outlines the many dimensions of ethics. Although only a few theories are addressed in this text, ethics is a rich and diverse discipline devoted to helping us make better ethical decisions and live better lives.

computer technology (computer ethics), and engineering (engineering ethics), to name a few.[2]

Normative ethics, however, raises important questions: Is morality discoverable by all humans in an objective and universal way? Is morality relative to each particular culture? Are moral laws discoverable like the laws of physics? What role does God and religion play in determining moral rules? These questions fall under the area of **metaethics.** Metaethics focuses on the very status and nature of morality. Metaethics also concerns itself with questions about the meaning of moral concepts. What do "good" and "evil" mean? What is "happiness?" What is the "good life?" What does it mean to tell a "lie"? But notice, normative ethics and metaethics cannot truly be separated, because in order to determine how we ought to behave, we often have to make reference to the meaning of moral concepts or how morality is derived. The first two readings in this chapter directly address the metaethical issues of whether morality is derived from God or from culture; the other readings are, strictly speaking, normative ethical theories. However, I will highlight the metaethical and normative aspects of each theory so you get a better understanding of how they are interrelated.

The normative ethical theories we will look at can be generally broken down into two types or kinds: consequentialist and deontological theories. **Consequentialist**, also known as teleological, theories are derived from the Greek word *telos* which means "end or goal". Accordingly, an act is right or wrong depending on the consequences produced or end/goal achieved. We will look at one consequentialist theory: utilitarianism. According to utilitarianism, an act is morally right if it maximizes the greatest happiness for the greatest number of people. **Deontological** theories are derived from the Greek word *deon*, which means "duty." For deontologists, the consequences of one's actions are irrelevant to whether an act is right or wrong. The rightness or wrongness of an act is determined by whether it conforms to a person's duties and obligations. We will look Kantian ethics as a representative sample of deontological ethics.[3] We must be careful here—I am not suggesting that consequentialist

theories do not have explicit duties and obligations; the duty of a utilitarian is to maximize happiness. Likewise, for deontologists, we have a duty to be dutiful. What's important here is that consequentialist and deontological theories highlight what they consider to be of value, and it's from what they value that duties and obligations are derived. For example, the duty to maximize happiness, say utilitarians, stems from the value that maximizing happiness is good and to not maximize happiness is bad. For Kant, he values the intentions and motives behind the actions themselves—specifically, duty. And it's through values of duty that we can determine what we ought to do. An act that conforms to duty is right and an act that does not conform to duty is wrong. "Moral duty must be done solely for its own sake ('Duty for duty's sake')" (Pojman 96). Normative ethical theories, then, are a complex mixture of values and duties that ultimately inform what we ought to do.

Let us start this chapter by looking at the relation between God and morality.

God and Morality

Fear is the mother of morality.
—Friedrich Nietzsche

Discussion Questions

1. In the Biblical chapter of Genesis, Abraham is ordered to sacrifice his only son Isaac as a way of expressing his love and obedience to God. Should Abraham obey such a command? Should any father sacrifice his son or daughter if ordered? Now imagine you are a Nazi SS officer during the Second World War ordered to exterminate the lives of Jews. Should you follow such orders? What does this say, if anything, about the divine command theory of ethics?

2. Millions of people know right from wrong, yet no god or religious scripture determines their moral convictions. Best described as a way of living devoted to eliminating suffering and attaining enlightenment, Buddhism provides an interesting example. Siddhartha Guatama,

Buddha, was born in 563 B.C.E. in what is now Nepal. Through meditation, Guatama discovered that suffering can be eliminated by learning to control and transform greedy and hateful thoughts, words, and actions into compassionate and loving ones (Koller and Koller 139). He outlined four guiding principles, known as the Four Nobel Truths, on how to eliminate pain and suffering and achieve peace and harmony. Deep meditation is used to transcend desires and cravings and thereby reach a higher state of consciousness known as *nirvana*, in which desires and cravings cease to exist and so too does the pain and suffering that go along with them. Because Buddhists don't believe in god but espouse ideas similar to Christianity and Islam (love, compassion, self-discipline), does this show that a person can be moral without God? Why or why not? Would Buddhism show that the divine command theory is false? Does it show that morality is really a human creation based on, in part, emulating the actions of other people who live ethically exemplary lives? Why or why not?

3. A main objection against the divine command theory is that it makes morality arbitrary to the will of God; good acts such as helping the poor and not committing murder could be morally wrong. However, why should we think that God's will is arbitrary? Although it is logically possible for God to command cruelty for its own sake, surely, if God loves us, God would never will this to happen. In other words, commanding cruelty would be inconsistent or contradictory to God's love (Berg 528). If it is true that God loves us, is it impossible for God to will bad acts good and good acts bad? Give reasons for your answer.

I Command You to ... Sit ... Good Boy

From a metaethical perspective, and for billions of people around the world, religion plays a significant role in determining our moral actions.

For Christians, ethical guidance is most explicitly expressed in the form of the Ten Commandments. According to the Old Testament (known as the Hebrew Scriptures in some denominations), the commandments represent the will of God inscribed into stone tablets and given to Moses on Mount Sinai. But Christian ethics includes more than the Ten Commandments. Christian ethics is based on the teachings found in the Old Testament and in the teachings of Jesus Christ.

Although human nature was created good, it was corrupted by Adam and Eve's fall from grace in the Garden of Eden. Eating the forbidden fruit violated God's laws. As punishment, Adam and Eve and their descendants were banished from the Garden, to live in suffering and misery. To help us correct our ways, and live up to the Ten Commandments, God sent us his son Jesus. Jesus is the incarnation of God himself, sent to us in order to save us from the misery of this world and help us find eternal happiness in the next world. Jesus also teaches us how to live a meaningful ethical life in the here and now. To do this, humans must love God and each other. If we conform our actions to the will of God, through the teachings of Christ, our reward is entrance into the kingdom of heaven (Wall 140).

The roots of Christian ethics are found in the ministry of Jesus, specifically the Biblical gospels of Mark, Matthew, Luke, and John. What's important in the gospels is the idea of love. Jesus manifests love in many ways including miracles—curing leprosy and deafness, casting out demons, and bringing the dead to life—and interacting with the underclass and outcasts of society (Preston 94). For Jesus, it did not matter if a person was poor or rich, educated or ignorant, sinner or saint—they all deserved love. In this way, the key to righteousness is love. God's love and devotion to us require giving love and devotion to God, but, moreover, we must extend our love to our neighbours and enemies. As Norman Melchert explains, "To love your neighbor as yourself is to have compassion, to 'feel with' your fellow human being, and to act in accord with that feeling. Just as we feel our own desires, anxieties, cares, pains, and joys, so are we to 'feel with' the desires, anxieties, cares, pains and joys of others" (223). This idea of compassion is nicely expressed in the golden rule (always treat others as you would like them to treat you [Matthew 7:12]), which is the cornerstone of Christian ethics. But what's important here is that "it is in universal compassion that we will find the kingdom of God" (Melchert 224). It's through love that we create peace and harmony in the world. The corollary of this is that we ought (normatively) to love all of humanity including the poor, uneducated, and sinner, as God loves us. The live and death of Jesus is an example of God's love and serves a model for an ethical life. Ethical failure is punishable by eternal damnation (hell), whereas ethical success is rewarded by eternal peace and happiness (heaven). Although other religious perspectives have comparable views regarding reward and punishment for ethical/unethical behaviour, what sets Jesus' ethical teachings apart is its radial nature (Preston 95). There is no limit to forgiveness for injuries suffered. We ought to forgive those to have injured us, not because we can win over the offender, but because God has forgiven us for our sins. We ought to love our enemies, not for personal gain, but because God loves his enemies. As Ronald Preston explains:

> [Jesus'] ethics is very different from an everyday ethic of doing good turns to those who do good turns to you; that is to say an ethic of reciprocity … Jesus goes much deeper, explicitly warning against loving only those who love you, and saying there is nothing extraordinary in that … Jesus calls for a certain flair in life, a certain creative recklessness at crucial points. (95–96)

Why is love important? Because Jesus did not give precise rules for guidance on ethical issues such as discrimination, slavery, or contraception, to name a few; instead, Jesus focused on establishing an ethical foundation of love. We are to love God and our neighbours. Once we understand this, obeying God's will—in the form of the Ten Commandments—will come naturally.

Islamic ethics is also based on divine will. Like Christianity, Islam's beginnings are based on the idea of establishing a moral order for humans based on divine commands (Nanji 107). The word of God is most explicitly expressed in the Quran (Koran). The Quran embodies the message of God revealed to the prophet Muhammad. Ethics, in this sense, is derived from the Quran itself and revealed through the actions, sayings, and norms of Muhammad. It is the relationship between the Quran and the model behaviour of the Prophet, with the help of reason, that rules and principles of moral conduct can be derived.

But God also created humans with the ability to do good or evil. Human free will can often usurp ethical behaviour. Thus, one must perpetually seek balance between free action and submission to God's will. The concept that best expresses this relationship is that of *taqwa*. *Taqwa* represents "on the one hand, the moral grounding that underlies human actions, while on the other hand, it signifies the ethical conscience which makes human beings aware of their responsibilities to God and society" (Nanji 108). The community (*ummah*) is seen as the instrument through which God's commands are translated at a social level. It is through the community that the relationship between humans and God is maintained. For example, the Quran emphasizes redistribution of wealth from individuals and society to the poor. Individuals are supposed to spend their wealth on family and relatives, orphans, the poor, the homeless, the enslaved, and others in need (Nanji 108). "For Muslims, the message of the Quran and the example of the Prophet's life thus remain inseparably related through all of history as paradigms for moral and ethical behaviour" (Nanji 110).

Central to the Muslim faith is peace. After all, *Islam* means "peace through submission." Peace on earth means living in accord with God's will; and living in accord with God's will means fulfilling one's duty to other people (Hassan 428). This duty to others is expressed in a number of beliefs and values including that human life is a gift from God; all humans are to be respected and regarded as having intrinsic worth; justice is based on merit or righteousness, not equal treatment (a poor child who stole food would be given a lesser punishment than a rich child with plenty of money to buy food); and humans are free and must work to ensure they are not bound by racism, sexism, slavery, and other forms of repression (Hassan 428–430). Although much more could be said about Muslim values, without the elimination of inequalities, inequities, and injustices, peace is not possible (Hassan 431).

Many of these ethical values have been codified in Islamic Shari'a law. Shari'a law is a legal framework that guides everyday practices, such as sexuality, economic, politics, theft, adultery, and so on. In this sense, Shari'a is more than a strict code of conduct, "it is also the right teaching, the right way to go in life, and the power that stands behind what is right" (Denny 187). Shari'a law, generally speaking, provides direction, security, and order to one's world for success as an individual, as a community, and in the hereafter.

It is impossible to do justice to both Christianity and Islam in such limited space. My sweeping generalizations will not suffice for those looking to understand the subtle complexity of each religion. However, what is important is that Christian and Muslim ethics are, at heart, based on what is known as the **divine command theory** (see Box 5.3). According to the divine command theory, the rightness or wrongness of an action is related to the fact that God either commands it or forbids it. After all, given God's omniscience, omnipotence, and omnibenevolence, God knows what is good, has the power to make acts good or bad, and, because of his goodness, we can be assured that the acts are morally correct. We can put the argument as follows:

1. Morality (i.e., rightness and wrongness) originates in God.
2. *Moral rightness* simply means "willed by God," and *moral wrongness* means "being against the will of God."
3. Because morality essentially is based on divine will—not on independently existing reasons for action—no further reasons for actions are necessary. (Pojman 181–182)

Morality is determined by God's will or command. To go against the will of God is immoral; to live by the will of God is moral. Let's clarify this ethical theory by looking at the issue of abortion (Thomas and Waluchow, "When a Couple" 75–76).

Bob and Linda are a happily married, middle-class couple living in Calgary. Bob is a 35-year-old professor at a local college. Linda is a 32-year-old petroleum engineer and has stayed at home the past few years to raise their two children. After the birth of their second child, Linda and Bob agreed to have no more children. Despite their best contraceptive efforts, however, Linda becomes pregnant. Linda's pregnancy was not detected right way because she mistook morning sickness as having the flu. As a result, she is diagnosed three months' pregnant.

Bob is overjoyed about having another child, while Linda is miserable. Linda was hoping to return to the workforce and pick up her career where she left off. The thoughts of staying at home with another child, and delay her career again, is highly unpalatable. Linda demands an abortion; after all, it's her body and she can do whatever she wants with it. Bob, on the other hand, argues that abortion is murder. All life is sacred and to abort a fetus is to kill an innocent human being. Life begins, says Bob, at conception and thus to abort the fetus is tantamount to murder (Thomas and Waluchow, "When a Couple" 75–76). If you were Linda or Bob, what would you do? Is abortion murder? What would a Christian or Muslim do?

If the divine command theory of ethics is correct, Linda should be able to turn to God's will for guidance about whether to have an abortion. At first glance, abortion, from a Christian perspective, is immoral because it violates God's commandment not to kill. From a Muslim perspective, abortion is also immoral because it violates God's will that all life has intrinsic value. Linda, in other words, ought not to have an abortion.

The divine command theory has certain advantages (Rauhut 226–227). First, if morality is dependent upon God's will, then morality will be independent of subjective preferences and cultural norms. If someone believes, for example, that abortion is morally right, we can appeal to God's will

Box 5.3 The Ten Commandments: Christianity and Islam

The Ten Commandments (Exodus 12: 1–17 & Deuteronomy 5: 6–21)	Confirmation in the Quran (Chapter: Verse)
1. Thou shall not take any God except one God.	1. There is no God except one God. (47:19)
2. Thou shall make no image of God.	2. There is nothing whatsoever like unto Him. (42:11)
3. Thou shall not use God's name in vain.	3. Do not subject GOD's name to your casual swearing, that you may appear righteous, pious, or to attain credibility among the people. (2:224)
4. Thou shall honor thy mother and father.	4. ...and your parents shall be honored. As long as one or both of them live, you shall never say to them, "Uff" [the slightest gesture of annoyance], nor shall you shout at them; you shall treat them amicably. (17:23)
5. Thou shall not steal.	5. The thief, male or female, you shall mark their hands as a punishment for their crime, and to serve as an example from GOD. GOD is Almighty, Most Wise. (5:38–39)
6. Thou shall not lie or give false testimony.	6. Do not withhold any testimony by concealing what you had witnessed. Anyone who withholds a testimony is sinful at heart. (2:283)
7. Thou shall not kill.	7. If anyone has killed one person it is as if he had killed the whole mankind. (5:32)
8. Thou shall not commit adultery.	8. You shall not commit adultery; it is a gross sin, and an evil behavior. (17:32)
9. Thou shall not covet thy neighbor's wife or possessions.	9. Do good to your parents, relatives and neighbors. (4:36) Saying of the Prophet Muhammad (P) "One of the greatest sins is to have illicit sex with your neighbor's wife."
10. Thou shall keep the Sabbath holy.	10. O you who believe, when the Congregational Prayer (Salat Al-Jumu`ah) is announced on Friday, you shall hasten to the commemoration of GOD, and drop all business. (62:9)

Source: Adapted from Rashad Khalifa. "The Ten Commandments in the Quran." *Submission.Org.* n.d. 20 June 2007 <http://www.submission.org/quran/ten.html>.

to show otherwise. Second, the will of God gives us motivation to be moral. To live a moral life by adhering to God's word means that you will go to heaven and attain peace and harmony in the afterlife. To not adhere to God's will is to be cast into the fires of hell. As Carl Henry states,

"The moral law that lays an imperative on the human conscience is nothing more or less than the manifested will of God. For man nothing is good but union with the sovereign will of God.... According to Christianity, to be morally good is to obey God's commands. The performance of God's will alone constitute man's highest good" (78–79). And finally, the divine command theory gives us a sense of security that these decisions are already made for us. We don't have to wrestle intellectually and emotionally about whether abortion (or keeping promises, stealing, etc.) is morally right or wrong. God has decided for us what constitutes morality. No worries; be happy.

Following Orders Is No Excuse

There are, unfortunately, significant problems with the divine command theory. First, being right and being commanded by God is hardly the same thing. I may want my children to do the right thing, but just because I command it, doesn't mean it's right (John Arthur 85). I may command my children to steal money for me, but this command, clearly, doesn't make stealing right, anymore than if God commands something to be right. Charles Manson, for example, ordered some of his followers to murder but this does not make murderous actions right because he commanded it. However, as Stanley Milgram's experiments showed in the 1960s, the majority of people (62 percent) will cause significant pain and suffering to others in obedience to authority.[4] If the divine command theory is true, then something is right because God commands it, and wrong because he forbids it. But the problem is that just because God commands something as being right or wrong does not make it so. God could have commanded what is "right" to be "wrong." This means what is "moral" or "immoral" is merely an arbitrary decision based on God's will. Thus, the Ten Commandments could look radically different than previously stated. It is possible for God to decree the virtues of kindness and courage as vices, while the vices of cruelty and cowardice could be decreed as right (John Arthur 85). So if torturing innocent children is morally right by virtue of God's command, then we would have an obligation to increase the pain and suffering amongst innocent children. This makes morality arbitrary and subject to the whim of God. And if God could have made torturing innocent children morally right, the sheer abhorrent nature of such

Figure 5.2 Does the Will of God Make Morality Arbitrary?

"You have nothing to be ashamed of. If it were not the Will of God, those obscene profits wouldn't be up for grabs."

a command would surely make God unworthy of worship and prayer. But theists and atheists would insist that torturing innocent children is morally wrong, regardless of who commands it. If so, then morality must be independent, not dependent, of God's will (see Figure 5.2). This was the point made by Socrates in his dialogue *Euthyphro*.

Socrates and Euthyphro meet at court and strike up a conversation regarding justice. Euthyphro is prosecuting his father for murder. A day-labourer on the family farm got into a fight with one of Euthyphro's servants, killing him. Euthyphro's father bound the murderer's hands and feet and threw him in a ditch. After sending a messenger to find out what to do about the labourer, Euthyphro's father forgot about the man and the murderer died from exposure. Needless to say, Euthyphro's family is unhappy about him prosecuting his father. But Euthyphro is emphatic that his actions are morally right or holy because the gods say they are. What is agreeable (commanded) by the gods is holy (right) and what is not agreeable (not commanded) by the gods is unholy (wrong). But then Socrates asks: Do the gods love holiness (what is right/moral) because it is holy (right/moral), or is it holy (right/moral) because the gods love it? In other words, *does the loving of the gods cause an action to be moral, or do moral actions cause the gods to love it?*

This question is crucial to the dialogue because Socrates' question has two possible answers: 1) If what is morally right/wrong is dependent upon the gods, then "good" and "bad" are arbitrary labels. As we have seen, the gods could, by virtue of their commands, will murder, adultery, or rape to be moral. 2) If the gods command what is morally right because some actions are right (wrong) independent of their will, then we should be able to approve or disapprove of them like the gods do. In other words, we don't need to look to the gods for moral guidance because we can determine what is morally right or wrong ourselves. And if we can determine what is right or wrong without looking to the gods, then morality must be independent of the gods' will and not determined by it. In short, morality must be independent of the gods.

To illustrate his question, Socrates uses a number of examples (see Box 5.4). "Being carried" is the state of an object that is carried. A book, for example, is in the state of "being carried" because someone acts upon it and picks it up. That is, it's by virtue of someone carrying that the book is "being carried." Likewise, "being led" is the state of an object that is led. A band is in the state of being led because a conductor is acting upon or causing that state. It's by virtue of the conductor's leading, that the band is led. Similarly, something is in the

state of being loved because someone loves it. For Euthyphro, something is holy (moral) because it is caused or loved by the gods. And if what is moral is because the gods love it, then morality is dependent on the gods' will.

But then Socrates asks Euthyphro why he thinks the act of the gods' loving causes something to be holy (moral)? Fatally, Euthyphro says some actions are holy (right) *because they are holy (right),* not because the gods love them. Why does Euthyphro make the fatal mistake of agreeing that the gods love holiness because it is holy? Because Euthyphro is caught in a dilemma: either morality is based on the arbitrary whims of the gods, which, as we have seen, is problematic, or it is not. If morality is not based on the gods' love or command, then this means that some actions are holy (right) because of their intrinsic nature or worth, and this is what causes the gods to love them. The only conclusion, says Socrates, is that morality is independent of the gods. And if morality is independent of the gods, then right or wrong actions are equally discoverable by humans. Unfortunately, from a Judeo-Christian or Islamic perspective, if Socrates is right, this places limits on omnipotence because morality is something beyond God's power to create and, as such, it makes God hardly worth worshipping (John Arthur 86) (see Box 5.5).

A second problem is that of defining "good." Theists often defend morality as a derivative of God's will on the basis that "God is good." Again, if God is good, it is reasonable to assume that God will have our best interests at heart when deciding what is right or wrong. God would never make murder, incest, or rape morally acceptable. For many theists, to think that God is not good would "be like a man shipwrecked, lost in a vast and indifferent universe" (Nielsen 6). So, how do we know that God is good? What grounds do we have to believing that God is good? The problem is twofold: 1) If we define goodness by virtue of the will of God, then there is no meaning of goodness independent of God. That is, there are no standards of good besides the dictates of God. Therefore, if God commands torture or incest to be morally good, we would have to acquiesce. This is something most theists would not accept.

Box 5.4   Is "Being Carried" the Same as "Carrying"?

Object Affected by a Causal Agent (Passive)	Causal Agent Affecting an Object (Active)
X is being carried	Carrying
X is being led	Leading
X is being seen	Seeing
X is being loved	Loving

Box 5.5 Argument Against the Divine Command Theory

1. Suppose God commands us to do what is right. Then *either* (a) the right actions are right because he commands them or (b) he commands them because they are right.

2. If we take option (a), then God's commands are, from a moral point of view, arbitrary; moreover, the doctrine of the goodness of God is rendered meaningless.

3. If we take (b), then we have admitted there is a standard of right and wrong that is independent of God's will.

4. Therefore, we must *either* regard God's commands as arbitrary, and we give up the doctrine of the goodness of God, *or* admit that there is a standard of right and wrong that is independent of his will, and give up the theological definition of rightness and wrongness.

5. From a religious point of view, it is undesirable to regard God's command as arbitrary or to give up the doctrine of the goodness of God.

6. Therefore, even from a religious point of view, a standard to right or wrong that is independent of God's will must be accepted.

Source: James Rachels. (2003). *The Elements of Moral Philosophy.* 4th ed. New York: McGraw-Hill, 52–53.

In response, a theist might argue that God cannot do certain things like make morally abhorrent acts, such as torture or incest, morally right. But this is problematic for the theist because: a) it shows that morality is independent of God (again). If God cannot make bad acts moral, then these acts must be immoral prior to God's will; b) If God cannot

make torture or incest morally right actions, then God is not omnipotent. 2) In order to know that God is good, we need independent moral criteria of God's goodness. That is, the experience of God's goodness through his acts is not sufficient to know that God is good. In order to know that God's acts are, in fact, good, we need an understanding goodness independent of God. As Kai Nielsen explains, "in order to know that [God] is good or to have any grounds for believing that [God] is good, we must have independent moral criterion which we use in making this prediction of God" (7). So if knowing God's goodness requires an independent moral criterion, then morality cannot be based on God. That is, we must have an understanding of good ness that is logically prior to any understanding or acknowledgment of God (Nielsen 11).

A third problem is that it is difficult to find specific moral guidance in the Bible or Quran. Clearly, the issues faced in today's society are, in many respects, vastly different than those faced in ancient times. For example, religious scriptures tell us nothing about the morality of drug-testing of employees, whistle-blowing on corporate wrongdoing, monitoring employee e-mail, cloning, global warming, extinction of species, genetically modified food, shipping of toxins to third-world countries, and so forth. It's true that religion can give us general guidelines, but this is hardly helpful when we come to make specific moral decisions. This lack of moral guidance, in part, is due to another problem, namely, religious texts can be interpreted in biased ways to support one's subjective point of view.

The fourth problem with the divine command theory is that of biased interpretation. Even if we know what God wants, there are problems of how to interpret God's word. Is all killing wrong? Christians, for example, both defend and criticize capital punishment based on traditional texts. On the one hand, the Old Testament says, "Eye for an eye and tooth for a tooth," and, on the other hand, it says "Judge not least ye be judged" and "Thou shalt not kill." Which ought you to follow to make the morally right choice? It's too hard to tell. The interpretive problems of religious scriptures make moral guidance impossible. The trouble with using scripture to guide morality is that, because of its generality, it can be interpreted to support both sides of issues. The point of scripture, ideally, is to use it in an objective way to determine what we believe about specific moral issues. But most people use scripture not for objective guidance but to reinforce their already deeply held moral convictions. And they do this while ignoring the same or other parts of the scripture that contradict their conclusions. As James Rachels explains:

> Thus when people claim that their moral views are derived from religious commitments, they are often mistaken. In reality, something very different is going on. They are making up their minds about the moral issues first and then interpreting the Scriptures, or church tradition, in such a way as to support the moral conclusion they have already reached. (Rachels 58)

Let's consider abortion again. According to many Christians, the Bible tells us that a human being exists at conception. "Now the word of the Lord came to me, saying, 'Before I formed you in the womb I knew you, and before you were born, I consecrated you'..." (Jeremiah 1:4–5). Unfortunately, as Joyce Arthur explains in her article, "Anti-Choicers Don't Have a Biblical Leg To Stand On: The Bible is Pro-Choice," anti-abortionists usually forget to include the rest of the passage which states, "...'and I appointed you a prophet to the nations.'" Unless taken out of context, it is hard to see how this could be interpreted as God's word against abortion. This passage is really about how God has given Jeremiah permission to speak on his behalf. Another Biblical quotation used by anti-abortion supporters, says Joyce Arthur, is the following:

> In those days, Mary arose and went with haste into the hill country, to a city of Judah, and she entered the house of Zechariah and greeted Elizabeth. And when Elizabeth heard the greeting of Mary, the babe leaped in her womb, and Elizabeth was filled with the Holy Spirit. (Luke 1:39–41)

But it's very difficult to directly see this as a story about the sins of abortion. This is merely a story of Elizabeth, the mother of John the Baptist, being greeted by Mary, the mother of Jesus, and the kicking of the fetus in the womb. Interestingly, there are other Biblical passages, says Arthur, supporting abortion. Here is one such example:[5]

> If a man begets a hundred children, and lives many years, so that the days of his years are many, but he does not enjoy life's good things, and also has no burial, I say that an untimely birth is better off than he. For it comes into vanity and goes into darkness, and in darkness its name is covered; moreover it has not seen the sun or known anything; yet it finds rest rather than he. (Ecclesiastes 6:3–5)

Again, it's hard to see this as a proof of God's condemnation of abortion. The passage seems to be appealing to the quality of life, not the mere fact of being alive. Hence, this scripture seems, from a pro-choice perspective, to offer evidence of the morality of abortion. My point is that all of these quotations can be interpreted in ways to support one's moral convictions.

And what about Islam? Generally speaking, most Muslims consider all life sacrosanct, including the life of fetuses. The Quran explicitly states, "God has made life sacred" (17:33). It also states, "You shall not kill your children due to fear of poverty. We provide for them, as well as for you. Killing them is a gross offense" (17:31). Accordingly, Islamic law says that when a woman has a spontaneous abortion, such as a miscarriage, it is considered to be the will of God. However, despite what the Quran says, the moral justification depends on the notion of ensoulment. Ensoulment is the creation or placing of a soul in a fetus, usually taking place 120 days or 4 months after conception. At the time of ensoulment, the fetus is considered a person with full rights. For some Muslims, abortion is immoral, even before ensoulment, except in cases where a woman's life is at risk or the child is seriously malformed (Kyriakides-Yeldham 217). For other contemporary scholars, abortion is permissible for any valid reasons, in addition to the threat to a mother's life, before ensoulment. And for other Muslim scholars, abortion is never morally acceptable, even if a mother's life is at risk (Hussain 247). Again, the morality of abortion is based on subjective interpretation of ensoulment.

My point here is not to suggest that religious beliefs play no role in morality (see Box 5.6) or

Box 5.6 Hindu Ethics

The divine command theory runs into another problem. Millions of people are morally good but do not believe that morality comes from God or God's will. Hinduism is an interesting example of ethics without God.

Hinduism is one of the oldest religions in the world and much of its beliefs and values come from the writings called the Vedas, especially the Upanishads. Religion writing tells us that although Hinduism is considered a polytheistic religion, this is not entirely accurate. There are many gods in Hinduism including *Vishnu* (preserver of the universe), *Siva* (destroyer of the universe), *Kali* (destroyer of Ignorance; maintainer of world order), and *Krishna* (embodiment of joy; destroyer of sin), but there is only one supreme god named *Brahman*. *Brahman* is the ultimate reality, a being who is "great" or "expansive"; a being who is indivisible, all knowing, all powerful, immoral, loving, and good (Lawhead 370). These attributes make *Brahman* sound similar to our Judeo-Christian God but it is not. *Brahman*, it is said, has no properties, is indefinable; and, in many respects, is unknowable. For lack of better words, *Brahman* is identical to the world. All reality is unified under one divine entity. In this sense, all of the other gods are really just a manifestation of *Brahman*.

Although Christianity holds that God is immanent—throughout the universe—God is not physical. For example, if God made a chair, God would not be the chair. In Hinduism, however, *Brahman*, the creator is his creation (Flesher). *Brahman* and universe are one and the same. This means that in a world of multiple gods, humans, and animals, there is unity beyond our immediate senses. What humans see on the daily basis is *maya*; our goal is to transcend what we see with our senses and perceive *Brahman*. Like thinking you see a snake, when it is only a rope; the world we experience does not truly resemble reality the way it actually is. Likewise, *Brahman* is

not something "in the world" independent of us to be discovered. Each human soul or true self (*atman*) is *Brahman*; each individual soul is identical with a larger god of the cosmos (Flesher). Thus one of life's goals is to "overcome the illusion of this duality and separateness and to realize our oneness with the Absolute Being [*Brahman*]" (Lawhead 374).

But how do we achieve oneness? Well, it's a long and complicated process but ultimately it's tied to four life goals each having intrinsic value: *artha* (success, material gain), *kama* (pleasure), *dharma* (virtue, individual duties), and *moksha* (bliss, consciousness, liberation). The first two goals, generally speaking, are easy to attain by, for example, being successful in business or taking pleasure in passing your philosophy course. However, it's much more difficult to be virtuous and attain liberation. Trying to be virtuous is difficult when we are tempted by sins on a daily basis. Unfortunately, we sometimes give into sin. *Dharma* is, therefore, closely connected with the concept of *karma*. *Karma* literally means "action" but more to the point it "denotes the moral, psychological spiritual and physical causal consequences of morally significant past choices" (Ranganathan). *Karma* is the moral law that governs our actions and soul. Given the temptations in life, we can fully control whether we act virtuously and in doing so determine our destiny in future lives. That is, moral or immoral actions will determine how a person is reincarnated. Depending on whether you do good or bad in this life, you could be reincarnated into a dog, politician, movie star, rat, and so forth in your next life. The idea is that each rebirth ought to reflect higher moral development. And with each successive life, you will be one step closer to attaining *moksha*. That is, by being virtuous, you will come to understand reality as it *really is*; you will come to know freedom; and you will come to know *Braham* (Flesher).

that religious beliefs are irrational. My aim is to show that religious beliefs and scripture can be interpreted in such a way that is both for and against abortion. Although religion can help support one's position regarding abortion, to conclude one's religion dictates its moral status is unconvincing. In many respects, biased beliefs are superimposed on religion through which scriptures are interpreted (Rachels 62). Part of the difficulty of knowing God's commands is that they are often viewed through a historically and culturally biased lens. The challenge for moral philosophers is to read through those biases, be attentive to their own, and reflect upon issues with care and sensitivity.

25

Plato (427–347 B.C.)

The son of Ariston and Perictione, Plato was born in Athens in 427 B.C. Although originally named Aristocles, he was given the nickname of Plato because of his wrestler-like broad shoulders. Plato's father died when he was young and his mother remarried Pyrilampes, in whose house Plato grew up. His early years were devoted to receiving the best education Athens had to offer and being groomed for a life in politics. During the Peloponnesian wars with Sparta, Plato served in the military from 409 to 404 B.C. After the defeat of Athens, Plato became part of the oligarchy of the Thirty Tyrants that ruled

the country by force. The violence inflicted upon the people of Athens by the oligarchy disillusioned Plato, causing him to leave politics, becoming instead a student of Socrates in search of the truth. After Socrates' death in 399 B.C., Plato travelled for the next twelve years, studying philosophy in various countries. He returned to Athens in 387 B.C. and founded the Academy, Europe's first university, where philosophy, astronomy, and mathematics were taught and studied. Plato's writings include the Apology, Crito, Euthyphro, Meno, Phaedo, *and, most famously, the* Republic. *Plato died in 347 B.C.*

Euthyphro

E: Well then, what is dear to the gods is pious, what is not is impious.

S: Splendid, Euthyphro! You have now answered in the way I wanted. Whether your answer is true I do not know yet, but you will obviously show me that what you say is true.

E: Certainly.

S: Come then, let us examine what we mean. An action or a man dear to the gods is pious, but an action or a man hated by the gods is impious. They are not the same, but quite opposite, the pious and the impious. Is that so?

E: It is indeed.

S: And that seems to be a good statement?

E: I think so, Socrates.

S. We have also stated that the gods are in a state of discord, that they are at odds with each other, Euthyphro, and that they are at enmity with each other. Has that, too, been said?

E: It has.

S: What are the subjects of difference that cause hatred and anger? Let us look at it this way. If you and I were to differ about numbers as to which is the greater, would this difference make us enemies and angry with each other, or would we proceed to count and soon resolve our difference about this?

E: We would certainly do so.

S: Again, if we differed about the larger and the smaller, we would turn to measurement and soon cease to differ.

E: That is so.

S: And about the heavier and the lighter, we would resort to weighing and be reconciled.

E: Of course.

S: What subject of difference would make us angry and hostile to each other if we were unable to come to a decision? Perhaps you do not have an answer ready, but examine as I tell you whether these subjects are the just and unjust, the beautiful and the ugly, the good and the bad. Are these not the subjects of difference about which, when we are unable to come to a satisfactory decision, you and I and other men become hostile to each other whenever we do?

E: That is the difference, Socrates, about those subjects.

S: What about the gods, Euthyphro? If indeed they have differences, will it not be about these same subjects?

E: It certainly must be so.

S: The according to your argument, my good Euthyphro, different gods consider different things to be just, beautiful, ugly, good, and bad, for they would not be at odds with one another unless they differed about these subjects, would they?

E: You are right.

S: And they like what each of them considers beautiful, good, and just, and hate the opposites of these?

E: Certainly.

S: But you say that the same things are considered just by some gods and unjust by others, and as they dispute about these things they are at odds and at war with each other. Is that not so?

E: It is.

S: The same things then are loved by the gods and hated by the gods, and would be both god-loved and god-hated.

E: It seems likely.

S: And the same things would be both pious and impious, according to this argument?

E: I'm afraid so.

S: So you did not answer my question, you surprising man. I did not ask you what same thing is both pious and impious, and it appears that what is loved by the gods is also hated by them. So it is in no way surprising if your present action, namely punishing your father, may be pleasing to Zeus but displeasing to Kronos and Ouranos, pleasing to Hephaestus but displeasing to Hera, and so with any other gods who differ from each other on this subject.

E: I think, Socrates, that on this subject no gods would differ from one another, that whoever has killed anyone unjustly should pay the penalty.

S: Well now, Euthyphro, have you ever heard any man maintaining that one who has killed or done anything else unjustly should not pay the penalty?

E: They never cease to dispute on this subject, both elsewhere and in the courts, for when they have committed many wrongs they do and say anything to avoid the penalty.

S: Do they agree they have done wrong, Euthyphro, and in spite of so agreeing do they nevertheless say they should not be punished?

E: No, they do not agree on that point.

S: So they do not say or do anything. For they do not venture to say this, or dispute that they must not pay the penalty if they have done wrong, but I think they deny doing wrong. Is that not so?

E: That is true.

S: Then they do not dispute that the wrong-doer must be punished, but they may disagree as to who the wrongdoer is, what he did and when.

E: You are right.

S: Do not the gods have the same experience, if indeed they are at odds with each other about the just and unjust, as your argument maintains? Some assert that they wrong one another, while others deny it, but no one among gods or men ventures to say that the wrongdoer must not be punished.

E: Yes, that is true, Socrates, as to the main point.

S: And those who disagree, whether men or gods, dispute about each action, if indeed the gods disagree. Some say it is done justly, others unjustly. Is that not so?

E: Yes, indeed.

S: Come now, my dear Euthyphro, tell me, too, that I may become wiser, what proof you have that all the gods consider that man to have been killed unjustly who became a murderer while in your service, was bound by the master of his victim, and died in his bonds before the one who bound him found out from the seers what was to be done with him, and that it is right for a son to denounce and to prosecute his father on behalf of such a man. Come, try to show me a clear sign that all the gods definitely believe this action to be right. If you can give me adequate proof of this, I shall never cease to extol your wisdom.

E: This perhaps no light task, Socrates, though I could show you very clearly.

S: I understand that you think me more dull-witted than the jury, as you will obviously show them that these actions were unjust and that all the gods hate such actions.

E: I will show it to them clearly, Socrates, if only they will listen to me.

S: They will listen if they think you show them well. But this thought came to me as you were speaking, and I am examining it, saying to myself: "If Euthyphro shows me conclusively that all the gods consider such a death unjust, to what greater extent have I learned from him the nature of piety and impiety? This action would then, it seems, be hated by the gods, but the pious and the impious were not now defined, for what is hated by the gods has also been shown to be loved by them." So I will not insist on this point; let us assume, if you wish, that all the gods consider this unjust and that they all hate it. However, is this the correction we are making in our discussion, that what all the gods hate is impious, and what they all love is pious, and that what some gods love and others hate is neither or both? Is that how you now wish us to define piety and impiety?

E: What prevents us from doing so, Socrates?

S: For my part nothing, Euthyphro, but you look whether on your part this proposal will enable you to teach me most easily what you promised.

E: I would certainly say that the pious is what all the gods love, and the opposite, what all the gods hate, is the impious.

S: Then let us again examine whether that is a sound statement, or do we let it pass, and if one of us, or someone else, merely says that something is so, do we accept that it is so? Or should we examine what the speaker means?

E: We must examine it, but I certainly think that this is now a fine statement.

S: We shall soon know better whether it is. Consider this: It is the pious loved by the gods because it is pious, or is it pious because it is loved by the gods?

E: I don't know what you mean, Socrates.

S: I shall try to explain more clearly; we speak of something being carried[1] and something carrying, of something being led and something leading, of something being seen and something seeing, and you understand that these things are all different from one another and how they differ?

E: I think I do.

S: So there is something being loved and something loving, and the loving is a different thing.

E: Of course.

S: Tell me then whether that which is being carried is being carried because someone carries it or for some other reason.

E: No, that is the reason.

S: And that which is being led is so because someone leads it, and that which is being seen because someone sees it?

E: Certainly.

S: It is not seen by someone because it is being seen but on the contrary it is being seen because someone sees it, nor is it because it is being led that someone leads it but because someone leads it that it is being led; nor does someone carry an object because it is being carried, but it is being carried because someone carries it. Is what I want to say clear, Euthyphro? I want to say this, namely, that if anything comes to be, or is affected, it does not come to be because it is coming to be, but it is coming to be because it comes to be; nor is it affected because it is being affected but because something affects it. Or do you not agree?

E: I do.

S: What is being loved is either something that comes to be or something that is affected by something?

E: Certainly.

S: So it is in the same case as the things just mentioned; it is not loved by those who love it because it is being loved, but it is being loved because they love it?

E: Necessarily.

S: What then do we say about the pious, Euthyphro? Surely that it is loved by all the gods, according to what you say?

E: Yes.

S: Is it loved because it is pious, or for some other reason.

E: For no other reason.

S: It is loved then because it is pious, but it is not pious because it is loved?[2]

E: Apparently.

S: And because it is loved by the gods it is being loved and it is dear to the gods?

E: Of course.

S: The god-beloved is then not the same as the pious, Euthyphro, nor the pious the same as the god-beloved, as you say it is, but one differs from the other.

E: How so, Socrates?

S: Because we agree that the pious is beloved for the reason that it is pious, but it is not pious because it is loved. Is that not so?

E: Yes.

S: And that the god-beloved, on the other hand, is so because it is loved by the gods, by the very fact of being loved, but it is not loved because it is god-beloved.

E: True.

S: But if the god-beloved and the pious were the same, my dear Euthyphro, and the pious were loved because it was pious, then the god-beloved would be loved because it was god-beloved, and if the god-beloved was god-beloved because it was loved by the gods, then the pious would also be pious because it was loved by the gods; but now you see that they are in opposite cases as being altogether different from each other: the one is of a nature to be loved because it is loved, the other is loved because it is of a nature to be loved. I'm afraid, Euthyphro, that when you were asked what piety is, you did not wish to make its nature clear to me, but you told me an affect or quality of it, that the pious has the quality of being loved by all the gods, but you have not yet told me what the pious is. Now, if you will, do not hide things from me but tell me again from the beginning what piety is, whether loved by the gods or having some other quality—we shall not quarrel about that—but be keen to tell me what the pious and the impious is.

E: But Socrates, I have no way of telling you what I have in mind, for whatever proposition we put forward goes around and refuses to stay put where we establish it. [...]

Notes

1. This is the present participle form of the verb *phenomenon*, literally *being-carried*. The following passage is somewhat obscure, especially in translation, but the general meaning is clear. Plato points out that this participle simply indicates the object of an action of carrying, seeing, loving, etc. It follows from the action and adds nothing new, the action being prior to it, not following from it, and a thing is said to be loved because someone loves it, not vice versa. To say therefore that the pious is being loved by the gods says no more than the gods love it. Euthyphro, however, also agrees that the pious is loved by the gods because of its nature (because it is pious), but the fact of its being loved by the gods does not define that nature, and as a definition is therefore unsatisfactory. It only indicates a quality or affect of the pious, and the pious is therefore still to be defined (11a7).

2. I quote an earlier comment of mine on this passage: "...it gives in a nutshell a point of view from which Plato never departed. Whatever the gods may be, they must by their very nature love the right because it is right." They have no choice in the matter. "This separation of the dynamic power of the gods from the ultimate reality, this setting up of absolute values above the gods themselves was not as unnatural to a Greek as it would be to us ... The gods who rule on Olympus ... were not creators but created beings. As in Homer, Zeus must obey the balance of Necessity, so the Platonic gods must conform to an eternal scale of values. They did not create them, cannot alter them, cannot indeed wish to do so." (*Plato's Thought*, Indianapolis: Hacket Publishing Co., 1980, pp. 152–3.)

Ethical Relativism

The idea of cultural relativism is nothing but an excuse to violate human rights.

—Shirin Ebadi

Discussion Questions

1. Imagine you live in an African, Asian, or Middle Eastern country where female circumcision—the partial or complete remove of the clitoris[6]—also known as female genital mutilation (FGM), is socially and morally acceptable. According to

the World Health Organization, 100–140 million girls and women have been circumcised and another 2 million girls aged four to twelve face the procedure each year. The health consequences vary with the type of circumcision but include extreme pain, infection, haemorrhage, ulceration, cysts, abscesses, and psychosexual trauma, which is why most countries have outlawed this surgical practice. In Canada, female circumcision violates the Charter of Rights and Freedom and is considered aggravated assault under the Criminal Code (LeBourdais). It also violates the *United Nations Declaration of Human Rights* and the *Declaration of the Rights of the Child*. Imagine that your 12-year-old daughter is near puberty and social custom requires her circumcision. If conventional ethical relativism is right, do you have a moral obligation to follow the customs of the country? What about immigrants arriving in Canada and requesting circumcision for their daughters? Setting aside the legal ramifications, if morality is relative, would physicians have an obligation to do the procedure? Give reasons for your answers.

2. An issue that brings conventional relativism into light is bribery. An Oakville, Ontario, engineering consulting firm Acres International has worked in over 100 countries on numerous construction projects including power stations and water treatment facilities. In 1986, Lesotho and South Africa wanted to build a dam to generate electricity. Acres bid on the project and the following year they were awarded a contract. In subsequent years, Acres was awarded additional lucrative contracts. Acres was making substantial payments to Zaliswango Mini Bam, a local agent hired to oversee the project, and to Masupha Sole, the chief executive in charge of contracts and a close friend of Bam. Documents revealed that Acres was giving bribe money to Bam, who forwarded just over half to Sole, who then awarded the contract to Acres (Karakowsky, Carroll, and Buchholtz 593–594). In 2002,

Acres International was fined $2.2 million for giving $266,000 to Sole in exchange for a $21 million contract on the $21 billion multidam project (Powers 13). If bribery is common practice in some countries, should we fault the relativist for doing "as the Romans do"? If bribery is the only way to do business in some countries, should we consider it immoral?[7] Give reasons for your answers.

When in Rome Do as the Romans

The second metaethical theory we will look at is ethical relativism. Put simply, ethical relativism claims that there are no universal (objective) moral values that hold for all people everywhere. In contrast, ethical objectivists claim that universal moral values exist and, most importantly, can be used to judge the moral standing of behaviour. Objectivist claims regarding morality, say relativists, are problematic because it's obvious that different cultures have different ways of living, including different moral codes. For ethical relativists, morality is either determined by virtue of the culture in which one lives (conventional ethical relativism) or individually (subjective ethical relativism). Let us start by looking at examples of **conventional ethical relativism**.

Examples of relativism are abundant. In January 2005, Dr. Shazia Khalid, a physician working for Pakistan Petroleum Limited, was asleep in her bedroom when a masked intruder broke into her home and repeatedly beat and raped her. The rape caused serous injury, leaving her unconscious. When she came to, she sought help and was taken to a local hospital. Instead of treating her wounds, doctors asked her not to report the rape to the police, gave her some sedatives, and then shipped her off to another hospital. Although the police eventually did take a statement from her, she was told that there was nothing they could do about her case. When Dr. Khalid's husband, who was working in Libya at the time of the assault, returned, the two were put under house arrest for two months. Pakistan authorities allegedly pressured Dr. Khalid and her husband to leave the country or face death, as her husband's father suggested she be killed for dishonouring the family. (The couple is now living in London and seeking refugee status in Canada where she has family and friends. The Canadian government has, so far, refused her entry [McCarthy A2]). As for the case, the rapist has been identified as a Pakistan army officer. But according to Sharia'a law (known as the Hudood Ordinance), a woman's alleged rape must be supported by four adult males who witnessed the "act of penetration." Failure to provide witnesses is subject to prosecution of adultery. The penalty for adultery is death by stoning or imprisonment.[8] From a Western perspective, this impossible standard of evidence is surely unjustified. Moreover, to then accuse the victim of adultery because she cannot provide four witnesses seems morally abhorrent and smacks of paternalism. However, although Canadians may condemn the Pakistani law, if relativism is correct, we would have to accept such practices as morally acceptable.

In March 2006, Abdul Rahman was arrested and charged in an Afghan court for converting to Christianity from Islam. Although Rahman converted to Christianity over 14 years ago, according to Afghan law, conversation from Islam to Christianity is punishable by death. Not surprisingly, there has been international outcry over this case. But what makes this case even more troubling is that Canadian and other NATO (North Atlantic Treaty Organization) troops are risking their lives and dying to bring freedom to the Afghan people, including the right of religious freedom. But according to cultural relativists, Westerners would have to accept this practice as being morally acceptable (Tandt and Oziewicz A1).

The point should be clear. Although we might think these examples morally deviant, from a conventional ethical relativist perspective, these actions are morally right if they are accepted in these cultures. That is, morality is derived from culture itself, and given the diversity of cultures worldwide, we ought not to expect universal agreement about what is right or wrong. If so, then "when in Rome do as the Romans." That is, we ought to conform to the moral codes in force in a particular culture, even if they differ from our own.

The idea of conventional ethical relativism stems from what is known as cultural relativism. **Cultural relativism** is the anthropological claim that cultures differ regarding what is morally right and wrong. Moreover, cultural relativism requires we be respectful and tolerant of these differences. The idea of respect and tolerance towards different cultures is in direct contrast to the disrespect and intolerance demonstrated by many Western cultures over the centuries. In fact, many Western cultures took an ethical **ethnocentric** view; namely, Western beliefs and values were the right and ought to be imposed on other cultures. Ethnocentrism often had devastating effects on indigenous populations. The Spanish, for example, in the sixteenth century, colonized the Aztecs in Mexico, destroying their culture and imposing Christian beliefs and values (Harrison, Sullivan, and Sherman 386). The French colonized Quebec, United States (Louisiana), and other territories in West Indies and Africa, while the British colonized the rest of North America, Barbados, Jamaica, India, amongst others. Although colonizing brought benefits to aboriginal groups such as tools, clothing, and rifles, it also brought diseases like small pox and alcohol, which devastated many indigenous cultures and populations. The British treatment of aboriginal peoples was particular troubling, especially in the United States. As settlers moved onto aboriginal lands, resistance became inevitable, "In the effort to protect their land, the Indians fought back savagely. Their resistance nourished a feeling among the colonists that the native Americans were inferior savages whose extermination would best serve everyone's interest" (Harrison, Sullivan, and Sherman 457). The American government took an offensive role in dealing with their "Indian" problem, while the Canadian government took a subtler, but equally devastating approach. For example, residential schools popped up across the country, forcing, by law, Native children to attend (see Photo 5.1). The goal was to try to assimilate First Nations people into the white community. Although residential schools were government funded, they were church-run and systematically forced First Nations children to give up their traditional beliefs and ways of life. Children were often physically and emotionally abused for being "Indian," and, in some cases, they were also sexually abused. As of 2006, there are currently 17,000 lawsuits filed against various church organizations that ran the schools and against the Canadian government; 4,500 lawsuits have been resolved. Total financial compensation to the victims is estimated at $113 million.

These kinds of ethnocentric abusive attitudes eventually gave way to the idea of ethical relativism, thanks, in part, to the work of anthologists. Morality ought not to be forced on other cultures but, instead, we ought to show tolerance and respect for all belief systems, even those we disagree with. After all, given the difference between cultures, we cannot say that one culture is superior or inferior about what is right or wrong, just different. As the anthropologist William Graham Sumner states,

The "right" way is the way which the ancestors used and which has been handed down. The tradition is its own warrant. It is not held subject to verification by experience. The notion of right is in the folkways. It is not outside of them, or independent origin, and brought to them to test them. In the folkways, whatever is, is right. This is because they are traditional, and therefore contain in themselves the authority of the ancestral ghosts. (5)

We must see the right way as being handed down through the folkways of a culture. Morality is not determined by some external or independent set of objective moral codes but is determined by cultural traditions. If ethical relativists are correct, then there are no objective truths that will guide human behaviour to achieve comparable moral ends. This is a metaethical thesis. And given the lack of objective moral truths, this, then, leads to the normative thesis: an act is right if it conforms to the moral codes in a society and an act is wrong if it goes against the moral code in a society. Morality, it is said, is relative.

James Rachels' article outlines a number of important objections against relativism. Let's start with what we can call the *non sequitur* problem.

The Romans Are Wrong

Conventional ethical relativism is based on the logical move from the idea of cultural diversity to the claim that there are no objective truths. It's from the fact that different cultures have different beliefs about morality that relativists claim that morality is culturally determined and, therefore,

Photo 5.1 Native Residential Schools

Residential schools were found across Canada, except in New Brunswick, Newfoundland, and Prince Edward Island. The schools were an attempt by the government to "aggressively assimilate" aboriginal children into mainstream "white" culture. Of the 130 church-run institutions, the Roman Catholic Church operated 70 percent of them. The first residential school opened in British Columbia in 1861 and the last school closed in 1996. Unfortunately, many students in residential schools suffered physical, sexual, and emotional abuse.

no universal moral truths exist that hold true for all people everywhere. This is not so, says Rachels. The problem is that diversity in moral practices does not mean that there are no objective moral truths. It could turn out that someone is simply wrong about his or her moral beliefs. Racist and sexist attitudes may be based on mistaken assumptions about the intellectual and rational facilities of specific people, for example. And if a person's moral beliefs are wrong, perhaps we have a duty to try and correct them. But we should be careful about what Rachels is saying. He is not suggesting that our Western cultural values are right and that we ought to impose them on others (ethical ethnocentrism). What he is arguing is that there are universal moral truths that everyone ought to accept as morally right or wrong. And, over time, everyone will come to see specific actions as morally agreeable or disagreeable based on independent reasons and justifications.

A second problem is that if relativism is true, we cannot criticize other ethical practices as right or wrong. This leads to some very disturbing consequences. Two hundred and forty years ago, for example, slavery was considered morally and legally acceptable. The taking of slaves goes back to ancient Greece and Rome, but we normally associate slavery with Dutch and British colonization during the seventeenth century, specifically the first slaves brought to the United States in 1619 as a means of cheap labour (Harrison, Sullivan, and Sherman 609). In Canada, slavery was morally accepted and common in New France (Quebec) starting in the late seventeenth century. Although most slaves were used as domestic servants, rather than forced labour, their lives were equally bleak and short[9] (Moore 166). Slavery was abolished in the United States in 1866. Abolition, in Canada, was a gradual process but slavery was formally outlawed within the British Empire in 1833. In today's society, we consider slavery morally repugnant, but if were living hundreds of years ago, given slavery was morally acceptable, we could not criticize such practices as wrong and evil.[10] Likewise, if we were living in Germany during the Second World War, the humiliation, torture, and extermination of Jews would be morally acceptable. In his book, *Hitler's Willing Executioners*, Daniel Goldhagen argues that German culture was highly anti-Semitic. Far from being morally repulsed with Hitler's "final solution," most Germans embraced it (see Photo 5.2). In short, the Jewish holocaust was a reflection of German morality. Again, if relativism is true we could not criticize Nazi Germany for their anti-Semitic practices. The extermination of six million Jews is merely different, not morally wrong.

Rachels, however, disagrees. Failure to condemn these practices, he says, is not "enlightened." What he is driving at is that these acts are cruel, pointless, and grossly unjust;

Photo 5.2   Hitler's Final Solution

If you were an ethical relativist, and living in Nazi Germany during the Second World War, would you have to accept Hitler's "final solution" to what he called the "Jewish problem"?

to inflict pain and suffering unnecessarily on individuals undermines the point and purpose of morality. Very roughly, the point of morality is to ensure a stable society, prevent human suffering, motivate humans to be the best people they can be, allow them to find meaning and happiness in life, create peace and freedom, and resolve conflicts of interests in just ways (Pojman 14). Minimally, to be moral is to be concerned impartially with everyone's interest that might be affected by our behaviour (Rachels 13–14). The study of ethics helps us determine what we ought to do, by integrating and learning from past mistakes. Slavery and genocide are two examples that undermine this intellectual tradition.

A third problem is that relativism prevents us from criticizing our own culture. If you are wondering if abortion, euthanasia, smoking marijuana, cheating on exams, and so forth are morally right or wrong, all you have to do is "look out the window," so to speak. That is, all you have to do is consult the standards of society. How do we do this? Well, we can ask friends and family, consult moral experts, and survey people on the street. And if the people on the street say that torturing innocent children, slavery, and bribery are morally acceptable, there would be nothing we could do or say about it. In short, we are prevented from criticizing the moral standards in our own society because to go against them is to act immorally. But, as Rachels points out, most of us rarely think the moral codes in our own society are perfect. If so, surely we have a duty to speak out against those things that we feel are morally wrong.

A fourth, and related argument, is that relativism leads to moral stultification. In other words, relativism impedes moral progress. Moral progress is based on individuals within and outside of society criticizing and pointing out what is wrong with current mores. Martin Luther King Jr. fought for the moral and legal right to vote in the United States; Gandhi forced the British government to give India independence; Nelson Mandela sought the end of racial discrimination in South Africa; and Nellie McClung, Emily Murphy, Henrietta Muir Edwards, Louise McKinney, and Irene Parlby (the group of five) fought for the recognition of women as persons under the British North America Act (see Box 5.7). But if relativism were correct, then we could not change society for the better.

Moral reformers could not challenge the morals of their own society because it's society that defines what is right or wrong. To go against society's moral code is to act unethically. And since, according to relativists, we must always abide by a society's moral code, reform is impossible. However, the fact of the matter is that morality does progress, often slowly and inconsistently, to end immoral practices like slavery, child labour, discrimination, racism, sexism, and so forth. Relativism would, however, prevent society from becoming better.

Relativism also raises another problem, not addressed by Rachels. Given that most cultures are pluralistic, which moral code do we live by or accept? Although most of us belong to a general culture with general moral norms, we also belong to various subcultures that can have conflicting moral perspectives. In March 2006, for example, South Dakota passed a new law banning all abortions, even in the case of rape or incest, except when a woman's life is at risk. Doctors found guilty of doing illegal abortions can face up to five years in jail and a $5,000 fine (Freeman A1). Now imagine you are an American, South Dakotan, feminist, and catholic. Which moral values do you choose to accept as morally correct? American culture, generally speaking, has accepted abortion as both morally acceptable and a legal right thanks to the 1973 *Roe v. Wade* landmark decision. Imagine you accept the *Roe v. Wade* decision but, as a South Dakotan, abortion is morally wrong except in the most extreme cases. Imagine further that you are feminist and volunteer at a organization supporting women's rights, including the right for access to abortion on demand. Furthermore, imagine you are a devoted Catholic, which means that abortion is immoral. Which cultural values do you accept? In this case, there are numerous cultural mores to follow and each would be right or wrong depending upon your perspective. There is no reason to choose one over the other if morality is based on cultural relativism. If correct, then relativism leads to moral ambiguity. Given

Box 5.7　Women's Rights in Canada: Some Notable Achievements

1875	Grace Lockhart is the first woman to be awarded a university degree (Mount Allison University).
1881	Charlotte Ross becomes the first woman to practise medicine in Western Canada.
1897	Clara Martin is the first woman to be admitted into the law profession in the British Empire.
1916	Manitoba becomes the first province to grant the right to vote and hold office to women.
1916	Alberta and Saskatchewan grant women the right to vote. Emily Murphy is appointed the first magistrate in the British Empire.
1917	B.C. and Ontario grant women the right to vote. Louise Mckinney and Roberta MacAdams become the first women to be elected into a provincial legislature (Alberta).
1918	Canadian government grant women the right to vote if over 21 years of age.

1921	Agnus McPhail is the first women elected to the House of Commons.
1930	Cairine Wilson becomes the first woman senator.
1940	Quebec grants women the right to vote and hold office.
1951	Charlotte Whitton becomes Canada's first mayor (Ottawa).
1984	Jeanne Sauvé appointed the first woman governor general of Canada.
1993	Catherine Callbeck is the first premier elected in Canada (Prince Edward Island).
1993	Following a party leadership convention, Kim Campbell becomes the first female Canadian prime minister.
1995	Christine Silverberg is the first female police chief in a major Canadian city (Calgary).
2002	Approximately one third of the Canadian Senate are women.

Source: "The Famous 5: Heroes for Today." *Heritage Community Foundation.* 2004. 3 November 2006 <http://www.abheritage.ca/famous5/timeline_text.html>.

this conflict, morality seems to have lost its action guiding purpose (Pojman 26).[11]

And how many people must hold the same view in order for a culture to accept it as morally correct? The quantitative value of morality becomes ambiguous if relativism is true. In other words, if morality is dependent upon society, what percentage of the population must agree with a moral code for it to be right and vice versa? Would 51 percent (60 percent? 75? 95?) be enough to establish moral norms? Consider the United States' invasion of Iraq. In 2003, when President George Bush decided to invade Iraq, according to opinions polls, over 70 percent of American people supported his decision. However, according to a CNN poll in 2006, support for the Iraq war had dropped to approximately 35 percent ("Poll"). But the moral pendulum could switch back the other way next week, month, or year. If relativism is correct, then the morality of the Iraq war will change, if the majority of the American population changes their minds. But surely the justification of moral issues cannot merely rest on the fact that a population changes its opinion. Again, what we need here is good argument and reasons to justify our moral opinions. One solution is to dispense with culture norms altogether. After all, isn't morality really a matter of personal preference and opinion?

Let me raise another objection not discussed by Rachels. Ethical relativism leads us to what is known as **subjective ethical relativism**: morality is not dependent on society but on the individual. That is, if there are no objectively valid norms of morality, then perhaps morality is merely a matter of personal taste and opinion. If so, for example, then a salesperson who helps only Asian customers; a worker who steals corporate secrets or bribes government officials; and a teacher who fails all of her students would all be morally acceptable according to their own personal subjective standards. In short, there would be no difference between Hitler and Mother Teresa if morality were merely a subjective opinion. If Mother Teresa believes helping the poor is moral and Hitler believes killing Jews is moral, then each opinion would be morally correct. But surely this is a mistake. If morality is merely a matter of personal opinion—if there is no objective morality—there can be no interpersonal comparison or argument about what is right or wrong. This means subjective ethical relativism is the antitheses of morality. As Wilfred Waluchow states in his *The Dimensions of Ethics*, "By its very nature morality is a means of helping to resolve disputes among people and of answering fundamental questions about how they should lead their lives. Subjectivism, which effectively says that the right moral standards are whatever ones happen to accept, seems to rob morality of its critical, action-guiding character"(77). The action-guiding character, then, must not come from personal opinion or culture but from an objective morality itself.

The last objection to ethical relativism is based on proof of some kind of objective morality. This idea is appealing because if we can find some objective moral truths that universally hold for all humans, regardless of culture, then relativism is clearly mistaken.

Consider infanticide, says Rachels. Did the Inuit, historically speaking, really have a fundamentally different set of moral beliefs and values than Canadians? Although it's true the Inuit did commit infanticide when hunting was poor, we ought not conclude their moral values were radically different from ours. The Inuit care for their children as much as any other culture.[12] As Rachels points out, if people did not care for their young, society's members would not be replaced and, over time, the society would die out. Therefore, cultures that exist must have a

moral prohibition against infanticide. This same reasoning, says Rachels, applies to a prohibition on murder and telling the truth. If societies did not have prohibitions against murder, people would try to isolate themselves from everyone else and society would collapse. A moral code against murder is the only way humans can cooperate and flourish together. In regards to telling the truth, a society with no prohibition on lying would find communication difficult, if not impossible, because communication is based on truthfulness. And without communication we would have great difficulty coordinating our collective actions to achieve various ends such as food, shelter, building roads, cars, computers, and so forth. In short, the success of society and business is based on truthfulness in our communicative exchanges.

The point here is that there are universal rules necessary for societies to exist and flourish.[13] For moral objectivists, like Rachels, objective moral principles must exist in order to have social order. Louis Pojman echoes these sentiments stating, "Principles like the Golden Rule, not killing innocent people, treating equals equally, telling the truth, keeping promises, and the like are central to the fluid progression of social interaction and the resolution of conflicts of which ethics are about…" (32). I don't know how many universal moral rules there are, but there would have to be enough to ensure a moral minimum so people could live in a stable society. The application of these moral values might also differ depending on a culture's environment, traditions, and customs. However, the point is that relativism is wrong. Not all moral beliefs are morally acceptable and it's wrong to conclude there are no objective ethical standards.

For ethical objectivists, morality does not depend on social custom or individual acceptance. If objectivism is true, then moral facts are independent of humans and potentially discoverable by everyone. So just as it was discovered that water boils at 100 degrees Celsius, we can discover that murder is wrong. But if moral objectivism is right, these supposed universal "moral facts" pose some very troubling questions: How do moral facts motivate us to act? How can we come to know moral facts? Which moral facts can we know? The famous English philosopher John Mackie argued against moral objectivism. He stated that if objectivism were true, moral facts would turn out to be very strange. First, moral facts would have to possess qualities different from anything else in the universe. Second, we would have to possess a special faculty or intuition to come and know these moral facts (Mackie 38–39). After all, morality is not like a table and chairs or other physical things that you can know via your senses. Nor can you do experiments to discover what is right or wrong. Moral facts would have to hold extraordinary (supernatural) power to motivate us to act and we would need to possess an equivalent sensory faculty. This strangeness regarding moral facts motivated Mackie to dismiss objectivism outright.

However, perhaps we ought not be so pessimistic. There may be widespread agreement regarding moral facts because we are all the same biological species and share the same evolutionary lineage. Or maybe we have discovered that certain agreed upon moral facts make life better and satisfies our basic needs. Either way, this is beyond present purposes. I will leave it up to you to explore the problems of objectivism on your own.

institutions including Duke University, New York University, and University of Miami before moving to the University of Alabama at Birmingham in 1977 to become chair of the philosophy department. His books include The Elements of Moral Philosophy *(1986),* The End of Life: Euthanasia and Morality *(1986),* Created from Animals: The Moral Implications of Darwinism *(1990),* Can Ethics Provide Answers? And Other Essays in Moral Philosophy *(1997), and* Problems from Philosophy *(2005). A kind and generous man, Rachels was considered one of the best moral philosophers of his generation with a passion for writing and a talent of making the most complex philosophical ideas easy to understand for students. His early textbook* Moral Problems *sold more than 100,000 copies and his most popular book,* The Elements of Moral Philosophy, *consistently outsells every other philosophy text on the market today. In conjunction to his books, he wrote over 85 essays dealing with many ethical issues, including euthanasia, animal rights, and ethical theory generally. He died of cancer on September 5, 2003.*

26

James Rachels

(1941–2003)

Born in Columbus, Georgia in 1941, James Rachels received his undergraduate degree from Mercer University and his Ph.D. from the University of North Carolina. He taught at a number of

The Challenge of Cultural Relativism

Morality differs in every society, and is a convenient term for socially approved habits.
—Ruth Benedict, *Patterns of Culture* (1934)

2.1. How Different Cultures Have Different Moral Codes

Darius, a king of ancient Persia, was intrigued by the variety of cultures he encountered in his travels. He had found, for example, that the Callatians (a tribe of Indians) customarily ate the bodies of their dead fathers. The Greeks, of course, did not do that—the Greeks practiced cremation and regarded the funeral pyre as the natural and fitting way to dispose of the dead. Darius thought that a sophisticated understanding of the world must include an appreciation of such differences between cultures. One day, to teach this lesson, he summoned some Greeks who happened to be present at his court and asked them what they would take to eat the bodies of their dead fathers. They were shocked, as Darius knew they would be, and replied that no amount of money could persuade them to do such a thing. Then Darius called in some Callatians, and while the Greeks listened asked them what they would take to burn their dead fathers' bodies. The Callatians were horrified and told Darius not even to mention such a dreadful thing.

This story, recounted by Herodotus in his *History*, illustrates a recurring theme in the literature of social science: different cultures have different moral codes. What is thought right within one group may be utterly abhorrent to the members of another group, and vice versa. Should we eat the bodies of the dead or burn them? If you were a Greek, one answer would seem obviously correct; but if you were a Callatian, the opposite would seem equally certain.

It is easy to give additional examples of the same kind. Consider the Eskimos. They are a remote and inaccessible people. Numbering only about 25,000, they live in small, isolated settlements scattered mostly along the northern fringes of North America and Greenland. Until the beginning of this century, the outside world knew little about them. Then explorers began to bring back strange tales.

Eskimo customs turned out to be very different from our own. The men often had more than one wife, and they would share their wives with guests, lending them for the night as a sign of hospitality. Moreover, within a community, a dominant male might demand—and

get—regular sexual access to other men's wives. The women, however, were free to break these arrangements simply by leaving their husbands and taking up with new partners—free, that is, so long as their former husbands chose not to make trouble. All in all, the Eskimo practice was a volatile scheme that bore little resemblance to what we call marriage.

But it was not only their marriage and sexual practices that were different. The Eskimos also seemed to have less regard for human life. Infanticide, for example, was common. Knud Rasmussen, one of the most famous early explorers, reported that he met one woman who had borne twenty children but had killed ten of them at birth. Female babies, he found were especially liable to be destroyed, and this was permitted simply at the parents' discretion, with no social stigma attached to it. Old people also, when they became too feeble to contribute to the family, were left out in the snow to die. So there seemed to be, in this society, remarkably little respect for life.

To the general public, these were disturbing revelations. Our own way of living seems so natural and right that for many for us it is hard to conceive of others living so differently. And when we do hear of such things, we tend immediately to categorize those other peoples as "backward" or "primitive." But to anthropologists and sociologists, there was nothing particularly surprising about the Eskimos. Since the time of Herodotus, enlightened observers have been accustomed to the idea that conceptions of right and wrong differ from culture to culture. If we assume that *our* ideas of right and wrong will be shared by all peoples at all times, we are merely naïve.

2.2. Cultural Relativism

To many thinkers, this observation—"Different cultures have different moral codes"—has seemed to be the key to understanding morality.

The idea of universal truth in ethics, they say, is a myth. The customs of different societies are all that exist. These customs cannot be said to be "correct" or "incorrect," for that implies we have an independent standard of right and wrong by which they may be judged. But there is no such independent standard; every standard is culture-bound. The great pioneering sociologist William Graham Sumner, writing in 1906, put the point like this:

> The "right" way is the way which the ancestors used and which has been handed down. The tradition is its own warrant. It is not held subject to verification by experience. The notion of right is in the folkways. It is not outside of them, of independent origin, and brought to test them. In the folkways, whatever is, is right. This is because they are traditional, and therefore contain in themselves the authority of the ancestral ghosts. When we come to the folkways we are at the end of our analysis.

This line of thought has probably persuaded more people to be skeptical about ethics than any other single thing. *Cultural Relativism*, as it has been called, challenges our ordinary belief in the objectivity and universality of moral truth. It says, in effect, that there is no such thing as universal truth in ethics; there are only the various cultural codes, and nothing more. Moreover, our own code has no special status; it is merely one among many.

As we shall see, this basic idea is really a compound of several different thoughts. It is important to separate the various elements of the theory because, on analysis, some parts of the theory turn out to be correct, whereas others seem to be mistaken. As a beginning, we may distinguish the following claims, all of which have been made by cultural relativists:

1. Different societies have different moral codes.
2. There is no objective standard that can be used to judge one societal code better than one another.
3. The moral code of our own society has no special status; it is merely one among many.
4. There is no "universal truth" in ethics—that is, there are no moral truths that hold for all people at all times.
5. The moral code of a society determines what is right within that society; that is, if the moral code of a society says that a certain action is right, then that action *is* right, at least within that society.
6. It is mere arrogance for us to try to judge the conduct of other peoples. We should adopt an attitude of tolerance toward the practices of other cultures.

Although, it may seem that these six propositions go naturally together, they are independent of one another, in the sense that some of them might be true even if others are false. In what follows, we will try to identify what is correct in Cultural Relativism, but we will also be concerned to expose what is mistaken about it.

2.3. The Cultural Differences Argument

Cultural Relativism is a theory about the nature of morality. At first blush it seems quite plausible. However, like all such theories, it may be evaluated by subjecting it to rational analysis; and when we analyze Cultural Relativism we find that it is not so plausible as it first appears to be.

The first thing we need to notice is that at the heart of Cultural Relativism there is a certain *form of argument.* The strategy used by cultural relativism is to argue from facts about the differences between cultural outlooks to a conclusion about the status of morality. Thus we are invited to accept this reasoning:

1. The Greeks believed it was wrong to eat the dead, whereas the Callatians believed it was right to eat the dead.
2. Therefore, eating the dead is neither objectively right nor objectively wrong. It is merely a matter of opinion, which varies from culture to culture.

Or, alternatively:

1. The Eskimos see nothing wrong with infanticide, whereas Americans believe infanticide is immoral.
2. Therefore, infanticide is neither objectively right nor objectively wrong. It is merely a matter of opinion, which varies from culture to culture.

Clearly, these arguments are variations of one fundamental idea. They are both special cases of a more general argument, which says:

1. Different cultures have different moral codes.
2. Therefore, there is no objective "truth" in morality. Right and wrong are only matters of opinion, and opinions vary from culture to culture.

We may call this the *Cultural Differences Argument*. To many people, it is very persuasive. But from a logical point of view, is it s *sound* argument?

It is not sound. The trouble is that the conclusion does not really follow from the premise— that is, even if the premise is true, the conclusion still might be false. The premise concerns what people *believe*: in some societies, people believe one thing; in other societies, people believe differently. The conclusion, however, concerns *what really is the case*. The trouble is that this sort of conclusion does not follow logically from this sort of premise.

Consider again the example of the Greeks and Callatians. The Greeks believed it was wrong to eat the dead; the Callatians believed it was right. Does it follow, *from the mere fact that they disagreed*, that there is no objective truth in the matter? No, it does not follow; for it *could* be that the practice was objectively right (or wrong) and that one or the other of them was simply mistaken.

To make the point clearer, consider a very different matter. In some societies, people believe the earth is flat. In other societies, such as our own, people believe this earth is (roughly) spherical. Does it follow, *from the mere fact that they disagree*, that there is no "objective truth" in geography? Of course not; we would never draw such a conclusion because we realize that, in their beliefs about the world, the members of some societies might simply be wrong. There is no reason to think that if the world is round everyone must know it. Similarly, there is no reason to think that if there is moral truth everyone must know it. The fundamental mistake in the Cultural Differences Argument is that it attempts to derive a substantive conclusion about a subject (morality) from the mere facts that people disagree about it.

It is important to understand the nature of the point that is being made here. We are *not* saying (not yet, anyway) that the conclusion of the argument is false. Insofar as anything being said here is concerned, it is still an open question whether the conclusion is true. We *are* making a purely logical point and saying that the conclusion does not *follow from* the premise. This is important, because in order to determine whether the conclusion is true, we need arguments in its support. Cultural Relativism proposes this argument, but unfortunately the argument turns out to be fallacious. So it proves nothing.

2.4. The Consequences of Taking Cultural Relativism Seriously

Even if the Cultural Differences Argument is invalid, Cultural Relativism might still be true. What would it be like if it were true?

In the passage quoted above, William Graham Sumner summarizes the essence of Cultural Relativism. He says that there is no measure of right and wrong other than the standards of one's society: "The notion of right is in the folkways. It is not outside of them, of independent origin, and brought to test them. In the folkways, whatever is, is right."

Suppose we took this seriously. What would be some of the consequences?

1. *We could no longer say that the customs of other societies are morally inferior to our own.* This, of course, is one of the main points stressed by Cultural Relativism. We would have to stop condemning other societies merely because they are "different." So long as we concentrate on certain examples, such as the funerary practices of the Greeks and Callatians, this may seem to be sophisticated, enlightened attitude.

However, we would also be stopped from criticizing other, less benign practices. Suppose a society waged war on its neighbors for the purpose of taking slaves. Or suppose a society was violently anti-Semitic and its leaders set out to destroy the Jews. Cultural Relativism would preclude us from saying that either of these practices was wrong. We would not even be able to say that a society tolerant of Jews is *better* than the

anti-Semitic society, for that would imply some sort of transcultural standard of comparison. The failure to condemn *these* practices does not seem "enlightened"; on the contrary, slavery and anti-Semitism seem wrong *wherever* they occur. Nevertheless, if we took Cultural Relativism seriously, we would have to admit that these social practices also are immune from criticism.

2. *We could decide whether actions are right or wrong just by consulting the standards of our society.* Cultural Relativism suggests a simple test for determining what is right and what is wrong; all one has to do is ask whether the action is in accordance with the code of one's society. Suppose a resident of South Africa is wondering whether his country's policy of *apartheid*—rigid racial segregation—is morally correct. All he has to do is ask whether this policy conforms to his society's moral code. If it does, there is nothing to worry about, at least from a moral point of view.

This implication of Cultural Relativism is disturbing because few of us think that our society's code is perfect—we can think of ways it might be improved. Yet Cultural Relativism would not only forbid us from criticizing the codes of *other* societies; it would stop us from criticizing our *own*. After all, if right and wrong are relative to culture, this must be true for our own culture just as much as for others.

3. *The idea of moral progress is called into doubt.* Usually, we think that at least some changes in our society have been for the better. (Some, of course, may have been changes for the worse.) Consider this example: Throughout most of Western history the place of women in society was very narrowly circumscribed. They could not own property; they could not vote or hold political office; with a few exceptions, they were not permitted to have paying jobs; and generally they were under the almost absolute

control of their husbands. Recently much of this has changed, and most people think of it as progress.

If Cultural Relativism is correct, can we legitimately think of this as progress? Progress means replacing a way of doing things with a *better* way. But by what standard do we judge the new ways as better? If the old ways were in accordance with the social standards of their time, then Cultural Relativism would say it is a mistake to judge them by the standards of a different time. Eighteenth-century society was, in effect, a different society from the one we have now. To say that we have made progress implies a judgment that present-day society is better, and that is just the sort of transcultural judgment that, according to Cultural Relativism, is impermissible.

Our idea of social *reform* will also have to be reconsidered. A reformer such as Martin Luther King, Jr., seeks to change his society for the better. Within the constraints imposed by Cultural Relativism, there is one way this might be done. If a society is not living up to its own ideals, the reformer may be regarded as acting for the best; the ideals of the society are the standard by which we judge his or her proposals as worthwhile. But the "reformer" may not challenge the ideals themselves, for those ideals are by definition correct. According to Cultural Relativism, then, the idea of social reform makes sense only in this very limited way.

These three consequences of Cultural Relativism have led many thinkers to reject it as implausible on its face. It does make sense, they say, to condemn some practices, such as slavery and anti-Semitism, wherever they occur. It makes sense to think that our own society has made some moral progress, while admitting that it is still imperfect and in need of reform. Because Cultural Relativism

says that these judgment make no sense, the argument goes, it cannot be right.

2.5. Why There Is Less Disagreement Than It Seems

The original impetus for Cultural Relativism comes from the observation that cultures differ dramatically in their views of right and wrong. But just how much do they differ? It is true that there are differences. However, it is easy to overestimate the extent of those differences. Often, when we examine what *seems* to be a dramatic difference, we find that the cultures do not differ nearly as much as it appears.

Consider a culture in which people believe it is wrong to eat cows. This may even be a poor culture, in which there is not enough food; still, the cows are not to be touched. Such a society would *appear* to have values very different from our own. But does it? We have not yet asked why these people will not eat cows. Suppose it is because they believe that after death that souls of humans inhabit the bodies of animals, especially cows, so that a cow may be someone's grandmother. Now do we want to say that their values are different from ours? No; the difference lies elsewhere. The difference is in our belief systems, not in our values. We agree that we shouldn't eat Grandma; we simply disagree about whether the cow *is* (or could be) Grandma.

The general point is this. Many factors work together to produce the customs of a society. The society's values are only one of them. Other matters, such as the religious and factual beliefs held by its members and the physical circumstances in which they must live, are also important. We cannot conclude, then, merely because customs differ, that there is a disagreement about *values*. The difference is customs may be attributable to some other aspect of social life. Thus there may be less disagreement about values than there appears to be.

Consider the Eskimos again. They often kill perfectly normal infants, especially girls. We do not approve of this at all; a parent who did this in our society would be locked up. Thus there appears to be a great difference in the values of our two cultures. But suppose we ask *why* the Eskimos do this. The explanation is not that they have less affection for their children or less respect for human life. An Eskimo family will always protect its babies if conditions permit. But they live in a harsh environment, where food is often in short supply. A fundamental postulate of Eskimo thought is: "Life is hard, and the margin of safety small." A family may want to nourish its babies but be unable to do so.

As in many "primitive" societies, Eskimo mothers will nurse their infants over a much longer period of time than mothers in our culture. The child will take nourishment from its mother's breast for four years, perhaps even longer. So even in the best of times there are limits to the number of infants that one mother can sustain. Moreover, the Eskimos are a nomadic people—unable to farm, they must move about in search of food. Infants must be carried, and a mother can carry only one baby in her parka as she travels and goes about her outdoor work. Other family members can help, but this is not always possible.

Infant girls are more readily disposed of because, first, in this society the males are the primary food providers—they are the hunters, according to the traditional division of labor—and it is obviously important to maintain a sufficient number of food gatherers. But there is an important second reason as well. Because the hunters suffer a high casualty rate, the adult men who die prematurely far outnumber the women who die early. Thus if male and female infants survived in equal numbers, the female adult population would greatly outnumber the male population. Examining the available statistics, one writer concluded that "were it not for female infanticide . . . there would be approximates one-and-a-half as many females in the average Eskimo local group as there are food-producing males."

So among the Eskimos, infanticide does not signal a fundamentally different attitude toward children. Instead, it is a recognition that drastic measures are sometimes needed to ensure the family's survival. Even then, however, killing the baby is not the first option considered. Adoption is common; childless couples are especially happy to take a more fertile couple's "surplus." Killing is only the last resort. I emphasize this in order to show that the raw data of the anthropologists can be misleading; it can make the differences in values between the cultures appear greater than they are. The Eskimos' values are not all that different from our values. It is only that life forces upon them choices that we do not have to make.

2.6. How All Cultures Have Some Values in Common

It should not be surprising that, despite appearances, the Eskimos are protective of their children. How could it be otherwise? How could a group survive that did *not* value its young? This suggests a certain argument, one which shows that all cultural groups must be protective of their infants:

1. Human infants are helpless and cannot survive if they are not given extensive care for a period of years.
2. Therefore, if a group did not care for its young, the young would not survive, and

the older members of the group would not be replaced. After a while the group would die out.

3. Therefore, any cultural group that continues to exist must care for its young. Infants that are *not* cared for must be the exception rather than the rule.

Similar reasoning shows that other values must be more or less universal. Imagine what it would be like for a society to place no value at all on truth telling. When one person spoke to another, there would be no presumption at all that he was telling the truth—for he could just as easily be speaking falsely. Within that society, there would be no reason to pay attention to what anyone says. (I ask you what time it is, and say "Four o'clock." But there is no presumption that you are speaking truly; you could just as easily have say the first thing that came into your head. So I have no reason to pay attention to your answer—in fact, there was no point in my asking you in the first place!) Communication would then be extremely difficult, if not impossible. And because complex societies cannot exist without regular communication among their members, society would become impossible. It follows that in any complex society there *must* be a presumption in favor of truthfulness. There may of course be exceptions to this rule: there may be situations in which it is thought to be permissible to lie. Nevertheless, these will be exceptions to a rule that *is* in force in the society.

Let me give one further example of the same type. Could a society exist in which there was no prohibition on murder? What would this be like? Suppose people were free to kill other people at will, and no one thought there was anything wrong with it. In such a "society," no one could feel secure. Everyone would have to be constantly on guard. People who wanted to survive would have to avoid other people as much as possible. This would inevitably result in individuals trying to become as self-sufficient as possible—after all, associating with others would be dangerous. Society on any large scale would collapse. Of course, people might band together in smaller groups with others that they *could* trust not to harm them. But notice what this means: they would be forming smaller societies that *did* acknowledge a rule against murder. The prohibitions of murder, then, is a necessary feature of all societies.

There is a general theoretical point here, namely, that *there are some moral rules that all societies will have in common, because those rules are necessary for society to exist.* The rules against lying and murder are two examples. And in fact, we do find these rules in force in all viable cultures. Cultures may differ in what they regard as legitimate exceptions to the rules, but this disagreement exists against a background of agreement on the larger issues. Therefore, it is a mistake to overestimate the amount of difference between cultures. Not *every* moral rule can vary from society to society.

2.7. What Can Be Learned from Cultural Relativism

At the outset, I said that we are going to identify both what is right and what is wrong in Cultural Relativism. Thus far I have mentioned only its mistakes: I have said that it rests on an invalid argument, that it has consequences that make it implausible on its face, and that the extent of cultural disagreement is far less that it implies. This all adds up to a pretty thorough repudiation of the theory. Nevertheless, it is still a very appealing idea, and the reader may have the feeling that all this is a little unfair. The theory *must* have something going for it, or else why has it been so influential? In fact, I think there *is* something right about Cultural Relativism, and now I want to say what that is. There are two lessons we should learn from the theory, even if we ultimately reject it.

1. Cultural Relativism warns us, quite rightly, about the danger of assuming that all our preferences are based on some absolute rational standard. They are not. Many (but not all) of our practices are merely peculiar to our society, and it is easy to lose sight of that fact. In reminding us of it, the theory does a service.

Funerary practices are one example. The Callatians, according to Herodotus, were "men who eat their fathers"—a shocking idea, to us at least. But eating the flesh of the dead could be understood as a sign of respect. It could be taken as a symbolic act that says: We wish this person's spirit to dwell within us. Perhaps this was the understanding of the Callatians. On such a way of thinking, burying the dead could be seen as an act of rejection, and burning the corpse as positively scornful. If this is hard to imagine, then we may need to have our imaginations stretched. Of course we may feel in visceral repugnance at the idea of eating human flesh in any circumstances. But what of it? This repugnance may be, as the relativists say, only a matter of what is customary in our particular society.

There are many other matters that we tend to think of in terms of objective right and wrong, but that are really nothing more than social conventions. Should women cover their breasts? A publicly exposed breast is scandalous in our society, whereas in other cultures it is unremarkable. Objectively speaking, it is neither right nor wrong—there is no objective reason why either custom is better. Cultural Relativism beings with the valuable insight that many of our practices are like this—they are only cultural products. Then it goes wrong by concluding that, because *some* practices are like this, *all* must be.

2. The second lesson has to do with keeping an open mind. In the course of growing up, each of us has acquired some strong feelings: we have learned to think of some types of conduct as acceptable, and others we have learned to regard as simply unacceptable. Occasionally, we may find those feelings challenged. We may encounter someone who claims that our feelings are mistaken. For example, we may have been taught that homosexuality is immoral, and we may feel quite uncomfortable around gay people and see them as alien and "different." Now someone suggests that this may be a mere prejudice; that there is nothing evil about homosexuality; that gay people are just people, like anyone else, who happen, through no choice of their own, to be attracted to others of the same sex. But because we feel so strongly about the matter, we find it hard to take this seriously. Even after we listen to the arguments, we may still have the unshakable feeling that homosexuals *must*, somehow be an unsavory lot.

Cultural Relativism, by stressing that our moral views can reflect the prejudices of our society, provides an antidote for this kind of dogmatism. When he tells the story of the Greeks and Callatians, Herodotus adds:

> For if anyone, no matter who, were given the opportunity of choosing from amongst all the nations of the world the set of beliefs which he thought best, he would

inevitably, after careful consideration of their relative merits, choose that of his own country. Everyone without exception believes his own native customs, and the religion he was brought up in, to be the best.

Realizing this can result in our having more open minds. We can come to understand that our feelings are not necessarily perceptions of the truth—they may be nothing more than the result of cultural condition. Thus when we hear it suggested that some element of our social code is *not* really the best and we find ourselves instinctively resisting the suggestion, we might stop and remember this. Then we may be more open to discovering the truth, whatever that might be.

We can understand the appeal of Cultural Relativism, then, even though the theory has serious shortcomings. It is an attractive theory because it is based on a genuine insight—that many of the practice and attitudes we think so natural are really only cultural products. Moreover, keeping this insight firmly in view is important if we want to avoid arrogance and have open minds. These are important points, not to be taken lightly. But we can accept these points without going on to accept the whole theory.

Notes

The story of the Greeks and the Callatians is from Herodotus, *The Histories*, translated by Audrey de Selincourt, revised by A. R. Burn (Harmondsworth, Middlesex: Penguin Books, 1972), pp. 219–220. The quotation from Herodotus toward the end of the chapter is from the same source.

Information about the Eskimos was taken from Peter Freuschen, *Book of the Eskimos* (New York: Fawcett, 1961); and E. Adamson Hoebel, *The Law of Primitive Man* (Cambridge: Harvard University Press, 1954), Chapter 5.

The estimate of how female infanticide affects the male/female ratio in the adult Eskimo population is from Hoebel's work.

The William Graham Sumner quotation is from his *Folkways* (Boston: Ginn and Compay, 1906), p. 28.

Utilitarianism

Nature has placed mankind under the governance of two sovereign masters, pain and pleasure. It is for them alone to point out what we ought to do, as well as to determine what we shall do.

—Jeremy Bentham

Discussion Questions

1. More than 4,000 Canadians are waiting for organ transplants at any one time of year. In 2005, 1,805 organ transplants were performed in Canada, but 195 people died while awaiting surgery ("Organ and Tissue"). Now imagine you are a transplant surgeon frustrated by the fact that many of your patients will die waiting for organs. One day on your way to work, you walk by a homeless person. You stop and talk to him and discover that he is relatively healthy, has no family or friends, and is not addicted to drugs or alcohol. Imagine further that you have five patients waiting for different specific organs: kidney, heart, lung, liver, and pancreas. You invite the man to the hospital for a hot lunch. You slip him a sedative in his soup, take him to an operating room, and begin to remove his organs to give to your patients. As a utilitarian, you figure that killing this innocent man and distributing his healthy organs to your patients will maximize happiness (Harman 156). In what ways might this be morally justified? How might a rule utilitarian respond?

2. If you are a utilitarian, you are to act in way that will maximize happiness. But does utilitarianism

require too much effort and sacrifice (Harman 157)? If you are reading this book, chances are you are in university or college and have spent considerable money to take this course and get an education. But if we take utilitarianism seriously, all the money you spent on books and tuition would maximize more happiness if it was donated to charity. Moreover, you could maximize more utility if you stopped pursuing your educational goals and instead volunteered your time helping African AIDS victims or raising money to prevent children dying of malnutrition and malaria.[14] In other words, if you take utilitarianism seriously, by reading this book (or getting an education, going to movies, watching TV, hanging out with friends, etc.) you are not doing what you *ought* to be doing, which is maximizing happiness. In short, reading this book is morally wrong. Would you agree with this? Does utilitarianism require us to do too much? Why or why not? How might a utilitarian respond to this criticism?

The Greatest Happiness for the Greatest Number

Utilitarianism is a normative teleological theory which focuses on the consequences of a person's actions to determine what is right or wrong. Historically, Jeremy Bentham (1748–1832) and John Stuart Mill (1806–1873) were the strongest supporters of utilitarianism. Put simply, an act is morally right if it produces the greatest amount of happiness for the greatest amount of people. Utilitarianism, generally speaking, comes in two forms: act and rule. Before I get into specifics, let's look at a few examples of **act utilitarianism** since this is what is espoused by Bentham and Mill.

Let's go back to the example at the beginning of this chapter. You see two boys set fire to a cat and you are desperately trying to explain to the boys what they did was wrong. From a utilitarian perspective, setting a cat on fire is wrong because of the pain and suffering it causes to the cat, the

cat's owner, and also to the boys. According to the Canadian Criminal Code, cruelty to animals is punishable by up to six months in jail and a $2,000 fine.[15] This would mean that if the boys were charged, arrested, and convicted of their crimes, they would go to jail and/or pay a fine. These punishments are certain to cause unhappiness since they, or their parents, will be out thousands of dollars; their parents may be mad, humiliated, and embarrassed at their son's behaviour; and if they go to jail, the boys will be deprived of various privileges, including playing video games, going to the movies, and hanging out with their school friends. If the boys were utilitarians, despite the fact that the boys derived a certain amount of happiness from burning the cat, they would have reasoned that their actions caused substantially more unhappiness than happiness. In short, they ought not to have burned the cat.

Let's consider another example. Imagine you are struggling with this course and are contemplating whether to cheat on an upcoming exam. If you successfully cheat (do not get caught) on the exam, you might pass the course with a high mark; a great mark might increase your grade point average (GPA); a high GPA might get you into law school and ultimately fulfill your dreams of becoming a lawyer; and your parents and friends might be proud of you. In short, everyone will be happy. However, if you unsuccessfully cheat (get caught), then you would fail the test and class; your GPA would suffer and your dream of law school would be dashed; and your parents and friends might be unhappy and humiliated by your actions. From a utilitarian perspective, cheating on the exam is wrong because the total amount of potential unhappiness outweighs the potential happiness and, therefore, you ought not cheat.

Or consider infidelity. Imagine Fred is happily married with two children, living in a middle-class neighbourhood in Montreal. As a sales representative for a multinational company, he is often away from home, travelling to conferences and trade shows. One night, after a long day of making sales, he sits in the hotel's bar alone, when a gorgeous woman sits down beside him for a drink. They begin to talk, and after a few drinks, she invites Fred up to her room. Although Fred is deeply tempted sexually, he reasons that if he were to commit infidelity it would cause more unhappiness than happiness. Fred takes into consideration not only the act of sexual gratification itself, which would bring him and her happiness, but also the pain and unhappiness of his wife if she were to find out (and the impending divorce); the guilt he would feel; the pain and suffering of his children; and the financial costs of alimony and child support. In this case, if Fred were a utilitarian, although flattered, he ought to turn down her request. In short, cheating on his wife would create more unhappiness than happiness for everyone involved. Infidelity is immoral.

Utilitarian theory has two key points: 1) human happiness is the ultimate moral good; and 2) actions should be evaluated by virtue of their consequences. In other words, for utilitarianism, we ought to maximize utility. Utility means any object or act that produces a benefit, good, pleasure, or happiness (these words are used synonymously). Let's take each point in turn. For Bentham and Mill, happiness or pleasure is the only goal in life that has intrinsic value. That is, we ought to seek pleasure/happiness and avoid pain/unhappiness. This is also known as **hedonism**. It should also be pointed out that there is no difference between happiness and pleasure; both are considered a state of satisfaction that can be attained through food, sex, education, art, poetry, music, and so forth. Since happiness is the main goal, this means the motives behind a person's actions, and the nature of the acts themselves, are irrelevant to determining if an act is right or wrong. We determine what is right or wrong by looking at the most reasonable consequences given the circumstances in which you find yourself, and the various alternative courses of action you could have taken. So, if not setting the cat on fire, not cheating on an exam, or staying faithful to your spouse all have the consequence of increasing the total amount of happiness for everyone affected by your actions, then this is the morally correct act. The converse is also true. If setting fire to the cat, cheating on the exam,

and committing infidelity all decrease the total amount of happiness for everyone affected by your actions, then this act is morally incorrect. In other words, taking into consideration the greatest happiness principle, an act is right if it produces greater proportion of utility (happiness) over disutility (unhappiness).

However, situations might arise when no matter what we do we will cause more disutility than utility. In other words, there will be time when we are damned if we do X and damned if we don't do X. What do we do then? In such cases, for utilitarian, we must act in ways that will produce the smallest amount of unhappiness or disutility. That is, we must minimize suffering.

Let's consider euthanasia. Sue Rodriguez lived in Victoria, B.C. At age 40, she was diagnosed with Amyotrophic Lateral Sclerosis (ALS) (also know as Lou Gehrig's disease after the famous baseball player). ALS is a progressively fatal neurodegenerative disease that affects the central nervous system. The disease causes muscle weakness and atrophy, which, over time, means ALS sufferers lose the ability to walk, talk, swallow, physically move, and, eventually, breathe. It is a slow, painful death. But what makes this disease so hideous is that ALS does not affect the mind. The individual's memories, intelligence, and personality remain intact. Knowing that a painful death was inevitable, Rodriguez decided to try and attain some control over how she died. She would enjoy live for as long as the disease would allow, but she did not want to experience the painful final stages of disease (Thomas and Waluchow 183). She decided to commit suicide. By committing suicide she would mitigate or lessen her pain and suffering. The problem was that by the time she was unable to enjoy life, she would be unable to physically terminate her own life. She petitioned the Canadian courts to allow a medical practitioner to assist her in her death "by her own hand." Notice, Rodriguez was not asking for someone else to take her own life (euthanasia) but only asking for assistance in committing suicide (physician-assisted suicide). Unfortunately, according to the Criminal Code of Canada, aiding and abetting a person to commit suicide is a criminal offence. Rodriquez decided to challenge the law. The Supreme Court of Canada rejected her legal request for physician-assisted suicide. (Shortly after the ruling, Rodriguez took her own life with the help of an unidentified physician [Thomas and Waluchow 184]). The Rodriguez case raises some fundamental moral issues: Do we have a right to hasten our own or another's death? Should we respect an individual's right and autonomy to die with dignity? Does helping another commit suicide violate a physician's duty to never harm a patient? Would permitting physician-assisted suicide lead to involuntary euthanasia? The moral and legal issues get complicated, but for our concerns, a utilitarian might argue that physician-assisted suicide is morally justified. If a physician does help Rodriquez commit suicide, the physician might go to jail, feel guilt, or lose his or her medical licence. However, if a physician does not help Rodriguez, allowing the disease to progress naturally, this will cause even greater suffering than losing one's medical licence. Helping Rodriquez take her life, despite the unhappy consequences of jail, guilt, or losing one's licence to practise medicine, minimizes the overall the pain and suffering once all affected parties are considered. In other words, physician-assisted suicide is moral.

However, despite the fact that Mill and Bentham both believe that happiness and pleasure is the ultimate goal for humans, they differ in one significant way. For Bentham, we must only consider the *quantity* of pleasure produced by an act, whereas for Mill, we must consider the *quantity* and *quality* of the pleasure produced by an act. This is important because, if Bentham is right, then that there is no difference between pushpin[16] and poetry. That is, reading a book, going out with friends for dinner, attending philosophy class, watching TV, attending the latest exhibit at the museum, and getting drunk at a party are of equal value so long as they generate the same quantity of pleasure. This means that if you get 6 units of pleasure by going out with friends for dinner, and attending philosophy class gives you 2 units of pleasure, then attending three philosophy classes will give you the equal

quantitative amount of happiness as going out once with friends. In short, it's the quantity of happiness that matters nothing else.

The problem with Bentham's utilitarian approach, says Mill, is that if there is no difference between the "intellectual" pleasures (aesthetic, poetry, philosophy, literature, etc.) and the "sensual" pleasures (food, drink, sex, etc.), we will be hard pressed to achieve our end goal of happiness. Why? Because some things have a qualitative value that makes them more pleasurable. Attending philosophy class, for example, has greater qualitative value than getting drunk because it will lead to greater happiness in the long run. Although getting drunk may produce immediate pleasure, it's ultimately fleeting in nature, and you also have to put up with a hangover. Attending philosophy class, on the other hand, can give you the intellectual pleasures of searching for truth, justice, and the meaning of life. Moreover, attending philosophy class will allow you to finish the course as part of a degree requirement and graduate. Graduating with your degree has itself qualitative value. Let's face it, college and university is hard work. There is a tremendous amount of reading and assignments; you have to put of with bad teachers; exams are stressful; and it costs lots of money, meaning most students graduate with substantial debts.[17] However, completing your degree can give you such a deep sense of happiness it outstrips the more sensual pleasures. As we said earlier, Socrates spent much of his life in frustration looking for various philosophical truths, of which he claimed to find none. But his dogged pursuit of truth gave him a deep sense of happiness that nothing comparable could be derived from more beastly pleasures. Likewise, for Mill, "It's better to be a human being dissatisfied than a pig satisfied"; humans would not be happy or satisfied with what satisfies a pig (Pojman 77). Thus, when it comes to determining what actions are morally right and wrong, we must consider the pleasure and happiness produced in others and ourselves both quantitatively and qualitatively. So, for example, in Fred's decision whether to commit infidelity he must compare the immediate sensual pleasure of the sexual act and the long-term deep, caring relationship he is putting at risk. In other words, the quantity and quality of pleasure derived from a loving and caring relationship with his wife and children will outweigh the immediate quantity and quality of the illicit affair. In short, infidelity is immoral.

With this in mind we can formulate what is known as classic or act utilitarianism (see Box 5.8).

Box 5.8 Six Theses of Utilitarianism

1. Consequentialism: The rightness of an act is determined solely by their consequences.

2. Hedonism: The theory is identified with seeking pleasure (happiness) and avoiding pain (unhappiness).

3. Maximalism: A right action must produce the greatest amount of good consequences when the bad consequences are taken into consideration.

4. Universalism: In determining the morality of an action, we must take into consideration the happiness and unhappiness of everyone affected by the action equally and impartially.

5. No Absolutism: Utilitarian theory is not absolutist. That is, lying, breaking one's promises, murder, or stealing, for example, are not always wrong. Such acts can be moral so long as they maximize overall net happiness.

6. Look at Present and Future Consequences: Utilitarianism requires us to consider both immediate and future foreseeable consequences. For each action we must take into account the long-term happiness and unhappiness of each person who is affected by the action.

Source: Adapted from John Boatright. (2007*). Ethics and the Conduct of Business.* 5th Edition. Upper Saddle River, New Jersey: Pearson Prentice Hall, 34.

As Richard Brandt states in his article, "If doing *A* has, amongst all the things X can do, the maximum net expectable utility, then it is X's objective duty to do *A*." In other words, from an ethical point of view, an act is right, if and only if, the sum total of utilities produced by that act is greater than another act. For act utilitarians, we must balance one set of pleasures and pain against other alternative courses of action. If an act will produce good consequences, it should be taken; if it produces bad consequences, it should not be taken. Moreover, sometimes we may have to do things that are counterintuitive, like lying, cheating, stealing, etc., in order to maximize happiness. As Brandt points out, utilitarianism leaves little room for absolutist moral maxims like "Keep your promises" and "Always tell the truth." We can, given the circumstances, break these maxims if in doing so we maximize overall net utility.[18]

For Brandt, utilitarianism is an attractive theory for a number of reasons. First, it fits nicely with our moral intuitions about trying to maximize the overall welfare of society. That is, we have a duty to try to improve the lives of others when we can. To put a finer point on Brandt's claim, people often talk about the rightness or wrongness of a specific action based on its harms and benefits. For example, lying and breaking promises are wrong because you end up hurting others. Saving a child from a burning building is right because the child will be alive and continue to enjoy life (Velasquez, *Business Ethics* 74–75). Second, most people don't feel they are obligated to follow strict rules such as keeping promises, telling the truth, and so forth. The problem, says Brandt, is that rules can conflict with each other, leaving us morally impotent. For example, during the Second World War, Dutch fisherman would often smuggle Jews to England from Europe and occasionally the Nazi navy would stop these boats. When asked who was on board and where they were bound, the Dutch fishermen would lie in order to protect the lives of innocent people. In this case, we have a conflict of two rules: "Always tell the truth" and "Always protect innocent lives." And if we were to strictly follow both rules,[19] this leaves us in an unacceptable position, since we would not know which rule ought to take priority. But, for act utilitarianism, this is not a problem. We ought to act in ways that maximize the general welfare, and if this means lying to protect innocent lives, then lying is morally acceptable (Rachels 126–127). However, on a more general level, lying is generally wrong because of its cost to human welfare. If everyone lied, then we would be less apt to trust each other and cooperate with each other, which would have a negative effect on the welfare of humans. Conversely, telling the truth strengthens relationships and cooperation, thereby increasing overall welfare of humans. But utilitarians would not say that lying is never wrong. After all, in some situations lying may be moral if it brings about good consequences. And there is one more advantage we can add to Brandt's list. Utilitarianism fits well when discussing government policy and public goods. The Canadian government, for example, receives approximately $228 billion in revenue from taxes. The government, in turn, then decides how to spend the money (health care, roads, military, national parks, education, etc.) to benefit the maximum number of Canadians. I think most Canadians would agree, in deciding how our taxes should be spent, it makes sense to spend our money in such a way that it increases the overall utility of most Canadians, rather than, say, giving the money to one province. This would be blatantly unfair (Velasquez, *Business Ethics* 74–75).

Problems with Utilitarianism

In his article, Brandt outlines a number of problems with act utilitarianism. First, some actions are intrinsically wrong despite maximizing happiness. That is, utilitarianism allows people to escape their moral obligations to others. To see this, using a different example from Brandt, let's consider this well-worn hypothetical situation.

Imagine you and your friend Mary are stranded alone on a desert island. Having been on the island for a number of weeks, you have explored it thoroughly and discover hidden treasure. Once rescued, both of you will be rich beyond your wildest dreams. Unfortunately, Mary has been infected with a deadly disease known as *plasmodium falciparum* malaria. With no help forthcoming, you spend weeks beside Mary tending to her illness. As the headache, vomiting, diarrhea, and muscle pain take their toll, Mary turns to you saying, "When I die, give my half of the fortune to my nephew. He is the only relative I have and want him to enjoy what I will not." You reply, "Don't be silly, we will be rescued any day and when we do you will get medial help." "Be realistic," says Mary. "I know I am on my deathbed and I want you to promise me you will give the money to my nephew. Do you promise?" "Yes," you say. The next day, Mary slips into a coma and dies. A few days later you are rescued. Having cashed in the fortune, you track down Mary's nephew at a local drop-in centre. He is high on methamphetamine and has a prostitute in his arms. You talk to him about his Aunt Mary and how you were stranded, found the treasure, and how you promised to give him Mary's money. The nephew is so high he does not comprehend what you have just told him. Disgusted, you leave the drop-in centre to figure out what to do. As you walk down the street, you see an advertisement for a local university scientist who has almost found a cure for childhood leukemia but needs more research money to complete his work. What do you do? Should you keep your promise to Mary or give the money to the scientist? A utilitarian would, of course, despite making a promise to Mary, give the money to the scientist because finding a cure would maximize the happiness for countless children and their families. After all, the thoughts of giving million of dollars to Mary's drug addicted and prostitute-buying nephew turns your stomach. Besides, no one would know that you were breaking your promise, since Mary is dead and she told no one else. In short, breaking promises to maximize utility is morally justifiable. Still, say critics, you made a promise to Mary and, therefore, are obligated to give the money to her nephew. Keeping promises is intrinsically valuable regardless of the consequences it produces. The same can be said for telling the truth, treating people equally, justice, not stealing, not killing, fidelity, and so forth. Utilitarianism fails to take into consideration the intrinsic nature of morality. Rightness or wrongness is not merely determined by the consequences of a person's actions but by the nature of the act itself.

Another way of looking at this problem is that utilitarianism's forward-looking nature prevents us from keeping our moral commitments. That is, whether we ought to keep our promises is often based on past action and commitment. So if Mary had kept promises to you in the past, then you ought to keep her promise now and give the money to her nephew. But utilitarians don't see it his way. Past commitments and duties are irrelevant. And this, say critics, cannot make act utilitarian theory right (Waluchow 155).

A second problem, says Brandt, is that utilitarianism does not take into consideration special relationships including things like loyalty, fidelity, and family obligations. To see this, using a different example than Brandt, imagine that you and your mother are on a tropical cruise through the Caribbean. Unfortunately, the ship has just run into a coral reef, cracking open its hull. The order is given to abandon ship, and in the subsequent chaos of passengers trying to find a life raft, you lose your mother in the panicked crowd. Distraught, but wanting to save your own life, you find a life raft with others on board. The life raft is lowered into the sea, the engine is started, and the small vessel slowly moves away from the rapidly sinking ship. The life raft holds 40 passengers, 39 seats of which are full. For some reason, you are named captain of the boat. As the boat makes its way through the water, you stumble upon two people in need of rescue: your mother and a famous brain surgeon. As a utilitarian, which person do you decide to save (you can only save one and your mother does not hold a special job or status in society)? From a utilitarian perspective, it's easy; you save the brain surgeon because in doing so she will save more lives and produce more happiness than your mother. In short, you must condemn your mother to death. But surely this

is not how most of us make moral decisions. If we could only save one person, unless you hated your mother, you would pick her over the brain surgeon. That is, those we love and have special relationship with have moral priority over strangers; but this is not the case for utilitarianism. There is something wrong with a moral theory that forces us to value strangers over loved ones.

Third, utilitarianism conflicts with our obligations to social and economic justice. Consider insider trading. In 2005, Andrew Rankin was charged with ten counts of illegal insider trading or "tipping"—the largest case in Canadian history.[20] Rankin worked for the Royal Bank of Canada Dominion Securities as a managing director. Rankin leaked information about corporate secrets, before they were made public to other shareholders, to his childhood friend Danial Duic, who reaped more than $4.5 million by investing in companies ahead of takeover news. Duic was eventually arrested and made a deal with Crown prosecutors. Duic agreed to pay back most of the $4.5 million, accepted a lifetime ban on trading and, in doing so, he would become a witness against Rankin (McNish and Won B3).

Insider trading is illegal, but is it immoral? What is wrong with using privileged insider information about corporate secrets to benefit oneself, family, and friends? From a utilitarian perspective, it could be argued that insider trading is morally justified. If everyone could take advantage of insider information, then those best informed or able to gain information will benefit. Outsiders are not harmed by not having this information and can only benefit from insider trading. To put another way, Rankin gave Duic corporate secrets for their own gain and benefit. No one else knew secrets were being passed; therefore, no one was getting hurt. In fact, most people in Duic's situation would probably have done the same thing. Hence, because no one is getting hurt, and there is only money to gain, insider trading is moral. Insider trading maximizes the overall net benefit to those affected by this decision.

Unfortunately, insider trading violates the principles of economic justice. How? Capitalist markets work on the fundamental principles of equality and fairness. That is, markets are most efficient under the notion of free and open competition to all citizens. But in order to be free and open, all parties have to be, more or less, on equal footing. That is, equal access to the same information at the same time. Insider trading violates these principles. Insider trading gives some people more knowledge than others. This puts other stockholders at a disadvantage because they do not have equal access to this secret "insider" information and, therefore, cannot benefit from it. Insider trading is unfair and unjust. It violates the very idea of free, open, and fair competition upon which our economy is based; by not having access to the same information, it precludes stockholders from the market process (Werhane 238). If so, then insider trading is immoral.[21]

A fourth problem is known as the free rider problem. Suppose the government tells us that we must conserve electricity in order to prevent the system from being overloaded, which could result in citywide blackouts. Everyone dutifully adheres to the government's request. But as a utilitarian, knowing that everyone will conserve electricity, I reason that it's okay for me to use more electricity than everyone else since it makes my life better and no one is harmed. That is, my using electricity will not cause a blackout. In other words, so long as happiness is maximized and no disutility is produced, then violating the government request is morally acceptable. But critics point out that this unjust and unfair. If everyone has to conserve electricity, utilitarians ought not to be exempt. In short, a moral theory that allows people to ride freely on the coattails of others while they reap the benefits is surely problematic.

Here is one more objection, not addressed by Brandt. A fifth problem is based on our ability to measure and calculate pleasure and pain. Although most of us don't personally have a problem calculating which actions will produce the greatest pleasure or happiness for ourselves (some of us will value opera over rock concerts, chocolate over strawberry ice cream, etc.), it's often very difficult

to determine and compare the pleasure and pain of others. Imagine you are the human resources director for an engineering firm in need of hiring a civil engineer. In front of you are the resumes of Sally and Beth, who are both suitable candidates for the job. How do you measure the utility Sally would gain from the job against the utility Beth would gain from the job? Since the utility Sally would get out of the job may be greater or lesser than what Beth would get out of the job, there is no way to objectively decide who should get the job (Velasquez, *Business Ethics* 76). In other words, there is no way you can truly know what happiness Sally and Beth will feel in getting the job, and given the differences and degrees to which people can be happy, a comparative measure of happiness cannot be made. And since you cannot know if hiring Sally or Beth will produce the greatest amount of happiness, we cannot apply utilitarian (Velasquez, *Business Ethics* 76). In short, utilitarianism fails.[22]

Can Utilitarianism Be Defended?

There are a number of ways utilitarians have defended their position. Let's look at two. One way, says Brandt, that utilitarianism can avoid some of the previous objections is by developing various rules and principles, which if universalized, maximize the overall utility. This is known as **rule utilitarianism**. Rule utilitarianism can be used to avoid the problems of rights and justice and the intrinsic nature of morality objections. To see this, let's revisit some of the earlier examples. It was argued that insider trading could be justified from a utilitarian perspective because in violating economic justice it maximizes happiness. But does it? Imagine a world in which the rule "Always engage in insider trading" was generally accepted. What kind of world would it be? Well, as hinted at earlier, it would undermine the principles of equality and fairness. It would unjustly allow insiders to become wealthy at the expense of other investors; undermine trust in the marketplace; hinder foreign investment in Canada; and if our economy slowed because of it, everyone would be worse off. In other words, a moral rule against insider trading maximizes happiness if generally accepted. Or consider the desert island example. Although an act utilitarian would justify breaking promises, consider what would happen if everyone broke promises—that is, if everyone followed the rule "Always break your promises." Following such a rule wouldn't maximize happiness because if everyone broke their promises, we would not trust what people said, and people would stop making promises in the first place (Rawls 17). In other words, if "Always keep your promises" is generally accepted by society, it promotes more happiness than unhappiness and, therefore, is moral.

One significant problem with rule utilitarianism, not discussed by Brandt, is that it seems to collapse into act utilitarianism. If rule utilitarianism is correct, then, for example, keeping promises will maximize overall utility. Now if the goal of utilitarianism is to maximize happiness, then there might be situations in which breaking promises achieves this goal. So although strictly keeping your promise to Mary and giving the money to her nephew will maximize happiness, we must remember that no one will ever find out that you broke your promise to Mary since she is dead. Here we have a situation where we could follow a rule that says, "Always keep your promises unless not doing so will have no ill effect on society." And since not keeping your promise will have no ill effects on society, and if the goal is to maximize happiness, then you ought not to keep your promise. That is, when we follow the rule of promise-keeping in this particular situation, rule utilitarianism collapses into act utilitarianism if we are obligated to maximize happiness. In other words, rule utilitarianism will not maximize happiness in this case, and thus we must look at the specific consequences of the act itself to achieve this goal. If so, then rule utilitarianism collapses into act utilitarianism.

We saw earlier that utilitarianism suffers from the problem of trying to measure pleasure and pains. A potential solution, not discussed by Brandt, is the use of a **cost-benefit analysis**. Cost-benefit analysis is important for attempting to quantify pleasures and pains. Consider the classic Ford Pinto example. When Ford made the Pinto back in the early 1970s, engineers put the gas tank behind the rear axle of the car, which made the car potentially lethal if hit from behind. Crash tests revealed that if the car was struck from behind at 20 miles per hour or more, the tank could rupture and burst into flames. Ford managers decided to push ahead with the car despite the test results. How could they justify this? Simply, they used a utilitarian approach or a cost-benefit analysis. They figured that the overall utility of the car (it was cheap and economical) outweighed the potential dangers. In fact, the Pinto met all government safety regulations at the time. According to Ford's cost-benefit analysis, to modify the tank would cost the company $137 million or $11 per car (there were 12.5 million built). They also analyzed the potential benefits (lives saved) based on insurance costs at the time. Ford determined that each fatality per year would cost approximately $200,000. They determined there would be 180 deaths per year at $200,000; 180 injuries at $67,000; and 2,000 burned vehicles at $700. In total, if Ford fixed the car, approximately $49 million could be saved (Shaw 77). In other words, if the car was redesigned, lives would be saved and insurance companies would not have paid out millions of dollars. By weighting the costs and benefits, Ford decided not to fix the car despite the potential loss of life. In short, the company felt it wasn't right to spend $137 million if the benefit was only $49 million (net cost of −$88 million). In total, according to Ford, 23 deaths were related to the Pinto; its critics put the death toll around 500 (Shaw 77). (In 1978, Ford eventually recalled and fixed the Pinto and was eventually phased out of production.) My point is that many companies use this type of cost-benefit approach when making business decisions. The morally right thing to do is to produce the greatest net benefits for society while imposing the least cost on the company.

The problem with the cost-benefit approach is that some things seem not to fit into this kind of analysis. Take, for example, human life or health. How do we put a price on these intrinsically valuable things? Are these not benefits for their own sake? Ford did place a value on human life, by assigning a dollar value to it, but placing such a value on human life is arbitrary and subjective. Remember, Ford decided that the cost of human life didn't warrant fixing the potentially dangerous gas tank. But surely we can't place a price on life, can we? Is this not morally inappropriate? And, as Steve Kelman argues, by placing a monetary value on such items we actually reduce their perceived value. For example, consummating love with sex has a very different value than paying for sex with a prostitute. Yet, if we take cost-benefit analysis seriously, we could potentially compute the value of sex based on cost of prostitute services (460). But it would be inappropriate to equate the two because in doing so, it undermines the value that sex plays between two people who are deeply in love.

27

John Stuart Mill

(1806–1873)

John Stuart Mill was born in London in 1806 to James and Harriet Mill. James Mill, John's father, was a well-known philosopher, economist, and senior official with the East India Com-  *pany. His father homeschooled John, resulting in an educational experience that was disciplined, intense, and lacked the fun-loving playfulness of most children. By age 3, John had learned Greek; by age 8, Latin; at age 12, he was a competent logician; and by age 16, he knew the fundamentals of economics.*

In 1823, his father secured him a junior position with the East India Company. Mill moved up the corporate ranks and eventually took over his father's position as Chief Examiner. At the age of 20, he had a nervous breakdown. It is said that his father's rigorous analytical training and lack of emotional attachment eventually lead to his emotional crisis. He recovered within in a few months. In 1830, Mill met Harriet Taylor. Although she was married at the time, Mill and Taylor developed a very personal (supposedly non-sexual) relationship. However, they eventually married in 1851, two years after the death of Taylor's husband. Harriet had a significant impact on Mill's philosophy, especially her advocacy of women's rights. Unfortunately, she fell fatally ill with tuberculosis while travelling in Avignon, France, and died in 1858. Mill, it is said, was inconsolable at the loss of his wife, so much so that he spent half of each remaining year of his life in Avignon so he could be near her grave. Mill stayed with the East India Company until the government dissolved the company in 1858, at which time he retired with pension. Seven years later he was elected to the House of Commons in 1865. A man of principle, Mill soon found himself at odds with his constituents and failed at his attempt to be re-elected. Mill died in Avignon in 1873 and was buried next to his wife. John Stuart Mill's major works include Systems of Logic *(1843),* Principles of Economy *(1848),* On Liberty *(1859),* Utilitarianism *(1861),* Considerations on Representational Government *(1851), and* The Subjection of Women *(1869).*

Utilitarianism

A passing remark is all that needs be given to the ignorant blunder of supposing that those who stand up for utility as the test of right and wrong, use the term in that restricted and merely colloquial sense in which utility is opposed to pleasure. An apology is due to the philosophical opponents of utilitarianism, for even the momentary appearance of confounding them with any one capable of so absurd a misconception; which is the more extraordinary, inasmuch as the contrary accusation, of referring everything to pleasure, and that too in its grossest form, is another of the common charges against utilitarianism: and, as has been pointedly remarked by an able writer, the same sort of persons, and often the very same persons, denounce the theory 'as impracticably dry when the word utility precedes the word pleasure, and as too practicably voluptuous when the word pleasure precedes the word utility.' Those who know anything about the matter are aware that every writer, from Epicurus to Bentham, who maintained the theory of utility, meant by it, not something to be contradistinguished from pleasure, but pleasure itself, together with exemption from pain; and instead of opposing the useful to the agreeable or the ornamental, have always declared that the useful means these, among other things. Yet the common herd, including the herd of writers, not only in newspapers and periodicals, but in books of weight and pretension, are perpetually falling into this shallow mistake. Having caught up the word utilitarian, while knowing nothing whatever about it but its sound, they habitually express by it the rejection, or the neglect, of pleasure in some of its forms; of beauty, of ornament, or of amusement. Nor is the term thus ignorantly misapplied solely in disparagement, but occasionally in compliment; as though it implied superiority to frivolity and the mere pleasures of the moment. And this perverted use is the only one in which the word is popularly known, and the one from which the new generation are acquiring their sole notion of its meaning. Those who introduced the word, but who had for many years discontinued it as a distinctive appellation, may well feel themselves called upon to resume it, if by doing so they can hope to contribute anything towards rescuing it from this utter degradation.

The creed which accepts as the foundation of morals, Utility, or the Greatest Happiness Principle, holds that actions are right in proportion as they tend to promote happiness, wrong as they tend to produce the reverse of happiness. By happiness is intended pleasure, and the absence of pain; by unhappiness, pain, and the privation of pleasure. To give a clear view of the moral standard set up by the theory, much more requires to be said; in particular, what things it includes in the ideas of pain and pleasure; and to what extent this is left an open question. But these supplementary explanations do not affect the theory of life on which this theory of morality is grounded—namely, that pleasure, and freedom from pain, are the only things desirable as ends; and that all desirable things (which are as numerous in the utilitarian as in any other scheme) are desirable either for the pleasure inherent in themselves, or as means to the promotion of pleasure and the prevention of pain.

Now, such a theory of life excites in many minds, and among them in some of the most estimable in feeling and purpose, inveterate dislike. To suppose that life has (as they express it) no higher end than pleasure—no better and nobler object of desire and pursuit—they designate as utterly mean and grovelling; as a doctrine worthy only of swine, to whom the followers of Epicurus were, at a very early period, contemptuously likened; and modern holders of the doctrine are occasionally made the subject of equally polite comparisons by its German, French, and English assailants.

When thus attacked, the Epicureans have always answered, that it is not they, but their accusers, who represent human nature in a degrading light; since the accusation supposes human beings to be capable of no pleasures except those of which swine are capable. If this supposition were true, the charge could not be gainsaid, but would then be no longer an imputation; for if the sources of pleasure were precisely the same to human beings and to swine, the rule of life which is good enough for the one would be good enough for the other. The comparison of the Epicurean life to that of beasts is felt as degrading, precisely because a beast's pleasures do not satisfy a human being's conceptions of happiness. Human beings have faculties more elevated than the animal appetites, and when once made conscious of them, do not regard anything as happiness which does not include their gratification. I do not, indeed, consider the Epicureans to have been by any means faultless in drawing out their schemes of consequences from the utilitarian principle. To do this in any sufficient manner, many Stoic, as well as Christian elements require to be included. But there is no known Epicurean theory of life which does not assign to the pleasures of the intellect, of the feelings and imagination, and of the moral sentiments, a much higher value as pleasures than to those of mere sensation. It must be admitted, however, that utilitarian writers in general have placed the superiority of mental over bodily pleasures chiefly in the greater permanency, safety, uncostliness, etc., of the former—that is, in their circumstantial advantages rather than in their intrinsic nature. And on all these points utilitarians have fully proved their case; but they might have taken the other, and, as it may be called, higher ground, with entire consistency. It is quite compatible with the principle of utility to recognise the fact, that some *kinds* of pleasure are more desirable and more valuable than others. It would be absurd that while, in estimating all other things, quality is considered as well as quantity, the estimation of pleasures should be supposed to depend on quantity alone.[1]

If I am asked, what I mean by difference of quality in pleasures, or what makes one pleasure more valuable than another, merely as a pleasure, except its being greater in amount, there is but one possible answer. Of two pleasures, if there be one to which all or almost all who have experience of both give a decided preference, irrespective of any feeling of moral obligation to prefer it, that is the more desirable pleasure. If one of the two is, by those who are competently acquainted with both, placed so far above the other that they prefer it, even though knowing it to be attended with a greater amount of discontent, and would not resign it for any quantity of the other pleasure which their nature is capable of, we are justified in ascribing to the preferred enjoyment a superiority in quality, so far outweighing quantity as to render it, in comparison, of small account.

Now it is an unquestionable fact that those who are equally acquainted with, and equally capable of appreciating and enjoying, both, do give a most marked preference to the manner of existence which employs their higher faculties. Few human creatures would consent to be changed into any of the lower animals, for a promise of the fullest allowance of a beast's pleasures; no intelligent human being would consent to be a fool, no instructed person would be an ignoramus, no person of feeling and conscience would be selfish and base, even though they should be persuaded that the fool, the dunce, or the rascal is better satisfied with his lot than they are with theirs. They would not resign what they possess more than he for the most complete satisfaction of all the desires which they have in common with him. If they ever fancy they would, it is only in cases of unhappiness so extreme, that to escape from it they would exchange their lot for almost any other, however undesirable in their own eyes. A being of higher faculties requires more to make him happy, is capable probably of more acute suffering, and certainly accessible to it at more points, than one of an inferior type; but in spite of these liabilities, he can never really wish to sink into what he feels to be a lower grade of existence. We may give what explanation we please of this unwillingness; we may attribute it to pride, a name which is given indiscriminately to some of the most and to some of the least estimable feelings of which mankind are capable: we may refer it to the love of liberty and personal independence, an appeal to which was with the Stoics one of the most effective means for the inculcation of it; to the love of power, or to the love of excitement, both of which do really enter into and contribute to it: but its most appropriate appellation is a sense of dignity, which all human beings possess in one form or other, and in some, though by no means in exact, proportion to their higher faculties, and which is so essential a part of the happiness of those in whom it is strong, that nothing which conflicts with it could be, otherwise than momentarily, an object of desire to them. Whoever supposes that this preference takes place at a sacrifice of happiness—that the superior being, in anything like equal circumstances, is not happier than the inferior—confounds the two very different ideas, of happiness, and content. It is indisputable that the being whose capacities of enjoyment are low, has the greatest chance of having

them fully satisfied; and a highly endowed being will always feel that any happiness which he can look for, as the world is constituted, is imperfect. But he can learn to bear its imperfections, if they are at all bearable; and they will not make him envy the being who is indeed unconscious of the imperfections, but only because he feels not at all the good which those imperfections qualify. It is better to be a human being dissatisfied than a pig satisfied; better to be Socrates dissatisfied than a fool satisfied. And if the fool, or the pig, are a different opinion, it is because they only know their own side of the question. The other party to the comparison knows both sides.[2]

It may be objected, that many who are capable of the higher pleasures, occasionally, under the influence of temptation, postpone them to the lower. But this is quite compatible with a full appreciation of the intrinsic superiority of the higher. Men often, from infirmity of character, make their election for the nearer good, though they know it to be the less valuable; and this no less when the choice is between two bodily pleasures, than when it is between bodily and mental. They pursue sensual indulgences to the injury of health, though perfectly aware that health is the greater good. It may be further objected, that many who begin with youthful enthusiasm for everything noble, as they advance in years sink into indolence and selfishness. But I do not believe that those who undergo this very common change, voluntarily choose the lower description of pleasures in preference to the higher. I believe that before they devote themselves exclusively to the one, they have already become incapable of the other. Capacity for the nobler feelings is in most natures a very tender plant, easily killed, not only by hostile influences, but by mere want of sustenance; and in the majority of young persons it speedily dies away if the occupations to which their position in life has devoted them, and the society into which it has thrown them, are not favourable to keeping that higher capacity in exercise. Men lose their high aspirations as they lose their intellectual tastes, because they have not time or opportunity for indulging them; and they addict themselves to inferior pleasures, not because they deliberately prefer them, but because they are either the only ones to which they have access, or the only ones which they are any longer capable of enjoying. It may be questioned whether anyone who has remained equally susceptible to both classes of pleasures, ever knowingly and calmly preferred the lower; though many, in all ages, have broken down in an ineffectual attempt to combine both.

From this verdict of the only competent judges, I apprehend there can be no appeal. On a question which is the best worth having of two pleasures, or which of two modes of existence is the most grateful to the feelings, apart from its moral attributes and from its consequences, the judgment of those who are qualified by knowledge of both, or, if they differ, that of the majority among them, must be admitted as final. And there needs be the less hesitation to accept this judgment respecting the quality of pleasures, since there is no other tribunal to be referred to even on the question of quantity. What means are there of determining which is the acutest of two pains, or the intensest of two pleasurable sensations, except the general suffrage of those who are familiar with both? Neither pains nor pleasures are homogeneous, and pain is always heterogeneous with pleasure. What is there to decide whether a particular pleasure is worth purchasing at the cost of a particular pain, except

the feelings and judgment of the experienced? When, therefore, those feelings and judgment declare the pleasures derived from the higher faculties to be preferable *in kind,* apart from the question of intensity, to those of which the animal nature, disjoined from the higher faculties, is suspectible, they are entitled on this subject to the same regard.

I have dwelt on this point, as being a necessary part of a perfectly just conception of Utility or Happiness, considered as the directive rule of human conduct. But it is by no means an indispensable condition to the acceptance of the utilitarian standard; for that standard is not the agent's own greatest happiness, but the greatest amount of happiness altogether; and if it may possibly be doubted whether a noble character is always the happier for its nobleness, there can be no doubt that it makes other people happier, and that the world in general is immensely a gainer by it. Utilitarianism, therefore, could only attain its end by the general cultivation of nobleness of character, even if each individual were only benefited by the nobleness of others, and his own, so far as happiness is concerned, were a sheer deduction from the benefit. But the bare enunciation of such an absurdity as this last, renders refutation superfluous.

According to the Greatest Happiness Principle, as above explained, the ultimate end, with reference to and for the sake of which all other things are desirable (whether we are considering our own good or that of other people), is an existence exempt as far as possible from pain, and as rich as possible in enjoyments, both in point of quantity and quality; the test of quality, and the rule for measuring it against quantity, being the preference felt by those who in their opportunities of experience, to which must be added their habits of self-consciousness and self-observation, are best furnished with the means of comparison. This, being, according to the utilitarian opinion, the end of human action, is necessarily also the standard of morality; which may accordingly be defined, the rules and precepts for human conduct, by the observance of which an existence such as has been described might be, to the greatest extent possible, secured to all mankind; and not to them only, but, so far as the nature of things admits, to the whole sentient creation. [...]

I must again repeat, what the assailants of utilitarianism seldom have the justice to acknowledge, that the happiness which forms the utilitarian standard of what is right in conduct, is not the agent's own happiness, but that of all concerned. As between his own happiness and that of others, utilitarianism requires him to be as strictly impartial as a disinterested and benevolent spectator. In the golden rule of Jesus of Nazareth, we read the complete spirit of the ethics of utility.[3] To do as you would be done by, and to love your neighbour as yourself, constitute the ideal perfection of utilitarian morality. As the means of making the nearest approach to this ideal, utility would enjoin, first, that laws and social arrangements should place the happiness, or (as speaking practically it may be called) the interest, of every individual, as nearly as possible in harmony with the interest of the whole; and secondly, that education and opinion,[4] which have so vast a power over human character, should so use that power as to establish in the mind of every individual an indissoluble association between his own happiness and the good of the whole; especially

between his own happiness and the practice of such modes of conduct, negative and positive, as regard for the universal happiness prescribes; so that not only he may be unable to conceive the possibility of happiness to himself, consistently with conduct opposed to the general good, but also that a direct impulse to promote the general good may be in every individual one of the habitual motives of action, and the sentiments connected therewith may fill a large and prominent place in every human being's sentient existence. If the impugners of the utilitarian morality represented it to their own minds in this its true character, I know not what recommendation possessed by any other morality they could possibly affirm to be wanting to it; what more beautiful or more exalted developments of human nature any other ethical system can be supposed to foster, or what springs of action, not accessible to the utilitarian, such systems rely on for giving effect to their mandates.

Notes

1. p. 8. See Introduction, p. xiii. 'Quality' is ambiguous. It sometimes mens 'good *quality*', as when the aristocracy were called 'the quality' or the *Sunday Express* includes itself among 'the quality papers'. It also means the what or *quale* of something, its characteristics or properties. Mill works with both meanings. Higher pleasures are good quality pleasures. But pleasures are distinguished from one another in respect of the qualities or characteristics of their objects. There are 'kinds' of pleasure corresponding to kinds of action of kinds of objects or sources of pleasure.

2. p. 10. Plato in the *Republic*, Book IX, argues that the philosopher who has intelligence as well as sensation and aggression, is the only one qualified to judge the preferability of the types of pleasure associated with each of three 'parts' of the soul. Mill's reference to 'higher faculties' suggests he had this passage in mind.

3. p. 18. Mill is suggesting that justice and fairness are somehow contained in the utilitarian standard. See Chapter 5 below, especially p. 64.

4. p. 18. Later (p. 34) Mill writes of a religion. See Introduction, p. xi.

28

Richard Brandt

(1910–1997)

Considered one of the most influential moral philosophers of the twentieth century, Richard Brandt was born on October 17, 1910, in Wilmington, Ohio. His undergraduate degrees were from Denison University and Trinity College, Cambridge University. He received his Ph.D. in philosophy from Yale University in 1936. He taught philosophy at Swarthmore College until he assumed the chairmanship of the Department of Philosophy at the University of Michigan in 1964, where he later was named the Roy Wood Sellars Distinguished College Professor of Philosophy. He was a fellow of the Guggenheim Foundation, a fellow at the Center for Advanced Studies in the Behavioral Sciences in Stanford, California, and a senior fellow of the National Endowment for the Humanities. He served as president of the American Philosophical Association (western division), and was a member of the American Academy of Arts and Sciences. Brandt was the author of nearly 100 articles and six books, including Ethical Theory: The Problems of Normative and Critical Ethics *(1959),* Social Injustice *(1963),* Moral Philosophy and the Analysis of Language, Freedom and Morality *(1976), and* A Theory of the Good and the Right *(1979). He died on September 10, 1997 at the age of 86 years old.*

Moral Obligation and General Welfare

The most important problem of normative ethics now faces us: a choice among the major theories about when we are morally obligated to do something—among the result theories (excluding the egoisms) and the formalist theories. The central problem (but not the only one) to be solved is that of the exact relevance of general welfare for moral obligation.

If we look at the concrete teaching about moral obligation common in our society, we get the impression that the general welfare is at best only of secondary relevance for obligation. The Ten Commandments do not mention it explicitly (nor does the Golden Rule, although it is closer). Rather, they tell us not to worship (or build) "graven images," to keep the Sabbath day holy, to honor our fathers and mothers, not to kill or steal or commit adultery or bear false witness or covet anything belonging to our neighbors. Similarly, the advice we give our children is at least partly in the form of rather specific directives or prohibitions, which do not mention general welfare—for example, "Don't ask people personal questions"; "Don't take another person's property"; "Always tell the truth except . . . "

Are specific principles like these the ultimate principles of obligation or duty? Or is it true, as some hold, that there is only one true principle about duty—such as that we ought to act so as to maximize welfare?

1. Act Utilitarianism: Its Force and Problems

The simplest answer to these questions is that of two kinds of utilitarian theory: hedonistic utilitarianism and ideal utilitarianism. These two forms of universal result theory [...] we shall group together under the title of "act-utilitarianism." What they have in common is roughly the view that it is an agent's duty (in the objective sense) to perform a specific act on a specific occasion if and only if so doing will (actually or probably) produce a state of conscious beings that is of maximum intrinsic worth, as compared with what would have been produced by other acts the agent could have performed instead. The two types differ between themselves about what states of conscious beings are intrinsically desirable: the hedonist holds that only states of pleasure are so, whereas the ideal utilitarian holds that other states of conscious beings are also intrinsically worthwhile, as we have seen in earlier chapters. We shall ignore this difference in the present chapter.[1]

We begin with an examination of act-utilitarianism. The first thing we must do is state the theory precisely. To do this may seen simple, but unfortunately there is a problem we must face. Roughly, the problem is as follows: Shall we construe the act-utilitarian theory as saying *(a)* that a person's (objective) duty is to perform that act whose performance will *actually* produce a state of conscious beings of maximum intrinsic worth, as compared with what would in fact be produced by other actions he could perform instead? Or, *(b)* is it saying that a person's (objective) duty is to perform that act whose

performance will, roughly, *on the available evidence probably* produce a state of conscious beings of maximum intrinsic worth (and so on as before)? Consider an example. Suppose a surgeon is weighing whether to perform a certain operation on a patient's heart. The basic known facts are that a successful operation will work a complete cure, whereas without the operation the patient must be permanently confined to bed; but the operation is a dangerous one, the mortality rate being 60 per cent. Now, is the act-utilitarian saying that the surgeon's (objective) duty is to perform the operation if and only if *in fact* so doing will produce the best results (namely, if and only if the patient will in fact survive)? Or, is he saying that the surgeon's (objective) duty is to perform the operation if and only if so doing is the "best bet," has the "best promise," has the highest "product" of probability X value? Or, to use a phrase we shall employ, if and only if operating has *maximal net expectable utility*?

There would be a gain in consistency and neatness if we interpreted it in the former way.[2] But there is a considerable advantage in construing the theory in the second way. Partly the gain is pragmatic: in that our discussion will better illumine the reasoning we all have to perform in life. Partly the gain is in historical truth, for we shall be assessing a theory closer to what the great utilitarians, such as Bentham, actually held. We shall, therefore, construe the theory in the *second* way.

Let us then state the thesis of act-utilitarianism as follows: "If doing *A* has among all the things X can do, the maximum net expectable utility, then it is X's objective duty to do *A*."

But what exactly, is "maximum net expectable utility"? How shall we, in principle, decide that doing a particular *A* has maximum net expectable utility? To give the proposed formulation of the utilitarian thesis definite content, we must explain this.

We can limit our explanation to a definition of what it means to say that doing *A* has "greater net expectable utility" than has doing *B,* since "maximum" merely means "not smaller than that of any other course of action."

In order to determine which has "greater net expectable utility" (and the procedure for determining this may be taken as defining the meaning of the phrase), the first thing to do is consider the things that, on the basis of available evidence, have more than a negligible probability of happening if *A* is done, and which are different from what probably will happen if *B* is done. All the things that will in all probability be the same, whatever we do, may be ignored; so, although what we do now may have important repercussions a thousand years from now—like the statements of Jesus, or the writings of Plato and Aristotle—the probability now that such things will occur is negligible. So we consider, then, two sets of things: events likely to happen (with the estimated probabilities attached) if *A* but not *B* is done, and events likely happen if *B* but not *A* is done. This gives us a view of what difference it makes which course of action is taken.

Let us call one set "the expectable consequences of *A*" and the other set the "expectable consequences of *B.*" How, then, do we decide which has the greater net expectable utility? [...] That set of consequences (with probabilities attached) has greater net expectable utility which is *better,* that is, which would be the object of a justified preference. [...] There can be a justified preference, we have already noted, not only for one situation over another, but for one situation with a probability attached, over another situation with another probability attached.

Whichever set of expectable consequences has the capacity of eliciting such justified preference, we shall say has "greater net expectable utility." Whether one set of consequences has a greater net expectable utility than another, then, is a matter of fact about which a person can have a correct or incorrect opinion.[3]

The utilitarian must concede that it may be no easy matter to decide which act has maximum net expectable utility, that is, which one from the sets of states of conscious organisms that would result from different possible actions (and ignoring questions of distribution, that is, which conscious organisms were affected) is best, that is, would be justifiably preferred.[4] In order to be as accurate as possible in one's estimate of which act has maximum net expectable utility, one will naturally use all the devices of matching, and the other principles formulated at the end of Chapter 13. The hedonist, of course, because he holds that only states of pleasure are of intrinsic worth, can say that for him the problem is somewhat simplified, since a preference for one state can be justified on the basis of an examination of the intensities and durations of pleasure-effects alone. But the hedonist—and this point is an important one—cannot regard the problem of determining maximum net expectable utility as simply one of deciding which course of action will produce *most pleasure* and viewing this course as one's obligation. He must concede that the problem is one of balancing one set of pleasures with certain probabilities attached against another set of pleasures with different probabilities, so that, except in special cases, ability to compare situations for "greater pleasure" will not solve the relevant problem, and he must, like nonhedonists, appeal to preferences for a decision as to which action has maximum net expectable utility.

The foregoing complications in the utilitarian theses are unfortunate but necessary. It is important to see that they *are* necessary. Many people have been attracted by the utilitarian thesis because they supposed that, once general decisions about what general kinds of thing are intrinsically worthwhile have been made, the utilitarian can leave the job of deciding what is one's duty to empirical science. But this is mistaken, at least for all those cases in which the intrinsic values of sets of consequences have to be balanced against probabilities of getting them. In the cases where such comparisons are required, it is not easy to see how the utilitarian's procedure for determining one's duty is in any respect simpler than that of nonutilitarians.

So much, then, by way of explanation of the utilitarian thesis that it is always a person's duty to do *A*, if only if doing *A* has, among all the things he can do, the maximum net expectable utility.

The utilitarian naturally thinks we must take into account the less obvious as well as the more obvious consequences. Suppose, for instance, Mr. X asks me whether I know the size of Mr. Y's salary, which I do. It would be an unfair caricature of utilitarianism to suppose it is committed to holding that it is my duty to lie, in view of the embarrassment that will arise if I admit I do know, but then have to explain that I prefer not to publicize my information. One of the utilities to be considered is that if mutual forthrightness among human beings. Another is the effect of a lie on my habits, the building up of a habit of taking the easy way. In general it is probably not often that the utilitarian formula implies that a lie is one's duty.

Does the utilitarian formula leave any place for moral maxims like "Keep your promises" and "Always tell the truth"? Yes, these maxims can be regarded as directives that for the most part point out what is a person's duty. They are rules of thumb. They are properly taught to children and used by everyday as a rough timesaving guide for ordinary decisions. Moreover, since we are all prone to rationalizing in our own favor, they are apt to be a better guide to our duty in complex cases than is our on-the-spot reflection. However, we are not to be enslaved to them. When there is good ground for thinking the maximum net expectable utility will be produced by an act that violates them, then we should depart from them. Such a rule is to be disregarded without hesitation, when it clearly conflicts. [...]

Now that we have explained what the act utilitarian thesis is, we must assess it.

How shall we decide whether the act-utilitarian thesis is true? Since the thesis is a universal normative statement, we must see whether there are exceptions, or probable exceptions to it. If there are, then it is false although it might be more nearly true than any one of the other major theories. Or contrariwise, we may find reasons for supposing that there are no exceptions to it. Finding exceptions to it, of course, presupposes that we have some method for determining what our duty is, aside from relying on the utilitarian formula. And we do. As we have seen, every statement of obligation must be tested against our "qualified" feelings of obligation or inclinations to demand certain behavior of all persons. It must be tested by whether it fits in with a system of consistent principles of duty, of universal form, which are coherent with our feelings of obligation and inclinations to make demands on others, as they are when we are fully informed, impartial, and in a normal frame of mind. So our question, roughly, is this: Are the acts that we must view as our obligation or duty, as a result of a process of thinking of his sort, identical with the ones that the thesis of utilitarianism asserts are our duty? Let us look at some pros and cons. We begin with points favorable to utilitarianism.

1. The most impressive line of reasoning is this. Many people have asked themselves: "How can it possibly be my duty to do something less than the most good I can do? How can it be wrong to do the greatest amount of good?" They have gone on in similar vein: "A person *explains* why he as a duty to do something if he shows that it is necessary in order to maximize the welfare of sentient beings. The utilitarian's thesis about duty, then, is an intelligible one. The nonutilitarian, however, has a bundle of rules about duty for which he can give no such explanation. And isn't one being just a slave to traditional rules if one doesn't demand that the rules be supported by showing their connection with welfare? Nonutilitarians are surely thoughtless worshippers of traditional rules."

This reasoning has force. It is doubtful whether we think any action is wrong if *nobody's* welfare is in any way adversely affected by it. Moreover, "qualified" feelings of obligation or of demand on others might surely be expected to be influenced by whether or not an action will cause harm—and perhaps by nothing else?

The point is sufficiently serious that we shall not try to assess it at the present stage. Rule-Utilitarianism has been in good part inspired by desire to formulate a near-formalist system that is not open, at least not as much, to this objection.

2. The second line of support for the utilitarian thesis is simply the question, "What is your alternative?" Obviously the alternative, if we ignore the possibility of rule-utilitarianism for the present, must be a *set* of rules, probably, including a rule about doing good where one can. But what will these rules be like? Moreover,

if there are several rules, the set must provide directions as to what we are to do when two rules conflict, for example, if "Your duty is always to tell the truth" conflicts with "Your duty is always to keep your promises." Evidently, the set must contain higher-order rules, telling us what do if the lower-order rules conflict; and so on up. One would like to see some plausible concrete proposals for such a set of rules.

Leaving aside the complications of higher-order rules, do we really know any nonutilitarian first-order rules that we can take seriously? No matter how such rules are framed, they seem objectionable. Take, for instance, "It is your prima facie duty (namely, duty when no stronger moral consideration override) to tell the truth." But do we really believe this rule? Suppose I am talking with a shrewd real-estate dealer about the purchase of a piece of property. He asks me to name a figure that is the highest I am prepared to offer, but expecting all the time that I shall only be making a *bargaining* offer, being willing to make some further concession if the seller makes one. Am I then bound prima facie to speak the truth? Or, if someone asks me a personal question, and I think of a way of giving a literally true answer, which, however, will lead him to infer something that is false, is there a prima facie obligation to avoid leading him into such inferences?

Much the same questions could be raised about the rule, "It is your prima facie obligation to keep your promises." Is this rule as stated to be applied to promises made under duress? Or promises made in a joking vein? Or promises made to a person who, since you made promises to him, has ignored his promises made to you? Or promises made on a mistaken assumption—for instance, if I promise to give $10,000 to a college for a certain purpose but, before the money is paid, a gift from another donor is announced, for the same purpose, and in the sum of $10,000,000, a sum sufficient to realize completely the goal I had in mind?

Suppose we had to agree the few, if any, non-utilitarian principles have been stated—much less a complete set of them, with higher-order rules giving directions for conflicts between the other rules—with all the qualifications and exceptions we think are necessary. Does this fact not destroy the case of the nonutilitarians, by showing that their own positive view does not even admit of being stated? This argument, again, has weight, and we postpone attempting to assess it.

Let us now look at the other side of the situation, at the problems of act-utilitarianism. The main, but not the only, difficulty is that act-utilitarianism has erroneous implications about what is obligatory. Let us consider some examples.

1. Let us suppose that Mr. X is considering whether it is his duty to hasten his father's death. Let us suppose further that Mr. X's father is well-to-do, whereas the son is poor. The father gives the son no money, and the son and his family are continually missing the joys of life because they do not have the means to pay for them. Furthermore, the father is ill and requires nursing care. The cost of nursing care is rapidly eating into the father's capital. Moreover, the father himself gets no joy from life. He must take drugs to make life tolerable, and his physician says that his condition will gradually become worse, although death is still several years away.

On the utilitarian theory, it can well be (and on the hedonistic form, certainly will be) the son's duty to bring about the demise of his father, provided he can do this so that his deed will be undetected (thereby avoiding legal calamities for himself and his family, and not weakening the general confidence of fathers in their sons). But would this in fact be his duty? It does not seem so. We may perhaps hesitate to say that the father would be wrong in ending his own life, and conceivably some will say it is duty to do so; but it is doubtful if anybody will say that the son's duty is to take the matter into his own hands as soon as it becomes clear that the public (primarily his own) welfare will be served by so doing.[5]

2. Suppose a widow with a ten-year-old daughter has been supporting herself and her child by her earnings as a teacher. However, her earnings are so low that she is not able to purchase adequate life insurance or save against the future. Let us suppose further that she has no near relatives, has recently moved into a large community, and that you and your family, her neighbors, are her only friends. Now suppose she is suddenly taken ill, and it is immediately clear that her illness will be fatal. She asks you if you will see to the care of her daughter, so that she will not have to go to an institution. Wisely or unwisely, you promise you will do so. The question then is: Does the making of such a promise affect your obligation to act more than utilitarian theory permits? Does the making of such a promise create a prima facie [...] obligation toward the child, whereas the act-utilitarian theory implies that it does not.

Most people, if not all persons, will agree that the making of the promise does create a prima facie obligation. Further, they will feel that it imposes a stronger obligation to provide for the girl than there is to care for other persons similarly circumstanced whom one has not promised to care for.

In contrast, the act-utilitarian formula holds that a promise is of weight only if and insofar as the fact of having made it affects the relative expectable utilities of various courses of action.

If it so happens that the fact of having made the promise does not affect the relative expectable utilities (for example, if no one knows about the promise, and hence will not be disappointed by failure to keep it), then the promise is of no moral effect whatever. Consequently, because sometimes it will not be of *any* weight for this reason, the act-utilitarian cannot say that there is a prima facie obligation to keep promises (that is, can't say it is *always* one's duty to keep them, when there is no conflicting prima facie obligation).

There are many parallel difficulties for the act-utilitarian. We think we have strong prima facie obligations to our children, our parents, and our wives, that we do not have to others, and that derive from the special relation in which we stand to them. We think that, if we have accidentally caused the injury of another person, we have a prima facie obligation to be solicitous, to send flowers, and so on, which we would not have if we merely read about the injury in the newspaper. Or, if a friend has done us a favor of reading and criticizing the manuscript of our book, we think we have a prima facie obligation to read and criticize the manuscript of his book, which we do not have toward others, even if we think the manuscripts of others would interest or profit us more. Furthermore, in all these cases, it is plausible to conclude not merely that we think we have these prima facie obligations, but that we really do have them—and that their duty is, therefore, affected by more things than net expectable utility. [...]

3. The act-utilitarian thesis is in conflict with the fact that we have certain obligations connected with social and economical justice. The matter is a complex one [...]. But it may be convincing to observe now that many people have thought that, if a divine being had the power to guide the distribution of joy in the world, he should distribute it equally (or perhaps compensate for the past, to virtuous people who have sacrificed themselves for the public good), and not arbitrarily favor individuals whom he happened to fancy—and this even if his playing favorites did not diminish the total amount of welfare in the world. On this question, however, the act-utilitarian must say that any distribution is equally satisfactory, as long as the total amount of joy is undiminished. Again, many people have thought that if a man had a family of four, but could increase the total amount of welfare by increasing it to eight, albeit at severe cost to the average welfare of the initial four, it would obviously be immoral for him to have a larger family. However, the act-utilitarian must say that any act that maximized the total welfare is one's duty.

4. Suppose that, in wartime England, people are requested, as a measure essential for the war effort, to conserve electricity and gas by having a maximum temperature of 50 degrees F. in their homes. A utilitarian Frenchman living in England at the time, however, argues as follows: "All the good moral British obviously will pay scrupulous attention to conforming with this request. The war effort is sure not to suffer from a shortage of electricity and gas. Now, it will make no difference to the war effort whether I personally use a bit more gas, but it will make a great deal of difference to my comfort. So, since the public welfare will be maximized by my using gas to keep the temperature up to 70 degrees F. in my home, it is my duty to use the gas."

According to the act-utilitarian theory, this argument is perfectly valid. But we should not take it seriously in fact. Why not? At least part of the reason is that we think that, if a sacrifice has to be made for the public good, all should share in it equally. Imagine the outcry in Britain, if it became known that members of the Cabinet, who knew that electricity and gas were in good supply because of the country's willingness to sacrifice used this argument to justify using whatever power was necessary to keep their homes comfortable.

5. The foregoing example discloses a further difficulty. *Every* Englishman can also argue that what he personally does will in all probability have a negligible effect on the war effort; and therefore; by the utilitarian principle, any substantial benefit from self-indulgent behavior will justify it. It is true that losing the war must be judged an enormous calamity that cannot be risked; if the chance were one in ten million that the war would be lost by one's self-indulgence, one should not take the risk. But this is not the case; if other people decide on self-indulgence, too, and the war is lost on the account, one will still conclude that it would have made no difference if one had abstained oneself. But, if *everybody* follows this act-utilitarian reasoning, the war will be lost, with disastrous effects for everybody. Thus, universal obedience of the act-utilitarian directive to seek the public good may well cause great public harm. The point may be put in a general way. Suppose there is some kind of behavior (for example, truthfulness) the practice of which by the vast majority of people is highly valuable although deviation by occasional individuals may have good effects, on balance. The act-utilitarian thesis justifies any individual in deviating from this practice whenever the net expectable utility of *his* deviation exceeds that of *his* conformity.

Suppose everyone followed the act-utilitarian principle in behavior. This would mean that every time one answered a question, even under oath, one must think it one's duty to answer falsely if one thinks so doing will serve the public (including one's own) good. It would mean that when one has contracted to do something and the time has arrived for performance, one must raise the question of whether performance will really have maximum net expectable utility, everything considered. It would mean that when one's parents fall ill and are in need of assistance, one must think one ought not to help them if the net expectable utility of so doing is less than net expectable utility of spending one's money and time in some other way. But if people really thought and acted in this way, no one could have assurance about what might happen on important occasions in the future. Institutions would be undermined. (Take marriage: A man would feel it his duty to commit adultery, if the net expectable utility assuming it could be kept secret—would exceed that of refraining!) A great number of people, if no everyone, would feel insecure. [...]

3. The Compromise: Rule Utilitarianism

Many philosophers today are convinced both by objections to formalism and by objections to act-utilitarianism. They are therefore attracted by a compromise theory, which we shall call "rule-utilitarianism."[6]

This theory, a product of the last decade, is not a novel one. We find statements of it in J.S. Mill and John Austin in the nineteenth century; and indeed we find at least traces of it much earlier, in discussions of the nature and function of law by the early Greeks. But in the earlier statements of it we do not find it sharply defined, as an alternative to act-utilitarianism. Clear formulations of it have been the work of the past few years.

Let us begin with as exact a statement of the theory as is possible. Unfortunately, no exact statement will represent accurately the views of all who advocate this general type of theory, for the precise suggestions they have put forward have varied considerably. But there is an exact formulation that is at least as convincing as any others that have been suggested.

The thesis of rule-utilitarianism may be formulated thus: "It is obligatory over all for an agent to perform an act *A* if and only if the prescription that it be performed ['Do *A*!'] follows logically from a complete description of the agent's situation plus ideal prescriptions for his community; and ideal prescriptions for his community are that set of universal imperatives [of the form 'Do *A* in circumstances *C*'] containing no proper names which is *(a)* complete[7] and as economical in distinct imperatives and in concepts as is compatible with completeness, and such that *(b)* a conscientious effort to obey it, by everyone in the agent's community, would have as least as great net expectable as similar effort to obey any other set of imperatives."[8]

A rough example of the application of this thesis is as follows. Suppose I have made a promise to do *A*, and I wonder whether I should really do *A*. Now, presumably the set of imperatives, universal conscientious effort to conform with which will have maximum net expectable utility in my community, will contain a directive rather like (but with some qualifications), "If a person has made a promise to do *x*, let him do *x*!" And, by the thesis, I am therefore obligated over all to do *A*.

It may be helpful to draw an analogy between this theory and the application of laws to particular cases. Laws are general, and they are made by legislators, undoubtedly with utilitarian considerations in mind. But when judges apply the law, they do not construe their job as one of

deciding particular cases by appeal to utilities (as if act-utilitarianism were the principle judges should follow); they regard their job as of following the direction of the general law for the particular case. Now, morality is an informal analogue of law, and the rule-utilitarian is saying that we should decide particular cases by following general prescriptions but that whether a given general prescription should be adopted depends roughly on the utility of its being generally obeyed.

Such a view to some extent avoids the main objection to formalism, for it links moral principles to welfare; general prescriptions are not to be adopted unless observance of them will probably do good. But it also escapes at least most of the objections to act-utilitarianism; its implications are closer to reflective conclusions about obligations. Take our second objection above, to the implications of act-utilitarian theory about the bindingness of promises. On the rule-utilitarian theory, if we make a promise to a widow to care for her daughter, we are bound not just to the extent that we must do whatever will produce consequences (so that e are bound, perhaps, to do just what we would otherwise have been bound to if we had not made the promise); we are bound to do whatever it would have the best consequences for *everyone* to do in similar situations. This—especially in view of the value of people being able to reply on promises—may be to honor the promise in many situations for which act-utilitarians would not prescribe honoring the promise. [...]

There are two more specific questions likely to be raised about such a theory, whose answer will help us understand it. These are the following. First, suppose a man thought that the best possible system of rules for his community would include the prescription that no individuals support their parents in their old age, but that all the elderly be supported by the state, out of taxes. (Perhaps he would be right in this.) The question is then this: If this is correct, is one then relieved of one's obligation to support one's parents, as the social system now stands? The correct answer is negative, for we must distinguish two questions. (1) Given a community in which it is established practice for children to support their parents and where there are no other institutional arrangements, would it have maximum net utility for everybody to stop supporting parents? The answer is obviously, "No." (2) But, given this same kind of community, would it have maximum net utility for everyone to start advocating and doing all in his power to introduce a legal system of institutional tax-supported care for the elderly? The answer to this may well be, "Yes." If we distinguish the two issues carefully, the theory does not lead to obviously wrong conclusions.

There is a second question, about the implications of the theory for cases such that the agent happens to know whether or not other people will in fact obey an ideal rule. Suppose to take a simple case, an agent knows that it would be better for everyone (except persons with some urgent business) to refrain from cutting across the grass of a park. But he also happens to know that no one (except possibly himself) will in fact hesitate to cut across the grass when it suits his convenience—and knows that in fact the grass in the park is going to be, or is already, in an unpleasing condition. Should their be a rule prescribing that he (anyone who knows this) now may walk on the grass also, since this will have most net utility in a society where the

grass will be spoiled anyway? Or, take the opposite case. Suppose he knows that practically everybody else will scrupulously avoid crossing the grass, and therefore nothing will be gained by his refraining from walking on it since the grass will be in fine shape anyway. Should there again be a special rule prescribing that he (anyone who knows this) walk on the grass if it suits his advantage, this time because so doing by everybody in a situation like his will produce a net gain in utility in a society where the grass is carefully provided for? The most thoughtful defenders of the theory who have considered the matter have answered both these questions in the affirmative.

Notes

1. One might urge that it would be more consistent to count "universalist impersonal pluralism" as a form of utilitarianism. It is more illuminating, however, to treat it separately, in connection with formalism. Its spirit is closer to formalism than to the other universalist theories.

Some writers are "utilitarian" to mean more specifically "hedonistic utilitarian." The reader should be alert to such specialized uses. Many "refutations" of utilitarianisms are aimed at the hedonistic features, and do not touch the utilitarianism at all.

2. Given the way in which we have explained "objective duty," it is more consistent, since we are construing utilitarianism as a theory about what our objective duty is, to interpret it in the *former* way. The reason why is complex, and we shall omit statement of it here. We interpret it in the second way mainly because so doing provides a better model of a reasonable way to decide what is one's duty (or probably one's duty), for readers who may have attracted by utilitarianism.

This decision makes no difference, however, to our appraisal of the theory. The arguments adduced in criticism of the theory are effective in whichever way we interpret it, although sometimes minor adjustments need to be made (usually simply striking the word "expectable" from the phrase "net expectable utility") in order for the reasoning to be equally effective against the theory, as construed in the first sense.

When we come to "rule-utilitarianism" later in the chapter, we shall construe it in a parallel way. There too, we have a choice. One could decide differently, and the arguments used in appraisal of the theory would be equally effective.

Incidentally, we could have defined "egoism" in this second way, but our objection to it would still have been fatal.

3. There is a necessary reservation about the use of the phrase "have a correct opinion." If we are relativists, the possibility is open that a course of action will be correctly said to have greater net expectable utility by one person, and less (than some alternative) by another person.

It may be suggested that the existence of a "correct" opinion is further compromised by the fact that probability is always relative to the available evidence. But at the time when a decision must be made, the "evidence available" will be approximately the same for any person involved; and we shall assume that there is, therefore, a fixed base of "evidence" for probability determinations, and hence that the probabilities correctly assigned any event in a given set will be determinate, for a given problem. If it is questioned whether probabilities can be assigned in an objective manner, then matters are not greatly altered; for now the choice is simply between sets of consequences, not now with a definite probability assigned each member of the set, but with a certain specifiable piece of evidence as the ground for explanation of each member of the set. In principle, there is still no question except that of what preferences are justified; indeed, this manner of stating the problem probably is closer to life—since no one ordinarily does us the favor of working out the probabilities of the members of the sets between which we choose, and we make the choices on the basis of rough familiarity with the favorable and unfavorable evidence.

The critical reader may wonder whether these qualifications do not go a long way toward erasing the difference between what is a person's "objective" duty and what is his "subjective" duty. And, of course, this is correct. But there is still a difference between the act which *has* maximum expectable net utility and the one the agent *thinks* has maximum net expectable utility.

4. It is assumed that the choice is made between sets of experiences, ignoring who has the experiences, and thus ignoring questions of one distribution of enjoyments being better than another. If this assumption is not made, the distinction between the utilitarian theories and universal impersonal pluralism is erased.

5. The act-utilitarian can consistently say we should *condemn* such an act, if it is detected, as a means of promoting the security of fathers.

6. On p. 253, it was formulated, not as a general statement about what acts are obligatory, but *as a method* for determining which acts are obligatory.

7. A "complete" set is one that does not fail to supply direction for any decision one may have to make.

8. The expectable utilities of everyone obeying a given rule will include not only direct benefits, but the indirect benefits of being able to plan on other people doing a certain thing in certain circumstances. An alternate formulation very similar to the foregoing is this: "If the doing of *A* by everyone in your community who might find himself in circumstances like yours would be greater net expectable utility than any other act that might be performed in such circumstances, then it is your obligation to do *A*."

Kantian Ethics

It is noble to be good; it is still nobler to teach others to be good—and less trouble.
—Mark Twain

Discussion Questions

1. Good will, contrary to Kant, is not always good without qualification. After all, the road to hell is often paved with good intentions. Robert Oppenheimer, the father of the atomic bomb, was motivated, in part, by the belief that building a nuclear bomb would end the Second World War quickly, thereby preventing countless deaths during an allied invasion of Japan. He was, in other words, doing his duty

to help the war effort. However, when the U.S. Air Force dropped the bomb on Hiroshima on August 6 and Nagasaki on August 9, 1945, it killed 200,000 people instantaneously and led to the deaths of thousands more due to radiation poisoning. The development of the atomic bomb also unleashed an arms race leading to the escalation of nuclear weapons. Did Oppenheimer's good intentions of trying to end the Second World War justify the thousands killed by the atomic bombs? Did the bombs' development justify the thousands of nuclear weapons currently throughout the world?[23] At what point do the consequences become relevant when it comes to the moral worth of our actions?

2. Imagine that the Canadian Securities and Intelligence Service (CSIS) has discovered a terrorist network. Suspects are arrested and interrogated. During the interrogation process, it is discovered that a "dirty" (nuclear) bomb has been placed somewhere in Toronto, armed and set to go off in one hour. The terrorists are unwilling to disclose the bomb's location; they are confident that it will cause significant damage and loss of life. Would security agents be morally justified in torturing the suspects in order to discover the bomb's location? Do they have a duty to ensure that the rights of terrorist suspects are not violated? Would a security agent's duty to protect the public usurp an individual's right not to be tortured, as outlined in the United Nations *Convention Against Torture*? Give reasons for your answers. If a duty to not torture and a duty to protect innocent life are in conflict, how could we solve this dilemma? What would Kant say about this situation?

Duty Is as Duty Does

Immanuel Kant offers a unique approach to moral reasoning. Kant, unlike utilitarians, is not a consequentialist. That is, he believed the rightness or wrongness of a moral action does not depend on the consequences it produces but on whether the act itself is morally right or wrong. In this sense, Kantian ethics is deontological in nature. Certain acts are themselves right or wrong, and, therefore, we are duty bound to follow them in all circumstances regardless of the consequences. To get a better understanding of Kantian reasoning, let's look at a real-life example.

Over the last 30 years, the Canadian International Development Agency (CIDA) has been instrumental in helping prevent river blindness. To date, CIDA has committed more than $25 million (USD) to fight the disease and Canada is ranked one of the top five donors worldwide (Canadian International Development Agency).

River blindness (*onchocerciasis*) is caused by the bite of a black fly, which breeds along riverbanks in tropical regions in Africa and Latin America, and in parts of the Middle East (The Business Enterprise Trust 238–239). When the fly bites its victims, it passes to them a tiny parasitic worm. The tiny worm burrows itself under the skin, where it can grow up to two-feet long curled inside an ugly round nodule. Inside the nodule, the worm reproduces by releasing millions of microscopic offspring called microfilariae, which wiggle their way through the body underneath the skin causing discolouring, lesions, and intense inching. The itching is so intense that some people have committed suicide because of it. The microfilariae eventually invade the eyes causing blindness.

In the late 1970s, river blindness affected approximately 18 million impoverished people living in remote villages worldwide and another 85 million people were at risk of being infected. William Campbell, a researcher working for the pharmaceutical company Merck & Co., discovered that one of the company's best-selling animal drugs, known as Ivomec (Ivermectin), might be useful in treating river blindness (The Business Enterprise Trust 242). Ivomec was used to cure a wide range of parasites in cattle, pigs, horses, and other animals. Further evidence revealed that Ivomec could provide a cure for river blindness at a relatively low cost. The total cost of making the human version of Ivomec was estimated at $100 million. This was cheap, considering the average cost of getting a drug to market at this time took 12 years and $200 million (The Business Enterprise Trust 240).

However, Merck quickly realized that even if the company produced the drug, the villagers would be too poor to afford it. There was no way that Merck could recover their expenses. And even if the villagers could afford it, it was impossible to distribute the drugs because of the remoteness of the villages and the lack of access to doctors, commercial outlets, or clinics. There was also a concern that if Merck donated the drug it might lead to comparable expectations in the future and thus hamper research into tropical diseases. Other executives pointed out that if the drug had side effects, it might lead to poor publicity for the animal version of the drug, which contributed over $300 million to company coffers. Moreover, even if a cheap human version of Ivermectin was available, it might be smuggled to black markets and sold for use on animals, which would undermine Merck's lucrative sales of Ivomec. And to top it all off, despite a net income of $1.98 billion, Merck's profits were being eroded due to legislation passed by the United States government to increase competition in the marketplace by allowing competitors to produce low-cost drugs originally developed by other companies. Hence, senior executives were unwilling to take on major projects, which had little economic promise,[24] and yet without the drugs millions of people would suffer (Velasquez, *Business Ethics* 3–4). What should Merck do? Should Merck make the drug regardless of cost? Does the company have a moral obligation? Should it shelve the project and forget the whole thing because of the costs?

After much debate, the senior executives at Merck decided to go ahead and produce the drug; the potential human benefits of the drug for river blindness were too significant to ignore. Many of the managers thought they were morally obligated to produce the drug despite the fact that there was little economic reward (Velasquez, *Business Ethics* 4). On February 24, 1981, in Dakar, Senegal, the first patient in the clinical trials of Mectizan received a single dose of the

medicine. During the next four years up until 1985, Merck researchers, in conjunction with the World Health Organization and academe, conducted trials in countries such as Ghana, Guatemala, Liberia, Senegal, and Togo. The trial proved the effectiveness of Mectizan in the treatment of river blindness. In short, after seven years of research, a single pill was developed that would eradicate from the body all traces of the parasite. An annual dose of Mectizan would effectively reduce microscopic worms in the skin to near zero in one month, and be successfully maintained for up to 12 months (Merck & Co.).

In October 1987, P. Roy Vagelos, Merck's chairman and CEO, announced that the company would donate Mectizan for the treatment of river blindness to all who needed it for as long as needed. In other words, so long as river blindness existed, Merck would donate the drug. Why did Merck do this? Why develop, manufacture, and distribute a drug that made no money? Vagelos argued that he had a duty to help these people. Merck also took the initiative and financed an international committee to provide the infrastructure for distribution and ensured the drug didn't end up on the black market. Although Mectizan is donated free of charge by Merck, it costs an average of 50 cents to get one dose into the hands of each infected person. To date, Merck has provided more than 1.8 billion tablets of Mectizan free of charge to people at risk for river blindness in some of the poorest countries in the world. Since the program began in 1987, it has grown to reach more than 40 million people annually in more than 30 countries where river blindness is endemic. The program has become an unparalleled worldwide endeavour that includes the World Health Organization, the World Bank, UNICEF, and numerous non-governmental organizations and ministries of health. Currently, there are approximately 120 million people worldwide who are at risk of contracting river blindness (Merck & Co).

Merck's decision to help prevent river blindness is very Kantian in flavour. Merck didn't develop the drug to maximize happiness of those impoverished people, to increase sales, boost morale for his employees, or ensure a greater return on investment for investors. Merck made the drug because it had a moral obligation to prevent suffering. In other words, the company did so out of duty. It is this sense of duty and obligation that is at the heart of Kant's moral theory. Let's look at some of its main features.

The Good Will

Kant wished to develop a moral theory based on the intrinsic rightness or wrongness of certain actions. In this sense, the morality of an action is determined, not by its consequences, but whether or not it conforms to and for the sake of the moral law. The moral law is a statement that is binding on all people unconditionally. In short, Kant is an **absolutist**. Some actions are right and some wrong—period. Moreover, determining what is morally right or wrong is based on reason and rationality. Rationality and morality go hand in hand, according to Kant. If we choose to be rational, we choose to follow the moral law. More specifically, morality is determined *a priori*. It's from pure reason and rationality, not experience, that our moral decisions are made.

Kant's *Groundwork for the Metaphysics of Morals* starts with asking this question: "What gives an act moral worth?" For Kant, an act has moral worth if it is done from the **good will**. That is, an act is right *only* if it is done out of duty. A person who acts from good will does so because it is the right thing to do. Our will is good if the motives behind our actions are morally good. Consider the river blindness example. Merck made the drug because it was motivated to prevent unnecessary suffering. Its actions were not only derived from a sense of duty but in accord with duty. In short, the company acted upon good will. Or consider Liviu Librescu. Librescu, a holocaust survivor and engineering professor, sacrificed his life to save his students during the worst killing spree in United States history, when 32 people died at Virginia Polytechnic Institute. As Cho Seung-Hui tried to shoot his way into Librescu's classroom, Librescu used his body to block the door, which allowed his students to jump out windows to safety below. Librescu was fatally shot and died

on the classroom floor. According to eyewitness counts, Librescu's actions were courageous and brave, but it was not out of character (Verma A1). He did it because it was the right thing to do. Notice, from a utilitarian point of view, Librescu's actions in saving his students would also be considered moral, not because he acted out of duty but because he maximized the overall happiness for his students. In contrast, from a Kantian point of view, Librescu's actions were right because it was done from the motive to fulfill his duty of helping others and preventing harm to innocent people. Even if Librescu had been unsuccessful at saving his students, his motives would still be good. As Kant says, his good will "like a jewel… would still shine by its own light." The consequences of achieving certain ends are irrelevant to whether Librescu's actions have moral worth; he acted from and in accord with his duty and this is all that counts.

If the moral worth of an action is determined by its underlying motivation of duty and the moral law, how do we know what the moral law is? How do we know which action is the right one to take? For Kant, we determine our moral action by testing maxims. A maxim is a general rule or principle that guides the action you intend to perform. For Kant, any maxim must be able to be applied universally. In other words, "acting upon a maxim commits me, as a rational moral agent, to a universal moral rule or principle governing all persons in situations like mine (in the relevant respects)" (Waluchow 176). For Kant, everyone must be prepared that if a maxim is a sufficient reason for him or her to act, it must be a sufficient reason for everyone else to act like him or her. For example, Kant asks us to imagine a situation in which we make a promise we know we will not be able to keep. Imagine Beth's business is near financial ruin. Her bank is hounding her to repay her loan. She promises to repay, knowing she will not be able to keep her promise. Her maxim might be something like, whenever I can avoid paying a loan by making a false promise I shall do so. But, again, this must be universalizable for Beth and everyone else in her situation. Maxims are merely descriptive principles that explain what action is intended to be performed. This differs from what Kant calls imperatives. Imperatives are normative; they tell us what we ought to do.

Hypothetical and Categorical Imperatives

The normative aspect of imperatives can be broken down into two kinds: the hypothetical and categorical. The **hypothetical imperative** tells us what we ought to do to achieve personal ends or goals. So, for example, if you want to get an 'A' in philosophy class, then you ought to study. If Vagelos wants to prevent river blindness, he ought to make Mectizan. If Librescu wants to save lives, he ought to hold the door shut. In this sense, we ought to do certain actions to achieve specific ends. In other words, the hypothetical imperative takes the form: If you want Z, then you ought to do Y. Of course, the converse will also be true. If you don't want to pass philosophy class, prevent suffering, or save lives, then by renouncing your desires, your duties no longer hold. From a moral point of view, this is problematic because no one will be obligated to do certain actions if morality is based on the whim of personal desires. If you suddenly stop desiring to prevent illness or save lives, then so be it. The hypothetical imperative undermines the point and purpose of morality. The point of morality is to get us to do things beyond or regardless of personal self-interested desires. If so, then the hypothetical imperative cannot be the basis of morality.

In contrast, Kant underwrites our moral obligations with the **categorical imperative**. The categorical imperative is objective, independent of personal desires, and holds universally. In this sense, it is law-like in nature—exceptionless and unconditional. The categorical imperative must be obeyed even if you don't feel like it. In this sense, the categorical imperative takes the form of a strict law: Do X—it is not based on the results (consequences) of an action but is itself the result. The categorical imperative holds universally valid for everyone regardless of the circumstances or situations. And because everyone is rational, says Kant, everyone will come up with the same categorical imperative about what is morally right or wrong. In other words, the categorical imperative prescribes or determines our moral obligations.

But what is the process by which we come up the categorical imperative? That is, how do we determine our universally binding moral obligations? For Kant, there are various formulations of the categorical imperative. Let's look at his two most famous formations, taking each in turn.

The First and Second Categorical Imperatives

Kant's **first formulation of the categorical imperative** states, "Act only on that maxim whereby you can at the same time will that it become a universal law." That is, act on a maxim only if it can be universalized. If the maxim can't be universalized, then we shouldn't act on it. This requires that each of us do a little thought experiment when deciding what our moral obligations are. For Kant, an immoral maxim will not be accepted under his categorical imperative, not because of the negative consequences, but because the maxim is logically impossible (inconsistent) or inconceivable. As Joshua Glasgow points out, in his article following Kant's, the first categorical imperative can be broken down into three steps:

1. Develop a maxim.
2. Universalize the maxim. That is, ask yourself what would happen if it became a universal law. In other words, what would happen if everyone universally followed the maxim.
3. Determine if the maxim is logically inconsistent or would contradict itself.

Let's look at some examples. Let me alter Kant's original example. Beth promises to pay back a loan, knowing full well she will be unable to fulfill this promise. Should she make a false promise in order to get the loan? The maxim in this case would be:

> When I think myself in want of money, I will borrow money and promise to repay it, although I know that I never can do so.

In other words, whenever Beth needs a loan, she promises to repay it, even though she knows she will never be able to do so. Now, take this maxim and now universalize it. What would happen if everyone followed this maxim? The maxim might look like this:

> Whenever anyone is in want of money, one will borrow the money and promise to repay it, although one knows that one will never do so.

Well, if this maxim were universalized, then no one would believe the promises made to them, and no one would give loans based on false promises. To put another way, promise-keeping would be meaningless, since whenever someone said "I promise," we simply would not believe what is being said. More importantly, there would be no point in making a promise or accepting a promise, since promises can only work against a background of people believing them. Promising requires trust on the part of the person to whom the promise is made, but in this situation, there is no trust, and so promises of this sort would be impossible. Hence, not keeping one's promises would be self-defeating or inconsistent because the very activity of promise-keeping would eliminate itself. To put another way, it is immoral for Beth to make a promise to the bank that she knows she can't keep.

Consider one more example. Let's pretend you are bidding for a construction project overseas. You need this contact because if you don't get it, then your business will go bankrupt. To ensure your company stays afloat, you contemplate whether to bribe the government official you are dealing with (see Box 5.9). What ought you to do? Well, your maxim might be:

> If I am facing bankruptcy, then I will bribe in order to get a needed contract.

Universalizing the maxim would look something like this:

> Whenever anyone is facing bankruptcy, one will bribe in order to get a needed contract.

> **Box 5.9** 2006 Transparent International Corruption Perception Index
>
> | Least Corrupt Countries | Most Corrupt Countries |
> |---|---|
> | 1. Finland | 1. Haiti |
> | 2. Iceland | 2. Myanmar |
> | 3. New Zealand | 3. Iraq |
> | 4. Denmark | 4. Guinea |
> | 5. Singapore | 5. Sudan |
> | 6. Sweden | 6. Congo |
> | 7. Switzerland | 7. Chad |
> | 8. Norway | 8. Bangladesh |
> | 9. Australia | 9. Uzbekistan |
> | 10. Netherlands | 10. Equatorial Guinea |
>
> **Source:** Transparency International. *Transparency International Corruption Perceptions Index 2006.* 28 May 2007 <http://www.transparency.org/policy_research/surveys_indices/cpi>.

What happens if everyone bribes to get contracts? It must be remembered that the point of bribery is to get special consideration. In other words, if I give you X, you will give me special consideration Y. But if everyone bribes, then the very idea of special consideration becomes inconsistent and irrational. You will never get special consideration if everyone bribes because everyone is seeking the same things. In other words, bribery can only work against a background of non-bribery. Hence, if universalized, bribery is immoral.

Applying maxims universally is important because it avoids the "free rider" problem discussed in the last section. It avoids double standards and hypocrisy. You cannot will an act be morally acceptable for you and, yet, immoral for someone else. For Kant, we also have duties against suicide and neglecting one's talents. Although I will not venture to universalize these maxims here, the idea should be clear; by universalizing maxims we can determine the categorical imperatives which will be universally binding on all rational people.

Kant's second categorical imperative is also a hallmark of his moral theory. Unfortunately, in our reading from Glasgow, he does not outline this crucial imperative. Let me do this now.

Show Me Some Respect

Kant's **second formulation of the categorical imperative** states, "So act as to treat humanity, whether in my own person or in that of another, in every case at the same time as an end, never as a means only." In short, never use people. People should be treated as rational creatures with dignity and **intrinsic value**. If I respect someone, I treat them the same as myself. That is, we ought to not treat people as merely having **instrumental value**. This is important. Whereas utilitarians can justify using other people as a means to maximizing happiness, for Kant, this would be morally unacceptable. People have value in themselves, not for the purpose they serve others. Similarly, we ought not let ourselves be used. No one should be under the will of another person. People are to treat each other as free and equal in the pursuit of their interests. Again, we ought to be careful here. Although it's true we often use people as a means to an end, say, using one's employer for a pay cheque or hiring someone to paint your house, we are not allowed to *merely* use them. As an employee, for example, we consent to working in exchange for a pay cheque every two weeks. We are usually told of the working conditions, hours, holidays, etc., and agree to them as part of the conditions when accepting a job. But one cannot manipulate or deceive others to achieve desired ends. An example of this kind of manipulation would be sexual harassment. If women were merely used as a form of sexual pleasure or gain, then this would be morally wrong. Or consider the Ford Pinto example from the last section. If Ford truly valued people with dignity and respect, they would have never allowed the faulty gas tank to

be put into the Pinto, and many lives would have been saved. In short, we are to treat people as an end in themselves and respect their autonomy and freedom. Kant also thinks that we should treat ourselves with respect and not merely as a means to some end. For example, Kant condemns suicide because you are using yourself as a means to an end. That is, by killing yourself you are trying to achieve some other end such as freedom from pain and suffering.

The Perils of Imperatives

Kant's moral theory has certain advantages: it is consistent, shows respect for others, and values fairness for all. But it also has some considerable problems.

First, Kant's moral theory is absolutist. He allows no exceptions to his categorical imperatives. Let's go back to our earlier example of Beth promising to pay back a loan, knowing full well she will be unable to fulfill this promise. Although Kant thinks making false promises is immoral, what he doesn't realize is that we can build various exceptions into a maxim whereby, once universalized, they become logically consistent, thus, moral. Consider Beth's original universalized maxim:

> Whenever anyone is in want of money, one will borrow the money and promise to repay it, although one know that one will never do so.

Notice, if we can alter this slightly to:

> Whenever anyone is in want of money, one will borrow the money and promise to repay it, except when one are faced with financial ruin.

In other words, always keep your promises, except when faced with financial ruin. What would happen if everyone paid his or her loan, except when faced with bankruptcy? Universalizing this maxim would be consistent. Why? Because, on average, only very few people would not be able to keep their promise due to bankruptcy. According to Industry Canada, there were

3.5 cases of bankruptcy per 1,000 businesses in 2006, a decrease of 0.6 percent from the previous year (Office of the Superintendent of Bankruptcy Canada). This means banks would continue to believe promises to repay loans, even if the person is lying, because the vast majority of people will repay them. In short, banks would loan money because they would believe their clients, and therefore lying to get a loan when you know you cannot pay it back is morally acceptable.

The building of exceptions into maxims highlights a fundamental problem with Kant's moral theory. As Glasgow points out, whether a maxim passes or fails the test of universalizability depends on how it is formulated. Consider this example not discussed by Glasgow. Imagine you are assigned a research paper in your philosophy class but you don't feel like writing it (Feldman 114). Instead, you consider buying a research paper off the Internet written by someone else and submitting it as your own. What would your maxim be? It might be:

> Whenever I need a term paper for my philosophy course, and don't feel like writing it, I will buy it off the Internet and submit it as my own.

Once universalized, it might read:

> Whenever anyone needs a term paper for a course, and one doesn't feel like writing it, one will buy one off the Internet and submit it as one's own.

Universalization means this maxim would be self-defeating because buying a paper off the Internet undermines the academic process. Writing papers are important because it helps professors determine a student's understanding of a specific subject area and his or her analytic and critical thinking skills. In buying papers off the Internet, professors wouldn't believe the work represented is really that of their students but someone else's. Therefore, it not only undermines the educational process, but professors wouldn't be so foolish to assign a writing assignment in the first place. In this sense, buying papers off the Internet and submitting it as one's

own is self-defeating. But what if the maxim was altered slightly to read:

> Whenever I, Sam Smith, student at X University, need a term paper for my philosophy course, and don't feel like writing it, I will buy it off the Internet and submit it as my own.

Once universalized it will read:

> Anyone named Sam Smith, who is also a student at X University, is in need of a term paper for a course, and doesn't feel like writing it, he will buy it off the Internet and submit it as his own.

In this formulation of the maxim, it is perfectly consistent. It is consistent because only those individuals named Sam Smith and who attend X University will follow the maxim. The academic process and educational process is not undermined. Professors will assign writing assignments because only those students named Sam Smith will find ways to cheat the system. In this case, Sam Smith can buy a paper off the Internet and submit it as his own without contradiction. In short, plagiarism is moral. The obvious problem is that all forms of plagiarism are wrong regardless of whether it can be willed to be a universal law. But by tinkering with Kantian maxims, plagiarism is morally acceptable. This surely cannot be right.

Now practice this objection yourself. Is it ethical to cheat a thief (see Box 5.10)?

Another problem with Kant, not discussed by Glasgow, is in how to solve conflicting maxims. I mentioned earlier that during the Second World War Dutch fishermen used to smuggle Jewish refugees to England. When stopped by Nazi patrol boats, according to Kant, the fisherman would be duty bound to follow two maxims: "Do not lie" and "Always protect innocent lives." The universalization of both maxims are consistent and, therefore, moral. The problem is that Kant gives us no way, no mechanism, to determine which categorical imperative takes priority[25] (Rachels 125). In short, there is no way out; we are damned if we do and damned if we don't.[26]

Box 5.10 Is It Ethical to Cheat a Thief?

"We could use a drink. I'll buy us a round of beer," I offered with a hesitant smile.

My two companions were slightly shocked: It was our first day in Oaxaca, Mexico, and we had just been mugged and were supposedly penniless.

We had wandered the city with a wide-eyed enthusiasm and naiveté typical of freshly arrived travellers, and found ourselves on the outskirts of the city in a park that the guidebook (we later read) recommended that visitors avoid because of thefts.

A man materialized in front of us on a dirt road void of people. I noticed him only a moment before we reached each other, and we did that awkward dance-like step people do to avoid each other's path, only to step in the same direction.

I gave a polite, apologetic laugh and moved to avoid him. I don't know what the man said as he stepped back in front of me, but the knife in the man's hand left little room for miscommunication. He hurriedly repeated his request for—obviously enough—money, the knife waving a few inches from our bellies.

A quick cost-benefit calculation evaporated thoughts of physically defending ourselves. We could run, but I figured it wasn't a sensible option to impose on my companions.

Another idea popped into my head. Is it ethical to cheat a thief? I didn't ponder this question for long. I opened my wallet and swiftly handed the man a wad of Canadian Tire cash, which a friend had suggested I carry for use as bribes.

If I had planned this swindle, I'm sure I would have blown it. But I did it with barely a thought and it worked; I left with my real money safe in my wallet.

The beer calmed our nerves, and before long my friends and I were chuckling and speculating about what our robber might do with a fistful of Canadian Tire bills. I privately mused whether he might eventually see a little humour in the situation. Who knows, but I sincerely hoped I would never have the occasion to find out.

(I should add that after the incident described here, I spent six crime-free months in beautiful Oaxaca, an exceptionally safe and friendly city.)

Source: Jamie Simpson. "How to Outsmart a Thief in Mexico: Carry Canadian Tire Money." *Globe and Mail* 20 Jan. 2007: T8.

Kant's second categorical imperative is also subject to criticism. Kant says we are always to treat people as an end and never as a means only. Using Kant's earlier example, if a person were to make a promise to get a loan, knowing that it would never be repaid, he or she would be treating the bank as a means to an end and not an end in itself. And if the bank were to find about the false promise, it would object to being treated this way, and refuse to loan the money. Generally speaking, people do not agree to being used and are upset if they are. But does this apply in all situations and contexts? Imagine Diane intends to steal Karen's motorcycle (Feldman 147). Karen finds out about Diane's plans and chains her motorcycle to a lamppost to prevent Diane from stealing it. In this sense, we could say that Karen is preventing Diane from achieving her goal, namely, stealing the motorcycle. Now if Diane knew what Karen was doing, Diane would object to being treated this way because it prevents her stealing the motorcycle. In this sense, we could say that Karen was using Diane as a means to an end by chaining up her motorcycle. Following Kant, this entails that what Karen was doing was wrong; that it was morally wrong to prevent her bike being stolen. And this is surely absurd (Feldman 148).

Kant's second categorical imperative is also too restricted to humans. Kant states, "the human being and in general every rational being exists as an end in itself, *not merely as a means* to be arbitrarily used by this or that will…[but] must always be regarded at the same time as an end." To have moral worth—to be treated as an end and not as a means—is restricted to those creatures that

Photo 5.3 Endangered Species

The Vancouver Island Marmot is Canada's most endangered species. Unfortunately the population is decreasing, from approximately 300 in the 1980s to just 205 today.

possess (or can potentially possess) rationality; namely, humans. This means that other animals are excluded from Kant's moral sphere. In other words, it's immoral to treat other humans or oneself as a means to an end, but it's morally acceptable to treat non-human animals, plants, and the ecosystem as a means to an end because they do not possess rationality. However, given the current state of our environment, a moral theory that does not take into consideration climate change, species extinction, and deforestation, to name a few problems, seems wholly incomplete (see Photo 5.3).[27]

Another problem, not discussed by Glasgow, is that Kant seems to place too much emphasis on duty as the only action of moral worth. An act is right only if it is from and in accord with duty, says Kant. An act has moral worth from duty, not out of inclination. Inclination means acting out of feeling, desire, or emotion. In this sense, if someone acts out of compassion or sympathy, his or her actions are not morally worthy, says Kant, because it was not in accord with duty. Consider someone who gives money to charity out of sorrow. Although the act may be beneficial to others, the motives are not pure but clouded by the sorrow in his or her heart. To act morally, and for an act to have moral worth, it must be done out of duty. But Kant's moral theory

seems too cold-hearted and unrealistic. Imagine your mother is in the hospital undergoing chemotherapy for breast cancer. You visit her one evening and have a lovely long conversation. As visiting hours come to an end, she turns to you expressing her deepest thanks for coming up to see her. Talking to her has taken her mind of the nauseating effects of chemotherapy and her outlook on life is more optimistic and happier. As a Kantian, you turn to her and say, "It was my duty to see you because it's the right thing to do; it has nothing to do with love, compassion, or sympathy. I merely came to see you because I was obligated and duty bound to do so." I suspect that your mother would be heartbroken. It seems that loving your mother is *itself* a prime motivator for going to see her. However, for Kant, if you did act out of love, not duty, your action would have no moral worth. But surely this can't be right. Love, compassion, and sympathy are just as legitimate a motivator as duty. There seems to be something wrong with a moral theory that doesn't take into consideration emotions, desires, or feeling into account as part of being a moral human being.[28]

29

Immanuel Kant

(1724–1804)

Born in 1724 in Königsberg, Prussia (now Kaliningrad, Russia), Immanuel Kant spent all of his life in this small provincial town. His parents were very religious, belonging to a sect known as the Pietists. They believed that in order to serve God, one

must be pure hearted, kind, and of strong moral conviction. Although unspectacular as an early student, Kant entered the University of Königsberg in 1740 at the age of sixteen, where he studied a number of disciplines including theology, physics, medicine, and philosophy. He eventually came under the influence of Martin Kuntzen, who not only emphasized human reason (rationalism) but also stimulated Kant's interest in Newtonian physics. Both the rationalist and empiricist schools of thought would later have a significant impact on Kant's philosophy. After graduation from university, Kant worked as a private tutor, eventually becoming a lecturer at the University of Königsberg in 1755. In 1770, Kant became a full professor. For the next decade, Kant published nothing, instead devoting his time to what many philosophers regard as one of greatest philosophical works: The Critique of Pure Reason *(1781). Over the next ten years he would also publish the* Prolegomena to Any Future Metaphysics *(1783),* The Foundations of the Metaphysics of Morals *(1785),* Critique of Pure Reason *(1788), and the* Critique of Judgment *(1790), to name a few. Kant died on February 12, 1804.*

Groundwork for the Metaphysics of Morals

Nothing can possibly be conceived in the world, or even out of it, which can be called good, without qualification, except a *good will*. Intelligence, wit, judgement, and the other *talents* of the mind, however they may be named, or courage, resolution, perseverance, as qualities of *temperament,* are undoubtedly good and desirable in many respects; but these gifts of nature may also become extremely bad and mischievous if the will which is to make use of them, and which, therefore, constitutes what is called *character,* is not good. It is the same with the *gifts of fortune.* Power, riches, honor, even health, and the general well-being and contentment with one's condition which is called *happiness,* inspire pride, and often presumption, if there is not a good will to correct the influence of these on the mind, and with this also to rectify the whole principle of acting and adapt it to its end. The sight of a being who is not adorned with a single feature of a pure and good will, enjoying unbroken prosperity, can never give pleasure to an impartial spectator. Thus a good will appears to constitute the indispensable condition even of being worthy of happiness.

There are even some qualities which are of service to this good will itself, and may facilitate its action, yet which have no inner unconditional value, but always presuppose a good will, and this qualifies the esteem that we justly have for them, and does not permit us to regard them as absolutely good. Moderation in the affections and passions, self-control, and calm deliberation are not only good in many respects, but even seem to constitute part of the *inner* worth of the person; but they are far from deserving to be called good without qualification, although they have been so unconditionally praised by the ancients. For without the principles of a good will, they may become extremely evil; and the coldness of a villain not only makes him far more dangerous, but also directly makes him more abominable in our eyes than he would have been without it.

A good will is good not because of what it accomplishes or effects, not by its aptness for the attainment of some proposed end, but simply by virtue of the volition—that is, it is good in itself, and considered by itself is to be esteemed much higher than all that can be brought about by it in favor of any inclination, or even the sum total of all inclinations. Even if it should happen that, owing to a step-motherly nature, this will should wholly lack power to accomplish its purpose, if with its greatest efforts it should yet achieve nothing, and there should remain only the good will (not, to be sure, a mere wish, but the summoning of all means in our power), then, like a jewel, it would still shine by its own light, as a thing which has its whole value in itself. Its usefulness or fruitfulness can neither add nor take away anything from this value. It would be, as it were, only the setting to enable us to handle it the more conveniently in common commerce, or to attract to it the attention of those who are not yet connoisseurs, but not to recommend it to true connoisseurs, or to determine its value. [...]

Thus the moral worth of an action does not lie in the effect expected from it, nor in any principle of action which needs to borrow its motive from this expected effect. For all these effects— agreeableness of one's condition, and even the promotion of the happiness of others—could have been also brought about by other causes, so that for this there would have been no need of the will of a rational being; whereas it is in this alone that the supreme and unconditional good can be found. The pre-eminent good which we call moral can therefore consist in nothing else than the *representation of law* in itself, *which certainly is only possible in a rational being,* insofar as this representation, and not the expected effect, determines the will. This is a good which is already present in the person who acts accordingly, and we have not to wait for it to appear first in the result.[1]

[The Categorical Imperative]

But what sort of law can that be, the conception of which must determine the will, even without paying any regard to the effect expected from it, in order that this will may be called good absolutely and without qualification? As I have deprived the will of every impulse which could arise to it from obedience to any particular law, there remains nothing but the universal conformity of its actions to law in general, which alone is to serve the will as a principle, that is, I am never to act otherwise than so *that I could also will that my maxim should become a universal law.* Here, now, it is the simple lawfulness in general, without assuming any particular law applicable to certain actions, that serves the will as its principle, and must so serve it if duty is not to be a vain delusion and a chimerical notion. The common reason of human beings in its practical judgments perfectly coincides with this, and always has in view the principle here suggested.

Let the question be, for example: May I when in distress make a promise with the intention not to keep it? I readily distinguish here between the two significations which the question may have: whether it is prudent or whether it is right to make a false promise. The former may undoubtedly often be the case. I see clearly indeed that it is not enough to extricate myself from a present difficulty by means of this subterfuge, but it must be well considered whether there may not hereafter spring from this lie much greater inconvenience than that from which I now seek to free myself, and as, with all my supposed *cunning,* the consequences cannot be so easily foreseen but that credit once lost may be much more injurious to me than any mischief which I seek to avoid at present, it should be considered whether it would not be *more prudent* to act herein according to a universal maxim and to make it a habit to promise nothing except with the intention of keeping it. But it is soon clear to me that such a maxim will still only be based on the fear of consequences.

Now it is a wholly different thing to be truthful from duty than to be so from apprehension of injurious consequences. In the first case, the very notion of the action already implies a law for me; in the second case, I must first look about elsewhere to see what results may be combined with it which would affect myself. For to deviate from the principle of duty is beyond all doubt evil; but to be unfaithful to my maxim of prudence may often be very advantageous to me, although to abide by it is certainly safer. The shortest way, however, and an unerring one, to discover the answer to this question whether a lying promise is consistent with duty, is to ask myself, Would I be content that my maxim (to extricate myself from difficulty by a false promise) should hold good as a universal law, for myself as well as for others? and should I be able to say to myself, "Everyone may make a deceitful promise when he finds himself in a difficulty from which he cannot otherwise extricate himself?" Then I presently become aware that while I can will the lie, I can by no means will that lying should be a universal law. For with such a law there would be no promises at all, since it would be in vain to allege my intention in regard to my future actions to those who would not believe this allegation, or if they over-hastily did so, would pay me back in my own coin. Hence my maxim, as soon as it should be made a universal law, would necessarily destroy itself. [...]

[The Hypothetical and Categorical Imperatives]

Everything in nature works according to laws. Rational beings alone have the capacity to act *in accordance with the representation of laws*—that is, according to principles, that is, have a *will*. Since the deduction of actions from principles requires *reason,* the will is nothing but practical reason. If reason infallibly determines the will, then the actions of such a being which are recognized as objectively necessary are subjectively necessary also, that is, the will is a capacity to choose *that only* which reason independent of inclination recognizes as practically necessary, that is, as good. But if reason of itself does not sufficiently determine the will, if the latter is subject also to subjective conditions (particular incentives) which do not always coincide with the objective conditions; in a word, if the will does not *in itself* completely accord with reason (which is actually the case with human beings), then the actions which objectively are recognized as necessary are subjectively contingent, and the determination of such a will according to objective laws is *necessitation*, that is to say, the relation of the objective laws to a will that is not thoroughly good is conceived as the determination of the will of a rational being by principles of reason, but which the will from its nature does not of necessity follow.

The conception of an objective principle, in so far as it is obligatory for a will, is called a command (of reason), and the formula of the command is called an **imperative**.

All imperatives are expressed through an *ought*, and thereby indicate the relation of an objective law of reason to a will which from its subjective constitution is not necessarily determined by it (a necessitation). They say that something would be good to do or to forbear, but they say it to a will which does not always do a thing because it is represented to be good to do it. That is *practically good,* however, which determines the will by means of the representations of reason, and consequently not from subjective causes, but objectively, that is, on principles which are valid for every rational being as such. It is distinguished from the agreeable, as that which influences the will only by means of feeling from merely subjective causes, valid only for the senses of this or that one, and not as a principle of reason, which holds for everyone.[2]

A perfectly good will would therefore be equally subject to objective laws (viz., laws of good), but could not be conceived as *necessitated* thereby to act lawfully, because of itself from its subjective constitution it can only be determined by the conception of good. Therefore no imperatives hold for the Divine will, or in general for a *holy* will; *ought* is here out of place because the volition is already of itself necessarily in unison with the law. Therefore imperatives are only formulae to express the relation of objective laws of all volition to the subjective imperfection of the will of this or that rational being, for example, the human will.

Now all imperatives command either *hypothetically* or *categorically*. The former represent the practical necessity of a possible action as means to something else that is willed (or at least which one might possibly will). The categorical imperative would be that which represented an action as necessary of itself without reference to another end, that is, as objectively necessary. [...]

[First Formulation of the Categorical Imperative]

There is therefore but one categorical imperative, namely, this: *Act only on that maxim whereby you can at the same time will that it should become a universal law.*

Now if all imperatives of duty can be deduced from this one imperative as their principle, then, although it should remain undecided what is called duty is not merely a vain notion, yet at least we shall be able to show what we understand by it and what this notion means.

Since the universality of the law according to which effects are produced constitutes what is properly called *nature* in the most general sense

(as to form)—that is, the existence of things so far as it is determined by general laws—the imperative of duty may be expressed thus: *Act as if the maxim of your action were to become by your will a **universal law of nature**.*

We will now enumerate a few duties, adopting the usual division of them into duties to ourselves and duties to others, and into perfect and imperfect duties.[3]

1. Someone reduced to despair by a series of misfortunes feels wearied of life, but is still so far in possession of his reason that he can ask himself whether it would not be contrary to his duty to himself to take his own life. Now he inquires whether the maxim of his action could become a universal law of nature. His maxim is: From self-love I adopt it as a principle to shorten my life when its longer duration is likely to bring more ill than satisfaction. It is asked then simply whether this principle founded on self-love can become a universal law of nature. Now we see at once that a system of nature of which it should be a law to destroy life by means of the very feeling whose vocation it is to impel to the improvement of life would contradict itself, and therefore, could not exist as a system of nature; hence that maxim cannot possibly exist as a universal law of nature, and consequently would be wholly inconsistent with the supreme principle of all duty.

2. Another finds himself forced by necessity to borrow money. He knows that he will not be able to repay it, but sees also that nothing will be lent to him unless he promises firmly to repay it within a determinate time. He wants to make this promise, but he has still so much conscience as to ask himself: Is it not unlawful and inconsistent with duty to get out of a difficulty this way? Suppose, however, that he resolves to do so, then the maxim of his action would be expressed thus: When I think myself in want of money, I will borrow money and

promise to repay it, although I know that I never can do so. Now this principle of self-love or of one's own advantage may perhaps be consistent with my whole future welfare; but the question now is, Is it right? I change then the suggestion of self-love into a universal law, and state the question thus: How would it be if my maxim were a universal law? Then I see at once that it could never hold as a universal law of nature, but would necessarily contradict itself. For supposing it to be a universal law that everyone when he thinks himself in a difficulty should be able to promise whatever he pleases, with the purpose of not keeping his promise, the promise itself would become impossible, as well as the end that he might have in view in it, since no one would consider that anything was promised to him, but would ridicule all such statements as vain pretences.

3. A third finds in himself a talent which with the help of some culture might make him a useful human being in many respects. But he finds himself in comfortable circumstances and prefers to indulge in pleasure rather than to take pains in enlarging and improving his fortunate natural predispositions. He asks, however, whether his maxim of neglect of his natural gifts, besides agreeing with his inclination to indulgence, agrees also with what is called duty. He sees then that a system of nature could indeed subsist with such a universal law, although human beings (like the South Sea islanders) should let their talents rest and resolve to devote their lives merely to idleness, amusement, and propagation of their species—in a word, to enjoyment; but he cannot possibly **will** that this should be a universal law of nature, or be implanted in us as such by a natural instinct. For as a rational being, he necessarily wills that his faculties be developed, since they serve him and have been given him, for all sorts of possible purposes.

4. Yet, a fourth, who is in prosperity, while he sees that others have to contend with great wretchedness and that he could help them, thinks: What concern is it of mine? Let everyone be as happy as heaven pleases, or as be can make himself; I will take nothing from him nor even envy him, only I do not wish to contribute anything to his welfare or to his assistance in need! Now no doubt, if such a mode of thinking were a universal law, the human race might very well subsist and doubtless even better than in a state in which everyone talks of sympathy and good-will, or even takes care occasionally to put it into practice, but, on the other side, also cheats when he can, betrays the rights of human beings, or otherwise violates them. But although it is possible that a universal law of nature might exist in accordance with that maxim, it is impossible to **will** that such a principle should have the universal validity of a law of nature. For a will which resolved this would contradict itself, inasmuch as many cases might occur in which one would have need of the love and sympathy of others, and in which, by such a law of nature, sprung from his own will, he would deprive himself of all hope of the aid he desires. [...]

[Second Formulation of the Categorical Imperative]

Now I say: the human being and in general every rational being exists as an end in itself, *not merely as a means* to be arbitrarily used by this or that will, but in all his actions, whether they concern himself or other rational beings, must be always regarded at the same time as an end. All objects of the inclinations have only a conditional worth; for if the inclinations and the needs founded on them did not exist, then their object would be without any value. But the inclinations themselves, being sources of needs, are so far from having an absolute worth for which they should be desired that, on the contrary, it must be the universal wish of every rational being to be wholly free from them. Thus the worth of any object which is *to be acquired* by our action is always conditional. Beings whose existence depends not on our will but on nature's, have nevertheless, if they are nonrational beings, only a relative value as means, and are therefore called *things*; rational beings, on the contrary, are called *persons,* because their very nature restricts all choice (and is an object of respect). These, therefore, are not merely subjective ends whose existence has a worth *for us* as an effect of our action, but *objective ends,* that is, things whose existence is an end in itself—an end, moreover, for which no other can be substituted, which they should serve *merely* as means, for otherwise nothing whatever would possess *absolute worth*; but if all worth were conditioned and therefore contingent, then there would be no supreme practical principle of reason whatever.

If then there is a supreme practical principle or, in respect of the human will, a categorical imperative, it must be one which, being drawn from the conception of that which is necessarily an end for everyone because it is *an end in itself,* constitutes an *objective* principle of will, and can therefore serve as a universal practical law. The foundation of this principle is: *rational nature exists as an end in itself.* The human being necessarily conceives his own existence as being so; so far then this is a *subjective* principle of human actions. But every other rational being regards its existence similarly, just on the same rational principle that holds for me;[4] so that it is at the same time an objective principle from which as a supreme practical law all laws of the will must be capable of being deduced. Accordingly the practical imperative will be as follows: *So act as to treat humanity, whether in your own person or in that of any other, in every case at the same time as an end, never as means only.* We will now inquire whether this can be practically carried out.

To abide by the previous examples:

First, under the head of necessary duty to oneself: Someone who contemplates suicide should ask himself whether his action can be consistent with the idea of humanity *as an end in itself.* If he destroys himself in order to escape from painful circumstances, he uses a person merely as a *means* to maintain a tolerable condition up to the end of life. But a human being is not a thing, that is to say, something which can be used merely as a means, but must in all his actions be always considered as an end in itself. I cannot, therefore, dispose in any way of a human being in my own person by mutilating, damaging, or killing him. (It belongs to morals proper to define this principle more precisely, so as to avoid all misunderstanding, for example, as to the amputation of the limbs in order to preserve myself; as to exposing my life to danger with a view to preserve it, etc. This question is therefore omitted here.)

Second, as regards necessary duties, or those of strict obligation, towards others: He who is thinking of making a lying promise to others will see at once that he would be using another human being *merely as a means,* without the latter at the same time containing in himself the end. For he whom I propose by such a promise to use for my own purposes cannot possibly assent to my mode of acting towards him, and therefore cannot himself contain the end of this action. This violation of the principle of humanity in other human beings is more obvious if we take in examples of attacks on the freedom and property of others. For then it is clear that he who transgresses the rights of human beings intends to use the person of others merely as a means, without considering that as rational beings they ought always to be esteemed also as ends, that is, as beings who must be capable of containing in themselves the end of the very same action.[5]

Third, as regards contingent (meritorious) duties to oneself: It is not enough that the action does not violate humanity in our own person as an end in itself, it must also *harmonize with it.* Now there are in humanity capacities of greater perfection which belong to the end that nature has in view in regard to humanity in ourselves as the subject; to neglect these might perhaps be consistent with the *maintenance* of humanity as an end in itself, but not with the *advancement* of this end.

Fourth, as regards meritorious duties toward others: The natural end which all human beings have is their own happiness. Now humanity might indeed subsist, although no one should contribute anything to the happiness of others, provided he did not intentionally withdraw any-thing from it; but after all this would only har-monize negatively not positively with *humanity as an end in itself,* if everyone does not also endeavor, as far as he can, to forward the ends of others. For the ends of any subject which is an end in itself ought as far as possible to be *my* ends also, if that conception is to have its *full* effect with me.

Notes

1. It might be here objected to me that I take refuge behind the word *respect* in an obscure feeling, instead of giving a distinct solution of the question by a concept of reason. But although respect is a feeling, it is not a feeling *received* through influence, but it *self-wrought* by a rational concept, and, therefore, is specifically distinct from all feelings of the former kind, which may

be referred either as inclination or fear. What I recognize immediately as a law for me, I recognize with respect. This merely signifies the consciousness that my will is *subordinate* to a law, without the intervention of other influences on my sense. The immediate determination of the will by the law, and the consciousness of this, is called respect, so that this is regarded as an *effect* of the law on the subject, and not as the *cause* of it. Respect is properly the conception of a worth that thwarts my self-love. Accordingly it is something which is considered neither an object of inclination nor of fear, although it has something analogous to both. The *object* of respect is the *law* only, that is, the law that we impose on *ourselves,* and yet recognize as necessary in itself. As a law, we are subjected to it without consulting self-love; as imposed by us on ourselves, it is a result of our will. In the former aspect it has an analogy to fear, in the latter to inclination. Respect for a person is properly only respect for the law (of honesty, etc.) of which he gives us an example. Since we also see in a person of talents, as it were, the *example of the law* (viz., to become like him in this by exercise), and this constitutes our respect. All so-called moral *interest* consists simply in *respect* for the law.

2. The dependence of the faculty of desire on sensations is called inclination, and this accordingly always indicates a *need.* The dependence of a contingently determinable will on principles of reason is called an *interest.* This, therefore, is found only in the case of a dependent will which does not always of itself conform to reason; in the Divine will we cannot conceive any interest. But the human will can also *take an interest* in a thing without therefore acting *from interest.* The former signifies the *practical* interest in the action, the latter the *pathological* interest in the object of the action. The former indicates only dependence on principles of reason for the sake of inclination, reason supplying only the practical rules how the requirement of the inclination may be satisfied. In the first case the action interests me; in the second the object of the action (because it is pleasant to me). We have seen in the first section that in an action done from duty we must look not to the interest in the object, but only that in the action itself, and in its rational principle (viz., the law).

3. It must be noted here that I reserve the division of duties for a future *metaphysics of morals;* so that I give

it here only as an arbitrary one (in order to arrange my examples). For the rest, I understand by a perfect duty one that admits no exception in favor of inclination, and then I have not merely external but also internal perfect duties. This is contrary to the use of the word adopted in the schools; but I do not intend to justify it here, as it is all one for my purpose whether it is admitted or not.

4. This proposition is here stated as a postulate. The ground of it will be found in the concluding section.

5. Let it not be thought that the common: *quod tibi no vis fieri, etc.,* [i.e., what you do not want others to do to you, do not do to them] could serve here as the rule or principle. For it is only a deduction from the former, though with several limitations; it cannot be a universal law, for it does not contain the principle of duties to oneself, nor of the duties of benevolence to others (for many a one would gladly consent that others should not benefit him, provided only that he might be excused from showing benevolence to them), nor finally that of duties of strict obligation to one another, for on this principle the criminal might argue against the judge who punishes him, and so on.

30

Joshua Glasgow

(1973–)

Originally from Portland, Oregon, Joshua Glasgow received his B.A. from the University of California, Santa Cruz, and his M.A. and Ph.D. from the University of Memphis.

He has taught at Occidental College in Los Angeles and at California State University, Bakersfield. He is currently Senior Lecturer at Victoria University of Wellington in New Zealand. Glasgow's main areas of research are in ethical theory and the philosophy of race. In addition to these issues, he has also published articles on supervenience and aesthetics. His research has been published in the Journal of Philosophy, Philosophical Studies, The Journal of Political Philosophy, The Journal of Aesthetics and Art Criticism *and the* Canadian Journal of Philosophy.

Kant's Principle of Universal Law

Introduction: The Good Will

Kant develops his theory of ethics by considering some of our most fundamental commonsense intuitions about the nature of morality. On the basis of such intuitions, he articulates a basic moral principle that is strikingly different from the principles of other moral theories, such as utilitarianism, egoism, or virtue ethics. In order to see how Kant arrives at this principle, which he calls the *Categorical Imperative*, we can begin where he begins, with the concept of the good will.

The first commonsense intuition that Kant notes is that we don't usually change our evaluation of how good someone is merely because of how successful she is in pursuing her ends, as long as she is in fact sincerely pursuing them. For instance, imagine that two of the President's Secret Service guards see a would-be assassin pull out a gun and aim it at the President. Each of the guards is standing the same distance from the president, one to the right and one to the left, and neither has time to prevent the shooter from pulling the trigger. Thus, the most each can do is to dive in front of the President, in the hopes of taking a bullet. They both dive at the same time; however, at just the same moment the Vice President, who is sitting between the guard on the left and the President, stretches his legs. As a result, the guard on the left trips and fails to stop the bullet, while the guard on the right, unobstructed, successfully prevents the assassination by taking the bullet in the shoulder.

Now we might bestow certain honors on the guard on the right that we do not give to the guard on the left. But Kant's question is a more basic one: just by virtue of being successful, is the guard on the right somehow *morally better* than the (unsuccessful) guard on the left? Kant believes that our intuitions here suggest that the two agents are morally equal, because, after all, their intentions were the same. As he puts it, even if a good will—that is, the will of an agent who is committed to doing her duty for the sake of duty—were unsuccessful in achieving its ends, "like a jewel, it would still shine by itself" nonetheless.[1] This, then, is the first commonsense intuition of Kant's ethics: whether or not an agent's will is good is independent of her actual success in achieving her ends.

Two Kinds of Principles: Maxims and Imperatives

The claim that the successful good will is as good as the unsuccessful good will suggests a second basic intuition we have about ethics, namely that our moral evaluations focus on the agent's *intentions*, rather than her outward behavior. (Contrast this with classical utilitarianism, which focuses on whether the agent's outward act actually brings about happiness.)

The term of art that Kant uses to capture the intentional feature of one's will is "maxim." A *maxim*, in brief, is an abstract description of the action one intends to perform. There are three things to note about maxims. First, when a maxim is explicitly formulated in Kant's technical sense, it will include three components. Namely, each maxim has (1) a description of the physical act you are performing (e.g., "washing my hair"); (2) a description of the circumstances in which you are performing the act (e.g., "when I'm in the shower getting ready for school"); and (3) the purpose or end of your action (e.g., to present myself in a cleanly manner"). With these three components, we can express the general form of all maxims as follows:[2]

GENERAL (ACE) FORM OF MAXIMS: I will do act A, in circumstances C, for end E

Before we consider the second main point about maxims, there are two more things to know about the ACE form of maxims, First, A, C, and E are *variables*—they can be replaced with whatever would accurately described the act you intend to perform, no matter what the action is. Second, the *end* (E) is different from the *motive* of an act. For instance, say that your end in diving into the ocean is to save a drowning person. This end might be aimed at from all sorts of motives: perhaps you see it because you think it is your duty, or simply because the drowning person is your friend, or perhaps because you believe that you'll get a reward for doing so. It doesn't matter here what the motive is; the point to keep in mind is that the motive is different from the end. In short, an end is what the agent hopes to achieve in a given action, while the motive is why the agent hopes to achieve it.

The second main point about maxims is that every action has some maxim, whether or not the agent explicitly thinks of it. For example, if you plan to see the dentist, you might explicitly think about what you are doing, and that thought will (barring cognitive error) contain your maxim. (You might not normally think of it in the precise ACE form, but of course it could be formulated in this way.) At the same time, as you go through the morning routine of washing your hair in the shower, you probably don't think about what you are doing. Nevertheless, that action still has a maxim—there is some description of what you are doing.

So far, then, we have seen that since the good will "shines like a jewel" independently of whether it succeeds in achieving its ends, moral evaluation focuses on intentions rather than outward bodily acts. We have also seen that every intended act has a maxim and that each maxim can be presented in the ACE format. The final main point to emphasize is that a maxim is a *description* of whatever action you intend to perform. It is not a principle about what you *should* do; rather it is a principle that describes the action you *actually intend*. Thus both the assassin and the guard and the guard have maxims (again, every action has an abstract description, or maxim). One reason for emphasizing the point that maxims are *descriptive* principles is that in this respect maxims differ from another main kind of principle. These principles are *prescriptive*, or *normative*. Rather than describing what we actually intend to do, they tell us what we *should* intend to do—they prescribe, rather than describe. Kant, following the tradition ways of talking, calls such normative principles, about what we ought to do, *imperatives*.

Two Kinds of Imperatives: Hypothetical and Categorical

Here is where a third ordinary intuition about morality enters into Kant's ethical theory: moral claims are imperatives, rather than maxims. That is, when we say "It is wrong to torture puppies just for kicks" or "The right thing to do is to donate some of my income to charity," we are not describing the way we act. (Though, of course, people do act in these ways.) Instead, when we use words like "right" and "wrong," we are expressing the thought that people *should* or *should not* act in certain ways, and claims about what people should or should not do can be expressed as imperatives.

To fully appreciate this point, we must consider a more basic claim that Kant makes, namely, that moral principles are *rational* principles. If you have a moral obligation to keep your promises, then keeping your promises is the rational thing to do. (To say that an action is the rational action to perform is to say that it is the one that you have *reason* to perform.) At the same time, of course, we do not always do what is rational; we sometimes let our "inclinations"—roughly, our desires and aversions—influence us independently of what reason tells us to do. Kant's way of making this point is to distinguish between imperfectly rational beings like us and perfectly rational or "holy" beings (such as God, if God exists). By definition, perfectly rational beings always and necessarily do what is rational. Imperfect rational beings like humans (and perhaps aliens or non-human animals that also have rational capacities) do not necessarily do what is rational.

This explains why moral principles come in the form of imperatives for creatures like us. A rational principle details what is rational to do, and as such it will simply *describe* the choices of a perfectly rational being. Since we are not perfectly rational (that is, we do not necessarily do what is rational), rational principles do not necessarily described what we do. Rather they detail what we *should* do and accordingly can be expressed in imperative form. So, since moral principles are rational principles, they too come in imperative form.

This brings us to the next main stage on the road to the Categorical Imperative, where Kant distinguishes between different kinds of imperatives. An imperative, remember, expresses an "ought-claim", a claim about what we should do. There are, of course, several kinds of ought-claims, of which Kant focuses on two: hypothetical and categorical imperatives.

A *hypothetical imperative* expresses an ought-claim that applies that you by virtue of your subjective (or personal) ends.[3] For instance, someone might say "if you want to get an 'A' on the exam, then you should study for it." In general, hypothetical imperatives all have this form: you should take all of the necessary, and some sufficient, means to your subjective ends. Thus, if you have the end of getting an 'A' on the exam, and if the means to that end involve studying for the exam, then you should study. But now imagine that you don't have the subjective end of getting an 'A', perhaps because you don't care about getting an 'A,' or perhaps because you are not even in school. If you lack such an end—one that is relevant to your studying, then you choose not to study, you aren't violating the hypothetical imperative to study.

A *categorical imperative*, by contract, expresses an ought-claim that applies to you independently of your subjective, personal ends. We will get to examples of categorical imperatives shortly. For now the key thing to note is the basic difference between the two kinds of imperatives: hypothetical imperatives apply to you because of your subjective ends, while categorical imperatives apply to you independently of your subjective ends.

Moral Principles or Categorical Imperatives

The next main stage in Kant's moral theory is to claim that moral principles must be (when formulated for imperfectly rather than perfectly rational beings) categorical imperatives. This claim is again supported by our ordinary thinking about moral obligation. Consider the hypothetical imperative "If you want to get an 'A', you should study." There is, again, an easy way to get yourself out from under such a hypothetical imperative: all you have to is abandon your end. That is, you can escape any hypothetical imperative simply by avoiding the ends that make it apply to you. If you do not have an end that requires studying, then you don't violate the hypothetical imperative to study when you end up spending the day hiking instead. If you do not seek to lose weight or improve your health, you don't have to change your diet. If you do not see to become a world-renowned pianist, you don't have to practice the piano for several hours per day. Again, the point is straightforward: the obligation placed on you by any given hypothetical imperative can be escaped simply by changing you subjective ends.

As Kant points out, however, ordinary thinking about ethics suggest that *moral* obligations are not like these hypothetical imperatives. If I have a moral duty to, say, keep my promise, I can't escape this obligation simply by changing my subjective ends so that this duty does apply to me. Even if I say, "I don't care if other people trust me," it is still the case that I have a moral duty to keep my promise. This, then, is the fourth ordinary moral intuition identified by Kant: moral imperatives obligate me independently of whatever subjective ends I might have. That is, moral obligations are categorical imperatives, rather than hypothetical imperatives.

The Categorical Imperative: Kant's Formula of Universal Law

Now that we have seen Kant's analysis of ordinary moral concepts, such that moral obligations are categorical imperatives, we can appreciate his supreme principle of morality. We can begin by clarifying a few more points.

Kant thinks that there is only *one* Categorical Imperative. That is, he thinks there is only one supreme principle of morality: whether an act is right or wrong will ultimately be determined by whether or not it accords with this single supreme principle. However, we must make two caveats to this point about there being only one supreme principle of morality. First there can be several derivative, or non-supreme, principles of morality. Thus while there can only be one Categorical Imperative (with a capital "C" and capital "I") as the *supreme* principle of morality, there can be several categorical imperatives (with a lower-case "c" and "i"), that is, several *derivative* principles that obligate us independently of our ends. These categorical imperatives are our moral *duties*, the specific types of act that we either must or must not perform (e.g., "be beneficent" or "do not make false promises"), and these duties are derived from the Categorical Imperative.

Secondly, Kant is also clear that while there is only one Categorical Imperative, it comes in several different formulations. Commentators have long puzzled over how to make sense of this claim and how to understand the relations between the different formulations. But here we need only note that while there are several formulations of the Categorical Imperative, we only are going to focus on two of them. The Kant scholar H. J. Paton dubbed the first formulation the "Formula of Universal Law," or FUL for short.[4] Let us now see how Kant arrives at FUL.

We already know that the supreme principle of morality cannot depend on our ends—for that would make it a hypothetical imperative, when we know it must be a categorical imperative. But here's the rub: if the supreme principle of morality cannot depend on our ends, it is hard to see what such a principle would demand of us. That is, it is often easy to identify hypothetical imperatives as long as we identify our ends—once you know that you want an 'A,' it follows pretty quickly that you need to study. But categorical imperatives (by definition) can't use our subjective ends to tell us what we need to do. According to Kant, what follows from this is that all we can say about the supreme principle, of morality (the Categorical Imperative) is that it must require our maxims to be compatible with its essential nature, and its essential nature has two parts. First, Kant thinks that morality's categorical nature has the force of *law:* unlike hypothetical imperatives, which don't necessarily obligate us (because we can avoid the ends that make them apply to us), moral imperatives bind us *necessarily*, like a law (because their applicability isn't contingent on our subjective ends). So this pushes the question one step further: What is the character of law? In a word, *universality.* All law (laws of nature, civil laws, etc.) are universal in the sense that within their domains (nature, civil society, etc.) they cover everything. Second, the Categorical Imperative is an *imperative*, that is, it prescribes to, or obligates, us. So, if we put these two ideas—the universality and necessity of law and the prescriptive nature of imperatives—together with the claim that morality focuses on maxims, then we get the result that the Categorical Imperative must categorically obligate us to have maxims that can be universal laws.[5]

The fact that the Categorical Imperative cannot use our subjective ends to generate our obligations, and so can only require us to act in a manner compatible with the universality of law, is the basis for FUL:

> FUL: "Act only in accordance with that maxim through which you can at the same time will that it become a universal law."[6]

Kant follows his presentation of FUL by noting that our actions take place in the natural world. So he gives us a second, related formulation of the Categorical Imperative, which Paton labeled the Formula of the Law of Nature (FLN):

> FLN: "Act as if the maxim of your action were to become by your will a universal law of nature."

So far, then, we have seen that from our basic intuitions about the categorical nature of morality Kant generates FUL and FLN as two ways of formulating the supreme moral principle, the Categorical Imperative. With this we can turn to two questions. First, how is the Categorical Imperative to be applied to our lives? That is, how can it function as a decision procedure, a way of determining the right thing to do? Second, are there any problems with this principle? These two questions are taken up in the next two sections.

FLN and Our Duties

Kant proceeds to discuss how we can get various duties (or categorical imperatives) from the Categorical Imperative. Rather than continuing on with FUL, he proceeds to use FLN, and we shall follow suit here.

When Kant says that we should act as if our maxims are going to become universal laws of nature, he is asking us to try to imagine a hypothetical world. That is, for any act you might perform, you should try to imagine a world where your maxim is going to be a law of nature, which everyone had to conform to, just like everyone in the real world must conform to the law of gravity. The question to ask, then, is whether your maxim could in fact be such a law, Kant's test for whether an act is morally permissible, then, is deceptively simple: if the maxim cannot be a universal law of nature, acting on it is morally forbidden. (Morally obligatory acts are the opposites of morally forbidden acts. For example, if it is forbidden to neglect the needs of others, then it is obligatory to attend to the needs of others.)

To see how this works, let's look at Kant's treatment of the duty to not make false promises. Kant has us imagine a person who has an urgent need to get some cash. This person knows that he cannot pay back a loan, but he also knows that the only way he can get the cash is if a second party loans it to him on the promise that he will repay it tomorrow. So, he decides to make a false promise to the second party to repay borrowed money knowing full well that he will not fulfill this promise.

According to FLN, what this person should do is try to imagine that the maxim of this action is a universal law of nature. That is, he should ask, "What if, as a law just like the law of gravity, everyone had to make false promises, when they needed money, to serve their own self-interest?" Kant's verdict is that *it is impossible to imagine this as a universal law of nature*. For if everyone had to do this when in need of money, we all would know that each of us was lying when we promised to pay back loans (just like we all know that none of us can fly simply by flapping our arms); in turn, this would mean that we wouldn't believe anyone's promises, which would mean that the practice of promising would collapse into nonexistence. So the "false promise" maxim cannot be universal law, because such a law would require that promises are possible (so that our false promisor can make his false promise) but also that promises are impossible (because the practice of promising collapses). The problem is not that we'd have a world with no promising; rather, the problem is that this hypothetical world would impossibly contain the *contradiction* that everyone makes false promises but false promises (indeed all promises) cannot be made. Therefore, since it is impossible to imagine a world with a contradiction like this, false promising is morally forbidden.

We cannot be more precise about this procedure for generating not only the duty to not make false promises, but any duty whatsoever. There are three steps to this procedure:

1. First, you must figure out your maxim. At its most precise, this will come in the ACE format.
2. Second, you must "universalize" your maxim. To *universalize* your maxim is just to pretend that it is a universal law of nature, like the law of gravity—to try to think of a world where everyone does what you are doing.
3. Finally, you then see if this universalization is successful. Again, if the maxim cannot be successful universalized, acting on it is morally wrong. If it can be successfully universalized, acting on it is morally permissible. Maxims that can be successfully universalized are called *universalizable* maxims.

One more point is crucial here. In step (3), when you examine whether your maxim can be successfully universalized, Kant means something very specific by this, namely, he means that you should see if you *run into a contradiction*. You are *not* supposed to ask, "Would *bad* results follow if everyone acted according to my maxim?" For example, a world were false promising was

universally practiced would contain some bad states of affairs, because some people might get used or hurt in the process. But on Kant's view bad results do not of themselves show that the action is immoral. Instead, what you should ask is, "Is it *contradictory* for everyone to act according to my maxim?" So Kant's point with the false promising maxim is not that universalizing it would have bad results, but that it is simply contradictory to imagine such a state of affairs. The contradiction that emerges upon universalizing the "false promise" maxim is that it entails a state of affairs where the following are both true:

(p) It must be possible to make promises. (After all, this is required if the agent is to make a false promise.)
(~p) Promises cannot be made. (Because upon universalizing the false promising maxim the practice of promising collapses.)

This is one place where Kant clearly differs with consequentialists. Roughly put, consequentialists say that it is wrong to do what would bring about bad states of affairs. Historically, the most prominent consequentialist view has been utilitarianism, so utilitarians say that the wrong act is the one the produces less than maximally available happiness.[7] For Kant, what reveals the wrongness of making false promises is not that it makes people unhappy (though it no doubt does in many cases); rather, false promising is shown to be wrong because it cannot be universal law. Kant's ethics is similarly distinguished from rule-consequentialism, which roughly holds that an act is wrong when it violates the rules that, when widely internalized, would best promote well-being. While both rule-consequentialism and Kantianism would prohibit false promising, each view offers a unique theoretical account of the wrongness of false promising. For rule-consequentialism, false promising is wrong because when widely internalized it wouldn't maximize well-being, and for Kantianism it is wrong because a maxim of false promising cannot be universalized.

It is worth recalling why we should care about whether or not a maxim is universalizable. For Kant, two ordinary intuitions about morality are particularly salient on this question. First, we ought to focus on the agent's maxims, rather than her outward acts. Second, moral obligations come in the from of categorical imperatives, and therefore moral requirements cannot depend on the agent's subjective ends, but only on whether her maxims have the form of law, that is, universality. (Later, Kant adds to the appeal of his principle by noting that what it shows is that it is wrong to be a "free rider." For instance, the only way you can make false promises is if everyone else plays by the rules and keeps their promises—false promising cannot be something that everyone always does a matter of universal law. Put more generally, people who act immorally are parasitically free riding on the morally upright behavior of others.[8])

The contradiction involved in the false promising maxim is what has become known as a *contradiction in conception*: what shows us that false promising is immoral is that it is impossible to even *conceive* of a world in which false promising is universally practiced as a way of securing loans. Kant has another duty that is generated by a contradiction in conception, namely, the duty to not commit suicide. Here Kant imagines someone who is, perhaps, feeling sorry for himself, and this person decides to commit suicide out of 'self-love.' But, Kant thinks that the purpose of self-love is to preserve the self. Many have questioned whether Kant is right to think

this about the purpose of self-love, but let's grant it here so that we may focus on how he generates the duty against suicide. If he were right that the purpose of self-love is self-preservation, then it would be impossible to imagine a world where the motive of self-preservation leads to self-examination. Therefore, suicide based on self-love is morally forbidden.

Kant thinks that when a duty is derived from contradiction in conception, that duty is a *narrow duty*. A narrow duty is narrow in the sense that the agent has no leeway in deciding when, how, and in what circumstances she will comply with it. So with means, for example, that an agent couldn't say "Well, I fulfilled my duty against suicide on Monday, so it's okay for me to commit suicide on Tuesday." But Kant also offers some *wide duties*. Wide duties allow latitude in deciding when, how, and in what circumstances the agent will fulfill them. Consider, for example, the duty of beneficence. One way of being beneficent is to give money to charity. Since this is a wide duty, the agent has leeway here—she can decide which (reputable) charity to give to, she can decide to do it only when she has the available wealth, and she can do it on Tuesday instead of Monday.

Just as narrow duties are derived from contradictions in conception, wide duties are derived from what are known as *contradiction in the will*. A contradiction in the will arises not when a potential hypothetical world is impossible to conceive (as with contradictions in conception); rather, a contradiction in the will arises when the maxim contradicts something else that the agent must will. To see this, consider the duty of beneficence.

Kant has us imagine a person who could help others, but decides not to. This agent won't place demands on others; rather, she merely wishes to not be burdened by the needs of others. So let's put it to Kant's test: could we imagine a world in which no one helps anyone else? In one sense, we can imagine such a world. It might not be a very nice world, but there's nothing contradictory about it in the way we cannot imagine a world where everybody makes false promises. So there is no contradiction in conception here. But there is a contradiction in the will. For, according to Kant, every agent at some point will need the love or aid of someone else. So the question becomes: Can one will the help of others in a world in which no one helps anyone else? The answer is that we cannot, because those two willings are incompatible: if no one is helping anyone, then our agent cannot receive help from others when she needs it. Thus, though a non-beneficent world is possible, and so there is no contradiction in conception, the maxim of non-beneficence would be contradicting her willing help for herself. Thus, non-beneficence is forbidden (and, therefore, beneficence is an obligation).

Finally, Kant holds that a maxim of neglecting one's talents generates a contradiction in the will. Again he offers a purposive premise about our talents (which, as with the purposive premise about self-love, many have questioned): the purpose of our talents is to enable us to handle any of the manifold tasks we might face in life. So now imagine someone who just wants to sit around all day, watching cartoons and letting her talents rust. Certainly it is *conceivable* that everyone could do this: even if it made for a pretty pathetic world with few resources and short life spans, there is no contradiction in conception here upon universalization. But the rusting-talents maxim contradicts something else that we must will, namely that we are able to handle life's challenges and tasks. So our agent gets a contradiction in the will: it is impossible both to completely neglect one's talents and to prepare oneself for life's challenges. This contradiction in the will generates a wide duty: we have to develop our talents, though we have leeway in determining which talents we want to develop (perhaps you're a better carpenter then violinist), when we'll work on our skills, and so forth.

What Kant offers, then, are four duties: prohibitions on false-promising, suicide, non-beneficence, and letting one's talents rust. Two are derived from contradictions in the will and are therefore narrow duties, while two are derived from contradictions in the will and are therefore wide duties. And two are duties to the self, while two are duties to others. The relationships between these concepts and duties are displayed in Figure 1. Given this system of duties, Kant thinks that his Categorical Imperative is quite fruitful as a way of guiding action. We can now proceed to examine whether there are any problems with this theory.

Figure 1 Categories of Duty in Kant's Ethics

	Duties to Others	Duties to Self
Narrow Duties	Prohibition on False Promising	Prohibition on Suicide
Wide Duties	Prohibition on Non-Beneficence	Prohibition on Neglecting One's Talents

Two Potential Problems

Commentators on Kant's ethics have long recognized two related problems facing Kant's universalizability test. The first problem is that it might generate erroneous results in some cases. Recall here the three-step procedure for determining moral permissibility: (1) formulate your maxim; (2) universalize it; and (3) look for a contradiction (if there is none, acting on that maxim is permissible).

But now consider, for instance, someone who likes to collect model trains.[9] Since she likes to collect (rather than trade) trains, when she goes to buy them her maxims will be "I will buy model trains and not sell them." But when she universalizes this maxim, she'll be imagining a world in which everybody buys model trains but nobody sells them. And this is impossible: it is contradictory to have a world where no one sells model trains but everyone buys them.

This is where the problem for Kant enters in: this contradiction means that collecting model trains is morally wrong according to FLN. But, of course, there is nothing morally wrong about collecting model trains. So something must be incorrect about FLN.

Cases like this are called *false negatives*, because they get a negative result from the test (i.e., they get a verdict of being morally wrong), but falsely so. We will see shortly that FLN also faces problem maxims in the form of *false positives*, that is, cases that get a positive result (of being morally permissible) from the test, but that are morally wrong.

Whether or not a maxim fails the universalizability test depends in part on how we formulate our maxims. The question of maxim formulation points us to the second problem with the universalizability rest, known as the *problem of*

relevant descriptions. This problem is that for any action, there are innumerable (perhaps infinite) ways of describing it. So, since a maxim is just a description of an action, there are innumerable maxims for any one action, and since it appears that we have no good way of figuring out which maxim to focus on, the potential problem is that we have no good way to run the FLN test. Let's look at an example.

Say that I intend to rob a bank. We could formulate the maxim for this action in several ways. Here are some, formulate in the ACE format:

a) "I will rob a bank at gun-point, when I am in need of cash, to satisfy my self-interest."

b) "I will get some money from the bank, I am in need of cash, to satisfy my self-interest."

c) I, Joshua Glasgow, author of the present article, will rob a bank at gun-point, when I am in need of cash, to satisfy my self-interest."

One problem here is that the universalization procedure yields different results for the three maxims. It seems that the universalization of maxim (a) would be contradictory, because of everyone robbed banks at gun-point when they needed cash, the banking system would collapse, in which case we'd be imagining a contradictory world in which there are banks (as required by maxim (a)) and there are no banks (because the banking system collapsed). Thus it seems FLM would imply that acting on maxim (a) morally forbidden.

But maxim (b), *which also describes the very same action of robbing the bank*, seems to pass the test. For what would happen if everyone got money from the bank when they needed it? Well, we can imagine such a world without contradiction—there is no impossibility in everyone doing this. (In fact, this maxim is followed with near universality in the real world.) But this means that we have a false positive: presumably it is wrong to rob a bank at gun-point, but the FLN test seems to imply that maxim (b), which is one way of formulating the bank-robbing maxim, is morally permissible.

Now consider maxim (c). What if everyone named Joshua Glasgow, who is also the author of this article, robs banks at gun-point to get some cash? Well, since I happen to be the only one who fits this description, and since the banking system won't collapse just from one person robbing banks, we won't get the contradiction that we got from maxim (a). So it seems possible that maxim (c) can be a universal law of nature without contradiction, which means that (c) is a false positive as well: if there is no contradiction, acting on maxim (c) would be morally permissible according to the FLN universalizability test, but it clearly is morally wrong.

The problem of relevant descriptions therefore actually generates three potential objections to FLN. First, the problem of relevant descriptions is at least one factor in the other main problem, the problem of false positives/negatives: until we know how to properly describe our actions, we'll keep getting objectionable results, such that it's morally wrong to collection model trains or permissible to rob banks at gun-point. Second, because any action, like robbing a bank, can be described in any number of ways, it can have different maxims, which means that in principle one action can get different results on the universalizability test. But this is a problem—robbing a bank is either right or wrong, but can't be both. If this objection is on target, then FLN will not satisfy the

desideratum of being *consistent*. Finally, if there are innumerable ways of describing my action, Kant's test seems woefully inadequate as a decision procedure, since I won't know which of my action's maxims to test. And the theory isn't very practical if we can't get *determinate* results. In short, it seems that FLN requires a *determinate and relevant* maxim for each action, and the problem is that it is not obvious that there is one determinate and relevant description for each action (hence the name "the problem of relevant descriptions"). Given the three objections involved in the problem of relevant descriptions, FLN seems problematic at best.

Conclusion

By way of conclusion, we should consider whether the problems of false negatives/positives and relevant descriptions are truly devastating for Kant's supreme principle of morality, as stated in FLN.[10] Two points are important here. First, recall that FLN is independently motivated, that is, we have a plausible basis for believing it. The basis for FUL and FLN is the ordinary intuition that moral obligations are categorical imperatives—they tell us what we should do independently of our subjective ends. And if our ends are made irrelevant, than all that is left to morally constrain our actions is to demand that our maxims have the form of law, or universality. So even if opponents of Kant can point out some problems for FLN, Kantians can always reply that their principle nevertheless captures some important features of morality. (Some who hold non-Kantian moral theories—such as perfectionists, including natural law theorists, who hold that right acts are those that realize the *objective* end of human perfection—maintain that their views also can generate categorical requirements. This remains a matter of ongoing debate in ethical theory.)

Second, there may be solutions to the two problems we have examined here. Ever since Onora O'Neill (then writing under the surname 'Nell') published her book, *Acting on Principle,* in 1975, in which she fully exposed the problems discussed here, Kantians have been working hard to find creative ways to solve them. This is an interesting area of research, and while it would be too ambitious to try to cover all the Kantian proposals, we can look at one of them.

Barbara Herman proposes dealing with the problem of relevant descriptions as follows.[11] She (plausibly) thinks that Kant's insight about morality focusing on maxims suggests that maxims are *general policies* for actions. This means that when we are formulating maxims for testing under FLN, we should think of them in a fairly general way. This would rule out, for instance, maxim (c) above, since it is *too specific* in referencing me in particular. Also, on this account, we must represent maxims *as they are willed*. This means, for example, that we cannot use maxim (b), since it *suppresses a basic fact about what I am willing*, namely that I am willing not merely to get money from the bank, but actually to rob it at gun-point.

Notice, then, that Herman's solution roles out maxims (b) and (c), and so it seems to rule out at least some of the false positives, which is a welcome result for Kantians. Now add to this a second virtue of Herman's account. Since FLN will be testing general policies only, we should not think of it as a decision procedure for *particular* actions. Rather, FLN will be used to get what Herman calls "deliberative presumptions," which are general duties about what is morally forbidden (such as "do not make promises"). For Herman, these deliberative presumptions set the ground rules that provide the starting point for deliberating about particular about particular cases' morality, though they can be overridden in some cases (much like Ross' *prima facie* duties and Aristotle's virtues). Then, if an act falls under two or more competing deliberative presumptions, we use judgment, rather than any algorithmic test, to determine whether or not it is morally permissible.[12] So Herman's account also avoids the problem of needed a determinate and relevant maxim for every specific action, since in her interpretation FLN is not to be used for specific actions. Instead, we simply use FLN in generate basic policies, which then would set the ground rules for further deliberation about the moral permissibility of our specific actions. Finally, this means that it won't suffer the third problem involved in the problem of relevant descriptions, namely that of getting incompatible results for different maxims that describe the same specific action. For again, what we will be testing are basic deliberative presumptions for general act-types, not maxims for specific actions.

In short, Herman's account seems to neutralize the three potential objections that stem from the problem of relevant descriptions. So, while Kant's principle of universality faces certain problems, it is independently motivated, and Kantians are presenting arguments to fully defend it.

Notes

1. Immanuel Kant, *Groundwork of the Meta-physics of Morals,* ed. and trans. Mary Gregor, (Cambridge: Cambridge University Press, 1997), p. 394. (Here, as elsewhere, I cite the standard Academy pagination.)

2. This way of formulating maxims was codified in Onora Nell, *Acting on Principle* (New York; Columbia University Press, 1975), p. 37.

3. For our purposes, we can roughly characterize *subjective* ends as the ends that depend on your personal constitution, while *objective* ends would those ends that are not particular to you but instead are common to all rational beings.

4. H. J. Paton, *The Categorical Imperative* (Philadelphia: University of Pennsylvania Press, 1947), p. 129.

5. I would be remiss not to note that commentators have long struggled with this argument. They often find it plausible to claim that morality involves prescriptivity, universality, and (more controversially) necessity. But it's an open question whether that then implies that the supreme principle simply states that one's maxims should be fit for universal law.

6. Immanuel Kant, *Groundwork*, p. 421.

7. More precisely, this is the claim of maximizing, act-utilitarians.

8. See Kant, *Groundwork*, p. 421.

9. This example is taken from Nell, *Acting on Principle*, p. 76.

10. There are, recall, other formulations of the Categorical Imperative. So even if these problems are devastating for FLN, one might turn to those other formulations to defend Kantian ethics.

11. See Barbra Herman, "Moral Deliberation and the Derivation of Duties," in Herman, *The Practice of Moral Judgment* (Cambridge, MA: Harvard University Press, 1993), Chapter 7.

12. Despite the prevalent stereotype, Kant (like Aristotle and Ross) placed a high premium on non-algorithmic judgment. For example, at one point Kant writes that moral philosophy furnishes "laws a priori, which no doubt still require a judgment sharpened by experience, partly to distinguish in what cases they are applicable and partly to provide them with access to the will of the human being and efficacy for his fulfillment of them"(*Groundwork*, p. 389).

Feminist Ethics

Men have defined the parameters of every subject. All feminist arguments, however radical in intent or consequence, are with or against assertions or premises implicit in the male system, which is made credible or authentic by the power of men to name.
                                            —Andrea Dworkin

Discussion Questions

1. Think back to the example from the beginning of this chapter of the two boys setting the cat on fire. Imagine you have a friend of the opposite sex with you as you confront the boys about their wrongdoing. Would each of you give different reasons for why the boys' actions are immoral? In other words, do males and females have fundamentally different characteristics? If one assumes that men and women do have different moral perspectives, how might these moral perspectives differ?

2. In 2005, two Canadian Great Lake freighters, the Canadian Venture and Canadian Trader, were sent to Alang, India, for shipbreaking. Decommissioned ships are increasingly sent to India, China, Bangladesh, Pakistan, and Turkey, where thousands of men and women cut, saw, and break them apart for $2–$5 a day. The steel is melted down and sold abroad or used for local construction. Old ships contain hazardous wastes such as PCBs, asbestos, lead, and oil, so that shipbreaking is dangerous, dirty, and toxic, and much of it is done by hand with little, if any, safety equipment. On average, four to five workers die every month from falls or explosions. Moreover, toxins pollute the water and leach into the soil, which can damage wildlife and the ecosystem.[29] Shipbreaking appears problematic for care ethics. A fundamental claim of care ethics is that we have duties and obligations only to specific individuals with whom we have a special relationship, such as family, friends, colleagues, and other people close to us. In other words, we would have no duty or obligation to protect the shipbreaking workers or their environment because, generally speaking, we do not have a relationship with them. Does this problem show that the moral theory of care ethics is inadequate? Why or why not? How might a supporter of care ethics respond to this objection?

The Problem with Traditional Moral Theories

Utilitarianism and Kantian ethics may leave some students feel unsatisfied; that something is missing from their moral perspective. Recall that one of the main objections against utilitarian theory is that it does not take into consideration special relationships—those we love and care for. For utilitarianisms, we are to base our moral decisions on the "greatest happiness principle." This means we are to be impartial in our decision-making processes. Individuals with whom we have deep emotions and relationships are to be given no more emphasis or priority over strangers. In fact, given the circumstances, we may have to act in ways that may benefit strangers over those we love. In regards to Kantian ethics, we discovered that we are to act from duty for duty's sake. Applying Kant's categorical imperative requires universalism and abstracting from situational specifics. Moreover, acting contrary to the motivation of duty—say, from compassion, sympathy, or love—is morally questionable. If you feel that both utilitarian and Kantian ethics are too cold, austere, impractical, abstract, objective, and unrealistic, then you are not alone. It's these concerns that have prompted many people, especially women, to challenge traditional ethics and moral reasoning. According to some feminists, we must recognize that the very things that traditional ethical theory leaves out are the very things that are crucially fundamental to morality—namely, caring, compassion, and relationships. Unfortunately, traditional moral thinking has been dominated by male biases and has failed to take into consideration women's point of view. It is this female point of view that is central to feminist ethics.

As Alison Jaggar points out in her article, women have been systemically considered inferior to men. Unfortunately, this is not only a historical fact but, in some cultures, a current reality. Women are often the subject of different norms and expectations leading to sexist and discriminatory actions and policies by men in order to keep women in subordinate positions. The result is often unequally treatment regarding reproductive rights, labour, and wages, just to name a few. Women have been systematically excluded from the "public" sphere and relegated to the "private" or domestic sphere. Although Jaggar points out that most Western democracies recognize women as equal to men, this domestic sphere, for some feminists, offers women a radically different view point from men, such that these differences are salient in developing alternative solutions to moral problems not couched in traditional moral reasoning. Carol Gilligan's research into moral development suggests significant gender differences in moral reasoning. This feminine perspective not only directly challenges many of the assumptions of traditional ethics but is also the foundation of a new ethic. Although there are various feminists ethical theories, my discussion will primarily concern itself with the **ethics of care** or, simply, "care ethics."

There are a number of problems with traditional moral theories. First, according to Jaggar, traditional theories are impoverished because they view humanity rationally and impartially. This narrow moral vision, for many feminists, is unrealistic since it's impossible to be intellectually detached from social context and relationships. Traditional theories are concerned with generating moral rules to guide behaviour (Cruzer 279). Both utilitarianism and Kantian ethics, for example, focus their energy on developing and explaining how such rules ought to be applied in, usually, abstract hypothetical situations. But, as we saw earlier, Kantian theory is problematic because it is absolutist; it abstracts from the particulars of each individual and situation and applies categorical imperatives universally. According to care ethics, focusing on general rules gives us little to no moral guidance because each person and situation is very different. By abstracting away from the particulars of a situation, we lose the very things that are salient to moral decision-making. Instead, we ought to focus on particular people in specific circumstances, while taking into account that people are not isolated beings but live within a larger network of relationships (family, friends, co-workers, etc.). Moreover, we also must take into consideration a person's interests, habits, family background, financial status, occupations, and so forth, when making moral decision-making. Unlike utilitarianism or Kantian ethics, partiality and particulars matter.

Second, says Jaggar, the rationalist approach of traditional ethics does not consider the body. This devaluation of the body fails to recognize moral issues that are salient to women's bodies, such as abortion, and issues that are related to the bodies of both men and women such as mandatory age retirement and discrimination. A person's physical being is important to understanding moral issues but irrelevant for traditional ethics.

Third, as Jaggar explains, traditional moral theories are problematic because they don't consider emotions as important to moral decision-making. This criticism stems from the fact that moral theories considered interpersonal relationships, and any emotional attachments within these relationships as inimical to rationally. In fact, appeals to maximizing utility or willing maxims to be a universal moral law requires impartiality and objectivity. The reason seems to be twofold. One, traditional theories require moral decisions to be made by people as rationally autonomous isolated individuals withdrawn from the wider network of family and friends. This is important since, according to utilitarianism and Kant, we are morally obligated, at times, to break our relationships if warranted under the application of objective rules. For example, the right thing to do may require us to help a stranger over our own children. Second, relationships threaten objectivity and impartiality (Cruzer 279). The problem is the emotional attachments we have with others. Emotions get in the way of rational judgment because they cloud the process of determining what is right and wrong. But these reasons seem misguided, says care ethics. Humans are social creatures by nature and the relationships we form over a lifetime are relevant, not only to who we are as people, but also to the moral dilemmas we face. It's those people with whom we have relationships with that ultimately determine our moral duties and obligations, not abstract rules. This is not to say traditional moral theories cannot take into consideration family or friends, it's just that such relationships are analyzed

in terms of implicit promises codified in rules or principles (Cruzer 280). For care ethics, impartiality is merely an unrealistic ideal. Morality is not about helping strangers; it's about understanding our responsibilities to family, friends, children, aunts, uncles, etc., and deriving moral obligations from these relationships. In this sense, we ought to try and fulfill our responsibilities within this relationship network.

It's equally mistaken to assume our emotions—such as love, compassion, and sympathy—bias moral judgments. Traditional moral theories do not require emotional attachment as part of the decision-making process but, for psychologist Carol Gilligan and philosopher Nel Noddings, morality begins with care and love (Cruzer 280). We care for different people in often very different ways. A person, generally speaking, will care for her husband and children very differently than her boss or strangers. In this sense, we may show very little regard or caring for strangers but show excessive amount to our children. This is not morally deviant, but a recognition of the role relationships play in our lives. This means we are under no moral obligation to help strangers over and above our children because they are not part of our relationship web. Moreover, a person motivated by duty appears cold, calculating, insincere, and emotionally detached. As mentioned in the last section, to visit your mother in the hospital merely out of duty, not care and love, fails to consider the reason why you should visit her in the first place. Visiting your mother is right because of the emotional attachment you have with her. For feminist ethics, the emotions of care and love, far from being unimportant to morality, are central to it.

Finally, for Jaggar, the alleged masculinity of traditional ethics fails to consider the psychological differences between men and women. Although very few feminists consider these differences innate, most feminists argue that there are socially constructed differences between men and women. The real problem is that such feminine characteristics are often devalued and not incorporated into moral analysis. The upshot is that we need a moral theory that takes into consideration the feminine point of view.

Caring as a Moral Imperative

The development of care ethics began in the 1980s with the work of Carol Gilligan. Gillian's research on the moral development of children suggests that males and females think differently about morality. Males tend to think about moral problems in abstract, objective, impartial, and emotionally detached terms, whereas females tend to think about moral problems in realistic, subjective, partial, emotional, and

relationship-based terms. To understand Gilligan's work, however, we must look at the research of Laurence Kohlberg.

Moral development in children seems to highlight the psychological differences between males and females. The Harvard psychologist Laurence Kohlberg argued that moral development occurs through a series of three levels (two stages in each level), each more complex than the other (see Box 5.11). At the preconventional level, children abide by the rules of society because they fear the

---

Box 5.11   Kohlberg's Stages of Moral Development

Level 1: Preconventional (Age 0 to 9)

Stage 1: Punishment and Obedience Orientation. Moral reasoning is based on obedience for its own sake or to avoid punishment. Children obey because they are told to obey.

Stage 2: Naïve Hedonism or Instrumental Orientation. Moral reasoning is based on rewards and self-interest. Children obey when it is in their self-interest (feels good or rewarded) to do so. Doing what is right serves their own needs or interests.

Level 2: Conventional (10 to Early Adolescence)

Stage 3: Good Boy and Good Girl Orientation. Moral reasoning is based on meeting the expectations of others. Adolescents try to live up to what other people generally expect from them as sons, daughters, friends, etc. Doing what is right is done to be a good person in the eyes of another. Being good means having good motives, showing concern and care, and following the "golden rule."

Stage 4: Law and Social Order Orientation. Moral reasoning is based on understanding social order, law, justice, and duty. Right behaviour consists in doing one's duty, respecting authority, and maintaining social order. For adolescents, laws are to be upheld or maintained unless they conflict

with other duties. It's also important to contribute to society, groups, or institutions. Obligation to the law overrides personal obligations to family, friends, or groups. Doing the right thing avoids the breakdown of social institutions and social order.

Level 3: Postconventional (Early Adolescence to Early Adulthood)

Stage 5: Social Contract and Individual Rights Orientation. The individual recognizes that values and laws are culturally relative and can also vary from person to person. However, relative rules should be upheld because they are the social contract. Some nonrelative values and rights, such as life and liberty, must be upheld in any society regardless of opinion. A person does the right thing because of one's social contract to make and abide by laws for the greater good of everyone and the protection of individual rights.

Stage 6: Universal Ethical Principles. Moral reasoning is based on individually developed moral principles based on universal human rights. A person does the right thing by acting in accord with these universal principles, including justice, human rights, and respect and dignity for others. A person acts out of personal commitment to these principles and follows his or her conscience. Very few people reach this stage of moral development.

Source: Based on John Santrock (1990). *Adolescence.* 4th ed. Dubuque, IA: Wm. C. Brown Publishers, 462–464; and Lawrence Kohlberg. (1976). "Moral Stages and Moralization: The Cognitive-Developmental Approach." *Moral Development and Behavior: Theory, Research and Social Issues.* Ed. T. Lickona. New York: Rinehart and Winston.

consequences of breaking them. In other words, the child behaves morally to avoid punishment or receive a reward. At the conventional level, adolescents are concerned with the approval or disapproval of others. At this level, an adolescent acts morally as defined by the expectations of others. At the postconventional level, which is reached by very few adults, people act morally in accord with universal moral principles that transcend the laws of society (Wortman and Loftus 251). So, for example, Martin Luther King Jr. and Mahatma Gandhi reached the postconventional level of moral development because they acted, at often risk to themselves, in accord with universal beliefs about freedom and justice.

The problem with Kohlberg's moral development theory, says Gilligan, is that it's male-biased. It fails to consider that men and women have different values that imbue moral attitudes and moral judgement. For Gilligan, women are more sensitive to the needs of others and often are responsible for the caring for others. The focus on relationships and responsibilities—care and concern for others—means that females often define themselves in context of human relationships (Gilligan 288). This means female moral development is different from males and, therefore, not represented in the literature. Kohlberg's theory of moral development was based on the study of 84 boys over 20 years. Although Kohlberg's moral theory is supposed to be universal, when females are compared to the scale, they come up morally deficient. Females' reasoning is associated with stage three: at this stage acting morally is equated to meeting the approval of others. In other words, "goodness" is defined in terms of a female's desire to help and please others and thereby maintain interrelations between people. But this puts females at odds with male thinking about morality. From a male perspective, people are supposed to be impartial, objective, formal, abstract, cold, unbiased, and logical in their moral deliberations. They are not supposed to be tainted by unfettered emotions or relationships with others. But this difference in thinking means, unfortunately, says Gilligan, that the female moral perspective

is often undermined and deemed not appropriate for reasoning about moral problems. A female's point of view, in other words, is deemed "second class." As Gilligan states, "the very traits that traditionally have defined the 'goodness' of women, their care for and sensitivity to the needs of others, are those that mark them as deficient in moral development" (289). Moreover, this difference in thinking would account for females not measuring up to Kohlberg's stages of moral development. Although females fail to reach the postconventional level of abstracting away from society, laws, family, friends, and other people in order to do the right thing, Kohlberg didn't realize that females do not think about morality this way. Therefore, for Gilligan, we ought not conclude that men are more morally sophisticated than women; they have a different voice.

To see the difference, let's consider this example from Kohlberg, known as Heinz's dilemma. Heinz's wife is near death from a rare cancer. The doctors tell Heinz that a newly discovered drug by a local pharmacist could save his wife. The drug, however, is expensive. Although the drug only costs $200 to produce, it costs $2,000 to buy. Heinz has only saved $1,000. Given his situation, he approaches the pharmacist in hopes the druggist would accept the $1,000 for the drug or let him pay the remaining amount later. The pharmacist refuses both options. Depressed, and seemingly out of options, Heinz breaks into the pharmacist's store to steal the drug for his wife. Would it be wrong for Heinz to steal the drug? One 11-year-old boy, named Jake, responded to this dilemma saying that Heinz should steal the drug:

> For one thing, a human life is worth more than money, and if the druggist only makes $1,000, he is still going to live, but if Heinz doesn't steal the drug, his wife is going to die. (*Why is life worth more than money?*) Because the druggist can get a thousand dollars later from rich people with cancer, but Heinz can't get his wife again. (*Why not?*) Because people are all different and so you couldn't get Heinz's wife again. (qtd. in Gilligan 291–292)

Jake's decision is based on the idea that life is more important than money. Heinz will be worst off if his wife dies than if the druggist loses some property. To put another way, Heinz's wife's right to life supersedes the pharmacist's property rights. For Gilligan, Jake's response is likened to a math problem by setting up an equation and working towards a solution (292). Jake's rule- or principle-based approach would fit into Kohlberg's level 4–5 moral development sequences. In contrast, consider Amy. She states:

> Well, I don't think so. I think there might be other ways besides stealing it, like if he could borrow the money or make a loan or something, but he really shouldn't steal the drug—but his wife shouldn't die either….If he stole the drug, he might save his wife then, but if he did, he might have to go to jail, and then his wife might get sicker again, and he couldn't get more of the drug, and it might not be good. So, they should really just talk it out and find some other way to make the money. (qtd. in Gilligan 292–293)

Amy's decision not to steal the drug is based on seeing humans within "a narrative of relationships that extends over time" (Gilligan 293). The dilemma is not worked out like a math problem but through recognizing the needs of Heinz, his wife, and druggist. In this sense, the world is viewed as comprising relationships, responsibilities, and trying to meet various exceptions imbued within these relations. Amy is putting relationships ahead of such objective principles as the right to life. Although saving the wife is important, it is done not by appealing to rules but by taking a caring and relationship-based approach. Amy's moral decision making fits into level three "good boy and good girl" orientation, according to Kohlberg.

The problem with Amy's response, says Gilligan, is that, in light of Kohlberg's development sequence, her appeal to relationships and communication to solve this moral dilemma appears naïve and cognitively immature (294). But there is no reason to think this. For Gilligan,

Jake's and Amy's moral decision-making merely reflects different modes of moral understanding. Generally speaking, males solve moral problems using a logical, abstract, and rule-based approach, whereas females solve moral problems by placing them within a web of relationships and then using communication as the vehicle to some kind of resolution. The difference in ethical approaches stems from the fact that women tend to see themselves as interdependent and responsible to others which necessitates care and nurturing, while men tend to see themselves as autonomous which necessitates rules and abstract formulas to extend the same consideration to others and self (Gilligan 295). For Gilligan, this means the process of solving moral problems will be very different for men and women.

Nel Noddings, in her book *Caring: A Feminine Approach to Ethics and Moral Education*, advanced Gilligan's work into a sophisticated moral theory:

> This commitment to care and to define oneself in terms of the capacity to care represent a feminine alternative to Kohlberg's "stage six" morality. At stage six, the moral thinker transcends particular moral principles by appealing to a highest principle—one that allows a rearrangement of the hierarchy in order to give proper place-value to human love, loyalty, and the relief of suffering. But women, as ones-caring, are not so much concerned with the rearrangement of priorities among principles; they are concerned, rather, with maintaining and enhancing caring. They do not abstract away from the concrete situation those elements that allow a formulation of deductive argument; rather, they remain in the situation as sensitive, receptive, and responsible agents. As a result of this caring orientation, they are perceived by Kohlberg as "being stuck" at stage three— that stage in which the moral agent wants to be a "good boy or girl." The desire to be good, however, to be one-caring in response to these cared-fors here and now,

provides a sound and lovely alternative foundation for ethical behavior…Her caring is the foundation of—and not a mere manifestation of—her morality. (42)

For Noddings, ethics must be seen in the context of particular relationships between "one-caring" and the "cared-for." The "one-caring" will thus be motivated to attend to the needs of the "cared-for." From this perspective, the relationship between Heinz (one-caring) and his wife (cared-for) will inform Heinz's decision as to whether to steal the drug. Stealing the drug may actually cause more harm if Heinz goes to jail or if his wife becomes sicker. Either result would not be an act of caring. Caring requires acting in ways to nurture and foster the relationship even if it's painfully obvious the pharmacist's exurbanite prices for his life-saving drug violates the universal principles of fairness and justice. By focusing on universal rules and principles, we abstract from the particulars of the case at hand and, thereby, miss situational nuances that can give rise to alternative moral solutions. From an ethics of care perspective, Heinz's wife's illness, their financial circumstances, drug cost, the pharmacist's time doing research, and his pride—and, perhaps, greed—must all be taken into consideration to reach an agreeable solution. In other words, Heinz can only find a solution through recognizing the various relationships and the responsibilities that he has to each party. And this recognition can only come from being genuinely concerned for the welfare of each relationship and being motivated to meet their needs—an ethics of care.[30]

In summary, the ethics of cares, following Jaggar, consists of the following:

1. Ethical propriety should be given to the values of mothering and nurturing (care), including emotional sensitivity, responding to the needs of others, intimacy, connectedness, and responsibility. In this sense, the virtues of the private domain ought to be more prevalent in society and in ethics.
2. Women's concept of self is relational. Moral problems, then, are seen as conflicts of

responsibility, not rights; resolutions should repair and strengthen relationships; we ought to practise caretaking, not respectful non-intervention, and love, caring, and attentiveness rather than impersonal equality, rights, and justice.
3. Care, in contrast to justice, is oriented towards particular persons in particular situations, instead of impersonal and impartial universal principles.

It is this sense of particularism, which is, perhaps, care ethics' most distinct feature. Moral situations are analyzed by looking at specific people, problems, relationships, personalities, and solutions. For care ethics, we meet the needs of others in concrete reality unmitigated by abstract moral principles.

Is it true that men and women think differently? If so, could this lead to different moral perspectives? Although Gilligan's work certainly inspired, and gave impetus to modern care ethics, the idea of a unique feminine ethic dates back to the eighteenth century. It was during this period that questions and concerns about femininity and female consciousness emerged. They emerged, in part, due to the idealistic status of women in society. As women became increasingly dependent on men for financial stability, a concept of the "ideal woman" emerged as one that stays at home and raises children (Grimshaw 491). The philosopher Jean-Jacques Rousseau, for example, argued in his work *Emile* that morality is not the same for men and women. For Rousseau, naturally different virtues for men and women ought to be enhanced through education. Males must be educated to enhance their rationality, temperance, justice, and fortitude (moral virtues); females, on the other hand, must be educated to enhance their patience, docility, and good humour (nonmoral virtues). Males ought to study the natural sciences, social sciences, and humanities; females ought to study those things relevant to domestic life, such as poetry, music, art, and fiction (Tong 31).

Mary Wollstonecraft, in her book *A Vindication of the Rights of Women*, rejects Rousseau's notion that men and women are different by nature. Instead she argues, although not explicitly, the different virtues between men and women are the result of enculturation and society. Put very generally, we could say that men are raised to be courageous, assertive, independent, hardy, rational, and emotionally controlled. Women, on the other hand, are raised to be gentle, modest, humble, supportive, empathetic, compassionate, tender, nurturing, intuitive, sensitive, and unselfish (Tong 29). For Wollstonecraft, women will only be considered moral if they display the psychological traits of men.

Although more could be said about Wollstonecraft's views, fundamentally underlying her objections against Rousseau is a healthy scepticism regarding the idea of a specific feminine virtue. And for good reason: it's these nonmoral virtues that have played a key role in keeping women in subordinate positions within historically and also within contemporary societies. I mentioned earlier that Canadian women were not granted the right to vote until 1918 (women of aboriginal or Asian descent were excluded from this legislative success). According to early Canadian law, only "persons" could vote and since "persons" were defined as "he" or male, women were excluded from voting. Women contested the legal definition of "persons" and won.

Women, it could be argued, are still devalued in today's society. Consider this: women make up over half of Canada's population and make up 46.6 percent of the workforce, yet their presence at top levels of Canadian business is virtually nonexistent (see Box 5.12). Here are some statistics from Anne Kingston's article "Why Women Can't Get Ahead":

- Only 19 women in 2004 led Canada's top 500 companies.
- The November 2005 issue of *Report on Business* magazine's top 25 most influential business leaders contained no women.
- 35 percent of students in the University of Toronto Master of Business Administration program in 2002 were women; this number has not changed since 1982.

Box 5.12   Canadian Women in Business

Companies in Canada headed by women	4.2%
Women as top earners	5.4%
Women on board of directors	12.0%
Women as corporate officers	15.1%
Women in management positions	36.3%
Women in Canadian labour force	46.9%

Source: Adapted from *2006 Catalyst Census of Women Corporate Officers and Top Earners of the FP 500 in Canada.* Toronto: Catalyst 2007. 3 July 2007 <http://www.catalyst.org/files/full/Canadian%20COTE%202006-%20FINAL.pdf>.

- In 2005, 51.4 percent of Canada's top 500 companies had no women on their boards; this number has not changed since 2001.
- 49 percent of women who are 40 and making more than $100,000 a year are childless, compared to only 19 percent of men in the same salary bracket.

Why are women underrepresented in the world of business? Is it due to choice, inaptitude, discrimination, or other factors? Well, if Gilligan is right, women will be hard-wired differently than men. Women are nurturers by nature and may not have the "killer instinct" or aggression necessary to succeed in the dog-eat-dog world of business. Men, in contrast, are natural leaders, taking charge and delegating responsibility. Women, because they can have children, are nurturers and, therefore, best suited to supportive roles in organizations where collaboration and teamwork are needed (Kingston 64–65). However, even if it is true that women have different natures, the problem is not that women have "soft skills" (interpersonal) and men "hard skills" (financial), but these supposed "soft skills" are devalued by the male-dominated corporate world. This devaluing of women's unique skills could account for the low representation of women in Canadian business. It could also explain why, according to Statistics Canada, women earn, on average, 64 cents for every dollar that a man earns. It may also account for the pressure some women feel deciding between taking the "mommy track" and the "fast track." The idea is that women who take the "fast track" are considered to be highly career focused, desire no children, and, therefore, will be rewarded with promotions and high pay. Women on the "mommy track" are considered moderately career focused, desire children, and, therefore, will receive limited raises and promotions. The mommy track is based on the outdated male-biased notion that women cannot have a high-paying successful career and a family. This supposed inability forces women to take the lesser-esteemed "mommy track" in exchange for a greater balance with family life. In short, a woman cannot be a CEO and a mother. Of course, why this obvious double standard doesn't apply to men ("father track") is beyond present purposes, but it should be clear that differences between men and women, given our patriarchal society, have been used in unjustifiable ways to devalue and oppress females.

Do men and women really think differently? Do they really reason differently about moral problems? Well, if men and women do differ in their moral reasoning, the differences could not be so great as to prevent understanding and comprehension. As James Rachels points out, it is probably a difference in emphasis rather than differences in values:

> It is not as though women make judgments that are incomprehensible to men or vice versa. Men can understand the value of caring relationships, empathy, and sensitivity easily enough, even if they sometimes have to be reminded; and they can agree with Amy that the happiest solution to Heinz's Dilemma would be for the two men somehow to work it out. (Not even the most reprobate male thinks theft would be the *best* thing that could happen.) For their part, women will hardly disagree with such notions as human life being worth more than money. Plainly, the two sexes do not inhabit different moral universes. (165).

It is also plain to see that not all women will solve moral dilemmas using care ethics and not all men will solve moral dilemmas using rules. Women can equally employ rules as men can equally care. In fact, men and women will probably use a mix of both rules and care to solve moral problems.

Interestingly, the empirical evidence does not seem to support Gilligan's claim that men favour rules and principles while women favour care ethics. M. Ford and C. Lowery's 1986 study of gender differences did not reveal any significant degree to which men have a rights orientation and women a care orientation. However, women were more consistent in their use of the care orientation and men were more consistent in their use of the rights orientation. Similarly, W. Friedman, et al., in their 1987 paper, also found little support for Gilligan's hypothesis. A more recent meta-analysis of 113 studies by Sara Jaffee and Janet Shibley Hyde on gender differences in moral reasoning, once again, reveals only a very small difference between care orientation for females and justice orientation for males. The authors recognize that although moral differences may exist, they are not strongly associated with gender. In fact, males and females probably use a mixture of care and justice in their moral reasoning. Most importantly, however, is that the use of care or justice reasoning is best accounted for by the context and content of the moral dilemma, not gender.

However, even if women are only somewhat different than men, for some feminist philosophers, these differences ought to be exploited to offer a very different ethical point of view. More specifically, much of the destruction of the planet, wars, corporate scandals, violence, terrorists attacks, and a host of other ills may stem, in part, from the male nature and male psyche which, unfortunately, dominates most societies and societal institutions around the world. The idea is that these unique female characteristics could be used in a positive way to offer alternative solutions to life's problems (Grimshaw 492). Let's consider the examples regarding the environment and abortion.

For feminists, like Karen Warren, environment problems, such as species extinction and global warming, call for a rethinking of their causes and solutions. Warren argues much of our environmental concerns can be connected to the oppression of women. More specifically, ecological feminism (ecofeminism) suggests we develop "an environmental ethic which takes seriously connections between the domination of nature and the domination of women" (Warren, "The Power and the Promise of Ecological Feminism" 322). Generally speaking, the goal of ecofeminism is to develop worldviews and practices that are free from male-biased models of domination. They argue that feminism and the ecological movement must unite in order to radically reshape the basic socioeconomic relationships and underlying values of society. But this is difficult since in patriarchal societies an oppressive conceptual framework justifies and maintains the subordination of women by men, and by extension, the subordination of nature by humans. It's this dual domination of women and nature that makes the environment an important issue for feminists. If feminists are motivated to end the oppression of women by men, then they must also be motivated to end the oppression of nature by humans. Warren states:

> By showing that the conceptual connections between the dual dominations of women and nature are located in an oppressive and, at least in Western societies, patriarchal conceptual framework characterized by a logic of domination, ecofeminism explain how and why feminism, conceived as a movement to end sexist oppression, must be expanded and reconceived as also a movement to end naturism [the domination or oppression of non-human nature]. ("The Power and the Promise of Ecological Feminism" 328)

The causes of this logic of domination are many. Carolyn Merchant, for example, argues the domination of women and nature can be explained by rise of the mechanical worldview in the sixteenth century. New technologies such as pumps, windmills, and watermills have allowed humans to mine, drain, and deforest nature and thereby dominate it. Joan Dunayer makes a linguistic connection. If it is true, as Ludwig Wittgenstein suggests, that language reflects concepts of self and world, then our linguistic practices have also led to, and sustain, harmful interconnections between women and nature. Women are continually described in pejorative animal terms such as chicks, dumb bunnies, cows, foxes, bitches, old hens, and vixens. Similarly, language is used to feminize nature, including the raping, mining, and conquering of nature. Nature's secrets are penetrated; virgin timber is cut; and fertile soil is ploughed (Warren, "Introduction" 258). Language reinforces the naturalizing of women and the feminizing of nature. The slide from oppressing women to nature is, therefore, authorized.

The environment is also a feminist issue because of the negative effects damaged ecosystems have on women and children. In 2007, the United Nations Intergovernmental Panel on Climate Change released its latest report on global warming. According to the world's top scientists, climate change is real, and humans, mostly the West, are the major emitters of greenhouse gases (carbon dioxide, nitrous oxide, methane, and fluorocarbons). According to the panel, unless the amount of greenhouse gases, especially carbon dioxide, is significantly reduced, we will see an increase in temperatures over the next century. The increase in temperatures could have a significant impact on the earth and humans, including rising sea levels, melting glaciers, drought, extreme weather, and species extinction. Climate change will affect the poor, women in particular, in developing countries the most. For example, according to experts, for every 1 degree increase in global temperature we could see crop yields decrease by 10 percent (Mittelstaedt A8). In developing countries, particularly in Asia and Africa where women are responsible for tending crops and paddies, 80 percent of food production is the responsibility of women, not men (Duncan 10). This means, any decrease in crop yield will most likely have a greater negative impact on women and their families. Global warming might also decrease water availability. In Kenya, for example, women are responsible for collecting household water. The responsibility of carrying water can consume up to 85 percent of a woman's daily energy intake (Duncan 10). Given the physical effort women exert to supply water, a decrease in water supply due to global warming may have untold consequences on women's health. Moreover, lack of access to clean water may force women to use dirty water, putting them and their children at risk of water-borne diseases (Denton 14). Fatma Denton states, "Women's active involvement in agriculture, and their dependence on biomass energy, makes them key stakeholders in effective environmental management. Hence, women and their livelihood activities are particularly vulnerable to the risks posed by environmental depletion" (11). Unfortunately, women are virtually absent from climate change decision-making processes. Women's lack of involvement stems, in part, due to gender inequities, specifically regarding paid labour, access to land, ownership of land, and, generally speaking, control over resources (Denton 17). And unless this changes, women will be disproportionably affected by climate change.

However, given the intimate connectedness that woman have to the earth, women will be in a unique position to know what effects environmental destruction may have and find ways to protect the environment. An excellent example of the environment and feminist activism is the Chipko Movement. *Chipko* comes from the Hindi word for "hugging." The northern mountainous region of India consists of small rural villages. The village people survive by subsistence farming, raising livestock, and trading forest products (Des Jardins 233). Traditionally, women would do much of the work including cooking, tending crops and livestock, raising children, gathering firewood, and so forth. The villages have lived off the land this way for centuries and had unfettered access to the forests. However, in the nineteenth century, the British government, and later the India

government, decided to use the forests for commercial logging and thus tightened its control over forest use. The Chipko Movement was sparked by two events. First, in the 1970s, this area was severely impacted by monsoons, causing flooding, landslides, erosion, and loss of life. Villagers recognized that increased deforestation was a major cause in the subsequent destruction. And because women were responsible for the collecting firewood and tending crops and livestock, they were significantly affected by the flooding. Second, local workers in the region formed a cooperative to help local business and local workers. In 1973, the cooperative put in a request to the government to cut down approximately one dozen ash trees to make tools. Their request was denied, while at the same time the government approved a commercial licence to cut down significantly more trees for sporting good equipment. The threat of protests from villagers prevented any logging, but one year later, the government announced it would start to log in the area again. While most of the men were away meeting with the government, loggers moved in and began cutting down the forest (Des Jardins 234). The women in the villages mobilized quickly and went into the forest and formed human chains about the trees, "hugging them." The women's actions not only forced the loggers to retreat but also saved countless trees from being felled. The Chipko Movement eventually resulted in a 15-year ban on logging in the area. In other words, the actions of the women were, at heart, based on the feminist concepts of care, compassion, and understanding the relations of the environment to the people affected by the potential logging.

The idea should be clear. Men are in a position of privilege and thus have systematically excluded the experiences of women and non-white groups through various forms of oppression, discrimination, and sexism (racism). But it's through their role as the oppressed that they have developed an understanding of reality and the world that is much truer and more accurate than those of the insulated male. So how can feminism transform into an environmental ethic? Warren suggests the following: First, feminist approaches towards environment must reject any logic, values, or attitudes that dominate or oppress non-human nature. Second, we must see ourselves within a larger network of relationships with the natural world. Third, we must recognize differences between humans and non-human nature. Fourth, the first-person narratives of women are important for learning about the connection between women and nature and environmental destruction. Fifth, we must include not only women's experiences of environmental harm but also indigenous people as well. Sixth, the domination of women and nature are social problems caused by historical, socioeconomic, and an oppressive patriarchal conceptual framework. Seventh, the values of care and love must be central to our relationships with nature in such a way that we care about and treat nature respectfully. Finally, we must recognize that to be human is, in part, defined by our relationship to the non-human environment (Warren, "The Power and the Promise of Ecological Feminism" 335–336). Ecological feminism seeks to understand our relationship to the earth as sustainer and provider for humans. The earth provides us with life and, thus, we must recognize this interconnectedness. Damage to the environment will not only harm non-humans but also lead to the destruction of humans if we remain recalcitrant. An ecofeminist approach to protecting the environment requires care, love, reciprocity, and by extension doing what is right.

Let's turn to abortion. As mentioned in chapter 2, arguments for and against abortion usually revolve the following key questions: Is the fetus a person with a right to life comparable to that of children or adults? Is the body of woman her own property to do with as she sees fit? From a feminist perspective, however, the question of abortion can be re-evaluated, not focusing on personhood or autonomy, but on the impact that abortion directly has on women.

Susan Sherwin's paper, "Abortion Through a Feminist Lens," explains how traditional discussions of abortion tend to revolve around questions about the moral and legal permissibility of abortion. Such discussions are usually couched in masculine terms of choice, privacy, and property rights. Most importantly, the issue of abortion tends to focus exclusively on the moral status of the embryo or fetus. Non-feminist approaches to abortion, however, fail to consider the interests and experiences of women. Women are rendered peripheral to most discussions of abortion.

For Sherwin, the obvious intimate relationship between the fetus and women must be brought back to centre stage, since abortion decisions have the greatest impact on the lives of women, not men. Women decide to have abortions for a variety of reasons such as illness, rape, incest, being poor, homeless, and so forth, but whatever the reason, pregnant women are usually the ones *best* able to make these decision within the specific context of their lives. As Sherwin states, "most feminists reject attempts to offer any abstract rules for determining when abortion is morally justified. Women's personal deliberations about abortion include contextually defined considerations reflecting her commitment to the needs and interests of everyone concerned—including herself, the fetus she carries, other members of her household, etc." (284). There is no single rule or principle to determine whether abortion is moral or immoral in all cases. Instead, abortion decisions ought to be based on each woman's experience; contrary to traditional moral theories, there are no objective or universal (dispassionate observer) ways of making such decisions. Bearing children has significant physical, psychological, financial, and social consequences usually not recognized by traditional moral theories. For feminists, by recognizing the impact of pregnancy on women's lives, abortion decisions will ultimately empower women.

Unfortunately, this is easier said than done, says Sherwin. Women's subordinate status in societies often prevents them from refusing a man's sexual advances. And if a woman cannot prevent pregnancy, her dependence on man, especially financially, increases. As Sherwin explains, using contraception or abstinence is not as easy as it seems, especially in patriarchal societies. Traditional non-feminist accounts of abortion have failed to consider how cultures oppress women and thereby ensure they have little control over their lives (Sherwin 285). A feminist account of abortion, however, demands that the contextual oppression of women be factored in to any abortion decision or policy.

For Sherwin, from a feminist point of view, the moral status of abortion must be broadened beyond traditional accounts to include the import of abortion on women's lives and connect abortion to the domination and subordination of women. Once we make this connection, we will see that reproductive freedom is couched in a much wider relational and specific context of empowerment, sexual freedom, and gender equality.

Problems with Feminist Ethics

As Jaggar points out in her article, feminist ethic is not immune from criticism. Although these criticisms are not exhaustive, let me highlight three of the most salient objections against care ethics.

First, there are problems concerning whether a moral theory can be built upon women's experiences. Women's experiences are so broad and varied it's questionable whether experiential consistency and agreement can be gleaned to build feminist ethics in the first place. In our complex modern societies, says Jaggar, generalizations about the experiences of women (and men) are unfounded given that societies vary so widely in regards to class, ethnicity, and even across generations. It is unrealistic to assume that women share the same moral experiences and thus share a radically different moral perspective from men. As we have seen previously, empirical research does not support the link between gender and caring.

Second, despite feminist calls for eliminating the domination of women by men, care ethics can actually reinforce such domination. If Nel Noddings is right in arguing that doing what is right comes from a responsibility of caring for others (Noddings), this may lead to an underlying obligation that women should always care no matter what. This makes care ethics disempowering and alienating, or, if you prefer, slave-like.

To always be the caregiver, rather than the care receiver, reinforces women's subordinate role, especially in patriarchal societies, since caring by nature requires a person to be in a supportive or helping role. Moreover, if women have a special understanding of morality because of their historical subordinate positions in society, then being oppressed is necessary to gain this special understanding of care. This would justify domination and oppression, not get rid of it.

Third, care ethics narrow focus on specific relationships often fails to consider the wider context of moral dilemmas. To put another way, some "philosophers have criticized the very idea of an ethics based on caring for specific individuals with whom we have a special relationship" (Velasquez, *Philosophy* 564). The problem is that care ethics limits our duties and obligations to those people within our immediate circle of family and friends. In other words, if you do not know or have a relationship with strangers, then you are under no moral obligation to care for them. So if, for example, a manufacturer exports toy trains painted with lead paint, which can be very harmful to children if the paint is ingested, this would be morally acceptable because the manufacturer is selling its product to children that it does not know; they are strangers, not family or friends, and, therefore, fall outside of manufacturer's moral concern. In short, it would be okay to sell harmful toys to children. This objection would also be applicable to non-human animals. Many people oppose eating meat because of the harm and suffering factory farms cause cows, chickens, and pigs. But since our relationship with animals is tenuous at best, except for those who maybe work on farms or own cats, dogs, etc., killing animals for human consumption would be morally justified. For vegetarians and vegans, care ethics would be an inappropriate moral theory. In response, the adoption of rights or utilitarian principles would fare much better in regards to protecting factory farm animals.[31] Care ethics seems to limit our moral obligations to those people we have a relationship with, and thus seems to be inadequate to account for the wider duties and obligation we may have to strangers and non-human animals.

Feminist ethics is an ongoing debate, but whatever you decide, it's clear that care ethics and its main themes have been denied by traditional ethical theories. It seems, then, for an ethical theory to be truly adequate it must take into consideration the moral perspectives of women as well as marginalized groups.

31

Alison Jaggar

(1942–)

Alison Jaggar received her Ph.D. from State University of New York at Buffalo in 1970. Since 1990, she has been Professor of Philosophy and Women's Studies at the University of Colorado

at Boulder. Previously, she was the Wilson Professor of Ethics at the University of Cincinnati and occupied the Laurie Chair in Women's Studies at Rutgers University. She has also held visiting appointments at the University of Illinois at Chicago, the University of California at Los Angeles, Victoria University of Wellington, New Zealand, and the University of Oslo. Jaggar's research in moral and political philosophy from a feminist perspective has earned her many awards and honours, including fellowships from the American Association of University Women, Edinburgh University's Institute for Advanced Studies in the Humanities, the Rockefeller Foundation, and

the National Endowment for the Humanities (twice). In 1995, she was awarded Distinguished Woman Philosopher by the Society of Women in Philosophy. Some of her works include Feminist Frameworks: Alternative Theoretical Accounts of the Relations Between Men and Women *(1978),* Feminist Politics and Human Nature *(1983),* Gender/Body/Knowledge: Feminist Reconstructions of Being and Knowing *(with Susan Bordo) (1989),* Living with Contradictions: Controversies in Feminist Social Ethics *(1994),* The Blackwell Companion to Feminist Philosophy *(edited with Iris M. Young) (1998), and* Just Methodologies: An Interdisciplinary Feminist Reader *(2007).*

Feminist Ethics

Throughout the history of western ethics, the moral status of women has been a persistent though rarely central topic of debate. A few isolated voices have contended that women are men's moral equals but most of the dominant figures in the tradition have offered ingenious arguments to justify women's subordination to men. Despite the long history of this controversy, the expression "feminist ethics" was coined only in the 1980s, after feminism's "second wave" had swept into the academies of North America—and, to a lesser extent, western Europe—a critical mass of philosophers for whom the status of women was an important ethical concern. The appearance of this expression not only signaled a perception that attention to women and gender was indispensable to adequately understanding many issued in practical ethics; it also reflected a new belief that women's subordination had far-reaching, though hitherto unnoticed, consequences for ethical theory.

Feminist ethical theory is distinguished by its exploration of the ways in which cultural devaluation of women and the feminine may be reflected and rationalized in the central concepts and methods of moral philosophy. Not all feminist philosophers are convinced that western ethical theory is deeply flawed by such devaluation; on the contrary, some propose that one or another existing theory—perhaps with a little fine tuning—is entirely adequate to address feminist ethical concerns. However, many feminist philosophers contend that western ethical theory is deeply male biased. Although they sometimes disagree with each other regarding the nature of this alleged bias and/or in their prescriptions of an alternative to it, their work is characterized by attention to certain recurrent themes. The present essay traces the evolution of those themes and in so doing offers a critical reconstruction of the development of western feminist ethical theory.

I. Including Women in Ethical Theory

Most of the great western philosophers assigned a higher ethical priority to men's interests than to women's, contending that women's proper role was to support men in men's undertakings. One theme continuing from ancient to modern times in that women's primary responsibility is to produce children for their husbands and the state, while providing their husbands with physical and emotional care. Aristotle, for example, asserts that a wife must obey and serve her husband because he has bought her with a great price; Aquinas writes that woman was made to be a helper to man "not indeed, as a helpmate in other works; as some say, since man can be more efficiently helped by another man in other works;

but as a helper in the work of generation," and Rousseau argues that "woman is intended to please man." Feminist philosophers have revealed what Susan Okin calls "functionalist" treatments of women by, among others, Plato, Aristotle, Aquinas, Hobbes, Locke, Rousseau, Kant, Hegel, Nietzsche, and Rawls (Okin 1979, 1989; Clark and Lange 1979).

Even though western philosophers generally treated women's interests as instrumental to men's, they regarded this treatment as standing in need of justification; their justifications typically took the form of arguing that women were in some important sense less fully or perfectly human than men. Some held that women were incapable of the same moral perfection as men: for instance, Aristotle says that women's temperance, courage and justice are of a different—and lesser—kind than men's; Rousseau asserts that women's merit consists in such "feminine" virtues as obedience, silence, and faithfulness; Kant writes: "The virtue of a woman is a *beautiful virtue*. That of the male sex should be a *noble virtue*." Many philosophers argued that women's capacity for reason was also different from and inferior to men's; major figures developing such arguments included Aristotle, Aquinas, Rousseau, Kant, Hegel, Nietzsche and Sartre. Since the western tradition typically regards rationality as the essential human characteristic, often defining moral agency in terms of the capacity for reason, arguments that women's reason is inferior to men's are deeply damaging to women's aspirations for equality. They suggest that women may be less morally valuable than men because their supposedly lesser rationality places them closer to animals and further from God; moreover, by entailing that women have less moral authority than men, they provide a strong rationale for placing women under men's political authority.

At the turn of the twenty-first century, when a commitment to women's equality is enshrined in United Nations declarations of human rights as well as in many national constitutions, it may seem hardly controversial to claim that women's interests should weigh equally with men's. Yet despite the lip service paid almost universally to the idea that persons should receive equal moral consideration regardless of their sex, feminists note that in practice public policies often accord less weight to women's interests than to men's. Sometimes this inequality of consideration may be attributed to faulty applications of ethical theory but sometimes feminists tract it to bias endemic in the theory itself.

(a) Utilizing "gender" in ethical analyses

One reason for public policy's frequent bias against women is that equality of consideration is often assumed to require treating men and women indistinguishably. Deliberately ignoring distinction of sex often has the consequence that ethical analyses fail to take account of morally salient differences between men and women.

Feminist research has revealed that many superficially sex-neutral issues in fact affect men and women differently and feminists insist that these differences must be addressed by any public policy that is ethically adequate. Examples of such differences abound; for instance, women often suffer more than men from war, even though men constitute most of the combatants. Over the twentieth century, as the proportion of civilian casualties has multiplied, women's share of the suffering has increased, since women who are not injured or killed directly are often displaced and became refugees; even in times of so-called peace, women

suffer disproportionately from the allocation of tax money to military expenditures rather than to social services and benefit least from job opportunities in the military and related industries. Many issues of global justice have significantly different implications for men and women. They include: population polices that target women's rather than men's fertility; economic development policies that invest in men's enterprises while failing to acknowledge the value of women's agricultural and domestic work; foreign investments in industries that exploit women's labor; and the increasing economic prominence of the global tourism industry and its concomitant sex trade.

The above examples illustrate that men and women are differently situated in all known societies; they are subjected to systematically different norms and expectations that govern virtually every aspect of their lives. All known societies assign different work to biological males and females, different family responsibilities, different standards of appropriate sexual behaviour, dress and diet, even different norms of physical deportment and patterns of speech. To distinguish these sets of social norms and expectations from biological differences between men and women, western feminists of the late 1960s appropriated the hitherto grammatical term "gender." They contended that, whereas sex differences were socially invariant, gender differences varied both among and within societies; they observed that masculinities and femininities, the social meanings assigned to being male and female, differed both in different societies and also among individuals of different castes, classes and ethnicities in any given society. More recent work in feminist theory has challenged the apparent clarity of the sex/gender distinction, especially the supposed naturalness and immutability of sex, but I shall not pursue that discussion here.

The realization that gender is a variable salient for much ethical practice has convinced some feminists that it is also a category indispensable to ethical theory. Those who hold this view argue that ethical theory cannot remain satisfied with conceptualizing humans on such a high level of abstraction that their inevitable differences, including their gender differences, become invisible. They contend that an adequate ethical theory cannot conceptualize human beings as undifferentiated, ignoring gender and related characteristics such as age, ability, class and race; instead, it requires a more complex conceptual apparatus that reflects the inevitable differences among people.

In opposition to this contention, other feminists object that what is required for more adequate analyses in practical ethics is not that ethical theory be revised but simply that those utilizing the theory take more account of the morally salient differences among individuals. Liberal feminists, in particular, often fear that elevating gender to the status of a concept in ethical theory would abandon feminism's traditional insistence that there exist no morally significant differences between men and women and so play dangerously into anti-feminist hands. These liberals endorse the older feminist position that sex difference should be conceived simply as "accidental" or inessential properties qualifying an underlying—and sex-neutral—human essence; they contend that ethics should address issues of gender on the level of first-order practice rather than second-order theory. Later in the essay, we shall see how this dispute has developed.

(b) Expanding the domain of ethics

Modern, although not ancient, moral philosophy has given little attention to many issues of special concern to women, most notably issues of sexuality and domestic life. This neglect has often been rationalized by a theoretical bifurcation of social life into a public domain, regulated by universal principles of right, and a private domain, in which varying goods may be properly pursued. Even philosophers like Aristotle, Hegel and Marx, who regard the home as having some ethical importance, portray it as an arena in which the most fully human excellences are incapable of being realized.

Inspired by the 1960s slogan, "The personal is political" (and, by extension, ethical), many feminist have challenged not only philosophers' neglect of the gendered aspects of most ethical issues but also their theoretical rationale for excluding some issues altogether. Feminists point out that the public/private dichotomy is covertly gendered, since women traditionally have been excluded from what is conceptualized as the public and restricted to what is defined as the private; the home, for instance, has become symbolically associated with the feminine, despite the fact that heads of households are paradigmatically male. Feminists argue that excluding the domestic realm from the moral domain is not only arbitrary but also covertly promotes masculine interests. For instance, by denying the conceptual resources for raising questions about the justice of the domestic division labor, it obscures the social necessity and arduousness of women's work in the home; moreover, by relegating intimate relationships to the domain of the personal or subjective, it screens and may even license the domestic abuse of women and girls.

Contemporary feminists have sought to expand the domain of ethics to embrace not only the domestic sphere but also many other aspects of social life. They have raised ethical questions concerning: abortion; sexuality, including compulsory heterosexuality, sexual harassment and rape; representation, including mass media and pornographic portrayals of women; self-presentation, including body image and fashion; and the role of language in reinforcing as well as reflecting women's subordination. Although mainstream ethics has given little attention to these issues until very recently, they all have ethically significant consequences for women's lives and are sometimes matters of life and death.

Although they may sometimes speak of including "women's issues" within the domain of ethics, feminists' use of this language does not imply that they recognize a category of women's ethical issues that is distinct from men's, much less from human issues. What are often categorized as women's issues are also in practice men's, since men's and women's lives are always enmeshed with each other; for instance, whether or not childcare or abortion is available significantly affects the lives of men as well as women. Men are involved in domestic, sexual and personal relations, just as women are involved in the economy, science and the military, despite the symbolic casting of the former as feminine and the latter as masculine. Most contemporary feminist contend that, if women are more preoccupied with or affected by certain matters than men, this is not natural or inevitable but instead reflects women's culturally assigned confinement to and/or responsibility for some areas of life and their relatively exclusion from others.

In order to give due weight to women's interests, many feminists asserts that ethical theory must operate with a more complex set of categories and virtually all agree that it must expand its domain.

The question of moral rationality and subjectivity is logical independent of the question of moral considerability; there is no logical reason why the interests of children, mentally disabled persons, animals or ecosystems should not count as morally equal to those of rational moral agents. However, western disregard for women's interests has often been justified by denying that women are full moral agents and so it often been thought necessary to validate women's moral subjectivity in order to demonstrate that women's claims to moral concern are equal with men's. Demonstrating that women should have equal political rights certainly requires establishing that they have equal moral authority.

Efforts to establish that women are full moral subjects long predate the emergence of contemporary feminist ethics. In the *Republic* (written in the fifth century BC, Plato declares that some women are capable of being guardians or rulers; in *The Book of the City of Ladies* (1405), Christine de Pisan argues that women are equal or even superior to men in such virtues as wisdom, courage, prudence, constance and chastity; in *A Vindication of the Rights of Woman* (1792), Mary Wollstonecraft denies the existence of virtues specific to one sex or the other and insists that women are as potentially rational and as fully human as men; in *The Subjection of Women* (1869), John Stuart Mill suggests that women's apparent inferiority in reasoning and principled morality is most likely due to their different socialization; and early in the twentieth century Bertrand Russell argued that women's intelligence and virtue varied in just the same ways as men's.

At the end of the twentieth century, contending that women are moral subjects equally with men may seem as superfluous as arguing that women are entitled to the same moral consideration. But although women now vote in all western democracies, their suffrage was achieved in many of these nations only during the lifetime of many people living today. British women received the vote after World War I but they did not receive it on the same terms as men until after World War II; French and Italian women received the vote only after World War II; Swiss women were unable to vote in national elections until 1973 and did not have suffrage in all cantons until the 1990s. The death of women political leaders suggests that western public still lack confidence in women's moral authority. Although women's potential for moral subjectivity is rarely disputed directly nowadays by respected authorities, recent moral psychology has claimed that women are less likely than men to actualize that potential and attain the highest levels of moral development (Kohlberg 1981). During the 1980s, however, some theorists altered feminism's traditional response to such claims; instead of continuing to insist that women were capable of reaching men's level of moral development, they began to challenge the standard by which moral rationally and subjectivity were judged. The following sections explore their challenges.

II. Is Modern Ethical Theory Male-Biased?

When western feminists criticize modern ethical theory, their usual targets are those liberal theories, rooted in the European Enlightenment, that still dominate contemporary western philosophy. Such theories include Kantianism and its various forms and, sometimes, existentialism. Few feminists whole-heartedly endorse neo-Aristotelian theories such as communitarianism and virtue ethics but their reservations about these theories as far have received less development than their reservations about these

theories so far have received less development than their reservations about liberal theory. This may be partly because their criticisms of modern liberal theory share common elements with neo-Aristotelian criticisms.

By setting aside traditional constraints on the realm of the ethical and paying attention to gender differences, some feminists have succeeded in utilizing liberal theory to illuminate a number of practical ethical issues of special concern to women; for example, Susan Okin uses Rawlsian contractarian theory to show how contemporary marriage practices discriminate against women (Okin 1989). Despite such achievements, many feminists argue that modern ethical theory is so thoroughly infected with masculine bias that it has only limited usefulness for feminism. The present section of this essay elaborates feminist criticism of modern ethical theory and the next section outlines an influential feminist alternative; in the following section, I offer some critical discussion of that alternative.

Despite their differences, Enlightenment ethical theories have much in common; most fundamentally they share a commitment to the equal moral value of every human individual. In the Kantian tradition, this value is expressed by recognizing the worth of each individual's autonomy; in the utilitarian tradition, it is expressed by assigning equal weight to each individual's happiness. In both traditions, realizing this value requires non-paternalism expressed by non-interference in the lives of others (Baier 1987).

Few feminists reject modern ethical values entirely and some have deployed them to good effect, arguing that women are entitled equally with men to respect and autonomy. However, even when feminists endorse modern values, they often propose that widely accepted interpretations of them should be revised; for instance, some fault common interpretations of Kantian theory for assuming that autonomy is a natural property possessed by all normal adults instead of recognizing that it is a potential realizable only in a community.

A more fundamental challenge to modern ethical theory is the charge that it often generates ethical prescriptions that, according to its critics, are morally repellent to many women. These critics do not attribute the alleged incompatibility between ethical theory and women's moral sensibilities to improper application of the theories, still less to deficient sensibilities in women. On the contrary, they assert that liberal values offer an impoverished ethical vision, providing a model of human interaction that is appropriate at best only for a limited domain of life and at worst may rationalize inhumanity to others. For instance, Baier notes that "noninterference can, especially for the relatively powerless, such as the very young, amount to neglect, and even between equals can be isolating and alienating" (Baier 1987: 48–9).

Impartially is a core value in modern ethical theory but, since about 1980, it has been challenged both by communitarians and by some feminists. Their criticisms overlap but are not identical. The ideal of impartiality requires that each individual receive equal consideration, regardless of an agent's subjective connections or loyalties to particular individuals. Some feminists have argued that this ideal is unrealizable, since it is psychologically impossible for human thinking to be detached from its context of origin or form its motivating passions and commitments (Noddings 1984; Young 1990; 103–5). Others, communitarians as well as feminists, have argued that the ideal of impartiality is morally defective, since it entails readiness to sacrifice those we love to abstract principles and absent strangers. Some argue that treating people as ethically equivalent denies the more significance if individually, which appreciates precisely the uniqueness of each person (Sherwin 1987). According to its feminist critics, too much emphasis on impartiality underrates those personal values that are more fundamental to a good human life.

Modern ethical theory typically utilizes a neo-Cartesian conception of the moral subject as an agent that essentially rational. Although the canonical theorists certainly assumed that moral agents were embodied members of communities, they regarded people's bodies and community memberships as "accidental" or contingent properties irrelevant to their claims to moral subjectivity.

Some feminists have found that the modern conception of the subject is a valuable resource for maintaining that women are full moral agents, disqualified neither by their female bodies nor by their frequently dependent social status. Accepting the modern conception, they insist that women are just as capable as men of transcending the limitations of their bodies and they argue that the western philosophical association of men with mind and women with body has no defensible basis. In their view, this association serves simply to rationalize men's political dominance, as well as social arrangements that assign to women the primary responsibility for taking care of bodily needs.

Other feminists are critical modern ethical theory's abstract, rationalistic and individualistic conception of the moral subject. These critics often focus on the modern devaluation of the body, charging that it has been an important contributor to what they perceive as flaws in Enlightenment ethical theory. They argue that devaluing the body in comparison with the mind has encouraged ethical theory to ignore many fundamental aspects of human life and to posit ideals unattainable by human beings. Disparagement of the body, they contend, turns theoretical attention away from bodily-related differences among individuals, such as age, sex and ability, and encourages regarding people as indistinguishable and interchangeable. Ethical reflection on embodiment would reveal that inequality, dependence and interdependence, specificity, social embeddedness and historical community must be recognized as permanent features of human social life and that seeking to transcend these is a waste of time. Instead of devoting so much ethical attention to abstractions such as equality, autonomy, generality, isolated individuals, ideal communities and the universal human condition, many feminists argue that ethical theory should pay more attention to people's bodies. This would enable it to recognize the central issues of vulnerability, development and morality rather than changelessness, of temporality and situatedness rather than timelessness and nonlocatedness, of particularity rather than universality and of interdependence and cooperation rather than independence and self-sufficiency.

Enlightenment ethical theory regards rationality both as a natural property belonging to all normal human adults and as the only reliable guide to distinguishing right from wrong action. Viewing emotions as contaminants of pure reason, it defines moral rationality in terms of individuals' to consider dispassionately the interests of all those affected in any situation, thus overcoming the supposedly normal human tendency towards self-interested bias. Some feminists dispute both the descriptive and prescriptive elements of this account. On the descriptive level, they challenge the assumption that people are predominately self-aggrandizing, an assumption they see as facilitated by liberalism's disregard for human embodiment. Instead, they contend that the social meanings attached to bodily characteristics such as parentage, age or sex result in embodied individuals developing moral identities that are not purely abstract and universal but also defined by the social relations involved in the meanings assigned to various specific bodies. Individuals with relational moral identities are unlikely to make a sharp separation between their own interests and those of others; they are more likely to be moved by considerations of particular attachment than by abstract concern for duty, more by care, more than by respect, and more by responsibility than by right.

For feminist critics of modern ethical theory, people's propensities to care for others and to regard their own interests as liked with those of others are not just weaknesses to be overcome by moral reason. Baier challenges what she calls the rationalism or intellectualism of modern moral theory, a rationalism that assumes that we need not worry what passions persons have, as long as their rational will can control them.

> This Kantian picture of a controlling reason dictating to possibility unruly passions also tends to seem less useful when we are led to consider what sort of person we need to fill the role of parent, or indeed want in any close relationship. It might be important for father figures to have rational control over their violent urges to beat to death the children whose screams enrage them, but more than control of such nasty passions seems needed in the mother or primary parent, or parent-substitute, by

most psychological theories. They need to love their children, not just to control their irritation. (Baier 1987: 55)

We shall see in the next section that not only do some feminists deny that emotions are necessarily subversive of moral reason; they regard them as indispensable to it.

In modern ethical theory, impartiality is not only a substantive ideal; it is also a defining characteristic of moral rationality, providing a necessary and sometimes sufficient condition of right action. We have seen already that some feminists challenge the substance of this ideal; others may accept the ethical intuition as its core but observe that the concept is too indeterminate to guide right action. Modern moral philosophers have offered a variety of recommendations for achieving impartiality, such as disregarding one's own self-interested motivations or adopting others' points of view, but a number of feminist critics have argued that these recommendations are quite unhelpful since they cannot be operationalized in practice. For instance, Marilyn Friedman notes that the limited nature of individuals' experience and of their familiarity with the thinking of others makes it highly unlikely that any real person (as opposed to an archangel) could project herself imaginatively into the standpoint of another, let alone of many others, nor could one who attempted this imaginative feat ever know how far she have been successful. Friedman concludes that available philosophical conceptions of impartiality offer no practical guide to moral justification. She recommends that people who wish to do the right thing should focus instead on partiality, concentrating on eliminating particular nameable biases from their thinking (Friedman 1993: 31).

Why do some feminists allege that the distinctive values of modern ethical theory, its conception of the moral subject and its conception of moral reason are characteristically masculine? What is specifically masculine about valuing equality, autonomy and respect, understanding human subjects in terms of their minds rather than their bodies, and construing moral reason in terms of dispassionate impartiality? Marxist critics have long argued that modern ethical theory is based on a "possessive individualist" conception of human nature that portrays humans as essentially separate from others, insatiably appetitive and with interests typically in conflict, and they have charged that this conception reflects the adversarial market relations of bourgeois society. Feminists have accepted much of this picture but they have added the claim that men are more likely than women to understand human nature in such adversarial terms (Gilligan 1982). Few feminists attribute this alleged difference in perspective to some innate psychological differences between the sexes; instead, they explain it by reference to the contingently different social situations of men and women. Some draw on neo-Freudian object relations theory, which appeals to gendered patterns of parenting to argue that a preoccupation with separation is distinctively masculine. Others argue that disregard of the body is the luxury available only to those whose bodies are normative and/or who are freed from primary responsibility for bodily maintenance.

Basing ethical theory on a model of human nature that reflects men's distinctive experiences and values is problematic most obviously because it valorizes the ethical perspectives of only one segment of the population. Feminists further contend that the dominant model fails to describe accurately the moral psychology not only of most women but also of many men. Basing ethical theory based on false empirical postulates is likely to result in unrealizable ideals and epistemologists. Moreover, an ethical theory based on a masculine image of human nature devalues the symbolically feminine dimensions of human life; it also neglects more "feminine" ethical visions, promoting an image of the ethical life that many find repellent, especially many women. In addition to advancing an exclusionary, limited, and—to many—repugnant ethical vision, modern ethical theory impugns the moral authority of those who disagree with it by labeling them as morally deviant, immature or irrational (Gilligan 1982). For its feminist critics, modern ethical theory proposes a male-biased ethical vision that justifies itself by an equally male-biased moral epistemology.

Some feminists charge that modern ethical theory is masculine, finally, in projecting its devaluation of women and of feminine experience onto the universe at large. It follows the larger western philosophical tradition that interprets reality through conceptual dichotomies such as culture/nature, transcendence/immanence, permanent/unchanging, universal/particular, mind/body, reason/emotion and public/private. By associating the more highly valued term with masculinity and the less valued with femininity, western ethical theory inscribes cultural hostility for women into its portrayal of ultimate reality.

III. Women's Experience as Paradigm for Ethical Theory

In response to the charge that modern ethical theory assumes masculine experience as normative, some feminist ethics has sought to take women's experience as its paradigm or at

least as its point of departure. The best known example of this approach is the ethics of care, which elaborates a moral perspective said to arise from women's characteristic experience of nurturing particular others, especially their experience of rearing children (Gilligan 1982; Noddings 1984; Ruddick 1989; Held 1993). Although the project of deriving ethics from women's experience is generally associated with the ethics of care, a few feminists reject care's emphasis on nurturing or mothering and seek to derive ethics from other facets of women's experience; for instance Sara Lucia Hoagland aims to derive new value from reflecting on lesbian lives (Hoagland 1989).

Since feminist ethical theory is often identified with the ethics of care, it is worth emphasizing that neither the ethics of care nor the project of basing ethical theory exclusively or primarily on women's experience should be taken as feminist orthodoxy. I have nevertheless chosen to devote considerably space to care ethics because it offers the best known, and believe, most radical challenge made by feminists to modern ethical theory. It contends that attention to women's moral experience advances values that are ethically superior to those characteristic of modernity and fosters more adequate conceptions of moral subjectivity and more rationality.

Proponents of care ethics characteristically advocate that ethical priority should be given to the values that they see as central to women's practices of nurturing and especially of mothering; these include the values of emotional sensitivity and responsiveness to the needs of particular others, intimacy and connection, responsibility and trust. Modern ethical theory has always feared the that justice would be subverted if too much weight were accorded to these values but it has accepted them in what it has seen as there proper place, namely, within the limited domain of intimate personal relations; on the epistemological level, it has accorded them a similarity personal relations; on the epistemological level, it has accorded them a similarly minor role as personal motivators to right action. Most care theorists reject this relegation to what Benhabib calls "the margins of ethical theory;" instead, they often propose that the values hitherto associated with the private domain should become more prominent both in ethical theory and in society at large. For instance, Virginia Held considers how to export to wider society the relations suitable for mothering persons and children (Held 1993). Sara Ruddick considers how "maternal thinking" may promote a politics (Ruddick 1989). Joan Tronto argues that care may be a political as well as an ethical ideal, describing "the qualities necessary for democratic citizens to live well together in a pluralistic society"(Tronto 1993: 161–2).

We have seen that modern ethical theory is dominated by a neo-Cartesian model of the subject as disembodied, asocial, unified, rational and essentially similar to all other selves; we have also seen that some feminists accept this model but that many challenge it. In developing their challenges, feminists have drawn insight from several traditions, such as Marxism, psychoanalysis, communitarianism and postmodernism, but they have been especially influenced by the work of psychologists such as Jean Baker Miller and Carol Gilligan. Gilligan asserted that women and girls tend to see themselves as connected to others and to fear isolation and abandonment, unlike men who are said to see themselves as separated from others and to fear connection and intimacy. She reported that women's conception of their selves as rational

gives them different moral preoccupations and encourages them to construe moral dilemmas in ways that will repair and strengthen relationships, to practice positive caretaking rather than respectful nonintervention, and to prioritize the personal values of care, trust, attentiveness and love for particular others above impersonal principles of equality, respect, rights and justice. Many feminists ethical theorists advocate a so-called relational model of the self. They contend that such a model is superior to the Cartesian conception for understanding not only women but also men; contrary to the view of human nature presupposed by modern ethical theory, all human beings in fact are interdependent, constrained and unequal. Thus some feminists argue that a relational conception of moral subjectivity is both more adequate empirically that an atomistic model and also generates a more acceptable ethics (Whitbeck 1984). For these theorists, "masculine" consciousness is false consciousness.

The "style" of moral reasoning associated with care ethics is often contrasted with that characteristic of justice ethics. Whereas justice thinking focuses primarily on the structure of an ethical situation, deliberately disregarding the specific identities of the individuals involved, care thinking is characterized by a distinctive ethical orientation toward particular persons. This orientation has both affective and cognitive dimensions: caring individuals are both concerned about the other's welfare and perceive insightfully how it is with the other. Contrary to justice thinking, which is portrayed as appealing to universalizable moral principles that guide impartial calculation of who is entitled to what, accounts of care thinking emphasize its responsiveness to particular situations whose morally salient features are perceived with an acuteness thought to be made possible by the carer's emotional posture of empathy, openness and receptiveness (Blum 1992).

Perhaps the most distinctive and controversial feature attributed to care thinking is its particularity; this means not only that it addresses that needs of others in their others as unique, irreplaceable individuals rather than as "generalized" others seen simply as representatives of a common humanity (Benhabib 1992). Such responsiveness requires paying as much attention to the ways in which people differ from each other as to the ways in which they are the same. Another aspect of care's particularity is that its conclusions are nonuniversalizable; that is, they carry no implication that someone else in a similar situation should act similarly. The radical particularism of care thinking challenges a fundamental assumption of modern ethical theory, namely, that appraising particular actions or practices requires appeal to general principles.

Proponents of care ethics resist reducing care to a simple emotional response; they consider it not simply as a motivator to right action, the latter determined through a process of rational calculation, but also a distinct moral capacity with cognitive dimensions necessary to determining what actions are morally appropriate (Blum 1992). Care is not rational in the senses of being egoistic, dispassionate or deductive, but Nel Noddings asserts that "rationally and reasoning involve more than the identification of principles and their deductive application"(Noddings 1990: 27). Proponents of care thinking regard care as rational in the broad sense of being a distinctively human way of engaging with others; it is both ethically

valuable in itself and tends to produce morally appropriate action.

IV. Ethical Theory: Feminine or Feminist?

The ethics of care has revealed some serious gaps and biases in modern ethical theory, many of which are attributable to that theory's exclusions of women's experience and concerns. A more adequate ethical theory must, in my view, develop some means of including the moral perspectives of women, as well the perspectives of other devalued or marginalized groups. Nevertheless, I find that the way the ethics of care so far has developed ethics from the perspective of women is problematic both in methodological principle and ethical practice.

Attempts to derive ethical theory from empirical experience reflect the naturalist conviction that philosophical ideals must be compatible with people's actual moral sensibilities; on this view, apparent divergence between ethical theory and ethical practice may not be dismissed immediately as a failure in practice. Moreover, an ethical theory that is responsive to feminist concerns requires that specific attention be paid to women's ethical experience in order to acknowledge women's hitherto devalued capacities as moral agents.

Although these contentions are, in my view, correct, it is necessary to remember that naturalistic approaches to ethical theory involve characteristic moral dangers. One is conventionalism, which takes accepted values and ways of thinking as self-justifying; linked with conventionalism is relativism, which asserts that what is morally permissible varies for different moral communities. Both conventionalism and relativism are problematic for feminism, because they conflict with its steadfast opposition to all forms of male dominance.

In addition to its moral dangers, ethical naturalism faces considerable methodological problems. One of these is that the term "ethical experience" is so broad that it is unclear how it should be investigated. Another is that what people say about ethics is notoriously unreliable as a guide to their actions. Moreover, it is difficult to find empirical confirmation for generalizations about the moral experience of large and diverse groups, such as women or lesbians, even when these generalizations are made by philosophers who themselves are women or lesbian.

Methodological problems underlie many feminist debates about how women's ethical experience should be characterized and they emerge with special clarity in the ethics of care. We have seen that care theorists assert that culturally feminine experiences such as nurturing provide the basis for an ethical vision quite distinct from that promoted by modern ethical theory. In a complex modern society, however, all unqualified generalizations about men's and women's experiences are *prima facie* dubious; the life situations of both women and men in contemporary western societies vary so widely by class, race/ethnicity and even generation that it seems quite unlikely that all or most women share a moral perspective different from that of all or most men. In fact, investigations into the empirical validity of care theorists' claims have often failed to confirm a link between gender and caring; when subjects are matched for education and occupation, women often achieve almost identical scores with men on justice-oriented tests of moral development, leaving women who work in the home as the main female representatives of the care perspectives.

Moreover, many men as well as women have been found to employ care thinking, especially lower-class men and men of color. For these reasons, Marilyn Friedman argues that the ethics of care is feminine in a sense that is more symbolic or normative then empirical; rather than reflecting empirical dispositions in women toward empathy, sensitivity and altruism, she suggests that care expresses the cultural expectation that women be more empathic, sensitive and altruistic than men (Friedman 1993: 123–4).

Recent advocates of an ethics of care acknowledge that some women think in terms of justice and some men in terms of care, but they nevertheless associate caring with women because they regard the care perspective as emerging from forms of socialization and practice that, in contemporary western society, are predominately feminine; these include raising children, tending to the elderly, maintaining a supportive home environment and nursing. Joan Tronto argues that the ethics of care is associated not only with gender, but also with race and class. She links the ethical perspective of care with the work of maintaining and cleaning the body, tasks that in western history have been relegated primarily to women but not to all women or to women exclusively; such caring work is done not only by women but also by the working classes and especially, in much of the West, by people of color (Tronto 1993). Tronto's analysis of the social genesis of care thinking fits well with Lawrence Blum's argument that justice ethics expresses a juridical-administrative perspective that is indeed masculine but which reflects the concerns not of all men but specifically of those in professional and administrative classes (Blum 1982). Together, Tronto's and Blum's arguments suggest that both ethics of justice and the ethics of care are not only gendered but simultaneously raced and classed.

In the preceding section, we noted some difficulties in determining just what is women's moral experience. But even if we grant that the ethics of care is in some sense *feminine*, this would not be sufficient to establish it as an ethics that is *feminist*, since feminism is often critical of the feminine. One necessary condition of an ethical theory's being feminist is that it should provide conceptual resources adequate for criticizing all forms of male dominance and some feminists, including myself, doubt that the ethics of care offers such resources.

One concern raised by a number of feminist philosophers is that the ethics of care is insufficiently suspicious of the characteristically feminine moral failing of self sacrifice. Arguing that care for one's abuser, for instance, may be morally pathological rather that virtuous, and nothing that Noddings justifies the responsibility to care for oneself only in the instrumental terms of maintaining one's capacity to care for others, some feminists have characterized care as a slave morality (Card 1990).

Other problems result from care's characteristic focus on the specific needs of particular individuals. The morally problematic situations described by care theorists typically involve only a few individuals and typically require the agent to respond to others perceived in their concrete particularity. A number of critics have wondered how this model of moral rationality can avoid partially to the particular others known to the agent. They have also questioned how care thinking can address large-scale social or global problems involving large numbers of people who could never be known personally by any single agent.

I have worried that care thinking may distort our understanding of some morally problematic situations. Care's narrow focus is valuable in encouraging awareness of moral complexity and individual responsibility in small-scale situations but it may well obscure perception of the macro-situations that provide the context for individual encounters. For instance, it may enable us to discern insensitivity or bullying on the part of particular individuals while diverting moral attention away from the social structures of privilege that legitimate their behaviour. Similarly, attending to an individual's immediate needs for food, shelter, comfort, or companionship may distract us from moral scrutiny of the structures that create those needs or leave them unfulfilled. Thus care thinking may encourage what are sometimes called band aid or social work approaches to moral problems, rather than encouraging efforts to address them institutionally or even to prevent their occurrence through social reform (Jaggar 1995).

A final problem that I find in the ethics of care is its lack of guidance in determining which caring responses are ethically appropriate. Most care theorists acknowledge the need to distinguish appropriate from inappropriate caring but they seem to assume that this distinction is self-evident or at least that the carer/cared-for dyad can be relied on to make it. However, such an assumption is evidently unwarranted; examples of morally inappropriate behaviour often rationalized as caring by both agents and recipients include over-indulgence or "spoiling," co-dependence, even domestic violence and incest. The care tradition may contain the conceptual resources of distinguishing appropriate from inappropriate caring but so far I have not found a convincing account (Jaggar 1995).

The ethics of care is often caricatured as a "feel good" situationist ethics that rejects justice and is concerned exclusively with personal relations; in fact most care theorists regard justice as necessary, though not sufficient, for feminist ethics; they also recognize that transforming personal relations requires transforming the larger society. Feminist ethical theory, in turn, is often equated with the ethics of care but in fact the only orthodoxy in feminist ethical theory is its broad commitment to eliminating male bias.

References

Baier, Annette C.: "The Need for More than Justice," *Science Morality and Feminist Theory*, eds. Marsha Hanen and Kai Nielsen (Calgary, Canada: University of Calgary Press, 1987).

Benhabib, Seyla: *Situating the Self: Gender, Community and Postmodernism in Contemporary Ethics* (New York: Routledge, 1992).

Blum, Lawrence A.: "Kant's and Hegel's Moral Rationalism: A Feminist Perspective," *Canadian Journal of Philosophy,* XII (1982): 2, 287-302.

—. "Care." *Encyclopedia of Ethics,* ed. Lawrence C. Becker (New York: Garland, 1992).

Card, Claudia: "Gender and Moral Luck," in *Identity, Character and Morality,* eds. Owen Flanagan and Amelie Rorty (Cambridge, MA: MIT Press, 1990).

Clark, Lorenne M.G. and Lynda Lange, eds.: *The Sexism of Social and Political Theory* (Toronto, Buffalo, London: University of Toronto Press, 1979).

Friedman, Marilyn: *What Are Friends For? Feminist Perspectives on Personal Relationships and Moral Theory* (Ithaca: Cornell University Press, 1993).

Gilligan, Carol: *In a Different Voice: Psychological Theory and Women's Development* (Cambridge, MA: Harvard University Press, 1982).

Held, Virginia: *Feminist Morality: Transforming Culture, Society, and Politics* (Chicago: University of Chicago Press, 1993).

Hoagland, Sarah Lucia: *Lesbian Ethics; Toward new Value* (Palo Alto, CA: Institute of Lesbian Studies, 1989).

Jaggar, Alison M.: "Caring as a Feminist Practice of Moral Reason," in Virginia Held, ed., *Justice and Care: Essential Readings in Feminist Ethics* (Boulder, Westview, 1995).

Kohlberg, Lawrence: *The Philosophy of Moral Development: Moral Stages and the Idea of Justice* (San Francisco: Harper and Row, 1981).

Noddings, Nel: *Caring: A feminine Approach to Ethics and Moral Education* (Berkeley: University of California Press, 1984).

—. "Feminist Fears in Ethics," *Journal of Social Philosophy,* 21 (1990): 2-3.

Okin, Susan Moller: *Women in Western Political Thought* (Princeton: Princeton University Press, 1979).

—. *Justice, Gender and the Family* (New York: Basic Books, 1989).

Ruddick, Sara: *Maternal Thinking: Towards a Politics of Peace* (New York: Beacon Press, 1989).

Sherwin, Susan: "A Feminist Approach to Ethics," *Resources for Feminist Research,* 16 (1987): 3.

Tronto, Joan C.: *Moral Boundaries: A Political Argument for an Ethic of Care* (New York: Routledge, 1993).

Whitbeck, Caroline: "A Different Reality: Feminist Ontology," in *Beyond Domination*, ed. Carol Gould (Totowa, NJ: Rowman and Allheld, 1984).

Young, Iris Marion: *Justice and the Politics of Difference* (Princeton University Press, 1990).

Key Terms and Concepts

Ethics

Morality

Normative ethics

Descriptive ethics

Applied ethics

Metaethics

Consequentialist

Deontological

Divine command theory

Conventional ethical relativism

Cultural relativism

Ethnocentrism

Subjective ethical relativism

Act utilitarianism

Hedonism

Rule utilitarianism

Cost-benefit analysis

Absolutism

Good will

Hypothetical imperative

Categorical imperative

First formulation of the categorical imperative

Second formulation of the categorical imperative
Intrinsic value
Instrumental value
Ethics of care

Study Questions

1. How does ethics differ from morality?
2. What is the difference between normative and descriptive ethics?
3. What is the difference between consequentialist and deontological ethics?
4. What is the strongest argument in favour of the divine command theory?
5. Socrates asks Euthyphro this question: "Is the holy loved by the gods because it is holy (right, moral)? Or is it holy (right, moral) because it is loved?" What is Socrates' purpose and point in asking this question?
6. If morality is based on God's will, how does this make morality arbitrary?
7. What is ethical relativism and how does it differ from cultural relativism?
8. Do you think that the fact the people disagree about morality shows that ethical relativism is true? Why or why not?
9. Why does ethical relativism prevent us from criticizing other cultures?
10. How does ethical relativism impede moral progress?
11. How does utilitarianism determine morally right action? What are its main principles?
12. Does utilitarianism allow us to escape our moral obligations? Why or why not?
13. Does utilitarianism take into consideration rights and justice?
14. Why does utilitarianism fail to take into consideration special relationships?
15. What is the free rider problem?
16. What is a cost-benefit analysis? Why is it problematic?
17. What is the good will?
18. Using Kant's first categorical imperative, would breaking promises be moral or immoral? Why?
19. What is Kant's second categorical imperative?
20. Explain why critics think Kant's emphasis on unconditional absolute moral principles is problematic.
21. Why does respect of persons pose challenges to Kant's moral theory?
22. What are the key features of care ethics?
23. Why do critics argue that care ethics reinforces the subordination of women?
24. Why do critics argue that care ethics fails to take strangers into consideration?
25. Could care ethics implement institutional change in society?

Further Reading

Harman, Gilbert. *The Nature of Morality: An Introduction to Ethics.* New York: Oxford University Press, 1977.
MacRae, Sinclair. *An Introduction to Ethics: Theories, Perspectives, and Issues.* Toronto: Pearson Education Canada, Inc., 2003.
Nielsen, Kai. *Ethics Without God.* New York: Prometheus Books, 1973.
Pojman, Louis. *Ethics: Discovering Right and Wrong.* Belmont, CA: Wadsworth, Inc., 1990.
—. *Ethical Theory: Classical and Contemporary Readings.* Belmont, CA: Wadsworth, 1989.
Rachels, James. *The Elements of Moral Philosophy.* 4th ed. New York: McGraw-Hill, 2003.
Singer, Peter. *A Companion to Ethics.* Oxford: Blackwell Publishing, Ltd., 1991.
Smart, J. J. C., and Bernard Williams. *Utilitarianism: For and Against.* New York: Cambridge University Press, 1973.
Tong, Rosemarie. *Feminine and Feminist Ethics.* Belmont, CA: Wadsworth Publishing Company, 1993.
Waluchow, Wilfrid. *The Dimensions of Ethics: An Introduction to Ethical Theory.* Peterborough, ON: Broadview Press, 2003.

Internet Resources

Fieser, James. "Ethics." *The Internet Encyclopedia of Philosophy.* Eds. James Fieser and Bradley Dowden. n.d. 28 May 2007 <http://www.iep.utm.edu/e/ethics.htm>.
Hinman, Lawrence. *Ethics Updates.* San Diego, CA: University of San Diego, n.d. 28 May 2007 <http://ethics.sandiego.edu/>.

The W. Maurice Young Centre for Applied Ethics. Vancouver: University of British Columbia, n.d. 28 May 2007 <http://www.ethics.ubc.ca/>.

Zalta, Edward. Ed. *Stanford Encyclopedia of Philosophy.* Stanford, CA: The Metaphysics Research Lab, Stanford University, n.d. 25 May 2007 <http://plato.stanford.edu/entries/>.

Notes

1. According to an Angus Reid poll, 59 percent of Canadians and 57 percent of Americans believe that possession of marijuana should not always result in a criminal record.

2. The application of specific rules and principles to concrete circumstances to make moral evaluations is known as casuistry.

3. Also see W. D. (William David) Ross' *The Right and the Good* as another example of deontological ethics.

4. Milgram's classic experiments are based on a series of electrical shocks being delivered by a "teacher" to a "learner." The learner memorizes a series of word pairs, such as "cat" and "dog" and the teacher tests the learner on his or her memorization. Mistaken word matches are punished by electrical shocks increasing in intensity with each wrong answer. The shocks range from mild to severe. Unbeknownst to the teacher, the learner is not really being shocked but is in collaboration with the "authoritarian" researcher in the experiment. As the shock intensity increases, causing cries of pain and help from the learner, the researcher cajoles and pressures the teacher to continue with the shocks. Although only 62 percent of the teachers administered shock to the very end of the experiment, it does highlight, for example, how Nazi officers could carry out the extermination Jews and other innocent civilians merely by following orders. However, this would not mitigate their moral responsibilities.

5. Other examples include: "Or why was I not as a hidden untimely birth, as infants that never see the light? There the wicked cease from troubling, and there the weary are at rest. There the prisoners are at ease together; they hear not the voice of the taskmaster. The small and the great are there, and the slave is free from his master" (Job 3:16–19). And, "The wicked go astray from the womb, they err from their birth, speaking lies. They have venom like the venom of a serpent. [...] Let them vanish like water that runs away, like grass let them be trodden down and wither. Let them be like the snail which dissolves into slime, like

the untimely birth that never sees the sun" (Psalms 58:3–8). These examples suggest that abortion was far from immoral, even in Biblical times. The use of biblical scriptures to support the anti-abortionist argument is highly spurious.

6. According to the World Health Organization, there are four main types of female circumcision: 1) Cut out or remove prepuce, with or without removing part or all of the clitoris; 2) Cut out or remove the clitoris with partial or total removal of the labia minora—this is the most common (80 percent) form of circumcision; 3) Cut out or remove part or all of the external genitalia and then narrowing the vaginal opening (infibulation)—this is the least common form, making up of only 5 percent of cases; 4) This includes such things as pricking, piercing, cutting, stretching, or burning of the clitoris and/or labia.

7. In 1997, the OECD (Organization for Economic Co-operation and Development) introduced an anti-corruption convention. That same year, Canada signed the OECD convention and promised to produce legislation to prevent corruption, including bribery. On February 14, 1999, the Corruption of Foreign Public Officials Act became law. It is now a criminal offence, punishable by up to five years in prison, for paying bribe to a foreign public official to gain a business advantage. Lesotho also ratified the OECD convention and implemented its own legislation. As a result, in 2002, Acres was charged and found guilty of bribery and fined $2.2 million (USD) (Karakowsky, Carroll & Buchholtz 595).

8. A comparable case is that of Mukhtaran Bibi, a women living in a rural village in the Muzaffargarh region of Pakistan, who was gang-raped because her brother was having relations with a woman of a higher caste. Village elders, in retaliation for her brother's moral indiscretion, ordered the rape. The perpetrators of the crime and the elders who ordered the rape have since been arrested, tried, and sentenced to death. The president of Pakistan, Pervez Musharraf, has just introduced legislation to overturn this law.

9. A notable example is that of Marie-Joseph Angelique, the slave of a wealthy Montreal businessman. On April 10, 1734, Angelique discovered that she was about to be sold; in defiance she burned down her owner's house in an attempt to escape and incidentally set fire to 46 other buildings. She was eventually captured, tortured, and hanged.

10. Most countries have laws against slavery, including the United Nations. It prohibited slavery in 1948 under the *Universal Declaration of Human*

Rights and the 1956 *UN Supplementary Convention on the Abolition of Slavery*. Unfortunately, slavery is still prevalent. According to Anti-Slavery International, the world's oldest international human rights organization (founded in 1839), there were approximately 12.3 million adults and 179 million children forced into labour in 2005. Slavery takes a variety of forms including child labour, sex slaves (forced prostitution), and human trafficking.

11. For a more extreme example, consider Neo-Nazis or "skin heads." This racist subculture has its own unique culture relative to general society. Should Neo-Nazis accept their own sub-cultural racist views as correct or the general culture's non-racist views? And if they accept their racist views as morally correct, given their subculture, do we have a right to criticize their view? If relativism is correct, it's not only difficult to choose which cultural norms are morally correct but, given pluralism and cultural diversity, non-racists would have to accept racist views and vice versa. In short, if we apply cultural relativism to our own cultures, we couldn't criticize the various subcultures in our own society as morally right or wrong, just different. But this seems reprehensible. Just because an action is morally accepted by a culture or subculture does not justify it.

12. For the Inuit, unfortunately, given the harsh climate of northern Canada, a poor hunting season could push families to the edge of destruction. Rather than face the demise of the whole family, a child might be sacrificed. The reasoning is simple: men (hunters) are most important to a family, for without them the family would not have food, women are second to men because women can bear children and bring new life to the people. Children are below men and women, and the elderly are considered the least important. When old age has sapped a man's strength and a women's ability to bear children, their dominance within a family ceases. If food were in short supply, an elder might commit suicide to ensure the survival of the family. The environment, in other words, determines the logic of death: who lives and dies. But this logic does not trump their love for children. If they did not love their children, their culture would have never survived.

13. William Shaw, in his article "Relativism and Objectivity in Ethics," argues that even though most philosophers have accepted the claim that ethical disagreement does not undermine the idea of universal moral truths, they have failed to consider the reverse: agreement on the universal ethical principles does not mean that metaethical relativism is false. Universal moral

agreement might be a happy coincidence of culture itself or it may be the result of some psychological aspect of all humans.

14. According to the Centers for Disease Control and Prevention, an estimated 700,000 to 1.5 million people die each year of malaria, 75 percent of which are children.

15. New legislation tabled in the House of Commons would increase the punishment for cruelty to animals to a maximum of five years and/or a $10,000 fine.

16. Push-pin is like the children's game "jacks."

17. According to Statistics Canada, students graduating with a bachelor's degree from university have an average debt of $19,500.

18. Let's look at one more example of utilitarianism. Jim is a botany professor at a local university. He is lost and finds himself in a small town in Central America (Smart and Williams 98–99). Tied up against a wall in the town square are twenty men with several armed men watching guard. An authoritative man in military uniform enters the town square and questions Jim about who he is, where he is from, and what he was doing in the area. Content with his answers, the man explains to Jim that he is a captain in the military and local indigenous groups have been protesting against the government. In response, the government seeks to stop the protests once and for all. They reason that if they randomly kidnap and execute twenty innocent locals, this will instill so much fear in the indigenous groups they will stop their protests. However, because Jim is an honoured visitor from out of town, the captain explains he gets the privilege of executing one local. If he does this, the rest of the people will be let go Jim, of course, refuses. But the captain further explains that if he refuses, his men will kill them all twenty locals as planned. What should Jim do? From utilitarian perspective, the answer is easy: kill the one innocent person.

19. I am assuming there is no other rule that tells us how to solve this conflict. For example, there is no rule, which says, "Protecting the lives of innocent people will take priority over always telling the truth."

20. The charges against Rankin were eventually thrown out. It is claimed that the trial judge made an error by not dealing with each of the ten charges against Rankin individually. The Ontario Securities Commission is now asking the courts to clarify the ground rules for future prosecutions (Blackwell B3).

21. Here is another example that demonstrates how utilitarianism conflicts with rights and justice (Rawls 10). Imagine you are a utilitarian sheriff of a small southern town in the United States

where racial tension and discrimination is prevalent. Imagine further a white woman is raped. Although you do not know who the offender is, you do know he is African-American. The white-majority in town are furious and take to the streets, starting race riots and engaging in vigilantly justice against the African-American community. Now in order to calm this explosive situation, and hence maximize utility, as sheriff, you might decide to apprehend an innocent African-American male with similar characteristics as the perpetrator and who has no alibi. In fact, imagine the only way to stop the town from sliding into anarchy is to concoct a case against this innocent man, have a quick trial, and put him in jail. Once word spreads that someone has paid for this crime, greater utility will be restored. In short, framing an innocent man will promote greater utility and, hence, is morally right. But this example, once again, highlights the problem of rights and justice for utilitarians. In this case, putting an innocent man in jail is clearly a violation of his rights to a fair trial and undermines the very idea of justice. There can be no justice if innocent people end up paying for crimes they did not commit. Failing to take into consideration individual rights and justice is a major problem with utilitarianism.

22. A sixth problem with utilitarianism is that the consequences are hard to measure. The consequences of an action are hard to predict because the happiness and unhappiness of an action are hard to measure. In other words, since it's hard to define happiness, it's hard to foresee what consequences an action will have. However, this objection can be weakened depending on the case. Most professors, for example, make it very clear to their students that the consequence of cheating on an exam is failure; and most people are aware that the infidelity is one of the leading causes of divorce. In short, we can know with reasonable accuracy the consequences of our actions in some cases and we are blind in the next. The best we can do is to reasonably foresee the potential consequences.

23. According to Greenpeace, there are approximately 30,000 nuclear weapons in the world today, with over one thousand ready to be launched in a moments notice.

24. Merck also investigated third-party payment options with the World Health Organization, the U.S. Agency for International Development, and the U.S. Department of State, but given budget cutbacks all were unwilling to fund the project.

25. A way around this problem would be to appeal to W. D. Ross's *prima facie* duties.

26. One potential solution to this problem is to apply the second categorical imperative. In situations where there are conflicting duties, we appeal to the idea of treating people with respect; having intrinsic value. Clearly, in this case, the Nazi treatment of Jews was far from respectful. The Nazi used Jews as a means to an end, rather than ends in themselves. In this case, it would be perfectly moral for the Dutch fisherman to lie to protect innocent lives.

27. In Paul Taylor's *Respect for Nature: A Theory of Environmental Ethics*, he puts forward a life-centred or biocentric ethical theory based on Kantian principles. From a life-centred theory, we have a *prima facie* (at first glance) moral obligation to wild plants and animals themselves as member of the earth's biotic community. Which means that we are morally bound to protect and promote their well-being for their own sakes in recognition of their inherent worth. We have to respect the integrity of the ecosystems, preserve endangered species, and avoid pollution because these are ways in which natural specie populations achieve and maintain their healthy existence. Their well-being are things to be realized as ends in themselves.

28. An alternative moral theory that takes into consideration emotions as part of our moral assessment is that of David Hume. For Hume, our moral assessments involve sympathetic feelings of pleasure and pain that is derived from observing the consequences of someone's actions. For example, if I witness someone being robbed, I will feel sympathetic pain for her, and this pain constitutes my moral condemnation of the robber's actions. Similarly, the pain and suffering of my mother's cancer will conjure up sympathetic feeling. Moreover, by visiting her in the hospital and seeing the pleasure she gets from my being will produce in me pleasure and this will constitute my moral approval of this action (Stumpf and Fieser 274–275).

29. From a corporate perspective, the sending of ships to be disposed of from developed countries to developing countries make economic sense. Companies pay to dispose of their old ships there at a fraction of what it costs in North America. Currently the U.S. government has approximately 450 ships in need of recycling. According to the Rand Corporation, a U.S.-based thinktank, to domestically recycle the 450 ships would cost approximately $1.9 billion, compared to $170 million if sent to India or China. Although some ships have been dismantled at local U.S. shipbreaking yards and in England, given the negative media attention shipbreaking has received over the years, the bulk of the fleet is still awaiting a decision by the U.S. government.

Unfortunately, international law to protect workers and the environment from the harmful consequences of shipbreaking is lacking. The Basel Convention (1989), which Canada signed, regulates the international trade of hazardous waste. The trading of hazardous waste is considered illegal. Under the Convention, ships *destined* to shipbreaking yards are considered hazardous waste. However, according to the Basel Action Network, a watchdog group based in Seattle, there are loopholes that companies consistently use to avoid the Convention. For example, an owner could sell a ship to a broker, not the actual ship yard, as "sale of ship" without disclosing it is being sold for shipbreaking disposal until after it is imported. In this way, the ship appears *as if* it is not destined for a shipbreaking yard, but merely being sold, and thereby avoid any legal ramifications. The international community is working towards closing up such loopholes.

30. Contrary to Gilligan, perhaps caring and justice are compatible rather than opposed to one another (Tong 92). In fact, we can look at personal relationships as a sort of social contract with implicit values such as support, mutual intimacy, and reciprocal concern about another's welfare. The problem is that if the caring relationship is one-sided between the giver and receiver, as in many heterosexual relationships, the caregiver can be exploited and oppressed. If women typically serve men's physical and psychological needs without being reciprocated, this act of injustice can turn "women's caring acts...into masochistic acts" (Tong 92). Therefore, if we take care ethics seriously, it must, at root, espouse some concept of justice to ensure equality and fairness.

31. See Peter Singer's "All Animals Are Equal" for a utilitarian approach to protecting animals against unnecessary pain and suffering.

Works Cited

Angus Reid. *Similar Views On Marijuana Arrests In Canada, U.S.* 11 May 2005. 17 October 2006 <http://www.angus-reid.com/polls/index.cfm?fuseaction=viewItem&itemID=7160>.

Arthur, John. "Morality Without God." *Conduct and Character: Readings in Moral Theory.* 3rd ed. Ed. Mark Timmons. Belmont, CA: Wadsworth, 1999.

Arthur, Joyce. "Anti-Choicers Don't Have a Biblical Leg to Stand On: The Bible Is Pro-Choice." n.d. 26 October 2006 <http://mypage.direct.ca/w/writer/abortion.html>.

Berg, Jonathan. "How Could Ethics Depend on Religion?" *A Companion to Ethics.* Ed. Peter Singer. Oxford: Blackwell Publishing, Ltd., 1991.

Blackwell, Richard. "OSC Seeks to Clarify Rules on Stock-tipping Cases." *The Globe and Mail,* 3 Feb. 2007: B3.

Boatright, John. *Ethics and the Conduct of Business.* 4th ed. Upper Saddle River, NJ: Prentice Hall, 2003.

Canadian International Development Agency. *River Blindness in West Africa Is Nearly Eradicated, Canada Is Key Donor to Expansion Efforts Across Africa.* 13 March 2007. 28 May 2007 <http://www.acdi-cida.gc.ca/cidaweb/acdicida.nsf/En/FRA-1012103248-K3K>.

Centers for Disease Control and Protection. *Malaria Facts.* Ottawa: Department of Health and Human Services. 11 April 2007. 25 May 2007 <http://www.cdc.gov/malaria/facts.htm>.

Cruzer, Howard. "Ethics of Care: Gilligan and Noddings." *Ethical Theory and Moral Problems.* Ed. Howard Cruzer. Belmont, CA: Wadsworth Publishing Company, 1999.

Des Jardins, Joseph. *Environmental Ethics: An Introduction to Environmental Philosophy.* 3rd ed. Belmont, CA: Wadsworth/Thomson Learning, 2001.

Denny, Frederick. *An Introduction to Islam.* 3rd ed. Upper Saddle River, NJ: Prentice Hall, 2006.

Denton, Fatma. "Climate Change Vulnerability, Imparts, and Adaptation." *Gender and Development* 10 (2002): 10–20.

Dunayer, Joan. "Sexist Words, Speciesist Roots." *Animals and Women: Feminist Theoretical Explorations.* Ed. Carol Adams and Josephine Donovan. Durham, NC: Duke University Press, 1995.

Duncan, Kristy. "Global Climate Change and Women's Health." *Women and Environments* 2007: 10–11.

Feldman, Fred. *Introductory Ethics.* Englewood Cliffs, NJ: Prentice-Hall, 1978.

Flesher, Paul. "Hinduism." *Exploring Religions.* University of Wyoming. n.d. 13 June 2007 <http://uwacadweb.uwyo.edu/religionet/er/hinduism/index.htm>.

Ford, M., and C. Lowery. "Gender Differences in Moral Reasoning: A Comparison of the Use of Justice and Care Orientations." *Journal of Personality and Social Psychology.* 50 (1986): 777–783.

Freeman, Alan. "S. Dakota Bans Most Abortions." *Globe and Mail,* 7 Mar. 2006: A1+.

Friedman, W., A. Robinson, and B. Friedman. "Sex Differences in Moral Judgments? A Test of Gilligan's Theory." *Psychology of Women Quarterly.* 11 (1987): 37–46.

Gilligan, Carol. "Women, Relationships, and Caring." *Ethical Theory and Moral Problems.* Ed. Howard Cruzer. Belmont, CA: Wadsworth Publishing Company, 1999.

Goldhagen, Daniel. *Hitler's Willing Executioners: Ordinary Germans and the Holocaust.* New York: Vintage Books, 1997.

Grimshaw, Jean. "The Idea of a Female Ethic." *A Companion to Ethics.* Ed. Peter Singer. Oxford: Blackwell Publishing, Ltd., 1991.

Harman, Gilbert. *The Nature of Morality.* New York: Oxford University Press, 1977.

Harrison, John, Richard Sullivan, and Dennis Sherman. *A Short History of Western Civilization.* 7th ed. New York: McGraw-Hill, 1990.

Hassan, Riffat. "On the Islamic View of Rights and Duties." *Philosophy and Choice: Selected Readings from Around the World.* 2nd ed. Ed. Kit Christensen. New York: McGraw-Hill, 2002.

Henry, Carl. "Good and Duty Determined by the Will of God." *Conduct and Character: Readings in Moral Theory.* Belmont, CA: Wadsworth, 1990.

Hussain, Arif Abdul. "Ensoulment and the Prohibition of Abortion in Islam." *Islam and Christian-Muslim Relations* 16 (2005): 239–250.

Jaffee, Sara, and Janet Shibley Hyde. "Gender Differences in Moral Orientation: A Meta-Analysis." *Psychological Bulletin.* 126 (2000): 703–726.

Karakowsky, Len, Archie Carroll, and Ann Buchholtz. *Business and Society: Ethics and Stakeholder Management.* Toronto: Thomson Nelson, 2005.

Kelman, Steve. "Cost-Benefit Analysis: An Ethical Critique." *Environmental Ethics: What Really Matters What Really Works.* New York: Oxford University Press, 2002.

Kingston, Anne. "Why Women Can't Get Ahead." *Report on Business* Dec. 2005: 57–71.

Koller, John, and Patricia Koller. *Asian Philosophies.* 3rd ed. Upper Saddle River, NJ: Prentice-Hall, Inc., 1998.

Kyriakides-Yeldham, Anthony. "Islamic Medical Ethics and the Straight Path of God." *Islam and Christian-Muslim Relations* 16 (2005): 213–225.

Lawhead, William F. *The Philosophical Journey: An Interactive Approach.* 2nd ed. New York: McGraw Hill, 2003.

LeBourdais, Eleanor. "Circumcision No Longer a 'Routine' Surgical Practice." *Canadian Medical Association Journal* 152 (1995): 1873–1976.

Mackie, John. *Ethics: Inventing Right and Wrong.* New York: Penguin Books, 1977.

McCarthy, Shawn. "Times Writer Blasts Canada for Rejecting Raped Refugee." *Globe and Mail,* 2 August 2005: A2.

McNish, Jacquie, and Shirley Won. "Rankin Found Guilty of Illegal Stock Tipping." *Globe and Mail,* 16 July 2005: B3.

Melchert, Norman. *The Great Conversation: A Historical Introduction to Philosophy.* 4th ed. New York: McGraw-Hill, 2002.

Merchant, Carolyn. "The Death of Nature." *Environmental Philosophy: From Animal Rights to Radical Ecology.* 3rd ed. Ed. Michael Zimmerman, J. Baird Callicott, George Sessions, Karen Warren, and John Clark. Upper Saddle River, NJ: Prentice Hall, 2001.

Merck & Co. "The Merck MECTIZAN Donation Program." n.d. 28 May 2007 <http://www.merck.com/cr/enabling_access/developing_world/mectizan/>.

Milgram, Stanley. *Obedience to Authority.* New York: Harper and Row, 1974.

Mittelstaedt, Martin. "How Global Warming Goes Against the Grain." *Globe and Mail,* 24 Feb. 2007: A8

Moore, Christopher. "Colonization and Conflict: New France and Its Rivals (1600–1760)." *The Illustrated History of Canada.* Ed. Craig Brown. Toronto: Key Porter Books Limited, 1997.

Nanji, Azim. "Islamic Ethics." *A Companion to Ethics.* Ed. Peter Singer. Oxford: Blackwell Publishing, Ltd., 1991.

Nielsen, Kai. *Ethics Without God.* New York: Prometheus Books, 1973.

Noddings, Nel. *Caring: A Feminine Approach to Ethics and Moral Education.* Berkeley, CA: University of California Press, 1984.

Office of the Superintendent of Bankruptcy Canada. *Insolvency in Canada in 2005.* Ottawa: Industry Canada, 2006. 28 May 2007 <http://strategis.ic.gc.ca/epic/internet/inbsf-osb.nsf/en/br01570e.html>.

"Organ and Tissue Donation." *Canadian Association of Transplantation.* n.d. 25 May 2007 <http://www.transplant.ca/pubinfo_orgtiss.htm>.

Preston, Ronald. "Christian Ethics." *A Companion to Ethics.* Ed. Peter Singer. Oxford: Blackwell Publishing, Ltd., 1991.

Poff, Deborah, and Wilfrid Waluchow, eds. *Business Ethics in Canada.* 3rd ed. Scarborough, ON: Prentice-Hall Canada Inc., 1999.

Pojman, Louis. *Ethics: Discovering Right and Wrong.* Belmont, CA: Wadsworth, Inc., 1990.

"Poll: Opposition to Iraq War at All Time High." *CNN.* 25 September 2006. 21 June 2007 <http://edition

.cnn.com/2006/POLITICS/08/21/iraq.poll/index .html>.

Powers, Mary Buckner. *ENR: Engineering News-Record* 249 (2002): 13. *Academic Search Premier*. EBSCO. University of Lethbridge, Lib., Lethbridge, AB. 25 Aug. 2007 <http://0-web.ebscohost.com.darius .uleth.ca>.

Rachels, James. *The Elements of Moral Philosophy*. 4th ed. New York: McGraw-Hill, 2003.

Ranganathan, Shyam. "Hindu Philosophy." *The Internet Encyclopaedia of Philosophy*. Eds. James Fieser and Bradley Dowden. 2005. 13 June 2007 <http://www .iep.utm.edu/h/hindu-ph.htm>.

Rauhut, Nils. *Ultimate Questions: Thinking about Philosophy*. New York: Pearson Longman, 2004.

Rawls, John. "Two Concepts of Rules." *Philosophical Review* 64 (1955): 3–32.

Ross, W. D. *The Right and the Good*. Oxford: Oxford University Press, 1930.

Senate of Canada. *Cannabis: Our Position for a Canadian Public Policy*. 2002. 17 October 2006 <http://www .parl.gc.ca/37/1/parlbus/commbus/senate/com-e/ ille-e/rep-e/summary-e.pdf>.

Shaw, William. *Business Ethics*. 3rd ed. Belmont, CA. Wadsworth Publishing Company, 1999.

Sherwin, Susan. "Abortion Through a Feminist Lens." *Readings in Health Care Ethics*. Ed. Elizabeth Boetzkes and Wilfrid Waluchow. Peterborough, ON: Broadview Press, 2000.

Singer, Peter. "All Animals Are Equal." *Environmental Philosophy: From Animal Rights to Radical Ecology*. 3rd ed. Ed. Michael Zimmerman, J. Baird Callicott, George Sessions, Karen Warren, and John Clark. Upper Saddle River, NJ: Prentice Hall, 2001.

Smart, J. J. C., and Bernard Williams. *Utilitarianism: For and Against*. New York: Cambridge University Press, 1973.

Sumner, William Graham. "Folkways." *Ethical Theory: A Concise Anthology*. Ed. Heimir Geirsson and Margaret Holmgren. Peterborough, ON: Broadview Press, 2000.

Tandt, Michael, and Estanislao Oziewicz. "Canadian Church Groups Furious Over Afghan's Trial for Converting." *Globe and Mail,* 22 Mar. 2006: A1.

Taylor, Paul. *Respect for Nature: A Theory of Environmental Ethics*. Princeton, NJ: Princeton University Press, 1986.

The Business Enterprise Trust. "Merck and Co., Inc." *Ethical Issues in Business: A Philosophical Approach.*

7th ed. Ed. Thomas Donaldson, Patricia Werhane, and Maragret Gording. Upper Saddle River, NJ: Prentice Hall, 2002.

Thomas, John, and Wilfrid Waluchow. "When A Couple Disagrees Over Abortion." *Well and Good: A Case Study Approach to Biomedical Ethics*. 3rd ed. Peterborough, ON: Broadview Press, 2002.

—. "Sue Rodriguez: 'Please Help Me to Die.'" *Well and Good: A Case Study Approach to Biomedical Ethics*. 3rd ed. Peterborough, ON: Broadview Press, 2002.

Tong, Rosemarie. *Feminine and Feminist Ethics*. Belmont, CA: Wadsworth Publishing Company, 1993.

Verma, Sonia. "The Hero." *Globe and Mail,* 18 April 2007: A1+.

Velasquez, Manuel. *Philosophy: A Text with Readings*. Belmont, CA: Wadsworth/Thomson Learning, 2002.

—. *Business Ethics: Concepts and Cases*. 4th ed. Upper Saddle River, NJ: Prentice-Hall, Inc., 1998.

Wall, Thomas. *On Human Nature: An Introduction to Philosophy*. Belmont, CA: Wadsworth, 2005.

Waluchow, Wilfrid. *The Dimensions of Ethics: An Introduction to Ethical Theory*. Peterborough, ON: Broadview Press, 2003.

—. "Introduction: Ethical Theory in Business." *Business Ethics in Canada*. 3rd ed. Eds. Deborah Poff and Wilfrid Waluchow. Scarborough, ON: Prentice-Hall Canada Inc., 1999.

Warren, Karen. "The Power and the Promise of Ecological Feminism." *Environmental Philosophy: From Animal Rights to Radical Ecology*. 3rd ed. Ed. Michael Zimmerman, J. Baird Callicott, George Sessions, Karen Warren, and John Clark. Upper Saddle River, NJ: Prentice Hall, 2001.

—. "Ecofeminism: Introduction." *Environmental Philosophy: From Animal Rights to Radical Ecology*. 3rd ed. Ed. Michael Zimmerman, J. Baird Callicott, George Sessions, Karen Warren, and John Clark. Upper Saddle River, NJ: Prentice Hall, 2001.

Werhane, Patricia. "The Ethics of Insider Trading." *Ethics in the Workplace: Selected Readings in Business Ethics*. 2nd ed. Ed. Robert Larmer. Belmont, CA: Wadsworth Thomson Learning, 2002.

World Health Organization. *Female Genital Mutilation*. June 2000. 9 November 2006 <http://www.who .int/mediacentre/factsheets/fs241/en/print.html>.

Wortman, Camille, and Elizabeth Loftus. *Psychology*. 3rd ed. New York: Alfred A. Knopf, 1988.

Credits

TEXT CREDITS

Chapter 1. 5: NON SEQUITUR © 1993 Wiley Miller. Dist. By UNIVERSAL PRESS SYNDICATE. Reprinted with permission. All rights reserved. **6:** Reprinted with permission from The American Philosophical Association. **7:** BIZARRO (NEW) © Dan Piraro. King Features Syndicate. **7:** *Journal of Economic Education*, 29 (1998), 377–79. Reprinted with permission of the Helen Dwight Reid Educational Foundation. Published by Heldref Publications, 1319 Eighteenth St., NW, Washington, DC 20036-1802. Copyright © 1998. **9:** Plato *The trial and death of Socrates: Euthyphro, Apology, Crito, death scene from Phaedo/Plato*; translated by G.M.A. Grube; revised by John M. Cooper - 3rd ed. Copyright © 2000 by Hackett Publishing Company, Inc. Reprinted by permission of Hackett Publishing Company, Inc. All rights reserved. **18:** Chapter- The Problems of Philosophy, pp. 89–94, "Extract circa -2000w" from *Problems of Philosophy* by Russell, Bertrand (1967). Reprinted by permission of Oxford University Press.

Chapter 2. 34: Descartes, Rene, 1596–1650. *Discourse on Method and Meditations on First Philosophy*, pp. 17–23. Translated by Donald A. Cress. Copyright © 1980 by Hackett Publishing Company, Inc. Reprinted by permission of Hackett Publishing Company, Inc. All rights reserved. **46:** National Aeronautics and Space Administration. *The Electromagnetic Spectrum*, 2007. 22 May 2007 <http://imagers.gsfc.nasa.gov/ems/visible.html> **49:** Cartoon copyrighted by Mark Parisi. Reprinted with permission. Visit offthemark.com **53:** From *An Essay Concerning Human Understanding* by John Locke. **58:** From *A Treatise Concerning the Principles of Human Knowledge* by George Berkeley. **65:** From *An Enquiry Concerning Human Understanding* by David Hume. **73:** Ludwig Wittgenstein ON CERTAINTY. Edited by G.E.M. Anscombe and G.H. von Wright. Translated by Denis Paul and G. E. M. Anscombe. Copyright © 1969 Blackwell. **77:** Von Wright, Georg Henrik "Wittgenstein on Certainty", *Wittgenstein*. Oxford: Blackwell Publishing Ltd (1982); pp. 165–182. **92:** Reprinted from Lorraine Code *What Can She Know?: Feminist Theory and the Construction of Knowledge*. Copyright © 1991 by Cornell University. Used by permission of the publisher, Cornell University Press.

Chapter 3. 103: Courtesy of Preston Hunter <www.adherents.com> **104:** "Top 10 religious denominations, Canada, 2001", adapted from the Statistics Canada publication *Analysis Series, 2001 Census*, Catalogue 96F0030XIE, released May 13, 2003, URL: http://www.www.statcan.ca/bsolc/english/bsolc?catno=96F0030XIE2001015. **112:** St. Anselm **114:** Yeager Hudson, *The Philosophy of Religion*, pp. 75–84. Reprinted by permission of The McGraw-Hill Companies, Inc. **125:** www.CartoonStock.com **126:** St. Thomas Aquinas **128:** Theodore Schick Jr. "The 'Big Bang' Argument for the Existence of God (1998*)", *Philo*. Published by Society of Humanist Philosophers, Center for Inquiry. Reproduced by permission of the publisher. **140:** Reprinted with permission from the Encyclopaedia Britannica, © 2005 by Encyclopaedia Britiannica, Inc. **143:** From *Natural Theology* by William Paley. **147:** From *Dialogues Concerning Natural Religion* by David Hume **152:** Richard Dawkins "The Improbability of God", *Free Inquiry*, vol. 18 no. 3. Published by Council for Secular Humanism <www.secularhumanism.org/library/fi/dawkins_18_3.html> Reprinted by permission of the publisher. **161:** Copyright Agence France-Presse **166:** From *Philosophy of Religion, An Introduction* 4th edition by ROWE. 2007. Reprinted with permission of Wadsworth, a division of Thomson Learning. www.thomsonrights.com. Fax 800 730-2215. **185:** Chapter- Infini-Rien, pp. 185–189, "Extract circa-1750w" from *A Compelling Introduction to Philosophy* by Blackburn, Simon (1999). Reprinted by permission of Oxford University Press. **187:** Copyright © 2001 by the New York Times Co. Reprinted with permission.

Chapter 4. 207: Descartes, Rene, 1596–1650. *Discourse on Method and Meditations on First Philosophy*, pp. 92–100. Translated by Donald A. Cress. Copyright © 1980 by Hackett Publishing Company, Inc. Reprinted by permission of Hackett Publishing Company, Inc. All rights reserved. **213:** Patricia Smith Churchland "8.2: Substance Dualism" *Neurophilosophy: Toward a Unified Science of the Mind-Brain*, The MIT Press, pp. 317–323. Copyright © 1986 by The Massachusetts Institute of Technology. All rights reserved. **220:** From THE CEREBRAL CORTEX OF MAN by Penfield/Rasmussen. 1950. Reprinted with permission of Gale, a division of Thomson Learning: www.thomsonrights.com. Fax 800 730-2215. **223:** © The New Yorker Collection 1989 Robert Weber from cartoonbank.com. All Rights Reserved. **224:** Copyright © 2001 from *Matters of the Mind* by William Lyons. Reproduced by permission of Routledge, a division of Taylor & Francis Group. **242:** © 1985, The Washington Post Writers Group. Reprinted with permission. **243:** Copyright © 2002. From *Doing Philosophy* by Theodore Schick, Jr. and Lewis Vaughn. Reproduced by permission

Index

Note: Page locators for key terms appear in boldface. The letter *T* attached to a page locator indicates that the entry is found in a table on that page. Refer to *Text Credits* for source information re articles, readings, extracts.